Lecture Notes in Computer Science 12215

More information about this series at http://www.springer.com/series/7409

Matthias Rauterberg (Ed.)

Culture and Computing

8th International Conference, C&C 2020
Held as Part of the 22nd HCI International Conference, HCII 2020
Copenhagen, Denmark, July 19–24, 2020
Proceedings

 Springer

Editor
Matthias Rauterberg
Eindhoven University of Technology
Eindhoven, The Netherlands

ISSN 0302-9743   ISSN 1611-3349 (electronic)
Lecture Notes in Computer Science
ISBN 978-3-030-50266-9   ISBN 978-3-030-50267-6 (eBook)
https://doi.org/10.1007/978-3-030-50267-6

LNCS Sublibrary: SL3 – Information Systems and Applications, incl. Internet/Web, and HCI

This Springer imprint is published by the registered company Springer Nature Switzerland AG
The registered company address is: Gewerbestrasse 11, 6330 Cham, Switzerland

Foreword

The 22nd International Conference on Human-Computer Interaction, HCI International 2020 (HCII 2020), was planned to be held at the AC Bella Sky Hotel and Bella Center, Copenhagen, Denmark, during July 19–24, 2020. Due to the COVID-19 coronavirus pandemic and the resolution of the Danish government not to allow events larger than 500 people to be hosted until September 1, 2020, HCII 2020 had to be held virtually. It incorporated the 21 thematic areas and affiliated conferences listed on the following page.

A total of 6,326 individuals from academia, research institutes, industry, and governmental agencies from 97 countries submitted contributions, and 1,439 papers and 238 posters were included in the conference proceedings. These contributions address the latest research and development efforts and highlight the human aspects of design and use of computing systems. The contributions thoroughly cover the entire field of human-computer interaction, addressing major advances in knowledge and effective use of computers in a variety of application areas. The volumes constituting the full set of the conference proceedings are listed in the following pages.

The HCI International (HCII) conference also offers the option of "late-breaking work" which applies both for papers and posters and the corresponding volume(s) of the proceedings will be published just after the conference. Full papers will be included in the "HCII 2020 - Late Breaking Papers" volume of the proceedings to be published in the Springer LNCS series, while poster extended abstracts will be included as short papers in the "HCII 2020 - Late Breaking Posters" volume to be published in the Springer CCIS series.

I would like to thank the program board chairs and the members of the program boards of all thematic areas and affiliated conferences for their contribution to the highest scientific quality and the overall success of the HCI International 2020 conference.

This conference would not have been possible without the continuous and unwavering support and advice of the founder, Conference General Chair Emeritus and Conference Scientific Advisor Prof. Gavriel Salvendy. For his outstanding efforts, I would like to express my appreciation to the communications chair and editor of HCI International News, Dr. Abbas Moallem.

July 2020   Constantine Stephanidis

HCI International 2020 Thematic Areas
and Affiliated Conferences

Thematic areas:

- HCI 2020: Human-Computer Interaction
- HIMI 2020: Human Interface and the Management of Information

Affiliated conferences:

- EPCE: 17th International Conference on Engineering Psychology and Cognitive Ergonomics
- UAHCI: 14th International Conference on Universal Access in Human-Computer Interaction
- VAMR: 12th International Conference on Virtual, Augmented and Mixed Reality
- CCD: 12th International Conference on Cross-Cultural Design
- SCSM: 12th International Conference on Social Computing and Social Media
- AC: 14th International Conference on Augmented Cognition
- DHM: 11th International Conference on Digital Human Modeling and Applications in Health, Safety, Ergonomics and Risk Management
- DUXU: 9th International Conference on Design, User Experience and Usability
- DAPI: 8th International Conference on Distributed, Ambient and Pervasive Interactions
- HCIBGO: 7th International Conference on HCI in Business, Government and Organizations
- LCT: 7th International Conference on Learning and Collaboration Technologies
- ITAP: 6th International Conference on Human Aspects of IT for the Aged Population
- HCI-CPT: Second International Conference on HCI for Cybersecurity, Privacy and Trust
- HCI-Games: Second International Conference on HCI in Games
- MobiTAS: Second International Conference on HCI in Mobility, Transport and Automotive Systems
- AIS: Second International Conference on Adaptive Instructional Systems
- C&C: 8th International Conference on Culture and Computing
- MOBILE: First International Conference on Design, Operation and Evaluation of Mobile Communications
- AI-HCI: First International Conference on Artificial Intelligence in HCI

Conference Proceedings Volumes Full List

38. CCIS 1224, HCI International 2020 Posters - Part I, edited by Constantine Stephanidis and Margherita Antona
39. CCIS 1225, HCI International 2020 Posters - Part II, edited by Constantine Stephanidis and Margherita Antona
40. CCIS 1226, HCI International 2020 Posters - Part III, edited by Constantine Stephanidis and Margherita Antona

http://2020.hci.international/proceedings

8th International Conference on Culture and Computing (C&C 2020)

Program Board Chair: **Matthias Rauterberg,**
Eindhoven University of Technology, The Netherlands

- Juan A. Barcelo, Spain
- Emmanuel G. Blanchard, Canada
- Jean-Pierre Briot, France
- Torkil Clemmensen, Denmark
- Nick Degens, The Netherlands
- Halina Gottlieb, Sweden
- Francisco Grimaldo, Spain
- Susan Hazan, Israel
- Rüdiger Heimgaertner, Germany
- Jean Ippolito, USA
- Toru Ishida, Japan
- Donghui Lin, Japan
- Yohei Murakami, Japan
- Ryohei Nakatsu, Japan
- Elisabet M. Nilsson, Sweden
- Jong-Il Park, South Korea
- Antonio Rodà, Italy
- Kasper Rodil, Denmark
- Pertti Saariluoma, Finland
- Mamiko Sakata, Japan
- Hooman Samani, Taiwan
- Vibeke Sørensen, Singapore
- Morishima Shigeo, Japan
- Alistair Swale, New Zealand
- Chaudhury Vikramshila, India

The full list with the Program Board Chairs and the members of the Program Boards of all thematic areas and affiliated conferences is available online at:

http://www.hci.international/board-members-2020.php

HCI International 2021

The 23rd International Conference on Human-Computer Interaction, HCI International 2021 (HCII 2021), will be held jointly with the affiliated conferences in Washington DC, USA, at the Washington Hilton Hotel, July 24–29, 2021. It will cover a broad spectrum of themes related to Human-Computer Interaction (HCI), including theoretical issues, methods, tools, processes, and case studies in HCI design, as well as novel interaction techniques, interfaces, and applications. The proceedings will be published by Springer. More information will be available on the conference website: http://2021.hci.international/.

General Chair
Prof. Constantine Stephanidis
University of Crete and ICS-FORTH
Heraklion, Crete, Greece
Email: general_chair@hcii2021.org

http://2021.hci.international/

Contents

Interactive and Immersive Cultural Heritage

HCI and Ethics in Cultural Contexts

Mood Boards as a Tool for Studying Emotions as Building Blocks of the Collective Unconscious

Huang-Ming Chang[1], Leonid Ivonin[2], Marta Diaz[3], Andreu Catala[3], and Matthias Rauterberg[4(✉)]

[1] Mendix Technology B.V., Rotterdam, The Netherlands
ahuang17@gmail.com
[2] Keytree Ltd., London, UK
leonid.ivonin@gmail.com
[3] Universitat Politècnica de Catalunya, Vilanova, Spain
{marta.diaz,andreu.catala}@upc.edu
[4] Eindhoven University of Technology, Eindhoven, The Netherlands
g.w.m.rauterberg@tue.nl

Abstract. We conducted an empirical study to answer the research question whether designers could generate richer affective content through mood boards when they are primed by archetypal media content, comparing to non-archetypal media content. Mood board making may stimulate more feedback from target users and help designers discover deeper insights about user needs and aspiration towards products. Today, mood board making has become an essential skill for designers. However, this technique did not gain adequate credits in terms of scientific evidence. It is necessary to assess the validity of mood boards to be an effective tool for studying unconscious emotions in design research. Four professional designers were asked to make mood boards for four different TV commercials ($2\times$ without archetypal content; $2\times$ with archetypal content). All 16 mood boards are made online available to a group of 141 raters. In a random order all raters had to click on each mood board to view the full-size and give a rating of 'attractiveness' [0–100 score]. The GLM results of all ratings indicate that the attractiveness of the mood boards for archetypal media content and non-archetypal media content are significantly different ($F = 15.674$, $df = 1$, $p < 0.001$). The mood boards primed by archetypal media content (Mean = 54.42, SE = 1.55) are significantly more attractive than the mood boards primed by non-archetypal media content (Mean = 51.37, SE = 1.47). We conclude that mood boards are a enough good tool to investigate and use unconscious emotions what is relevant for addressing design challenges in different contexts.

Keywords: Mood board · Industrial design · Unconscious emotions · Archetypes

1 Introduction

Emotion is an essential part of people's life. While psychological science strives for exploring the functionality and the ontology of emotion, other fields of study focus on

© Springer Nature Switzerland AG 2020
M. Rauterberg (Ed.): HCII 2020, LNCS 12215, pp. 3–18, 2020.
https://doi.org/10.1007/978-3-030-50267-6_1

how research on emotions can be applied in real-life applications and seek the possibilities to enhance the psychological wellbeing. In the engineer field, 'affective computing' was first proposed by Picard [1], who advocates the importance of emotion while the mainstream engineering studies focus more on machines and technologies rather than human perspectives. One of the visions of affective computing is that future computers (or machines) should be capable of sensing human emotions and acting accordingly, and, in an ideal scenario, computers should even be able to deliver emotional expressions to enhance their communication with human users Picard [2]. The current states of affective computing mainly focus on the development of precise and reliable measurements for emotion recognition and emotion modeling using computational algorithms. The obtained models can thus be applied to real-life applications that support a higher-level of human-computer interaction and even enrich human-human communication.

Although affective computing has grown vigorously and has achieved great success in recent years [3], its knowledge has not yet been used to support emotional design activities. This might since most designers rely on experience-based approaches rather than systematic approaches in order to cope with various design challenges. Experience based approaches are based on tacit knowledge that cannot be explicitly described and can only be gained through practices, especially for designers [4]. Experience based approaches are often used to deal with complex problems in which people can hardly solve through logical thinking and thus can only rely on their intuition for decision making [5]. On the contrary, systematic approaches are suitable for well-defined problems and less demanding on designers' experiences. Therefore, systematic approaches are mostly used for design evaluations rather than design practices [6].

The new challenge for design researchers is to integrate systematic approaches into experience-based approaches. Although experience-based approaches are powerful particularly for design practices, they are prone to biases and less consistency [7]. We have conducted three studies using affective computing techniques to explore the impact of archetypal media content on 'unconscious' emotions [8]. There were two primary findings. Firstly, we applied archetypal symbolism to meaning analysis on media content and developed a standard procedure for editing archetypal media content from commercial movies for psychological experiments. Secondly, the results of these three studies suggested that emotions induced by archetypal media content were either too complicated to express through self-reports or inaccessible to conscious awareness, but these emotions can be classified by using the predictive model obtained from the physiological data. Since experience-based design approaches toward emotional design are based on conscious introspection and self-reports, it appears that a wide range of emotions have not yet been discussed in emotional design. Thus, it is necessary to integrate affective computing into experience-based design approaches in order to facilitate emotional design. In this way, the design process would remain flexible and designers could get useful insights provided by scientific studies.

In order to initiate this undertaking, we started with mood board making, which was known as an experience-based technique used for communicating and visualizing emotional qualities. The use of mood boards is versatile. It has long been used for communicating emotional qualities between designers and clients [9]. The process of mood board making also serves as a resource for creative thinking [10]. While mood board making has become an essential skill for design practice, we have seen its potential to be a research tool specifically for investigating non-verbal emotional experience. In order to use mood board making as a research tool for studying emotions, it is necessary to apply psychological methodologies to verify its validity. This would reveal possible disadvantages of using mood board making for research purposes, but also help discover new opportunities to integrate affective computing into emotional design.

We first review the current development of emotion evaluation tools in design research, and then revisit the procedure of making mood boards from a psychological perspective to formulate a framework of mood board making as a research tool for emotional design. According to this framework, we conducted two experiments to examine the effectiveness of mood boards in expressing emotional qualities across interpretations of design background and non-design-background participants and the validity of mood board making for archetypal and non-archetypal media content. These two studies helped clarify the advantages and disadvantages of using mood board making as a research tool for studying emotion. Next, we developed an application by implementing affective computing technology for supporting the process of mood board making in order to enhance the validity of mood board making and remedy its deficiencies in visualizing the continuous emotional experiences in archetypal media content. A case study was reported for demonstrating the use of this application. Finally, we discuss the implications of this study for emotional design and look forward to future work in this direction.

2 Design Research on Emotions[1]

Similar to affective computing, Kansei Engineering is a consumer-oriented approach that is used to quantify emotional qualities particularly in products, and generalize design factors that allow designers to refine the current design and even explore new possibilities for design at the early stage of product development [11]. Researchers in Kansei Engineering intend to investigate the relationship between consumers' psychological feelings and product features, such form, shape, color, and any perceptual qualities. Designers can thus generate new product concepts by manipulating product features. This method can also be used to evaluate qualities of new concept at early stages of the design process [12]. The Japanese word 'Kansei' encompasses broad concepts, referring to all of which are conceived as mental responses to external stimuli, including emotion, senses, and aesthetics [11]. Although Kansei Engineering covered the issues about how customers feel about products, it was developed specifically for aesthetics and product design and did not draw much on psychological theories. This was probably because psychological theories put more emphasis on the functional views of emotions that facilitate the survival of human beings as a species, but rarely discuss non-utilitarian emotions, e.g. aesthetic emotion [13] and emotions in media content [14]. Therefore, design researchers cannot directly apply psychological theories to research on emotional design. This has led to the challenge for design researchers to mediate psychological theories and approaches into the context of design. Research in Kansei Engineering often uses semantic scales

---

[1] This paper is based on chapters 7 and 8 of the PhD thesis of H-M. Chang (2014).

with perceptual and emotional qualities, which may give rise to some concerns about cultural differences and product categories [15]. E.g., the expression in Japanese and English on certain perceptual qualities may differ; kitchen appliances and automobiles should use different sets of semantic scales.

The connection between emotion and design has drawn more attention since the term 'emotional design' was coined and popularized by Norman [16]. In recent years, pioneering design researchers have taken the initiative to extend existing psychological theories to build models particularly for product emotions [17–20]. Some researchers have shift the focus from physical products to user experience, exploring how emotions influence the overall experience under certain circumstances [16, 20, 21]. Jordan [22] developed a questionnaire specifically for evaluating positive emotional experience about products. This questionnaire encompasses 14 questions about specific emotions, such as entertained, excited, and satisfaction. Considering the feasibility across products and cultures, this questionnaire provided optional open-ended questions that allowed the experimenter and the subject to add new words. While Kansei Engineering and Jordan's questionnaire focused on physical products, several new evaluation tools for measuring user experience were proposed in recent years. User experience questionnaire (UEQ) [23] used a similar approach to Kansei Engineering but shifted the focus from products to users. Thus, UEQ removed adjectives describing physical appearance of physical products (e.g. shape and color) and included more words for describing cognitive load, emotions and preferences.

While most evaluation tools are intended to derive immediate responses from subjects, a tool called iScale [24] was developed for observing long-term, continuous user experiences. This tool requires users to recall their long-term experiences periodically while using a new product in their daily lives. Unlike other tools using Likert scales, iScale takes a novel approach, asking users to draw a curve to indicate the changes in their emotional experiences related to the product. However, this curve-drawing approach does not aim to acquire exact emotional qualities, but to serve as a reference for tracing pleasant or unpleasant events that occurred, which allows designers to 'reconstruct' the past and solve potential problems of the product accordingly. However, the abovementioned evaluation tools are language dependent. Although the interpretations in affective meaning are universal at a certain degree [25], various modalities of emotional responses are universally valid and might benefit non-verbal emotion communications, such as facial expressions [26]. PrEmo [27] was developed based on this assumption, using facial expressions and body gestures with animated cartoon characters to illustrate different emotional qualities. Subjects could thus fill this questionnaire through self-reports as an instrument for measuring consumers' emotional responses specifically to product appearance. In addition to the abovementioned tools, there are more new tools released in recent years [28, 29]. Most design researchers apply research-based approaches to investigate product emotions [16, 30] and endeavor to develop systematic procedures for evaluating emotional experience. However, how to study emotion in design practice is rarely discussed. Over the past years, designers have been using experience-based tools, such as mood boards, to study emotions. Comparing to systematic tools, experience based tools are usually quick-and-flexible solutions and do not have strict term of use [31]. On the other hand, the validity of experience-based tools is difficult to validate so that this kind of tool is rarely discussed in empirical studies [10, 30].

3 Revisit Mood Board Making

Considering integrating affective computing into emotional design, we start with mood board making because it is a design tool particularly for studying emotional qualities [32]. In order to verify the validity of mood board making, it is necessary to revisit its procedure and thereby look for possibilities to improve this experience-based tool using systematic approaches [33].

3.1 A Psychological Perspective

Mood boards are a collection of visual images gathered together to represent an emotional responses to a design brief [34]. It is a visual and sensory instrument for designers to communicate with each other and also with the clients [10]. This tool functions as a non-verbal medium communicating complex and delicate emotional qualities that are difficult to express through languages. The process of mood board making can stimulate insightful discussions, providing inspirations at the early stage of concept development [12]. In order to support mood board making, various modalities of interactive technologies were applied to developing digital mood board [35], which enable designers and clients to co-create mood boards effectively.

Mood board making were developed solely for designers. Since mood board making is technically easy and simple, some researchers have tried to use mood boards as a catalyst in focus groups [36]. Similar to the context-mapping approach [37], mood board making may stimulate more feedback from target users and help designers discover deeper insights about user needs and aspiration towards products. This has shown the potential of mood boards to be used as a tool for capturing emotional experiences in different contexts. Today, mood board making has become an essential skill for designers. Several studies have discussed how to teach and apply this technique in design education [9, 33, 34]. It appears that most designers are trained to translate emotional qualities into mood boards – a visual manifestation that associates with the given content, e.g. products and brands. However, this technique did not gain adequate credits in terms of scientific evidence. It is necessary to assess the validity of mood boards to be an effective tool for studying emotions in design research.

In the early stage of the design process, one of the primary tasks is to define emotional qualities of the new product. To initiate this undertaking, designers usually start with the 'design theme' of the given project, such as the brand image of the client and the marketing position of the new product. After a thorough understanding of the theme, designers can thus make mood boards to visualize predefined emotional qualities. These mood boards serve as part of the key references for later stages of product development. Designers must discuss with their clients about the mood boards to identify the common goal of the project, and also talk with target users in order to obtain useful insights. From a psychological perspective, the above process can be decomposed into two stimuli-response processes. The 'design theme' of the given project can be conceived as a mutual affective stimulus to bot designers and users/clients. After both have been primed with the emotional experience, designers make mood boards as a self-report outcome, and then users/clients provide their evaluation according to their subjective emotional experience. Designers need to modify their mood boards iteratively in order to reach a certain consensus among themselves and the target users [38]. If we intend to use mood board making as a research tool, it is necessary to assess the validity of these two processes - the making of mood boards and the evaluation of mood boards - in order to ensure that the final outcome (i.e. mood boards) successfully reflect the emotional qualities in the design theme.

3.2 Mood Boards as a Research Tool for Study Emotions

In order to take this initiative, we needed to first verify the validity of the evaluation of mood boards. If designers and target users share universal criteria on evaluating mood boards, the evaluation process would thus serve as the reference for testing the validity of mood board making.

For evaluation, previous studies have revealed that design students share a common perception of mood boards [33]. In this study a group of design students was recruited to create mood boards according to two general terms, 'masculine' and 'feminine', and asked them to give ratings to the mood boards created by other students depending on how well the mood boards represent the concept of masculine and feminine. The results suggested a consistency for both male and female students in terms of the concept of 'masculine' and 'feminine'. These studies have revealed promising results in this direction, encouraging us to make a step forward and taking into account more critical issues that are related to the validity of the evaluation process on mood boards [39].

First, it is necessary to verify if mood boards are emotionally meaningful for both designers and target users (i.e. individuals who are not trained as a designer). While most designers are trained to make mood boards, they are also experienced in interpreting and justifying mood boards. Although mood boards are assumed to be a non-verbal emotional communication tool, it has not yet clarified if users share the same underlying criteria in justifying mood boards with designers. In order to apply mood boards as a universal tool for evaluating emotions for the general population, it is important to examine whether mood boards can be self-explained affective content to both designers and users.

Second, in the study of McDonagh and Denton [33] the raters (i.e. the design students) also participated in the task of making mood boards. This would lead to a priming effect because the raters had thought attentively about the themes for creating mood boards and would have anticipated what elements might be included in the final mood boards. We propose to include users as the role of rater in order to avoid priming effects, and this setting is also closer to how mood board making is applied in design practices.

Lastly, the stimuli for eliciting emotions in designers and users should be more immersive, emotionally rich, and generic. Most previous studies used static pictures to demonstrate the visual appearance of products, such as keywords, color, shape, and materials [11, 18]. However, this content is too feature-specific, and is not suitable for the early stage of product development. Moreover, the selection of media type should also be considered. Several psychological studies have suggested that film clips are an effective media type for eliciting emotions [40–42]. Film clips are relatively short, intuitively powerful, and easily accessible; the clips and the procedure for viewing them can be standardized across participants [43].

In order to overcome the above-mentioned issues, we chose to use TV commercials as a proper resource for affective stimuli in our research. TV commercials have long been used in research on emotions specifically for consumer psychology [44]. TV commercials are suitable for our research because affective reactions to TV commercials are highly related to buying behaviors [45] and the symbolic meaning of advertisement is an essential element in visual communications between products and consumers [46]. Moreover, mood board making is closely related to the brand image of the product as it is often used in the early stage of product development [36]. TV commercials represent the spirit of the brand of the company and demonstrate the emotional qualities that the company intend to communicate with their potential customers. More importantly, TV commercials were considered as a fruitful resource of media content that contains represents archetypes [47–50].

While mood boards making is often used in design practice, we propose three research questions about the validity of using mood boards as a research tool for investigating emotions for the general population rather than just designers. The first research question is whether designers and non-design-background people had universal tendencies in judging the qualities of mood boards. In our first study [51] we examined whether design students and non-design students have similar criteria in evaluating mood boards. The results showed that the inter-rater reliability among all participants were considerably high, which suggested that mood boards have enough potential to be used as an evaluation tool for research on emotion.

Since the answer to the first research question is positive, the second research question is to ask whether individual designers could make equal quality of mood boards for different design themes, for example, different categories of archetypal media content. In the meantime, the third research question is to determine whether archetypal media content stimulated designers' creativity in making mood boards that contained richer emotional qualities. In order to answer the above two remaining questions, one additional study is conducted.

4 Empirical Comparison Between Archetypal and Non-archetypal Content

The results of our first mood board study [51] have confirmed that design students and non- design students had similar criteria on ranking mood boards. It was concluded that the participating students shared a similar competence in judging the qualities of mood boards even though some of them had no design backgrounds. Next, we proceed to answer the remaining research question - whether professional designers could make equal quality of mood boards for different categories of archetypal media content. Apart from the second research question, the other research question to be answered is whether archetypal media content stimulated designers' creativity in making mood boards that contain richer emotional qualities.

4.1 Approach

The archetypes Hero and Anima are widely manifested in stories, movies, and of course advertisements. Archetypes, such as Shadow, are less popular in advertisements (i.e. TV commercials) since they are not triggering positive emotions to stimulate purchasing behavior. Because of this, we can have more selection options among TV commercials if we focus on Hero and Anima. Two automobile TV commercials with non-archetypal content were selected for comparison. Both two commercials were made by the same advertising agency Wieden and Kennedy. One of the non-archetypal TV commercials, Honda Cog, utilized a chain of colliding parts taken from a disassembled automobile in order to demonstrate the motion qualities of the mechanical objects in an automobile [52]. The other commercial, Honda Everyday, used a series of daily routines behaviors, including driving a car, in order to emphasize the importance of owing a reliable car in modern people's lives [53]. Most of the content in the commercial of Honda Everyday was highly similar to the category of neutral emotions in IAPS and IADS, standardized databases for affective pictures and sounds [54, 55]. Both two commercials were archived on the Internet and received good reviews for their high qualities of aesthetics. Although these two commercials were considered well-made ones, they contained no archetypal symbolic meaning, and thus served as affective stimuli with non-archetypal media content in this study of mood boards.

In order to validate the reliability using mood boards as a research tool, the consistency of the mood board making should be considered. It is important to evaluate whether the designers can make equal quality of mood boards for different commercials. In the previous study, we invited twelve professional designers participated in mood board making. According to the ranking given by the participants, we invited two of the designers who made the top-ranked mood boards (designer E and K in Table 1) and two designers who made the lowest-ranked ones (designer C and I in Table 1) to contribute in this study. Their mood boards for archetypal media content continued to be used in the present study (i.e. mood boards for TV commercials of hero and anima archetypes). The task for these four designers in this study was to make mood boards for non-archetypal media content for comparison, i.e. the TV commercials of Honda Cog and Honda Everyday. Like the previous study, they first viewed one of the two commercials and made a mood board that described their emotions about it, and then repeated the same procedure for the other commercial. The mood boards made by the designers are shown in Figs. 1 and 2 for example; see Appendix D for all the mood boards in [8]. With this experimental design, we can examine whether the designers who made top-ranked mood boards in the previous study could still conduct better performance in this study.

Therefore, we collected 16 mood boards for this study, including mood boards for the hero archetype, the anima archetype, the mechanical object and the daily routines. Next, we conducted an online survey using these mood boards as affective stimuli. Different from the previous study, the primary goal of this study was to examine whether the mood boards for archetypal media content (the commercials of the hero archetype and the anima archetype) induced richer emotions than the mood boards for non-archetypal media content (the commercials of the mechanical object and the daily routines). According to Zajonc [56] and Dijksterhuis [5], it was suggested to use 'preferences' as an essential indicator for retrieving the richness of the emotions and preferences should not be influenced by inferences. In addition, some research also used preferences for evaluating archetypal content [57]. This leads to a key distinction between the present study and

Table 1. The results of the descriptive analysis and the post-hoc test for pairwise comparison on the rankings for the mood boards [average rank (standard deviation)]. Twelve designers participated [Identification (ID) is a capital letter from A to L for each designer]. The upper three rows show the highest ranked mood boards, while the lower three rows show the lowest ranked ones for both archetypal primes [rank 1 = highest, rank 12 = lowest].

BMW Commercial (Anima)			Jeep Commercial (Hero)		
ID	Mean (SD)	Post-hoc	ID	Mean (SD)	Post-hoc
K	4.80 (3.23)	K-H: p = 0.003	G	3.65 (2.79)	G-H: p < 0.001
E	4.92 (3.17)	K-B: p < 0.001	K	3.80 (2.87)	G- I: p < 0.001
		K-C: p < 0.001			G-C: p < 0.001
D	5.22 (3.01)	E-H: p = 0.006	E	4.33 (3.25)	K-H: p < 0.001
H	7.57 (3.13)	E-B: p < 0.001	H	8.82 (2.45)	K- I: p < 0.001
B	8.02 (3.25)	E-C: p < 0.001	I	9.55 (2.60)	K-C: p < 0.001
		D-H: p = 0.028			E-H: p < 0.001
C	8.43 (2.68)	D-B: p = 0.002	C	9.88 (2.44)	E- I: p < 0.001
		D-C: p < 0.001			E-C: p < 0.001

Fig. 1. One of the mood boards for the prime with the mechanical object commercial (made by designer G, see Table 1).

the previous study. In the previous study, the participants first viewed the TV commercials and used these viewing experiences as references for ranking mood boards, which involved inferences in that they had to compare what they perceived from the stimuli and their own emotional experiences with the mood boards. In order to remove the impact of inferences on the participants' preferences on the mood boards, we decided to exclude the viewing task and asked the participants to report their preferences on the mood boards without any given references. Since the participants were unaware of what content these mood boards were related to, the results would thus allow us to infer whether the mood boards for archetypal media content were more emotionally attractive than the mood boards for non-archetypal media content.

Fig. 2. One of the mood boards for the prime with the daily routine commercial (made by designer G, see Table 1).

4.2 Procedure

This study was less constrained because the participants did not need to view the commercials in a controlled setting. In order to facilitate data collection, we used webpage questionnaires, which were more accessible and more convenient for recruiting participants from different countries. Nevertheless, it is important to make this online survey similar to a physical one such as the previous experiment (see the right panel in Figure 7.2 on page 123 in [8]), which allows the participants to have an overview of all the mood boards for comparison and look closer at the details of an individual mood board when giving ratings. Therefore, we built an experimental webpage using a jQuery plugin Gridster which enabled participants to drag and drop mood boards in order to rearrange their positions for visual comparison. The participants could also click on a specific mood board to view the full-size of it and then give a rating of 'attractiveness' for the given mood board.

The invitation to this online questionnaire was spread out through Internet. Before entering the experimental page, the participant was required to read the informed consent form and provide demographic information (e.g. age, gender, nationality, and design or non-design professionals). The experiment started only if the individual participant agreed with the terms. Next, the participant would be led to a tutorial page with five fruit and vegetable pictures in order to get familiar with the drag-and-drop interface and the rating mechanism (see Figure 7.7 on page 129 in [8]). After the practice, the participant would enter the core part of the experiment–give ratings for all the sixteen mood boards. The initial screen showed an overview of all the sixteen mood boards and the positions of all mood boards were randomized (see Figure 7.8 on page 130 in [8]). The participant could click on one of the mood boards to enlarge the mood board to see the details and give a rating about the attractiveness of the selected one [rating: 0...100].

4.3 Results[2]

We applied the analysis on intra-class correlation using a two-way-random, average-measure model. The results indicated that the inter-rater reliability among all rankings

---

[2] We analyzed our data with IBM SPSS Statistics, version 25.

given by all participants is remarkably high (ICC(2, 178) = 0.945, F(15,2655) = 18.3, p < 0.001, 95% confidence interval for ICC population values: 0.899 < ICC < 0.977), which indicates that all of the participants had similar criteria in giving ratings on the attractiveness of the mood boards. The results were in accordance with the previous study, again confirmed the validity of using mood boards for communicating emotional qualities. We further investigated whether there were differences between the ratings on attractiveness of the mood boards given by the design-background participants and the non-design-background participants.

In order to validate the reliability using mood boards as a research tool, the consistency of the mood board making should also be considered. In the present study, two designers who made the top-ranked mood boards (designer E and K) and two for the lowest-ranked mood boards (designer C and I) in the previous study were invited to make mood boards for the other two commercials. Thus, we need to test if the mood boards made by designer E and K are more attractive than mood boards made by designer C and I respectively. In accordance with the previous study, we first transfer the ratings into ranking data and thus used the ranking for the following analyses. The same non-parametric repeated-measures analysis of variance, i.e. the Friedman Test [58] was used. The 'designer who made the mood board' served as a grouping variable. The results showed a significant effect of the designers on the ratings on attractiveness (X2(3) = 17.438, p < 0.001).

Next, we examined whether the mood boards for archetypal media content were more attractive than the mood boards for non-archetypal media content. The data are categorized into two groups ('archetype' as independent variable): archetypal (including the hero archetype and the anima archetype) and non-archetypal (including mechanical object and daily routines) media content. According to the results of a General Linear Model (GLM) analysis with repeated measures the factor 'archetype' is significant (F = 15.674, df = 1, p < 0.001), the mood boards for archetypal media content (mean = 54.42, SE = 1.55) are significantly more attractive than the mood boards for non-archetypal media content (mean = 51.37, SE = 1.47).

Among others, the interaction effect between factor 'designer' and factor 'archetype' is significant too (F = 3.248, df = 3, p < 0,022). We proceeded to post-hoc analyses using the Wilcoxon-Nemenyi-McDonald-Thompson test [59]. This Wilcoxon signed-rank test is considered to be an appropriate statistical analysis for answering the individual differences among the designers [60]. In Table 2 we present the results of our analyses and the pairwise comparisons among the mood boards made by the four professional designers. The results indicate that the mood boards made by designer K are significantly more attractive than all the others and there were no significant differences among the mood boards made by designer E, designer C and designer I. It appeared that designer E performed less well in creating mood boards for non-archetypal media content comparing to the mood boards he made for archetypal media content. These results allow us to answer our third research question, that individual designers might not perform equally well in making mood boards for different design themes. This to some extent reflects the nature of mood board making as an experience-based tool for extracting emotional qualities. Variations in the quality of mood board making still occurred even though these four professional designers were highly experienced.

Table 2. The results of the descriptive analyses and the post-hoc test for pairwise comparison on the rankings for the attractiveness of the mood boards [average ranking (standard deviation)]. Four of the twelve designers in the previous study participated in this study. Designer K and E made the top-ranked mood boards in the previous study; designer C and I made the lowest-ranked mood boards in the previous study

Designer	Mean (SD)	Post-hoc	
K	7.88 (4.63)	K-E: $p < 0.001$ ***	E-C: $p = 0.356$
E	9.00 (4.34)	K-C: $p = 0.013$ **	E-I: $p = 0.209$
C	8.60 (4.77)	K-I: $p = 0.039$ *	C-I: $p = 0.991$
I	8.53 (4.51)		

Furthermore, we conducted the Person's Chi-squared test to examine if there is a significant correlation between the number of the images in a mood board and its ranking. The analysis is showing that there is a significant but negative correlation between the numbers of images and rankings ($r = -0.046$, $n = 2848$, $p = 0.014$). In the previous study, the correlation analysis was meant to determine whether the number of images used in mood boards was correlated to the preciseness of using mood boards to communicate emotional qualities. On the other hand, the correlation analysis in the present study aimed to verify whether the number of images used in mood boards was correlated to the richness of the emotions in mood boards. Both analyses showed significant results, which suggested that designers should consider using more images in mood boards for communicating emotions and meanwhile enhancing the attractiveness of mood boards by exploiting archetypal content.

5 Discussion and Conclusion

Designers are usually assumed to be more sensitive to affective content than users and clients because designers are more experienced in visualizing emotional qualities. Although the participants with non-design backgrounds were less experienced in conceptualizing and visualizing emotional qualities, they share similar criteria with the design-background participants for judging the qualities of the mood boards because the inter-rater reliability among all the participants are noticeably high. However, it needs to be noted that these two studies are different in their judging mechanism in terms of psychology. In the first study, the participants were first presented with the TV commercials as references for judging the mood boards. For executing this task, two mental capabilities might get involved in the decision-making process. We assumed that the participants would use associations for judging the quality of the mood boards according to their own emotional experiences. However, it was also possible that the participants made inferences to compare the content of the commercials and the content of the mood boards and did not use their own emotional experience as the primary reference for ranking the mood boards. While inferences are considered to be part of the rational system of human mind, associations belong to the experiential system [7, 61]. It was unclear which of these two mental capabilities contributed more on their judgment about ranking and rating the quality of the mood boards. In order to clarify this confusion, in the second study the participants' judgment about the quality of the mood boards were solely based on their own preferences about the mood boards without viewing the TV commercials (single blind approach). Since several studies have used preferences as an indicator for measuring emotions in decision making tasks [5, 56], the results further confirm that the participants were utilizing their experiential systems rather than using the rational system for their decision making in the given task.

The results of these two studies have confirmed the validity of using mood boards as a tool for investigating emotional experience among a general population. Furthermore, since the mood boards used in our study were made without adding any text, it has revealed the capability of mood boards to express non-verbal emotional qualities. Traditional research on emotion tends to use direct measurement, such as self-reports on specific emotional qualities 'excited'. Although this approach is effective in most cases, it is prone to filter out trivial emotional qualities that are difficult to express through languages. The results of our studies suggest that mood boards have the potential to be used as an indirect measure using visual images as cues for associating complex, trivial emotional qualities. Since images are language independent, mood boards may overcome the limitation of traditional approaches for studying emotions in design. According to the results of the correlation analysis on the number of the images in the mood boards and the ranking of the mood boards, it is suggested to include more images in one mood board in order to enhance the richness of its emotional qualities. While this finding seems obvious, there are more factors that have not yet been considered, such as the layout of mood boards. The real challenge is to keep the balance between the number of the images and other factors related to mood boards in order to enhance the expressiveness of mood boards.

One of the underlying motivations for the two studies was to determine whether archetypal media content could stimulate designers' creativity in making mood boards with richer emotional qualities. In the second study, the statistical analysis revealed that the mood boards for the archetypal media content are more attractive than those for non- archetypal media content. Therefore, we can conclude that using archetypal media content as stimuli would help designers create emotionally richer content, e.g. mood boards in our study. However, the results of our studies could not answer the question about whether archetypal media content was emotionally richer comparing to non-archetypal media content. As we mentioned earlier, the nature of mood board making is an experience-based tool and the validity of the outcome (i.e. mood boards) would largely depend on the designer's expertise in dealing with various kinds of media content. In the second study, some designers performed equally well in extracting emotional qualities for both archetypal and non-archetypal media content (e.g. designer K) while other designers could not make equal-quality mood boards in both cases (e.g. designer E, C, I). It appears that using mood board making as a research tool for studying emotions requires the supports from systematic approaches such as affective computing.

Acknowledgements. The authors thank 'The Archive for Research in Archetypal Symbolism' (ARAS) for the help with identification and selection of archetypal stimuli.

Funding. This work was supported in part by the Erasmus Mundus Joint Doctorate (EMJD) in Interactive and Cognitive Environments (ICE), which is funded by Erasmus Mundus [FPA no. 2010–2012], by Industrial Design Department from Eindhoven University of Technology (Netherlands), and by Department of Management from Universitat Politècnica de Catalunya (Spain).

Ethics Statement. Written consent was acquired from each participant prior to the empirical sessions. This was a non-clinical study without any harming procedure and all data were collected anonymously. Therefore, according to the Netherlands Code of Conduct for Scientific Practice (principle 1.2 on page 5), ethical approval was not sought for execution of this study.

References

1. Picard, R.W.: Affective Computing. MIT Press, Cambridge (2000)
2. Picard, R.W.: Affective computing: challenges. Int. J. Hum.-Comput. Stud. **59**(1–2), 55–64 (2003)
3. Ivonin, L., et al.: Traces of unconscious mental processes in introspective reports and physiological responses. PLoS ONE **10**(4), e0124519 (2015)
4. Mareis, C.: The epistemology of the unspoken: On the concept of tacit knowledge in contemporary design research. Des. Issues **28**(2), 61–71 (2012)
5. Dijksterhuis, A.: Think different: the merits of unconscious thought in preference development and decision making. J. Personal. Soc. Psychol. **87**(5), 586–598 (2004)
6. Koskinen, I., et al.: Design Research Through Practice: From the Lab, Field, and Showroom. Elsevier, Amsterdam (2011)
7. Kahneman, D.: Maps of bounded rationality: psychology for behavioral economics. Am. Econ. Rev. **93**(5), 1449–1475 (2003)
8. Chang, H.-M., Emotions in archetypal media content. In: Industrial Design, p. 245. Eindhoven University of Technology, Eindhoven (2014)
9. Cassidy, T.D.: Mood boards: current practice in learning and teaching strategies and students' understanding of the process. Int. J. Fash. Des. **1**(1), 43–54 (2008)
10. McDonagh, D., Storer, I.: Mood boards as a design catalyst and resource: researching an under-researched area. Des. J. **7**(3), 16–31 (2004)
11. Nagamachi, M.: Kansei engineering: a new ergonomic consumer-oriented technology for product development. Int. J. Ind. Ergon. **15**(1), 3–11 (1995)
12. Barnes, C., Lillford, S.P.: Decision support for the design of affective products. J. Eng. Des. **20**(5), 477–492 (2009)
13. Scherer, K.R.: What are emotions? And how can they be measured? Soc. Sci. Inf. **44**(4), 695–729 (2005)
14. Wirth, W., Schramm, H.: Media and emotions. Commun. Res. Trends **24**(3), 3–39 (2005)
15. Khalid, H.M., Helander, M.G.: Customer emotional needs in product design. Concurr. Eng. **14**(3), 197–206 (2006)
16. Norman, D.A.: Emotional Design: Why We Love (or Hate) Everyday Things. Basic Books, New York (2004)
17. Desmet, P.M., Hekkert, P.: The basis of product emotions. In: Green, W.S., Jordan, P.W. (eds.) Pleasure with Products: Beyond Usability, pp. 58–66. Taylor & Francis, London (2002)
18. Desmet, P.: A multilayered model of product emotions. Des. J. **6**(2), 4–13 (2003)
19. Hassenzahl, M.: Aesthetics in interactive products: correlates and consequences of beauty. In: Product Experience, pp. 287–302. Elsevier (2008)

20. Diefenbach, S., Hassenzahl, M.: The dilemma of the hedonic: appreciated, but hard to justify. Interact. Comput. **23**(5), 461–472 (2011)
21. Hassenzahl, M., Diefenbach, S., Göritz, A.: Needs, affect, and interactive products: facets of user experience. Interact. Comput. **22**(5), 353–362 (2010)
22. Jordan, P.: Designing Pleasurable Products: An Introduction to the New Human Factors. Taylor & Francis, London (2000)
23. Laugwitz, B., Held, T., Schrepp, M.: Construction and evaluation of a user experience questionnaire. In: Holzinger, A. (ed.) USAB 2008. LNCS, vol. 5298, pp. 63–76. Springer, Heidelberg (2008). https://doi.org/10.1007/978-3-540-89350-9_6
24. Karapanos, E., Martens, J.-B., Hassenzahl, M.: Reconstructing experiences with iScale. Int. J. Hum.-Comput. Stud. **70**(11), 849–865 (2012)
25. Osgood, C.E., et al.: Cross-cultural universals of affective meaning. In: May, W.H., Miron, M.S. (eds.) vol. 1, p. 486. University of Illinois Press, Illinois (1975)
26. Ekman, P.: Strong evidence for universals in facial expressions: a reply to Russell's mistaken critique. Psychol. Bull. **115**(2), 268–287 (1994)
27. Desmet, P.: Measuring emotion: development and application of an instrument to measure emotional responses to products. In: Blythe, M.A., et al. (eds.) Funology: From Usability to Enjoyment, pp. 111–123. Kluwer Academic Publishers, Dordrecht (2003)
28. Huisman, G., et al.: LEMtool: measuring emotions in visual interfaces. In: Proceedings of the SIGCHI Conference on Human Factors in Computing Systems. ACM (2013)
29. Hole, L., Williams, O.M.: The emotion sampling device (ESD). In: Proceedings of the 21st British HCI Group Annual Conference on People and Computers: HCI but not as we know it. BCS Learning & Development Ltd. (2007)
30. Desmet, P.M., Porcelijn, R., Van Dijk, M.: Emotional design: application of a research-based design approach. Knowl. Technol. Policy **20**(3), 141–155 (2007)
31. Tanderup Gade, U.: Design boards as an alignment tool for cross-disciplinarity in engineering. In: Proceedings of the 18th International Conference on Engineering and Product Design Education (E&PDE 2016), Design Education: Collaboration and Cross-Disciplinarity. Institution of Engineering Designers, The Design Society, Aalborg (2016)
32. Zabotto, C.N., et al.: Automatic digital mood boards to connect users and designers with Kansei engineering. Int. J. Ind. Ergon. **74**, 1–11 (2019)
33. McDonagh, D., Denton, H.: Exploring the degree to which individual students share a common perception of specific mood boards: observations relating to teaching, learning and team-based design. Des. Stud. **26**(1), 35–53 (2005)
34. Garner, S., McDonagh-Philp, D.: Problem interpretation and resolution via visual stimuli: the use of 'mood boards' in design education. J. Art Des. Educ. **20**(1), 57–64 (2001)
35. Lucero, A., Aliakseyeu, D., Martens, J.-B.: Funky wall: presenting mood boards using gesture, speech and visuals. In: Proceedings of the Working Conference on Advanced Visual Interfaces. ACM (2008)
36. McDonagh, D., Bruseberg, A., Haslam, C.: Visual product evaluation: exploring users' emotional relationships with products. Appl. Ergon. **33**(3), 231–240 (2002)
37. Visser, F.S., et al.: Contextmapping: experiences from practice. CoDesign **1**(2), 119–149 (2005)
38. Zhu, L.: Application of service design tools in product development process. In: 3rd International Conference on Management Science and Innovative Education - MSIE 2017. DEStech Transactions on Social Science, Education and Human Science, Jinan (2017)
39. Nenkov, G.Y., Scott, M.L.: "So cute I could eat it up": priming effects of cute products on indulgent consumption. J. Consum. Res. **41**(2), 326–341 (2014)
40. Philippot, P.: Inducing and assessing differentiated emotion-feeling states in the laboratory. Cogn. Emot. **7**(2), 171–193 (1993)

41. Gross, J.J., Levenson, R.W.: Emotion elicitation using films. Cogn. Emot. **9**(1), 87–108 (1995)
42. Rottenberg, J., Ray, R.D., Gross, J.J.: Emotion elicitation using films. In: Coan, J.A., Allen, J.J.B. (eds.) Handbook of Emotion Elicitation and Assessment, pp. 9–28. Oxford University Press, Oxford (2007)
43. Lench, H.C., Flores, S.A., Bench, S.W.: Discrete emotions predict changes in cognition, judgment, experience, behavior, and physiology: a meta-analysis of experimental emotion elicitations. Psychol. Bull. **137**(5), 834–855 (2011)
44. Edell, J.A., Burke, M.C.: The power of feelings in understanding advertising effects. J. Consum. Res. **14**(3), 421–433 (1987)
45. Baumgartner, H., Sujan, M., Padgett, D.: Patterns of affective reactions to advertisements: the integration of moment-to-moment responses into overall judgments. J. Mark. Res. **34**(2), 219–232 (1997)
46. Van Rompay, T.J., Pruyn, A.T., Tieke, P.: Symbolic meaning integration in design and its influence on product and brand evaluation. Int. J. Des. **3**(2), 19–26 (2009)
47. Mark, B.M., Pearson, C.: The Hero and the Outlaw: Building Extraordinar Brands Through the Power of Archetypes. McGraw-Hill Books, New York (2001)
48. Rapaille, G.C.: 7 Secrets of Marketing in a Multi-Cultural World. Executive Excellence Publication, Provo (2001)
49. Tsai, S.-P.: Investigating archetype-icon transformation in brand marketing. Mark. Intell. Plan. **24**(6), 648–663 (2006)
50. Caldwell, M., Henry, P., Alman, A.: Constructing audio-visual representations of consumer archetypes. Qual. Mark. Res.: Int. J. **13**(1), 84–96 (2010)
51. Chang, H.-M., Díaz, M., Català, A., Chen, W., Rauterberg, M.: Mood boards as a universal tool for investigating emotional experience. In: Marcus, A. (ed.) DUXU 2014. LNCS, vol. 8520, pp. 220–231. Springer, Cham (2014). https://doi.org/10.1007/978-3-319-07638-6_22
52. Midi-Minuit, P., Bardou-Jacquet, A.: Honda - The Cog (2012). http://www.youtube.com/watch?v=bl2U1p3fVRk&hd=1. Accessed 6 Nov 2019
53. Wieden, Kennedy: Honda Civic - Everyday (2006). http://www.youtube.com/watch?v=rcyfVQ1eobM&hd=1. Accessed 6 Nov 2019
54. Lang, P.J., Bradley, M.M., Cuthbert, B.N.: International affective picture system (IAPS): technical manual and affective ratings. In: Technical Report, pp. 1–5. NIMH Center for the Study of Emotion and Attention, Gainesville (1997)
55. Bradley, M., Lang, P.: The international affective digitized sounds (IADS-2): affective ratings of sounds and instruction manual Gainesville. In: Technical Report. The Center for Research in Psychophysiology, Florida (2007)
56. Zajonc, R.B.: Feeling and thinking: preferences need no inferences. Am. Psychol. **35**(2), 151–175 (1980)
57. Maloney, A.: Preference ratings of images representing archetypal themes: an empirical study of the concept of archetypes. J. Anal. Psychol. **44**(1), 101–116 (1999)
58. Friedman, M.: The use of ranks to avoid the assumption of normality implicit in the analysis of variance. J. Am. Stat. Assoc. **32**(200), 675–701 (1937)
59. Hollander, M., Wolfe, D.A., Chicken, E.: Nonparametric Statistical Methods. Wiley Series in Probability and Statistics, vol. 751, 3rd edn, p. 848. Wiley, Hoboken (2013)
60. Wilcoxon, F.: Individual comparisons by ranking methods (1945). In: Kotz, S., Johnson, N.L. (eds.) Breakthroughs in Statistics, pp. 196–202. Springer, New York (1992). https://doi.org/10.1007/978-1-4612-4380-9_16
61. Epstein, S.: Integration of the cognitive and the psychodynamic unconscious. Am. Psychol. **49**(8), 709 (1994)

Research on Consumers' Decision-Making Factors of Cultural and Creative Products of the Palace Museum Under the Background of New Media

Ziwei Chen, Jiaqian Xu, and Bing Xiao[✉]

Shanghai Jiao Tong University, Shanghai 200240, China
chenzw95@sjtu.edu.cn, daphneqian@qq.com, xbingdesign@163.com

Abstract. With the development of social economy, new media platform has gradually become an important channel for people to communicate. The cultural and creative industry of the Palace Museum has attracted more and more people's attention through the publicity of new media. It not only successfully creates a young Museum brand, but also better inherits and develops traditional Chinese culture. Therefore, this paper studies the influence of various factors on consumers' purchase of cultural and creative products in the context of new media by using Decision-making Trial and Evaluation Laboratory (DEMATEL), which leads cultural and creative workers to rethink the intrinsic value of cultural and creative products, and summarizes the more optimized development direction of cultural and creative products in combination with the development of new media. The result of the experimental test indicated that the most important factor influencing consumers' purchase decisions is the commemorative collection of cultural and creative products. It is suggested that using multimedia technology together with brand effects to enhance the memorial and collectible significance of products can strengthen the interaction and bring better development.

Keywords: The Palace Museum · Cultural and creative products · New media

1 Introduction

Because of the development of regional brand culture and the construction of intangible cultural heritage, cultural and creative industry is increasingly rising under the dual influence of national policies and markets. Both tourism and museum cultural and creative products are deeply loved by consumers. Under the background of new media, the cultural and creative products of the Palace Museum are not only sold in the physical store, but also popular by costumers online. Combined with multimedia communication and cross-branding collaborations, the annual revenue of cultural and creative products of the Palace Museum have reached 1.5 billion in 2017 [1]. In early 2020, the cultural and creative industry of the Palace Museum together with a cosmetics brand launching a series of lipsticks called 'Hebao' has been followed with numerous interests through

© Springer Nature Switzerland AG 2020
M. Rauterberg (Ed.): HCII 2020, LNCS 12215, pp. 19–30, 2020.
https://doi.org/10.1007/978-3-030-50267-6_2

WeChat Subscription. The number of readers broke through 20000 rapidly which brings a great promotion before the sale. It can be seen that the cultural and creative industry of the Palace Museum is well-known, influential and has a huge consumption market under the influence of new media. As a new economic form, the cultural and creative industry is paid more and more attention to the new marketing model. At the same time, the mode will also affect and change consumers' purchasing decision-making factors. It is hoped that this research can summarize the advantages of the development model of cultural and creative products of the Palace Museum in the context of new media through the consumers' decision-making factors, and bring useful enlightenment for the development of cultural and creative products.

2   Literature Review

In the field of cultural and creative industry, numerous studies have been conducted by researchers.

Through literature research and observation of the current situation of cultural and creative products, it is found that as early as 2002, the Taiwan government proposed to take the cultural and creative industry as one of the most important development industries to inherit regional culture and promote cultural and artistic vitality, which is a trend of globalization. It includes three aspects: cultural and art core industry, design industry, creative support and derivative creation industries [2].

The meaning of 'cultural and creative products' is extremely wide, and UNESCO defines it as consumer goods with ideas, symbols and lifestyles. Chen defines it as a product transforming through creativity with market value, which originates from cultural themes. In short, the obvious difference between cultural and creative products and ordinary products is that cultural products have cultural functions and cultural symbols [3]. Through the retrieval and integration of a large number of documents, the classification of cultural and creative products can be divided into three main categories: Museum Cultural and creative products, regional cultural and creative products and derivative cultural and creative products [4].

Plenty of scholars have already explored the design and development of cultural and creative products as follows. In terms of design, Wu believes that 'creativity' can be the use function beyond the expectation of the product, innovation in the selection of materials and technology, new interpretation of the cultural connotation of the product itself, etc. In addition to the artistry of the products, the essence of cultural and creative products is still a commodity. We should improve the cost-performance ratio of the products except for broadening its consumers [5]. After studying the Japanese tourism market, Ruan discussed the design of cultural and creative products in four aspects: cultural history, market demand, manufacturing technology, and sales channels [6]. In terms of development, Wang believes that cultural and creative products can be divided into two categories: one is the interpretation and reconstruction of art, the other is the substance and the non-material service to meet people's needs. He mentioned that the product should also be designed according to the living environment. In the relatively undeveloped areas, the information on material loss and cost should be fed back to users in time to avoid unnecessary burdens on them. For users in developed areas, designers can pay more attention to the combination of cultural and creative products and modern science and technology. In this way, the design method can promote the intelligent development of cultural and creative products [7].

New media is one of the dissemination ways for the development of cultural and creative products in the new era. Therefore, in the context of new media, scholars have carried out the following research: He classified the communication path of the cultural brand of the Palace Museum in the new media era into three categories: Micro communication, e-commerce products, and TV program production [8]. Shi integrated the cooperation cases of cultural and creative products and crossover brands in the Palace Museum and defined this marketing method as an open crossover development mode [9]. Luo believes that the cultural creation of the Palace Museum has made a breakthrough in the new media social age through emotional expression, art and culture restart, and narrative integration [10]. Cao believes that with the arrival of the new media marketing era, the museum has also begun to pay attention to the use of new media for the marketing and promotion of cultural and creative products, and meanwhile, it is a good way to promote its history and culture when promoting products [11]. Zheng believes that the Palace Museum can move from electronic screens to broad consumers through new media. In this way of marketing, it is more necessary to combine the actual situation of production to achieve the high cost-performance ratio of cultural and creative products in order to show the traditional culture vividly in a new way [12].

In the study of consumers' decisions, Qian studies the internal causes of consumers' decisions of cultural and creative products from comprehensive creativity, exterior design, manufacturing techniques, local characteristics, collectible value, functions and cost-performance ratio [13]. Guo studies on Customer-perceived Value by five dimensions: perception of culture, perception of usefulness, perception of purchase cost, satisfaction and intention of consumption [14]. When investigating cultural and creative products in remote areas, Ying-Jye Lee asked subjects to evaluate cultural and creative products through four dimensions: cultural image, utility, preference, and intention to purchase [15].

Through the collection and collation of the literature, it is found that the existing literature on customer decision-making mainly studied on the product itself and consumer perception, but few quantitative studies combined with the new media background. In the context of new media, online publicity and marketing will play a certain role in the decision-making of users. The point of this paper is how the product marketing model in the new era will affect the traditional model and how the traditional culture will be inherited. Therefore, this paper studies the influence of various factors on consumers' purchase of cultural and creative products in the context of new media by using Decision-making Trial and Evaluation Laboratory (DEMATEL), which leads cultural and creative workers to rethink the intrinsic value of cultural and creative products, and summarizes the more optimized development direction of cultural and creative products in combination with the development of new media.

3 Research Design

3.1 Method

This study uses Decision-making Trial and Evaluation Laboratory (DEMATEL) to analyze the data collected by the questionnaire. DEMATEL can analyze the correlation between various factors to find out the key decision-making factors for consumers to buy cultural and creative products of the Palace Museum and the relationship between various decision-making factors. Besides, in order to ensure the effectiveness of the questionnaire collection, the data are obtained through personal in-depth interviews and one-to-one questionnaire survey.

DEMATEL was proposed by scholars A. Gabus and E. Fontela of Battelle laboratory in the United States at a conference in Geneva in 1971 [16]. It is a systematic analysis method using graph theory and matrix tools. DEMATEL's experimental steps are as follows: (1) Determine the main influencing factors of consumers' purchasing decision and establish the scale; (2) Subjects were invited to estimate the direction of influence and the priority of each major factor when compared with other major factors by one of the five levels; (3) Deal with the questionnaire data and establish the direct relation matrix; (4) By normalizing the original relation matrix, the normalization direct influence matrix is obtained; (5) By normalizing the direct influence matrix, the direct/indirect relation matrix is calculated; (6) From the direct/indirect relation matrix, the Influence Value (D), Affected Value (R), Prominence Value (D+R) and Relation Value (D–R) of each element are obtained; and (7) Draw the causal diagram to extract the key influencing factors and find out the relationships between the main factors.

3.2 Questionnaire Design

In order to mine the information on what factors have strong effects when consumers make purchase decisions, a large number of consumers who are interested in culture and creative products are investigated by multiple user research methods such as brainstorming, observation and in-depth interview. Meanwhile, numerous information has been analyzed by reviewing related literatures and news interviews.

After a large quantity of information and suggestions gathered by channels motioned above are processed and analyzed, thirteen factors are summarized and defined as the preliminary influencing factors. In the earlier interview, it is found that in the dimension of marketing models under the background of new media, the factors of 'Micro communication' and 'TV program production' are close to each other. So, these two factors have been combined into 'Multimedia communication'.

At last, this study divides consumers' purchasing decision-making factors of cultural and creative products of the Palace Museum under the background of new media into 12 factors, 3 dimensions in total, which are the attributes of cultural and creative products, the characteristics of the Palace Museum and the marketing models under the background of new media. The attributes of cultural and creative products consist of artistry (whether the shape and exterior are creative and aesthetic), connotation (whether the connotation is creative), manufacturability (whether the material is satisfactory and the manufacturing process is exquisite), utilitarian functionality (whether the function meets the customer's requirements), commemorative collection (whether it has collection value and commemorative significance), cost-performance ratio (whether the pricing is reasonable compared with its quality). The characteristics of the Palace Museum include local characteristics (local characteristics of Beijing), historic value (cultural relic value, architectural value, historic value), brand (brand rejuvenation of the Palace Museum). The marketing models under the background of new media contain multichannel selling (the physical store and online store), multimedia communication (WeChat, Weibo, TV programs, etc.) and cross-branding collaborations (such as selling products or designing limited packaging in cooperation with other brands, etc.), as shown in Table 1:

Table 1. List of factors.

Dimensions	Factors
Attributes of cultural and creative products	Factor 1 – 'artistry'
	Factor 2 – 'connotation'
	Factor 3 – 'manufacturability'
	Factor 4 – 'utilitarian functionality'
	Factor 5 – 'commemorative collection'
	Factor 6 – 'cost-performance ratio'
Characteristics of the Palace Museum	Factor 7 – 'local characteristics'
	Factor 8 – 'historic value'
	Factor 9 – 'brand'
Marketing models under the background of new media	Factor 10 – 'multichannel selling'
	Factor 11 – 'multimedia communication'
	Factor 12 – 'cross-branding collaborations'

Subjects need to compare and score each factor. The scale of this study is divided into five measures, namely "no impact (0 point)", "low impact (1 point)", "moderate impact (2 points)", "high impact (3 points)", "extremely high impact (4 points)". This questionnaire survey received 24 valid answers.

3.3 Experimental Analysis and Discussion

After sorting out and normalizing the questionnaire data, the normalization direct impact matrix of consumers' purchasing decision-making factors for cultural and creative products of the Palace Museum can be derived, as shown in Table 2:

Calculate with developed DEMATEL tool [17] to find out the relationships among various factors and get the direct/indirect relation matrix, as shown in Table 3. The threshold of 0.52 is calculated by quartile method, so Factor 4 ('utilitarian functionality'), Factor 6 ('cost-performance ratio') and Factor 10 ('multichannel selling') that do not reach the threshold are deleted in the table.

Table 2. The factors in direct relation matrix.

	1	2	3	4	5	6	7	8	9	10	11	12
1	0.00	0.11	0.11	0.08	0.10	0.08	0.11	0.09	0.10	0.05	0.08	0.09
2	0.11	0.00	0.07	0.08	0.11	0.08	0.11	0.09	0.10	0.07	0.09	0.07
3	0.11	0.08	0.00	0.08	0.10	0.09	0.08	0.07	0.09	0.05	0.06	0.08
4	0.08	0.08	0.09	0.00	0.05	0.10	0.05	0.05	0.06	0.07	0.06	0.07
5	0.11	0.11	0.11	0.05	0.00	0.06	0.10	0.11	0.10	0.05	0.06	0.08
6	0.07	0.05	0.09	0.09	0.06	0.00	0.05	0.05	0.07	0.08	0.06	0.07
7	0.08	0.09	0.06	0.04	0.10	0.05	0.00	0.11	0.11	0.06	0.08	0.07
8	0.08	0.10	0.06	0.04	0.12	0.05	0.11	0.00	0.11	0.04	0.07	0.07
9	0.08	0.07	0.06	0.04	0.09	0.06	0.09	0.07	0.00	0.08	0.09	0.11
10	0.04	0.04	0.04	0.04	0.05	0.07	0.05	0.04	0.07	0.00	0.09	0.09
11	0.03	0.04	0.03	0.03	0.05	0.04	0.06	0.05	0.10	0.09	0.00	0.10
12	0.09	0.08	0.07	0.07	0.10	0.07	0.08	0.06	0.12	0.09	0.11	0.00

Table 3. The factors in direct/indirect relation matrix.

	1	2	3	4	5	6	7	8	9	10	11	12
1	0.48	**0.57**	**0.54**		**0.61**		**0.59**	0.53	**0.65**		**0.54**	**0.57**
2	**0.57**	0.46	0.50		**0.61**		**0.59**	0.53	**0.63**		**0.53**	**0.55**
3	**0.53**	0.49	0.40		**0.56**		0.51	0.47	**0.58**		0.47	0.51
4												
5	**0.56**	**0.55**	0.51		0.50		**0.57**	0.53	**0.62**		0.50	**0.54**
6												
7	0.49	0.49	0.44		**0.54**		0.43	0.49	**0.58**		0.47	0.50
8	0.49	0.50	0.44		**0.56**		0.53	0.39	**0.58**		0.47	0.49
9	0.48	0.47	0.43		**0.53**		0.50	0.45	0.47		0.48	**0.52**
10												
11	0.34	0.34	0.31		0.38		0.37	0.33	0.44		0.30	0.41
12	**0.52**	0.50	0.47		**0.56**		**0.52**	0.47	**0.62**		**0.52**	0.45

Note: The elements in bold type indicate those with values above the threshold of 0.52.

The Prominence Value (D+R) and the Relation Value (D–R) are calculated and listed in Table 4.

Table 4. Prominence and relation values.

Prominence (D+R)		Relation (D–R)	
Factor 5	**12.232**	Factor 4	0.938
Factor 1	**12.116**	Factor 1	0.756
Factor 9	**12.033**	Factor 2	0.736
Factor 2	**11.843**	Factor 3	0.563
Factor 12	**11.713**	Factor 8	0.288
Factor 7	**11.375**	Factor 12	0.078
Factor 3	**10.929**	Factor 6	0.032
Factor 8	**10.854**	Factor 5	0.000
Factor 11	9.589	Factor 7	–0.244
Factor 6	9.500	Factor 10	–0.667
Factor 4	9.027	Factor 9	–1.091
Factor 10	8.773	Factor 11	–1.389

Note: The elements in light grey form indicate those with values under the threshold of 0.52 in direct/indirect relation matrix. Data in bold type indicate Prominence Values above the mean value, 10.83.

In the overall valuation, the larger the Prominence Value (D+R) is, the more important the factor is. Chosen the factors above the mean value of 10.83, the rank in importance of decision-making and evaluation factors for consumers to buy cultural and creative products of the Palace Museum is Factor 5 ('commemorative collection'), Factor 1 ('artistry'), Factor 9 ('brand'), Factor 2 ('connotation'), Factor 12 ('cross-branding collaborations'), Factor 7 ('local characteristics'), Factor 3 ('manufacturability') and Factor 8 ('historic value').

In the table of Relation Value, when the positive value of the Relation Value (D–R) is larger, it means that this factor directly affects other factors, while when the negative value of the Relation Value (D–R) is larger, it means that this factor is affected by other factors. As the value of Factor 4 ('utilitarian functionality') does not reach the threshold 0.52 in the direct/indirect relation matrix, it has been excluded from results. As a result, Factor 1 ('artistry') is the main factor affecting other factors, Factor 11 ('multimedia communication') is mainly affected by other factors.

The following table shows the first three items and the last three items of Prominence Values and Relation Values.

According to the direct/indirect relation matrix (Table 3), the causal diagram (Fig. 1) is drawn above by Prominence Value (D+R) as X-axis and Relation Value (D–R) as Y-axis. In the causal diagram, the author distinguished the factors in different dimensions through different colors. Yellow represents the dimension of Attributes of cultural and creative products, orange represents the dimension of Characteristics of the Palace Museum and blue represents the dimension of marketing models in the context of new media.

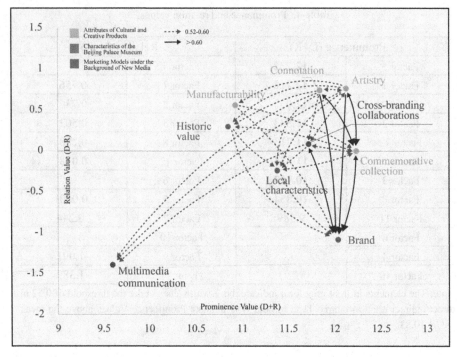

Fig. 1. The causal diagram (Color figure online)

Table 5. The top and the last three factors in Prominence.

The top three factors in Prominence	The last three factors in Prominence
Factor 5 – 'commemorative collection'	Factor 11 – 'multimedia communication'
Factor 1 – 'artistry'	Factor 8 – 'historic value'
Factor 9 – 'brand'	Factor 3 – 'manufacturability'

Table 6. The top three factors (>0) and the last three factors (<0) in Relation.

The top three factors in Relation (>0)	The last three factors in Relation (<0)
Factor 1 – 'artistry'	Factor 11 – 'multimedia communication'
Factor 2 – 'connotation'	Factor 9 – 'brand'
Factor 3 – 'manufacturability'	Factor 7 – 'local characteristics'

The arrows indicate the direction in which one factor affects the other. The solid line and the dotted line show strong influence relation (>0.6) and sub strong influence relation (0.52–0.6). Figure 1 in combination with Table 5 and Table 6 shows:

- Factor 5 ('commemorative collection'), Factor 1 ('artistry') and Factor 9 ('brand') are the most important key purchase decision-making factors because of the top three values in Prominence Values. Factor 5 ('commemorative collection') is the maximum value of Prominence Value (D+R), which shows that the most critical decision-making factor is the commemorative collection of cultural and creative products of the Palace Museum. Therefore, we need to focus on strengthening the collectible and commemorative significance of the Palace Museum. On the other hand, Factor 1 ('artistry'), Factor 2 ('connotation'), Factor 3 ('manufacturability'), Factor 7 ('local characteristics'), Factor 8 ('historic value'), Factor 9 ('brand') and Factor 12 ('cross-branding collaborations') have sub strong influence on it. Meanwhile, Factor 5 ('commemorative collection') has a strong impact on Factor 9 ('brand'), and has a sub strong influence on Factor 1 ('artistry'), Factor 2 ('connotation'), Factor 7 ('local characteristics'), Factor 8 ('historic value') and Factor 12 ('cross-branding collaborations'). Therefore, we can combine other factors to find design methods which can make products more worthy of collection and commemoration, so as to better promote consumption. The improvement of products' collection and commemoration can also assist the development of other factors. In addition, it can also improve the exterior of products, create more artistic products and adhere to the existing style to maintain a young brand image.
- Factor 11 ('multimedia communication'), Factor 8 ('historic value') and Factor 3 ('manufacturability') are the last three values in Prominence Value (D+R), indicating that these three factors have little impact on other factors.
- The top three positive Relation Value, Factor 1 ('artistry'), Factor 2 ('connotation') and Factor 3 ('manufacturability') which have more influence on other factors are the casual elements. While the last three negative Relation Value, Factor 11 ('multimedia communication'), Factor 9 ('brand') and Factor 7 ('local characteristics') which are more likely to be affected by other factors are the result factors. Factor 1 ('artistry'), Factor 2 ('connotation'), Factor 5 ('commemorative collection') and Factor 12 ('cross-branding collaborations') all have a strong impact on Factor 9 ('brand'), in addition, the factor's centrality ranking is also very high, so it can be seen that the promotion of brand is very important for the development of cultural and creative products.
- It can be seen from Fig. 1 that in addition to the influence of Factor 12 ('cross-branding collaborations') on Factor 9 ('brand'), the rest of the association lines can form a secondary association diagram shown in Fig. 2. Factor 1 ('artistry') and Factor 2 ('connotation') can directly and strongly affect the Factor 9 ('brand'), or first have a strong impact on Factor 5 ('commemorative collection'), and then strongly affect the development of Factor 5. This phenomenon shows that the design of cultural and creative products can start from the exterior and connotation of the products. This way can not only give the products more cultural significance, but also enhance its commemorative value and brand image. It can be seen that these four factors are closely related.

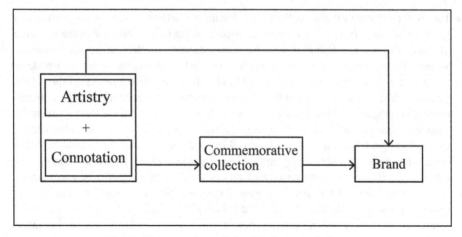

Fig. 2. The secondary relationship in strong influence

4   Conclusion and Suggestion

4.1   Conclusion

- **Conclusion 1.** Research shows that Factor 5 ('commemorative collection') is the most critical factor in all consumers' purchase decisions. Consumers think that cultural creation with the value of collection and commemoration can enhance the historic value, local characteristics and brand image of the Beijing Palace in their mind. Therefore, how to better enhance the value of commemorative collection through innovative technical means has become an important way to lift the purchasing decision-making ability.

- **Conclusion 2.** According to the Fig. 1, the attributes of cultural and creative products will affect consumers' cognition of the characteristics of the Palace Museum. We can publicize the cultural characteristics of the Beijing Palace and build the brand more effectively by enriching the exterior and connotation of cultural and creative products, refining its technology and assisting with the sales mode under the new media.

- **Conclusion 3.** As a new marketing model in the context of new media, Factor 12 ('cross-branding collaborations') is very important, which has a direct impact on the products, On the other hand, Factor 11 ('multimedia communication') is the resulting factor, which is more influenced by other factors. Enhancing the effects of these two factors by using multimedia technology to increase the interaction between products and consumers can promote consumers' awareness of cultural and creative products in the Palace Museum and lift their purchasing decision-making ability. With the help of innovative forms, the value of the cultural and creative products itself will be enlarged to get better benefits.

4.2 Discussion and Suggestion

- The results show that multichannel selling and multimedia communication, which were originally predicted to have a great impact on consumers' decision-making, do not have a strong impact on other factors. However, as an effective marketing model, they do play important roles in building image of the Palace Museum and improving consumption. The reason is mainly as follows: DEMATEL is a method to study the relationships among various factors. While multichannel selling and multimedia communication are both promotion models based on the overall products, so it will lack the relationships among the details of cultural and creative products. Based on DEMATEL, it is suggested to strengthen the relationship among Factor 10 ('multichannel selling'), Factor 11 ('multimedia communication') and other factors, such as promoting the limited products by multichannel selling in order to improve the purchasing power of consumers, or using multimedia technology together with brand effect to strengthen the interaction between products and consumers.
- It can still expand the sample size in order to get more accurate conclusions during the questionnaire collection. Meanwhile, the division of factors is overly detail and the questionnaire is too long, which is easy to make the subjects lose patience. It is suggested that the follow-up research should be simplified.

References

1. Song, Y., Zhang, Y.: Research on the development of museum cultural and creative products under the background of new media. New Media Res. **5**(06), 124–126+137 (2019)
2. Kang, Y.-Y., Wang, M.-S., Hung, W.-S., Lin, H.-Y.: The cultural creative of product design for pingtung county in Taiwan. In: Aykin, N. (ed.) IDGD 2009. LNCS, vol. 5623, pp. 366–375. Springer, Heidelberg (2009). https://doi.org/10.1007/978-3-642-02767-3_41
3. Chen, Z.: Culture to take away'—definition and classification of cultural and creative products and '3C resonance principle. Mod. Commun. **2017**(02), 103–105 (2017)
4. Li, J.-C., Ho, M.-C.: Rethinking about the cultural products of a museum: perspectives across disciplines. J. Des. **14**(4), 69–84 (2009)
5. Wu, Y.: A brief analysis of the new development of the design of cultural and creative products. Pop. Lit. Art **2019**(06), 133 (2019)
6. Ruan, C.: Analysis of design methods for cultural and creative products in Japanese tourism market. Ind. Des. **2016**(03), 92+95 (2016)
7. Wang, A., Qin, S.: Research and exploration of product customization of cultural and creative products. Art Educ. **2019**(05), 178–179 (2019)
8. He, Y.: Analysis of cultural brand communication path of the palace museum in the new media era. New Media Res. **5**(04), 54–56 (2019)
9. Shi, Y.: Analysis on the development trend of cultural and creative products in museums: a case study of the palace museum. China Newsp. Ind. **2019**(08), 10–11 (2019)
10. Luo, H.: The narrative way of brand stories in the social era—a case study of the palace museum. Radio TV J. **2018**(11), 138–139 (2018)
11. Cao, Y.: Marketing and promotion of cultural and creative products with new media in museums: a case study of taobao online store of the palace museum. New Media Res. **4**(09), 54–55 (2018)

12. Zheng, B.: The integration of new media and traditional culture promotes the development of cultural and creative industry: a case study of the innovative marketing strategy of the cultural and creative museum of the imperial palace. Public Commun. Sci. Technol. **10**(19), 169–171+188 (2018)
13. Qian, F., Yin, Z., Ding, N.: The relationship between comprehensive evaluation on products and purchasing behavior. Packag. Eng. **39**(24), 183–188 (2018)
14. Guo, M.: Perceived values and purchase intention of museum cultural and creative products. Packag. Eng. **39**(16), 223–227 (2018)
15. Lee, Y.-J.: Evaluation of involvement and multi-dimensions for cultural creativity products in remote districts. Anthropol. **17**(3), 795–809 (2014)
16. Li, Y., Yin, B.: Study on the influencing factors of enterprise environmental behavior based on DEMATEL. J. GuangXi Cadres Univ. Econ. Manag. **31**(01), 26–33 (2019)
17. Liu, C., Jin, Y., Zhu, X.: Extraction of key factors and its interrelationship critical to determining the satisfaction degree of user experience in taxi passenger service using DEMATEL. In: Marcus, A., Wang, W. (eds.) DUXU 2018. LNCS, vol. 10920, pp. 299–313. Springer, Cham (2018). https://doi.org/10.1007/978-3-319-91806-8_23

Computer Science Intersects Humanities: Visualization Projects for Liberal Arts Undergraduate Students Through an Interdisciplinary Approach Using Software Development Skills and Japanese Cultural Knowledge

Hiroko Chiba[✉] and Dave Berque

DePauw University, Greencastle, IN, USA
{hchiba,dberque}@depauw.edu

Abstract. This paper demonstrates how computer science can intersect with the humanities and the arts in a way that is tangible for students. Specifically, we provide four examples of interdisciplinary student projects that sit at the intersection of software design, Japanese culture, and art. Steve Jobs once said "—technology alone is not enough—it's technology married with liberal arts, married with the humanities, that yields us the results that make our heart sing" [1]. The projects we report demonstrate how students can experience this synergy first-hand.

Keywords: Computer science · Liberal arts

1 Introduction

Computer science in liberal arts contexts has been discussed among computer science academics as well as scholars in humanities during the last three decades. With increasing opportunities for global collaborations, students should learn effective communications, critical thinking, and problem solving no matter what discipline they pursue. Computer science is no exception. Shannon argues "—many of the successes in computer science applications spring directly from applications of theoretical results in multiple disciplines" [2]. In other words, the vitality of the discipline can be maintained through an interdisciplinary approach. Computer scientists in liberal arts colleges advocate the importance of bringing multiple perspectives to their discipline through the breadth of liberal arts education (arts, language, history, philosophy, psychology mathematics, sciences, and social sciences) [3, 4].

Technology itself has been actively implemented in classroom teaching, course materials, group projects, homework assignments and other activities to supplement the environment for the humanities. The digital humanities have supported a wide array of activities; maintaining databases, creating interactive learning environments, and producing

© Springer Nature Switzerland AG 2020
M. Rauterberg (Ed.): HCII 2020, LNCS 12215, pp. 31–41, 2020.
https://doi.org/10.1007/978-3-030-50267-6_3

artwork to name a few. Given these many previous examples, our projects are designed to bring software development, language, and art together more intentionally. The following projects are rooted in the symbiotic relationship between Computer Science and liberal arts education.

2 Project Overview

A team of two professors, one in computer science and one in Japanese Studies, and two undergraduate students designed and implemented four art products that leveraged software development skills, knowledge of the Japanese writing scripts, and Japanese art work. The students who worked on the following four projects majored in computer science and were well-versed in Japanese language and culture as well as software development. For one of the projects, the team was augmented by additional collaborators with backgrounds in visualization, art history and museum curation.

Project 1 and Project 2, as described below, were inspired by the work that a group called teamLab created. The teamLab was founded in 2001 in Tokyo and consists of artists, programmers, engineers, CG animators and mathematicians [5]. The team has two digital museums, teamLab Planets and teamLab Borderless, both in Tokyo, in which they showcase large-scale digital art created by the team. Their works embody interdisciplinary collaborations that integrate art, science, technology, and the natural world [5]. This approach naturally fits liberal arts education and our liberal arts vision.

3 Project Detail

3.1 Project I Overview: Falling Kanji on Touch-Sensitive Display

The first project involved visualizing one of the Japanese writing scripts called Kanji (or Chinese characters). The Japanese language employs three writing scripts; Hiragana, Katakana, and Kanji. Hiragana and Katakana are phonetic whereas Kanji is meaning based, i.e., each Kanji represents a meaning. There are a little over two thousand Kanji that one needs to know for daily use in Japan. This collection of Kanji is called jōyō Kanji [6]. Kanji can be divided roughly into four categories; pictograms, ideograms, compound ideograms, and phonetic-ideographic characters. Approximately 10% of Kanji are pictographic, meaning that these Kanji were created through drawings of objects. For example, the Kanji for mountain is 山 which stemmed from a visual image of mountain. Ideograms indicate somewhat abstract concepts such as numbers and spatial locations. For example, the number two is written in two lines 二. Compound ideograms generally consist of two or more basic Kanji such as 森 "forest" in which we see three trees. The last group mentioned above, phonetic-ideographic characters are a combination of a constituent that expresses the meaning and another that provides a phonological cue. We selected Kanji that show concrete objects among these categories.

Kanji also has been an artistic subject in Shodō, Japanese calligraphy, during many centuries and the following projects illustrate a way to appreciate the writing script coupled with technology. We envisioned and designed the visualization to draw the audience's attention to modern artwork just as traditional calligraphic works have done.

3.2 Falling Kanji Design, Implementation and Interface

The student learned the programming language, Unity, and selected the kanji characters to be used. All of the kanji selected are concrete objects such as hana 花"flower," tori 鳥"bird," and ame 雨"rain." The student then selected a video from YouTube that represents each object. For example, the video associated with "rain" depicts a rainy scene.

When running the software, Kanji characters float down a screen (See Fig. 1). When a user touches a Kanji, the screen plays a video of the object indicated by the Kanji. Thus, this project helps users experience the meaning of each kanji in an enjoyable way.

After watching the visualization of the meaning of each kanji through the video, we wanted the user to see how to write the Kanji. To accomplish this, the software plays a second video in a box and this video shows the stroke order of the Kanji stroke by stroke (See Fig. 2). Each Kanji has a specific stroke order and it is very helpful to learn the correct stroke order in order to write a well-balanced kanji. Finally, to engage the user, the system next displays four Kanji and invites the user to actually draw the Kanji on the touch sensitive screen (See Fig. 3).

The program runs in a public space on a 60-in. touch-sensitive interactive display so multiple users can gather around the screen to touch falling kanji which transforms them into videos as described above (see Fig. 4).

Fig. 1. Falling Kanji image one

Fig. 2. Falling Kanji showing stroke order

Fig. 3. Falling Kanji drawing practice

Fig. 4. Users exploring Falling Kanji on a large format display

3.3   Project II Overview: Floating Kanji in a Virtual Museum

At the suggestion of one of the student team members, the Kanji visualization was re-implemented using a HTC Vive head-mounted display. When a user wears the head-mounted display, the user is standing inside a virtual museum gallery with picture frames displayed on each of the four walls (Fig. 5). The content of each picture frame shows a still of an object such as rain, dog, flower, mountain, fish and so on. The user finds virtual Kanji floating in the air around in the VR space. When the user grabs a Kanji with a handheld controller (Fig. 6), the audio for the pronunciation of the kanji is played. Then, the user throws the grabbed Kanji to the picture that matches the meaning of the Kanji (Fig. 7). When the image and Kanji match correctly, the user sees the video of the corresponding object in the frame and the Kanji is planed in the caption box below the video (Fig. 8). For example, when the user catches the Kanji for "flower" and throw it to the frame that matches the image of a flower, a video of flowers blowing in the wind starts to play. The example below is the visualization of "rain." Although this program was designed as an artistic work, it also enables the user to both experience and learn the Kanji in the VR environment.

Fig. 5. Kanji Floating in the VR museum gallery

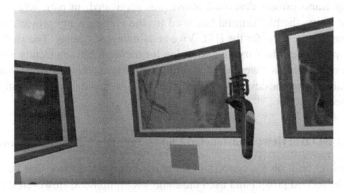

Fig. 6. Handheld controller grabs a Kanji for "Rain"

Fig. 7. Throwing the Kanji "Rain" to the frame

Fig. 8. The rain video starts showing with the right Kanji under the frame

3.4 Floating Kanji in Virtual Museum Design, Implementation and Interface

The Floating Kanji project described above was motivated, in part, when a student realized that Unity, the platform he had used for the Falling Kanji project, could also be used to develop systems for the HTC Vive head-mounted display. The student asked if he could spend a few days trying to develop for the Vive and the faculty supervisors eagerly agreed. In fact, we were thrilled with the initiative shown by this student and with his ability to imagine developing a program that leveraged a head-mounted display and associated controller.

3.5 Project III Overview: Constructed Landscapes in a VR Environment

The third project built on the concept of the virtual museum gallery that was conceptualized in the second project and used the same VR equipment. However, the original project team was now joined by collaborators with experience in art history, visualization and museum curation and we collectively took an approach that was more firmly rooted in the arts.

We learned that the University gallery planned to host an exhibit from February 1st through August 1st, 2019, entitled "Constructed Landscapes" which planned to highlight over 50 works drawn from the university permanent art collection. The motivation for the exhibit stemmed from the inquiry about the artists' and viewer's reality. It planned to ask participants to question whether an artistic landscape is a true representation of reality or whether it is simply a construct of the artist? As a part of this intellectual pursuit, we were invited to collaborate on a project that attempted to examine this complex balancing act between artistic/creative control and viewer's constructed reality through the emotional transformation of virtual landscapes.

3.6 Constructed Landscapes Design, Implementation and Interface

The team consisted of faculty from art history, computer science, Japanese studies, the director of the technology center, and two students from art history and computer science. The team met in person several times to discuss the theme, content, art materials, and visual and sound effects. The two students envisioned then designed and implemented a virtual museum display based on the discussions and feedback they received. Leveraging experience from previous projects they implemented their ideas using Unity and an HTC Vive Head Mounted Display and even repurposed some of the code from earlier projects.

The virtual museum gallery displayed four famous Asian landscape paintings in the picture frames on its walls. In addition, emoticons float in the air around the user. The user tries to catch an emoticon using an HTC Vive Controller and then throws the emoticon at one of the landscape paintings. When the emoticon hits a painting, the software applies the appropriate emotion to the landscape using a graphical transformation. For example, if the user throws an angry emotion at a painting, the landscape becomes redder, which is accomplished through a bit-wise manipulation of the original image. If the user thrown a sleepy emoticon at a painting, the landscape comes blurrier, which is accomplished by averaging nearby pixels. The target emotions included sad, happy, angry, and sleepy.

Each change is also accompanied by music that reinforces the target emotion. Feedback from users was very positive with regard to both technological excitement and aesthetic enjoyment. Some students, especially computer science majors, were inspired and presented their own project ideas.

Figure 9 shows how a user experiences the emotional landscape in the VR environment. When a user stands in the VR environment, a series of emoticons start floating nearby (Fig. 10). The user can pick an emotion with the handheld controller (See Fig. 11 for "angry" emotion) and throw it at one of the landscape paintings. Then the landscape is transformed to show the emotion that was applied.

Fig. 9. Constructed landscapes in action

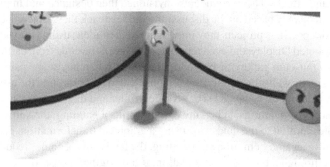

Fig. 10. Constructed landscape view through head mounted display

Fig. 11. Constructed landscapes view of the angry emoticon

3.7   Project IV Overview: KoroKoroll

KoroKoroll is a mobile game app that helps students practice learning Japanese expressions. Korokoro is a Japanese onomatopoetic expression that describes something rolling. The name of this game is a combination of "koroko" in Japanese and "roll" in English. For this exercise, the writing script called Hiragana, syllabic characters, was used because in learning Japanese, Hiragana is introduced first among the three writing scripts (Hiragana, Katakana, and Kanji) and the target audience consists of novice Japanese learners.

The game space was constructed as a castle. At the gate to the castle, the level options (Level 1, Level 2, and Level 3) are presented (See Fig. 12). When the user selects a level, the gate opens and Hiragana characters are placed on the stones on the ground (See Fig. 13). A prompt such as "Thank you for the meal (after eating)" appears on top of the screen as shown in Fig. 14. The user then tilts the phone in various direction to roll a block over the appropriate Hiragana to spell out the appropriate Japanese response, rolling the block from cell to cell by tilting the phone. As the block rolls over Japanese characters, the accumulated Japanese text is displayed. When the text is correctly formed, castle doors open and the user can proceed to the next level.

While the original version of KoroKoroll was designed to run on a phone, the game was ported to run on an HTC Vive head-mounted display. In this version, the user is placed in the castle and sees an open gate. Hiragana characters appear on the castle floor and the user physically walks over characters to select them. When the answer is correct, an elevator takes the user to the next level of the game which is represented by a higher floor of the castle. From the higher floors, the user can see the bottom of the castle, which creates an eerily surreal experience. Thus, the learner experiences a fun and compelling imaginary world while learning Japanese.

Fig. 12. KoroKoroll opening level selection

3.8 KoroKoroll Design, Implementation and Interface

KoroKoroll was, once again, developed in Unity. As described in the previous section, one version was developed to run on mobile devices that incorporate accelerometers to detect tilt, while the second version was developed for the HTC Vive. Importantly, many graphics and audio assets could be shared between the versions which made the dual development effort more manageable by a single student.

Fig. 13. KoroKoroll castle gates opening

Fig. 14. KoroKoroll Hiragana characters to roll over

4   Conclusion

Each of these projects was carried out by undergraduate students with assistance from faculty. The Kanji visualization remains on display in a public space on campus. The VR projects have been experienced by many students, faculty, staff members, and visitors. Through this interdisciplinary set of projects, the student designers, as well as the various audiences, have come to understand how technology and the arts can work together synergistically. These projects are the outcomes of computer science embedded in liberal arts education.

Acknowledgements. We want to thank Michael Boyles (Director of the Tenzer Technology Center, DePauw University), Craig Hadley (former Director and Curator of Exhibitions and University Collections, DePauw University), Keisuke Ohtani, (DePauw University '2019), Pauline Ota (Associate Professor of Art History, DePauw University), and Jinzhi Qin (DePauw University '2020) who made these projects possible.

References

1. Lehner, J.: Steve Jobs: Technology Alone is Not Enough. The New Yorker, 7 October 2011. https://www.newyorker.com/news/news-desk/steve-jobs-technology-alone-is-not-enough. Accessed 23 Feb 2020
2. Shannon, C.: Computer science and the liberal arts: computer science and the liberal arts have much to offer each other. Liberal Educ. **96**(4), 42–45 (2010)
3. Tenenberg, J., McCartney, R.: Computer science in a liberal arts context. J. Educ. Resour. Comput. **7**(2) (2007)
4. Walker, H., Kelemen, C.: Computer science and the liberal arts: a philosophical examination. ACM Trans. Comput. Educ. **10**(1), 1–10 (2010)
5. teamLab Homepage. https://www.teamlab.art/about/. Accessed 23 Feb 2020
6. Agency, Cultural Affairs, Government of Japan Homepage. https://www.bunka.go.jp/kokugo_nihongo/sisaku/joho/joho/kijun/naikaku/kanji/. Accessed 23 Feb 2020

Research on the Design and Method of Innovation System of Cultural and Creative Industries Based on Social Development

Wei Ding, Qianyu Zhang, Junnan Ye[✉], Dadi An, and Jie Zhou

East China University of Science and Technology, 130 Meilong Road, Xuhui District,
Shanghai, China
dw.6789@163.com, 1395320526@qq.com, 2723241@qq.com,
61915633@qq.com, wy_zj2009@163.com

Abstract. Under the background of economic globalization, the cultural and creative industries have received great attention from people as soon as they appear. At the same time, it have played an increasingly important role in society. But cultural and creative product categories are cluttered at present. The related creative products have more imitation and less innovation, low technical content. Most of the research and practice of the cultural and creative industry are based on particular point-like or face-shaped research ideas. But they did not build an innovative design system from the macro level. So that it is impossible to form a regular and general theoretical framework. What's more, it is also not possible to balance the relationship between the universality of the innovation theory system and the regional differences.

In view of the problems and shortcomings of the innovation and development, this paper will base on the dynamic analysis of social development and the poor county of Songxi, Fujian as an example. Explore the new system and new model for the innovation system and method research of cultural and creative products. First of all, through market research and analysis, information retrieval and social practice, this paper uses inductive and comparative methods for many systems in the creative industries at home and abroad. Then, combined with the development trend of the world creative industries and the current situation of China's. And summarize the design methods and principles that can be implemented on the ground. Finally, the scientific and practical implementation of this system is verified by the example of promoting the development of poverty-stricken counties by design, such as Songxi in Fujian Province. Based on the current situation of social development, this paper integrates the phenomenon of the following industry. Defining the cultural and creative industries in a new way by providing a rich theoretical basis and establishing a network. And put forward a set of operational procedures which can be implemented, so that the system method forms a complete closed loop from research to application. It can provides powerful theoretical support for the "logical" application of the creative design method in different design fields.

Keywords: The cultural and creative industries · Innovation systems · Design methods · Social development

© Springer Nature Switzerland AG 2020
M. Rauterberg (Ed.): HCII 2020, LNCS 12215, pp. 42–53, 2020.
https://doi.org/10.1007/978-3-030-50267-6_4

1   Theoretical Research on the Innovation System and Method of Cultural and Creative Industries in China and Abroad

The cultural and creative industries originated from the Cultural and Creative Industries Special Working Group established in the United Kingdom in 1997. And the next year, the United Kingdom published the *British Creative Industry Pathway Document* [1]. The development of cultural and creative products is an important branch of the cultural and creative industry in recent years [7]. At the same time, China's widely distributed and unique regional cultural resources provide a basic guarantee for the development of cultural and creative products. At this stage, the issues that the cultural and creative industry requires consideration about how to discover unique cultural resources, implement them through art and design activities, as well as incorporate products into the platform of industrial sales and dissemination. At the same time, through the construction of innovative systems and methods based on social development, the integration and development of the primary, secondary and tertiary industries can be achieved, thus realizing the transformation of economic value.

1.1   Literature Review of Theoretical Research in China and Abroad

Chinese scholars' research on theories of cultural and creative industries can be roughly divided into three aspects: industrial strategies, cultural and creative product design systems, and cultural and creative design methods.

Cultural and Creative Industry Strategy. Cultural and creative industry strategy research mainly involves the strategy discussion of the cultural and creative industries and related policies in the context of relevant policy interpretation. Guangnan Huang [2] started with the concept of cultural and creative industries, systematically combed the cultural and creative industries and policies in Europe, America, and Asia. He explained the current and future development direction of cultural and creative industries [2]. Yao Zhang (2015) analyzed the current situation of the cultural and creative industry of modern museums from the perspective of design. This article analyzed the advantages and influencing factors of its cultural and creative product development based on museum resources and discussed the development direction of future design. Huiwen Zhang (2018) discussed the positioning of the relationship between new media technology and traditional cultural and creative industries, and promoted brand development through cultural mining, product services, and other methods.

Cultural and Creative Product Design System. The research of cultural and creative product design systems from the perspectives of design and tourism, is to put forward cultural and creative system models. Zhimin Zhuang [12] took Shanghai as an example to outline the situation of cultural and creative products in the field of innovation design in the era of experience economy. Mo Lian (2016) discussed the design strategies of tourism souvenirs and related cultural and creative products in order to achieve the purpose of promoting the design and development of local cultural and creative products. In terms of cultural system research, Jianxin Cheng [1] proposed the "research-interpretation-innovation" design system, which is to draw "inspiring information" from classical art, traditional culture or regional culture [3]. Based on the theory of soft innovation and research on cultural and creative industries, Tingting Jiang [11] et al. logically construct a system model of cultural and creative industries, which has theoretical significance. From the perspective of art design, Zhi Yang [6] summarized the social innovation and regional development trends of cultural and creative design, and outlined the sustainable development model of it. And he puts forward the sustainable development theory of "cultural and creative design plus lifestyle".

Cultural and Creative Design Methods. It mainly involves subject areas such as tourism, management, and industrial product design, including improvement suggestions for specific cases, cultural and creative product design methods, and future development trends. Wenzhi Wu and Zhimin Zhuang [12] in the context of the experience economy, aimed at the problems that consumers have high expectations for tourism products but insufficient development, and proposed a system framework for experiential innovation of tourism products in ancient villages. He explained the methods and approaches for experiential design of tourism cultural and creative products. Xueling Miao (2004) redefined the definition of cultural and creative products and believed that it should become the material carrier characteristics of certain places. Yaqi Zhou [9] discussed the design principles, ideas and methods in the process of cultural transformation by exploring the forms and characteristics of traditional folk culture and combining the development of cultural and creative products. At the same time, she summarized the methods of applying traditional culture to modern cultural and creative design.

From the academic history, we can find out the question of further thinking is how to provide a universal logical framework for the cultural and creative industry innovation system for social development, and propose a design method that can be implemented on the ground. Under the background of service design ideas, the purpose of successful industrial upgrading and regional coordinated development is a considerable question.

2 Research on the Strategy of Cultural and Creative Industries Based on Social Development

It is necessary to dig deep into local characteristic culture. Firstly, through the cultural archeology, taking the characteristic cultural resources as the core carrier. And according to the brand culture, historical archeology is carried out on multiple dimension such as regional history, industry and art works. Excavate and reproduce the unique cultural elements of the region, including the multi-dimensional culture such as the brand area, history, enterprise, and artistic works, etc. It is necessary to select from a large number of cultural resources to extract a truly representative culture as a carrier. The second is cultural interpretation, through various promotion methods, improve the affinity and popularity of the brand, so as to achieve the purpose of perfect communication. Interpretation, research and interpretation of the selected cultural elements. This simplifies the complex cultural connotation, clarifies the implicit cultural value, and embodies the abstract cultural reference. By grafting today's cultural semantics, it is more adapted to the modern social environment. Finally, it is cultural innovation, integrating human and environment, behavior, and material elements to give cultural elements new vitality on the basis of fully interpreting culture. Re-design by modern artistic methods, which to form a unique IP element. By introducing cutting-edge cultural and creative industry resources, realize the coordinated development of three sections: cultural and creative design, supply chain management, and service operation. So that a basic model for the integrated development of the cultural and creative industries can be formed and the power of design to tap cultural value can be utilized, and to make the perfect combination of design service and experience operation.

3 Research on the Innovation System Design of Cultural and Creative Industries Based on Social Development

3.1 Design Forces Promote Product Development

Through design forces to drive product development, and after in-depth investigation and analysis of the characteristics and historical status of distinctive cultural resources, which can draw the style map of different cultural and creative derivatives. Based on local cultural characteristics, define category of popular products and develop cultural tourism products that meet the current interests of the public, and reinvent the cultural brand image by developing innovative derivatives.

Data Mining. Use big data platforms to determine future consumer hotspots and trends, and use this as a basis to define design themes and identify the creative products that the market is concerned about. And by segmenting the population and evaluating data, propose and define the development direction of online and offline product lines, and stimulate consumer demand by different product combinations.

Category Planning. In order to define the category of cultural and creative derivatives more accurately, online and offline three-dimensional surveys based on user behavior and big data are required to accurately analyze the characteristics of the entire cultural and creative product category. According to the user needs, re-adjust the differences in product categories online, offline, and between platforms. In terms of online sales, the different sales characteristics of each platform have led to differences in product categories. In terms of offline sales, we plan the categories through field interviews, physical store sales status and specific performance, and promote the formation of cultural and creative popular products.

Content Definition. Product content definition needs to start from the perspective of cultural and creative brands and consumers. Conduct targeted research and analysis on product requirements, market segmentation, product positioning, product design, and product development, etc., and summarize a category system that integrates selling points, quality, and image. In the process of research, we should always take the user as the center and rely on the brand culture to analyze the importance and urgency of market capacity and demand. The design team relies on the category planning theory. Develop a creatively thinking of the brand and theme, and finally determines the content plan. At the same time, it needs to consider the feasibility of the design, including factors such as process, materials, construction period and cost, and adjust the design content according to the actual situation.

3.2 Cultural and Creative Product Development and Design Innovation Platform

Establish cultural and creative product development and design innovation platforms. And expand the influence of regional culture through multi-faceted form such as experience space (Fig. 1 shows an example), service operation, and brand building. Achieve multi-platform operation for cultural and product design, which can stimulate the new vitality of local cultural and creative design. Then through service design and experience design, create a humanized consumer experience (Fig. 2).

Fig. 1. Cultural and creative product experience space

Fig. 2. Cultural and creative vertical innovation model

3.3 Creative Industry Block

The creative industry block is an important carrier for the development of cultural and creative industries, sometimes it is used as a "city card" to attract more creative inspiration and consumer groups [5]. Constructing a new type of creative industry block, which needs to borrowing characteristic historical culture as the background, and integrating the development model of cultural and creative industries. Based on modern cultural creativity and life experience, it promotes the development of cultural and creative industries and the protection and dissemination of distinctive culture. The establishment of creative industry blocks can not only drive the growth of the local economy through the consumption capital chain and make up for the lack of funds for the development of cultural and creative industries; it can also improve the local characteristic cultural and creative product service chain through creative industrial blocks to adapt to the new trend of socialized consumption.

3.4 New Town Model: Design Drives Integrated Development of Primary, Secondary and Tertiary Industries

The essence of cultural and creative industry innovation is to establish a two-way interaction between regional concepts and resources [10]. In the short term, it will increase the value of the industry between creative products and tourism destinations. In the medium term, it will establish an innovative long-term mechanism and operating system. And in the long term, it is about forming an innovative culture, habits and conscious attitude. Committed to promoting the coordinated and integrated development of primary, secondary and tertiary industries, and provide targeted design services based on the different characteristics of the three main industries. Firstly, add design concepts to the primary industry, forge peasant culture and develop experiential agricultural economy, which can promote agricultural revitalization [8]. Secondly, provide systematic design services for the secondary industry, apply vertical innovation to traditional manufacturing, and create design exhibition centers, maker spaces, and talent education exchange

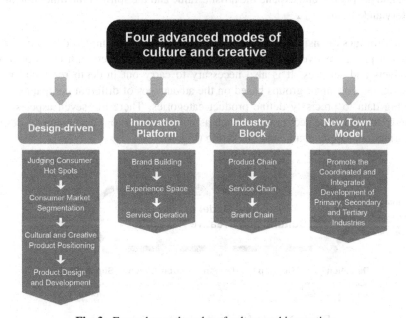

Fig. 3. Four advanced modes of culture and innovation

platforms. Finally, put design power into the tertiary industry, create unique urban and historical cultural IP for cities to revitalize traditional cultural resources. At the same time, the commercial value, design value and service value are organically integrated to form a new service system (Fig. 3).

4 Research on the Innovation System of Cultural and Creative Industries

Through cultural excavation to develop unique products, reshape the regional cultural and creative industries, and realize the multiple coordinated development of cultural industries. To provide cultural and creative industries in different regions with universal applicability of cultural and creative industry strategies and implementation plans. Committed to excavating the local culture of tourist destinations and giving them new vitality. At the same time, connect the cutting-edge cultural and creative industry resource, and complete the coordinated development of cultural and creative design, supply chain management, and service operation to form a basic model for the integrated development in the field of cultural creativity.

4.1 Cultural and Creative Design Innovation Methods

Grasp the Essence of Culture. Through research on the basic design of the industry and users, as well as grasp the essence of history and culture, find the direction of derivative research and development, define and innovate product categories. Using characteristic cultural resources as a carrier, extract the core of cultural and historical values, and deeply dig and expand the artistic value and the spirit of the times contained in history and culture.

New Advantages of Insight Research. The innovation of cultural and creative products is not just a creative and symbolic transform to the aesthetic attributes or forms of products and services. It is also necessary to carry out in-depth research on the corresponding consumer groups based on the advantages of different companies. And using big data to precisely define product categories. There are seven aspects have gradually formed in project practice, such as insight, definition, development, design, transformation, supply chain, and marketing (Fig. 4).

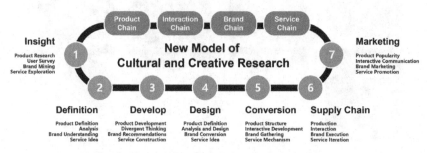

Fig. 4. New model of cultural and creative research

Combining Hotspot Development and Utilization. In product development, we combine cultural elements with consumer needs to define hot product categories and develop cultural products that meet current public interests. Through in-depth consumer research, using big data to precisely define product categories and improve product lines [4]. Make full use of product design advantages to create differentiated cultural and creative derivatives. At the same time, it has carried out strategic cooperation with a number of high-quality suppliers to integrate the supply chain.

4.2 Establishing an Ecological Supply Chain System

To establish a complete and strong execution system for cultural and creative products, we are facing with the problem of breaking the barriers of various channels. The supply chains are closely connected and interacting with each other. This requires us to opening up and connecting the channels of various parties to build a local innovation platform-"Design Center" (Fig. 5 shows an example). Bringing the strength and resources of various disciplines together to establish effective systems and models. By establishing a cultural and creative product supply chain resource platform, realize the continuous integration and development of creative resources and industry. In order to provide more effective design services, it requires improving conversion efficiency, accelerate the industrialization process, and help to build a creative ecological cycle system. At the same time, a complete vertically integrated cultural and creative design industry innovation system is formed, which one from regional cultural excavation to cultural and creative brand establishment, and another one from product development to business model.

Fig. 5. Design center

4.3 Service Design Provides New Marketing Strategies

The new retail model integrates online and offline resources, redefines the relationship between people, goods and venues in the new consumption scenario. Therefore, it can meet the individual needs of customers in a multi-touch and three-dimensional manner. Under this model, the local characteristic cultural and creative product service chain is more reasonable, which can adapt to the new trend of socialized consumption. And establishing a new strategy method that is applicable to most cultural and creative product design systems, and redefining cultural and creative design.

In terms of service operation, it expands regional cultural influence through multi-directional communication methods such as experience space, platform operation, and brand building. The online and offline multi-platform operation model helps the cultural and creative brand to rapidly expand its sales scale. By redesigning retail space and pinpointing the market, the cultural and creative industry is not limited to traditional stores, which can attract consumers with the times and create a humanized consumer experience.

4.4 Establish a Complete Closed Loop that Can Be Implemented from Research to Application

Apply the design methodology summarized in practice to the new practice project, which can form a complete creative ecological cycle system. Add vertical innovation thinking to practical activities to build a collaborative innovation system for cultural and creative products. Create a closed loop of the cultural and creative design industry with cultural mining, design and development, space structure, and service operations as the core, and

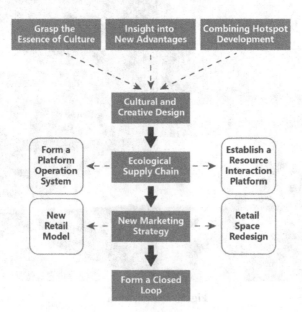

Fig. 6. Cultural and creative industry innovation system approach

establish a complete cultural and creative design and innovation system. At the same time, by loading the value of the platform and supporting the tourism base, gather a large number of individual designers, groups and companies. Use the platform to link the supply and demand sides of design, connect design and manufacturing, professional designers and universities, creativity and capital to form a complete closed loop from research to application (Fig. 6).

5   The Practice of "Design and Method of Cultural and Creative Industry Innovation System" in Promoting Social Development—Taking Songxi County, Fujian Province as an Example

Songxi County of Fujian Province was identified as a key county for poverty alleviation and development in 2012. Local fixed assets cannot bring wealth to local residents. Resources need to be combined with talents to use the "Cultural and Creative Product Innovation System Design and Method" to develop the local economy. By proposing the brand slogan of "Millennium Songxi Centennial Sugarcane", the local people used the Centennial Sugarcane to drive the Songxi regional brand. It connects urban designer

"Millennium Songxi Centennial Sugarcane" Cultural Tourism Festival   Songxi Tea House Cultural and Creative Experience Space

"Millennium Songxi Centennial Sugarcane" Cultural and Creative Product Design Competition

Fig. 7. Empowered innovation model

resources and integrates technology, design, channels and platforms to inject vitality into Songxi's characteristic products and realize the closed loop of cultural and creative value. Since 2018, empowered innovation has been carried out through the "Millennium Songxi Centennial Sugarcane" Cultural Tourism Festival, Songxi Tea House Cultural and Creative Experience Space, and tourism cultural product design competitions. Within a year, the local centennial sugarcane brown sugar sales increased by 18.7%, and Songxi green tea sales increased by 13.9%, which were reported by more than ten media including the Central Broadcasting Network and Youth Daily. With the support of national policies and schools, promoting local social and economic development through a cultural and creative product innovation system, Songxi County officially got rid of the title of provincial poor county in June 2019 (Fig. 7).

6 Conclusion

This article is based on the current status of the cultural and creative industries, and taking Songxi County, Fujian Province as an example. It develops local resources and specialty goods, reshapes regional brands, to realize multiple coordinated development of cultural industries. At the same time, research on the innovation system design of cultural and creative products, and proposed four advanced models of cultural and creative. In this way, establish a norm and model for the development of cultural and creative industries based on social development. And based on tourism cultural and creative product design, production, sales chain, etc., summarize the design method of implementability. Deeply understand the scientific connotation of culture and creative design and the requirements of practical innovation. By constructing an evaluation mechanism and quality standards, so as to realize the innovation of academic value, theoretical value and application value.

References

1. Cheng, J., Xi, L., Ye, J., Xiao, W.: The research of regional culture characteristics of tourism commodities based on cross-cultural experience. In: Rau, P.L.P. (ed.) CCD 2014. LNCS, vol. 8528, pp. 24–34. Springer, Cham (2014). https://doi.org/10.1007/978-3-319-07308-8_3
2. Huang, G., Yong, W.C.J.: An Analysis of Cultural and Creative Industries. Archives Art Family Co., Ltd., Taipei (2013)
3. Xi, L., Cheng, J., Ye, J., Xiao, W.: The effects of regional culture on user interface experience: a case study of Xin'an Hangu Guan in China. In: Stephanidis, C. (ed.) HCI 2015. CCIS, vol. 528, pp. 270–275. Springer, Cham (2015). https://doi.org/10.1007/978-3-319-21380-4_47
4. Sun, G.: Research on the Category Management in Fast Moving Consumer Goods Industry and its Application. Shanghai Jiao Tong University, Shanghai (2009)
5. Li, S., Liu, J.: Research on historic streets renovation and promotion based on cultural creativity industry: A case study of Nanluogu Lane in Beijing. Hum. Geogr. 28(1), 135–140 (2013)
6. Yang, Z.: Study on sustainable development mechanism of cultural and creative design incorporating social innovation. China Academy of Art, Hangzhou (2018)
7. Zhang, X., Hu, H., Zhang, J.: China Cultural Industry Development Report, vol. 2. Social Science Literature Press, Beijing (2011)

8. Yang, Y., Zhao, S.: an analysis of tourism cultural and creative design to promote the role of rural culture, taking rural tourism in Baodi area as an example. Art Des. **2**(04), 105–107 (2018)
9. Zhou, Y.: Study on the Application of Beijing Folk in Cultural and Creative Design. Beijing Institute of Technology Press, Beijing (2015)
10. Ding, W., Lai, H., Zhang, Z.: Design and transformation: the development path and the ten models of "the design strategy of the county plan"—Shanghai–Yangtze river delta industrial design project outsourcing services platform design county planning as an example. Design **07**, 118–120 (2014)
11. Jiang, T., Xie, F., Zhang, Y., Huang, Q.: Industries innovation system of culture and creativity: based on soft innovation theory. Forum Sci. Technol. China **09**, 34–39 (2014)
12. Wenzhi, W., Zhuang, Z.: The layout and innovation of tourism products in experience economy era–a case study on experience-exploitation of ancient village tourism product. Tour. Trib. **06**, 66–70 (2003)

How AI Systems Challenge the Conditions of Moral Agency?

Jaana Hallamaa[ID] and Taina Kalliokoski[(✉)] [ID]

University of Helsinki, 00014 Helsinki, Finland
{jaana.hallamaa,taina.kalliokoski}@helsinki.fi

Abstract. The article explores the effects increasing automation has on our conceptions of human agency. We conceptualize the central features of human agency as ableness, intentionality, and rationality and define responsibility as a central feature of moral agency. We discuss suggestions in favor of holding AI systems moral agents for their functions but join those who refute this view. We consider the possibility of assigning moral agency to automated AI systems in settings of machine-human cooperation but come to the conclusion that AI systems are not genuine participants in joint action and cannot be held morally responsible. Philosophical issues notwithstanding, the functions of AI systems change human agency as they affect our goal setting and pursuing by influencing our conceptions of the attainable. Recommendation algorithms on news sites, social media platforms, and in search engines modify our possibilities to receive accurate and comprehensive information, hence influencing our decision making. Sophisticated AI systems replace human workforce even in such demanding fields as medical surgery, language translation, visual arts, and composing music. Being second to a machine in an increasing number of fields of expertise will affect how human beings regard their own abilities. We need a deeper understanding of how technological progress takes place and how it is intertwined with economic and political realities. Moral responsibility remains a human characteristic. It is our duty to develop AI to serve morally good ends and purposes. Protecting and strengthening the conditions of human agency in any AI environment is part of this task.

Keywords: Moral agency · AI system · Human-computer interaction

1 Introduction

Human dignity and moral responsibility are the two moral features central to our view of humanity. Respect for human dignity also forms one of the cornerstones of moral action. In Immanuel Kant's words, human beings must never be treated as means only but always also as ends in themselves [11]. The basic assumption that human beings are morally responsible for their deeds makes them legally accountable. Within societies in which human rights form the core of the legal thinking, historical developments tend to be inspired by these fundamental values.

An ever-widening variety of artificial intelligence (AI) systems plays a central role in our professional, economic, and social activities. There are high hopes that, in the near

© Springer Nature Switzerland AG 2020
M. Rauterberg (Ed.): HCII 2020, LNCS 12215, pp. 54–64, 2020.
https://doi.org/10.1007/978-3-030-50267-6_5

future, autonomous and adaptive robots and AI systems will take over a diverse set of demanding or dangerous tasks. Complex webs of human–machine cooperation emerge as AI systems continuously collect information from their users and apply it as material for their learning algorithms, resulting in changes in their functioning in relation to their tasks and users.

Acting in interaction with an AI-modified environment may change the basic conditions of human agency and, therefore, affect the conditions of maintaining the intrinsic value of human dignity. In the following study, we explore how we can conceptualize the changes in human agency that a life closely tied to and connected with different types of AI are likely to bring forth.

2 Technologies Are Designed for Instrumental Uses

Artifacts and technologies are designed for instrumental uses; as such, we evaluate their goodness—that is, their suitability, usefulness, and efficiency—in terms of the functions they were designed to serve [32, 33]. If a tool is useless in its instrumental task, we may scrupulously replace it with something better. It is not morally blameworthy to treat artifacts and technological systems simply and solely as a means to an end; as such, should an artifact or technology be ill suited for its use, we need not feel guilty for abandoning them and replacing them with something better. We may lament the lost time and resources, but as consumer legislation indicates, the objects of blame are the designers or manufacturers of the artifacts rather than the artifacts themselves. If there is any harm involved in the use of an artifact, we seek human actors on which to place the blame.

Currently, we are experiencing another period of hype related to the development of AI and its applications. National governments and multinational organizations anticipate that AI will not only save the economy but also provide solutions to all sorts of problems, ranging from the climate change crisis to elderly care. These expectations seem to rely on assigning a large role to AI systems in an increasing number of fields of human activity [7, 17].

Autonomous and adaptive robots and AI systems are likely to take over a growing variety of tasks that are hazardous to human actors or so complicated that their performance involves a high probability of failure [16]. Rescue robots, for example, can accomplish life-saving actions that are too risky for human rescue workers; similarly, surgical robots can carry out an increasing number of different types of operations that require precision or durability that surpass human capacity. Most complicated calculations, data collection, and data management operations are already run by AI systems and would be impossible to perform without them. Energy, lighting, and water supply, maintenance, and delivery are also already run by AI-regulated systems [17]. The development of machine learning will multiply the number of fields that are based on AI-run procedures.

While AI helps to effectuate a vast number of human activities, it also renders human communities and societies extremely dependent on AI systems and their smooth functioning. Unlike mechanical machines, AI systems are not straightforward in their running, and the cause of their possible failure may be difficult to detect and both time-consuming and expensive to fix. The probability of responsibility gaps—that is, situations in which it becomes impossible to assign moral responsibility for perilous outcomes on any specific agent—also increases with the broader use of AI systems [8]. The view of an AI-regulated world that humans are unable to control and direct may not be just a remote dystopia.

Agency is a basic human good and closely related to the conception of dignity [10, 26, 32, 33]. Acting in interaction with an AI-modified environment may change the basic conditions of human action and, therefore, the intrinsic value of human dignity. How can we conceptualize the changes in human agency and protect the terms of human dignity? The unpredictable nature of cooperation in the AI environment involves the danger that the categories of instrumental and technical goodness [32] will overrule intrinsic moral values.

Previous moral philosophical [10] and psychological research [15, 20] shows that three features characterize human agency: ableness, intentionality, and rationality. In the following section, we use these three concepts to analyze human–AI cooperation in order to detect and explore the possible impacts of AI systems on human agency and their effects on conceptualizations of human dignity.

3 Agency and Moral Agency

3.1 Conditions of Agency

For decades, academics have studied how human–computer interaction situations— involving, particularly, the sense of control humans have over actions and their conse- quences—may change the way in which we conceptualize human agency [2, 15, 20]. Although the discussion has been in many ways insightful, the results of these studies cannot be straightforwardly applied to human interaction with AI systems, and even less so to AI with designed learning capacities.

Traditionally, human–computer interaction has been understood as a form of bilateral communication. The problem with this approach is that it disregards the features in the relationship that give rise to conceptualizing it as a cooperative situation between a single actor or a group of human agents and an AI system. From the perspective of users, AI systems appear to be environments in which they cannot foresee what will take place or how to control the environment. The unpredictable nature of moves and countermoves is accentuated in systems where human and machine partners form a cooperative collective [19]. As AI systems and their functioning become more complex with interactive elements and learning capacities, the number of problematic issues related to human–computer interaction grows.

Human beings tend to personify their environment; boats are given names, and engines are cursed at for not working properly. It is then no wonder that we attach personified characteristics to complex AI systems [1, 23]. Does our proneness to anthro- pomorphize the world in which we act mislead us, to give artifacts and technology roles and positions that will eventually make us less human? To better grasp the issue at hand, let us first discuss the conditions for calling a performing capacity "agency."

Aviation safety has improved immensely in virtue of various detection technologies and autonomous steering systems [4]. As these findings are translated into applications in the development of mass-manufactured motor vehicles, the role of human drivers is gradually decreasing. A fleet of self-driving cars in everyday use is no longer science fiction but an integral part of the prospect of improved road safety [16]. For a human being, such vehicles seem to make decisions and act upon them; as such, the question arises of whether we should view a self-driving car as an agent.

Historically, the concept of agency has been tightly tied to human beings and their capacities. There is, however, no consensus about the necessary or sufficient features defining the concept. It is safe to say that, in humans, agency is not a binary property but that its emergence takes place gradually during the physical, social, and psychological development of a child.

Even newborns, whose needs are provided for by parents and other caregivers, start to notice that what they do has an impact on those around them; for example, crying will usually summon someone to come to check on them, while gurgling or smiling will make the caregiver coo and caress them. Little by little, babies learn how to control their movements and the sounds they utter in a way that will enable them to make certain things happen [25].

The same aspects that are crucial in child development reflect two features that are central to the conception of agency. An agent must be able to do things that will, in some way, change how things are in the world. Part of these functions relates to oneself (e.g., babies learn how to put their thumb in their mouth), but more importantly, these functions can influence the outside world. Being able to affect reality is a necessary condition for agency [10]. Let us call this the "ableness condition" (for examples of the use of this term, see Morriss 2002, 80–86) [21].

The second feature related to the notion of agency that is already visible in early childhood is the purposefulness of activities [25]. Our needs must be satisfied; one's wants and wishes indicate that there is a will to change how things are in reality. Even a rudimentary sense of oneself and a vague understanding of one's abilities form a basis for intentionality. An act is based on a goal that an actor pursues, using their activity as a means by which to reach it. Achieving almost any goal necessitates performing a series of acts that, together, form the action for pursuing or realizing an end. For an activity to be a manifestation of agency, the "intentionality condition" states that the activity must be a means designed for achieving the desired end [10, 19].

Intentionality connects the aim and the action for achieving it, but this connection cannot be arbitrary. If there is no real possibility of reaching the goal or making its realization more probable, the activity is useless for furthering one's chosen end. To tie the goal to the action, agents must therefore be rational, in the minimal sense that they can discern fanciful ideas from realizable plans and have an idea of at least some of the actions that they are able to carry out. Let us call this requirement the "rationality condition" [10, 25, 30].

3.2 Features of Moral Agency

After having sketched central conditions of agency, let us consider the features of moral agency. As a starting point, we can use Thomas Aquinas's first principle of practical reason, a guiding norm of action (i.e., morality): "Bonum est faciendum et prosequendum et malum vitandum," meaning, "Good must be done and pursued and evil avoided" (Summa Theologiae I-II, 94:2) [28].

The main features central to moral agency serve as the presuppositions for the first principle of practical reason, as it is not possible to follow the norm without them. First, the principle expresses a positive and a negative norm. The positive norm exhorts the agent to do certain types of deeds and pursue certain types of ends; the negative norm tells the agent to avoid certain types of deeds and, implicitly, certain types of ends. The negative norm could also be expressed in a more categorical way by forbidding the agent to carrying out certain types of deeds and pursuing certain types of ends.

Second, morality presupposes that agents pay attention to discerning the types of actions they are supposed to do—that is, discerning good actions from those they must avoid doing, and good ends worth pursuing from those that are evil or bad. Third, agents must commit themselves to following both the positive and the negative norm in their acting as they choose the goals and means of their actions. It is the willingness to do so and to commit oneself to following the first principle of practical reason that makes an agent moral.

What Thomas Aquinas's definition does not express is the social nature of morality. An implicit presupposition in morality is that humans naturally aim at their (subjectively supposed) good and do not need any specific norm to motivate them to do so. What makes ends and deeds morally good or evil is their effect on other people and their wellbeing [26]. An important part of the social aspect of morality is that moral agents can be blamed and praised for what they do and what their actions cause. The social practices of blaming and praising indicate that the agents are being held responsible for what they do and cause by their deeds.

The central features of moral agency tie actors together into a community of other moral actors in which they are bound to each other, forming an intertwining web of relationships in virtue of the effects of their actions on each other and everyone [10]. Communities form and dissolve for various reasons; in between, they exist for some purpose that ties the members to each other and to the community [30]. Acting based on this purpose and being mutually connected create communication and meaning—a group culture that takes place in time, forming a common history for the members. In this way, belonging to and being part of any community is historically constituted [9].

"Moral responsibility" is acknowledging one's role in the moral community and committing oneself to doing one's share as a part of the whole. Being morally responsible involves moral agents identifying themselves as givers and receivers of various goods within a network of mutual interdependency. To adopt the role and viewpoint of a moral agent implies that one is willing to widen one's individual perspective and consider things from a universalizable moral point of view.

To sum up the central features of moral agency, we can say that moral agents (are willing and challenge themselves to) discern what is good from what is evil, and they commit themselves to doing and pursuing good and avoiding evil. In doing so, they commit themselves to extending their consideration not just to themselves but also to others. They identify themselves as members of a socially and historically constituted moral community within which they take and bear responsibility for their actions and the consequences of their actions. In which sense, then, can we speak of AI as having features of moral agency? Can human–AI interaction change the features of moral agency in humans?

3.3 Do AI-Systems Count as Moral Agents?

The development of AI systems has made the boundaries between instrumental technologies and human agents opaque. Human agents tend to interact more efficiently with AI systems when they perceive them to be humanlike entities. Social robots and bots developed for social contexts resemble human actors both in their functions and in their given identities: designers give names to technologies operated by social AI and share narratives of their history. Learning machines develop their own functioning. This development has led to claims that we should attribute agency to complex self-learning AI systems and assign at least partial responsibility to AI agents functioning in interaction with human agents [1, 6, 9].

Hakli and Mäkelä (2019) present a multifaceted argument against the view that AI systems are moral agents that can be held responsible for their actions. They introduce various arguments in the current discussion on the subject but maintain that not even future developments of the technology could furnish AI systems with the conditions necessary for moral agency. Their ground for arguing against extending moral responsibility—a feature central to moral agency—to AI systems and robots is that they lack—and will always lack, no matter how intricate their technology—autonomy and reflective self-control [9].

Such a view is based on Alfred R. Mele's (1995) [18] contention that both autonomy and responsibility are features that gradually develop during the lived history of an agent. It is not just the intentional attitudes, values (i.e., the view of certain behaviors as intrinsically good, or "pro-attitudes") and capacities of an agent that matter but the causal history through which they were formed. In contrast, every AI system and robot, those with in-built learning capacities included, are initially brought into existence—or produced—by someone who programmed them. It then follows that the values and preferences displayed as the pro-attitudes that direct or determine the goals of an AI system or a robot can be traced back to the initial engineering design of the system. From a moral point of view, engineering counts as manipulation that undermines moral autonomy. Even when AI systems display pro-attitudes that direct their functioning and, in this sense, simulate goal-oriented agents, their intentionality is not authentic for the reason of its origin as a programmed propensity. As such, AI systems cannot be held responsible for the outcomes of their functions and therefore cannot count as moral agents either [9].

What Hakli and Mäkelä's conclusion implies in terms of moral agency and human responsibility is that the complexity and self-learning features of machines and artifacts do have an impact on responsibility assessment, opening such considerations to responsibility gaps and making it harder to determine where both praise and blame lie. The way forward, then, is not to attribute moral responsibility to AI systems but to assess anew the nature and boundaries of human moral agency.

3.4   Is Human–AI Interaction Collective Action?

Another approach to considering whether AI systems can be held morally accountable is to examine human–AI interaction. An important part of human agency takes place in the context of multiple agents. A strong theme in an ongoing discussion concerns whether human interaction with AI systems counts as collective action involving shared responsibility [19, 27].

Whatever stance we take to the matter, AI systems and their various applications form a growing number of complex webs of human–machine systems: the AI systems continuously collect information about their users and apply it as material for their learning algorithms that again change their functioning in relation to the users, and so on.

It is hoped that AI-assisted data analysis will not only help in achieving goals set by human users of AI systems but that the systems themselves will pave the way for new findings, such as in medical diagnostics and the prevention of social issues [3]. Different types of data records could be used to improve both health and social wellbeing on a national, and even global, level. Not all researchers are equally enthusiastic about such prospects. Some claim that this new type of technology (i.e., AI systems) necessarily changes our view of humanity and morality and, therefore, also changes our conceptual terms of human action [24, 31].

Hakli and Mäkelä [9] consider whether human–machine interaction could be viewed as joint or collective action, as they discuss the possibility of holding AI agents at least partially responsible for the outcomes and consequences of their workings. According to their argument, the causal history of an AI system makes it implausible to regard the system as a moral agent capable of moral responsibility. They refute Latours's (2005) [13] view that collective agents, some of which are human beings and some artifacts, could be ascribed partial responsibility.

Hakli and Mäkelä back up their claim by referring to the philosophy of social action. Here, the definition of "joint action" reads as follows: two or more individuals perform a joint action if each of them intentionally performs an individual action but does so with the (true) belief that in performing the action, they will jointly realize an end that each of them has. The definition ascribes joint responsibility to the individuals partaking in the action. The notion of joint action implies that every group member is individually morally responsible for the joint action and its outcomes but also individually responsible, jointly and interdependently with the other members of the group [9, 30]. As AI systems cannot be held morally responsible agents, they also do not fulfill the conditions of joint responsibility.

Could programming AI systems to perform morally favorable preferences serve as a counter claim to the negative view concerning responsibility and moral agency in AI systems? Let us consider a simple example. There are AI-monitored systems for assigning doctor appointments to patients. Such a system's designers can program the system to discern the patients whose need for medical examination or care is urgent from those whose condition allows for a longer waiting time before the appointment. It is possible to include different types of parameters in the preference algorithm, such as the patients' age, social status, and indicators concerning vulnerability, to increase the moral sensitivity of the algorithmic principles concerning the administration of consultation times.

Adding such features into the algorithm would improve the monitoring of appointments in medical care in terms of fairness—which is a moral characteristic—but it would not make the AI system morally responsible for placing the patients in a preferential order. Those who feel they have unjustly been left waiting in the patient queue would, rightly, blame those who designed the code for the monitoring system rather than the AI application itself.

From the viewpoint of an AI system, the programming that produces the morally favorable features is in no way different from any other piece of code in its algorithm. It would be justified to call such an appointment monitoring application a well-functioning AI system, but it would not make the system a moral agent.

So far, there are no convincing arguments for assigning moral agency or responsibility to AI systems or robots, and if Hakli and Mäkelä are correct, there are conceptual reasons that prevent us from doing so notwithstanding any future developments in AI. For this reason, human–AI interaction is not genuinely or fully collective action.

4 Moral Agency Within Human–AI System Interaction

Let us now scrutinize how acting within an AI system or AI-monitored scheme may affect the notion of human agency by relying on the three characteristics of agency featured in Sect. 2 (i.e., the ableness condition, the intentionality condition, and the rationality condition).

Technology is always designed to serve some purpose; it is therefore never value neutral. The ends that artifacts are supposed to fulfill or further become visible through their uses and hoped-for effects. Technology plays a causal, not an intrinsic, role even in interactive settings between humans and AI systems [9].

As part of technology, AI is designed to assist human beings in their various enterprises. Machines are there to do the work that is too hard—in any sense of the word—for people. During the era of industrialization, motorized engines have replaced human labor in a growing number of tasks. Machines take care of chores that involve the use of physical power or repetitive actions. When machines take over human tasks, at each phase of the process, there are people who lose their jobs and positions. In the beginning of the process of industrialization, the development of technology replaced those doing manual labor. However, during recent decades, AI systems have begun to replace the skilled human workforce; in the coming years, an increasing number of professions are likely to become futile.

So far, machines have not become superior to human labor in terms of its most valued human features, and it has been consoling to think that human beings still take care of the highest functions of any activity and that machines only perform auxiliary tasks. The development of autonomous and self-leaning AI systems changes this. For example, the improvement of aviation safety now strongly relies on lessening the impact of human perception and decision making in managing an aircraft [12]. The same development is already in progress for sea and land traffic [14, 17]. The latest findings show that AI-based screening programs are able to detect tumors that doctors do not notice [3].

There is no prospect any time soon of a limit to the things that AI systems can do better than human agents. So, at what point does widening the range of technology become a form of paternalism that inhibits people from performing tasks for the sake of protecting their own interest? It is likely that being second to a machine in an increasing number of fields of expertise will affect how human beings regard their own abilities, and the use of self-learning AI will accelerate this process. The more human beings—who get ill and grow old, err and fail—can be replaced by robots and AI systems, the more they will look like a source of unnecessary cost.

Even artists may notice that robots can take over their jobs. Musical robots can be programmed to have a touch for any genre of music; from a large set of data about popular hits, they can produce an endless variety of new ones [23]. There is no characteristic as such that could be called "creativity" that would help to discern a human-composed piece from one produced by AI [29]. Linguistic programs are already versatile enough to complete many tasks, and the speed with which translation machines have improved predicts that, someday, AI systems will master linguistic skills that have traditionally been thought to make people unique. There are fewer and fewer human abilities that make human beings superior to machines. What, then, is the locus of human agency?

AI-regulated environments also modify the conditions of human intentionality. Unknowingly to the users, systems run by algorithms fix the available goals or set them in a preferential order. For example, recommender algorithms used by social media platforms, music and movie streaming companies, online marketing agencies, and dating applications, collect user data such as previous online behavior and preferences and make recommendations or dictate what content users see [16]. Consequently, the users may cherish false expectations, pursue unachievable goals, or disinvest their time, money, and energy, just because they are not fully aware of the algorithmic terms of the system.

Such developments are often unintentional; it is not a part of the concept of AI to curb human agency but to enhance it. The effects of activities in AI-regulated environments are unpredictable, but they may have wide-ranging implications in terms of how we perceive ourselves and treat other humans as intentional agents. There is already psychological evidence that performing computer-assisted tasks weakens the experience of being fully in charge of one's actions [2]. People show different personality traits when communicating with an AI than when interacting with another human [22]. Cooperating with AI and robots may therefore deteriorate the conditions that accentuate the feeling of moral responsibility in human agents.

Reliable, relevant, and wide-ranging information is important for any meaningful and responsible—and, in this sense, rational—decision-making process. Multinational giants such as Google, Facebook, and Twitter apply algorithms that have a huge impact on national and international politics and economies, as well as on ordinary people's private lives [17]. The ways in which the systems direct and manage the flows of information may remain a mystery even to their designers. There are already ample examples of how algorithms can be prejudiced in terms of the sources of available knowledge and how they can boost disinformation, thereby distorting the rational decision-making processes of human agents.

As the above examples show, it is not difficult to find cases of AI-regulated environments in which even the present use of AI technology impairs the conditions of human agency. It is, therefore, not exaggerating the risks to fear that such developments may weaken the terms on which our sense of human dignity and the institutions that support it rely.

5 Conclusions

There is already evidence of the effect that cooperation with AI systems has on humans' perception of the conditions of their agency. Great expectations concerning the instrumental benefits of AI-enhanced activities and their economic value direct the development of the AI industry. This may overshadow the implicit effects that living and working in various AI environments have on human agency and moral responsibility.

Listing ethical principles for AI development and use is not enough; they are abstract ideals, hard to apply in actual design and use. It is necessary, therefore, to obtain a deeper understanding of how technological progress takes place and how it is intertwined with economic and political realities in different types of societies and in the global community.

No matter how skillfully, diligently, and creatively AI systems can be designed to work, moral responsibility remains a human characteristic. It is therefore our duty to develop AI to serve morally good ends and purposes. Protecting and strengthening the conditions of human agency in any AI environment is part of this task.

Acknowledgement. This research was supported by the project Ethical AI for the Governance of Society (ETAIROS, grant #327352) funded by the Strategic Research Council (Academy of Finland).

References

1. Brożek, B., Janik, B.: Can artificial intelligence be moral agents? New Ideas Psychol. **54**, 101–106 (2019)
2. Ciardo, F., De Tommaso, D., Beyer, F., Wykowska, A.: Reduced sense of agency in human-robot interaction. In: Ge, S.S., et al. (eds.) ICSR 2018. LNCS (LNAI), vol. 11357, pp. 441–450. Springer, Cham (2018). https://doi.org/10.1007/978-3-030-05204-1_43
3. Esteva, A., Kuprel, B., Novoa, R., et al.: Dermatologist-level classification of skin cancer with deep neural networks. Nature **542**, 115–118 (2017)
4. FAA: Operational Use of Flight Path Management Systems. Final Report. FAA (2013)
5. https://www.faa.gov/aircraft/air_cert/design_approvals/human_factors/media/oufpms_rep ort.pdf. Accessed 28 Jan 2020
6. Fossa, F.: Artificial moral agents: moral mentors or sensible tools? Ethics Inf. Technol. **20**, 115–126 (2018)
7. Grace, K., Salvatier, J., Dafoe, A., Zhang, B., Evans, O.: Viewpoint: when will AI exceed human performance? Evidence from AI experts. J. Artif. Intell. Res. **62**, 729–754 (2018)
8. Gunkel, D.J.: The Machine Question: Critical Perspectives on AI, Robots, and Ethics. MIT Press, Cambridge (2012)
9. Hakli, R., Mäkelä, P.: Moral responsibility of robots and hybrid agents. Monist **102**(2), 259–275 (2019)

10. Hallamaa, J.: Yhdessä toimimisen etiikka [The Ethics of cooperation]. Gaudeamus, Helsinki (2017)
11. Kant, I.: Grundlegung zur Metaphysik der Sitten. Schriften zur Ethik und Religionsphilosophie. Erster Teil. Wissenschaftliche Buchgesellschaft, Darmstadt (1983)
12. Landry, S.J., Karwowski, W.: Advances in Human Factors and Ergonomics Series: Advances in Human Aspects of Aviation. CRC Press LLC, London (2012)
13. Latour, B.: Reassembling the Social: An Introduction to Actor-Network Theory. Oxford University Press, New York (2005)
14. Leikas, J., Koivisto, R., Gotcheva, N.: Ethical framework for designing autonomous intelligent systems. J. Open Innov. Technol. Mark. Complex. 5(1), 18–30 (2019)
15. Limerick, H., Coyle, D., Moore, J.W.: The experience of agency in human-computer interactions: a review. Front. Hum. Neurosci. 8, 643 (2014)
16. Lin, P., Abney, K., Jenkins, R. (eds.): Robot ethics 2.0: From Autonomous Cars to Artificial Intelligence. Oxford Scholarship Online (2017)
17. Marr, B.: Artificial Intelligence in Practice: How 50 Successful Companies Used AI and Machine Learning to Solve Problems. Wiley, Chichester (2019)
18. Mele, A.R.: Autonomous Agents: From Self-Control to Autonomy. Oxford University Press, New York (1995)
19. Misselhorn, C.: Collective agency and cooperation in natural and artificial systems. In: Misselhorn, C. (ed.) Collective Agency and Cooperation in Natural and Artificial Systems. PSS, vol. 122, pp. 3–24. Springer, Cham (2015). https://doi.org/10.1007/978-3-319-15515-9_1
20. Moore, J.W.: What is a sense of agency and why does it matter? Front. Psychol. 7, 1272 (2016)
21. Morriss, P.: Power. A Philosophical Approach, 2nd edn. Manchester University Press, Manchester (2002)
22. Mou, Y., Xu, K.: The Media inequality: comparing the initial human-human and human-AI social interactions. Comput. Hum. Behav. 72, 432–440 (2017)
23. Needham, J.: We are the robots: is the future of music artificial? FACT Magazine. https://www.factmag.com/2017/02/19/we-are-the-robots-could-the-future-of-music-be-artificial. Accessed 28 Jan 2020
24. Ollila, M.-R: Tekoälyn etiikkaa [Ethics of artificial intelligence]. Otava, Helsinki (2019)
25. Rochat, P.: Others in Mind: Social Origins of Self-consciousness. Cambridge University Press, New York (2009)
26. Smith, C.: To Flourish or Destruct: A Personalist Theory of Human Goods, Motivations, Failure and Evil. The University of Chicago Press, Chicago (2015)
27. Strasser, A.: Can artificial systems be part of a collective action? In: Misselhorn, C. (ed.) Collective Agency and Cooperation in Natural and Artificial Systems. PSS, vol. 122, pp. 205–218. Springer, Cham (2015). https://doi.org/10.1007/978-3-319-15515-9_11
28. Thomas of Aquinas: Summa Theologiae. Pars prima et prima secundae. Marietti, Torino (1952)
29. Thompson, Clive: What will happen when machines write songs just as well as your favorite musician? Mother Jones. https://www.motherjones.com/media/2019/03/what-will-happen-when-machines-write-songs-just-as-well-as-your-favorite-musician. Accessed 28 Jan 2020
30. Tuomela, R.: The Philosophy of Sociality: A Shared Point of View. Oxford University Press, Oxford (2007)
31. Visala, A.: Tekoälyn teologiasta [Remarks on theology of artificial intelligence]. Teologinen Aikakauskirja 123(5), 402–417 (2018)
32. von Wright, G.H.: The Varieties of Goodness. Routledge and Kegan Paul, London (1968)
33. Zdravkova, K.: Reconsidering human dignity in the new era. New Ideas Psychol. 54, 112–117 (2019)

Deep Fake and Cultural Truth - Custodians of Cultural Heritage in the Age of a Digital Reproduction

Susan Hazan[✉]

Digital Heritage, Jerusalem, Israel
Susan.hazan@gmail.com

Abstract. How can we tell if we are looking at authentic video footage – a video that has not been manipulated, or altered in any way [1]? How do we know that a news item reflects a truthful perspective? Sadly, in an age of pervasive digital reproduction we can't – we simply go through life hoping not to be lied to, spinned or even scammed – in an era of deep fake we simply no longer have the skillsets required to be able tell truth from falsity. And spun we are. Politically spin has become the norm for many of us and, while we may choose to go to a cinema for a moment of welcome knowing escapism, when we seek to walk a simple path of veracity the sound track of our lives is constantly punctured by advertising, political pundits and news articles strung before us across am endless stream of information that confuses and contradicts truth and the lies; and more often or not confounds all that is in between.

But we *do* need to be able to separate the real from the false for ourselves; especially when delivered digitally. We rely on information, daily news, and social interaction online, but do we really have the competency to be able to discern fact from fiction while peering through our screens throughout the day. The 100-dollar question is who are the purveyors of the truth? In reality there is more than often more than one perspective on any given issue; even the physical object in a museum may informed by more than one narrative in its provenance. But at least in a Museum you know that there is a professional group of fact-checkers behind the scenes who have done their very best to deliver reliable information to their public; the curators, conservators and educators whose role it is to interpret collections based on their own academic background. 'This is 'as truthful' as it gets, and while the act of telling a truth is highly complex and often disputed, we do tend to place our trust in a museum when we visit an exhibition [2]. While the museum traditionally represents a place of 'true' discovery, once collections are delivered digitally; abstracted from their physical envelope, can we presume that have the power to transmit those same eternal truths? This chapter will explore these polar opposites of deep fakery and cultural truth through two case studies, a 'visit' to the California-based Museum of Jurassic Technology and an overview of the Damien Hirst works in *The True Artist* exhibition held at the Haifa Museum of Art during the summer of 2019. Museums, like libraries and archives are institutions known for their devotion to the truth through the representation of unique objects; each with their own embedded memories; each telling their own story. These are not the typical places we would expect to struggle with notions of and falsity and fiction;

© Springer Nature Switzerland AG 2020
M. Rauterberg (Ed.): HCII 2020, LNCS 12215, pp. 65–80, 2020.
https://doi.org/10.1007/978-3-030-50267-6_6

reality and fantasy but when they do take up the challenge, we have plenty to learn from them.

Keywords: Cultural heritage · Fakery · Deep fake · Jurassic technology · Big data · Facial recognition · Surveillance capitalism

1   Deeply Fake, Deeply Disturbing

Have you noticed how many things we're now describing with the word 'deep'? Deep mind, deep medicine, deep war, deep fake, deep surveillance, deep insights, deep climate, deep adaptation. We keep applying this adjective 'deep' to describe our newfound abilities to hit targets in medicine or war, to identify leverage points in research, to find needles in haystacks of data or to fake any face, voice or image with an accuracy or at a depth and with an impact that was simply unimaginable just a decade ago. (Thomas Friedman, 2019) [3].

The adjective 'deep' denotes all that is embedded below our horizons. They are the invisible articulations of big data that only machines can read and are already affecting the decisions and actions that are permeating our lives in so many ways. This could be harmless algorithms that invite us to purchase something that has been informed by our profiles as something we would probably like to purchase; a series of [fake] articles that appear spontaneously in our newsfeed; or even a welcome automated cross check of medications interactions we take informed by the intelligent agent in the automated pharmaceutical system. We seed data about our personal and professional selves at an alarming rate, often unaware that our information has very deep, yet unwitting con-sequences in our lives such as; unknowingly appearing on a no-fly list – that is until we get to the airport; refusal of health benefits or the purchase of health insurance at a higher premium for smokers [4] or the result of a background check in the local bank that determines whether we are eligible, or not-eligible for a mortgage. These decisions were traditionally processed by humans; gatekeepers schooled in the proficiency of their expertise and have now been given over to algorithms who invisibly crunch the chunks of big data required to open the gate. But in an alarming exposé of the business model that drives the digital world Shoshana Zuboff argues that this seeding of personal and professional data poses a whole new challenge; processes she has called "surveillance capitalism". *It works*, she argues *by providing free services that billions of people cheer-fully use, enabling the providers of those services to monitor the behaviour of those users in astonishing detail – often without their explicit consent* [5].

Apart from the obvious concerns we might have about our personal well-being, there are just as critical concerns at a societal level. These are deep underlying process that are unseen to us and in reality, managed by a very few. The gap between our inability not only to access this kind of information, but to control it, is forever growing and well-illustrated in the movie *I, Daniel Blake*, 2016 [6], directed by Ken Loach where both protagonists; widower Daniel Blake, a 59-year-old joiner from Newcastle, and Katie, a struggling single mother whom Daniel befriends lack the digital skills and knowhow to navigate the myriad social systems needed to literally survive. But as Zuboff warns, digital natives avail themselves with unbridled enthusiasm to these systems; especially with the all the free services available to everyone, but, by the end of the day, do we all really fully understand the results of these immeasurable interactions? Zuboff forewarns …..

> In nearly every case the agents of institutionalization present their novel practices as if they are one thing, when they are, in fact, something altogether different. The realpolitik of commercial surveillance operations is concealed offstage while the chorus of actors singing and dancing under the spotlights holds our attention and sometimes even our enthusiasm. They sweat under the stage lights for the sake of one aim: that we fail to notice the answers or, better yet, forget to ask the questions: Who knows? Who decides? Who decides who decides? (Zuboff, 2019, P.231).

This is the crucial question and while I wouldn't even try to unravel the alarming repercussions that are looming on our global horizons – this is far too complex for a single author and a single chapter, I would like to unpack a more manageable question from my own field of expertise - who is responsible for cultural truths? And as Zuboff posits in her own research – who decides who decides? And in the management of culture; and especially digital culture, who are the actors who get to determine the truth? And this, I would argue is where custodians of cultural heritage need to step in, and especially in an age of digital reproduction where everything is reduced to a flat screen or a matrix of billions of points on a cloud.

Never before has reality been so easily reproducible. The deep fake seepage into our daily lives is often intended to beguile as, for example, with the self-promoting Trump tweet of a dog. October 2019, Trump posted a photo of himself awarding a medal of honor to the military dog that was involved in the raid that killed the Islamic State leader Abu Bakr al-Baghdadi [7], and in addition he appears to have declassified its name. This seemingly innocuous tweet may have slipped past our critical capabilities to disserve real from false – the image is so cute that it immediately enchants us. But it was, in fact an altered version of an Associated Press photograph of Trump awarding the medal of honor in 2017 to James McCloughan, a retired army medic who was honored for saving the lives of 10 people during the Vietnam war. According to a New York Times follow up [8] to the tweet, *Mr. McCloughan, 73, who had not seen the image before a reporter sent it to him, said that he interpreted it as Mr. Trump recognizing the dog's heroism. He certainly was not offended and laughed when he compared the two images.* Even though McCloughan took the fakery in good nature, the traction that Trump gained from the tweet was at the expense of the hero, the readers (as well as the dog)!

One could argue that we have already honed the critical faculties for telling fake from un-fake after decades of Photoshop artifacts, and even before that what we have experienced from the composite image created by photographic montage. The trouble is we don't yet have the capacity for critical evaluation of deep fake video. The most popular example of this kind of deception is usually the Obama manipulated video often touted as an emblematic illustration of deep fake. Researchers at the University of Washington produced a photorealistic Barack Obama [9] and by putting words into his mouth had the former President sharing ideas that were not his in the making. This particular video was not created for nefarious reasons, but rather because the researchers had found it interesting to enforce Obama's lip-synced statements to create more convincing photorealistic results and was, in fact, authored as an experiential artifact to be published in a Siggraph 2017 paper [10].

Since the early days of video manipulation, the sector has taken to these technologies with great zeal and building on years of computer-generated imagery (CGI) in animation and Sci-fiction films we are now beginning to welcome digital (human) actors onto the silver screen. Some of these CGI actors, however, are contemporary manifestations of long dead actors. For example, according to the New Scientist in a January 2020 article [11] *late in 2019, it was announced that US actor James Dean, who died in 1955, will star in a Vietnam war film slated for release later this year. Dean will be recreated on screen with CGI based on old footage and photographs, with another actor voicing him.* This opens up major ethical and financial questions both for the heirs of the estates as well as the public, and, in addition to these conundrums is that the eerie quality of these virtual humans is often disquieting. This weirdness factor was a major issue when the young Carrie Fisher was recreated for the film *Rogue One*, Lucas Film Ltd/Walt Disney Company Ltd. The uncanny quality was mostly notable around the eyes and mouth which people found disturbing and were not sure how to relate to a screen character which was not quite animated, yet not quite human.

Beyond the silver screen, digital artifacts may represent not only people but buildings and even entire neighborhoods; generating, yet again, a whole new range of a conceptual and ethical challenges and creating new kinds of realities. Once reduced to a point cloud, such as with light detection and ranging (LiDAR) laser scanners, every object, building or monument can be instantly re-purposed, morphed into 3D CAD models that can be manipulated and stored for posterity; and presented as a source for re-visualization; persuasive animation; creative rendering; and entirely new entities that can be disseminated throughout the mass media and directed to persuade you and I of new realities. It is as easy as baking a cake. Throw the ingredients into a cooking pan, stir for a few minutes and bake until done. But the gaps between original and clones are permeable, and the possibilities of infidelities that can creep into the system are challenging.

In the same way we need to navigate fakery in still and moving images, and, in order to recognize these kinds of interventions we have to produce new tools for forensic evaluation. With not only virtual dogs being conjured out thin air thin air but also (dead) people, and celebrities at that, we have to find ways to manage our surroundings and learn how to determine fact from fiction. New skill sets are being developed by professionals and academics around the world, for example at the L'Ecole Polytechnique Fédérale de Lausanne (EPFL), in Switzerland [12],

> The game between deepfake creators and the experts who try to catch them is one of cat and mouse. And the deepfakers tend to be one step ahead, since they can come up with an almost unlimited number of new contents that the experts must then try to detect. As soon as word gets out that deepfakes can be identified because people's mouths don't move naturally, for example, a malicious programmer will develop an algorithm to remedy that problem (Cécilia Carron, EPFL).

Also based in the EPFL is the Center for Digital Trust (C4DT) a research team startup that provides expertise in multimedia signal processing based on their many years of experience in detecting fake images. According to Olivier Crochat, Executive Director of the C4DT [13], *detection of image and video forgery to fight against malicious manipulations is clearly one of the applications where Artificial Intelligence helps to regain trust.*

Barak Obama lip-syncs, Trump's agile dog, and James Deans' digital resurrection, which all look disturbingly real have all been (re)born as a result of artificial intelligence and have since been amplified and multiplied exponentially across social media. Although we might take it all as a humorous prank the risk of commercial fraud is more than real....

The biggest fear that most people face vis-a-vis deepfakes is that they will be used to steal their identity. But the threat actually runs much deeper – fraudulent contents can also be used to deceive manufacturers, insurers, and even customs officials. For instance, goods can be digitally added to or removed from a cargo ship before it leaves the dock, or transactions could be approved using photos that have been counterfeited. *(*Cécilia Carron, EPFL CH-1015 Lausanne, 20.09.19).

Perhaps when we wake up to the fact that there may be a risk of fraud resulting in serious financial, or personal loss, more people might have to stand up and take notice. In 2019 the BBC took up the gauntlet and partnered with tech firms join forces to fight disinformation [14]. The educational program was set up and drew-up new plans including:

- Early warning system: creating a system so that organisations can alert each other rapidly when they discover disinformation that threatens human life or disrupts democracy during elections. The emphasis will be on moving quickly and collectively to undermine disinformation before it can take hold.
- Media education: a joint online media education campaign to support and promote media education messages.
- Voter information: co-operation on civic information around elections, so there is a common way to explain how and where to vote.
- Shared learning: particularly around high-profile elections.

These kinds of pro-active steps have been echoed around the world. In Finland, and other Nordic countries high school children are being taught new kinds of skillsets [15] in digital literacy and critical thinking in order to be able to discern misinformation and hoaxes, and help them confront these challenges by teaching them fact-checking methods. The Italian-based social awareness project, *Parole O_Stili* [16] focuses their efforts against the use of hostile language and supporting school children to redefine the way they handle online interactions and encourage them to choose their words carefully and responsibly.

They caution ...

Words are extremely powerful. They express thoughts, transmit knowledge, encourage cooperation, build visions, enchant, heal, and foster love. But words can also hurt, offend, vilify, deceive, destroy and marginalise, dehumanising their speakers. We must therefore choose words well and wisely, both in the real world and online. Since the Internet and social networks are virtual places where real people meet, we need to question who we are and how we should communicate and behave when we use them.

According to *Parole O_Stili* the Manifesto of Non-Hostile Communication is a commitment of shared responsibility to create a respectful and civilized Internet space that represents us and offers a sense of security and it is a charter of 10 practical principles to guide online behaviour. The Manifesto has been translated so far into 42 languages, including Emoji [17] introducing the principles of critical thinking that is both fun and relevant. In addition to the Manifesto, there are educational materials available with training events for teachers and educational courses for students. The original contributors to *Parole O_Stili* included approximately 300 professional business and political communicators, teachers, entrepreneurs, influencers and bloggers: a diverse group of passionate people sharing a desire to make the Internet a better, less hostile place, and one of respect and civilized behaviour.

These are encouraging inroads both in increasing awareness about the deep fake environment that is permeating and polluting our social, and educational ecosystem as well as developing tools for critical thinking for students and teachers. But who can act as gatekeepers on a global scale to monitor and modify the trillions of data points created every second? Who can verify the truth in a point cloud? Architects and urban planners who depend on its fidelity, might be concerned if there was a powercut with the resulting loss of data but might not even be aware of a bug in in the machine that subtly created undetectable falsities. What would happen to those CAD drawings that were committed to the next step – to physical reality if these falsities become invisibly embedded in silent practices? Our reliance on mechanical and digital processes is a reflection of our era. Medical diagnostics imaging [18] some claim overrides human frailty with so much big data to crunch. When it comes to big data, us highly limited humans don't even stand a chance.

The examples of false realities described above are may have been inspired with creative and benevolent intentions; less so if by mistake but, they are especially concerning when deep fakery is driven by profit. To return to the main theme of this chapter, the management of cultural heritage, we need to look to the gatekeepers of cultural heritage and ask the same question that Zuboff asks - *Who decides? Who decides who decides?* (Zuboff 2019, p. 231). What are the custodians of our heritage doing about deep fakery, for example in the Museum world?

2   The Museum as Truth

In an age of "alternative facts" and contested versions of history, museums provide the material evidence of our shared past and can use that evidence to host debate and narratives on a range of topics from the historical to the contemporary and, in so doing, may prompt reflection and critical interpretation. Museums help us negotiate the complex world around us; *they are safe and trusted spaces for exploring challenging and difficult ideas* [19] and, therefore, the ideal setting of discourse for these ideas. The following section will discuss two such opportunities: one an exhibition based on Damien Hirst's fantastic works, and the other a wholly fictitious, yet totally physical museum (Fig. 1).

2.1 Somewhere Between the Lies and the Truth Lies the Truth

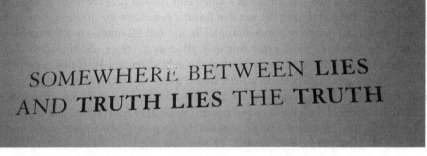

SOMEWHERE BETWEEN LIES AND TRUTH LIES THE TRUTH

Fig. 1. Damien Hirst exhibitions wall text © Susan Hazan, 2019

Describing the 2019 exhibition, presented by Haifa Museum of Art, *Fake News Fake Truth*, exhibition curator, Svetlana Reingold commented… *The radical blurring of boundaries between fiction and reality, in a world dominated by post-truth politics, is at the focus of this cluster of exhibitions. The works presented in it emphasize that truth itself has become just one option amongst a wide variety of perspectives, in an age of open conflict between those attempting to formulate a solid order, and their vocal opponents.* Reingold goes on to explain –

The exhibiting artists use diverse strategies of deception and fabrication – such as the use of fictitious figures, pranks, and interventions in real life by means of impersonation. These practices are intended mostly to illuminate the loss of faith in the media culture, particularly under the decisive influence of online communication. They train us in skepticism and doubt, yet also encourage a discussion geared towards the possibility of regaining our trust.

Artists listed in this exhibition included *200 works from 48 local and international artists* [20] *and this chapter will focus on the exhibition within an exhibition that included Damien Hirst's works in Treasures from the Wreck of the Unbelievable.*

The exhibition and the video documentary that accompanied it was originally presented at the Venice Biennale in 2017, conceived as a riveting spectacle but not particularly well received by everyone. As reported for Hyperallergic in reference to Damian Hirst's Venice debut of his exhibition, Tiernan Morgan wrote:—*Damien Hirst's Treasures from the Wreck of the Unbelievable is not an exhibition. It's a showroom for oligarchs. Comprised of about 190 works, including gold, silver, bronze, and marble sculptures, the show is undoubtedly the most expensive artistic flop in living memory*

[21]. The Biennale exhibition was located in two of Venice's prestigious museums, the Punta Della Dogan and the Palazzo Grassi, with 189 works in bronze, marble, malachite, rock crystal, silver, gold. The back story told of a non-existent collector and his sunken treasure hidden in a shipwreck, ready to be hauled to the surface by, nonother than Damien Hirst himself—or at least funded by him. The treasures were said to be dated from the first or second century, the belongings of a former slave who became fabulously wealthy and was named Cif Amotan II. The name is an anagram of "I am fiction."

In the online Netflix mockumentary video clip version [22] the artist proclaims he discovered amazing objects in the sea *that has not been seen for lifetimes* – something he professes to be *completely unbelievable*! In the full 90-minute mockumentary we learn that the Venice biennale exhibition took 10 years to create, and some $65 million to produce but was not the expected comeback exhibition that Hirst had been hoping for. The much more modest Haifa exhibit staged many of the key works, but in spite of the downscaling it was just as unbelievable. The exhibition opened with a video of the fictional discovery of the ancient shipwreck off the coast of East Africa, that supposedly took place in 2008, setting the scene and making for a very convincing entrée into the exhibition (Figs. 2 and 3).

Fig. 2. Recovering Micky, Photo of video, *Treasures from the Wreck of the Unbelievable,* released on Netflix, © Susan Hazan, 2019

Fig. 3. *Micky Mouse*, resin coated to appear bronze and encrusted with aquatic debris, © Susan Hazan, 2019

Hirst reportedly spent $65 million to stage a fictional shipwreck and the complex recovery operation of the antique sculptures, he claimed were ancient artifacts found at sea. Divers pull a barnacle-encrusted Micky-Mouse-like form from the seabed, to carefully stow it away amongst the rest of the precious cargo; of their long-lost treasures; including a monkey apparently sculpted in gold, and Medusa, snakes twisting sinuously from her head looking more like diver's air pipes.

Arranged in the Haifa gallery visitors could make the obvious connection from the sea-drenched artworks to the meticulously shiny objects perched on their exquisitely lit pedestals. Micky Mouse's corals and barnacles had been sculpted to perfection, making the trompe d'oeil sculpture highly persuasive (Figs. 4 and 5).

Fig. 4. Golden Monkey, © Susan Hazan, 2019

Fig. 5. The newly discovered *Medusa*, Photo of video in the gallery, *Treasures from the Wreck of the Unbelievable,* released on Netflix, © Susan Hazan, 2019

Through this lavish display of art and artist, Damien Hirst tricks us into believing the veracity of our own eyes, as well as institutional framing of a work of art in a museum – exploiting our implicit trust; yet confounding the truth in such institutions. Sadly, at the end of the day, what he is saying is that ultimately the truth no longer exists anywhere, anymore and no institutional framing can persuade us otherwise.

In Hist's own words ... *Its unbelievable to start with, but that is what makes it believable.*

2.2   Faked Reality - the Museum of Jurassic Technology

The notions of truth and veracity in the Museum are inherently bewildering. As inscribed in legislation, and through their traditions of integrity and open-door policy, museums assure their public of their authority to collect, conserve and exhibit the cultural heritage on behalf of their public. Through this social contract we are also required suspend our disbelief as soon as we walk through the door and tune into the narratives spread out before us; taking in the concrete proof of the physical object as the undeniable evidence that convinces us of the storyline. Confounding the very notion of the integrity of the museum to tell *the truth*, however, the Museum of Jurassic Technology in Los Angeles, California tells another story. Promoted as an educational institution dedicated to the advancement of knowledge and the public appreciation of the Lower Jurassic, their narratives do not fall into any known museum category [23]. This is David Wilson's Museum, whose institutional mission reads (Fig. 6):

> Like a coat of two colours, the Museum serves dual functions. On the one hand the Museum provides the academic community with a specialized repository of relics and artefacts from the Lower Jurassic, with an emphasis on those that demonstrate unusual or curious technological qualities. On the other hand, the Museum serves the general public by providing the visitor with a hands-on experience of "life in the Jurassic"

> Wilson, the Museum of Jurassic Technology website [24]

The street address, 9341 Venice Blvd., Culver City, CA, 90212, attests to its material presence, and by its portrayal in Lawrence Weschler's book, published in 1995, *Mr. Wilson's Cabinet of Wonder: Pronged Ants, Horned Humans, Mice on Toast, and Other Marvels of Jurassic Technology* [26]. The publication not only described the Museum of Jurassic Technology but also the history and the role of museums. According to information on the museum's website, the museum is open four days a week: Thursdays from 2:00 PM to 8:00 PM., and Fridays, Saturdays and Sundays from 12:00 noon to 6:00 PM, which I include here as the evidence of a physical museum, in that the museums seems to keep regimented opening hours. I must, however, admit that I gathered this information from the website, and have not had an opportunity to actually visit the museum myself. In this case I have to double my trust; firstly, that the museum actually exists, and secondly that the museum website is telling the truth. I have since been assured by more than one person that the place does exist and does keep regular opening hours.

On the Museum website, Mary Rose Canon, (her sepia photo is included) recounts the history of the museum in an essay that describes the founders of the museum, *The Thums: Gardeners and Botanists.* Canon provides information on the lives of two central figures in the history of the Museum, Owen Thum and Owen Thum the Younger, who have been

Fig. 6. , Museum of Jurassic Technology Facade - 9341 Venice Blvd. in Culver City, CA [25]

variously identified in the narrative as living in Xenia, Ohio, Rodenta, Nebraska, and in Plat, Nebraska in 1919. Their obscure history tells a tale of the Thum's botanical gardens, their gardening careers and their passion for collecting, and alludes to the Tradescants [27] with a specific reference, noting how during the ten years in which the Thums had inhabited South Platt, their house and garden had become renowned as *Thum's Ark* (an echo of the Tradescant Ark?), throughout the county and, in fact, the entire state [28].

The artefacts on display are no less confounding. The exhibition in the Thum Gallery, *Tell the Bees… Belief Knowledge and Hypersymbolic Cognition,* offers a rambling narrative that starts with Alexander Fleming's remedy, his extraordinary fungal cure (penicillin), and explains how Fleming had spent years investigating a range of home remedies, folk lore, and vulgar remedies. In Weschler's account, he dons a pair of headphones in the company of Mr Wilson, and sits down to the audio portion of the slide show that accompanied the exhibition, to listen to Fleming's own voice, or what Wescher describes as 'a Scottish voice of raspy, wire-recorder quality'. Weschler evidently was impressed with the first-rate production qualities of the tape, 'blending subtle music, crisp sound effects and a solid-seeming narrative' (1995: 100). *The go tell the bees* tale goes on to recount *the numerous healing traditions, pharmaceutical advances, superstitions, and folk remedies that all seem to relate (in the anonymous narrative's terminology) to vulgar knowledge, which, the voice of authority in the recording laments, has since been ghettoized and denigrated.*

The message of the narrative resembles the Hellenistic Greek tradition of tying a piece of funeral crepe to a beehive and the practice of bringing 'funeral sweet hives for the bees to feed upon' (see museum website). According to the Hellenistic Greek/*Jurassic* tradition, in this way, the bees are then invariably invited to the funeral and have, on a number of recorded occasions, seen fit to attend. The narrative ends in a plea: *Like the bees from which this exhibition has drawn its name, we are individuals, yet we are, most surely, like the bees, a group, and as a group we have, over the millennia, built ourselves a hive, our home, not to turn our backs on this carefully and beautifully constructed home especially now, in these uncertain and unsettling times. (*Museum of Jurassic Technology website narrative). You can, of course purchase the *Tell the Bees* T-shirt from the museum shop for less than $20 [29] (Fig. 7).

Fig. 7. *Tell the Bees* T-shirt, Museum shop, Museum of Jurassic Technology shop

The permanent collections in Gallery I includes the *Megolaponera Foetens*, the stink ant of the Cameroon of West Central Africa. Besides the photograph of the very weird looking insect, the visitor is beguiled by another strange tale… the stink ant, one of the very few to produce a cry audible to the human ear, while looking for food, is infected by inhaling a microscopic spore from a fungus of the genus *Tomentella*, which causes changes in the ant's patterns of behaviour. Driven on by the growth of the fungus, the ant climbs a tree where it impales the plant with its mandibles and waits to die. The fungus continues to consume first the nerve cells and finally all the soft tissue that remains of the ant. After approximately two weeks, a spike appears from what had been the head of the ant (Fig. 8).

Fig. 8. *Megolaponera Foetens*, the stink ant of the Cameroon of West Central Africa [30]

According to the Museum label, this spike is about an inch and a half in length and has a bright orange tip heavy with spores, which rain down onto the rain forest floor for other unsuspecting ants to inhale. Interestingly, in a *Google* search on the *stink ant,* apart from the direct links to the Museum of Jurassic Technology, several links lead to well organized entomology and biology websites, which all in turn link to the Museum of Jurassic technology and the one and only reference to the *Megolaponera Foetens.* (This does not in any way preclude either the existence of the ant or its strange tale, but in an effort to forage for further information, I did write to the museum for further information on this point, but, as yet, received no answer). Exhibiting the bizarre, paranormal, beguiling, and merely baffling, Mr. Wilson's museum no doubt captures the imagination of all who visit; the blur between the astonishingly real and the fabulously fake, however, is likely to leave the visitor dizzy and perplexed.

3   Conclusion

While The Museum of Jurassic Technology could be read more as a highly elaborate and sophisticated form of performance art, in that it deliberately sets out to beguile, in doing so, it also confounds the visitor as it transgresses with impunity the very integrity of a museum – the institutional mission to tell the truth. Just in the same way that Hirst frames his unbelievable artefacts in the gallery as true fiction, the visitor to the Museum of Jurassic Technology finds himself alternating between truth and fake; scratching his or her head and wondering whether any of this could possibly be true. *And it's that very capacity for delicious confusion,* Wilson suggests, *that may constitute the most blessedly wonderful thing about being human.* (1995: 60) However, the poetic license granted to art and artists, however, takes into account the crossing of boundaries, and in doing so is able to frame these kinds of performances as a 'stretching' of reality, rather than the 'representation of reality,' as the traditional museum would demand.

In conclusion, learning to decipher truth from deep fake demands new skills and new critical capabilities, such as those being taught to our children in Scandinavia and Italy. New kinds of research that is evolving in companies and universities has begun to confront technological challenges in combating deep fakery is also crucial. At the same time while the museum traditional frames physical realities, and canonical chronologies under its' institutional umbrella, in the case of artistic creatively there is more leverage to act, confident of the stamp of integrity and authority that is almost universally bestowed upon collections and exhibitions in, and by the museum.

The museum, in fact, has a vital role to play in mounting exhibitions to enable these kinds of conversations and opens up discourse by physically locating these kinds of exhibitions in the museum gallery where 'truth' is of prime value. This chapter has considered deep fake in binary opposition to cultural truth, but of course, things are more complicated than that. When an artist or even an entire museum crosses that Rubicon, alarm bells start ringing, especially when custodians of cultural heritage take action in the age of a digital reproduction.

References

1. Video manipulations. https://en.wikipedia.org/wiki/Video_manipulation
2. Golding, V.: Museums and truths: the elephant in the room. In: Fromm, A.B., Golding, V., Rekdal, P.B. (eds.) Museums and Truth. Cambridge Scholars Publishing, Cambridge (2014)
3. After the Flat World, Comes the Deep World: A Conversation with Thomas Friedman. https://www.haaretz.com/us-news/.premium-thomas-friedman-for-our-deep-world-to-win-u-s-and-china-must-rise-toget-1.7914948
4. How a smoker can buy health insurance, Economic Times (2019). https://economictimes.indiatimes.com/wealth/insure/health-insurance/how-a-smoker-can-buy-health-insurance/articleshow/69953046.cms?from=mdr
5. Zuboff, S.: The Age of Surveillance Capitalism: The Fight for a Human Future at the New Frontier of Power. Public Affairs-Hachette Book Group, New York (2019)
6. I Daniel Blake (2016). https://en.wikipedia.org/wiki/I,_Daniel_Blake
7. Trump tweets fake photo of Isis raid dog, and appears to declassify its name, Guardian Online, 30 October 2019. https://www.theguardian.com/us-news/2019/oct/30/trump-latest-news-tweet-dog-isis
8. Trump Tweets Faked Photo of Hero Dog Getting a Medal, New York Times, 30 October 2019. https://www.nytimes.com/2019/10/30/us/politics/trump-dog.html?auth=linked-google1tap
9. Fake Obama created using AI tool to make phoney speeches. https://www.bbc.com/news/av/technology-40598465/fake-obama-created-using-ai-tool-to-make-phoney-speeches
10. Synthesizing Obama: Learning Lip Sync from Audio. http://grail.cs.washington.edu/projects/AudioToObama/

11. What are the ethics of CGI actors – and will they replace real ones? New Scientist, January 2020. https://www.newscientist.com/article/2230205-what-are-the-ethics-of-cgi-actors-and-will-they-replace-real-ones/#ixzz6BYTQH000

12. EPFL develops solution for detecting deepfakes https://actu.epfl.ch/news/epfl-develops-solution-for-detecting-deepfakes/

13. Center for Digital Trust, (C4dt) EPFL, Lausanne, brings together 12 founding partners, 34 laboratories, civil society, and policy actors to collaborate, share insight, and to gain early access to trust-building technologies, building on state-of-the-art research at EPFL and beyond. https://www.c4dt.org/

14. Fake news: BBC and tech firms join forces to fight disinformation, BBC online, September 2019. https://www.bbc.com/news/technology-49615771

15. How Finland is fighting fake news - in the classroom. https://www.weforum.org/agenda/2019/05/how-finland-is-fighting-fake-news-in-the-classroom/

16. Parole O_Stili. Social awareness project against the use of hostile language. https://paroleostili.it/?lang=en

17. Translations - Parole Ostili.https://paroleostili.it/translations/?lang=en

18. Medical imaging, Wikepedia. https://en.wikipedia.org/wiki/Medical_imaging

19. The Museums Taskforce report and Recommendations, Museums Association, UK (2016). www.museumsassociation.org https://www.museumsassociation.org/download?id=1246

20. Haifa Museum of Art: Fake News Fake Truth. https://www.hma.org.il/eng/Exhibitions/6964/%22Fake_News_%E2%80%93_Fake_Truth%22

21. Damien Hirst's Shipwreck Fantasy Sinks in Venice https://hyperallergic.com/391158/damien-hirst-treasures-from-the-wreck-of-the-unbelievable-venice-punta-della-dogana-palazzo-grassi/

22. 'Treasures from the Wreck of the Unbelievable' released on Netflix https://vimeo.com/248348102

23. Museum of Jurassic Technology http://www.mjt.org

24. The Museum of Jurassic Technology. http://www.mjt.org/themainpage/main2.html

25. Museum of Jurassic Technology. https://commons.wikimedia.org/wiki/File:Museum_of_Jurassic_Technology_Facade_-_9341_Venice_Blvd._in_Culver_City,_CA.jpg

26. Weschler, L.: Mr. Wilson's Cabinet of Wonder: Pronged Ants, Horned Humans, Mice on Toast, and Other Marvels of Jurassic Technology, Random House (1995)

27. John Tradescant the Elder (1570s – 15–16 April 1638), and father of John Tradescant the Younger, was an English naturalist, gardener, collector and traveller. The Tradescant Ark was the prototypical "Cabinet of Curiosity", a collection of rare and strange objects, that became the first museum open to the public in England, the Musaeum Tradescantianum. https://en.wikipedia.org/wiki/John_Tradescant_the_Elder

28. The first Museum in Britain was John Tradescant's Ark in Lambeth. The Tradescants (father and son) were plant hunters and collectors of Curiosities. The Museum included natural history objects as well as antiquities, and ethnography. The collection was eventually, and somewhat controversially, inherited by Elias Ashmole, who set up the Ashmolean Museum in Oxford using Tradescant's Ark

29. Tell the Bees: T-shirt from the Museum shop. https://www.mjtgiftshop.org/products/tell-the-bees-t-shirt

30. Megolaponera Foetens: the stink ant of the Cameroon of West Central Africa. http://www.mjt.org/exhibits/foundation_collections/stink_ant/stinkant.html

Experiencing the Conditions of Trust: A Practice-Based Exploration of Trust Formation Through an Artificial Society Environment

Michael Heidt[1]([⊠]) and Andreas Bischof[2]

[1] GeDIS, University of Kassel, Pfannkuchstraße 1, 34121 Kassel, Germany
`mrbheidt@gmail.com`
[2] Chair Media Informatics, Chemnitz University of Technology,
Straße der Nationen 62, 09111 Chemnitz, Germany
`andreas.bischof@informatik.tu-chemnitz.de`

Abstract. Blockchain systems promise to establish novel patterns of interaction within the spheres of commerce, governance, politics, and art. They allow for novel practices of contract formation, facilitating transactions in a quick, transparent, and verifiable manner. Their ability to establish self-enforcing smart contracts would likely lead to fundamental changes within everyday interpersonal interactions. Specifically, it would likely upend the position of *trust* within existing social practices. In this paper, we explore this problematic through the medium of generative art, embedded into a practice-based research strategy. The approach employs artificial societies as generative readymades which ground and inform practices of speculative design.

Keywords: Blockchain · Trust · Practice-based research · Critical technical practice · Artificial societies · Generative art

1 Introduction

Innovative technologies allow for new systems of practice to supersede established ones, thus changing not only the set of skills and actions required to operate respective devices but also causing shifts in our attitudes and mental processes. We as technology makers thus bear the obligation not to limit ourselves to the design of useful artefacts but to also reflect on the whole range of consequences brought about by the establishment of new practice.

Social practices in themselves are complex structures, comprising both directly observable actions and inner attitudes and mental states [51,58]. Changes in systems of practice by extension stretch across the realms of bodily and mental activities, thereby affecting our attitudes and ways of relating to each other. Consequently, the potential transformatory effect of technologies such as Blockchain-based smart contract systems or artificial intelligence extends far beyond their immediate impact on everyday practices.

© Springer Nature Switzerland AG 2020
M. Rauterberg (Ed.): HCII 2020, LNCS 12215, pp. 81–94, 2020.
https://doi.org/10.1007/978-3-030-50267-6_7

Hence, it is reasonable to assume that induced fundamental changes in practice are only possible in a process of co-evolution with profound transformations on the level of attitudes. Anticipating possible patterns of technology use is thus only possible when imagining coextensive changes on the levels of mental processes, emotions, and sentiments. This is already apparent in the disruptive aspirations of those technologies themselves while complicating our efforts to sensibly negotiate their potentials and dangers.

In order to respond to these challenges, technology designers have to account both for the future directedness of artefacts in question and for the far reaching character of effected social transformations. This creates novel methodological problems for design processes which strain the boundaries of existing design methods. In response to these intricacies, practice-based design and speculative design have emerged as promising methodological candidates. Digital art offers productive ways to render these transformations observable, thus making them accessible to reflection and discourse.

In this paper, we describe an exploration of the aforementioned problematic through the medium of generative digital art. The designerly process discussed explores the interrelationship of the social phenomenon of *trust* and Blockchain technology. We furthermore detail the methodological position occupied by respective artefacts within an overarching process of practice-based research.

2   Blockchain, Trust, Trustlessness

Our research is driven by an interest in possible relationships between the technology of the Blockchain and the social phenomenon of trust. We will give a brief account of both objects in isolation before describing their interrelatedness.

2.1   Blockchain Technology

A Blockchain acts as a distributed database, allowing secure transactions in the absence of trusted intermediaries [49]. Every system participant is able to verify the legitimacy of every transaction made while being able to inspect the full history of transactions conducted within the system. No actor within the network is able to forge information or disregard information once it has been approved. Crucially, blockchain systems allow for the transference of digital property in a manner ensuring that transfers are "safe and secure, everyone knows that the transfer has taken place, and nobody can challenge the legitimacy of the transfer" [1].

The class of values which can be transferred within a Blockchain backed system encompasses "birth and death certificates, marriage licenses, deeds and titles of ownership, educational degrees, financial accounts, medical procedures, insurance claims, votes, provenance of food" [62].

2.2   Trust

Trust is a crucial ingredient in many contemporary social practices, indeed its presence is integral to the coherence of the social fabric. According to moral philosopher Annette Baier "[w]e inhabit a climate of trust as we inhabit an atmosphere and notice it as we notice air, only when it becomes scarce or polluted." [3].

Trust as a social mechanism evolves in response to vulnerabilities inhering within social situations: Whenever we turn our back to others, expect them to keep their word, to care for loved ones, return lended items or respect a compact, we expend trust.

In a climate of utter unpredictability, trust would not be possible. Nor is it possible without avowal of vulnerability. In the absence of vulnerability, no trust relationships are able to emerge. "The truster sees in his own vulnerability the instrument whereby a trust relationship may be created" ([43, p. 48]). An exchange based on trust comes into play where subjects realise their vulnerability to others and respond in a way signalling confidence into a trustee not to exploit this state of affairs.

Trust thereby facilitates acceptance of vulnerability, and thus allows exchanges and situations to unfold in which participants are susceptible to future harm by others: It makes it possible for us to fall asleep on a train, allows us to rely on directions obtained from strangers, store spare keys with a neighbour, place our child in the care of a friend, leave the house unarmed and unarmoured.

Crucially, vulnerabilities can be induced through lack of information: We might need to ask for directions in a foreign city or airport, be offered food we are not familiar with or rely on a friend's counsel when filling out immigration forms.

Contracts can be construed as device for making explicit arrangements which otherwise would be covered by more amorphous and implicit expectations for trust. They stipulate what is expected and allow for the provision of damages, should a contracting party renege on their commitment. Contracts, however, still need to be enforced should the underlying trust relationship break down. If the other party shows itself unwilling to comply with stipulated provisions, mechanisms such as courts come into play.

Smart Contracts

Blockchain systems introduce a socially consequential innovation by allowing for the operation of *smart contracts* [8,61]. Conflicts are decided not by means of human arbitrators but by encoding conditions in the medium of formal language. The respective mode of operation endows smart-contracts with a self-enforcing capability, automatically and securely transferring assets once certain formalized criteria are met. As an example, the smart lock of a rental apartment might automatically grant access to a guest once payment is detected; a smart fridge within the apartment might automatically charge the guest for any item consumed during the stay. Crucially, the integrity of smart-contract operation is guaranteed by the same mechanisms used for verifying transactions within the Blockchain. Hence, they cannot be hacked and their outcome is open for inspection to all parties involved. Consequently, systems built using smart contracts are described as being *trustless* [11,60].

3   Method

We approach the developed problematic of *trust* in relationship to Blockchain technology by means of a practice-based research strategy. In order to render artistic practices productive within this research context, we propose to combine methods of practice-based research and speculative design. This is in line with studies such as that of Elsden et al. [16] who explicitly call for combining design-led, speculative, and artistic methods in order to account for the specific set of challenges posed by Blockchain systems.

3.1   Practice-Based Research

Practice-based research is a methodology for achieving knowledge through the careful conduct of a constructive designerly or artistic process [56]. Following the principle of "Knowing through Making" [45], concepts are formed and explored through continuous engagement with constructed artefacts, paired with ongoing processes of reflection and observation.

The approach adopted here calls for continuous practices of writing and discussion [27,30] in order to hone a conceptual apparatus able to describe the object of study, *trust*, in its relationship to blockchain technology.

The practice-based process itself is structured in an iterative manner [28]: It continuously develops a conceptual apparatus which informs communications within individual research activities. Within each iteration clear expectations are articulated, in order to facilitate surprise in line with received practices of doing practice based research [55,56].

The practice-based process subsequently extends and revises its conceptual apparatus in order to further penetrate into the object of study. The extended apparatus facilitates novel observations, allows the process to discover facets of its objects not previously describable. At the same time, novel concepts create a coextensive lack within the object itself: they induce novel questions, highlighting aspects of the object which are not known and whose uncharted character was not expressible before the concept itself injected itself into the practice based process.

3.2   Speculative Design

Speculative Design [15] and Research through Design Fictions [6,7,59] are methodological tools for extending the reach of design activities into the realm of the future.

They are employed in the context of the present research project in order to account for the future directedness of research questions within the project.

4   Conceptual Apparatus

Trust as a social phenomenon appears to be as ubiquituous as it is hard to account for. Difficulties in grasping the nature of trust persist despite considerable interdisciplinary efforts to come to terms with the concept [23]. It has been described as conceptual "anomaly" [35] defying attempts of subsuming it into preexisting discursive frameworks. At the same time, trust by no accounts constitutes a novel phenomenon. Its evolution is seen to be temporally coextensive with civilization itself [54], while there is a long history of philosophical interest and sustained academic treatment of the topic [48].

In order to do justice to the phenomenon, the practice based process necessarily has to draw on a range of seeminlgy incommensurable references. Consequently, seemingly antagonistic discourses have to be brought into dialogue in order to effect an effective interplay of conceptual elements. There are unique challenges when accounting for formal objects such as Blockchain structures or artificial societies in relationship to the social phenomenon of trust. Especially, relating concepts stemming from the realm of computing with those received from the fields of sociology and philosophy poses challenges.

4.1 Complexity and Complication

In order to effect a critique regarding the capabilities and limitations of artificial societies within a practice-based research process, we have to secure the conceptual conditions for describing their specificity. To this end, we draw on the conceptual differentiation of *complexity* and *complication*.

The notion of complexity provides a first intellectual bridge, able to connect seemingly disparate discourses. It departs from a systems theoretic perspective. Sociologist Niklas Luhmann provides an account of *trust*, identifying it as a specific mechanism for reduction of social complexity [43].

Firstly, complexity in itself presents conceptual challenges. As a concept complexity stretches disciplinary boundaries; the signifier is known within the domains of psychology, computer-science, human-computer-interaction, sociology, science and technology studies, among others. As goes without saying, such a diverse pattern of intellectual proliferation does not reproduce without effecting equivoctions and ambiguities in usage: Computational complexity theory [25,63] might understand the concept very differently from sociological systems theory [42], science and technology studies [36,38], or design theory [64].

However, as a conceptual starting point, the concept remains useful. Where it is not accompanied by clear or congruent concepts, it at least triggers associations relating to relevant notions, which subsequently can be employed in order to bootstrap a discussion process.

4.2 Complication

Science and technology studies scholar Bruno Latour proposes distinguishing between *complexity and complication*: Complicated phenomena can be analysed in the form of a countable set of variables, while complex phenomena either consist of non-countable sets of variables or resist description through variables altogether [36,37].

Latour introduces complexity as a specific need for coordination: A complex situation forces us to take into account a large number of variables simultaneously

[36, 233]. ""Complex" will signify the simultaneous presence in all interactions of a great number of variables, which cannot be treated discretely" ([36, p. 233]).

Complexity is hence seen as characteristic of forms of social integration based on continuous interaction and negotiation. *Complication* on the other hand, refers to a process decomposable into a limited set of discrete variables, which, in principle, can be treated successively. "By contrast, we'll call "complicated" all those relation[s] which, at any given point, consider only a very small number of variables that can be listed and counted" [37, p. 30]. It is not significant whether relevant operations are indeed performed sequentially or in parallel, but that they can, in principle, be performed in sequence, without interfering with one another. Examples of complicated situations can be found in bureaucratic processes such as scheduling or in scripted repetitive interactions such as buying stamps from a postal clerk [37, pp. 30–31][36, pp. 233–234].

Distinguishing complexity and complication in this manner, allows for a characterisation of computing level processes as well as social complexity, employing a theoretical vocabulary already received within the field of HCI [4,5,10,19,20].

It has to be stressed, how Latour's approach contains an implicit valuation of complexity and complication. While he points out how evaluation of contemporary social structures entailed a development from complexity to complication, complex phenomena are repeatedly referred to as rich, while complicated procedures are associated with bureaucratic processes.

This construal further substantiates the role of Blockchain artefacts as complicating material frames. In their capacity of imposing regularity in the form of repeatable patterns of action, they formulate a complicated response to the problematic of trust.

5   Materiality

There has been renewed interest into questions of materiality, across the spheres of interaction design [14,24,32,52], sociology, political theory, cultural studies, philosophy [9], and art. The latter can be read as counterreaction to earlier 20th century developments of abstracting from the material qualities of art objects [41]. Generally, the turn to material can be read as counterreaction to intellectual movements such as post-structuralism and cultural formations such as postmodernism which focussed on underlying discursive structures, whereas treating objects as surface effects.

Practice-based research strategies naturally align themselves with a focus on materiality [33][46, p. 87], for practices of making implicitly always already depend on an understanding of material. Within the context of the practice-based process, the materialities of Blockchain structures were conceptualised based on notions of *digital materiality*.

5.1   Digital Materiality

One of the most influential concepts of digital materiality was formulated by Leonardi [39,40]. Leonardi shifts emphasis away from the realm of the physical, instead focussing on questions of practical instantiation and significance. No ontological difference exists between physical and formal artefacts, they are material insofar as they make a difference, insofar as "they matter". This allows a discussion of digital artefacts on par with other objects of study, for the only relevant question is which kind of impact a relevant artefact has on observable practice.

Blockchain structures thus become material through their remodulation of practices. Their material impact on trust expresses itself by displacing or reconfiguring practices of trusting. The materialization of blockchain systems thus can be thought as gradual proliferation of trustless systems which render trust obsolete or by effecting a changed position for mental attitudes of trust within emerging systems of practice.

However, while situated firmly within the practice paradigm, Leonardi's characterisation cannot be immediately related to a practice-based process concerned with construction of digital artefacts. Leonardi's is the perspective of social research, observing the effects of digital artefacts, not one of crafting them. Within the context of digital art production, we thus relate Leonardi's concept to positions developed by digital artists and researchers Nake and Grabowski [50].

In their account, material is conceptualised as that what offers resistance. The materiality of digital artefacts is *experienced* when creating them, through their recalcitrance. Software or systems of formal rules are material since they offer resistance to our efforts to shape them. Resultingly, work is required to bend them into the shapes required for interactive artefacts. Digital materiality is involved when work is expended in order to shape digital structures. The resulting concept of materiality is in line with Deleuzian conceptions of resistance as primary [12]. It thus aligns well with respective new materialist approaches to creative research [33].

5.2 Speculative Methods and Materialist Approaches

Conceptually, the notions of speculation and materialism appear to be at odds. While speculation appears to mark the emancipation of ideas from their immediate surroundings, the material turn effects a highlighting of the material conditions of technology development.

6 Generative Readymades: Artificial Societies of Practice

Artificial societies (AS) constitute agent based computational models that facilitate the simulation of social dynamics over time [17, 22].

Artificial Societies as Agents of Practice-Based Research

Artificial societies do not immediately present themselves as natural candidates for inclusion into processes of practice-based research. They might appear as self-contained structures, separating formal rule systems from systems of practice surrounding them. However, they are the result of productive continued interrelationship between creative and research practices.

Since their inception, artificial societies have been employed in order to ground predictions regarding future social transformation. Apart from their history in the field of generative art [2], they have been employed in order to study market behaviour [18], opinion dynamics [26], or the formation of political identities [44]. Simulated dynamics however always have to be embedded into critical processes of discussion for their complexity necessarily cannot compare to that of actual global social systems.

Through their projective character, artificial societies allow for future directedness. At the same time, the inner consistency of the simulation prevents discussion processes from descending into unfounded speculation, helps to detect bias, while providing novel impulses and facilitating surprise.

6.1 Simulations Studied

In order to inquire into the role of trust within emerging systems of Blockchain related practices, we incorporated artificial societies into the practice-based process. In [34] Holtz develops a model for evolution of practices that serves as generative ready-made within the practice-based process.

According to the approach by Holtz [34], individuals are treated as bearers of practices, while practices are first-order citizens within the simulation. Following Shove and Pantzar [58], and Røpke [53], Holtz models three levels of practice within the simulation: *material, meaning,* and *competence.*

On the basis of practice theoretic modelling, requisite conditions for the success of Blockchain based practices can be formulated. In order for Blockchain systems to become a viable source for instantiation of practices:

- the *material* requirements of respective practices have to be met,
- individuals have to combine actions with respective *meaning* of Blockchain linked actions,
- individuals need to possess adequate levels of *competence* with respect to the practice in question.

Simulated processes such as habituation and materialization allow for characteristic patterns of practices to emerge as objects of observation and discussion (see Fig. 1). Within a creative research context, modelled societies can in turn inform processes of narrativization and scenario building.

6.2 Phases

Burn-In. Simulations usually exhibit a *burn-in* phase at the beginning in which strong habits have not yet developed. Thus, simulated agents make deliberate choices, matching their competence with material. Coherence is low, while the model exhibits high dynamism. There is frequent change on the level of material.

Through an often non-linear increase in habituation, deliberate choice is gradually replaced by habitual action. With respect to Blockchain related dynamics, the burn-in can be used to pose the question whether current patterns of Blockchain adoption fit the simulated burn-in dynamics or not.

Development. The burn-in phase produces conditions in which the distribution of materials remains comparatively stable. Coherence is high. Individuals act habitually, with occasional occurences of deliberate action. However, there are occasional occurences of deliberate action. Subsequent adaptions of material can further stabilise existing clusters.

Lock-In. Not all models culminate into a pattern of stable clustering. In the context of certain models (e.g. those with a low number of materials), clustering remains low while overall coherence is high.

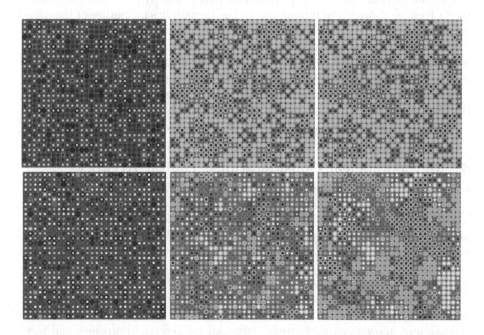

Fig. 1. Two simulation runs exhibiting a different number of materials. The top row depicts a simulation containing 2 materials. The bottom row depicts a simulation containing 5 materials. The leftmost grid in each row depicts the initial state. The state at $t = 200$ is shown in the middle, while the rightmost grid depicts the state at $t = 10000$. Each cell within the grid shows a material component by virtue of a coloured circle. Colours refer to individual materials. Coherence is visualised by virtue of background brightness: a minimum brightness background refers to a coherence level of 0 while a maximum brightness background refers to a coherence of 1. For a detailed explanation of underlying modelling dynamics, refer to [34]. (Color figure online)

7 Related Work

There is no shortage of artistic works referencing the Blockchain, for the technology constituted one of the more fashionable topics before becoming mainstream.

The `terra0` system builds a "self-owning" forest, able to reproduce itself through Blockchain technology [57]. Through smart contracts, the forest generates revenue by selling licenses to log trees, thereby compensating for running costs. It provides social commentary on ideas connected to Blockchain technologies in the context of an artistic project. The self-referential nature of the system (selling parts of itself) points towards the problematic of complexity while highlighting the economic implications of Blockchain technologies.

Bittercoin [21] "The World's Worst Bitcoin Miner" serves to illustrate the computational work embodied within Blockchain systems. The system consists of a mechanical calculator performing computations as dictated by Bitcoin's Blockchain protocol. Results are printed on paper. The system does not constitute a feasible approach to mining due to the incredibly slow nature of the computation. Instead it renders Blockchain's formal procedures tangible by virtue of mechanisation. It thus points both to the materiality of Blockchain technologies while facilitating critical perspectives through implicit reference to phenomena such as the enormous energy consumption of the Bitcoin system.

Di Battista et al. describe a system for visualization of flows within the Bitcoin system [13].

McGinn et al. describe visualizations of Bitcoin transaction patterns [47].

8 Methodological Considerations: Digital Artworks and Practice-Based Research

The digital artwork designed occupies a specific position within the overarching process of practice-based research. It functions as discursive reference point, allowing for observations to be made and predictions to be related to simulated structures.

Despite the exploratory and creative character of processes of art creation, when conducted in the context of practice-based research processes it is of paramount importance to formulate clear expectations. Only clearly articulated expectations allow researchers to be surprised by observed outcomes and new data [29,31,56].

8.1 Materiality of Artificial Societies

In order to develop an artificial society, makers have to craft formal material into an adequate shape. Not any rule based system will lend itself to requisite processes of interpretation, even if processs of simulation and interpretation at times appear to be only loosely coupled. Furthermore, the artificial society does not only consist in its formal rule-based components. In order to exist as artificial society, signifiers have to be attached that allow for interpretation of created dynamics as social processes.

Resistance thus occurs on multiple levels: Formal materials exhibit resistance while makers try to find serviceable configurations. The semiotic material gives rise to resistance of its own, for interpretations are confronted with the task of relating complex social processes with complicated formal simulations.

8.2 Role of Artworks

Artworks can point towards the possibility of a world in which the constitutive vulnerability of thinking and feeling subjects no longer appears as troubling. Likewise they can paint the picture of a world in which technology has become a means for disavowal of vulnerability.

The specific function of a digital artwork might be to escalate the constitutive antagonism between the compulsory function of formal methods and the emancipatory potentials of technologies in which these methods are embodied. Understood in this manner, the artwork would have to give an account of both the precarious pleasure of subjugating oneself under the rule of algorithm and formal procedures and the desire to transcend its trammels into the world of complexity.

Artificial societies are an especially interesting candidate for expressing this problematic due to the tortuous relationship they exhibit between complexity and complication. Situated firmly within the terrain of complication they want to shed light on the complex.

Their failures are thus as artistically productive as their successes: If the simulation of practices and the coordinate simulation of trust fails, this might tell us something substantial regarding our capacities to predict social dynamics. At the same time, a success in modelling trust can point towards a suspicion that what we thought was complex already has become complicated.

9 Outcome: Artificial Societies as Method of Inquiry

Generative artworks in the form of artificial societies allow for future scenarios of practice to be experienced. They render predictions tangible and serve to illustrate otherwise abstract hypotheses regarding the future status of social phenomena such as *trust*. Accordingly, they can stimulate imaginative activities within paradigms such as speculative design.

At the same time, the inner consistency of the simulation prevents discussion processes from descending into unfounded speculation, helps to detect bias, while providing novel impulses and facilitating surprise. Paired with a principled application of the practice-based research paradigm artificial societies thus constitute a productive approach to inquiries into future systems of practice.

Acknowledgments. This work was supported in part by the Andrea von Braun Foundation, Munich, under the grant "Blockchain – A Practice-Based Inquiry Into a Future Agent of Social Transformation".

References

1. Andreessen, M.: Why bitcoin matters. New York Times **21** (2014)
2. Annunziato, M., Pierucci, P. Towards artificial societies. In: Proceedings of the Third International Conference on Generative Art (2000)
3. Baier, A.: Trust and antitrust. Ethics **96**(2), 231–260 (1986)
4. Berger, A., Heidt, M.: Exploring prototypes in interaction design – qualitative analysis & playful design method. In: Proceedings of the International Association of Societies of Design Research Conference 2015 - Interplay, Brisbane, Australia 2015
5. Berger, A., Heidt, M., Eibl, M.: Conduplicated symmetries: renegotiating the material basis of prototype research. In: Chakrabarti, A. (ed.) ICoRD 2015 – Research into Design Across Boundaries Volume 1. SIST, vol. 34, pp. 71–78. Springer, New Delhi (2015). https://doi.org/10.1007/978-81-322-2232-3_7
6. Bleecker, J.: Design fiction: a short essay on design, science, fact and fiction. Near Future Laboratory 29 (2009)
7. Blythe, M.: Research through design fiction: narrative in real and imaginary abstracts. In Proceedings of the SIGCHI Conference on Human Factors in Computing Systems, CHI 2014, pp. 703–712. ACM, New York (2014)
8. Buterin, V.: A next-generation smart contract and decentralized application platform. White Paper (2014)
9. Coole, D., Frost, S.: New Materialisms: Ontology, Agency, and Politics. Duke University Press, London (2010)
10. Cordella, A., Shaikh, M.: Actor-network theory and after: what's new for IS research. In: European Conference on Information Systems 2003, Naples, Italy, June 2003
11. Dannen, C.: Introducing Ethereum and Solidity. Springer, Berlin (2017). https://doi.org/10.1007/978-1-4842-2535-6
12. Deleuze, G.: Foucault. University of Minnesota Press, Minneapolis (1988)
13. Di Battista, G., Di Donato, V., Patrignani, M., Pizzonia, M., Roselli, V., Tamassia, R.: Bitconeview: visualization of flows in the bitcoin transaction graph. In: 2015 IEEE Symposium on Visualization for Cyber Security (VizSec), pp. 1–8, October 2015
14. Doering, T.: Material-centered design and evaluation of tangible user interfaces. In: Proceedings of the Fifth International Conference on Tangible, Embedded, and Embodied Interaction - TEI 2011, p. 437 (2011)
15. Dunne, A., Raby, F.: Speculative Everything: Design, Fiction, and Social Dreaming. MIT Press, Cambridge (2013)
16. Elsden, C., Manohar, A., Briggs, J., Harding, M., Speed, C., Vines, J.: Making sense of blockchain applications: a typology for HCI. In: Proceedings of the 2018 CHI Conference on Human Factors in Computing Systems, CHI 2018, pp. 458:1–458:14. ACM, New York (2018)
17. Epstein, J.M., Axtell, R.: Growing Artificial Societies: Social Science from the Bottom Up. Brookings Institution Press, London (1996)
18. Filatova, T., Parker, D., Van der Veen, A.: Agent-based urban land markets: agent's pricing behavior, land prices and urban land use change. J. Artif. Soc. Soc. Simul. **12**(1), 3 (2009)
19. Fuchsberger, V.: Generational divides in terms of actor-network theory: potential crises and the potential of crises. In: Online Proceedings of the 7th Media in Transition Conference. MIT, Cambridge (2011)

20. Fuchsberger, V., Murer, M., Tscheligi, M.: Human-computer non-interaction: the activity of non-use. In: Proceedings of the 2014 Companion Publication on Designing Interactive Systems, DIS Companion 2014, pp. 57–60. ACM, New York (2014)
21. Garrett, M., Catlow, R., Skinner, S., Jones, N. (eds.): Artists Re: Thinking the Blockchain, 1st edn. Liverpool University Press, London (2018)
22. Gilbert, N., Conte, R.: Artificial Societies: The Computer Simulation of Social Life. Routledge, Abingdon (2006)
23. Grøn, A., Welz, C. (eds.): Trust, Sociality, Selfhood. Religion in Philosophy and Theology. Mohr Siebeck, Tübingen (2010)
24. Gross, S., Bardzell, J., Bardzell, S.: Structures, forms, and stuff: the materiality and medium of interaction. Personal Ubiquitous Comput. **18**(3), 637–649 (2014)
25. Hartmanis, J., Stearns, R.E.: On the computational complexity of algorithms. Trans. Am. Math. Soc. **117**, 285–306 (1965)
26. Hegselmann, R., Krause, U.: Opinion dynamics and bounded confidence models, analysis, and simulation. J. Artif. Soc. Soc. Simul. **5**, 3 (2002)
27. Heidt, M.: Examining interdisciplinary prototyping in the context of cultural communication. In: Marcus, A. (ed.) DUXU 2013. LNCS, vol. 8013, pp. 54–61. Springer, Heidelberg (2013). https://doi.org/10.1007/978-3-642-39241-2_7
28. Heidt, M., Berger, A., Bischof, A.: Blockchain and trust: a practice-based inquiry. In: Nah, F.F.-H., Siau, K. (eds.) HCII 2019. LNCS, vol. 11588, pp. 148–158. Springer, Cham (2019). https://doi.org/10.1007/978-3-030-22335-9_10
29. Heidt, M., Bischof, A., Berger, A.: Interactional aesthetics of blockchain technology. In: Nah, F.F.-H., Siau, K. (eds.) HCII 2019. LNCS, vol. 11588, pp. 137–147. Springer, Cham (2019). https://doi.org/10.1007/978-3-030-22335-9_9
30. Heidt, M., Kanellopoulos, K., Berger, A., Rosenthal, P.: Incommensurable writings - examining the status of gender difference within HCI coding practices. In: Marcus, A. (ed.) DUXU 2015. LNCS, vol. 9187, pp. 196–205. Springer, Cham (2015). https://doi.org/10.1007/978-3-319-20898-5_19
31. Heidt, M., Kanellopoulos, K., Pfeiffer, L., Rosenthal, P.: Diverse ecologies – interdisciplinary development for cultural education. In: Kotzé, P., Marsden, G., Lindgaard, G., Wesson, J., Winckler, M. (eds.) INTERACT 2013. LNCS, vol. 8120, pp. 539–546. Springer, Heidelberg (2013). https://doi.org/10.1007/978-3-642-40498-6_43
32. Heidt, M., Pfeiffer, L., Bischof, A., Rosenthal, P.: Tangible disparity - different notions of the material as catalyst of interdisciplinary communication. In: Kurosu, M. (ed.) HCI 2014. LNCS, vol. 8510, pp. 199–206. Springer, Cham (2014). https://doi.org/10.1007/978-3-319-07233-3_19
33. Hickey-Moody, A., Page, T.: Arts, Pedagogy and Cultural Resistance: New Materialisms. Rowman & Littlefield International, Lanham (2015)
34. Holtz, G.: Generating social practices. J. Artif. Soc. Soc. Simul. **17**(1), 17 (2014)
35. Hosmer, L.T.: Trust: the connecting link between organizational theory and philosophical ethics. Acad. Manag. Rev. **20**(2), 379–403 (1995)
36. Latour, B.: On interobjectivity. Mind Culture Activ. **3**(4), 228–245 (1996)
37. Latour, B., Hermant, E., Shannon, S.: Paris Ville Invisible. La Découverte Paris, Paris (1998)
38. Law, J.: After ANT: complexity, naming and topology. In: Law, J., Hassard, J. (eds.) Actor Network Theory and After, pp. 1–14. Wiley, Oxford (1999)
39. Leonardi, P.M.: Digital materiality? How artifacts without matter, matter. First Monday **15**, 6 (2010)
40. Leonardi, P.M., Barley, S.R.: Materiality and change: challenges to building better theory about technology and organizing. Inf. Organ. **18**(3), 159–176 (2008)

41. Lippard, L.R.: Six Years: The Dematerialization of the Art Object from 1966 to 1972. University of California Press, Berkley (1973)
42. Luhmann, N.: Social Systems. Stanford University Press, Palo Alto (1995)
43. Luhmann, N.: Trust and Power. Wiley, Hoboken (2018)
44. Lustick, I.S.: Agent-based modelling of collective identity: testing constructivist theory. J. Artif. Soc. Soc. Simul. **3**(1), 1 (2000)
45. Mäkelä, M.: Knowing through making: the role of the artefact in practice-led research. Knowl. Technol. Policy **20**(3), 157–163 (2007)
46. Manning, E., Massumi, B.: Thought in the Act: Passages in the Ecology of Experience. University of Minnesota Press, Minneapolis (2014)
47. McGinn, D., Birch, D., Akroyd, D., Molina-Solana, M., Guo, Y., Knottenbelt, W.J.: Visualizing dynamic bitcoin transaction patterns. Big Data **4**(2), 109–119 (2016)
48. Misztal, B.: Trust in Modern Societies: The Search for the Bases of Social Order. Wiley, Hoboken (2013)
49. Nakamoto, S.: Bitcoin: A Peer-to-Peer Electronic Cash System. Springer, Heidelberg (2008)
50. Nake, F., Grabowski, S.: Aesthetics and algorithmics. In: Aesthetic Computing. MIT Press (2002)
51. Reckwitz, A.: Toward a theory of social practices a development in culturalist theorizing. Eur. J. Soc. Theory **5**(2), 243–263 (2002)
52. Robles, E., and Wiberg, M. Texturing the "material turn" in interaction design. In Proceedings of the Fourth International Conference on Tangible, Embedded, and Embodied Interaction, TEI '10, ACM (New York, NY, USA, 2010), 137–144
53. Røpke, I.: Theories of practice—New inspiration for ecological economic studies on consumption. Ecol. Econ. **68**(10), 2490–2497 (2009)
54. Schneier, B.: Liars and Outliers: Enabling the Trust That Society Needs to Thrive, 1st edn. Wiley, Hoboken (2012)
55. Scrivener, S.: Reflection in and on action and practice in creative-production doctoral projects in art and design. Working Papers in Art and Design, January 2000
56. Scrivener, S., Chapman, P.: The practical implications of applying a theory of practice based research: a case study. Working Papers in Art and Design, March 2004
57. Seidler, P., Kolling, P., Hampshire, M.: Terra0: can an augmented forest own and utilise itself? Technical report, May 2016
58. Shove, E., Pantzar, M.: Consumers, producers and practices: understanding the invention and reinvention of nordic walking. J. Consum. C. **5**, 43–64 (2016)
59. Sterling, B.: Design fiction. Interactions **16**(3), 20–24 (2009)
60. Swan, M.: Blockchain: Blueprint for a New Economy, 1st edn. O'Reilly Media, Sebastopol (2015)
61. Szabo, N.: Formalizing and securing relationships on public networks. First Monday **2**, 9 (1997)
62. Tapscott, D., Tapscott, A.: Blockchain Revolution: How the Technology Behind Bitcoin is Changing Money, Business, and the World. Portfolio, New York (2016)
63. Turing, A.M.: On computable numbers, with an application to the Entscheidungsproblem. Proc. London Math. Soc. **s2–42**(1), 230–265 (1937)
64. Wakkary, R.: Framing complexity, design and experience: a reflective analysis. Digit. Creativity **16**(2), 65–78 (2005)

Cognitive Mimetics for AI Ethics: Tacit Knowledge, Action Ontologies and Problem Restructuring

Antero Karvonen[✉]

University of Jyväskylä, Jyväskylä, Finland
`antero.i.karvonen@jyu.fi`

Abstract. Ethics and ethical information processing are an important problem for AI development. It is important for self-evident reasons, but also challenging in its' implications and should be welcomed by designers and developers as an interesting technical challenge. This article explores AI ethics as a design problem and lays out how cognitive mimetics could be used a method for its design. AI ethics is conceptualized as a problem of implementation on the one hand, and as a problem of ethical contents on the other. From the viewpoint of human information processing, ethics becomes a special case of *ethical* information processing - one that has deep implications in terms of AI abilities and information contents. Here we focus on ethical information processing as a property of the system (rather as a general constraint on it). We explore three specific concepts relevant for cognitive mimetics from the perspective of ethics: tacit knowledge, ontologies, and problem restructuring. We close with a general discussion on the difference between abilities and mental contents noted as relevant in previous articles on cognitive mimetics and reiterate its importance in this context as well.

Keywords: AI ethics · AI design · Cognitive mimetics · Mimetic design

1 Introduction

At least in theory, artificial intelligence gives artefacts the ability to display ethical behavior. For example, the ability to set goals and reason a variety of means to achieve them that result in certain ends always contains some ethical dimensions. Another may be the capacity to actively detect specific moments during instantiated behavior which have ethical dimensions – an ethical situation awareness. One may think this a radical departure from traditional artefacts, which gain their ethical dimensions from use patterns and from design purposes. However, as AI systems are designed and used as well, it is clear that they retain all ethical questions that relate to traditional artefacts. They also introduce new dimensions to the question of ethical design in proportion to their autonomy in goalsetting, planning, decision-making and implementation, among others. At the very moment an AI system can set goals and reason a course of action and implement it, it is engaging in ethical behavior. It is a different question whether the

© Springer Nature Switzerland AG 2020
M. Rauterberg (Ed.): HCII 2020, LNCS 12215, pp. 95–104, 2020.
https://doi.org/10.1007/978-3-030-50267-6_8

designer has explicitly considered the system from an ethical perspective or taken steps to ensure that ethical abilities are implemented as part of the AI system itself.

Taking the ethical stance towards AI design naturally cascades into problems of implementation and to sources of ethics (see [1], for example). These are problems which must be tackled or at least acknowledged simultaneously. Two key questions arise. The first is how to design and implement such abilities into AI systems. The second is where to look for the basis for ethical reasoning – where should "ethics modules" derive their contents and their basis for reasoning? This article offers a conceptual discussion on these issues and then lays out how cognitive mimetics [2–6] can be used in the context of AI ethics.

2   AI Ethics as a Design Problem

Ethics and the achievement of ethical behavior in AI systems is fundamentally a design problem. Design is about satisfying design goals, requirements, and constraints – and in this context specifically the requirements set by ethical standards for AI systems. Here, as elsewhere in design, the general task is to achieve a good fit between the form of the design and its context [7]. In this particular case, the "form" of the AI system should fit well to general ethical standards and practices given by the context. The context consists of the task, the task environment and the task- or domain-specific culture and practice, as well as the wider culture in which the AI system will be nested.

There are at least two senses in which ethics play a role in AI development: as extrinsic or intrinsic to the AI system. A good example of extrinsic ethics are provided by the guidelines set forth by the EU, the seven requirements for achieving 'trustworthy AI': human agency and oversight; robustness and safety; privacy and data governance; transparency; diversity, non-discrimination and fairness, societal and environmental well-being; and accountability. While these requirements can (and will) result in particular kinds of implementations, they are more focused on the use of AI and are directed at the designers as general obligations rather than specific instructions – they are, as it were, "outside" the technical system. By intrinsic we mean that the AI system itself has some capacity to evaluate its own behavior (or its outcomes) or external events from an ethical standpoint.

The question of values and ethics in information system design have been around for a while, a prominent example of which is Value Sensitive Design (VSD) [8–10]. VSD has spawned numerous articles over the decades. As a design framework for values, VSD has a tripartite structure consisting of conceptual, empirical, and technical investigations. While sound in principle, the framework has drawn also criticism, for example, Albrechtslund [11] has critiqued VSD for not sufficiently distinguishing between ethical design goals and non-ethical use patterns. For a response and further development of VSD see [12]. Van de Poel [13] has sought to fill the gap between VSD and implementation by way of a method for transforming values into design requirements. Van Wynsberghe and Robbins [14] call for a pragmatic approach to bring together ethicists and engineers in the lab to formulate values into technical systems. This is all sound in principle. However, not much has been written on the application of VSD in the context of AI [15], and it is possible the framework is not as such suited for the special problems of AI where the question of ethical information processing in the machine itself becomes central. The typical outputs of a VSD process are what we have called extrinsic ethics – general guidelines, constraints, and requirements.

What is crucial going forward, is to begin considering the ways in which human values, norms and ethics can be embedded into the systems, namely, how to implement moral reasoning *into* the AI system itself (steps towards this direction have been taken for example in [1]). This has been called machine morality or machine ethics [1, 16, 17]. This is closer to what we have called intrinsic ethics. The question for machine ethics is fundamentally about how machines could support or replace humans in performing ethical reasoning [18]. This makes the problem a special question within the general discourse of AI, but one that has a wide range of implications beyond the its own specific problems. In fact, ethical dilemmas and design problems have a surprising similarity: they are often open-ended and ill-structured. This means that in both, there are many acceptable solutions and in neither is there a routine process by which one can reach a solution. This is of course the primary source of trouble for AI systems – and the problems go far beyond ethics-specific questions. Thus, we have truly a wicked design problem at hand: the only thing we know perhaps is that universal formal ethical systems are surprisingly feeble for real-world reasoning and at any rate contested by philosophers. The tension is that given the operating principles of computers, those are (when formal, axiomatic and rules-based) the best suited for machine implementation. On the other hand, one might take the "bottom-up" approach [16] and seek to model in a neural network the patterns of behavior immanent in some context in a sub-symbolic fashion. However, if a machine (or an evaluating human for that matter) cannot justify and provide reasons for its behavior, can it be called ethical at all? The questions go deep into the foundations of AI and indeed push the envelope for AI development. The point is that ambitious designers and engineers should welcome, rather than shun as problematic, the challenge of intrinsic machine ethics. As the problem is far from being solved, as is the case for AI in general [19], there is also room in the discourse for fresh approaches and machine ethics provides as challenging a framework as any to advance these questions.

We take the primary purpose of AI to be to replace or support human information processing. We further take it to be the case that ethics are an instantiation of human information processing. Thus, in principle, this means that the system should somehow be able to evaluate situations and behaviors from an ethical standpoint (thus displaying a form of intelligence in this context). Typically, this would mean that it should not only be able to perform the objective task but engage in ethical information processing as well. The system should possess a functioning "ethics module".

If the machine is controlling the joining and disjoining of railway lines, and people happen to be strapped in uneven numbers on both paths the train is headed, it should be able to engage in a form of moral reasoning [20]. However, artificial toy problems such as the trolley problem easily box our thinking in. For AI design, it is important to understand *actual* ethical information processing in humans. As the trolley problem and its variations show, actual human ethical judgement is a complex affair which integrates many kinds of information processes and contents together against open-ended problems with many possible solutions. An AI system built around a single variable as the target of an ethical evaluation function may work for many cases but fail (from an ethical standpoint) for others because it has not mimicked [2–6] the actual information process in humans. For example, human beings judge based on emotions, or concepts like allowing vs. doing harm [20]. More importantly perhaps, examples like the trolley problem are artificially limited and designed to summon specific moral dilemmas. In real world situations (and even in toy problems), humans have the ability to restructure the problems beyond what the experimenter has in mind. In the trolley problem, for example, the choice to sacrifice oneself rather than harm others, is typically forbidden for artificial reasons, but in fact shows the highest moral virtue. Thus, accessing by empirical means (without artificial limitations) how humans restructure problems [21] can give crucial hints on how to build similar abilities into AI systems, and discover usable patterns for moral problem solving. The empirical route sketched in cognitive mimetics [2–6] provides implementation cues for both general abilities and specific contents and patterns [see 6]. The whole point of the trolley problem is that within its limitations there *is no* right answer, and in such unfortunate circumstances it is difficult to see how either humans or machines should be forced to consider ethical questions, as both making the choice and not-making it result in an unethical action in one sense or another. The right answer to the trolley problem is of course to stop the train from moving or perhaps to remove the people from the tracks. As a speculative example, the design answer to the problem should *not* be to have the machine calculate least number of victims (perhaps modulo age, health, etc.) and cause their death. We should simply build a remote control which can stop any train in its tracks within the needed timeframe. This is what ethical design thinking *should* be about when dealing with complex real-world problems that in reality admit to many different solutions. The focus for AI designers should perhaps be less on developing a moral calculus, and more on problem restructuring that requires none. From this perspective, a moral calculus may be more of a warning signal that problem restructuring is needed.

3   Cognitive Mimetics for Ethics

Cognitive Mimetics is an idea for a design method for intelligent systems introduced by Kujala and Saariluoma and elaborated over a series of papers [2–6]. Mimetic design means using a source in the natural or artificial worlds as an inspiration for technological solutions. In biomimetics one typically imitates the biological structures found in nature. However, in creating intelligent technologies designers can use existing organizational and individual information processes as the source of ideas. Designing intelligent systems by utilizing existing human information processes as the source of solutions we have termed 'cognitive mimetics' [2–6]. Cognitive mimetics differs from typical and established biomimetics as it has different source of mimicking: human shared and individual cognitive processes, as well as the mental contents, representations, and constraints that establish the boundaries and forms it takes. It analyses how people carry out intelligent tasks today and uses this information in designing novel technological solutions.

From the perspective of cognitive mimetics, ethics in action is fundamentally an instance of human information processing. Thus, the basic rationale of cognitive mimetics works here as well. The logical structure of mimetic design consists of three main parts [6]. To be an instance of mimetic design, there must be a source domain. The logical corollary to the source is the target domain. Furthermore, there is a process of interpretation or translation between the source and target domain, which can be called mimetic transfer. Implicit here is the designer who can extract and implement design-goal- relevant information from a source. Important to note is that the process of interpretation is observer-relative given that designers with different backgrounds and knowledge observe different aspects in the source [22]. Thus, as noted by Van Wynsberghe and Robbins [14] in the context of VBD, it is important to involve experts from different domains into the design process (ethicists and engineers). In cognitive mimetics, one would also include subject matter experts from the domain into which AI is being developed (whose actual ethical information processing is being supported or replaced) and ethicists, and then take both the content and the processes of their thinking into account in developing intelligent technology. The mimetic perspective is about finding out what makes the source an effective solution [6], which in the context of human thinking typically implicates concepts such as problem spaces [21], their construction and structure, heuristics, reasons, and mental representations in general. Here effectiveness can mean the mental representation's effectiveness as a solution to a moral dilemma. A very effective solution removes moral considerations completely or mitigates them significantly.

3.1 Tacit Knowledge in Ethics

Tacit knowledge is of special interest for cognitive mimetics [4]. Human information processing, ethical or otherwise, is typically grounded in a complex web of tacit knowledge. This forms a significant corollary to the mere "figure" of our thought readily available for introspection and verbal reporting. Indeed, much of the norms that guide ordinary life recede into the background so long as no one violates them. Tacit knowledge is essentially non-codified, disembodied know-how whose take up is often informal [23]. This sort of knowledge comes in various grades, some outside the possibility of explication and others not. For instance, while it is very difficult if not impossible to describe and transfer the smell of coffee to someone who does not have the same sensory experience, guiding another person to make coffee is relatively straightforward even though the process is quite automatic for most people in ordinary circumstances. Of course, in the latter example one can imagine how much tacit knowledge and skills is required for someone to be able to follow the instructions, and in this sense tacit knowledge provides a key which opens the pandora's box of how much is taken for granted in ordinary human life. The ability to follow instructions typically presupposes a vast amount of knowledge and skills in the tacit domain. This is very important for AI development, where such things cannot be taken for granted but must typically be programmed into the system [24]. Of course, recent developments in machine learning may in some sense lessen the burden of programming minutiae into the system, but equally clearly simply assuming the form of human behavior is not ethical in any real sense, and in fact one can imagine the opposite to be the case. A middle ground is likely to be necessary, least burdensome and most fruitful.

Ethical questions are likely to follow this tacit quality. With respect to previous work on cognitive mimetics, in the ontological schema [5] ethical questions are most likely to occur in the space of reasons (for action). It should be noted that action can be understood also as non-action and still remain intentional. These typically answer the question "why?" or "why not?". In the seafaring context studied in previous research [4, 5], ethics are in fact absolutely central. In the research we did not even conceptualize the reasons for avoiding the ships on collision course from an ethical standpoint, although it is obviously at root an ethical and moral reason for behavior. Thus, in future research we can assume that much of ethical reasoning will follow this pattern and have deep tacit dimensions. It is also likely that we can't know these simply from our armchairs but must investigate actual activities.

"Why?" is the central guiding question for mimetic design. In terms of ethical information processing, this would typically lead through a succession of layers of meaning and lands at the ground of axiomatic assumptions. This type of investigation reveals the structure of ordinary knowledge, much of it tacit, and provides a central insight into the ontology (knowledge structure and contents) of the domain under investigation and its culture and norms.

3.2 Action Ontologies for Ethics

Ontologies are central for AI [25]. As all information systems – human, AI, or other – traffic in knowledge, it is important to be able to describe and organize domain-relevant information. Typically, some parts of the ontology are task-specific and others general [25]. What is relevant and sufficient in a particular case must be determined case-by-case. In all cases, it is necessary to enter into empirical investigation. Thus, the necessary ontology for ship steering [5] is probably different from the ontology of governmental complaint handling. And most certainly the contents will be different. Nevertheless, in all cases we can ask the question "What does the system know?" [25]. For cognitive mimetics this question is posed for the human operators (and other subject-matter experts) and later transformed into "what does the system *need* to know?" for AI systems.

In [5], we outlined a simple ontological structure for ship steering consisting of *observing, handling, and reasons.* It seems likely that with relatively minor adjustments this general ontology can work in many other contexts. Observation and interpretation are likely to be important in all AI contexts. Same applies to handling when conceptualized as behavior and action. By analogy these can be thought of as possible moves in a game. Reasons are perhaps the most crucial when it comes to ethics. Here, ethics can be thought of as a property of actions, as a constraint on actions, or as a goal for actions. They also provide a partial basis for what is interpreted in observation. Implicitly ethics can structure the whole ontology. For example, in autonomous cars a salient example is the interpretation of the visual scene of a ball bouncing from behind a car. Here the technical challenge is how to interpret the bouncing ball in terms of something that is not immediately seen (a child playing with the ball with the likely intention of running after it). The dilemma is of course completely ethical and has to do with reasoning beyond the immediately visible environment. Thus, the problems posed by ethics can often cascade into challenging technical questions that are in part answered by knowledge systems or ontologies. Here causal reasoning is implied in terms of a general ability for the AI system [19], but equally necessary are knowledge contents that give meaning to such interpretations.

3.3 Problem Restructuring

Problem spaces [21, 26] offer another perspective on the ethics problem in AI. A problem space is a mental construct in which the human operates by what Newell and Simon called 'heuristic search'. The problem space is a representation of the possible solutions that a solver might consider for a given problem [26]. It is specified by the mental representation of the problem, the goal to accomplished and a set of actions (or operators) [26]. When applied the result is a solution path or a trajectory through the problem space.

Moral reasoning can be conceptualized in many senses: as goals, as constraints, or as problems. For example, I may have a more-or-less amoral goal (get ice cream), but the means by which I go about obtaining ice cream are constrained by ethical standards (I will buy it, not steal for example). One might say I have then a general high-level goal of ethical virtue (do not steal) which constrains some parts of my normal day to day life. Whether I know it or not (see previous on tacit knowledge and ontologies), ethical demands have thus operationally narrowed my problem space in the ice cream problem.

Let us consider moral dilemmas vis a vis problem spaces and problem space restructuring. Two perspectives are crucial. The first is to discover empirically in specified task environments the problem spaces individuals construct, as well as the paths they take to achieve their goals in an ethical fashion. What gave Newell and Simon [21] trouble, was the discovery of "significant interpersonal differences in processing", which made it difficult to describe problem-solving by a single computer model [26]. However, in moral dilemmas, as illustrated by the ability of people to reconstruct the problem spaces, this carries a clear benefit: by non-restrictive experimental settings, we may discover problem restructuring in action and thus different ethical problem-solving methods and problem representations for AI implementation. The single model paradigm should thus be shifted into another level and discover (as a likely distant goal for AI) how problem restructuring can take place in natural and artificial systems. The lesson for AI development is to focus less on myopic single-model or ethical paradigm solutions to moral dilemmas, and rather go beyond to the different ways in which actual humans restructure problems. This shifts the design focus away from moral calculus based on, for example, factors and weights, structured perhaps around a moral system. A moral calculus may be important, but one can argue that problem restructuring is both a more pragmatic approach by way of the contents and problem-solving methods it can provide, and also a deep long-term challenge in terms of an *ability* for the AI system.

3.4 Cognitive Abilities and Mental Contents

Cognitive mimetics makes a conceptual distinction between cognitive abilities and contents [6]. Abilities here are general and necessary for all cognitive acts. Contents are domain-specific and learned or picked up by cognitive subjects over time. Take the example of problem restructuring. The ability of human subjects to restructure problem spaces is an ability we have. But the form and contents of our thinking that results in a problem space or the problem space itself are mental contents. We have suggested [6] the latter as a pragmatic starting point for AI design, since it is not clear whether the *ability* is a at present a realistic goal for actual current needs. The underlying idea is that mimetic design is based on the concept of multiple realizability, and in AI the common ground between computers and humans is to be found at the information level [2, 3]. This information level can be realized to some extent in both platforms, even though their qualitative nature is very different.

As there seem to be fundamental limits to computational processes [27, 28], the mimetic design process is about finding the common ground and representation form and accepting a large difference in implementation. Thus, cognitive mimetics begins with domain- and task-specific mental contents, ontologies, and thought processes rather than general abilities. General abilities, like problem restructuring, become implicated but the approach of cognitive mimetics leaves plenty of room for implementation strategies. Cognitive mimetics highlights the importance of domain-specific mental contents as starting point for AI development. Foundational work on AI abilities can then be fitted to the needs of this common ground. The approach in cognitive mimetics is no more about the material basis of information processes than a Turing Machine is about brain cells *or* transistors. The level at which cognitive mimetics approaches design problems in AI is the level of information processing and contents. The ethics problem in particular highlights that the correct level at which to look for ethics is not to be found in neurons, transistors, or even algorithms as such but at a higher level of abstraction.

4 Conclusion

The purpose of this article was to conceptualize ethical action and thought via the lens of human information processing and explore how some of the ideas in cognitive mimetics could be used in the context of AI ethics. Although no empirical work has yet been carried out, it seems clear that some of the key viewpoints in cognitive mimetics can be used to formulate ideas for designing ethics into AI. Tacit knowledge, action ontologies and problem structuring in ethical thinking are some clear examples of how concepts from the sciences around human information processing can be reflected onto the problem of ethics in AI.

Ethics and ethical information processing is an important problem for AI development. It is both important for obvious reasons, but also challenging in its' implications and should thus be welcomed by designers and developers as a major technical challenge. Cognitive mimetics may be useful in plotting out and providing contents for solutions in the intersection between man and machine and laying out necessary abilities that must be implemented for ethical information processing in machines to become a reality.

Acknowledgements. This work is funded by the Finnish Academy through the ETAIROS (https://etairos.fi/en/front-page/) project.

References

1. The IEEE Global Initiative on Ethics of Autonomous and Intelligent Systems. Ethically Aligned Design: A Vision for Prioritizing Human Well-being with Autonomous and Intelligent Systems, 1st edn. IEEE (2019)
2. Kujala, T., Saariluoma, P.: Cognitive mimetics for designing intelligent technologies. Adv. Hum. Comput. Interact. (2018)

3. Saariluoma, P., Kujala, T., Karvonen, A., Ahonen, M.: Cognitive mimetics - main ideas. In: Proceedings on the International Conference on Artificial Intelligence (ICAI), pp. 202–206. The Steering Committee of the World Congress in Computer Science, Computer Engineering and Applied Computing (WorldComp) (2018)

4. Saariluoma, P., Karvonen, A., Wahlstrom, M., Happonen, K., Puustinen, R., Kujala, T.: Challenge of tacit knowledge in acquiring information in cognitive mimetics. In: Karwowski, W., Ahram, T. (eds.) IHSI 2019. AISC, vol. 903, pp. 228–233. Springer, Cham (2019). https://doi.org/10.1007/978-3-030-11051-2_35

5. Saariluoma, P., Wahlström, M., Kujala, T., Puustinen, R., Karvonen, A., Happonen, K.: An ontology for cognitive mimetics. In: 2018 International Conference on Computational Science and Computational Intelligence (CSCI), pp. 1188–1192. IEEE (2018)

6. Karvonen, A., Kujala, T., Saariluoma, P.: Types of mimetics for the design of intelligent technologies. In: Ahram, T., Karwowski, W., Pickl, S., Taiar, R. (eds.) IHSED 2019. AISC, vol. 1026, pp. 40–46. Springer, Cham (2020). https://doi.org/10.1007/978-3-030-27928-8_7

7. Alexander, C.: Notes on the Synthesis of Form, vol. 5. Harvard University Press, Cambridge (1964)

8. Friedman, B., Kahn Jr., P.H.: Human values, ethics, and design. In: The Human-Computer Interaction Handbook, pp. 1209–1233. CRC Press (2002)

9. Friedman, B.: Value-sensitive design. Interactions 3(6), 16–23 (1996)

10. Friedman, B., Kahn, P.H., Borning, A., Huldtgren, A.: Value sensitive design and information systems. In: Doorn, N., Schuurbiers, D., van de Poel, I., Gorman, Michael E. (eds.) Early engagement and new technologies: opening up the laboratory. PET, vol. 16, pp. 55–95. Springer, Dordrecht (2013). https://doi.org/10.1007/978-94-007-7844-3_4

11. Albrechtslund, A.: Ethics and technology design. Ethics Inf. Technol. 9(1), 63–72 (2007)

12. Borning, A., Muller, M.: Next steps for value sensitive design. In: Proceedings of the SIGCHI Conference on Human Factors in Computing Systems, pp. 1125–1134. ACM (2012)

13. Poel, I.: Translating values into design requirements. In: Michelfelder, D.P., McCarthy, N., Goldberg, D.E. (eds.) Philosophy and Engineering: Reflections on Practice, Principles and Process. PET, vol. 15, pp. 253–266. Springer, Dordrecht (2013). https://doi.org/10.1007/978-94-007-7762-0_20

14. Van Wynsberghe, A., Robbins, S.: Ethicist as designer: a pragmatic approach to ethics in the lab. Sci. Eng. Ethics 20(4), 947–961 (2014)

15. Umbrello, S.: Beneficial artificial intelligence coordination by means of a value sensitive design approach. Big Data and Cognitive Computing 3(1), 5 (2019)

16. Wallach, W., Allen, C.: Moral Machines: Teaching Robots Right from Wrong. Oxford University Press, New York (2008)

17. Anderson, M., Anderson, S.L.: Machine Ethics. Cambridge University Press, New York (2011)

18. McLaren, B.M.: Computational models of ethical reasoning: challenges, initial steps, and future directions. IEEE Intell. Syst. 21(4), 29–37 (2006)

19. Lake, B.M., Ullman, T.D., Tenenbaum, J.B., Gershman, S.J.: Building machines that learn and think like people. Behav. Brain Sci. 40 (2017)

20. Woollard, F., Howard-Snyder, F.: Doing vs. allowing harm. In: Zalta, E.N. (ed.) The Stanford Encyclopedia of Philosophy. https://plato.stanford.edu/archives/win2016/entries/doing-allowing/. Winter 2016 Edition

21. Newell, A., Simon, H.A.: Human Problem Solving, vol. 104, no. 9. Prentice-hall, Englewood Cliffs (1972)

22. Floridi, L.: The logic of design as a conceptual logic of information. Mind. Mach. 27(3), 495–519 (2017)

23. Howells, J.: Tacit knowledge. Technol. Anal. Strat. Manag. 8(2), 91–106 (1996)

24. Dennett, D.C.: Cognitive wheels: the frame problem of AI. In: Boden, M.A. (ed.) The Philosophy of Artificial Intelligence, pp. 147–170. Oxford University Press, New York (1990)
25. Chandrasekaran, B., Josephson, J.R., Benjamins, V.R.: What are ontologies, and why do we need them? IEEE Intell. Syst. Appl. **14**(1), 20–26 (1999)
26. Ohlsson, S.: The problems with problem solving: Reflections on the rise, current status, and possible future of a cognitive research paradigm. J. Probl. Solv. **5**(1), 7 (2012)
27. Saariluoma, P., Rauterberg, M.: Turing test does not work in theory but in practice. In: Proceedings on the International Conference on Artificial Intelligence (ICAI), p. 433. The Steering Committee of The World Congress in Computer Science, Computer Engineering and Applied Computing (WorldComp) (2015)
28. Saariluoma, P., Rauterberg, M.: Turing's error-revised. Int. J. Philos. Study **4** (2016)

Good Life Ecosystems – Ethics and Responsibility in the Silver Market

Jaana Leikas[1]([⊠]), Anton Sigfrids[1], Jari Stenvall[2], and Mika Nieminen[1]

[1] VTT Technical Research Centre of Finland Ltd., Espoo, Finland
jaana.leikas@vtt.fi
[2] Tampere University, Tampere, Finland

Abstract. Population ageing is creating challenges for societies to seek innovative ways and technologies to support home care. Amid fast-developing emerging technologies, there is a need for ways to ensure that technical solutions and services really serve the good of the individual and society, and thus promote the good life. In this paper, a practical ecosystem based design and assessment framework for ethically acceptable services for the silver economy is introduced. The framework is based on life-based design (LBD), a holistic design approach that stresses understanding about people's life as the basis of the creation of design concepts, and on the idea of service and business ecosystems as a source of multi-dimensional value creation. We connect the ethical thinking and social responsibility aspects at the core of the ecosystem concept and analyse the dynamics of home care service ecosystems from the perspective of ethics and the good life. We suggest an iterative co-design process starting with identification of change needs in service production, followed by value mapping of services, and systematic analysis of the ethical issues related to the chosen services.

Keywords: Ethics · Values · Ecosystem · Ageing · AI · Home care

1 Introduction

Population ageing is creating challenges for societies to seek innovative ways to improve the independent living of older people. Spurred on by demographic change and rapid development of emerging technologies, services for older people are being developed eagerly and in abundance, inspired by promising prospects for the silver market economy. The focus of technology and service design has extended from individual products to continuously evolving ecosystems that are composed of human actors in different roles, technical artefacts and applications, as well as physical, social and information environments. The growth of the silver market, also called the silver economy, i.e., products and services for the ageing population [1, 2], opens up many new challenges for the development of new services and ecosystems.

The silver economy relies on the promises of emerging technologies to support the everyday life of older people and to improve quality of life. However, while many technological innovations can be explained by a 'user need', not all technical solutions

M. Rauterberg (Ed.): HCII 2020, LNCS 12215, pp. 105–122, 2020.
https://doi.org/10.1007/978-3-030-50267-6_9

can be justified in terms of the benefits of the good life. Ethical issues raised by the design, development, implementation and use of emerging technologies and especially artificial intelligence have significant consequences for human wellbeing, and should thus be a substantial part of designing 'good life' and a prerequisite for successful implementation of technology for the silver economy.

The challenge of creating ethically sustainable services concerns the entire service ecosystem. As application and software designers have a distinctive ethical responsibility in developing technology for the good of humanity, what kind of ethical guidelines can be offered to support their work? A crucial question is also how different actors in the service delivery ecosystem can act to ensure the fulfilment of responsibility and ethical values. Furthermore, what kind of design framework for ethically acceptable services, frameworks and practices could be used by application and software designers as well as public actors to foster ethically sustainable services for the ageing society?

In this paper, we focus on the ecosystems of home care services for older people as an example. The purpose of this paper is to enhance the understanding of ethics as a prerequisite for sustainable home care ecosystems. We start in Sect. 2 by presenting an overview of emerging home care technologies aimed at supporting the independent living of older people. This includes a preliminary reflection on the ethical issues related to AI. In Sect. 3, we discuss the preconditions for the good life of older people. Section 4 describes technology ethics in the context of home care, and draws on the preliminary ethical guidelines and principles introduced in the current literature. Section 5 then presents our idea of *good life ecosystems*, that is, silver market ecosystems that are ethical and responsible and aim at producing services that improve the quality of life of older people. Finally, on the grounds of this deliberation, we conclude by outlining and justifying a design framework for ethically acceptable services for home care ecosystems.

2 Emerging Technologies in Home Care

Home care is considered here as the care provided by professionals to people in their own homes with the ultimate goal of not only contributing to their life quality and functional health status, but also replacing institutionalized care with care in the home for societal reasons [3]. Home care covers a variety of activities, from preventive visits to end-of-life care. Home care services include (a) daily social services such as help with dressing, cleaning, shopping, and cooking, (b) homecare medical services such as nursing and rehabilitation, (c) provision of alert, alarm and assistive technologies to support independent, assisted living, including technologies for sensing, reasoning, acting, communication, and interaction [4], and (d) links to ambient services outside the home such as community organizations, transport services, security, and education and leisure. The twin aims of this approach are to support independent living and to continue senior citizens' roles as members of society.

As the number of older people in Western societies continues to grow, pressure to emphasize home care is increasing and consideration is being given to new monitoring technologies and artificial intelligence (AI). AI enables the collection of diverse data from home care clients, including genomics, historical, diagnosis, physiological and behavioural data. In addition, communication, wearable solutions and mobile health technologies provide new opportunities for 24/7 health monitoring at home. The combination of AI and big health data has the potential to reveal new knowledge relating to, e.g., prevention, early intervention and optimal care of home care clients [5, 6].

Application of AI will have significant potential in home care during the next decades. It will not only change the content of home care work but also change professions and jobs, and will have potentially extensive economic impacts. Consequently, the development of AI has provoked ethical discussions in home care with the recognition that, along with its positive effects, utilization of AI may also entail many risks. Ethical questions related to home care are associated with the data mass that intelligent systems will collect and share with each other in the future, and concerns regarding, for example, security, privacy, confidentiality, data protection, prevention of harm, and informed consent.

While the discussion on the ethics of AI is still in its early stages, the discourse on AI itself has already arrived at the requirement for user-friendliness and the *explainability* of AI. The latter refers to the concept of 'explainable AI' coined by the European Commission [7]. The concept should be used to promote understanding of the functioning of AI systems and the decisions generated as a result of those functions. Explainability captures the need for accountability and transparency. It is necessary in building and maintaining citizen's trust and is the precondition for achieving informed consent from individuals. The fundamental questions are: Who defines 'explainability'? Who is doing the explaining and who the listening? From whose perspective is the explanation of the significance of technology generated? and What values and conception of humanity are the viewpoints of the explainers based on?

3   Preconditions for the Good Life of Older People

Aristotle says that the good life is a goal that should be pursued by everyone. In practical life, this is not a goal that can materialize irrespective of our everyday activities. The good life is made up of good actions. Thus, individual actions taken to realize this goal are part of the goal itself (Aristotle, n.d., trans. 1984, 1097a30–1097b6) [8].

Very often technology is evaluated in terms of efficiency, rationality, and productivity. In these cases the starting point for discussion is the autonomy of technology. Even the discussion around information society is technology-driven in the way that the main criterion for 'goodness' seems to be the amount of computers, internet connections and smart phones. Talk about the content of technology-supported services and the relation between technology and people's quality of life is much more seldom heard.

As mentioned in the previous chapter, emerging technologies are considered to have a lot of potential in home care. As regards AI, we easily fall into looking for ethical problems related to the essence of AI, when we should be asking how emerging technologies could be used for good and for improving the quality of life. In ethical thinking, the main question is the interpretation of 'good' [9, 10]. What are the central values of good older age, and who can define them? One way to examine 'the good of older people' is to focus on the concept of the good life. The preconditions for the good life of older people are based on biological, socio-cultural and psychological factors.

From the technology ethics point of view, the good life can be examined in connection with the development of the information society: what kind of future do we want to build?

What role should technology play in this future? Consideration should be given to how technology can help in perceiving and improving the elements of good life. This is the meaningfulness of technology. In the case of older people, the key questions concern the maintenance of basic everyday attributes, such as independent living, security, trust in society, meaningful roles and agency, self-efficacy, social relationships, equal availability of services, possibility to be heard, and justifying decisions from the perspectives of human dignity, welfare, flourishing and sustainability [11].

4 Ethics of Home Care Technology

Ethics is concerned with the justification of moral norms. Moral refers to people's selective behaviour based on values, and the beliefs and contract systems related to this behaviour, as well as norms concerning good and evil, right and wrong, valuable and worthless, and acceptance and rejection. Moral also includes those perceptions of good and evil and right and wrong of individuals and societies that are culture-bound. Moral norms are created when we as agents consider the impact of our actions on those close to us and on humankind as a whole [11, 12].

Norms and values as mental contents direct our goals and activities and have a crucial role in the design and adoption of technologies. Values are culturally predominant perceptions of the central goals of the good life of individuals, society and humankind, and they guide decision-making [13, 14]. Besides individual and (multi)cultural values, there are also critical universal values that transcend cultural and national borders, such as the fundamental values laid down in the Universal Declaration of Human Rights [15], the EU Treaties [16] and the EU Charter of Fundamental Rights [17].

Technology has long been seen as value neutral and factual, whereas ethics has been associated with normative beliefs and subjective norms. Now this way of thinking is moving aside. Technology is no longer considered to be outside ethics, on the contrary, every technical device has its ethical dimensions [18–20]. According to van den Hoven [21], ICT technology has become a constitutive technology. It partly constitutes the things to which it is applied. It shapes practices, institutions, and discourses in important ways.

Dealing with technology ethics is always contextual [22]. Ethical issues arise regarding the introduction and adoption of technology and services rather than the inherent characteristics of the technology. Thus, the impact of technology concerns not only the direct usage situation, but also the actions of different stakeholders who may have conflicting interests. Ethical issues in home care technology ecosystems can be perceived on three levels. Firstly, they concern good design practices and the rights of older people and relevant stakeholders to participate in the design. Secondly, ethics relates to the foreseen impacts of design and development: what kind of possible applications and services are envisaged and whether these solutions are ethically acceptable and sustainable. Thirdly, there are ethical implications concerning the use and ownership of stored personal data. The ethical issues in this case are linked, for example, with trust, privacy and data protection.

Literature provides very little reading on ethical design and assessment of service ecosystems. So far, academic studies have been primarily concerned with the implementation of ethics in the design of products and applications. Value-sensitive design (VSD) holds that artefacts are value-laden and design can be value-sensitive [23, 24]. The app-roach refers to the need to identify early implicit values embedded in new technologies by focusing on the usage situations of technology.

As to ethics of AI, many public, private and civil organizations and expert groups have introduced visions for designing ethical technology and ethical AI. The most prominent ones are probably the guidelines of the European Group on Ethics in Science and New Technologies [25], the European Commission's High-Level Expert Group on Artificial Intelligence [7], and AI4People [26], to mention but a few.

The impact of technology can be assessed against a number of ethical principles that are considered universal ethical values [27]. These principles help in creating questions and finding and organizing answers to questions. However, none of them can alone offer clear answers to all design questions. In technology design, principles can often run into conflict. One of the reasons for this is that ethical issues are contextual by nature and are always case specific [27, 28]. The impact of technology concerns not only the direct usage situation, but also the many different stakeholders who may have conflicting interests. In the following, we introduce briefly the basic principles that should be considered when assessing the ethical impact of technology in home care.

Integrity and Dignity: Individuals should be respected, and technical solutions should not violate their dignity as human beings [29].

Autonomy is the perceived ability to control, cope with and make personal decisions about how to live on a day-to-day basis, according to one's own rules and preferences [30, 31]. An individual has the right to decide how (and for what purposes) they are using a technology.

Informed Consent & Right to Decline. This principle is a prerequisite for any imple-mentation of technology, and is especially significant for vulnerable older people. It means that people have the right to consent to technological intervention (adoption and usage of technology) [32].

Privacy. An individual should be able to control access to their personal information and protect their own space [30, 33–35].

Reliability. Technical solutions should be sufficiently reliable for the purposes for which they are being used [36]. Users of monitoring systems need to be confident that the collected data is reliable, and that the system does not forward the data to anyone who should not have it.

Justification and e-inclusion. Services should be accessible to all user groups irre-spective of physical or mental deficiencies. This principle of (social) justice goes hand-in-hand with the principle of beneficence [37].

Meaningfulness. The role of technology in the life of an individual [38]. Meaningfulness does not only refer to the usefulness of a technology, but the experienced or perceived impact of the technology on quality of life on an individual level, i.e. meaningful added value for the individual.

The Responsible Industry project, which explored how private corporations can conduct their research and innovation activities responsibly, listed principles and values that should be considered when developing ICT products for older persons in need of care, i.e. as vulnerable consumers. These are [39]:

- Individual rights and liberties
- Personal safety and health
- Autonomy, authenticity and identity
- Implications for quality of life (QoL)
- Social integration vs. isolation
- Integrity and dignity
- Bodily integrity (self-determination of human beings over their own bodies)
- Social safety
- Justice (distributive) and access to developed technology
- Equality
- Dual use of developed technologies.

Consideration of the above-mentioned principles and values means conscious reflection on them with respect to design decisions and reflection on the design process and methodologies (including the moral norms of the designers themselves as they may greatly influence the design). Designing for good life thus requires placing the human being and human life at the very centre as a starting point for technology design. For this reason, the role of human sciences has become increasingly important in innovation.

5 Good Life Ecosystems

Ecosystems thinking can be used to define a set of actors and their dynamically evolving interconnectedness in relation to a set of technologies or value propositions. Formally, ecosystems contain a conceptual dimension (the perspective through which the system is examined, as well as its boundaries, type and scope), a structure (the relationships and hierarchies between and among system actors), and a temporal dimension (function of dynamics and co-evolution over time). Investigation of such dimension require rigorous research involving the relevant stakeholders. This paper presents the conceptual dimension of an ecosystem and tentative structure [40].

Ecosystem is a biological metaphor featuring self-organizing agents constituting, along with the environment, a system. Generally speaking, an ecosystem is a collection of actors – such as organizations – engaged in joint production, whose choices and actions are interdependent [41]. Complexity theory uses the metaphor of ecosystems to suggest a diversity of autonomous parts responding to external stimuli and to the decisions and actions of other agents to create emergence-based action. Emergences become patterns in human ecosystems and constitute governances, what Arthur [42] terms *messy vitality*. Holland [43] shows how *fan-out* and *hierarchy* result in *loops* or routines resulting in governance emergence in ecosystems. These are always non-linear [44] and have unintended consequences.

Numerous uses of the ecosystem metaphor can be found, such as business and service ecosystems, innovation ecosystems and knowledge ecosystems [45]. However, many authors base their view on Moore's [46] classic definition and add their own ideas to it [47]. The baseline of the concept is value creation through a network of different actors that are interdependent [48]. While in these conceptualizations value is usually taken to mean economic value, the concept can be widened to also include social and environmental values, which are produced by a group of various interdependent actors.

The service- and knowledge-based economy has already changed the concept of value, making it increasingly intangible and complex [49]. However, the concept of value will become increasingly multi-dimensional as it develops to include ideas of ethicality, sustainability, and desirability. The ecosystem concept is also wide in the sense that it covers a community of various organizations, institutions, and individuals, such as firms and their customers, suppliers, and complementors, as well as different stakeholders and governmental institutions [50].

By *good life ecosystem*, we mean silver market ecosystems that are ethical and responsible and aim at producing services that improve the quality of life of older people. In good life ecosystems, the main aim is to generate more goodness in the everyday life of older people. That is, to serve their good both as individuals and as valued contributors to society. Understanding biological, psychological and socio-cultural aspects of the forms of life of older people [11] can bring a competitive edge to companies operating on silver markets.

Both public and private actors are taking part in the digital transformation of home care by offering service solutions that enable older people to live independently and safely at home, hence reducing public healthcare expenses. Future ecosystems of home care technology will utilize disrupting technologies such as big data and AI, which will create new business opportunities not only for current gerontechnology companies, but also for new players, from start-ups to existing players with core competence in ICT and AI technologies. Disrupting technologies can also provide opportunities for home care organizations to further develop their operations; however, it does not guarantee the responsible development of home care operations. Home care management and development should therefore be based on the question of how responsible and ethical development of home care services can be secured amid the growing demand for resource efficiency [51].

To generate goodness, an ecosystem has to operate in an ethical way. This means conscious reflection on ethical values and choices with respect to the design, development and delivery of goods and services. It means reflection on the design process and the choice of design methodologies. In addition, it means conscious consideration of the impact of technology and what impact is ethically acceptable. Moreover, an ethical ecosystem must define what is ethical, i.e. what constitutes the good of older people and the good of humanity.

The moral norms of the actors in the ecosystem, i.e., designers, service providers, home care personnel and other relevant stakeholders, may greatly influence the design and adoption of services. The designer and the care professionals do not work in a vacuum, and their personal values and worldview will also influence their design decisions.

When this is fully acknowledged, values can be incorporated as an integral part of the design and value-oriented methodologies can be exploited.

The general structure of the proposed ecosystem can be described in relation to the technology use layers within home care services, and the service integration between layers (see Fig. 1). The focus is on technologies and services that increasingly rely on utilizing intelligent technologies to collect, process, share and interpret data to support individual and organization level operations and decision making. The proposed ecosystem description connects a set of more or less loosely linked actors, institutions and technologies that relate to the use or provision of home care services. Thus, this kind of ecosystem facilitates shared understanding of the system and its co-created values among stakeholders, and functions as part of an ethical ecosystem design method.

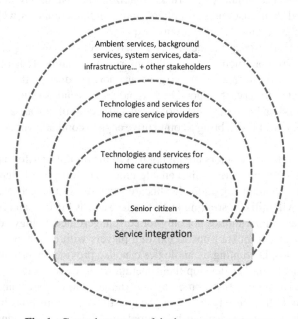

Fig. 1. General structure of the home care ecosystem.

The middle layer depicts the senior citizen as a user of smart home- and gerontechnology. The second layer includes the technologies provided for the senior citizen by home-care service providers as part of the service. In-house technologies for the use of senior citizens and service providers might range from self-acquired smart home technologies to services formally part of organized home care, such as support for daily living such as cleaning, meal, and transport services, as well as nursing and physician services (see Sect. 2). Related technology applications include alarm devices, smart door locks, automated medicine dispensers, smart walkers, various sensors and detectors integrated into lights, refrigerators, doors, rugs, and beds. Audio-visual technology supports telephone support and safety services, remote care, as well as remote dining groups and remote physical activity.

The third layer includes the technologies used by the immediate service providers (and manufacturers) in enabling the service, service optimization, and decision-making. Home care personnel might use enterprise resource planning (ERP) to optimize human resources, smart locks to enter homes easily and remote support to replace physical care. The service provider uses customer-interface sensor and health data for increased customer monitoring, care optimization and personalization. This includes the use of machine learning to monitor and predict deviations in customer behaviour and health to enable preventive care.

The fourth layer depicts the potential connections to ambient services in the near community, background services for customer support, system services to enable data-system functions, and the larger data infrastructure. The integration of a multitude of home-care and cross-sectoral services into a unified system requires service integrators that enable cooperation between various service providers in the public, private and third sector, as well as the voluntary sector and family members, and ambient services.

6 Design Framework for Ethically Acceptable Services

In the previous chapters, we have highlighted that while emerging technologies and especially AI can have many positive effects on home care, they also give rise to many yet unseen ethical issues. Consequently, solving ethical issues can bring a competitive edge to companies operating on the silver market. This creates pressure for home care ecosystems to carry out systematic consideration of ethical issues when implementing emerging technologies.

In the following, we present a framework for designing ethically acceptable services for home care. Our framework is based on three phases complementary to each other: (A) *Assessment of change needs in service production*; (B) *Value mapping of services*; and (C) *Ethical assessment of service production*. In our research, phases A and B were carried out in co-design sessions with experts in service development, while Phase C was conducted as co-design with care personnel and older citizens. The different phases of the framework are introduced in the following.

Phase A. Assessment of Change Needs in Service Production. In the first phase, change needs for home care services were investigated. We brought together a cross-section of stakeholders to discuss home care technology in order to build a shared understanding of future challenges and ethical issues related to acceptance, delivery and exploitation of emerging technologies in home care.

The study was carried out using a workshop as a practical tool that was complemented by interviews. Participants represented a municipal enterprise service centre, home care services development management in a metropolitan area, a national financial regulation and decision-making organization, and research organizations.

Table 1. Change needs of services for older citizens.

	2020–2021	2022–2025
Challenges, possibilities and needs	**Challenges:** Availability and funding of services. Resources limited in small communities with a majority elderly population Services comprise multiple technologies **Possibilities and needs:** Developing the governance of service delivery Private-public partnerships Technology increasingly located at home: how to handle maintenance, ownership, training, GDPR? Living at home for as long as possible: dignity/costs/scarce resources Sustainability	**Challenges:** Imbalance between increasing numbers of older people and amount of resources Imbalance between the needs of older people and the amount of care personnel The more technology, the less human contact? How to guarantee intimacy and physical contact? Grounds for granting services: inequality? Exclusion? Loss of privacy? Multiple problem clients and increasing numbers of people with memory impairment **Possibilities and needs:** Digitalization of home care Technology know-how increasing Proactivity needed in assessment of care needs Fast service for those living at home Role of family care givers diminishing; loneliness: pressure to increase communality How to ensure rich and meaningful life?
Central views and actors	**Central views:** Difference between 'housing' and 'home' Services to home: what is included in good living? Freedom of choice: services and living environment How to ensure autonomy? **Actors:** Elderly, disabled and special groups Family caregivers take more responsibility	**Central views:** Safety, identification and running errands Needs-based services: by whom, how and on what grounds are needs defined? Democratic service provision vs. solvency of the client Public vs. market-based services Urbanization and meaningfulness How to build a memory-friendly city? **Actors:** Elderly, voluntary people & associations, cultural services, social care professionals, family care givers, city dwellers
Actions and goals	Active and healthy life; increasing retirement age Generations act together Regulations for data collection and usage	Robots take care of heavy work Knowledge-based care Holistic wellbeing: cultural & social services Voluntary work in elderly care Remote groups, remote family care
Wishes for technology	Inclusive technology Sensors, IOT, video-based services Smart locks and keys	Robots, sensors, data analysis Ethical concerns of smarter AI, machine learning, self-learning algorithms AI to ensure better usability

Change needs in service production were discussed with the help of canvas drawings to trigger questions among participants about possibilities, challenges and needs for home care services for the next two and five years. After that, relevant stakeholders, their roles and the goals of actions were identified. Finally, expectations for future technology were identified. Table 1 above summarizes the outcomes of phase A.

Phase B. Value Mapping of Services. In phase B, we focused on understanding a home care ecosystem from the point of view of fulfilled, lost and new values with the help of a value mapping tool. The value mapping tool [52–54] was originally developed for business modelling for sustainability. When used for understanding responsibility, it helps actors in embedding responsibility and ethics into the core of the business model through improved understanding of the value proposition. It takes the network perspective and helps in analysing value creation opportunities from a multi-stakeholder perspective and understanding the positive and negative aspects of the value proposition of the value network [54].

Ideally, each stakeholder group considered relevant to the home care ecosystem would also be represented in the workshop [54]. In our study, the value mapping tool was utilized in the service provision process to help identify and explore the values of stakeholders, i.e. how they would benefit from the new service and what negative outcomes there might be for them. The goal of our exercise was to recognize stakeholder groups relevant to the home care context and to prioritize them according to their level of interests and power. After introducing the tool, the context in which the tool was used, i.e. home care as a service, was defined. The stakeholder groups were then identified and placed in segments using the value mapping tool. The benefits and challenges from the viewpoints of the different stakeholder groups were then discussed and documented. The key result of this value mapping discussion was the provision of a broad overview of the stakeholders and the positive and negative value that they could experience (see Fig. 2).

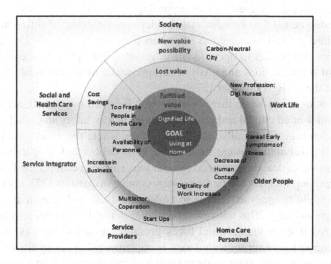

Fig. 2. The completed value map.

This case study gave us the possibility to explore and analyse the multiple value perspectives and interests of stakeholders from the viewpoint of responsible service development. Involving stakeholder representatives more broadly in this discussion would have been even more beneficial [52].

In good life ecosystems, it is necessary to find the right balance between value for the customer (the old person and the home care personnel) and value for the home care service provider. This calls for understanding among designers of the forms of life of the older people, how they live and act, but also the work environment of home care personnel [38]. The focal questions are: What is the problem that the technology has been introduced to address? Why? For whom is it a problem? What interventions have been tried to address this problem? Who decided on the technology and whose needs does it serve? What are the benefits of the technology for the actors in the ecosystem What are the benefits/drawbacks of the technology for the person(s) in question? Are the older people/home care organization ready and willing to adopt the technology?

Implementing a technology in home care does not only concern the immediate usage environment, i.e., the home, but changes the ways of working on an organizational level. For example, work and communication practices and management will need to change in step with changes in the technological environment. Changes in the technological environment often also require changes in attitudes towards new technologies and thus also concern public policy. The know-how of care personnel should be ensured along with the adoption of new technology [55, 56].

Phase C. Ethical Assessment of Service Production. In phase C, we focused on a selected service development and delivery, and studied this case in more detail. The aim was to understand what ethical principles and values should define the boundaries of the technology. This deliberation can be carried out with the help of a socio-technical scenario. A scenario can be used as a discussion tool to capture the different relevant aspects of the service and the actors and technology bound to it [57]. Socio-technical scenarios can also be used to broaden stakeholder understanding of different roles in shaping the future, as well as awareness of stakeholder interdependence [58]. With the help of scenarios, it is easier to operationalize 'good' in the design concepts from the point of view of actors, actions and goals of actions, and thus systematically assess the ethical value of the design outcomes [27].

An ethical issue arises when there is a dilemma between two simultaneous values (two ethical values or an ethical and practical value, such as safety and efficiency). For this reason, technology ethics calls for a broader view where the agents, the goal, and the context of the technology usage are discussed and deliberated in order to analyse, argue and report the ethical dilemma and its solution. This also enables the formulation of additional design principles for the technology context in question [27]. Finally, these ethical issues should be analysed further to understand them, solve them and translate them into design language. This outcome contributes to the design requirements [27].

We organized three human-centred focus group discussions focusing on a home monitoring scenario where sensor technology is implemented in senior citizens' homes to create an intelligent ambient environment that gathers information on how the inhabitant manages to perform her usual activities, and reveals possible changes in daily routines [38]. This information enables any variations in activity level to be detected and visualized. The data complement traditional health-related information, producing an integrated understanding of the person's daily performance. The technology is expected to reveal acute or gradual changes that may indicate a need for medical or other professional intervention. The scenario involves formal home care and a variety of stakeholders, and raises ethical questions of, e.g., integrity, autonomy and privacy.

Focus Group 1 consisted of older people living in their own home in a service house for seniors, with ubiquitous technology used in the home for study purposes. Focus

Group 2 consisted of professionals in the home care field. Focus Group 3 consisted of home care personnel, project coordinators, teachers and students acting in the field of home care and health care. It was found useful to study the possibilities for ethically sound service concepts by integrating older people and relevant stakeholders into the design discussion. Both sides are needed, as they weigh ethical principles and values differently. The participation of older people in the focus group revealed that they are relevant co-designers of the meaningfulness of technology in their own lives and in society [38].

The generic goals of the technology or service to be designed were discussed and analysed in the light of each identified ethical value. As the context of home care technology is always situated in a cultural environment [59], values for technology design and assessment naturally reflect the ethical values and norms of the given community. The results of the focus groups are summarized in tables below (Table 2 and Table 3).

Tables 2 and 3 illustrate that the groups emphasize slightly different issues. While older people value autonomy over privacy, home care professionals are highly concerned about the privacy of their clients and trust in technology. Meaningfulness was emphasized

Table 2. Stakeholders' appreciation of principles and values [38].

Mostly put forward by **older people**	Autonomy Meaningfulness E-inclusion
Mostly put forward by **home care planning officers**	Privacy Meaningfulness Trust
Mostly put forward by **home care personnel, academics and students**	Autonomy Informed consent Role of technology in society

Table 3. Main concerns about home monitoring technology [38].

Group 1	Group 2	Group 3
How to keep living independently? How to bring peace of mind to family and friends? How to guarantee that everyone can afford the technology? How to guarantee safety: quick help in acute need? How to avoid loss of social contacts?	How to guarantee the positive impact of technology on everyday home care work? How to modify the work of care workers in accordance with the efficient use of technology? How to find the best possible solution for each individual to ensure a better quality of life?	How to make people live a more active life? How to properly receive informed consent? How to make people aware of the need to nominate a trustee to decide on behalf of a person with memory impairment? How to define a trustee's qualifications? What kind of education is needed?

in groups 1 and 2. For older people, meaningfulness of monitoring technology is strongly linked with safety, a factor which they see as a prerequisite for independent living.

7 Conclusions

In this paper, we have discussed life-based design (LBD) [11, 60] in relation to a service ecosystem producing services for elderly people. In life-based design, the measure of technology is in its ability to enhance the quality of life for people. In LBD, design ideas are thoroughly examined to consider how they would support or inhibit the realization of a good life. LBD aims at identifying human requirements for services and defining how individuals' lives could be best improved with respect to their specific life circumstances. This information provides the *whys* and *what fors* that should guide the design process from the beginning to the very end [60].

A new perspective on LBD is to study it in the context of interdependent actors in a service ecosystem. This network of interdependent actors produces the needed services. While it is normal to consider that ecosystems produce economic or economy-related values, we have extended this approach by arguing that service and business ecosystems should be seen as sources of multi-dimensional value creation including social and environmental values. By arguing this, we were able to connect the ethical thinking and social responsibility aspects at the core of the ecosystem concept and analyse the dynamics of the service ecosystem from the perspective of ethics and the good life.

On this basis, we introduced an ecosystem based design and assessment framework for ethically acceptable services for the silver economy. Our case has been home care technology. We claim that successful implementation of ethics can create shared value [61] by providing sustainable solutions for older people, increased competitiveness for companies, and positive societal impact for society.

Our approach has three components: (A) Assessment of change needs in service production; (B) Value mapping of services; and (C) Ethical assessment of service production. In our research, phases A and B were carried out in co-design sessions with experts in service development, while Phase C was conducted as co-design with care personnel and older citizens.

Our study indicated how the assessment of ethical issues should take place in a dialogue where the impacts as well as positive and negative outcomes of technology innovations are anticipated. Deliberation of the ethical impacts of technology requires a multidisciplinary approach and the involvement of various experts and stakeholders.

Ethical questions related to the use and installation of technology require asking questions, consideration and debate from versatile perspectives and at different levels. This is particularly important when making decisions about people whose voice is not always heard when decisions on the use of technology are made. Human-centred multi-stakeholder co-design sessions bring all stakeholders together to discuss various socio-technical scenarios and design concepts. In this way, possible contradictory needs, attitudes and experiences concerning technology and ethics can be identified and understood.

Caring for older people is a social issue, and the use of technology should foster a community response, such as facilitating communication between individuals, instead of attempting to attend to the issue with technology alone [62]. In other words, the speed and efficiency of progress are not the only values. It is also necessary to know which direction to take and how to predict negative consequences.

Finally, successful implementation of ethics calls for changes in the ways all the organizations and actors in the service ecosystem operate and how they create value by their activity. In the creation of shared value, the voice of older people is needed as innovators of new ethical, needs-driven and demand-driven concepts for home care services.

References

1. Kohlbacher, F., Herstatt, C. (eds.): The Silver Market Phenomenon: Business Opportunities in an Era of Demographic Change. Springer, Berlin (2008). https://doi.org/10.1007/978-3-540-75331-5
2. Kohlbacher, F., Herstatt, C. (eds.): The Silver Market Phenomenon: Marketing and Innovation in the Aging Society, 2nd edn. Springer, Heidelberg (2011). https://doi.org/10.1007/978-3-642-14338-0
3. Thomé, B., Dykes, A.-K., Rahm Hallberg, I.: Home care with regard to definition, care recipients, content and outcome: systemic literature review. J. Clin. Nurs. **12**, 860–872 (2003)
4. van den Broek, G., Cavallo, F., Wehrmann, C.: AALIANCE Ambient Assisted Living Roadmap. IOS Press, Amsterdam (2019)
5. Andreu-Perez, J., Poon, C.C.Y., Merrifield, R.D., Wong, S.T.C., Yang, G.Z.: Big data for health. IEEE J. Biomed. Health Inf. **19**(4), 1193–1208 (2015)
6. Godman, B., et al.: Personalizing health care: feasibility and future implications. BMC Med. **11**, 179 (2013)
7. AI HLEG - European Commission's high-level expert group on artificial intelligence. Ethics guidelines for trustworthy AI, April 2019. https://ec.europa.eu/digital-single-market/en/news/ethics-guidelines-trustworthy-ai. Accessed 20 Jan 2020
8. Aristotle: Nicomachean ethics. In: Barnes, J. (ed.) The Complete Works of Aristotle. The Revised Oxford Translation, vol. 2. Princeton University Press, Princeton (1984). (n.d., trans. 1984)
9. Bowen, W.R.: Engineering Ethics. Outline of an Aspirational Approach. Springer, London (2009). https://doi.org/10.1007/978-1-84882-224-5
10. Stahl, B.C., et al.: Identifying the ethics of emerging information and communication technologies: an essay on issues, concepts and method. Int. J. Technoethics (IJT) **1**(4), 20–38 (2010)
11. Leikas, J.: Life-Based Design - A Holistic Approach to Designing Human-Technology Interaction. VTT Publications 726. Edita Prima, Helsinki (2009)
12. Westermarck, E.: The Origin and Development of the Moral Ideas, vol. 2. Macmillan and Company, New York (1908)
13. Rokeach, M.: Understanding Human Values: Individual and Societal. The Free Press, New York (1979)
14. Schwartz, S., Melech, G., Lehmann, A., Burgess, S., Harris, M., Owens, V.: Extending the cross-cultural validity of the theory of basic human values with a different method of measurement. J. Cross-C. Psychol. **32**, 519–542 (2001)
15. UN United Nations. Universal Declaration of Human Rights UDHR. http://www.un.org/en/universal-declaration-human-rights/. Accessed 5 Jan 2020
16. EU Treaties. https://europa.eu/european-union/law/treaties_en. Accessed 5 Jan 2020

17. EU Charter of Fundamental Rights 2000/C 364/01. http://www.europarl.europa.eu/charter/pdf/text_en.pdf. Accessed 5 Jan 2020
18. Pieper, R.: Technology and the social triangle of home care. In: Bjorneby, S., van Berlo, A. (eds.) Ethical Issues in Use of Technology for Dementia Care, pp. 1–30. Akontes Publishing, Knegsel (1997)
19. Stahl, C.B.: Ethics and research on information technology. Int. J. Technol. Hum. Interact. **1**. https://pdfs.semanticscholar.org/d0af/2913a54b9de6af8e0d3fd97af6e16f233ff8.pdf. Accessed 10 Jan 2020. Editorial Preface
20. Widdershoven, G.A.M.: Ethics and gerontechnology: a plea for integration. In: Graafmans, J., Taipale, V., Charness, N. (eds.) Gerontechnology. A Sustainable Investment in the Future, pp. 105–111. IOS Press, Amsterdam (1998)
21. van den Hoven, J.: Values, design and information technology: the front loading of ethics. In: Proceedings of ETHICOMP 2005, September 2005, Linköping University, Linköping, Sweden, pp. 12–15 (2005)
22. Eccles, A., Damodaran, L., Olphert, W., Hardill, I., Gilhooly, M.: Assistive technologies: ethical practice, ethical research, and quality of life. In: Sixsmith, A., Gutman, G. (eds.) Technologies for Active Aging. International Perspectives on Aging, vol. 9, pp. 47–68. Springer, New York (2013). https://doi.org/10.1007/978-1-4419-8348-0_4
23. Friedman, B., Kahn, P.H., Borning, A.: Value sensitive design and information systems. In: Zhang, P., Galletta, D. (eds.) Human-Computer Interaction in Management Information Systems: Foundations. M.E. Sharpe, New York (2006)
24. Borning, A., Muller, M.: Next steps for value sensitive design. In: Proceedings of the SIGCHI Conference on Human Factors in Computing Systems, Austin, TX, USA, 5–10 May 2012, pp. 1125–1134 (2012)
25. EGE - European Group on ethics in science and new technologies. Statement on artificial intelligence, robotics and 'autonomous' systems. https://ec.europa.eu/research/ege/pdf/ege_ai_statement_2018.pdf. Accessed 15 Dec 2019
26. Floridi, L., et al.: AI4People—an ethical framework for a good AI society. Minds Mach. **28**, 689–707 (2018)
27. Leikas, J., Koivisto, R., Gotcheva, N.: Ethical framework for designing autonomous systems. J. Open Innov. Technol. Mark. Complex. **5**, 18 (2019). https://doi.org/10.3390/joitmc5010018
28. Hansson, S.O. (ed.): The Ethics of Technology: Methods and Approaches. Rowman & Littlefield, London (2017)
29. Pew, R.W., Van Hemel, S. (eds.): Technology for Adaptive Aging. National Academies Press, Washington (2004)
30. Blueprint. Digital transformation of health and care for the ageing society. Strategic vision developed by stakeholders, 15 January 2017. https://ec.europa.eu/digital-single-market/en/blueprint-digital-transformation-health-and-care-ageing-society. Accessed 15 Dec 2019
31. WHO World Health Organization. Active aging: a policy framework. http://whqlibdoc.who.int/hq/2002/WHO_NMH_NPH_02.8.pdf. Accessed 15 Dec 2019
32. Downs, M.: The emergence of the person in dementia research. Ageing Soc. **17**, 597–607 (1997)
33. Lorenzen-Huber, L., Boutain, M., Camp, L.J., Shankar, K., Connelly, K.H.: Privacy, technology, and aging: a proposed framework. Ageing Int. **36**, 232–252 (2011)
34. Diller, S., Lin, L., Tashjian, V.: The evolving role of security, privacy, and trust in a digitized world. In: Jacko, J.A., Sears, A. (eds.) The Human-Computer Interaction Handbook. Fundamentals, Evolving Technologies and Emerging Applications, pp. 1213–1225. Lawrence Erlbaum, Mahwah (2003)
35. Rauhala, M., Topo, P.: Independent living, technology and ethics. Technol. Disabil. **15**, 205–214 (2003)

36. Czaja, S.J., Lee, C.C.: Designing computer systems for older adults. In: Jacko, J.A., Sears, A. (eds.) The Human-Computer Interaction Handbook. Fundamentals, Evolving Technologies and Emerging Applications. Lawrence Erlbaum, Mahwah (2003)
37. Rauhala-Hayes, M.: Ethics of care work. In: Bjorneby, S., van Berlo, A. (eds.) Ethical Issues in Use of Technology for Dementia Care, pp. 73–86. Akontes Publishing, Knegsel (1997)
38. Leikas, J., Kulju, M.: Ethical consideration of home monitoring technology: a qualitative focus group study. Gerontechnology **17**(1), 38–47 (2018)
39. Porcari, A., Borsella, E., Mantovani, E. (eds.): Responsible-Industry. Executive Brief. Implementing Responsible Research and Innovation in ICT for an Ageing Society. Italian Association for Industrial Research, Rome (2015)
40. Phillips, M.A., Ritala, P.: A complex adaptive systems agenda for ecosystem research methodology. Technol. Forecast. Soc. Change **148**, 119739 (2019)
41. Boudreau, K.J., Hagiu, A.: Platform rules: multi-sided platforms as regulators. In: Gawer, A. (ed.) Platforms, Markets and Innovation, pp. 163–191. Edward Elgar Publishing Limited, Cheltenham (2018)
42. Arthur, W.B.: Complexity and the Economy. OUP, Oxford (2015)
43. Holland, J.H.: Complexity, A Very Short Introduction. OUP, Oxford (2014)
44. Nicolis, G., Prigogine, I.: Exploring Complexity: an Introduction. Freeman, New York (1989)
45. Valkokari, K.: Business, innovation, and knowledge ecosystems: how they differ and how to survive and thrive within them. Technol. Innov. Manag. Rev. **5**(8), 17–24 (2015)
46. Moore, J.F.: Predators and prey: a new ecology of competition. Harv. Bus. Rev. **71**(3), 75–83 (1993)
47. Adner, R., Kapoor, R.: Value creation in innovation ecosystems: How the structure of technological interdependence affects firm performance in new technology generations. Strateg. Manag. J. **31**(3), 306–333 (2010)
48. Autio, E., Thomas, L.D.W.: Innovation ecosystems. In: Oxford Handbook of Innovation Management, pp. 204–288 (2013)
49. Pitelis, C.: The co-evolution of organizational value capture, value creation and sustainable advantage. Organ. Stud. **10**(30), 1115–1139 (2009)
50. Peltoniemi, M., Vuori, E.: Business ecosystem as the new approach to complex adaptive business environments. In: Proceedings of eBusiness Research Forum, vol. 2, no. 22 (2004)
51. Miettinen, J., Mäkinen, M., Leikas, J., Jutila, T., Veko, T.: Responsible enterprise resource planning in home care. Finnish J. eHealth eWelf. (2020)
52. Palomäki, K., Rana, P.: Mapping multiple stakeholder value in service innovation: an industrial case study. Int. J. Serv. Sci. **6**(3/4), 218 (2017)
53. Short, S.W., Rana, P., Bocken, N.M.P., Evans, S.: Embedding sustainability in business modelling through multi-stakeholder value innovation. In: Emmanouilidis, C., Taisch, M., Kiritsis, D. (eds.) APMS 2012. IAICT, vol. 397, pp. 175–183. Springer, Heidelberg (2013). https://doi.org/10.1007/978-3-642-40352-1_23
54. Bocken, N.M.P., Short, S., Rana, P., Evans, S.: A value mapping tool for sustainable business modelling. Corp. Gov. **13**(5), 482–497 (2013)
55. Karsh, B.T.: Beyond usability: designing effective technology implementation systems to promote patient safety. Qual. Saf. Health Care. http://dx.doi.org/10.1136/qshc.2004.010322. Accessed 5 Dec 2019
56. Kivisaari, S., Väyrynen, E., Saranummi, N.: Knowledge-intensive service activities in health care innovation. Case Pirkanmaa. VTT Research Notes 2267. VTT, Helsinki (2004). https://www.vtt.fi/inf/pdf/tiedotteet/2004/T2267.pdf. Accessed 2 Dec 2019
57. Carroll, J.M.: Five reasons for scenario-based design. Interact. Comput. **13**, 43–60 (2000)
58. Lucivero, F.: Ethical Assessments of Emerging Technologies: Appraising the Moral Plausibility of Technological Visions. The International Library of Ethics, Law and Technology, vol. 15. Springer, Heidelberg (2016). https://doi.org/10.1007/978-3-319-23282-9

59. Shrader-Frechette, K.S.: Environmental Justice: Creating Equality, Reclaiming Democracy. Oxford University Press, Oxford (2002)
60. Saariluoma, P., Cañas, J.J., Leikas, J.: Designing for Life - A Human Perspective on Technology Development. Palgrave MacMillan, London (2016)
61. Porter, M.E., Kramer, M.R.: Creating Shared Value: How to Reinvent Capitalism, pp. 2–17. Harvard Business Review, Watertown (2011)
62. Vermesan, O., et al.: Internet of things strategic research roadmap. European Commission (2009)

Hume's Guillotine Resolved

Pertti Saariluoma[✉]

Jyväskylä University, 40014 Jyväskylä, Finland
ps@jyu.fi

Abstract. According to Hume's guillotine, one cannot derive values from facts. Since intelligent systems are fact processors, one can ask how ethical machines can be possible. However, ethics is a real-life process. People analyze actions and situations emotionally and cognitively. Thus they learn rules, such as "this situation feels good/bad." The cognitive analysis of actions is associated with emotional analysis. The association of action, emotion and cognition can be termed a primary ethical schema. Through an ethical information process in which emotions and cognitions interact in social discourse, primary ethical schemas are refined into ethical norms. Each component of the process is different, but they cooperate to construct an ethical approach to thinking.

Hume's guillotine mistakenly breaks down primary ethical schemas and juxtaposes emotions and cognitions. There is no ethics without coordinated emotional, cognitive and social analysis. Therefore, his theory can be seen as a pseudo problem.

In the future, ethical processes will involve intelligent systems that can make ethical choices. Weak ethical artificial intelligence (AI) systems can apply given ethical rules to data, while strong ethical AI systems can derive their own rules from data and knowledge about human emotions. Resolving Hume's guillotine introduces new ways to develop stronger forms of ethical AI.

Keywords: Hume's guillotine · Intelligent system · Ethical information processes

1 Introduction

Human living centers on satisfying basic human needs. People set goals and use technical artefacts (e.g. programs, machines and devices) to help them pursue these goals. Thus technical artefacts, and how people use them, are important to consider when constructing the future intelligent information society. Designers must fit new technologies into the basic contexts of human life.

People act in groups and unify their efforts to reach their goals socially. They constantly participate in an infinite number of explicit and implicit action systems – what I call "forms of life" – such as programmers, soccer fans, nurses, workers, newspaper readers, elevens and executives. The concept of a form of life allows us to apply a I recommend clarifying what you mean by this.

Single concept to discuss kindergartens as well as parliaments and religious cultures [1, 2]. Given the structure of human actions, it is helpful to consider human technology

© Springer Nature Switzerland AG 2020
M. Rauterberg (Ed.): HCII 2020, LNCS 12215, pp. 123–132, 2020.
https://doi.org/10.1007/978-3-030-50267-6_10

interaction (HTI) problems from the human point of view. One of the central issues related to HTI today is ethics for intelligent systems.

Ethics can be seen as a system of ethical or moral rules and principles or laws [3]. However, the concept can also be considered as a system of real human actions [4]. For example, one can use ethical rules to ethically regulate marriage (i.e. normative ethics or norm-oriented ethics), but it is also possible to investigate how people in different cultures *really* act in their marriages (i.e. real-life or life-based ethics) [4].

When ethically regulating the human use of (or interaction with) intelligent systems, both axiological and action-based thinking are relevant. However, if researchers take the latter path, it will be essential to understand ethics as human information processing, i.e., thinking about what happens in human minds when they interact with intelligent systems among other people.

Human actions are controlled by mental processes: the mind tells the body what to do. Experience provides people with conscious representations of situations, actions and feelings; underlying these experiences, the mind operates as an information processing system in a broad sense [5, 6]. People experience *cognition*, which refers to information-related processes such as perceiving, attending, remembering and using language and thinking, and *emotions*, which include feeling and appraising the goodness and badness of things and events in relation to oneself [7]; researchers and designers must keep in mind social information processing [1, 8]. The human mind forms mental representations [5], which control every aspect of actions, from thoughts to motor movements. The information content of mental representations is called mental content. It is the basic theoretical concept in analyzing HTI issues from a human point of view [5]. Understanding how people mentally represent can be clarified by understanding the relevant mental content. Through teaching and training, people can find and use new mental content.

Ethical and moral information is a good example of mental content that is important in human HTI analysis. Ethical practices, rules, norms and tacit principles constitute mental content. If a person does not engage in truthful net communication practices, it is a value system, and it is mentally represented. In the opposite case, the information is also represented in the individual's mental content. Thus, explaining ethical information processing can be grounded in mental content. The prevailing mental content, with its emotional and cognitive aspects, explains how people act.

Consequently, investigations of ethical issues related to HTI can be approached from an information processing point of view. Thus researchers investigate how the human mind operates in different ways when people participate in different forms of life. From this point of view, it is also possible to reconsider classical problems of ethics such as Hume's guillotine [9], or the "is–ought to" problem.

Hume's problem is tricky in several senses when we think about how ethical AI life should be designed. First, it discusses the relationship between facts and values. This problem is important, as intelligent systems are fact processors. Second, his moral theories are firmly grounded in empiricist psychological thinking. Sentiments or emotions and reasons or cognitions are a central part of his thinking. As discussed in more detail below, resolving Hume's problem has important implications for the modern ethics of intelligent systems, their social use and technology design thinking.

2 Intelligent Systems and Hume's Guillotine

Technologies are developed and justified to help people achieve their goals and to improve the quality of human life or wellness [9]. The objective of a new technology is to make people's lives easier than before. Making something happen is a form of *emancipation*, which means expanding the possibilities of life. Historically, emancipation refers to breaking free from the social conditions that enslave people [1]. Life can be restricted by many kinds of necessities, difficulties, limitations and non-ideal living conditions that prevent people from increasing their happiness. But many of these problems can be solved or improved through technological advancements. Intelligent systems hold particular promise in their capacity to improve human life by emancipating people from routine tasks.

Intelligent technologies represent a new technological revolution, like stone-cutting tools, the printing press, steam technology, electricity, and nuclear energy generated new forms of work and social organization in the past [9]. Modern intelligent systems such as AI, autonomous systems and robots can carry out complex tasks that previously required information processing from a human mind. These emerging technological applications have revolutionary implications for the industrial processes, office automation, intelligent medicine, teaching, autonomous traffic systems and intelligent finance of the future [10].

In addition to fast routine processing logical inferences, intelligent systems can make decisions between alternative sense-making courses of action. They can even learn to make classifications of their own, so people cannot predict the information states that they can generate. Their capacity to engage in selective information processing makes it possible for modern AI-based systems to compare the values of different information states to select the one that is most fit for purpose.

Ethics introduces a very specific way to think about intelligent choices. Some information states are more ethical than others, and thus it makes sense to discuss ethics in the context of acting intelligent machines. They can select some courses of action based on the justification that they are more ethical than others. Thus, intelligent technologies can make operational decisions on ethical grounds. They can choose between different courses of action based on defined ethical principles. For example, intelligent systems can prioritize children over middle-aged people in making decisions about the order of medical operations.

Over 250 years ago David Hume identified an important problem in attempts to identify a relationship between facts and values: "It is impossible that the distinction between for all good and evil can be made by reason" [12]. This dilemma, known as Hume's guillotine or the "is-ought to problem", is central to the study of modern ethics. Hume's guillotine claims that one cannot determine how things *should be* based on how they *are*. When designing ethically intelligent machines, this is a relevant conceptual problem. One can justly ask: Can machines that process facts do so ethically, and if so, how is this possible?

The difference between how things are and how they should be plays a central role in ethical design thinking about how to improve things. Ethical design focuses on how to move from a given system of prevailing values to a system that improves the quality of human life. Scientific knowledge about human information processing is vital to this work.

Real-life ethics involves studying how human information processes, emotions, cognitions and social information processing can be used to analyze the emergence of ethical norms, rules and actions. How it is possible for the human mind to create new ethical norms and practices? Of course, people have developed ethical norms such as laws and ethically regulated action patterns. One way to approach real-life ethics is to evaluate how different aspects of human information processes have been used to discuss the nature of ethics.

3 Emotions and Cognitions

Emotive ethics or emotivism serve as a good starting point for the present analysis of the ethical relevance of information processes. In human information processing, emotions represent an evolutionarily more basic system of thinking than cognition. Emotional areas of the brain develop earlier than cognition, and especially higher-level cognition such as thinking.

Emotional ethics considers emotions to be fundamental components of ethical thinking. It was central to British empiricism. Smith [13] and Hume [12], for example, recognized the importance of emotional processes or passions and sentiments. In the last century many important researchers such as Moore [14] and Ayer [15] have also supported emotivism in different forms.

In information processing concepts, a key feature of emotions is valence, which refers to the positivity or negativity of emotions [7]. Pleasure and pain, good and bad, sorrow and joy, warmth and coldness are examples of opposite valences. In ethics and information processing, valence defines the goodness of actions and situations, and thus is essential to deciding how positive or negative actions and respective situations are from an individual's point of view.

The problem of Hume's guillotine arises from the difference between emotions and reason or cognition. Hume discussed the differences between reason and passion. He argued that the function of reason is to decide whether something is true or false. Emotions or passions with morals "produce or prevent actions." The two units are separate in the sense that truth and falsehood, i.e. reason, cannot dictate emotions. A typical consequence is the differentiation between the theoretical (i.e. reason based and practical) and the philosophical (i.e., passion dominated). Moreover, the distinction between an act that is morally good or bad cannot be made based solely on reason [12]. Hume views ethics as human mental activity that entails how people feel and reason – not simply as a system of rules.

Cognitive and human cognition refers to how people process knowledge [16]. Individuals take information from their environment, and store and manipulate it; in turn, it regulates their actions. Cognition registers actions and thoughts that have led people to a particular situation, and stores this information as memories. Thus, cognition provides mental representations of situations and the actions that have led to these situations.

Several ethics frameworks have grounded prior thinking about cognition. Typical examples are Kantian [17] and deontological ethics and Moses's ethics or Ten Commandments [18]. These directions present explicated norms of behavior that define how one should act to act correctly. All such norms and principles are expressed in the cognitive mind.

Emotional processes are closely linked to cognition. Emotional states are based on an individual's understanding of the current situation. If the situation is cognitively understood to be risky or threatening, the emotional states are constructed based on danger-related emotions, such as excitement, fear and courage. If positive cognitions dominate the situation, emotional states are characterized by relaxation, happiness, humor and benevolence. Before the situation-related emotional representation is constructed in the human mind, its cognitive content must be clear to the individual [7].

The psychological process of linking a situation's cognitive and emotional representations is called appraisal. Appraisal is a core process in the psychology of emotions [7], which is often defined as the representation of an individual's emotional significance, and the associated emotional value of cognitions and actions. Emotions associated with the use of technologies are relevant in the study of technology-related and AI ethics.

Cognitions provide cognitive aspects of ethical experiences in particular situations. Emotions provide evaluative information about these situations – for instance whether situations are pleasant or unpleasant, and good or bad for the person experiencing them. Thus, ethical experiences arise both from cognitions and emotions. The two systems encode different aspects of experiences and the respective mental representations.

People learn from experience to associate their actions with the situations the actions have led to. Based on these learned experiences, they encode rules of good conduct in interacting with technologies, including intelligent technologies. People learn to use them, which generates memory representations about the consequences of their actions and reasons why particular types of actions should be avoided or pursued, i.e., are the actions or duties allowed or forbidden. The representation of an action, its end situation and the emotional analysis of this situation can be called primary ethical representation.

4 Social Discourse

Ethics is social because people are social. Aristotle's [19] concept of "Zoon Politicon" expresses this aspect of human nature effectively. In their social actions, people organize themselves into an infinite number of types of social circles including sports clubs, house societies, non-governmental organizations, states, schools, religious communities, campers, families, entrepreneurs and taxpayers. Any social group that organizes a participant's actions around some system of rule-following actions can be thought of as a *form of life* [1, 2].

Forms of life are organized systems of action in which individuals can participate, and ethics is essential to forming them. If one is Catholic, they typically participate in the ceremonies of the holy week. People follow the norms and traditions of the event. In families, most people strive to take care of their children and speak with them about the way people should live. Such discourses belong to the family form of life.

Forms of life have rules, but these rules keep changing. A key mechanism of such changes is social discourse in its numerous forms [19]. Social discourse entails communicating individual ethical rules and norms. People feel that something causes pain and identify the mechanism of action that led to those unpleasant feelings. The discourses in different contexts give people the ability to create common norms within society, which in turn shape the forms of life.

Social discourse entails both free and normed forms. For example, discussions among friends are different from discourses in enterprise executive boards. Much social discourse now takes place via social media and other media. Even academic and political disputes on ethical issues can be seen as aspects of social discourse. Yet, these discourses create many types of actions that regulate ethical rules, such as company policies. How to express oneself in meetings and how to group in restaurants are typical examples of rules that regulate actions in organizational forms of life. Social discourse creates various social norms to guide how people act when participating in different forms of life.

Ethical discourse is in many ways beginning to define how people should act in different forms of life. It creates basic regulatory norms and values. However, societies are often regulated by laws. Of course, law making is an outcome of social discourse that is private as well as administrative or political. The forms of these discourses can vary from one society to another; democracies organize their discourses differently from oligarchies or dictatorships. Nevertheless, there are always groups of people who create new forms of life through thinking and discourse.

The social process of creating informal, tacit and formal regulatory rules and principles for different forms of life has been analyzed in detail in discourse ethics. A key issue is that the ideas are submitted for social discourse in different forms. Ideally, ideas are analyzed by assessing the argumentation. If arguments are valid, it is possible to continue norming. However, if they are no longer valid, e.g. historical changes have made them outdated, the rules should be replaced [19].

A very large "sea of social discourses" creates socially shared norms and renews them constantly. Social attitudes keep changing, social experiences are communicated to other people, and the discourse converges into systems of tacit and explicit norms and values. As a whole, the system of emotional valences, social analysis of related actions and action types, as well as social discourse formulate the ethical process. This process creates the values people follow in their everyday lives.

Individuals' primary ethical schemas form the basis of social discourse. Through small and large, formal and informal discussions, people form their views about what are the most important and fundamental ethical experiences and respective rules. Discourse ethics has investigated this process [19].

In discourse ethics, representations are submitted to argumentative or foundational analysis. Each primary representation or ethical rule will be submitted to the foundational discourse. Any ethical rules that cannot be argumentatively supported will be rejected. The discourse itself has layers and sub-discourses. The main outcome is a system of ethical concepts, rules and principles. The unification of emotional, cognitive and social analysis can be called an ethical process.

5 Ethical Information Process and Process Ethics

The ethical information process is the source of practical ethics in life: It creates values and norms. Research on ethical processes is valuable, as it creates a picture of a society's ethical thinking. Understanding the ethical process also makes it possible to solve the problem of Hume's guillotine. It appears to be a result of insufficient analysis of the relationship between people's minds and actions.

The analysis of ethical processes represents a specific approach to the study of ethics, which can be supported by its importance in designing an ethical world. For example, instead of representing external norms for the right kind of patient care, designers can work to understand how people are *really taken care of*, for example in units for senior citizens, and what norms they follow in their daily lives.

This type of empirical ethics is intimately connected to the analysis of ethical processes, but it has an important difference. The former moves the focus from academic discussions to life as people live it, which leads to the tacit and explicit development of a society's ethics, while the latter refers to the analysis of how norms are created. It is thus an empirical model of metaethical processes in real life. Westermarck [4] studied the norms and values of empirical ethics, while the analysis of ethical information processes presented here concentrates on the process of creating values. In ethical information processes, the creation of values and following them are both important. I refer to ethics based on the analysis of real-life value creation processes as "process ethics" to distinguish it from earlier approaches to ethics.

Value creation is important for design thinking. If researchers understand the value creation process, they can improve it by providing empirical information on different aspects of the process. This shift from reflective to active involvement and influence is vital in designing ethical AI processes.

Ethical information processes can help circumvent Hume's guillotine. Hume makes the fundamental (unsupported) assumption that emotions and cognitions are opposites in some sense, and that reason cannot affect sentiments or emotions. However, there is no support for such a conceptual differentiation in modern research on the mind. One cannot derive that the two concepts are opposites based on the fact they are different. In this case, they can complement each other.

Human actions are jointly regulated by both emotions and cognitions. They have different functions, and both are necessary. Emotions determine the goodness or badness of actions and attribute personal meaning to individuals [7], while cognitions analyze actions and consequential situations. Thus, the two faculties together can construct ethical experience and primary ethical schemas. Social discourse turns these primary ethical experiences and schemas into socially agreed rules and even laws. In this way they perform functions within relevant forms of life. Thus, Hume's guillotine is a pseudo problem that arises from a mistaken conceptualization of the mind and actions. The next section considers what ethical information processes and their analysis can add to our understanding of ethical machines.

6 Weak and Strong Ethical Intelligence

Improved computing speeds and the fast growth of data have made it possible to design technical artefacts with the ability to perform tasks that previously only people could carry out. Such machines are called intelligent systems as they execute tasks that demand intelligence from people. In addition to fast routine processing logical inferences, machines can decide between alternative courses of action. They can even learn to make classifications of their own, so that people are not able to predict the information states that intelligent systems can generate. Consequently, intelligent systems can select between different sense-making courses of action.

The capacity to engage in selective information processing makes it possible for modern AI and machine-based systems to compare the values of different information states on sense-making grounds. A chess-playing computer, for example, can find the best sequences of moves among millions of legal alternatives. Intelligent choices make machine actions intelligent. Similarly, ethical rules can be used as heuristics in selecting between different tasks.

For these reasons, one can speak of ethics typical to using intelligent technologies in two senses: (1) the ethical use of technical artefacts in society or (2) the development of systems with ethical capacities of some type. Here I investigate what it means to have ethical machines and technical artefacts.

Intelligent machines can be either weakly ethical (machines implement heuristics created by humans) or strongly ethical (machines can generate their own new ethical rules and principles). Hume's guillotine is easier to solve based on the former case. However, it is important to first ask how ethical information processing is possible, and then to evaluate how weak and strong ethical AI differ from each other.

The fall of Hume's guillotine paves the way for the development of strong ethical AI systems. It is possible to analyze data and see its connections to actions. Machines can also help determine if the resulting situations are emotionally pleasant or unpleasant. By combining the facts with emotional valence information concerning particular situations, machines can discover new primary values for social discourse. They can construct primary ethical schemas and thus develop stronger ethical AI. Human social discourse would be required to decide whether these new primary schemas are valid.

7   Ethics in Designing Intelligent Systems

Intelligent technologies introduce a new element of human actions and forms of life. Intelligent systems will perform an increasingly larger share of actions. Such systems can process ethical information and carry out ethics-requiring tasks. For example, social services or migration offices must analyze masses of applications for services, but they have to decide which can be accepted at least partly on ethical grounds.

Ethical processes must thus be studied using human research methods and approaches, but they should also be designed and improved. Importantly, intelligent technologies can help us understand how to design ethical processes. Value-based design and ethically aligned design are examples of how design thinking can help create ethical social processes or forms of life.

A core problem associated with designing ethical processes is how to implement ethics in machines. Weak AI is not a difficult case. Ethical norms can be implemented in AI programs by defining ethics-requiring situations and their factual properties. Intelligent systems can extract key information from data, and associated ethical norms can be followed in actions. For example, an underage person applying for a driving license can be taken out of line to return a year later. Designers of ethical processes and forms of life can build recognition–association type action models with ethical content.

Strong AI in ethical processes is a more challenging case. In principle, such systems can suggest primary ethical schemas. Therefore, they have the capacity to develop strong AI. However, as primary ethical schemas are always accepted by social discourse, the primary schemas suggested by intelligent systems must also be subsumed under social discourse before their acceptance.

The border between weak and strong AI is not absolute, but systems can differ in their strength. The strength of an ethical AI system is based on its capacity to create new ethical norms without human process time involvement. First, it is possible by means of data analysis to study possible pain- or negative-valence-causing situations. For example, data mining can identify new factors that cause illnesses. Such research has existed for a long time. For example, Durkheim [10] found a link between religion, social discourse, and suicide, and a connection between smoking and lung cancer was found in the 1960s. There is no logical obstacle to using intelligent systems to find such associations. Thus, human-supported AI and data mining can be used to find novel factual grounds for new ways of behaving. This kind of ethical AI system is known as machine-supported AI.

Another possibility is to ask machines to recognize features that are known to cause emotionally negative experiences. Human responses to different types of situations would first be registered to classify them as emotionally negative. AI programmes could actively search for new combinations. The information found can be associated with actions that produce negative situations, and thus new information can be used to create new ethical rules.

Finally, the core issue is whether intelligent systems can create new ethical norms without human involvement to process based on their factual data. Machines can use different approaches to analyze emotional valences typical to some situations, and associate the results of this emotional analysis with the actions. They can even analyze general social attitudes in these situations to gradually increase the autonomy of ethical systems. But human involvement can be relatively direct in creating new ethical rules.

Since information systems are involved in carrying out increasingly complicated actions, it is essential to develop ethical capacities for these systems. Their operational roles can be very independent, and thus it is essential that they can follow sense-making ethical practices.

Apparently, Hume's guillotine can make it hard to develop ethical autonomy for future systems. Intelligent systems are primarily factual information processing devices, and it is not easy to see how one could derive values from facts. Despite conceptual difficulties, it is important to investigate how intelligent systems can follow ethical norms in their actions.

Thus ethical information processing can be conceived as a spectrum with weak and strong ethical AI at either end. Weak AI systems can recognize critical features in situations and apply given ethical rules in these situations. In such cases, ethics are just a human-implanted feature in a recognition action system.

Yet despite Hume's guillotine, people are able to create ethical thoughts and information processes. Thus, it must be possible to create machine-supported ethical processes with greater autonomy. Analyzing the ethical process also provides clues about how machines can be used to improve existing ethical processes and create new ones. Thus, strong ethical AI systems can collect data, associate it with situations, and link these situations to emotional valence and respective actions. Such systems could develop new ethical principles to follow.

Finally, the outcome of Hume's guillotine is the unnecessary and mistaken juxta-position of emotions and cognitions. People associate emotions with cognitive plans and experience the outcome of a situation as either positive or negative. Based on their experience, they create primary ethical schemas and practices, which through social discourse become general ethical principles and even juridical laws.

Social norms can be implemented in machines, which can in turn be part of ethical information processes. Intelligent systems can recognize situations and be aware of ethical feelings associated with these situations – and thus make ethics-based decisions about their actions. Intelligent systems can also identify new types of properties in situations and determine whether they are emotionally positive or negative. Thus, designers can move from weak to strong AI. Yet, designers are still necessary, and ethical processes aided by intelligent systems are not created for systems but for people.

References

1. Saariluoma, P., Cañas, J., Leikas, J.: Designing for Life. Macmillan, London (2016)
2. Wittgenstein, L.: Philosophical Investigations. Basil Blackwell, Oxford (1953)
3. Kant, I.: Kritik der reinen Vernunft. [The critique of pure reason]. Felix Meiner, Hamburg (1781/1976)
4. Westermarck, E.: The Origins and Development of Moral Ideas. MacMillan, London (1906)
5. Newell, A., Simon, H.A.: Human Problem Solving. Prentice-Hall, Engelwood Cliffs (1972)
6. Neisser, U.: Cognition and Reality. Freeman, San Francisco (1976)
7. Frijda, N.H.: The Emotions. Cambridge University Press, Cambridge (1986)
8. Moscovici, S.: Social Representations. Polity Press, Cambridge (2000)
9. Bernal, J.D.: Science in History. Penguin Books, Harmondsworth (1969)
10. Tegmark, M.: Life 3.0. Penguin Books, Harmondsworth (2017)
11. von Wright, G.H.: Explanation and Understanding. Routledge and Kegan Paul, London (1971)
12. Hume, D.: A Treatise of Human Nature. Dent, London (1972)
13. Smith, A.: The Wealth of Nations. Dent, London (1975)
14. Moore, G.E.: Principia Ethica. Cambridge University Press, Cambridge (1996)
15. Ayer, A.: Language, Truth and Logic. Victor Collanz, London (1936)
16. Anderson, J.R.: Rules of the Mind. Erlbaum, Hillsdale (1993)
17. Malik, K.: A Quest for a Moral Compass. Atlantic Books, London (2014)
18. Habermas, J.: Diskursethik (Discourse ethics). Surkamp, Frankfurth am Main (2018)

Influences on Livestreaming Usage in China: Contents, Motivations, and Engagements

Yisi Yang[(⊠)]

Department of Asia-Pacific Studies, Waseda University, Tokyo, Japan
yangyisi@fuji.waseda.jp

Abstract. Viewing livestreams has already become a popular media habitus in China. The overall purpose of this research is to gain a better understanding of user motivation to view different livestreaming content in China. Therefore, this study adopts affective, cognitive, personal integrative, social integrative, and tension release to study the reasons behind this impulse. An analysis of 416 valid participants was established through the online questionnaire responded to by Chinese livestreaming users analyzed by linear regression. The results of this research indicated that Chinese audiences had different motivations for watching Esports, entertainment, knowledge-sharing, and E-commerce livestreams. The main reason Chinese audiences watch livestreams is that watching livestreaming can bring them joyfulness, self-pleasure, cognitive satisfaction, and pressure release, while social needs can explain more of audiences' emotional engagements. Furthermore, this study also explored the motivations behind audiences' deeper engagements. This study also represents an attempt to quantify unexplored differences in various livestreaming contents' perceptions of viewer motivations in China, which not only can offer the hint to the livestreaming industry and company but also influence the audiences and streamers in China. This research is among the first to explore the various livestreaming users' motivations based on motivational factors in China.

Keywords: Live streaming · Motivation · Content · Engagement

1 Introduction

The development of mobile Internet technology has interpenetrated the users' entertainment needs and consumption behaviours. Specifically, online live streaming has already become a popular entertaining application. Live streaming services such as Twitch, Douyu TV, YY Live, and Taobao Live have created a platform where audiences can interact with the streamers by commenting, chatting, donating paid gifts, and so on [22]. Live streaming also has shown diversity in content beyond game streaming and Esports, offering options such as e-commerce, social eating, dancing, singing, tattooing, etc. [12]. In the Chinese live-streaming market, the genres of live streaming can be generally dived into entertainment, e-commerce, Esports, and knowledge sharing [24].

Although there has been research on the motivations and engagements of streaming users, there is little understanding of audiences' motivations and engagements as they

© Springer Nature Switzerland AG 2020
M. Rauterberg (Ed.): HCII 2020, LNCS 12215, pp. 133–142, 2020.
https://doi.org/10.1007/978-3-030-50267-6_11

relate to different types of live-streaming content is different. This study will adopt a Uses and Gratification theory theoretical approach to explore Chinese live-streaming users' motivations and engagements with particular attention to the relationship of the live-streaming content. The overall target of this research is to acquire a better understanding of why Chinese streaming audiences engage in various types of live streaming media by conducting an online investigation in China.

2   Background

There have already accumulated a certain number of research studies about the live streaming industry. The majority of studies on live streaming can be divided into two schools. One research tendency is concentrating on the humanistic study, including the motivation research of the audiences and the broadcasters; meanwhile, the other one is more concerned with the media studies covering the live streaming content analysis, the application of media theory, and so on.

2.1   Research on the Live Streaming Participants

The nature of live streaming is not only about the media content but also the social interaction in line with the streaming platform. The social attribute of the live stream has been leading one of the research directions in the last few years. Scheibe, Fietkiewicz, and Stock [14] proposed the definition of Social Live Streaming Services (SLSSs) which underlines the interactive function of the live-streaming platform. Specifically, the audiences are able to communicate while watching the live broadcast. This human participation in the streaming has been studied from various perspectives. The most popular research topic is based on the reason why audiences choose to watch live streaming [2, 5–8, 15–18].

Among these researches, Sjöblom and Hamari [15] attempted to study the motivation of Esports users by designing the questionnaire, highlighting the definition of Esports as follows: 'its input and output are mediated by human-computer interfaces.' Then, they came to the conclusion that escapism and acquiring knowledge were the two prominent viewers' motivations for Esports. Except for the researches focusing on Esports motivation studies, Todd and Melancon [19] tried to consider the gender influence both on the live-streaming audience and the broadcaster with the results that there was a significant difference between male and female users when they choose to watch live-streamers. Furthermore, researchers also tried to explain users' motivations from a social psychological perspective [8]. Additionally, Chen and Lin [2] took the four factors (flow, entertainment, social interaction, and endorsement) into account to comprehend live-streaming motives.

Furthermore, Uses and Gratification theory [9, 10, 13] is a mainstreaming theoretical application among the recent researches on live-stream participants' motivation. Sjöblom and Hamari [15] conducted a survey on the video game streaming user on Twitch. By using the U&G theory, they tried to explore the relationship between the user motivation and the four usages, including hours watched, streamers followed, streamers watched, and streamers subscribed. This research team also made a comparative study on the live-streaming content and genres based on UG theory. Hilvert-Bruce and his team further set up the socio-motivational model to verify the audiences' engagement of live broadcasting [7]. Therefore, this research also based on this theoretical foundation to conduct the investigation.

2.2 Studies on the Media Content of Live Streaming

Esports and Entertainment Live Streaming

Another strand of research focuses on live-streaming media attributes, including the various live-streaming platforms and the different content information. Sjöblom and his research team [16] explored that various kinds of video games and streaming show types had different engagement motivations in Twitch. Zimmer [23] examined social live-streaming services (N = 7667) across genders, countries, platforms, and contents and found that various streaming contents had an impact on genders, countries, and motivations. Regarding the research on Chinese streaming, in the investigation conducted by Lu and his research team [24], they highlighted that the audiences' motivations in watching and participating in streaming platforms were different from audiences in North America, and they analyzed the top streaming content that interested Chinese audiences. Fan and Zhang [3] also testified that they designed an experiment showing that Chinese audiences had a different willingness to donate paid gifts when they were watching Esports and entertainment (talent shows) streaming contents. Based on the previous research, the different types and content of streaming media platforms had different influences on audiences' motivations and engagements.

Furthermore, researchers have demonstrated that there were differences in motivation among Esports and entertainment streaming users. For example, Chen and Lin [2] figured out that a majority of the studies on live streaming have been focused on the Esports area, and less attention has been put on other kinds of live streaming content, such as entertainment. Referring to the Chinese live streaming market, Hu, Zhang, and Wang [8] tried to analyze the two main live streaming platforms separately—Douyu and YY Live. Douyu contains more Esports content, while YY Live pays more attention to personal performances, including dancing, singing, and so on. Based on these previous streaming studies, this research focuses on the entire population of streaming users and the streaming industry's different contents. On the basis of prior studies on Esports and entertainment streaming contents, this study also includes these two contents of streaming into the investigation.

Live Streaming E-commerce and Knowledge Sharing

The existing researches have already explored that different contexts of live streaming have relationships among users' motivations for watching and engaging. With China's development of the live streaming industry, relatively new kinds of live streaming channels have been generated, especially e-commerce streaming. Sites such as Taobao.com, JD.com, and VIP.com have already provided live streaming services for their online brands [1]. Taking Taobao as an example, e-commerce streamers demonstrate and promote brands and products by explaining and experiencing them and communicating with audiences. Meanwhile, there are online shopping links showing up on the streaming screen, which the audiences can click and buy the products during the streaming time. Cai, Wohn, and their research team tried to explore the relationship between shopping motivations, such as hedonic and utilitarian and shopping intentions [1]. Limited researches of streaming have mentioned about knowledge sharing streaming type such as studying companion live streaming, investment live streaming, and so on. Therefore, this research also tries to study the reasons why audiences watch e-commerce and knowledge sharing streaming channels.

3 Conceptual Framework and Research Questions

3.1 Motivation Studies—Uses and Gratification Theory

U&G theory [9, 10, 13] has been applied in many Internet studies, such as the motivation of the viewer of online advertisement [11], the usage of e-books, online communities, and so on. This theory also has been applied to study participants' motivation in the live-streaming industry [11, 15, 16, 20]. To be more specific, 'Affective' indicates the media's attractiveness to the users, including entertainment, interests, and so on. 'Cognitive' is the motivation that people need to gain and learn about new information. 'Personal integrative' highlights the people using and watching media to create and solidify identity traits. 'Social integrative' is also very necessary to consider, indicating that communicating with others and being part of society are quite important. 'Tension release' shows the needs of people to escape from the pressure of their daily life.

3.2 Research Questions

RQ1: What are the motivations for watching and participating live streaming and in China? How do the motivations explain the intention of the audiences to watch and participate live streaming?
RQ2: How do the motivations differ from live streaming Esports, entertainment, E-commerce, and knowledge sharing media?

4 Methodology

4.1 Survey

An online investigation was adopted for this research. For the motivation study in the streaming area, this study conducted a similar online investigation as Todd and Melancon [19] did in the general streaming area. Since the questionnaire was about the audiences watching and engaging in live streaming, and to avoiding missing data, a qualifier question was set: "As a live streaming user, have you ever heard of, watched or participated in live streaming before?" Participants who answered that they never heard of live streaming were not qualified. The questionnaire included multiple-choice and 5-point Likert scale questions, through which this study attempted to gain information about the Chinese audiences' demographics, motivations, attitudes, engagements, and watching frequency of various live streaming content.

4.2 Recruitment

In order to avoid the data results being biased by limited platforms or certain groups of users [24], this study adopted the services from SoJump.com for recruiting participants in China. Thus, after two weeks in January 2020 of the online questionnaire being active, 433 participants responded to the online investigation; however, 3.93% of these interviewees' responses were removed because they chose the answer that they never watched entertainment live-streams (4) and finished the survey under 1 min (13), leading to a final sample of 416 participants. There were 154 male (37.02%) and 262 females (62.98%). Among these age groups, the group aged below 30 shared the largest proportion (62.26%), while the age group above 60 was the smallest proportion (0.05%). The educational background differentiated into four groups. The largest percentage was the undergraduate degree (including the junior college degree), which included 340 participants (81.73%). The remaining three groups accounted for smaller proportions, like the graduate degree and above had 43 participants (10.34%), the junior school degree group and below had 8 (1.92%), and the high school degree (including professional school) had 25 (6.01%).

4.3 Survey Measures

Data from 12 questions were gathered using the online questionnaire targeted at evaluating the Chinese entertainment live-streaming users' motivations and their engagement information by using 5-point Likert scale questions. The Kaiser-Meyer Olkin measure of the sampling adequacy was 0.86, which was higher than the level of 0.6. Bartlett's test of sphericity was significant ($p < 0.05$), which showed that the sample was able to do the factor analysis. All the items adopted a principal component analysis by setting a Varimax rotation with an eigenvalue > 1.00 as a criterion to decide the number of factors. The results showed that three factors accounted for 75.53% of the variance.

The details were indicated as Table 1, all the item loadings on each of the three factors and all the results were over the recommended thresholds (>0.40). The measurement reliability and validity were estimated through Cronbach's alpha. The Cronbach's alphas of the variables were over 0.6.

All the items for motivational model and emotional reactions were adopted from prior researches. Each variable of motivation was made up of two items including "Affective" (M = 3.81, SD = 0.71), "Cognitive" (M = 3.76, SD = 0.83), "Personal integrative" (M = 3.87, SD = 0.75), "Social integrative" (M = 3.84, SD = 0.83), and "Tension release" (M = 3.02, SD = 1.11).

For the dependent variables, this study measured the consumption of different content streaming by adopting a frequency scale with 5-point Likert scale indicating how frequently the user watches that kind of streaming content [15] including 5 responses (never, rarely, sometimes, often, and always). Furthermore, the emotional engagement (M = 3.02, SD = 1.14) was also a measure of the deeper engagement of the streaming audiences. This variable was made up of keeping a relationship with streamers and donating paid gifts to the streamers, and it has already been figured out that those kinds of engagements have emotional elements [6, 22, 24].

Table 1. Factor analysis with 6 factors derived.

Variable	Items	Cronbach's alpha	Factor loading					
Affective	Enjoyment	0.61	0.79					
	Excitement		0.74					
Cognitive	Learning knowledge	0.63		0.73				
	Gaining information			0.85				
Personal integrative	For me, watching streaming has positive influences	0.62			0.77			
	Watching streaming is valuable				0.71			
Social integrative	Communicating with the streamer	0.61				0.76		
	Keeping in touch with other audience					0.85		
Tension release	Getting away from the rest of my family	0.73					0.84	
	Forgetting about work, school, or others						0.85	
Emotional engagement	Sending paid gifts to streamers	0.72						0.84
	Keeping relationship with streamers							0.77

4.4 Findings

Streaming Topics Categories

For the content that Chinese streaming users were most interested in, Fig. 1 shows the various topics audiences were willing to watch. The most fundamental issue included in this study of content categories was based on Lu and his research conclusions [24]. Secondly, this study observed the 50 most popular pieces of streaming content in Douyu and on YY Live streaming platforms. This study then tried to cross-reference these findings and discovered that entertainment-related topics—such as daily life, singing, and dancing—were the most interesting streaming topics for Chinese audiences, partially

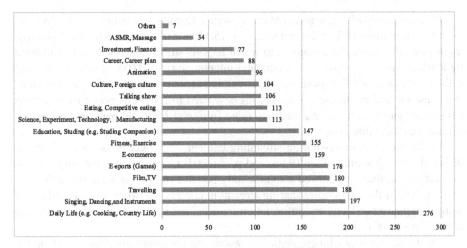

Fig. 1. Streaming topics most interested in Chinese audience.

confirming previous research teams' results. Then, the topics included in Games and E-commerce also ranked high in the research results. The topics related to knowledge-sharing streaming channels—such as education, science, and career—ranked relatively lower in Fig. 1.

Content and Motivations

As to the relationship between motivations and engagements, this research put five motivations as independent variables; it also put frequency of watching four types of streaming and emotional engagement as dependent variables. More details are shown in Table 2.

Table 2. Linear regression models explaining motivations to watch and engage live streaming in China.

	Affective	Cognitive	Personal integrative	Social integrative	Tension release	Adjusted R^2
Esports	+0.24***	−0.10	+0.144*	+0.046	+0.15**	0.15***
Knowledge sharing	−0.05	+0.22***	+0.07	+0.08	+0.06	0.09***
Entertainment	+0.21***	+0.05	+0.28***	+0.00	+0.09	0.23***
E-commerce	+0.07	+0.21***	+0.15**	+0.08	+0.11*	0.19***
Emotional reactions	+0.12*	+0.01	+0.24***	+0.17***	+0.30***	0.37***

*$p < 0.05$, **$p < 0.01$, ***$p < 0.001$. Values are standardized beta coefficients.

To understand why Chinese audiences watch Esports streaming, the motivation model could explain 15% of the variance, $F = 15.15$, $p < 0.001$. Affective had a positive impact on influencing the audiences to watch Esports streaming ($p < 0.001$), followed by tension release ($p < 0.01$) and personal integrative ($p < 0.05$), indicating that the audience chose to watch Esports-related streaming content because of the game streaming's interest and attractions. Also, the users wanted to release pressure by watching Esports streaming content and find self-value from watching and participating in this interactive media platform.

As for the knowledge-sharing streaming content, the U&G model accounted for 9% of the total variance, $F = 19.98$, and $p < 0.001$. Cognitive was the only type of motivation variable that showed a significantly positive impact on when the audiences chose to watch the knowledge-sharing streaming content, showing that the audiences wanted to gain knowledge and information by watching knowledge-sharing streaming content ($p < 0.001$).

For the reason why Chinese audiences watch entertainment streaming, U&G motivations could explain 23% of the variance, $F = 26.03$, $p < 0.001$. Affective and personal integrative motivations both showed significant impacts on the audience's decision to watch entertainment streaming ($p < 0.001$). The results manifested that the audience chose to watch entertainment-related streaming content because these streaming shows were attractive and watching these contents could bring the audiences a feeling of self-satisfaction.

In reference to the E-commerce streaming, U&G motivations could explain 19% of the variance, $F = 15.15$, $p < 0.001$. Cognitive had a positive effect on influencing the audiences to watch Esports streaming ($p < 0.001$), followed by personal integrative ($p < 0.01$), and tension release ($p < 0.05$), indicating that the audiences chose to watch e-commerce channels due to being willing to receive information about the brand and products (such as price and function) ($p < 0.001$).

For the emotional reactions, U&G motivations could explain 37% of the variance, $F = 47.25$, $p < 0.001$. Personal integrative, social integrative, and tension release showed a significant positive impact on Chinese streaming users' emotional reactions to the streaming channels ($p < 0.001$). Affective also showed a positive influence on the audiences emotional engagement in streaming.

5   Conclusion

In this research, Chinese livestreaming users showed that watching different contents of livestreaming and emotional reactions were associated with various motivations. Specifically, personal integrative, affective, tension release, and cognitive had positive significance on Chinese streaming users' motivations to watch various streaming contents, which stated that the reasons behind Chinese audiences were related to self-accomplishment such as watching live streaming could help the viewer feel self-improvement. Meanwhile, social integrative showed more impact on Chinese users' deeper engagements to streaming channels, such as emotional reactions. For the Chinese streaming audiences, social integrative related motivates could explain that streaming media was different from other kinds of mass media in developing stronger social and community relationships, which confirmed with Hilvert-Bruce and his research teams' results based on Twitch [6].

This research also found that affective could interpret why Chinese audiences choose to watch Esports and entertainment streaming content, which also confirmed the results from Chen and Lin's research [2]. They explored that Taiwanese people's primary impression on entertainment streaming was due to the joviality which streaming could provide and the release of their pressure. Furthermore, the audience also choose to participate in streaming platforms because of attractiveness.

The cognitive motivation indicated that the Chinese audience choose to watch knowledge sharing and E-commerce streaming because they tried to touch with the new information and knowledge. This result might provide some supportive evidence for the future development of these two streaming areas. For example, the previous research in E-commerce investigation mentioned that streaming viewers watched and engaged in streaming because they like the product and its usefulness. The results of this research further prove that audiences also needed to gain new information and knowledge from the streaming channels. Compared to the other media, streaming had more timeliness of information and communicative characteristics. Georgen [4] theorised streaming as a form of 'participatory spectatorship', which meant that streaming audiences could actively engage with streamers and other audience members. During knowledge sharing and E-commerce streaming, the audience could communicate with the streamer and other viewers in real time and acquire more information.

This research did not fully tap the motivator elements. Each motivation variable had several aspects—for example, the social-integrative aspect could include companionship and shared emotional connection [5]. The next step of this research is to further explore the motivations of audiences. Additionally, this research has not deeply studied the influence of the streamer on the audience. The attractiveness of streamers also might have a strong influence on the audience's decision to watch or engage in streaming shows. Therefore, future research will take into consideration the personal attractive elements of the streamers in the streaming shows such as the appearance of streamers [21].

References

1. Cai, J., et al.: Utilitarian and hedonic motivations for live streaming shopping. In: Proceedings of the 2018 ACM International Conference on Interactive Experiences for TV and Online Video (2018)
2. Chen, C.-C., Lin, Y.-C.: What drives live-stream usage intention? The perspectives of flow, entertainment, social interaction, and endorsement. Telemat. Inform. 35(1), 293–303 (2018)
3. Fan, J., Zhang, Q.: The impact of interactivity on virtual gifts giving intent–based on live-streaming platforms. In: 2018 3rd International Conference on Humanities Science, Management and Education Technology (HSMET 2018). Atlantis Press (2018)
4. Georgen, C., Duncan, S.C., Cook, L.: From lurking to participatory spectatorship: understanding affordances of the Dota 2 noob stream. International Society of the Learning Sciences, Inc.[ISLS] (2015)
5. Hamari, J., Sjöblom, M.: What is eSports and why do people watch it? Internet Res. 27, 34 (2017)

6. Hamari, J., Keronen, L.: Why do people play games? A meta-analysis. Int. J. Inf. Manag. **37**(3), 125–141 (2017)
7. Hilvert-Bruce, Z., et al.: Social motivations of live-streaming viewer engagement on Twitch. Comput. Hum. Behav. **84**, 58–67 (2018)
8. Hu, M., Zhang, M., Wang, Yu.: Why do audiences choose to keep watching on live video streaming platforms? An explanation of dual identification framework. Comput. Hum. Behav. **75**, 594–606 (2017)
9. Katz, E., Haas, H., Gurevitch, M.: On the use of the mass media for important things. Am. Sociol. Rev. **38**, 164–181 (1973)
10. Katz, E., Blumler, J.G., Gurevitch, M.: Uses and gratifications research. Public Opin. Q. **37**(4), 509–523 (1973)
11. Lee, J., Lee, M.: Factors influencing the intention to watch online video advertising. Cyberpsychol. Behav. Soc. Netw. **14**(10), 619–624 (2011)
12. Recktenwald, D.: Toward a transcription and analysis of live streaming on Twitch. J. Pragmat. **115**, 68–81 (2017)
13. Ruggiero, T.E.: Uses and gratifications theory in the 21st century. Mass Commun. Soc. **3**(1), 3–37 (2000)
14. Scheibe, K., Fietkiewicz, K.J., Stock, W.G.: Information behavior on social live streaming services. J. Inf. Sci. Theory Practi. **4**(2), 6–20 (2016)
15. Sjöblom, M., Hamari, J.: Why do people watch others play video games? An empirical study on the motivations of Twitch users. Comput. Hum. Behav. **75**, 985–996 (2017)
16. Sjöblom, M., et al.: Content structure is king: an empirical study on gratifications, game genres and content type on Twitch. Comput. Hum. Behav. **73**, 161–171 (2017)
17. Sjöblom, M., et al.: The ingredients of Twitch streaming: affordances of game streams. Comput. Hum. Behav. **92**, 20–28 (2019)
18. Sjöblom, M.: Spectating play-investigating motivations for watching others play games (2019)
19. Todd, P.R., Melancon, J.: Gender and live-streaming: source credibility and motivation. J. Res. Interact. Market. **12**, 79–93 (2018)
20. Turner, L.H., West, R.: Introducing Communication Theory: Analysis and Application. Mc-Graw Hill, New York (2010)
21. Uszkoreit, L.: With great power comes great responsibility: video game live streaming and its potential risks and benefits for female gamers. In: Gray, K.L., Voorhees, G., Vossen, E. (eds.) Feminism in Play, pp. 163–181. Palgrave Macmillan, Cham (2018)
22. Zhang, X., Xiang, Y., Hao, L.: Virtual gifting on China's live streaming platforms: hijacking the online gift economy. Chin. J. Commun. **12**, 340–355 (2019)
23. Zimmer, F.: A content analysis of social live streaming services. In: Meiselwitz, G. (ed.) SCSM 2018. LNCS, vol. 10913, pp. 400–414. Springer, Cham (2018). https://doi.org/10.1007/978-3-319-91521-0_29
24. Lu, Z., Xia, H., Heo, S., Wigdor, D.: You watch, you give, and you engage: a study of live streaming practices in China. In: Mandryk, R., Hancock, M. (eds.) Proceedings of the 2018 CHI Conference on Human Factors in Computing Systems. Association for Computing Machinery, New York, April 2018

Interactive and Immersive Cultural Heritage

Archiving the Memory of the Holocaust

Ernst Feiler[1], Frank Govaere[1], Philipp Grieß[2], Simon Purk[2], Ralf Schäfer[3(✉)],
and Oliver Schreer[3]

[1] UFA Serial Drama, Potsdam, Germany
[2] UFA Show & Factual, Potsdam, Germany
[3] Fraunhofer Heinrich Hertz Institute (HHI), Berlin, Germany
ralf.schaefer@hhi.fraunhofer.de

Abstract. Volumetric Video is a rather new technology, which allows the creation of dynamic 3D models of persons, which can then be utilized like computer generated models in any 3D environment. In a recent project between UFA and Fraunhofer HHI a VR documentary about the last German survivor of the Holocaust Ernst Grube has been produced. It consists of six interviews with Ernst Grube lasting about 8–12 min each. The Jewish contemporary witness talks about his experience in Nazi Germany and his imprisonment in the concentration camp Theresienstadt. The VR experience allows the user to meet Ernst Grube and the young interviewer at different places, for which a thrilling virtual environment has been built. Additional interactive components provide the user with more detailed historical information, such as videos, images and text.

Keywords: Volumetric video · Virtual reality · Holocaust documentary

1 Introduction

Thanks to new head mounted displays (HMD) for virtual reality, such as Oculus Rift and HTC Vive, the creation of fully immersive environments has gained a tremendous push. In addition, new augmented reality glasses and mobile devices reach the market that allow for novel mixed reality experiences. With the ARKit by Apple and ARCore for Android, mobile devices are capable of registering their environment and put CGI objects at fixed positions in viewing space. Besides the entertainment industry, many other application domains have potential for immersive experiences based on virtual and augmented reality. In the industry sector, virtual prototyping, planning, and e-learning benefit significantly from this technology. VR and AR experiences in architecture, construction, chemistry, environmental studies, energy and edutainment offer new applications. Cultural heritage sites, which have been destroyed recently, can be experienced again. Finally yet importantly, therapy and rehabilitation are other important applications. For all these application domains, a realistic and lively representation of human beings is desired. However, current character animation techniques do not offer the necessary level of realism. The motion capture process is time consuming and cannot represent all detailed motions of an actor, especially facial expressions and the motion

© Springer Nature Switzerland AG 2020
M. Rauterberg (Ed.): HCII 2020, LNCS 12215, pp. 145–155, 2020.
https://doi.org/10.1007/978-3-030-50267-6_12

of clothes. This can be achieved with Volumetric Video. The main idea is to capture an actor with multiple cameras from all directions and to create a dynamic 3D model.

With the availability of this technology the idea was born, to use Volumetric Video also for recording live persons and to archive their memory for future generations, when they will no longer be alive. This becomes extremely important, if the memory of such persons reflects an important period of history and as it is the case for the Holocaust. Although this dark period of German history is only 75 years ago, it disappears out of the thoughts especially of young people. Therefore, it is important to preserve the memories of contemporary witnesses in such a way, that it can be presented in an appealing way to young audiences.

This reflection was the starting point for the documentary about one of the last German survivors of the Holocaust Ernst Grube named "ERNST GRUBE – THE LEGACY", which will be described in this paper. In Sect. 2 the story board of the production is presented, while in Sect. 3 the technologies for generation of volumetric 3D models are explained. In Sect. 4 the construction of the virtual environment, in which the recorded persons are presented and in Sect. 5 the interactive experience will be described. Finally the results of an evaluation of the production will be presented in Sect. 6 before summarizing the paper and giving an outlook in Sect. 7.

2 The Story Board Volumetric Video Production

The short VR film "ERNST GRUBE – THE LEGACY" consists of six interviews with Ernst Grube lasting about 8–12 min each. These interviews have been carried out by a young person, because the idea is to show these short films in schools, museums and memorials and to especially attract a young public in order to inform them about this dark chapter of German history (Fig. 1).

Fig. 1. Student Phil Carstensen with Ernst Grube in the volumetric studio. Photo: UFA

The Jewish eyewitness talks about his experience in Nazi Germany and his imprisonment in the concentration camp Theresienstadt. This "walkable film" represents a time document of compelling authenticity.

Altogether six stations of his life are told, which are: (1) the exclusion of the Jewish population by the Nazi regime, (2) the Jewish life in Nazi Germany, (3) his life in the ghetto in Munich, (4) the fear of deportation, (5) the concentration camp Theresienstadt and (6) his life in Germany after the Second World War.

3 Volumetric Video Production

There are several companies worldwide offering volumetric capture systems, such as Microsoft with its Mixed Reality Capture Studio [1], 8i [2], Uncorporeal Systems [3] and 4D Views [4]. Compared to these approaches, the presented capture and processing system for volumetric video distinguishes in several key aspects, which will be explained in the next sections. Concerning multi-view video-based 3D reconstruction, several research groups work in this area. A complete workflow for volumetric video production based on RGB and depth sensors is presented in [5]. In [6], a spatio-temporal integration is presented for refinement of surface reconstruction. This approach is based on 68 4M pixel Cameras requiring approx. 20 min/frame processing time to achieve a 3M faces mesh. Robertini et al. [7] present an approach focusing on surface detail refinement by maximizing photo-temporal consistency. Vlasic et al. [8] present a dynamic shape capture pipeline using eight 1k cameras and a complex dynamic lighting system that allow for controllable light and acquisition at 240 frames/sec. The high-quality processing requires 65 min/frame and a Graphics Processing Units (GPU) based implementation with reduced quality achieves 15 min/frame processing time.

In Sect. 3.1, the volumetric capture system is presented with its main feature of a combined capturing and lighting approach. In Sect. 3.2, the underlying multi-view video processing workflow is presented.

3.1 Volumetric Capture

A novel integrated multi-camera and lighting system for full 360-degree acquisition of living persons has been developed. It consists of a metal truss system forming a cylinder of 6 m diameter and 4 m height. On this system, 32 cameras are arranged in 16 stereo pairs and equally distributed at the cylindrical plane in order to capture full 360-degree volumetric video. In Fig. 2, left, the construction drawing of the studio is presented. 120 KinoFlo LED panels are mounted outside the truss system and a semi-transparent tissue is covering the inside to provide diffuse lighting from any direction and automatic keying. The avoidance of green screen and provision of diffuse lighting from all directions offers best possible conditions for relighting of the dynamic 3D models afterwards at design stage of the VR experience. This combination of integrated lighting and background is unique. All other currently existing volumetric video studios use green screen and directed light from discrete directions.

The system completely relies on a vision-based stereo approach for multi-view 3D reconstruction and omits separate active 3D sensors. The cameras are equipped with a

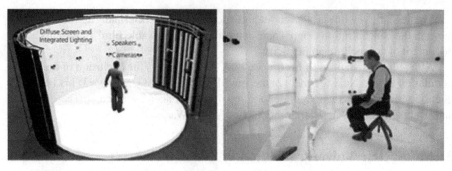

Fig. 2. Drawing of the capture and light stage (left) and first prototype (right)

high-quality 20 MPixel sensor at 30 frames per second. This is another key difference compared to other existing capture systems. The overall ultra-high resolution video information from all cameras leads to a challenging amount of data, resulting in 1.6 TB per minute. In Fig. 2, right, a view inside the rotunda is shown, with an actor sitting in the center.

For the multi-view camera system, the aim was to find the best possible arrangement of least possible number of cameras, with the largest possible capture volume and minimum amount of occlusions. In Fig. 3, a sample view of all 32 cameras is presented that represents our solution for the multi-dimensional optimization problem. Four pairs are mounted on the ceiling and on the bottom, while eight pairs are distributed equally at middle height in the cylinder.

Fig. 3. 32 camera views

3.2 Processing of Volumetric Video

Now, the complete volumetric video workflow is described, consisting of pre-processing, stereo depth estimation, point-cloud fusion, meshing and mesh reduction (see Fig. 4).

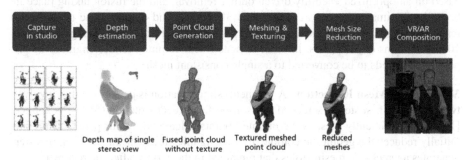

Fig. 4. Production pipeline for volumetric video

Pre-processing. In the first step, a pre-processing of the multi-view input is performed. It consists of a color matching to guarantee consistent colors in all camera views. This has significant impact on stereo depth estimation, but even more important, it improves the overall texture during the final texturing of the 3D object. In addition, color grading can be applied as well to match the colors of the object with artistic and creative expectations. E.g. colors of shirts can be further manipulated to get a different look. After that, the foreground object is segmented from background in order to reduce the amount of data to be processed. The segmentation approach is a combination of difference and depth keying supported by the active background lighting.

Stereo Depth Estimation. The next step is stereo depth estimation. As mentioned before, the cameras are arranged in stereo pairs that are equally distributed in the cylinder. These stereo base systems offer the relevant 3D information from their viewing direction. A stereo video approach is applied that is based on the IPSweep algorithm [9, 10]. In contrast to many other approaches that evaluate a fixed disparity range, a set of spatial candidates and a statistically guided update for comparison is used in this algorithm, which significantly speeds up correspondence search. Once all candidates are evaluated for a given similarity measure, the best candidate is selected as final depth candidate. Compared to standard block-matching approaches, spatial 3D patches are projected from the left to the right image (as well as from the right to left) in order to consider perspective distortions. After that, a consistency check is performed between both depth maps and a consistency map is produced. This is used to hinder inconsistent matches to propagate in the next iteration and to penalize their selection. The iterative structure of the algorithm allows for propagation of results to their local neighborhood, while keeping pixel independent processing, which enables highly efficient parallel implementation on GPU.

Point Cloud Fusion. For each 2D depth map, initial patches of neighbored 2D points can be calculated straight away including information about the normal on the surface for each 3D point. The resulting 3D information from all stereo pairs is then fused with a visibility-driven patch-group generation algorithm [11]. In brief, all 3D points occluding any other depth map are filtered out resulting in an advanced foreground segmentation. The efficiency of this approach is given through the application of fusion rules that are based on an optimized visibility driven outlier removal, and the fusion taking place in both, the 2D image domain as well as the 3D point cloud domain. Due to the high-resolution original images, the resulting 3D point cloud per frame is in a range of several 10 s of millions of 3D points. In order to match with common render engines, the 3D point cloud needs to be converted to a single consistent mesh.

Meshing and Mesh Reduction. A geometry simplification is performed that involves two parts: In a first step, a screened Poisson Surface Reconstruction (SPSR) is applied [12]. SPSR efficiently meshes the oriented points calculated by our patch fusion and initially reduces the geometric complexity to a significant extent. In addition, this step generates a watertight mesh. Holes that remained in the surface after the reconstruction due to complete occlusion or data imperfections are closed. Secondly, the resulting mesh is elementally trimmed and cleaned based on the sampling density values of each vertex obtained by SPSR. In contrast to the common approaches introduced earlier, we do not require an extensive intersection of the resulting surface with the visual hull. Outliers and artifacts are already reliably removed by our patch fusion.

Subsequently, the triangulated surface is simplified even further to an appropriate number of triangles by iterative contraction of edges based on Quadric Error Metrics [13]. Thus, detailed areas of the surface are represented by more triangles than simple regions. During this stage, we ensure the preservation of mesh topology and boundaries in order to improve the quality of the simplified meshes. Another important aspect is the possibility to define the target resolution of meshes. Depending on the target device, a different mesh resolution is necessary in order to match with the rendering and memory capabilities. To recover details lost during simplification, we compute UV coordinates

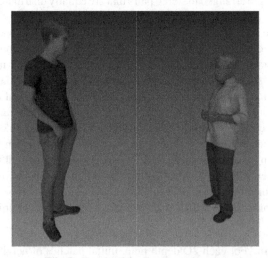

Fig. 5. Result of final volumetric asset

for each vertex and create a texture of suitable size [14]. In Fig. 5, an example of the final volumetric 3D model of both persons is presented.

The final sequence of meshes is then further manipulated in standardized post-production workflows, but also be rendered directly in virtual reality applications, created with 3D engines like Unity3D [15] or Unreal Engine [16].

4   Building the Virtual Environment

The challenge was to recreate the historical sites as locations for the interviews. We believe the eyewitness report will have more impact, when it is told in a convincing reconstruction of the actual historical environment. Some of these locations are no longer in existence and in some cases picture material is scarce. It was therefore necessary to conduct a substantial amount of historical research. As a first step in building the virtual environment concept art was created using these historical references. The tools for this were rather low-tec: pencil and paper (Figs. 6, 7 and 8).

These concept art sketches and the existing photo material were the base for our 3D-artists to start modelling the environments in Autodesks 3DS Max. In order to enable the real time performance, we used low-polygon modelling techniques. Textures were made in Adobe Photoshop, using the Quixel Plugin, which helped us to create so called PBR materials (physically based rendering). This was essential to achieve a photo-realistic result in Unity 3D, a real time engine in which we combine the environment, characters and interactive content (Fig. 9).

5   The Interactive Experience

The final VR experience will allow the user to meet Ernst Grube and the young inter-viewer at all these different places mentioned in Sect. 2, for which the virtual environment described in Sect. 4 has been built. Additional interactive components provide the user with more detailed historical information, such as videos, images and text.

The life story of Ernst Grube is told in different stations. The various locations are arranged along a path in the form of vignettes (Fig. 10). On the other side of the path are stele-shaped milestones (Fig. 11). These milestones represent the interactive content

Fig. 6. Concept art of apartment in Munich (left) and children's home (right)

that the user can access. Thus, the set is also the user interface. The user can teleport into the various time segments along the way and control the interactive elements. Archive material is displayed on floating, transparent screens.

Fig. 7. Concept art of freight yard (left) and deportation camp (right)

Fig. 8. Concept art of main gate of Theresienstadt

Fig. 9. Screenshot of the VR scene of the children's home

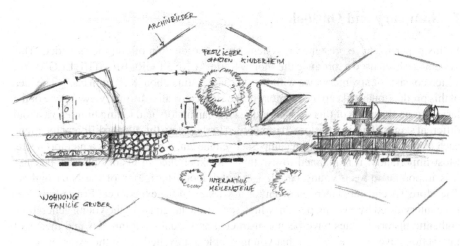

Fig. 10. Interactive set (top view)

Fig. 11. Drawing of interactive steles (left) and final 3D model (right)

6 Evaluation

One objective of the collaboration between Fraunhofer HHI and UFA GmbH is to evaluate the acceptance and level of experience. Hence, a proof-of-concept VR experience is developed, where the user joins the contemporary witness Ernst Grube and the young student in the garden of the children's home. This proof-of-concept will last for three minutes and will be presented to different audiences and to the public. It will be presented in the visitor center of the memorial site Sachsenhausen, Germany. The VR experience is also demonstrated to executives from the foundation of Brandenburg memorials (Stiftung Brandenburgische Gedenkstätten). One major objective is to use this new concept of interactive storytelling of historical content in secondary schools during history lessons. Therefore, the VR experience will be brought to a Berlin secondary school to let the pupils experience the story of Ernst Grube.

Based on the outcome of the evaluation, the VR experience will be further adopted. With this first proof-of-concept, the general public shall be attracted and convinced that further investment in this new technology is required.

7   Summary and Outlook

In this paper we have presented a system for the production of volumetric video. This system has been used to produce the short VR film "ERNST GRUBE – THE LEGACY", which consists of six interviews with Ernst Grube lasting about 8–12 min each. The idea of this production is to keep the memory of the Holocaust alive by interviewing one of the last German survivors of this dark period in German history and letting him report about different stages of his martyrdom. It is intended to showcase this film at different locations such as the former concentration camp Sachsenhausen, which today is a memorial site. Most importantly, it is planned to use this VR experience in history classes, because it is important to keep young people informed about the felony of the Nazi regime. Therefore, special care has been taken for the design of the experience. Ernst Grube has been interviewed by a young person, which speaks the language of the young generation, authentic historical sites have been constructed as virtual environments and means of interaction have been added, so that young people get excited about the experience.

At this stage only the first of the planned six episodes has been produced, but the other five will follow in the future. Some novel interaction tools are currently under development, which may be added. One option is to establish eye contact between the viewer and the 3D model of Ernst Grube for viewing positions, where the users looks into his face. It is expected, that the feeling of immersion can be further increased by such means.

In addition, UFA expects to perform additional productions with other Holocaust survivors or other individuals of public interest in the future and with it create a new documentary format. As time goes by, this new way of interactive experience of contemporary witnesses plays a significant role to preserve cultural heritage and history of human being.

References

1. https://www.microsoft.com/en-us/mixed-reality/capture-studios
2. https://8i.com/
3. http://uncorporeal.com/
4. 4D View Solutions. http://www.4dviews.com
5. Collet, A., et al.: High-quality streamable free-viewpoint video. ACM Trans. Graph. **34**(4) (2015). https://doi.org/10.1145/2766945. Article 69
6. Leroy, V., Franco, J.-S., Boyer, E.: Multi-view dynamic shape refinement using local temporal integration. In: IEEE International Conference on Computer Vision 2017 (October 2017)
7. Robertini, N., Casas, D., De Aguiar, E., Theobalt, C.: Multi-view performance capture of surface details. Int. J. Comput. Vis. (IJCV) **124**, 96–113 (2017)
8. Vlasic, D., Peers, P., Baran, I., Debevec, P., Popovic, J., Rusinkiewicz, S.: Dynamic shape capture using multi-view photometric stereo. ACM Trans. Graph. **28**(5), 174 (2009)
9. Waizenegger, W., Feldmann, I., Schreer, O.: Real-time patch sweeping for high-quality depth estimation in 3D videoconferencing applications. In: SPIE Conference on Real-Time Image and Video Processing, San Francisco, USA, (2011). https://doi.org/10.1117/12.872868
10. Waizenegger, W., Feldmann, I., Schreer, O., Kauff, P., Eisert, P.: Real-time 3D body reconstruction for immersive TV. In: Proceedings of 23rd International Conference on Image Processing (ICIP 2016), Phoenix, Arizona, USA, September 25–28 (2016)

11. Ebel, S., Waizenegger, W., Reinhardt, M., Schreer, O., Feldmann, I.: Visibility-driven patch group generation. In: IEEE International Conference on 3D Imaging (IC3D), Liege, Belgium, December 2014, Best Paper Award (2014)
12. Kazhdan, M., Hoppe, H.: Screened poisson surface reconstruction. ACM Trans. Graph. (TOG) **32**(3), 1–13 (2013). https://doi.org/10.1145/2487228.2487237
13. Garland, M., Heckbert, P.S.: Surface simplification using quadric error metrics. In: Proceedings of the 24th Annual Conference on Computer Graphics and Interactive Techniques, SIGGRAPH 1997, pp. 209–216. ACM Press/Addison-Wesley Publishing Co., New York (1997) https://doi.org/10.1145/258734.258849
14. Ebner, T., Feldmann, I., Renault, S., Schreer, O.: 46-2: distinguished paper: dynamic real world objects in augmented and virtual reality applications. In: SID Symposium Digest of Technical Papers, Los Angeles, USA, vol. 48, no. 1, pp. 673–676, May 2017, Distinguished Paper Award. https://doi.org/10.1002/sdtp.11726
15. https://www.unity3d.com/
16. https://www.unrealengine.com/

Open City Museum: Unveiling the Cultural Heritage of Athens Through an -Augmented Reality Based- Time Leap

Georgios Kallergis[(✉)], Marios Christoulakis, Aimilios Diakakis, Marios Ioannidis,
Iasonas Paterakis, Nefeli Manoudaki, Marianthi Liapi,
and Konstantinos-Alketas Oungrinis

Transformable Intelligent Environments Laboratory, School of Architecture,
Technical University of Crete, Chania, Greece
gkallergis7@gmail.com

Abstract. A nation's cultural heritage is of great importance both for indigenous people as well as for foreigners as it is a nation's contribution to humanity and global civilization. As the spark to discover that treasure has ignited and travelling around the world has become much easier, it is necessary to enhance the way that monuments are exhibited and communicated. Current technology offers the capability to alter the way that information is provided and represented. Augmented reality (AR) is the most characteristic example as it surpasses the limits that exist in other media offering a unique experience to the user. A great challenge for AR is to shed a new light on monuments, especially in cities like Athens, filled with historical monuments. In this paper we describe the methodology that was followed in order to create an AR application that will provide users with a virtual time leap experience in the past depicting the monument's history in its social context. Thus, the issues emerging during the development of an AR app is discussed, as well as solutions to common problems regarding its utilization in outdoors space. Aiming to shed light on its importance throughout the centuries, an interdisciplinary research has been conducted combining fields like architecture and psychology in order to inform and in parallel, arouse emotions to visitors and thus, intensify the experience. Supporting that, user experience has been enhanced following a UI/UX approach, which provides the appropriate tools between easy-to-use and following a narrative.

Keywords: Augmented reality · Navigation · Cultural heritage · Mobile application

1 Introduction

Cultural heritage, which is described as the values, knowledge and customs passed from one generation to the next one, is of paramount importance as it shapes national identity [1]. However, as humanity proceeds in a globalized culture with common principles, that heritage turns out to be crucial, contributing to the new common value system

© Springer Nature Switzerland AG 2020
M. Rauterberg (Ed.): HCII 2020, LNCS 12215, pp. 156–171, 2020.
https://doi.org/10.1007/978-3-030-50267-6_13

that is currently shaping [2]. Monuments are the main focus for both tourists and local people, as a way to learn more about their place and its history. Having reached a great technological point and surpassing the era of personal Digital Assistants (PDAs) the question seems to be how we could provide people with a better medium to get informed and experience the history of a monument.

One of the most promising technologies, thought to prevail and change the way that people interact with others as well as with their environment is Augmented Reality (AR) [3], especially considering the fact that smartphones have a growing processing power to facilitate that technology. It is known that has a great impact on people's daily lives like retail [4], education [5, 6] and tourism [7]. As a result, a great challenge for this technology is to redefine the experience of visiting a monument or cultural heritage in general [8], providing more information, entertainment and in essence, a better understanding of the monument. In this context, Open City Museum (O.C.M.) is designed and developed through an holistic approach to achieve these goals.

O.C.M. is an AR application trying to feature Athens' immovable cultural heritage through a virtual time leap. This project provides a more interactive way to explore and enjoy the city's array of cultural heritage monuments through the overlaid information that AR provides. It includes predefined routes based on criteria like the historical era, the distance or even user's available time. In those, the included monuments are not the most famous ones like Parthenon or Erechtheion; instead they are those "hidden" in neighborhoods of Athens that people may walk by them without paying much attention. The intention is to shed light on their history and redefine their importance for the locals and in parallel, make visitors enrich their experience with the cultural "weight" of these sites, as they wander around the city. In this way, not only do they discover these antiquities while making a virtual time leap but they also explore the city and its overlapping layers of history; its streets, its people and its vibes. A shared belief is that monuments' significance can only be experienced in the context of the culture and the people surrounding them, a preconception that we try to utilize to create a unique sensation through our app.

Focusing more on time leap, which distinguishes this app from any other, it utilizes an abstract representation of how monuments looked like instead to the usual efforts of strict accurate representation, by processing layers of visual information in a different way. The advantages of this lie on the fact that more techniques in imaging can be used as well as it can utilize AR better and thus, have a more powerful result. Instead of focusing on excessive details that also require more resources to run properly, it focuses on expressionistic tools that aim to address also the emotional part of the brain. In this way, the user not only gets informed but also has an emotional arousal, an emotional connection with it creating a unique experience that makes him understand the area's *Genius-loci* [9].

Apart from that, the basic principles of UI/UX were deployed while designing the app, intending to maximize user experience in the application. Discovering visitors' needs and wills and how they can be satisfied was crucial leading to having interviews with people that could be O.C.M.'s users according to their personas. Implementation of the app was of paramount importance given the fact that markerless object recognition was utilized and what is more, in outdoor space, approaches which are still very challenging in this field. Moreover, the suggested utilities from UI/UX had to be implemented, too, such as navigating users to the monument.

As it becomes evident, our clear goals regarding the representation of the monuments and the gain of the user, urged us to do cross-disciplinary research, trying to achieve the best possible human computer interaction. In the following pages, methodology and workflow are analyzed; achieving the virtual time leap, designing a user friendly AR application focusing on cultural heritage and its implementation with state of the art game engine and AR libraries.

2 Spatial Cognition and Visual Representation

2.1 Visual Layering Theory

The approach presented for the creation of AR apps is based on the way the human brain receives, perceives and memorizes environmental information. Since AR applications superimpose information on "top" of reality, the created mixed visual experience could lead to the assigning of meanings and connotations, enriching the ability of images to become memories. An individual memory is comprised by a collection of data that combines explicit and implicit information. A memory carries information that mixes logic and emotion creating a bit of a *place*, that holds a very specific value for an individual, and can be the initiation of an immersive experience, meaning that it can start the process of "daydreaming".

In this perspective, the main target of the applied methodology is to augment the ability to retrieve personal memories through visual "triggers" and facilitating the initiation of small immersive personal narratives to each viewer. The main tool to achieve that is to enhance the perceptible visual information by decomposing the info-rich structure of an image and reconstructing it in six discrete visual layers. Kaplan & Kaplan in their attention and restoration theory (ART) mention the limited capacity of a person's voluntary attention [10]. Voluntary attention focuses on the important parts of a composition and rules out the irrelevant background information. This visual layering process, that was developed at the Transformable Intelligent Environments Lab of T.U.C., is based on the limited capacity of the human brain to process visual information and provides an abstraction tool with the ability to optimize the communication between the context and the user (Fig. 1).

More specifically, image layers are characterized as active or passive based on the characteristics of the contained information, as well as their semantic value. Images are composed of at least three active and three passive layers. The importance is determined by the ability of the human brain to recognize dominant figures, moving objects and foreground action as the more dominant elements of a scene and the surrounding information as a background [11].

Animated objects are considered as the protagonistic elements of a visual scene and belong in the first and in some instances second layer of an image. Fundamental structural elements supporting the main action (e.g. cars, objects, etc.) belong to the third active layer. The active layers construct the main action and are easily perceived by the human brain.

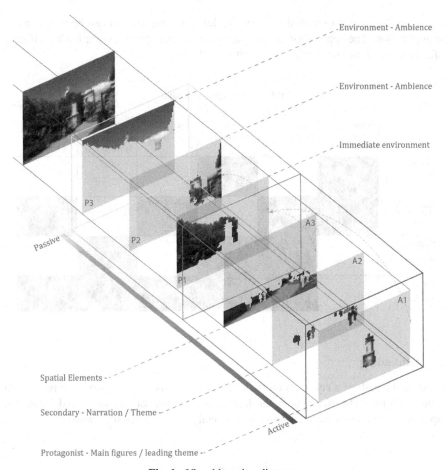

Fig. 1. Visual layering diagram

The passive layers provide points of reference that address the right frontal lobe of the human brain and create the general atmosphere of the theme. The overall atmosphere of a place is a synthesis of multiple factors, often involving more than the five Aristotelian senses [12]. Surrounding elements, such as colors and textures, are also classified as ambient background information and provide the "sense of place".

The visual layering methodology aims to enhance and alter the semantics of each layer and immerse the user via an educational visual experience. In order to make each visual layer more prominent, a blur effect is used on the surrounding elements [13]. The immersion is enhanced by introducing different visual styles according to the era each photo refers to. These stylistic approaches are selected according to the color, texture, and style that represent each historic period.

2.2 Strategic Approach

According to Table 1, research in historical archives, literature review, and interviews with locals take place before the first app development stage. During the third stage, the content has already reached the required level of analysis and can be tested inside the application. The application is being developed since stage 2, since further effort is required to integrate the graphical content with the app.

Table 1. Strategic approach

	Stage 1: Analysis	Stage 2: Start	Stage 3: Process	Stage 4: App Testing	Stage 5: Content Testing	Stage 6: Final Result
Research Literature Historical archives						
Visit Field Analysis Image Capturing						
Content Collage Visual Layering						
AR App Development Field Testing						

2.3 Pathfinding

Based on the path of a common touristic route in Athens, close to the more prominent monuments (i.e. The Acropolis), the least prevalent and often overlooked - but still important-monuments were chosen for this analysis. Accessibility (walking distance,

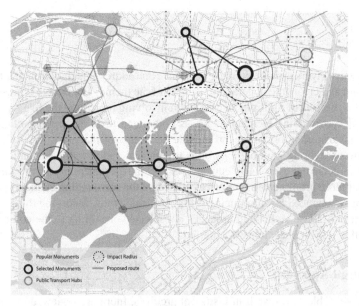

Fig. 2. Pathfinding diagram.

cycle, bus, and adjacent public transport hubs) is a major classification factor. The impact radius of each monument, which refers to the influence it has on the surrounding areas, is also holding an important role in the selection process (Fig. 2).

2.4 Topological Analysis (Fig. 3)

After the determination of the proposed routes, each monument is classified according to these factors:

1. Location
2. Relation to other monuments
3. Accessibility
4. Surrounding environment
5. Viewpoints
6. Current Decay and Restoration Status

2.5 Processing of Historical Data

Historical archives and archeological services offer the most accurate representations regarding the evolution of each monument in time. However, O.C.M. recognizes the numerous challenges in accurately portraying a significant piece of architecture in different chronological periods. The materiality, the surroundings, and the sound represent some of the most significant parts of the environmental composition. These elements along with colors, textures and artistic styles, are able to achieve the anticipated holistic experience which will immerse the user into the scene (Fig. 4).

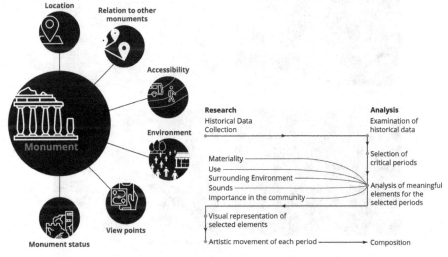

Fig. 3. Topological analysis.   **Fig. 4.** Historical data diagram.

2.6 Visual Representation Timeline

The sequence to present the visual transition to separate historic periods is presented below:

1. the monument is isolated from the surrounding environment
2. the background is blurred directing the attention to the central theme
3. a sepia effect is applied to the image
4. the characteristics of the first era are emphasized by outlining the main differences
5. an abstract collage composed of old pictures overlaying the present situation is introduced
   1st time leap
6. the blur and sepia effects are reduced
7. an abstract collage composed of old pictures overlaying the present situation is introduced the characteristics of the second era are emphasized by outlining the main differences (this step refers to the fourth step)
   2nd time leap
8. the blur and sepia effects are further reduced-color saturation is closer to the original image
9. a collage composed of old pictures overlaying the present situation is introduced elements from the specific era are added into the scene (e.g. people and vehicles from that era)

Original Photo - 2019   Ancient Greece - 335 b.C.

Original Photo -1669   Neoclassicism -1900

Fig. 5. Visual representation sequence example. The Choragic Monument of Lysicrates, Plaka, Athens

This process briefly describes the timeline of events during the AR representation and not the post-processing steps of the visual layering methodology (Fig. 5).

3 Design Using UI/UX

Nowadays, it is essential to deploy a UX/UI plan to make applications as friendly as possible for the user. User experience (UX) assists people to achieve their goals and take value from the product based on their needs. To make this happen, design thinking is utilized. In the first phase which is called "Empathize" or "Strategy", a plan is made in order to discover users' needs and set business goals. The second is called "Define" or "Scope" in which the findings from the previous step are collected and analyzed, the problem statement is defined alongside with the content and the requirements of the application. Then, we move to "Ideate" where brainstorming takes place. The solutions from the previous steps lead to prototypes which are given to users for feedback. On the other hand, user interface (UI) is not only about how the app looks like or the colors but it handles the interaction between user and the application; is the design of interfaces of machines in order to accomplish an easy and efficient experience for the user in terms of accomplishing their goals.

O.C.M. with the above process achieves a more interactive, friendly user experience with easy interactions for all different types of users (Fig. 6).

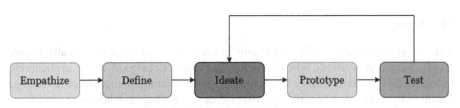

Fig. 6. UI/UX flow diagram.

3.1 Empathize

When tourists and travellers search for a new attraction, they are trying to learn the history of a place or to get some intriguing facts. Searching on the web about famous attractions in the city proves to be a hard and time consuming process. Furthermore, the amount and the content of information is not sufficient as it is obsolete or shortly described so, people can not feel the vibe of the ancient period. The lack of interaction in that is evident and should be upgraded. In addition, navigating in the city and getting informed demands more than one application which is certainly not practical. All these state some of the problems that a tourist has to face when visiting a monument.

At this point, it is meaningful to proceed with the Competitive analysis. The last few years there is a growing number of applications using AR in cultural heritage. There are two kinds of applications: the first one is used indoors, in places like museums and the second one outdoors. Being interested in the second category, one of the most noticeable projects is ARCHEOGUIDE which creates routes and reconstructs the ruins of ancient monuments [14]. In addition, more similar applications have been proposed like Chang's et al. who proposed a geo context based embedding visiting system pointing out that augmented reality had a major impact on the experience [15]. Another interesting approach was project AR-CIMUVE Augmented Reality for the Walled Cities of the Veneto which had educational purposes for primary and middle school students which among others incorporated 3D models [16]. In their application, Pacheco's et al. [17] used orientation sensors and GPS to track the user's position and also navigated the user in order to point out the differences in an old german concentration camp. A project that included multiple types of interaction that were used in order to create a story-telling by visiting multiple locations was VisAge [18] offering a quite different experience to the user by having its own content. Last but not least, recently, Panou designed and implemented an AR application that could be used as tourist guide for the city of Chania, superimposing 3D models of monuments in the real ones [19].

Having carried out the research about similar applications, the next step was to have stakeholder interviews. The aim of that was to make clear of the business goals and also, have the same perception about the application: its objectives and the way to achieve them. As a result, some initial goals and functions were set, an outline of the technologies to use and what is more, the type of the customers: tourists and citizens of Athens who want to discover the ancient places of the city. To be our app effective, an important step was to learn from them: what they desire and most importantly, what they need.

3.2 Define

Hence, it was necessary to delve deeper into the user's behavior. More specifically, to find out pain points, motivations, how they define an experience as good, which applications are mainly used and how the user solves the emerged problems before and during visiting. The interviews included 7 people with experience of traveling and they were conducted through telephone. Most of the people search for the most famous places and they group them together making a "day trip" list so they have a plan for each day. They usually pin famous places on Google Maps, which they also use to navigate. Almost everyone uses Trip Advisor to find museums, attractions and places according to their interests around the city. When they were asked about problems on the procedure or pain points, they answered that they need more filters about the exact pricing, the opening hours they can visit and the public transportation. As it seems, choosing a monument to visit is a complex decision based on a lot of information and apart from this, an important factor is the monument's proximity to their accommodation. Regarding their experience during the visit some of them mentioned that they get only the basic information from the guide or from a travelling site. As a result, they do not engage, even though they are trying to imagine how it was in the past. Interestingly, one of the participants suggested that a podcast would be a good idea (resembles the PDAs) while another participant said that he had used AR based on QR codes on the exhibits of a museum finding it a nice experience. From that it becomes apparent that users need a more vivid interaction, especially if it includes multimedia like audio and visual representations. Based on their answers and on the previous phases, two personas were created, one of which is described in Fig. 7.

Before moving to UI testing and to UI implementation, it is important to grasp all the possible constraints that can affect how the O.C.M. is structured and implemented. The first restriction was the size of the time leap feature. The size could not be very large as it would raise an issue regarding storage and battery from the increased energy consumption. So, the decision was made to have a sequence of pictures, as described before. Another significant restriction could be the constant changing conditions in outdoor spaces where differences in ambient lighting, whether conditions and people passing by could affect the AR recognition of the monument. The application will need to inform users about potential environmental restrictions.

3.3 Ideate

The above process of personas and the problem statement offered a good insight about the users' needs and selecting the business goals for the project. One of the most important requirements was that the application should spark the users interest instead of just providing historical information. This can be achieved with the use of AR and by creating the emotion of time leap. Another requirement was to add a navigation feature in the application. This way the users do not need another application for navigating to the monument, like Google maps or similar applications. When setting the business goals, a new requirement emerged where users should have the ability to review and upload

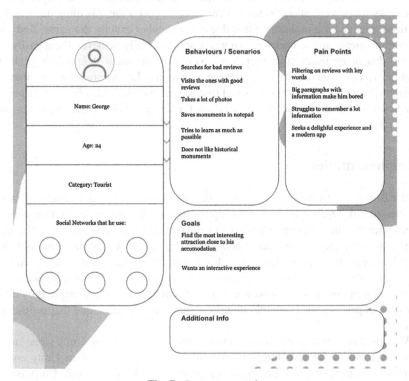

Fig. 7. Persona example

photos of the monument in order to have more information to decide if it is worth visiting or not. It was crucial to prioritize the needs and emphasize on those features that would characterize O.C.M. and make it distinguish from the competitors. Consequently, in this first version of O.C.M. the first two requirements were implemented whereas the last one, was chosen for a later version, as extra features that will provide added value. Having the review of the first release, would help us assess their importance and also, fix any existing bugs.

3.4 Prototypes

At this point, the examination of the architecture of the application is the next step. For that reason were generated prototypes of the application based on the previous phases that include users needs and requirements.

3.5 Testing

In the last phase of design, there are Hi-Fidelity prototypes which should be tested. Through this process the usability of the app is checked and the ability of the user to complete the main scenarios. Hence, user scenarios were written and the user was trying to accomplish them. If one of them takes a lot of time for the user to find out or searches for it without success, then this is considered as failure and must be redesigned. Some of the tasks users were about to implement were to visit a famous monument and get directions, search for a monument that doesn't remember exactly the name, find some nearby monuments and to find some routes. Users generally achieved them easily. The scenario that made users more sceptical was one of the main stakeholder goals, the predefined routes. One reason is that users are not used to having predefined monuments or famous places included, thus, this had to change. Overall, in this way, users pointed us out how this app can be functional and cover their needs, which made implementation more clear.

4 Implementation

In order to select a technology for the application implementation a variety of factors were considered. One of the main considerations was the ease of integration with AR technologies that the application was going to use, since AR is a core feature of the application. Another factor to consider was the extensibility and cross platform publishing of the developed application. Even though the first version has been tested on Android only, in the future it will be made available for other platforms. This application tries to enrich the environment of the monument with visual effects that are inspired by different historical periods and by employing the visual layering technique that is described above.

   With these factors in mind the decision was made to make use of Unity game engine. Many AR frameworks have integrations with Unity, so the choice of Unity enabled the application to have flexibility in the selection of the AR framework. Unity is cross platform and allows publishing an application in many platforms. So, combining this with the ease of use and the community size of Unity made this a solid choice to develop the application.

Another very important feature of the application was the map integration. The first tests for integrating maps used google maps API. During the first stages of development it was discovered that the Google Maps integration with Unity is not targeted for small (indie) developers and it is not free. Also from information on public forums [20] it seems that there is some middleware code that needs to be developed to make the google maps easy to use it Unity. Another final drawback is that even though Unity supports a variety of deployment platforms the use of google maps API supports only Android and IOS [21], which restricts the future expansions of the application. This led the development team to research alternative map apis to use for the application. The alternative chosen was Mapbox which uses OpenStreetMap as source data for the Mapbox Streets [22]. The integration of Mapbox in the application code was very simple and the getting started information that was provided was very accurate. This made the decision to switch the original maps framework easy to implement and test. Finally the last major component of the application that needs to be analyzed is the database that will contain all the information about the users and the monuments. The framework that was chosen for the database is Firebase realtime database [23]. The greatest benefit of this framework is that it does not require any backend server setup. It is a no-SQL database that works with JSON (Javascript Object Notation) objects that requires minimal setup to get started and it has support for Unity. So this made it very easy to integrate in the application code.

The AR framework that was selected was Wikitude SDK, due to the cross platform support and Scene Recognition ability. It enables the tracking of large objects that are viewed from a variety of angles. The generation of the Tracking Object is made in Wikitude Studio, an online application of Wikitude. The generation follows the principles of photogrammetry. The final object is a 3d representation of the model, that can be tracked form a variety of angles and distances, even in a noisy background. The Object Tracker of the monument was generated by a set of photographs. Each one of the photographs was from a different angle or distance. The first step was to remove the background from the photographs, a process that was made in Photoshop. Before the generation of the Object Tracker in Wikitude Studio (Fig. 8), the set of the photographs were tested in 3df Zephyr (photogrammetry software), in order to evaluate the extracted model and supplement with extra photographs if needed. The final step was to generate the Object Tracker in Wikitude Studio and import the exported model (.wtc) into Unity.

Fig. 8. Point cloud of object target of monument, in Wikitude Studio.

The AR framework that was initially selected was Vuforia AR SDK. During testing the first versions of the application with this framework it was discovered that it is not working efficiently in outdoor spaces where the target has changing weather and lighting conditions. So the decision was made to switch the AR framework to Wikitude AR SDK.

The following activity diagram (Fig. 9) analyzes the high level activities that a user can perform in the O.C.M. application. The first screen of the application is a welcome screen that prompts the user to login or register (Fig. 10a). In case of a new registration the application supports three ways to register a new user. The available registration options are: direct registration, register with a Google account and register with Facebook. Once

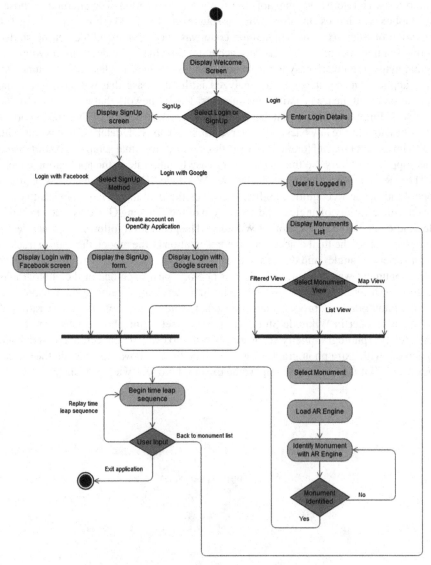

Fig. 9. High level activity diagram of O.C.M. application.

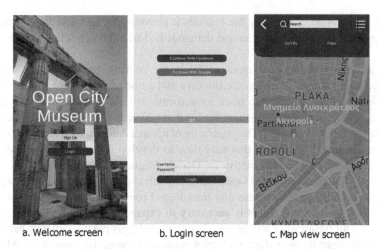

a. Welcome screen   b. Login screen   c. Map view screen

Fig. 10. O.C.M. application screenshots.

a user is registered and logged in they have access to the monument list. From this screen a user can see the map of the monuments that are nearby (Fig. 10c) and is able to select the monument that will be loaded to start the time leap sequence.

The software minimum requirements for the O.C.M. application on android is Android 7.0 (API level 24). This is enforced by the external APIs that the application depends on. Mapbox has this minimum android requirement. Where Wikitude sets the minimum version to Android 5.0 (API Level 21). For hardware minimum requirements a mobile phone needs to have a camera, a gps module and a gyroscope, support for OpenGL 2.0 (or newer) and a CPU a capable armv7a with NEON support (or armv8a).

5   Conclusions

This paper describes the design and development of an AR application that focuses on unveiling the cultural heritage of Athens using a virtual time leap. The proposed application suggests an innovative way to suggest which monuments a user should visit, navigate in the city and represent monuments' history providing users with a unique interaction.

The visual representation of the monument originates from TIE Lab's Visual Layering Theory which takes advantage of passive and active image layers in order to assign different meanings and semantics to each one of them. Those play a key role in the creation of visual scenes as they project the desired atmosphere for the virtual time leap. Of course, the choice of the monument is important as it relies on historical data as well as on the social context of a time period and its surrounding environment. These affect the representation and are taken into account to the creation of small emergent narratives.

In parallel, O.C.M. does not focus only on the provided experience by AR but also utilizes UI/UX principles in order to discover and fulfil user's needs. Performing interviews with potential users contributed to draw useful conclusions regarding what they need before and during their visits in the monument leading to develop a more complete application concerning the features it provides. In addition, it was easier to implement it as the goals, the plan and demands had become very clear thanks to this process.

The progress that has been made so far in the field of AR assists a lot to create innovative applications. Open source libraries and game engines can be really crucial for the development enabling to track monuments and also superimpose the desired information. Wikitude seems trustworthy for that task and this is the reason that more and more developers use it [19]. The popularity of iOs and Android increases our outreach to more users and Unity makes that very easy to develop for both operating systems. Mapbox seems also a good alternative for Google Maps.

Currently, the first version of Open City Museum is developed containing key parts that shape its character like routes and time leap. From the interviews and our study based on UX, it is known that it is necessary to expand to social media and create a community. Our future work will be based on that: make people interact with each other and also encourage them to share their own personal view of the monument. Allowing users to generate their own content could be a crucial step to increase engagement and interaction with it. This shall be the next crucial update in a later version alongside with suggested improvements that will emerge later by using the application. Still, the proposed application is a characteristic example of human computer interaction enabling people to enjoy the long history of Athens' monuments and engage them with a more interactive and emotional way offering a unique experience.

Acknowledgements. It is essential to express our gratitude to all these people that have worked for this project the last few years: Neamoniti Sophia, Marianna Pavlopoulou, Arguraki Aikaterini and Vgontzas Ioannis. In addition, I would like to thank Marinella Teliou and Sapountzi Despoina for their guidance and assistance in the very early stages of this project. This project is supported by Athens Digital Lab, an organization of Municipality of Athens, supported by NOKIA and Cosmote and funded by Stavros Niarchos Foundation.

References

1. Blake, J.: On defining the cultural heritage. Int. Comp. Law Quart. **49**(1), 61–85 (2000). Accessed 23 Feb 2020
2. Harrison, R.: Heritage and globalization. In: Waterton, E., Watson, S. (eds.) The Palgrave Handbook of Contemporary Heritage Research. Palgrave Macmillan, London (2015)
3. Sutherland, I.E.: A head-mounted three dimensional display. In: Proceedings of the Fall Joint Computer Conference, Part I, AFIPS 1968 (Fall, Part I), 9–11 December 1968, pp. 757–764, ACM, New York (1968)
4. Poushneh, A., Vasquez-Parraga, A.Z.: Discernible impact of augmented reality on retail customer's experience, satisfaction and willingness to buy. J. Retail. Consum. Serv. **34**, 229–234 (2017)
5. Lee, K.: Augmented reality in education and training. Techtrends Tech Trends **56**, 13–21 (2012)
6. Bower, M., Howe, C., McCrefdie, N., Robinson, A., Grover, D.: Augmented reality in education - cases, places and potentials. Educ. Media Int. **51**(1), 1–15 (2014)

7. Yung, R., Khoo-Lattimore, C.: New realities: a systematic literature review on virtual reality and augmented reality in tourism research. Curr. Issues Tourism **22**, 1–26 (2017). https://doi.org/10.180/13683500.2017.1417359

8. Berndt, E., Carlos, J.: Cultural heritage in the mature era of computer graphics. IEEE Comput. Graph. Appl. **20**(1), 36–37 (2000)

9. Norberg-Schulz, C.: Genius Loci: Towards a Phenomenology of Architecture. Rizzoli, New York (1979)

10. Kaplan, R., Kaplan, S.: The Experience of Nature: A Psychological Perspective. Cambridge University Press, Cambridge (1989)

11. Oungrinis, K.A., Liapi, M., Christoulakis, M., Paterakis, I., Manoudaki, N.: Hybrid environmental-projection platform (HEPP). An enhanced-reality installation that facilitates immersive learning experiences. In: EDULEARN 2018 Proceedings, pp. 8215–8224 (2018)

12. Pallasmaa, J.: Space, place and atmosphere. Emotion and peripherical perception in architectural experience. Lebenswelt Aesthet. Philos. Exp. (2014). https://doi.org/10.13130/2240-9599/4202

13. Peterson, J.: The effect of blur on visual selective attention (2016). https://doi.org/10.13140/rg.2.2.23844.68489

14. Vlahakis, V., et al.: ARCHEOGUIDE: first results of an augmented reality, mobile computing system in cultural heritage sites, 131–140 (2001). https://doi.org/10.1145/584993.585015

15. Chang, Y.-L., et al.: Apply an augmented reality in a mobile guidance to increase sense of place for heritage places. J. Educ. Technol. Soc. **18**(2), 166–178 (2015). JSTOR, http://www.jstor.org/stable/jeductechsoci.18.2.166. Accessed 23 Feb 2020

16. Petrucco, C., Agostini, D.: Teaching our cultural heritage using mobile augmented reality. Je-LKS: J. E-Learn. Knowl. Soc. **12**, 115–128 (2016). https://doi.org/10.20368/1971-8829/1180

17. Pacheco, D., et al.: Spatializing experience: a framework for the geolocalization, visualization and exploration of historical data using VR/AR technologies. In: Proceedings of the Virtual Reality International Conference, Laval, France, pp. 9–11 (2014)

18. Julier, S.J. et al.: VisAge: augmented reality for heritage. In: Proceedings of the 5th PerDis 2016 ACM International Symposium on Pervasive Displays, Oulu, Finland, pp. 20–22 (2016)

19. Panou, C., Ragia, L., Dimelli, D., Mania, K.: An architecture for mobile outdoors augmented reality for cultural heritage. ISPRS Int. J. Geo-Inf. **7**, 463 (2018). https://doi.org/10.3390/ijgi7120463

20. Unity forums. https://forum.unity.com/threads/announcement-google-maps-unity-sdk-for-gaming.534265. Accessed 21 Feb 2020

21. Google Developers. https://developers.google.com/maps/documentation/gaming/overview_musk. Accessed 21 Feb 2020

22. Mapbox documentation. https://docs.mapbox.com/help/glossary/osm. Accessed 21 Feb 2020

23. Firebase realtime database. https://firebase.google.com/products/realtime-database. Accessed 24 Feb 2020

Research on Cultural Tourism Experience Design Based on Augmented Reality

Meiyu Lv[1,2], Lei Wang[1(✉)] [iD], and Ke Yan[1]

[1] School of Digital Media and Design Arts,
Beijing University of Posts and Telecommunications, Beijing 100876, China
wl_bupt@163.com
[2] Beijing Key Laboratory of Network and Network Culture, Beijing
University of Posts and Telecommunications, Beijing 100876, China

Abstract. Following the continuous development of the internet and the widespread use of mobile devices, tourism products and services have experienced three different stages: 1.0 stage of group tours, 2.0 stage of independent travel, and 3.0 stage of in-depth tours. In addition to in-depth experience tours to meet the independent travel needs of tourists, it also needs to meet the needs of tourists for more in-depth understanding of the culture of attractions. In order to better integrate modern technology with China's cultural heritage, the use of augmented reality (AR) to enhance a tourism experience is studied here. Firstly, the characteristics of AR technology are analysed, and its advantages of application in the design of cultural tourism activities is discussed. This includes advantages such as extended dimensions of perception, enhanced cognitive depths and aesthetic experiences. This is also extended to summarise the mechanism that makes up a tourist's experience, and a framework of user experience design for AR tourism application is identified. Specifically, a tourism experience is designed from the sensory layer to the cognitive, the interactive, and finally the emotive layer, and the corresponding design strategies are given. Lastly, feasibility is verified by the design scheme.

Keywords: Augmented reality · Cultural tourism · Experience design

1 Introduction

When an individual's quality of life improves, travelling to different locations becomes increasingly possible, and generally, more and more people have the ability and free-time to travel. Modern tourists are not drawn to exclusive tourism, but place a greater importance on understanding the history of their destination, and taking part in an experience that offers more emotional depth. Furthermore, they hope to interact with surrounding environment and appreciate local historical culture, leading to a more depth cultural experience. Many scenic spots in China have rich cultural and historical relevance. Consequently, how to better integrate digital technology in tourism alongside this profound cultural heritage, creating a more emotive, intelligent travel experience has become a popular topic of discussion.

© Springer Nature Switzerland AG 2020
M. Rauterberg (Ed.): HCII 2020, LNCS 12215, pp. 172–183, 2020.
https://doi.org/10.1007/978-3-030-50267-6_14

Zhang Guohong proposed that cultural tourism is the observation, feeling and experience of different places or heterogeneous cultures that leave people's living environment caused by people's knowledge and longing for different places or heterogeneous cultures to meet cultural intervention or participation needs impulsive process [1]. "Cultural tourism" here refers to travelling for the purpose of appreciating the traditional culture of a place, such as by searching for famous historical remains or participating in cultural events.

In the past, the development of historical and cultural tourism products and cross-cultural communication has not been able to progress beyond special effects videos and animations. However, in recent years, a large number of universities and enterprises have invested in the exploration of emerging technology applications, including the use of augmented reality technology to realise building restoration and tour navigation for tourists [2]. Previous research on areas of tourism product focused on practical and theoretical research, and the applications of the technology. The findings emphasised that effectiveness of products relies on the content and functions provided by technology, but there was a lack of research into user emotion and experience.

The aesthetics and interactivity of AR technology aid its perception by users, which in turn helps to enhance the cognitive experience. Furthermore, incorporating enhanced display technology in cultural tourism can help create an improved travel experience.

The remainder of this paper is organized as follows: First, we analyze the characteristics of AR technology and its advantages in tourism applications. Secondly, it summarizes the process of tourism experience formation, and refines the design framework and design strategies that affect the tourism experience. It is then applied in design practice. The last part is the summary and future research directions.

2   AR Technology Analysis

2.1   AR Technology Features

AR technology refers to technology that superimposes virtual information into real scenes and allows people to interact with this information. It supplements the real world and enhances an individual's perception of reality [3]. Specifically, using the following characteristics:

Fusion of Virtual with Reality. In AR, virtual information and the real world are displayed in the same visual space. Computer-generated virtual images are superimposed into the real world, making the real and virtual known to the subject at the same time, blurring the boundary between these states to a certain extent.

Understand and Track Real-Life Scenarios. The position of the camera is calculated so that the virtual object is properly placed in the real world. The basis for correctly displaying virtual information lies in the positioning and tracking of real scenes, while accurate understanding of input information by the AR system enables tourists to interact with the technology [4].

Human-Computer Interaction Is Multi-dimensional and Efficient. Human-computer interaction technology is an important part of an AR system. It recognises and processes the instructions from users through interactive operations, and feeds back the results through audio, visual and other sensory responses. Virtual digital information supported by AR technology is interactive, and user input and information output are synchronized, ensuring the timeliness of user perception.

2.2 Advantages of the Application of AR Technology in a Travel Experience

Expanding the Perception Dimension. Most cultural tourism experiences mainly serve tourists visually, lacking items and activities that serve other senses. Moreover, Explanation of cultural content is tedious and leads to creating an uninteresting atmosphere. When used in a tourism setting, AR technology will ensure that the participant's understanding of objects/the area is not limited to static text materials. The augmented reality interactive mode presents information in a variety of forms including through text, video, graphics, and models in both two-dimensional and three-dimensional planes; this expands the scope of information, meeting the need for multi-dimensional displays [5]. In addition, AR provides the possibility for multi-channel interaction. A fusion of virtual visual, auditory, taste, and tactile sensations with real world objects using AR technology will increase the dimension of user perception.

Increase Cognitive Depth. An augmented reality interaction mode, with its unique characteristics and creative information, influences the mechanisms of perception, attention, and memory related to information processing [5]. Generally, tourist activities enable the process of communication between tourists and other individuals, objects, and situations [6]. AR equipped with internet technology provides a way to explore, discover and gain an in-depth understanding of the surrounding environment at any time during, for example, a tour. It could also display up-to-date information about the tourist's geographic location, increasing their awareness and comfort. The content is no longer limited to real situations such as the current time. It can cross time through virtual means, and present the features of cultural relics in the real space through augmented reality, so as to achieve time span in content. In addition, AR increases enthusiasm in tourists by providing vivid experiences, leading to the formation of deeper, more meaningful memories.

Increase the Aesthetic Experience
Immersion. Immersion is often referred to in research into virtual reality. A high level of immersiveness in virtual reality comes from the complete separation of a user's awareness and their real environment. The purpose of augmented reality is not to change the objective feeling of the user in their real environment, but rather to utilize an augmented reality environment to help users complete tasks and goals in the real world. The immersive characteristics of augmented reality are reflected in the real space, in that an immersion in augmented reality leads to greater immersion in the real environment.

Pleasure. The amount of pleasure derived from a particular experience is dependent upon the behaviour, feelings and overall experiences. People can obtain pleasure from interacting with an environment and exploring its history [7]. In this way, tourists can use AR technology to obtain narrative information not present in their physical reality, assigning a deeper meaning to the space around them. Furthermore, augmented reality technology can provide tourists with unlimited interaction possibilities. The significance of these two aspects suggests there can be significantly more pleasure derived from taking part in a digitally designed tourism experience.

Satisfaction. In the process of tourism, tourists are in the mood of curiosity, aesthetics and other psychology, which will have a strong demand for sensory information in the tourist environment space. A digital design for tourism experiences including AR technology can make up for the lack of sensory resources in traditional activities, better satisfying tourist needs [8].

3 Design Elements that Influence the Travel Experience

3.1 Tourism Experience Formation Mechanism

In essence, the term "experience" refers to a series of facts that an individual recollects after a period of time [9]. Therefore, the "tourist experience" can be thought of as the process of interaction between tourists and tourism products, often through activities, and the feeling generated by these activities [10].

First, tourists in a particular environmental space passively receive various pieces of information through their own sense organs (sight, hearing, smell, taste, and touch). A positive perception of the tourist experience can affect selective perception of the environment and overall cognition and evaluation.

After receiving information by interacting with their environment, cognitive objects are selected and the information is processed and fed back. The human cognitive process includes three stages: assimilation, adaptation, and balance. Through different tourism activities, that is, the interaction between tourists and different environments, the cognitive process will achieve balance through self-regulation, thereby generating cognition in the constant balance. The quality of interactive activities directly affects perception of the environment, hence the design of interaction methods is particularly important.

At the end of the tourist experience, cognitive results can be evaluated to obtain an overall travel experience. This includes the emotional and aesthetic experiences. A positive emotional experience may be the result of a high level of interaction with environments, enabling tourists to resonate spiritually with a location, meeting their psychological needs. Aesthetic experience is a comprehensive evaluation of an entire activity. A positive aesthetic experience can allow tourists to satisfy their desires, release their emotions, and find their superego value.

3.2 Design Elements Affecting Tourism Experience

The main difference between AR cultural tourism products and general tourism products is that AR relies on a specific device to implement the virtual interactive travel experience. The design of virtual digital content and the presentation of the augmented reality technology will directly determine enjoyment of the tourist experience. Yin Diange analysed the factors that affect the tourist experience from the perspective of both the subject and object. The subject of experience is the internal factor of the tourist, and the object of experience is the factor of scenic spots and tourism products, including scenic area resources, product characteristics, tourist routes, service quality, and tourist atmosphere [11]. Moreover, from the perspective of AR application, Liu jinhong found that elements which users attach the most importance to in AR products are the emotional experience, sensory experience, interactive experience, and reliability experience, in this order [12].

This article aims to combine the characteristics of AR technology with the formation of a tourist experience from the perspective of tourists. It proposes the factors that affect the perception of AR tourism products including sensory experience, cognitive experience, operation experience and emotional experience. Then, the four design levels that influence the travel experience are perceived, cognitive, interaction and emotional.

The perception layer must meet the user's multi-channel needs, including sight, hearing, and touch. The cognitive layer means that the design has to conform to the human cognitive law. In other words, it should use knowledge of the human cognitive experience to choose a reasonable form of presentation that ensures user cognition is efficient and effective. The operation layer needs to satisfy usability to provide smooth operation. The emotional layer emphasises the importance of spiritual identity and aesthetic experience, in that tourists wish to establish emotional connections with the cultural space of their destination, meaning AR products should consider emotional factors such as sociality, interaction, and narrative (Fig. 1).

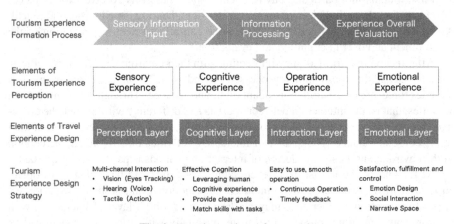

Fig. 1. Travel experience framework

3.3 Design Strategy of AR in a Tourism Experience

Provide Multi-channel Interactive Experience. A multi-dimensional interactive experience brings together text, pictures, sounds, and more to combine visual, auditory, tactile, and interactive outputs and present users with a multi-channel, multi-sensory experience. Purely digital products are limited by time of use, the environment and other factors, meaning the user's attention can easily be diverted. Multi-channel interaction can help users better distribute their attention. On the other hand, multi-channel design allows effective communication of information by combining multiple sensations. The user can select a suitable method according to the environment, unaffected by physical constraints and other factors. This accurately transmits information, improves operation efficiency and creates a more immersive experience.

Provide Clear Goals and Tasks that Match Skills. Tourism is an extended experience, consisting of a variety of goals and tasks to achieve. Breaking down these goals into periodic tasks can help users more clearly control the entire operation process and can be adjusted in real time as needed. This can also lead to matching tasks according to corresponding skills of the user, further improving their sense of control and achievement.

Provide a Continuous Operation Experience. Scenic environments are complex and subject to change. In a tourism experience, this is very susceptible to external factors making it difficult for participants to concentrate. Because it is easy to be disturbed by factors such as talking, walking, and sightseeing, it is difficult for users to complete a certain operation continuously. Therefore, it is better to record the location and operational steps taken by the user to provide a continuous experience, reduce repeated operations and improve efficiency.

Provide Timely Feedback. Timely and accurate feedback is a prerequisite for an immersive experience. Timely feedback can reduce anxiety of the user when waiting. Periodic feedback can guide the user through the next stage of operation and feedback. This helps users to understand whether they are operating correctly. In turn, this ensures continuity and fluency of user operation, improving product experience and overall immersiveness.

Incorporate Social Interaction Elements. Tourism has a certain social significance. Travelling individuals are able to better understand their peers through interactive experiences, and provide online and offline interactive experiences based on attractions by publishing events or comments. Users are more willing to interact with people with similar interests, sharing their experience of achieving a desired emotional feeling.

Emotional Design. There are three levels of design that must be considered in design psychology: instinctive, behavioral, and reflective. In the design of a cultural tourism experience, we should therefore focus on the design of these three levels. The product design and link to its cultural background are the main aspects affecting the tourist's emotional feelings toward a destination. In the design of a cultural tourism experience, narrative content should be created. Information can be transmitted through this narrative, triggering an emotional reaction in the tourist, leading to a better experience.

4 Design Practice

4.1 Design Background

Confucian culture is at the heart of Chinese culture. It is the source of China's ancient feudal society and has influenced thinking for more than 2,000 years. It has a complete ideological and cultural system, and has widely affected today's Chinese politics, economy, military, education, culture and arts and even folklore. In recent years, with the continuous growing interest of Confucianism and the opening of Confucius Institutes around the world, the international popularity of "Confucianism" has continued to increase. Qufu City, as the birthplace of the Confucian saint, has world-class cultural tourism resources: the Confucian Temple, Confucian Mansion, and Confucius Forest (San Kong). It is of great significance to further explore and capitalize on this rich cultural heritage.

Qufu City has obvious advantages in terms of cultural tourism resources and tourism transportation. However, in recent years, with the trend of the tourism industry upgrading, the development of Sankong Scenic Area also faces many problems. On one hand, the information services of scenic spots are flawed, and dynamic navigation and real-time information interaction are lacking – so tourists' information needs are often not met. On the other hand, as a cultural scenic spot with profound historical and cultural heritage, the SanKong Scenic Spot has a singular model for the process of cultural transmission, which lacks distinctive and interesting forms of communication and media. AR technology could virtually superimpose information, that was difficult to experience in the real world, in the original scenic area to add an unprecedented sensory experience for tourists and better understand the Confucian culture.

4.2 Scheme Design

The preliminary project design is shown in Fig. 2. The target users are young adults aged 18–35. Their basic characteristics are that they are curious about new things, willing to try them, and that they advocate freedom. This design solution integrates the fun of cultural factors into the tour through AR interaction, and creates a personal participation experience with the design of several typical scenes. This better meets the needs of tourists looking for an understanding of the culture of the scenic spot. The whole plan is divided into three parts: before travel, during travel, and after travel. Before the tour, the brand of the scenic spot is mainly promoted via publicity and advertising. The tour includes three modules of tour, explanation and interactive experience activities. After the tour, it includes online and offline memorials. This section analyzes the application of design elements and strategies in travel scenarios through actual design cases that can enhance users' sensory, cognitive, interactive, and emotional experiences.

Navigation Module. In the context of navigation and positioning, tourists' physical perceptions are dominated by their visual perception and azimuth. Visual recognition participates in the identification and positioning of things. Orientation enables subjects to judge physical coordinates in the tourism context. Additionally, the senses of smell, hearing, touch, body, and movement are also indispensable perception components for tourists to move, walk, and touch in navigation and positioning situations.

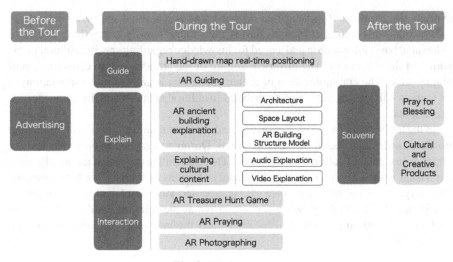

Fig. 2. Design scheme

The traditional travel APP navigation service information display is not intuitive enough. It is necessary for the tourists to align a two-dimensional plane with the three-dimensional physical world, which means tourists must perform a cognitive transformation. The introduction of AR technology can place virtual street signs, guidance arrows and other indicators in the scenic area without destroying the natural environment of the scenic spot. Based on the user's first-person perspective, the fusion of the virtual and real in the three-dimensional information display method eliminates cognitive human errors of tourists. This reduces the dependence on perception during tourism, improves the sense of security in the way-finding process, and brings a new geographical positioning experience (see Fig. 3).

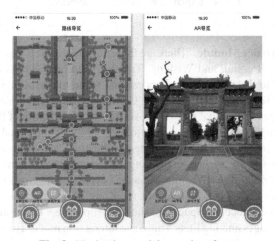

Fig. 3. Navigation module user interfaces

Explain the Module. Tourists often do not know much about the historical culture and customs surrounding attractions during their tours. However, they have a need to understand basic information and a need for knowledge regarding specific cultural information of the attractions. The historical culture of the attractions also constitutes their unique value. The communication of scenic backgrounds and cultural connotations is not tourists only desire, but it also contributes to cultural symbols and the uniqueness of scenic spots.

In the traditional context of explanation, cultural communication is mostly limited to brochures and notice boards on paper mediums. During tours, you can only view texts of related historical and cultural backgrounds. These cognitive processes are usually one-way visual inputs. To invoke the multi-sensory channels of tourists, we have designed three ways of AR explanation, voice explanation and video explanation. In the course of applying AR technology, when tourists arrive at the relevant building, the trigger mechanism based on geographical location starts the interactive explanation function (see Fig. 4).

Fig. 4. Explain the module user interfaces

Interactive Experience Module. There are three parts to the proposed AR interactions: Confucius Temple Blessing and Wishing, Treasure Hunting Game and Group Photo. These correspond to different physical spaces and game modes. Praying for blessings in the Confucius Temple is a highlight of Confucian Temple tourism. Based on the correlation between the physical and virtual situations, the function of flying Kongming lanterns and praying for wishes is designed to meet people's emotional needs and elicit emotional resonance. The interaction of Kongming Lantern's elements and flying accord with people's cognitive experiences of blessing. Based on LBS positioning, when tourists reach the blessing point, the "Wishing Message" event is triggered. This allows users to record their own voices and make exclusive Kong Ming Lanterns. Simultaneously, mobile phones can enhance the Space and show other people's Kongming lanterns, play other people's messages and facilitate a message interaction mode. The sliding operation simulates the process of flying Kongming lanterns, visually superimposing the dark night sky, and audibly simulating summer nights. Finally, the elements of Kongming lanterns and the dynamic changes of visual perception are integrated to enable visitors to experience immersion in the multi-channel interaction process (see Fig. 5).

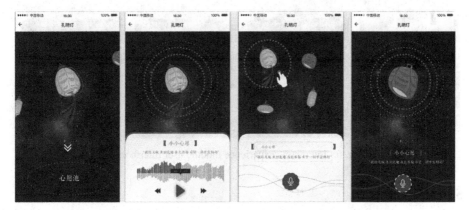

Fig. 5. Interactive experience module user interfaces

The AR treasure hunt game is based on LBS positioning. When visitors arrive at the specified location, they activate the AR interactive experience activity. This encourages them to search for "benevolence", "righteousness", "ceremonial", "wisdom", and "trustworthy" in the virtual scene. These are the "five constant virtues" of Confucianism. When you find the seal, you can learn the relevant knowledge content, and combine the science popularization of "Confucianism" with interactive games to enhance the fun. At the beginning of the game, visitors are informed about the game's background and gameplay, including experience suggestions (these are recommendations that affect the immersion of the AR application experience and guide users to have the best subsequent experience). The dialogue form enhances legibility and combines with the narrative elements of scenic culture to enhance tourists' memories. In the course of the game, the target tasks are decomposed, and step-by-step tasks are provided to improve the user's sense of control and achievement. Alongside this, it provides a visual display of progress and updates the task list as tasks are completed. The information that is required for a user to progress is proactively provided to enhance the user's perception. For example, some hidden functions can be selected by users to help them find the strategy (see Fig. 6).

At the end of the tour, when a visitor arrives at the entrance of the Confucian Temple and triggers a "Taking group photo" experience based on the geographic location, the photo template will provide images of Confucius and his disciples. When the user completes the photo and shares it on social media, the person and the attraction information will also be displayed. This helps users leave unforgettable memories and advertise the attraction.

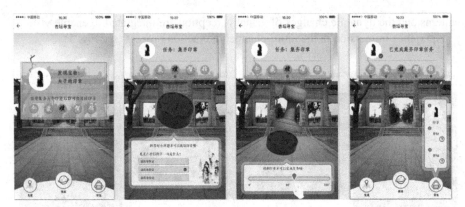

Fig. 6. Interactive experience module user interfaces

5 Conclusion

Current trends of technology around the world have seen advancements affecting a great number of industries internationally. This article will specifically focus on the tourism industry and how progress in AR technologies has enabled the tourism experiences to be enhanced. This article summarized the characteristics of AR technology and highlighted how the application of AR technology in cultural tourism has the potential to enhanced tourists' perception dimensions, cognitive depths and aesthetic experiences. Through analyzing the tourism experience, this article has examined how AR tech can bring a new form of digital experiences for tourists. In doing so, this article pointed out how the application of AR interactions in the tourism industry are designed with different layers in mind, these are the: sensory layer, cognitive layer, interaction layer and emotional layer. With focus on these, this article proposed a design strategy and applied it to a new application. Future research could build on this by developing design solutions and verifying if these are effective with experiments.

References

1. Guohong, Z.: Chinese Cultural Tourism: Theory Strategy, Practice. Nankai University Press, Tianjin (2001)
2. Guowei, S, Yongtian, W.: Application of augmented reality technology in digital protection of cultural heritage. J. Syst. Simul. (2009)
3. Azuma, R.T.: A survey of augmented reality. Presence Teleoperators Virtual Environ. **6**(4), 355–385 (1997)
4. Mei, Z.: Research on the application of AR interaction model in tourism situational experience from the perspective of embodiedness. Jiangnan University (2019)
5. Mei, Z., Li, Z.: Research on application of AR interactive mode for tourism experience. Packag. Eng. **40**(02), 191–195 (2019)
6. Hongjian, W., Jiangzhi, L.: A theoretical model of tourism experience generation path. Soc. Sci. Ser. **3**, 46–49 (2009)
7. Yong, J., Liangchuan, D.: Accessibility, pleasure, and sustainability: sociological value of urban road traffic environment design. Planner **21**(1), 17–20 (2005)

8. Zhi, L.: Research on digital tourism design and user experience based on augmented reality. Harbin Institute of Technology, (2013)
9. Pine, B.J., Gilmore, J.H.: The Experience economy. Harvard Business Press, Brighton (2011)
10. Yiyun, W.: Research on AR cultural tourism product development based on tourist experience. Hubei University (2018)
11. Diange, Y.: Research on marketing strategy of tourism scenic spots based on experience economy. Take Baiyangdian scenic spot as an example. Hebei University of Technology, Hebei (2008)
12. Jinhong, L.: Research on the construction of user experience model for augmented reality interactive games. Publ. Sci. (Bimon.) 2(23) (2015)

User Experience of Interaction Design in Local Cultural Heritage Museum Based on Digital Information Services and Navigation Support

Yidan Men[1,2], Robert Chen[1], and Xiaoping Hu[3(✉)]

[1] Faculty of Art, Design and Humanities, De Montfort University, Leicester, UK
[2] Art and Design, Guangdong University of Finance and Economics, Guangzhou, People's Republic of China
[3] School of Design, South China University of Technology, Guangzhou, People's Republic of China
huxp@scut.edu.cn

Abstract. Museum as a memory carrier of local heritage culture, it is a great significance to the cultural preservation and inheritance of countries and regions. In the 21st century, along with the transformation and development of information technology, digital technology is becoming more and more widely used in museum interactive navigation of information. However, due to the rapid and convenient acquisition method of digital information, it will lead to generalization and over-promotion of information dissemination in interactive navigation design. At the same time, the information formation system is fragment during the information transmission process. Fragmentation of information will weaken the accuracy and systematicity of information dissemination. It will cause difficulties for the audience to form a practical focus in the visiting process of mastering the information, thus causing obstacles to user experience and information collection in the museum.

This study was implemented using three methods: observation, questionnaire survey and interview. 1) Based on the museum user experience, determine the application of audience experience needs and preferences in interactive navigation design; 2) evaluate the existing museum information service design and navigation support system integrity And sustainability; 3) find and evaluate the critical factors of user experience in the museum interactive information service; 4) establish an 'RIRP' evaluation mode.

Keywords: User experience design · Service design · Interaction design

1 Introduction

1.1 Research Background and Motivation

The cultural heritage contains national spiritual characteristics and developmental genes. As a carrier of urban memory, the museum is of great significance for the collection, preservation, display and protection of tangible cultural heritage [1]. According

© Springer Nature Switzerland AG 2020
M. Rauterberg (Ed.): HCII 2020, LNCS 12215, pp. 184–194, 2020.
https://doi.org/10.1007/978-3-030-50267-6_15

to museum core activities including preservation, education, research, collections, networking, display, Renovation and communication to rejuvenate culture heritage [2]. Most museums are gradually improving the management and dissemination of information in the museum, but for local cultural heritage museums, a good information exchange platform still needs to be established. Therefore, the information service design is not only for the visitors to provide high-quality services, but also to provide useful information for the museum's development and future planning. Based on traditional museum information services, most of them are display in static display methods such as graphic display panels. Withing the advent of the experience era, it was changing in the needs of visitors and service design methods of the museum. Traditional information service methods might be unable to satisfy the various needs of visitors, such as perception and emotion. The involvement of new media and new interaction methods are leading to the emergence of a large number of new experiences in digital information service design.

Digital museums also have unique advantages in remotely accessing information and information. At present, China has established a digital museum of cultural heritage based on regions, exhibition halls for the protection of tangible cultural heritage in various provinces, and different local cultural display platforms. However, according to research, local exhibition venues existed as a small and medium-sized, private exhibition halls and events. Among them, most of the museum application objects are scientific researchers and experts in related fields. The information frame is modern flat as one-way communication. Lack of interactive experience considerations for information service design, establishing accurate and direct information services and navigation support that deliver features to the audience.

This research is based on the protection and dissemination of culture, focusing on the optimisation of user interaction experience and information expansion in the design of museum information services establish a 'R I R P' evaluation mode. Through the investigation and analysis of the existing information service design of multiple first-level museums, locked on the IoT information interconnection channel to share the data with official government consulting websites, social media website and travel information application, etc. via big data computing about museum information navigation. The study also provides a reference for the same type of cultural heritage museum in digital navigation support and information service application.

1.2 Aims and Objectives

This study is based on the problem of fragmented information in museum navigation, for a perspective of user experience behaviour in information acquired and information expansion in the museum, combined with the research and application in digital concepts used of navigation system in three types of National First-Class Museums in China, developed a 'R I R P' evaluation mode for enhancing the museum information feasibility and precisely, as well as audience felling of experience in interactive processing.

The objectives to achieve these aims are:

- To explore the relationship between museum functions and visitors needs
- To produce background research on the relationship between the information dissemination and the interaction processes in the museum through literature research.

- To investigate digital information services and navigation design in three types of National First-Class Museum.
- To analysis and Calculation application of Digital Information Service Design by Historical Heritage Museum in Guangdong Province
- To identify the main problems between the acquisition of audience information from museum dissemination
- To research the interactive experience needs of visitors and expectations of information acquisition.
- To establish 'R I R P' evaluation mode.

2 Method

The methodology is divided into three main aspects, namely secondary research, primary research and discussion.

1. Secondary Research:
   This is mainly for in-depth literature research to summarize the relationship between the functions of cultural heritage museums and the needs of visitors, and the relationship between the mechanism of information dissemination and interactive systems in the museum, to obtain the theory support, method and case studies for this research.
2. Primary Research:
   Interviews: 1) In-depth interviews with visitors to explore their needs for information services and interaction of cultural heritage museums, 2) In-depth interviews with curator and staff to gain relevant experience in concepts, methods, visitors behaviour and technologies in related professional fields.

   Observation: Examine the status quo of existing information service and navigation design cases in multiple museums, analyze and summarize the current status and problems of interaction between service and navigation design.

   Non-intervention observations: As a qualitative study, observations will be recorded to understand the movement paths, activity behaviours, and interactive feedback of public target groups.

3 The Function of Material Cultural Heritage Museum and the Cognitive Needs of the Audience

Cultural heritage is a precious wealth left to humanity by history. UNESCO (2016) from the presence of the substance into the form of cultural heritage (tangible cultural) and intangible cultural heritage (intangible heritage). For these two different types of cultural heritage forms, museums face considerable challenges in management and display. Traditional museums are more adept to managing and preservation of material objects, lack of experience in displaying spiritual beliefs with a living intangible heritage [3]. With the development of digital technology, more and more interactive experience design into the interior of the museum. Based on these two different types of heritage forms, the museum not only focuses on collecting, preserving and displaying past objects but also emphasizes the viewer's immersive experience. Adopt a people-oriented concept as the basis to encourage visitors to participate in the process as well as the museum's function [4]. Within the advancement and development of the times, the functions of museums are becoming more and more diverse. The museum's display could effectively enhance the awareness of the protection of public of intangible cultural heritage and is also an essential means of tourism development of intangible cultural heritage [5]. In China, the preservation and dissemination of local cultural heritage are carrying out in various cities. Local cities and towns are building museums related to their cultural heritage. Taking Guangdong Province as an example, Guangzhou, Shenzhen, Foshan, Shaoguan, Qingyuan, Conghua, Heyuan, Hezhou and many other cities are mining cultural heritage information within the region. Until 2018, the Department of Culture and Tourism of Guangdong released a catalogue of cultural Guangdong museums, recording a total of 313 museums in 37 cities. The following Table 1 gives a summarizes the percentage of local heritage museum in Guangdong Province different levels and types of museums.

Table 1. Utilization of museum digital information service system platforms

Museum level	Culture Heritage (state-owned)	Industry	Culture Heritage (Private)
Level 1	4	2	0
Level 2	18	2	0
Level 3	25	1	0
No level	97	25	92
Percentage	46.00%	9.58%	29.39%

A large number of new museums and traditional museums refurbished building, in addition to expanding the scale of the pavilion and the number of exhibits, it is more focus on digital information service design building. The following Table 2 gives a summarizes usage rate of museum existing digital information service system platforms in Guangdong Province. Most digital information services are including Positioning navigation, intelligent navigation, entertainment interaction and real-time data management in the museum, etc. and each additional features reflect a certain amount of audience demand.

Table 2. Utilization of museum digital information service system platforms

Information service		Percentage
Official website	177	56.54%
Weibo official account	72	23.00%
WeiChat official account	109	34.82%

The interview focuses on the audience from the local cultural heritage museum, 42 people interviewed, 27 were academic visitors. The main purpose was generally academic education, project research and observation. Fifteen people purpose of tourist visit as a family unit. According to questionnaire surveys and interviews, the needs of most viewers are divided into four categories: 1) Academic research, For researchers, the complete information and exhibits of local cultural heritage in the museum have research value and attractiveness. 2) Education. To achieve the educational significance of the museum, integrated with the curriculum of primary and secondary school, is a common practice in museums. Holding educational courses and workshops as museum short- term activities open to the public also preceded. 3) Entertainment, the museum has functional environmental space and equipment, which could meet the spiritual and emotional needs of the public. 4) Information, through the information in the museum, to perceive the outside world. Therefore, the needs of museum audiences could divide into cognitive needs, learning needs, and emotional needs. Therefore, the discussion of the relationship between museum functions and audience cognitive needs is the basis for the development of information services and navigation design.

4   Relationship Between Museum Information Dissemination and Interaction Processes

The application and integration of modern technology are changing the expression of cultural heritage, which represented and enhanced the interactive visual and non-abstract display of data [6]. Enter the era of information technology, the category of interaction design has gradually evolved from creative design to information interaction design, and the form of design objects also shifted from physical to virtualised information. This kind of shift in interaction design places higher requirements on information mobility, requiring mobility not only between users and products but even between users and users [7]. The digital information service platform provides audiences with more diversified knowledge navigation services. By using user experience design concepts to create a new model of museum visitors service, which based on the characteristics inside the museum, cultural relic collections, performances and activities,it could effectively and sincerely serve visitors. For example, the Museum of Terracotta Warriors and Horses Museum in China, using the "reservation – visit – navigation – interaction - feedback" service system. The contents include: visiting ticket purchase, a navigation system, smart navigation, voice album, interactive entertainment and other essential services while adding real-time monitoring of passenger flow analysis as an auxiliary service (see Fig. 1). This systematic information service will not only make the museum and the audience closer but also increase the interaction between people by adding interactive communication and entertainment services. Besides, by linking with the navigation system, the museum presents real-time traffic monitoring (see Fig. 2). By thermodynamic diagram analysis, following the time node to guide the comfort level of people in the region.

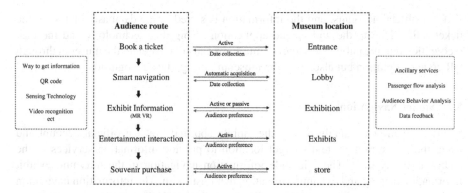

Fig. 1. Digital information service platform process.

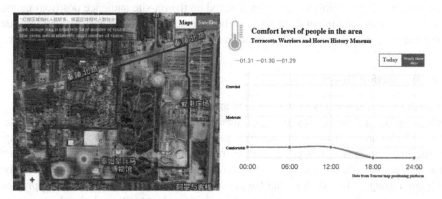

Fig. 2. Thermodynamic system diagram of Qin Shihuang Terracotta Warriors History Museum [8].

5   Results Analysis and Discussion

According to primary research of Three different types of national First-Level Museum Information service design in the local cultural heritage museum, which includes: Hunan Provincial Museum, Imperial Mausoleum of Qin Shi Huang Museum and Guangdong Province Museum. Furthermore, the local cultural heritage museums (mostly small and medium-sized museums) also conducted a field investigation. A few characteristics were found in the observations:

5.1   Visit Appointment

Museums generally provide online and offline reservation functions for museum tickets, events, guided rental and other services in order to achieve the purpose of monitoring the even distribution of passenger flow and visitor crowd. It could be improved the attraction and scientific management of the museum. After the audience has successfully booked, the QR code (including the date of visit, user name, ID card, contact information, etc. generated after the booking is successfully sent to the user via the SMS platform or

WeChat official accounts, and the information is stored in the database for Use at the ticket office. Due to the widespread application of big data technology and the face recognition into the public view, part of museums can not only enter the museum through QR code recognition but also enter the museum through face recognition.

5.2 Smart Navigation

Smart navigation is usually tied to the mobile app and WeChat official account and using the positioning system's target location to provide information services to the audience at any time. These include information navigation in the museum, exhibit information display and dynamic animation demonstration. The information navigation in the museum actively assists the audience to display the functional sections in the museum, such as toilets, rest areas, commodity areas or other specific exhibit guides. The display of the exhibit information is based on the on-site audience positioning and moving position, and it can instantly correlate the nearest exhibits nearby, and provide information retrieval or related information services.

5.3 Interaction Design

In recent years, museums in major cities are emerging to establish digital experience halls based on interactive design. Most museums have established online virtual museums, which can be browsed online through VR equipment or online virtual roaming. In the museum space, a large number of historical and cultural exhibits have added interactive QR codes to enhance the historical and cultural authenticity behind static exhibits through MR. Visitors can trigger interaction with the exhibits by tapping or playing games. The game-type interactive experience deepens the relationship between the museum, the exhibits and the audience, and through an entertaining and enjoyable interactive experience, the audience can also communicate and interact online, expanding the publicity of museum.

5.4 Base on Big Data Analysis of Audience Behavior

Most of the traditional museums use questionnaires or interviews to study the audience's visit routes, exhibit preferences and experience needs. In the natural behaviour patterns of the audience, by the information service in big data background and interactive experience, positioning the audience's preferences and behaviours of viewers label division. According to its behaviour habits, it can be associated with other related exhibit information or other types of museum navigation.

Based on the above studies, large national first-Level museums have relatively perfect designs in information services and navigation support. However, the regional cultural history museum is relatively weak. Excluding the problem of cost budget, the following are the problems presented by the local cultural heritage museum:

5.5 Incomplete Information Transmission Process

In order to comply with digital applications, most regional museums try to incorporate interactive experiential design to enhance the communication between the audience and the museum. Feedback from interviewed groups. First, it is not very easy to find relevant museum information. Most museums have the problem of inaccurate publicity information. Because the information has not been updated, the webpage is lost and misleading, resulting in visitors being unable to select valid information and causing the museum to lose visitor flow. Second, the information connection network is imperfect, and fragmented information in multiple cities cannot be energetically interconnected and transmitted. Due to the lack of publicity for small and medium-sized cultural heritage museums in townships, it is not very easy for visitors to locate related museums on the Internet or in tourism applications. This way of disseminating information on the Internet can now be captured by user behaviour preference systems in big data. By establishing a city-to-city museum information association network, the communication power of regional museums can be enhanced.

5.6 Targeted Audience

It was found in the questionnaire that in the regional cultural history museum, the main audiences were tourists and academic visitors. The gender, age, education level, economic level, and geographical origin of the audience determine the way of display and communication [5]. When setting up the information service and navigation system, we should design for the characteristics of these two groups. For tourist groups, most of them are families, with emotional needs as the mainstay, supplemented by cognitive needs. For academic visitors, most of them visit in the form of expert visits or organizational learning, and their study needs are mainly. According to the above two types of groups, the museum should divide the age level of visitors, points of interest and activity capabilities to meet their experience needs. Taking academic visitors as an example, in the information service, accurate information can be associated according to their preferences, and different cities but the same type of historical and cultural museums or exhibition halls can be interconnected to form a similar type of museum association network.

6   R I R P Evaluation Mode

Based on the above research and analysis to establish 'RIRP' evaluation model for the local museum of cultural heritage in the future development of information services design as a guiding role.

6.1 R-Relevance

Through the analysis and analysis of city information to build a precise classification. According to different levels of classes, associated with the relevant information to expand. The flow of information between the various museums can not only improve their dissemination of the museum, but they can also expand the initiative to provide information to the audience. At present, most local museums only establish links to private information, and rarely connect the information to other cities. For local small and medium-sized museums, effective interconnection could not be established to improve their dissemination. However, according to questionnaires and interviews, most of the visitors might not be satisfied with the services of museums in central cities and were eager to receive more relevant information, involving marginal cities or villages. The information about each city museum is fragmented and difficult to count. In the information collection and sorting, the provinces should be divided into regions and then spread to other cities centred on provincial capitals. According to the investigation, most of the cultural and heritage museums in provincial capitals are comprehensive types, with diversified contents, and the cities could be related according to their categories. For example, the Chaozhou wood carving art exhibition in the long-term exhibition hall in the Guangdong Museum should be linked to the Chaozhou Intangible Cultural Heritage Exhibition Hall, Chen Peixi Wood Carving Art Museum, Jinshi Tiezhi Puppet Art Heritage Center, Chao District Intangible Cultural Heritage Exhibition and other related museums. Therefore, the establishment of information links between cities can improve the dissemination of local cultural heritage museums and provide visitors with a variety of relevant information.

6.2 I- Initiative

Information services should actively serve the audience. In the traditional static display of museums, visitors are in a state of passively receiving information, which is a one-way transmission process, which reduces the diversity and accuracy of information transmission to a certain extent. As far as the status quo of Chinese museums is concerned, most national first-level museums provide an intelligent navigation system. Through the museum network, relevant exhibit information or navigation support can be pushed in real-time according to the audience's positioning, so that the audience can effectively receive relevant information and improve the dissemination of useful information.

6.3 R-Rationality

Design information services should have precise interaction logic and rationality. Through the investigation of multiple information services design in the museum, several museums create an online digital museum and provide virtual reality roaming services. It is lacs of fluidity in the information presented on apps and web; it should be considering the user experience requirements of the information framework and retrieval methods. The information of each exhibition hall is independent, and there are less connectivity instruction and guideline, which makes most visitors unable to use this information effectively. Therefore, interaction logic and rationality are reasonable to use in designing information services.

6.4 P- Preference

The positioning of the information service design is based on the research of museum and analysis of the audience; it should cater to the experience preferences of the visitor group. Each type of museum audience is slightly different when providing information services and navigation support. It should include orientation according to group preferences. A survey of visitors to the local cultural heritage museum found that the primary audience of the museum are tourists and academic visitors, and the proportion of the "parent-child relationship" model is increasing among into groups visiting the museum. This kind of service could achieve accurate information delivery based on big data estimation and information capture methods.

7 Conclusion

Local cultural heritage museums as an essential platform for displaying traditional human culture and spiritual civilization still need to strengthen their communication and inter-action functions. Most museums are already building the basic framework of a digital information service platform; however, database updates and connections still need to be strengthened. Based on the user experience design theory, forming a complete interactive logic sequence and accurate information delivery has become the main tasks of infor-mation service design. Among them, based on the information sharing in the original museum, the relationship between cities and villages is connected through information interconnection to achieve more effective and far-reaching dissemination.

The application of Big Data, the Internet of Things (IoT), and Artificial Intelligence could provide sharing and interconnecting data services for the information applications of local cultural heritage museum. The application of the technology of the Internet of things could provide visitors with proactive information services, thereby expanding the spread of information. Intelligent navigation in the context of big data could provide accurate information placement and expansion for viewers. This research analyzes and summarizes the existing information service design in the museum, and puts forward the "R I R P" evaluation mode to provide a particular reference for the future development and planning of digital information services and digital navigation.

Acknowledgements. This work was supported by a grant from the Innovative Talents Project of General Universities in Guangdong Province, NO.2019WQNCX035

References

1. Ambrose, T., Paine, C.: Museum Basics. Routledge, London (2012)
2. Stefano, M.L., Davis, P., Corsane, G. (eds.): Safeguarding Intangible Cultural Heritage, vol. 8. Boydell & Brewer Ltd., Suffolk (2014)
3. Kurin, R.: Museums and intangible heritage: culture dead or alive. ICOM News **57**(4), 7–9 (2004)
4. Pirnar, I., Sari, F.Ö.: The changing role of museums: for tourists or local people? (2013)
5. Yoshida, K.: The museum and the intangible cultural heritage. Museum Int. **56**(5), 8–10 (2004)

6. Card, M.: Readings in Information Visualization: Using Vision to Think. Morgan Kaufmann, Burlington (1999)
7. Dean, D.: Museum Exhibition: Theory and Practice. Routledge, London (2002)
8. Qin, S.: Terracotta Warriors History Museum Weichat official account. https://heat.qq.com/wap_qqmap_big_data/heatmap_embed.html?city=%E8%A5%BF%E5%AE%89%E5%B8%82&region=%E7%A7%A6%E5%A7%8B%E7%9A%87%E5%85%B5%E9%A9%AC%E4%BF%91%E5%8D%9A%E7%89%A9%E9%A6%86&from=singlemessage. Accessed 20 Jan 2010

Mixed Reality and Volumetric Video in Cultural Heritage: Expert Opinions on Augmented and Virtual Reality

Néill O'Dwyer$^{(\boxtimes)}$, Gareth W. Young , Nicholas Johnson ,
Emin Zerman , and Aljosa Smolic

Trinity College Dublin, Dublin, Ireland
{odwyernc,youngga,johnson,zermane,smolica}@tcd.ie

Abstract. Mixed reality (MR) technology is currently growing in popularity for applications in the cultural heritage domain. Furthermore, with the ability to be viewed with six degrees of freedom, volumetric video (VV) is presently being explored as a viable approach to content creation within this area. When combined, MR technology and VV present both practitioners and audiences with innovative approaches to the creation and consumption of both tangible and intangible representations of cultural significance. While there are some existing quantitative studies appraising these new technologies, the precise effects of MR in a cultural heritage context have yet to be fully explored. Here we show the results of a systematic evaluation of MR technology as applied in a cultural heritage context, where subject matter expert interviews were conducted to identify how virtual reality and augmented reality technologies are influencing the creative practices of domain experts and audience engagements with modern dramatic literature. Gathered from high-level stakeholders within the cultural heritage domain, our results highlighted the problems, concerns, and desires of users who must consider this technology in practice. We found that MR and VV content were considered by many to be disruptive technologies for the future of film, theater, and performance practice from the perspectives of both practitioners and audiences. We anticipate that these results will help future MR and VV projects to create meaningful content that is sympathetic to the needs and requirements of creators and audiences.

Keywords: Mixed reality · Cultural heritage · Subject matter expert interviews

1 Introduction

Samuel Beckett was one of the great innovators of technology in theater. He created works for all media, including radio, television, film, as well as experimenting with technological innovations on the live stage. He was interested in

---

N. O'Dwyer and G. W. Young—These authors contributed equally.

© Springer Nature Switzerland AG 2020
M. Rauterberg (Ed.): HCII 2020, LNCS 12215, pp. 195–214, 2020.
https://doi.org/10.1007/978-3-030-50267-6_16

the possibilities that new technologies open for creative expression. If Beckett had continued to work into this century, he would likely be curious about new digital technologies that did not exist during the analog age. A major artistic mission of the practice-based research trilogy underpinning this paper was to extend the idea of Beckett's theater into these new digital realms, affording audiences and artists extended capabilities in networking, immersion, interactivity, telepresence, and the new medium of volumetric video (VV)[1] for mixed reality (MR). As new technologies emerge, they compel new experiments in art-making and storytelling, and revisiting Beckett's texts asks what these plays will mean in the 21st century. As such, the epistemological significance of remaking Beckett's *Play* for virtual reality (VR) and augmented reality (AR) consists of a will to transmit his texts to forthcoming generations of art-going publics, who will increasingly access content via MR technologies, thereby responding to a cultural need for his works to be intergenerationally reactivated.

Virtual Play and *Augmented Play* are the second and third parts of a three-year practice-as-research trilogy, wherein Samuel Beckett's groundbreaking theatrical text, entitled *Play* (1963), was reimagined and reinterpreted for digital culture, as 1) a webcast (*Intermedial Play*), 2) a VR drama (*Virtual Play*), and 3) an AR drama (*Augmented Play*). This project reinterprets Beckett's classic modernist text in a way that is engaging for 21st-century audiences, by capturing actors using cutting-edge digital media recording techniques and then visualizing their corresponding characters using advanced VR and AR head-mounted displays (HMDs). The actors were recorded using a VV technique [23] which involved capturing action simultaneously on multiple video cameras "strategically placed, in an arc of about 150°, in a compromise between scene coverage and image overlap" [15]. Actors were recorded against a green-screen backdrop, which simplified segmentation (or chroma-keying) processes at the post-production stage.

For traditional video, viewers can only watch the captured content as framed on a 2D display in a way that was decided by the director and the cinematographer; for traditional theater and performance, there is the visceral and contingent experience of being present in the space of the live performance. MR technologies are distinct from both theater and film, but exhibit characteristics that overlap with existing modalities of content creation and consumption. MR technologies enable viewers to potentially interact with and explore content in ways that were not possible via traditional performance modes. Developments in VV capture techniques and MR display technologies create a mediatized content paradigm that can be, on the one hand, utilized by the content creators, and on the other, consumed openly by the audiences. However, this raises questions concerning the intent and realization for the dramatic arts, where one can discuss the relationship between the narrative, interaction, and perception.

This paper analyzes the results of a series of subject-matter expert (SME) interviews, which include the opinions of academics, researchers and practicing

---

[1] VV is a capture and display technique that generates 3D models; the audience can choose their own viewpoint within a scene, thus providing interactive free navigation.

artists who specialize in film, theater, and performance studies. The goal was to reflect on the relationship between emergent MR technologies and discuss opportunities and challenges for the domain. Specifically, we identify topics of novel, immersive, interactive imaging devices, cutting-edge live-action capture techniques, and the potential that they hold for creative artists as a means of expression, and for audiences as a means of engaging content. The qualitative data analysis of the SME interviews showed that specific improvements can be made to our MR experiences that can potentially benefit the broader domain.

2   Background and Related Work

The philosophies of mixed realities have been of interest and influence for creative technologists for many years. However, it is only recently that advanced AR and VR technology has become more readily accessible for broader research, commercial content creation, and widespread consumption. New developments in the area now focus on the creation of accessible content and the techniques MR designers and artists can apply in communicating their creative ideas.

2.1   Mixed Reality and Volumetric Video

The ubiquitous nature of digital technology in the everyday lives of many means that human-computer interactions take place more frequently, where "collective human perception meets the machines' view of pervasive computing" [20]. The idea that the digital world is constantly intervening in the real via technology is one of the driving philosophies of mixed reality, where technology channels data from the physical world into the virtual and vice versa. MR can be defined as the merging of the real world with the virtual, where both physical and digital objects exist in real time [13]. Therefore, MR can refer to a continuum that spans between real environments and virtual environments, encompassing both augmented reality and virtual reality. New developments in MR have presented users with options of engaging content in VR, where the user is placed within an immersive virtual environment (IVE), and AR, where virtual objects are superimposed on to the real-world view, using HMDs and mobile 'window on the world' technologies that employ spatial registers to anchor digital objects to the real world. Often, content is created for these platforms via proprietary and open-source cross-platform game engine technologies.

Capitalizing on developments made in 3D capture and reconstruction, VV technology enables content creators to reconstruct live action in 3D. This is done in dedicated studios where multiple cameras are placed around the edges of the studio looking inwards, although the setup may differ depending on limitations and requirements, using cameras ranging from 12 [19] to 106 [6]. In general, the 3D object in the scene is segmented via either chroma-keying [19], depth-keying [22], or their combination [6]. For *Virtual Play* and *Augmented Play*, the method proposed by Pagés et al. [19] was applied due to the low number of cameras required, which would be more feasible for many content creators.

2.2   Mixed Reality and Volumetric Video in Creative Practice

Following the emergence of consumer VR, one of the early innovators was journalism. This trend was led by the *New York Times*, "which distributed over a million cardboard viewers to its print subscribers and created a high-end, VR-specific smartphone application to distribute Times-related VR experiences" [2, p. 204]. Many of these experiences were filmed using 360 video technology, which has a fixed viewpoint and only affords three degrees of freedom (3DoF).

One of the pioneers of combining VV in VR and journalism was Nonny de la Peña, who created several VR experiences that allowed her audiences to immerse themselves in realistic six degrees of freedom (6DoF) VR. De la Peña is a "trained journalist who was drawn to VR for its immediacy and empathy-encouraging qualities" [2, p. 209]. There are several other examples of content creators who are attempting to write original fictional narratives for VV VR storytelling and to define a grammar thereof; see for example, *Awake: Episode One* [24], where the narrative drops the viewer into a series of scenes that are ambiguously situated somewhere between the protagonist's reality and unconscious - memory, hallucination, or both. The dominant narrative strategy for such experiences consists of placing the spectator into the middle of a scene, and some action ensues; however, at no point is the audience directly involved in the dialogue or action or addressed by the characters. The role of the viewer is reduced back into the same voyeuristic role of traditional media practice; there is no attempt to elicit the new interactive potentialities for narrative in VR. As of yet, there is very little investigation into combining interactive narrative techniques with VV, and affording the viewer significant agency in the unfolding of the narrative event. However, with the emergence of new MR and VV technologies, users are now permitted 6DoF, which affords a more naturalistic sense of presence.

As a new form of visual media, VV has started to be used more frequently in MR applications, including: remote communication and collaboration schemes [18], live-action reenactments for educational museum-guide applications for cultural heritage [17], and an AR version of the aforementioned *Play* by Samuel Beckett [16]. *Play* lends itself to MR because of Beckett's deep engagement of the notion of play. In the original script, the sequence of the actors speaking is determined by a moving spotlight, which Beckett calls the "inquisitor" [3, p. 318]; they speak when the light is on them and fall silent when the light is off. *Play* is a game of interaction between the light operator and the actor, mediated by the lighting technology of the time [15]. In the presented MR versions the spotlight is aligned with the user's gaze, and they are afforded the power to activate the characters into speaking. Thus, the user embodies the interrogator, a privilege originally withheld for the director or light operator. By directly involving the user in the cause-and-effect dynamics of shining a light upon the actors, the reinterpretation attempts to elicit the interactive opportunities afforded by the MR medium. Thus, *Play* offers a glimpse of the new opportunities for MR to break away from the predominant three-act narrative, as well as the fly-on-the-wall audience paradigm.

2.3   Narrative and Interactivity

The will to transpose old media processes and idiosyncrasies onto digital media is a tendency that formulates the theory of "remediation", which documents and theorizes the prolongation of old media characteristics in new media [4]. Historically speaking, this is evident in the progression of live-action storytelling from theater to film, where *1)* directors initially filmed using the proscenium format, and *2)* actors made broad gesticulation as if communicating with audiences in the back row of an auditorium, rather than a camera positioned close by. However, as the film medium became more established, a grammar gradually developed that allowed filmmakers and audiences to understand that film was not synonymous with theater, and that the working processes and finished artifacts were different. The theater-to-film transition shows us that it takes time for creative practitioners to exploit the potentialities of new interdisciplinary art forms, and those potentialities are subject to the indeterminacy of technological developments. This raises the fundamental question concerning the preference of MR audiences: is it better to observe narrative as a fly-on-the-wall, choosing a viewpoint without having any effect on the outcome of the story, or to embody a character who participates in the plot and impacts the narrative? The former paradigm, which appeals to empathy and emotions through a tightly regimented and efficient system of narrative disclosure, is the domain of Hollywood; the latter, concerning exploration, immersion, deep engagement, and repetition, is that of gaming.

The reinterpretation of Beckett's *Play* progresses a new "storyworlding" grammar [2, p. 225]. Beckett's original script had to be linear for it to work in the proscenium format; however, in some sort of prophetic act anticipating the destiny of storytelling, Beckett designed his script as circular and, therefore, potentially infinite. Furthermore, in a note entitled "Repeat", he says: "The repeat may be an exact replica of the first statement or it may present an element of variation" [3, p. 320], and in his own adaptation for radio, he allowed the actors to speak in a random order while ensuring that the sequential integrity of individual monologues was maintained [8, pp. 125–154]. In both *Augmented Play* and *Virtual Play*, this concept was pushed to its limits by putting control of the randomness in the hands of the audience. To explore the establishment of a storyworlding grammar, SME interviews were proposed to raise, present, and explore multiple issues of current interest and contention at the intersection of MR with film, theater, and performance.

In traditional productions, the stories being told are compelling because they often furtively reflect the audiences' previously lived experiences. AR and VR can be used in this context, because MR narratives are often delivered on a first-person experiential basis, and the innately immersive nature of the technology enhances these narrative experiences even further. However, this alone does not create engaging content, just as not everything that is performed on stage or captured for film is storytelling. Therefore, performance-audience resonance is required to impart a sense of inclusion within a narrative that is laid out explicitly for the role of the viewer. Although MR technology has seen many new developments in recent years, past theories of VR and storytelling that closely tie the roles of imagination, interaction, and immersion still hold today [5]. For example, to understand a story via MR the viewer must use their imagination to fill in any gaps perceived in the presented materials. A similar phenomenon was observed, revealing that the way in which an actors' representations of an imaginary narrative was judged by an audience was closely connected with the subjective attribution of the origin of their movements, attribution based purely upon the values, beliefs, and memories of the observer [10]. Creators of cultural content can, therefore, never remove subjective interpretation.

When multimodal sensory narratives are experienced in MR, the perceptions of the audience require some grounding in the real world; this is a central principle of Gestalt psychology – pattern recognition and previous experiences combine to engage the imagination [12]. When creating content for MR, new experiences must be created that exhibit some commonalities with the audience's previous experiences. Therefore, we sought to find which experiential practices had the most impact, and what was useful for achieving artistic goals and intentions. To test these ideas, data was collected and analyzed to learn and develop a heuristic for creating MR interpretations of existing works, exploring the technicalities of the processes undertaken to stage performances via AR and VR platforms, and improving experiences of MR practitioners and audiences in the future. The main goal of the presented work was to learn from previous practices, to discover what worked and what did not, and to use these data to inform future creative projects in the MR creative sector in an ongoing, iterative design process.

In terms of cultural heritage and human-computer interaction, this raises some questions: How aware are domain experts of the disruptive impact of MR on artistic practice and audience engagement? How can we establish a story-worlding grammar that allows makers to more easily create engaging VV-based MR content, and audiences to more enthusiastically engage with it? How can we make MR content that aligns better with the time-honored paradigm of story-telling as a communal (non-solipsistic) experience?

3 Interview Methodology

Data collection took place in the Republic of Ireland during December 2019 and January 2020. Participants were recruited via email, with potential respondents identified via a snowball method to identify an appropriately qualified peer user group from the UK and Ireland. Sessions of one hour were conducted face-to-face at locations and times that suited the individual. The session began with an introduction to the research, then a fully labeled 5-point Likert scale questionnaire was used to gather demographic and user-type identifier data. Following this, each participant experienced five minutes of both *Virtual Play* and *Augmented Play* to familiarize themselves with the material and platforms before being interviewed. For each session, a Dell Alienware Area 51 laptop (Intel i9k-9900K CPU, NVIDIA GeForce RTX 2080, and 64 GB DDR4 Memory) and an HTC Vive (a VR headset developed by HTC and Valve Corporation) was set up for *Virtual Play*, and a Magic Leap One was used for *Augmented Play*. The order of presentation was counterbalanced to control for ordering effects, and visible observation (GoPro Hero7) was started at this time. Participants were recorded throughout and observational notes logged.

An in-depth interview on topics relating to the use of MR in creative practice was then conducted. The interview followed a semi-structured design for continuity and repeatability, and employed an interview-laddering technique [9] to systematically explore the same core themes with each participant, whilst allowing them to elaborate on their chosen topics of interest. The interviews probed: the SMEs' previous knowledge and experience of state-of-the-art MR technology; the use of MR technology in their respective domains; current user requirements for technology applied in creative practice; the challenges of using new MR technology; and the receptiveness of the domain to MR technology. The interview section of the experiment took on average 20 min (M = 21:30; SD = 5:29). Finally, participants were debriefed and given the opportunity to ask further questions.

The interviews were transcribed and coded using a grounded theory approach. The data were first categorized into the core rungs of our laddering technique and first-level core categories were then derived from topics of interest raised in the interviews. In this way, our interview analysis was structured to provide a focused view that matched our initial hypothesis.

4   Results and Discussion

The study consisted of 13 interviews with experienced practitioners and scholars of film, theater, performance, and literature, 6 male and 7 female. The average age of the cohort was 46.92 (SD = 14.42), and the sum total of professional experience was 221 years, with a mean number of years' experience of 18.42 (SD = 13.28). The current interviewee occupation profiles consisted of academics (n = 9), artistic directors (n = 3), and performer (n = 1). Their work experiences included titles of Professor, Head of School, Postdoctoral Research Fellow, industry expert, and theater director. All participants had undertaken important roles in areas of: Modern Irish Literature or Beckett Studies; artistic, pedagogic, and administrative leadership; movement practice in performance; feminism, gender, and women in performance; representations of 3D space in literature; and history and theory of theater, cinema, and digital media.

As a manipulation check, participants self-identified their aptitude for new or novel technologies as being "Fair" to "Good" (M = 3.65, SD = 0.82). To further classify the participant pool as experts within their respective domain, a user-cube [14] was constructed, see Fig. 1. The participants rated their knowledge and experiences of MR technology as "Moderately Familiar" (M = 2.92, SD = 1.21), and their expertise in relation to the study of avant-garde, modern literature, and modernism, as "Above Average" (M = 4.08, SD = 0.80). In summary, the cohort self-identified as being sufficiently informed, technically competent users, who could be considered as having some familiarity with MR in practice, and above-average expertise within their domain.

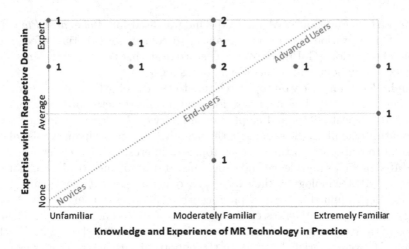

Fig. 1. User-cube identifying participant user-types (blue line representing the linear average and numbers representing the number of participants). (Color figure online)

To understand our cohort's opinions on MR in creative practice, interview data were analyzed applying inductive reasoning to generate codes relating to our core themes, see Fig. 2. The collected data were reviewed and repeated ideas and topics were extracted and categorized. This paper focuses on discussions around practitioners as content creators, and audiences as content consumers.

4.1   Previous Knowledge and Experiences of MR

A wide range of MR works had been previously developed and experienced by the cohort. This provided insight into how their involvement with MR influenced their opinions on future contexts of use and their expectations of the technology in practice. They commented on the genealogical reach of MR within the domain by referencing early AR and 3D performance experiments in Beckett's *Waiting for Godot* by George Coates Performance Works. Other early references were of an academic nature, such as the Annual Conference of Cyberspace ca. 1994/95, a period when the term "cyberspace" was first coined; as one SME explained, "There were a lot of artists working, at the time, using early virtual reality technologies".

The cohort's experiences of MR provoked comments on innovative and exploratory forms of artistic practice; for example, they supposed that MR was highly influential in helping artists to think differently about how new fiction is structured. Equally, it was perceived as a niche, experimental, and a counter-mainstream form of content creation and consumption, struggling to be integrated into conventional performance spaces: "It's its own thing. Like gaming, it's completely different". Participants speculated that MR would afford artists the ability to provide new types of imaginary worlds, reproduce specific historical scenarios, apply modern perspectives (e.g. feminism or postcolonialism) to

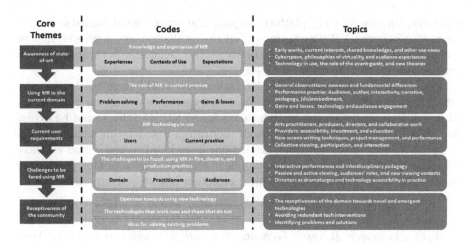

Fig. 2. Interview analysis of MR in film, theater, or performance practices.

narratives and allow viewers to reinterpret these events, and create new empathy-driven experiences that allow audiences to step into the shoes of another person and gain an understanding of their perspective.

Bridging both practice and audience perspectives, our participants were familiar with earlier performative VR works that concerned philosophies of "cyberspace" and the associated anxieties surrounding the nature of being. It was generally believed that these anxieties were somewhat quelled today: "We're now living in the virtual"; citing *Videodrome*, one participant jested, "Your reality is already half... hallucination" [7]. Historically, it was believed that scholars and practitioners were somewhat uncomfortable using new MR technologies, but in the current epoch people live much more of their lives in the virtual domain – "Whether it be in social media or banking, people aren't quite alarmed by that... it's just another extension of our existence". As such, it was felt that MR is now more readily accepted for creating layers of reality within artistic productions, and could be a disruptive technology for contemporary performances. Generally, it was believed that the new "theater" needs to explore digital technology to reconfigure the stage as a societal laboratory, where creatives can practice new techniques and better understand what it means to *be* in the digital space, and understand "...how stories or identities are recomposed in that space".

Participants were aware of the growing interest in AR and VR. However, it was reported that their access to MR experiences was primarily obtained through organized events in institutes of higher education, as a pedagogical tool, and cultural heritage sites or art museums/galleries, where it was used to represent historical narratives as installation art or bespoke applications. Notable public performances included works in which the mise-en-scène of virtual landscapes and dance choreographies played on new interactions between the reality of performance and the virtuality of digital worlds. It was generally agreed that these types of experiences were immersive, conducive to a feeling of presence, and offered a new viewing platform beyond the conventional formats. Partici-pants also believed VR was better suited to installation art, where immersing a viewer in a virtual space could facilitate surreal/avant-garde theater and new perspectives on performance.

Participants highlighted that MR technology would have to develop sig-nificantly to enable a collective audience to experience a singular production. Although technically feasible with location-based VR [15], this would be expen-sive/risky in terms of the established auditorium-based business model. The repeated failures of 3D cinema – a medium introduced, revised, and revisited since the 1960s – was given as an example of this phenomenon. One participant historicized the importance of technical evolution and shared experiences:

> *"When sound was introduced to the cinema, within a year every single cinema had to have sound in it, and you couldn't make a film that was silent any longer. It hasn't been like that with 3D, which is basically the precursor to what you are doing [with MR]." – (PW67)*

Shared CAVE experiences, where communal IVEs are simultaneously occu-pied by the performers and audience, were also discussed. These types of environ-ments highlighted the power of creating new, shared virtual landscapes, where the experience was unimpeded by the physicality of the real world. These prac-tices provided our SMEs with memorable, positive experiences that motivated them to explore MR in their respective domains, as one participant explained: "I felt like it had elevated beyond being an experiment in the art form; it was a very beautiful thing". While MR was described as "[Just] another technol-ogy to be employed... as simple as using lighting on the stage", it was also asserted that theater has always been virtual, and audiences are comfortable with that. Although a true disconnect from the physical world is not possible, the SMEs expected to be able to realize their imaginings and allow audiences to explore something new that would ordinarily be inaccessible. Moreover, the space between audiences and performers would also be transformed "By interac-tivity... between the user, performer, or creator", facilitating creations that are neither classical film nor stage performance. As per any disruptive technology, or a new mode of transposing concepts, "From creative moment to audience moment...", the discipline must expand its knowledge and expertise in a new way.

Some SMEs were particularly critical of current explorations of 360 video in stage production, while others described it as an interesting way of capturing a fundamentally ephemeral art form, one that is notoriously difficult to capture successfully on conventional video. One participant declared: "I would look at a lot of theater on video in my previous job and it was always horrendous; even the most wonderful shows were a torture to sit through". 360 recordings are attempting to create a sense of seeing the show live, and audiences are afforded the added advantage of being on stage among the performers. While it was predicted that original work made for 360 film would be genuinely impactful and interesting to the domain, it was also felt that 360 technology was lacking the communal experience of a classical performance, because each spectator is in their own world: "One of the great joys of theater and performance is that communal experience of being in an audience with other beating hearts".

4.2   Using MR in Current Practice

A major domain-specific, practice-related issue was the problem of novelty, and the uncertainty this creates in content creation and audience consumption. It was agreed that MR created a fundamentally different author–audience paradigm; for example, SMEs acknowledged: "There will be a period of audience learning" and "More of these problems will be solved as more and more people start to use it". Some were hesitant to align MR technology with existing performance formats, because the technology is neither film nor theater, which "...raises the question as to whether it is a completely new medium". Thus, MR introduces a new set of conditions; "It's an opportunity all by itself". In terms of the commercializing, "You would have to imagine something quite different... You are a long way off the three-act narrative". However, others were accepting of MR as an inevitable evolution of the domain, while remaining ambivalent about the benefits: "You can gain a lot... by allowing the viewer more agency; but you can lose a lot, because you still have the same problems [as film]: it's a one-off performance." Therefore, everything hinges on a quality take in the film studio as the actor is not permitted to refine their performance, resurrecting the live-versus-recorded debate. A Beckett director suggested that some spontaneous presence was lost, because the actors acted individually in the capture studio: "It really is between the three of them that the play is formed as a trialogue". However, another SME highlighted how the technological idiosyncrasies open new opportunities to challenge the audience engagement paradigm, and how to frame the art: "The future of VR is in content that's generated specifically for it and doesn't try to be either, and that acknowledges new opportunities that the new medium presents". SMEs generally acknowledged the variety and freshness that the interactivity provides to the audience: "Theoretically, it's the same performance, but you can change your method of engaging with it".

The film contingent problematized the difficulties that the MR viewer paradigm creates for storytelling, compared with the "mainstream". Controlling the viewer's gaze through framing and editing is crucial for narrative progression in complex or fast-moving plots, so "The question of gaze and where the user is directing their attention becomes a really important consideration". Audiences are not used to having the freedom to look around. The unedited choose-where-you-look viewer paradigm complicates the traditional narrative model, highlighting the need to establish a new grammar: "Because of the open-endedness... there needs to be ways to guide people through, so if you don't see everything you still understand what's happening". They concluded that slow, experimental, non-narrative stories are "Better suited to VR than fast-paced plots", because they are conducive to taking time, exploring and observing the surroundings. These observations accord with the aforementioned assertion of MR's suitability for installation and video art, where one could, for example, "Get to be in the shoes of someone... and see what it's like, for a few minutes".

The SMEs were excited by "...the possibility for directors to have real bodies... and virtual bodies together". They enthusiastically articulated creative ideas for experimenting with MR technologies along the lines of telepresence, interconnectivity, and the disembodied image. They suggested the technology could be useful for "Reanimating dead actors", expediting or supporting rehearsal processes, or solving "The problem of all performers not being available at the same time". These ideas support some of the anticipated future uses of the technology that are enthusiastically advocated by computer science researchers.

Practicing SMEs questioned the reliability of MR technology in performance: "You hope that the technology is going to work at the moment of the performance... I'm afraid of technological failure". Some SMEs advocated the dissemination benefits: "[MR] could help theater to boost its potential to immerse audiences in various sorts of realities", and help to solve the problem of universal access, for "[The] people who can't travel, or are not able-bodied". However, the converse view was also cautioned, as viewing theater in isolation could cause "A potential loss of communal experience". Generally, it was acknowledged that under the weight of new technologies "[The] performance changes... from whatever classical times have proceeded. It's not necessarily bad, it's just different". Where traditional works hinge on a passive empathy paradigm, MR offers a new active mode of empathizing, by putting the viewer in the place of the 'other' – potentially a group experiencing racial, gender, or religious oppression. MR was seen as "An opportunity to help build bridges and bring people together... in a world that is getting fragmented". SMEs also identified the potential to use the technology in "Site-specific theater and very immersive work, where it's often one-on-one between you and a performer". Specifically, performances by Anú Productions [1] and Punch Drunk [21] were described as championing storytelling paradigms ideally suited to these media, with one SME stating: "I think there are interesting opportunities there, where it creates another dimension within an existing world."

4.3   User Requirements

Our SMEs expected that current and next-generation practitioners and audiences will gain the most from MR, and it will play a crucial role in keeping stakeholders informed on contemporary media creation and consumption practices. Although it was acknowledged that current creative methodologies are openly engaging with 3D technologies, computer-generated models, and virtual environments, the role of MR and its integration into current practice was thought to impact upon several fundamental stakeholders in the wider domain, including:

"People who are interested in going to the theater, anybody who loves performance and theater, theater-makers, the actors, directors, designers, people who love tech, people who are performance and technology experts, students, obviously, and practitioners." (TQ44)

Discussions on the potential disruptions to practice explored the role of the producer, who must acquire new skills to yield professional MR content, as one participant highlighted: "It won't be someone who thinks purely in theatrical or cinematic modes". Thus, producers will have to think differently to understand the idiosyncrasies of immersion, how audiences will consume new content, and how this process will affect performance practices. While this role would suit directors/producers who have "A very distinct idea about what they are looking for in a performance", it may constrain some producers. It will provide a new platform for artists to express their imaginings and engage audiences as they envision in a more pure and controlled way – "The filters seem to be different and more manageable, from an artist's point of view". Effectively integrating MR into practice requires a rethinking of the relationship between screenwriting and directing to realize scripts with 6DoF. By maintaining elements of the existing "film-making perspective" and developing experimental practice, MR could push the boundaries of the current mainstream model. This would provide a new MR platform for content creators with "More experimental urges", like Jean-Luc Godard, to make full use of 6DoF formats – "To deconstruct aspects of style and our perception" – in very different ways to conventional Hollywood studios.

The requirements of MR in practice were compared to that of film production pipelines – a collaborative endeavor, where certain roles are critical and others peripheral. Where performances occur within 3D space, the "standard director model" would be challenged by scenographic considerations – "How they [the audience] are orientated and located [will be] really important". It was thought that this factor would be particularly disruptive, because the capture-to-consumption process would have to prioritize a more spatial "world-building" perspective over the dominant temporal one. For larger productions, a production designer would have to design exactly how the virtual world should look.

Participants repeatedly stated that MR was currently suited to avant-garde gallery installation (which already has an established grammar) above mainstream performance spaces, so platform-specific challenges would have to be addressed. It was also stressed that avant-garde cinema does not attract large, regular paying audiences; as such, work is carefully programmed by arthouse cinemas or film festivals. As embodied performances often take place in a spacious area in front of an audience, the constrained nature of the field of view in MR was potentially problematic for some practicing SMEs. In response, it was suggested that the producers of VV performances must carefully consider the space and the range of views available to the audience in an IVE; specifically, in AR, an audience "Could move through a space and discover" new perspectives. It would be more akin to reading the text, or "actually walking" through a physical scene, engaging with content, and interacting with the environment. MR has the potential to provide multimodal experiences for the audience, where they can "feel" the physicality of the mise-en-scène and move around it:

"They could feel the walls and hear the dripping, a physical thing that they are really experiencing and hearing Beckett's words at the same time... If you give the freedom to the body, you give the meaning to the body and it moves and crouches and stands. You create a choreography of the body while there are also experiences of the visual" – (UQ80).

MR technology will disrupt the traditional way of telling stories, as the audience has "The power to create the story" and complete it; for example, in *Virtual Play* and *Augmented Play*, the user becomes the "light", provoking the character's speech or reducing them to silence. This interactive narrative model points towards new ways creatives can approach storytelling, as the viewer becomes a type of director – not the author, but an experiencer with some authority. One SME observed: "We compel people to do something or not do something; to me, this is the most disrupting thing".

4.4   The Challenges of Using MR

The interviewees expressed that the role of MR within the domain brings many unique challenges to cultural industries. The advantages and disadvantages that were described by the SME cohort largely related to practitioners and audiences, or as one SME explained: "The ontology of the virtual is still incredibly interesting, and philosophically problematic, as to what it is and how we exist within these virtual domains".

The SMEs reaffirmed that there will be specific roles affected by the introduction of MR. Academic SMEs expressed interest in supporting MR production skills within the classroom. For other participants, this extended to related fields like motion capture, animation, and innovations in TV production, where there is a responsibility for institutes to keep up to date with new technologies as they emerge. For *Virtual Play* and *Augmented Play*, the work involved in the post-production stage (involving in the reconstruction, programming, and world-building within the game engine environment) far outweighed that of the brief period of filming real-life actors, at the beginning of the project, and one SME asked: "How useful is this in actually creating new theater, and evolving the art of acting?" Practicing SMEs also indicated that directors were now entering more dramaturgical roles. They believed directors were increasingly expected to draw out and distill the essence of a script, to allow for a more interactive performance that prioritizes the audience perspective. In this regard, "Directorial creative input would diminish hugely... It diminishes because what you are doing is putting the elements together, and then handing it over".

Although deeply interested in the future of actors, one pedagogue explained that apart from some work "...with the actors in the motion capture lab", there are few options that explicitly focus on the use of emergent technologies in practice. SMEs speculated on potential advantages and disadvantages resulting from the VV capture process. It would place increased demands on acting styles, as performances become "Even more intimate than even a big-screen closeup". From previous experiences and watching the MR performances of *Play*, SMEs commented that the opportunity to get up close and personal with the actor, without the weight of social constructs around bodily intimacy, meant that the nuance of the performance (like micro facial movements that indicate certain emotions) could be scrutinized more closely, and performers would become pressured by this level of dissection. "It's hard to say that this would negatively impact [actors] any more than film, or... existing hierarchies"; actors would more likely engage the challenge with zealous enthusiasm. It was also believed that experienced theater workers (e.g. technicians) will always develop new skills in line with technological evolution: "They'll be fine as long as they skill up", or, as another participant noted: "I don't want to take the position that technological advancement is necessarily going to destroy somebody's way of life. It's a disruption... but a lot of times people find ways of coping". Practitioners must, therefore, become more focused on idiosyncratic elements of the platform and how they relate to the work being created. "It should be simple, but effective... you have to think a lot more about the design and making sure it is palatable and really clear - concise!". In the planning stage of an MR project the creators will have to focus their creativity on world-building – "You are going to be storyboarding for a lot longer, taking longer to establish the world". MR was believed to be a very powerful way to show plays conceived in design-led practices that emphasize immersion and visual elements, akin to "Bringing a painting alive". Therefore, much excitement was expressed about its potential to engender new types of performance and extend existing visual practices.

One SME commented that VR installations in art galleries "[They] always seem to be an odd experience", because VR is a solo experience and if there are other people entering the same physical space, surrounding the user, it generates a vulnerability or anxiety. Additionally, by entering the experience on a temporal continuum, visitors determine the beginning and end: "You decide yourself when you are going to bow out". This practice influences how practitioners formulate their work, translating linear thoughts into non-linear practice. Some SMEs held that the works of Beckett, such as *Play*, were "Significant, major artwork[s]" and audiences should be allowed to experience them as the creator envisaged; the MR experiences are not necessarily better, as the audience may not have the capacity to reconstruct the complex narrative themselves. Most of the cohort's experiences were led by chance – "You look left, you look right; it's just an alternative subjective moment when you make that choice". This begs the question: "Do you enhance the Beckettian experience of that work or do you in some ways diminish it?". In a conventional performance the narrative is delivered in a linear fashion, like "A play function, where it just gives you the entire play, straight through", but these MR versions show how audiences can explore performances from multiple perspectives, attaining new levels of fascination with each viewing.

The cohort cogitated on the performance space where MR could be consumed collectively by audiences. They suggested that MR technology would have to evolve beyond the current individualistic mode of consumption to a more communal one, where mediated, interconnected audiences are engaged collectively. In naturalistic theater, a suspension of disbelief is often established by imagining a so-called "fourth wall" between a stage and an audience. The cohort emphasized that "At a live performance, the audience has a certain responsibility... When it's a conventional theater, the lights go down and the audience remains quiet"; whereas, in some performances, the audience accepts a contract of interacting, following prompts within the performance, or consenting to be moved around. Engaging with MR content was described as comparatively easy and accessible, as there are clear and explicit expectations of the user. It was, therefore, supposed that MR will contribute to removing these spatial thresholds: "You aren't in your own space anymore... that's transformative". VR performances can bring audiences into new spaces where they may not have previously been. Although AR was considered exciting on a technical level, the cohort quickly became accustomed to digital objects occupying their world; conversely, the sense of immersion afforded by VR gave the SME audience a deep sense of being "Transported to another place". They felt that, in VR, "The more interesting the material, the more you'll stop thinking about what you are wearing, and the wires don't stop you from moving". This led them to think about how to move audiences around an IVE without causing collisions, whereas they could easily imagine creative compositions for more mobile audiences in AR, because it mixes the imaginary with the real, without overburdening/isolating singular senses. Therefore, in relation to the audience–performer dialectic, most of the SMEs preferred AR because they could more easily imagine successful collective experiences.

Moving forward, SMEs suggested that the technology would have to provide an interactive space for the observer and performer, "Where performers are moving and interacting physically amongst themselves" and the audience. This prompted the question: Does that place the audience in the performance? In MR performances to date, the perspective of the audience is almost always directed and limited, and the viewer is often seen pivoting in a circle or looking for a macro-perspective over the entire scene. This may contradict the potential of walking around a performance space; however, if the performers were to start moving around the MR space, then the possibility to navigate around them presents itself, and "That starts to change your role... and your position within it, as an audience member, which opens up all kinds of interesting things".

4.5   Receptiveness of the Community

The cohort commented upon the receptiveness of the domain to new technology, including their openness to using novel technology in practice and the technologies that they were currently presenting with. The SMEs generally agreed that MR technology would have a positive impact on multiple domains within the cultural sector, particularly as the technology itself would be an attraction. While they generally advocated the use of technology, our SMEs were wary of the potential "suffocation" of theater, as "A unique form of art that relies on the corporeal presence of the actors", through excessive technological interventions. Although technology was sometimes seen as a detractor, AR and VR were described as "kind of fun", so while the novelty factor lasts, the technology was considered to be attractive. It was suggested that during this period of novelty, MR performances would see a boost to their profile and viewership. Furthermore, future advances in networked technology were identified as potentially providing MR audiences with distributed shared live experiences. The cohort predicted that more interesting work would emerge, particularly MR as an art form in and of itself, which does not impose a technological innovation upon other art forms. When the form of the artwork is a defining feature of what it is about, it raises philosophical questions about its nature. It was generally believed that for MR to be integrated into practice, the domain would have to be receptive and should use it as a resource to fulfill its intentions. But it may also provoke artists to think differently, as one participant suggested: "What is the thought that the virtual is thinking or inviting us to think? What happens inside the virtual... unto itself? Where does art collide with technology?".

The use of VV to represent characters within MR was described as a potentially disruptive intervention, comparable to that of video, due to the apparent "liveness" of the experience. Therefore, the space between live and mediated experiences will potentially become more problematic, as the mediated experience may precede the live. This was expressed as being particularly disruptive to the very nature of what theater is, as something "Here and now, and, all of a sudden... not here and not now"; the temporal and spatial configuration of the stage could be wildly disrupted. The possibility for technology to help develop a sense of intimacy and connection with the performer was described as a desirable way to engage with cultural content. As such, it was noted that MR technology has drastically improved audience engagements within the cultural heritage domain. However, AR HMDs were not thought of as being as advanced as VR, because they are not as freely available, and, as one participant pointed out: "[AR] feels nit-picky; it's cool! But it's not quite there yet". Furthermore, it was noted that areas of the emergent MR market are still in a state of flux and hard to predict, and different devices vie for prominent status and market share. As one SME explained:

> "If for example, Facebook's Oculus becomes the most popular, I can imagine a thousand news ways advertisements can be pumped straight into my brain. But if Microsoft's HoloLens becomes more popular... it really depends on the existing business models of the company..." – (GD38)

The cohort had predominantly experienced AR via "Window on the World" methods, as practiced on mobile phones and tablets. One SME described the mobile phone as a "companion; it's part of us", so the experience of using an AR HMD was "really disturbing". This conflict between existing human-computer interaction experiences and user expectations caused "uncanny" sensations. Using AR was described as "disruptive" to the overall experience, because the passage from watching *Play* in an IVE to the intrusion of physical reality, in AR, was "immersive breaking". The AR visual was described as "Glitchy", and the overall experience was "distracting", because reality encroached upon the performance. This included references to the emotional disconnect introduced via the physical space, as "...the context isn't as good". To improve immersion with AR, it was recommended to use site-specific locations, as one participant noted: "You could do cooler stuff with it if you find a cool building... or location to do it in". Furthermore, it was suggested that:

> *"It's not that AR failed to provide anything, because it did what I expected it to do... I like things that will really challenge me... and that's the type of thing that I want to get out of [VR]... I think that this technology captured that sense." – (YH87)*

Although lesser online virtual environments (e.g. Twitter, Facebook, etc.) provide a more streamlined experience, MR was still considered to be a vital, rich area for research in the arts. It was believed that advances in the next 20–30 years will be impressive and, as bandwidths increase, HMDs will become more desirable platforms for users. Although some potential resistance was predicted, research into creative practice in MR was still considered to be incredibly useful and productive within the cultural sector, as one SME noted: "I think, to a certain degree, the virtual has completely overloaded the traditional artform - drowned it out. So, the interesting work will be finding out what, within it, makes art?". Therefore, it was also suggested that the aesthetic theories applied in art practice would require some updating regarding what is disembodied and what is embodied within a performance.

5   Conclusion

The SMEs expressed an awareness of the disruptive nature of engaging with VV content through MR technologies and likened it to "watching the train coming at you in early cinema"; the technology is still emerging and, therefore, "still comically awkward". There still remains much work in making MR technologies more affordable and integrating the VV techniques into current film, theater, and performance practice workflows, so that practitioners are comfortable creating with it and audiences are more enthusiastic about engaging with it. Audiences currently experiencing MR struggle to suspend their disbelief; therefore, the performances and content being delivered can become overtaken by "the joy of watching the technology". The novelty of the technology currently makes it hard to measure its effect, as it is impossible for users to separate their awareness of the technology in assessing content. Nonetheless, in the short-term, this will drive the popularity of MR as an exciting and topical medium.

Our domain experts affirmed the potential for VV techniques in MR to significantly alter existing modes of artistic practice and audience engagement. They affirmed a contextual understanding of mixing realities with emergent MR platforms (within the film, theater, and performance domains) and provided insight into the disruption that could be caused by the widespread adoption of the technologies in future modes of creative practice and audience consumption. However, they highlighted the need to establish a new storytelling grammar that, from the maker's perspective, prioritizes specialization and mise-en-scène over the incumbent temporal paradigm, and from the audience's perspective, that facilitates enjoyment and engagement constituted by exploration and discovery over and above listening: "storyworlding". Therefore, further research is required to explore the idiosyncrasies of immersive technology that will dictate how this paradigm shift will affect the practice and consumption of creative cultural performances. Important factors that surfaced in discussion that will have to be carefully considered include the time, planning, and attention to detail needed to create both the IVE and the site of performance, in the case of AR. However, the specificities of the technology need to be linked to the content to avoid art being conflated with technical exhibitionism. From the perspective of keeping audiences engaged, performances will need to be reconceived on the basis of: timing and pace; existing, interactive narrative models (e.g. in gaming) that successfully employ user profiles, actions, rewards, etc.; and reconciling the shared communal experience.

There were warnings about attempting to overtake existing, effective, and time-honored modes of storytelling; MR should be explored as a stand-alone new media. Specifically relating to the cultural heritage of the playtext, there was considerable debate about the choice to reinterpret a play by Samuel Beckett for MR technologies, when the author originally and explicitly conceived it for the proscenium auditorium format. However, as argued elsewhere, any act of performance implies a translation that generates difference; the responsibility to maintain the integrity of the original (conceptually) coexists with strong incentives to innovate and push the boundaries of the work (practically) [11]. Modifying the medium of the work, while a fundamental shift, also serves to make the content accessible to contemporary audiences. This reactivation implies a survival of the literary work as a part of our intangible cultural heritage, but it does not guarantee that such survival will be mutation-free.

In this paper we focused on one strand of the SME discussions: those that related to practitioner versus audience viewing. Other topics of discussion related to cultural heritage and fidelity to the original, MR as a pedagogical tool, performance theory, and the (bio)Politics of access and data privacy. Therefore, the gathered data demands further reflection and research. Moreover, the potential of MR for developing empathy-building experiences will also require further exploration to help define the effects of this technology on perspective-taking.

Acknowledgments. This publication has emanated from research conducted with the financial support of Science Foundation Ireland (SFI) under Grant Number 15/RP/2776.

References

1. ANU_Productions: Anu productions (2020). http://anuproductions.ie/. Accessed 24 Feb 2020
2. Bailenson, J.: Experience on Demand: What Virtual Reality Is, How It Works, and What It Can Do. W.W. Norton & Company, New York (2018)
3. Beckett, S.: The Complete Dramatic Works. Faber and Faber, London (2006)

4. Bolter, J.D., Grusin, R., Grusin, R.A.: Remediation: Understanding New Media. MIT Press, Cambridge (2000)
5. Burdea, G.C., Coiffet, P.: Virtual Reality Technology. Wiley, Hoboken (2003)
6. Collet, A., et al.: High-quality streamable free-viewpoint video. ACM Trans. Graph. **34**(4), 1–13 (2015). https://doi.org/10.1145/2766945
7. Cronenberg, D.: Videodrome. Movie, 04 February 1983
8. Esslin, M.: Mediations: Essays on Brecht, Beckett, and the Media. Abacus, London (1983)
9. Hawley, M.: Laddering: a research interview technique for uncovering core values (2009). https://www.uxmatters.com/mt/archives/2009/07/laddering-a-research-interview-technique-for-uncovering-core-values.php. Accessed 27 Jan 2020
10. Heider, F., Simmel, M.: An experimental study of apparent behavior. Am. J. Psychol. **57**(2), 243–259 (1944)
11. Johnson, N.: A spectrum of fidelity, an ethic of impossibility: directing Beckett. In: The Plays of Samuel Beckett, pp. 152–164. Bloomsbury/Methuen Drama, London (2013)
12. Koffka, K.: Principles of Gestalt Psychology. Routledge, London (2013)
13. Milgram, P., Kishino, F.: A taxonomy of mixed reality visual displays. IEICE Trans. Inf. Syst. **77**(12), 1321–1329 (1994)
14. Nielsen, J.: Usability Engineering. Academic Press, Boston (1993)
15. O'Dwyer, N., et al.: Virtual play in free-viewpoint video: reinterpreting Samuel Beckett for virtual reality. In: IEEE International Symposium on Mixed and Augmented Reality (ISMAR-Adjunct), pp. 262–267 (2017)
16. O'Dwyer, N. et al.: Beckett in VR: exploring narrative using free viewpoint video. In: ACM SIGGRAPH 2018, pp. 1–2. ACM (2018). https://doi.org/10.1145/3230744.3230774
17. O'Dwyer, N., Ondřej, J., Pagés, R., Amplianitis, K., Smolić, A.: Jonathan Swift: augmented reality application for Trinity library's long room. In: Rouse, R., Koenitz, H., Haahr, M. (eds.) ICIDS 2018. LNCS, vol. 11318, pp. 348–351. Springer, Cham (2018). https://doi.org/10.1007/978-3-030-04028-4_39
18. Orts-Escolano, S., et al.: Holoportation: virtual 3D teleportation in real-time. In: Proceedings of the 29th Annual Symposium on User Interface Software and Technology, UIST 2016, pp. 741–754. Association for Computing Machinery, New York (2016). https://doi.org/10.1145/2984511.2984517
19. Pagés, R., Amplianitis, K., Monaghan, D., Ondřej, J., Smolić, A.: Affordable content creation for free-viewpoint video and VR/AR applications. J. Visual Commun. Image Represent. **53**, 192–201 (2018). https://doi.org/10.1016/j.jvcir.2018.03.012
20. Paradiso, J.A., Landay, J.A.: Guest editors' introduction: cross-reality environments. IEEE Pervasive Comput. **8**(3), 14–15 (2009). https://doi.org/10.1109/MPRV.2009.47
21. Punch_Drunk: Punch drunk international (2019). https://www.punchdrunk.org.uk/. Accessed 24 Feb 2020
22. Schreer, O., et al.: Capture and 3D video processing of volumetric video. In: IEEE International Conference on Image Processing (ICIP), pp. 4310–4314, September 2019. https://doi.org/10.1109/ICIP.2019.8803576
23. Smolic, A., et al.: 3D video and free viewpoint video - technologies, applications and MPEG standards. In: IEEE International Conference on Multimedia and Expo (ICME), pp. 2161–2164, July 2006. https://doi.org/10.1109/ICME.2006.262683
24. Start VR: Awake. https://startvr.co/project/awake/. Accessed 27 Jan 2020

The Effects of Interactive Digital Exhibits (IDEs) on Children's Experience in Science Museums

Qiang Li[1(✉)], Bohyeon Yoo[2], and Yong Ding[1]

[1] Shenyang Aerospace University, Shenyang, China
wudi95@hotmail.com
[2] Kyonggi University, Suwon, Gyeonggi-do, South Korea
byoo1@kyonggi.ac.kr

Abstract. The purpose of this study is to find the characteristics of Interactive Digital Exhibits (IDEs) and analyze the effects of these characteristics on children's experience in science museums. IDEs enable children not only to know science knowledge, but also to interact and operate, even to play, which can induce children to explore. 60 IDEs and more than 600 children from 6–11 years old were observed in two science museums. Through the analysis of the relationship between the types of IDEs and children's average holding time, games related IDEs were found to have the longest average holding time. And the IDEs with new technologies were found having a relatively long holding time. It indicates that games related IDEs are most attractive for children. And technological novelty is also important to hold children's attention or improve children's experiences. New HCI technologies used in IDEs are more attractive and can promote children's experience and holding time. The analysis also shows that the display screen plays an important role in children's understanding and attention.

Keywords: Interactive digital exhibits · Science museums · User experience · Children

1 Introduction

Science museums are a valuable resource, and they play a very important role in stimulating visitors, especially children's interest and understanding of science that often are not available for children in formal learning settings. With the development of science and technology, the exhibition (especially science exhibition) has evolved from the object-based and non-interactive, displaying real objects or using traditional exhibition media, to more of the information-based and interactive digital exhibition. The interactive exhibits make visitors especially children more involved in the process of scientific experience and learning. Therefore, exhibition designers and professionals are increasingly involved in the design of exhibits that make use of interactive digital technologies to engage visitors in novel ways.

Many previous studies have confirmed that interactive exhibits have a more significant impact on visitors' behavior and experience than non-interactive exhibits [1, 2].

© Springer Nature Switzerland AG 2020
M. Rauterberg (Ed.): HCII 2020, LNCS 12215, pp. 215–228, 2020.
https://doi.org/10.1007/978-3-030-50267-6_17

And the characteristics of interactive exhibits had been analyzed and classified by a few previous studies [3–6]. However, little research has been conducted to research the role of IDEs (Interactive Digital Exhibits) on visitor experiences and behavior in science museums. Therefore, it is meaningful to study the characteristics of IDE and to find how they affect children's experiences and behaviors in science museums.

2 Theoretical Foundation and Related Works

2.1 Museums Experience

Csikszentmihalyi and Robinson first proposed that experience in museum consists of four dimensions (Perceptual dimension; Emotional dimension; Intellectual dimension; Communication dimension.) [7]. Then Falk and Dierking proposed an interactive experience model in the context of museum [8]. And they evolved interactive experience model into a Contextual Learning Model in 2000 by adding the time dimension. Doering proposed four types of satisfying experiences: Object experiences, Cognitive experiences, Introspective experiences and Social experiences [9]. De Rojas and Camarero analyzed the relationship between visitors' expectation, perceived service quality and satisfaction and confirmed the positive relation among visitors' expectation, experience and satisfaction [10]. Packer and Bond stressed the psychological effects of restorative attributes which include fascination, being away, extent and compatibility [11].

2.2 Characteristics of Children

Rousseau documented that children and adults have an essential difference in behavior and psychology. The development of children is phased [12], and the development of children at each stage is different. Therefore, different educational methods should be adopted according to the psychological and behavioral characteristics of children. Froebel documented that children prefer self-activity and it is the essential method in education. Froebel also emphasized the values and nature of sensory experiences or play, especially in the free-choice context of science museums, play can immerse children in observation and thinking. Hodgkin stressed that when children are challenged by new or difficult tasks, children seem to be curious and try the new things (touch, play, smell, taste and see) [13]. And children learn from their mistakes.

For the children aged from 6–7 years old, they have become aware of their existence in the world and full of imagination. In addition, children of this age group are in the stage of motor development. For 8–11-year-olds, they already have certain language ability (listening, speaking, reading and writing), they are more inclined to socialize with others, or exchange information with others. And these children prefer to learn about the world through interactive experience (touch, smell, try, operation). In view of these characteristics, exploratory education is the ideal mode of education.

2.3 Digital Technology in Interactive Exhibits

Digital technology refers to the technology which includes a wide range of systems and devices and it is generally characterized, but not limited to, the use of computer

[14]. Similar words such as ICT (Information & Communication Technology) or IT (Information Technology) are often used in digital technologies related research. Pine and Gilmore asserted that new technologies, in particular, encourage whole new genres of experience, such as interactive games, motion-based simulators, and virtual reality [15]. T Jung and MC tom Dieck etc. also proposed that digital technologies have been used for the enhancement of visitor experiences in museums. And it is the exhibition interpretation medium that connects exhibition and audience [16]. McCarthy et al. proposed that videos and smart phones can enhance users' experience [17]. And Gagnebien et al. (2011) pointed out that multi-user touch-screen exhibits with AR technology can lengthen the visit and facilitate the behavior of reading [18]. Vom Lehn and Heath documented that visitors spend more time in museum due to the presence of mediation devices [19]. Szymanski et al. found that a handheld device which showed descriptions of artifacts in a historical exhibition hall to multiple users simultaneously can increase conversations around exhibits [20]. In another study, an AR (Augmented Reality) exhibit has been shown to increase young students' engagement and interest [21]. Hughes et al. found in a case study that an augmented dinosaur exhibit with a MR (Mixed-Reality) technology can enrich experiential learning for children in museum [6].

3 Research Method and Data Collection

In order to observe children's behavior in the process of experiencing interactive digital exhibits, find out the characteristics of interactive digital exhibits, and research the relationship between these characteristics and children's experience, this study selected two typical science museums, 60 interactive digital exhibits, and 600 children were observed. For the study of this project, several children centered museums were investigated in both Korea and China. Finally, the data collection procedures were being carried out in both Gwacheon National Science Museum (GM) and Liaoning Science and Technology Museum (LM). Different data collection strategies are employed to assess children's experiences and behaviors in each exhibition hall.

3.1 Observation Method

To understand children visitors' behavior and investigate the characteristics of interactive digital exhibits in the two selected science museums, unobtrusive observation is used in this research. The unobtrusive observation allows for the study of children behavior as it occurs in natural settings. With unobtrusive observation, the observer does not interfere with the subjects observed. And in the process of unobtrusive observation, subjects are more likely to behave naturally and it ensures the reliability and validity of the survey results. Two unobtrusive observation strategies were employed to identify how children use or experience IDEs in each exhibition hall: timing and tracking observations and focused observations.

Timing and Tracking Observation
Timing and tracking observation can provide insight into visitor behavior and provide quantitative data in relation to time related variables. In this study, children's "Average

Holding Time" on interactive digital exhibits is acquired by focused observation. The average holding time was measured by the average time that children spend at the IDE. Therefore, the highest popularity is the highest in both attractiveness and average holding time. However, in this study, the attracting power depends more on other factors, such as the location of exhibits, size and so on. And based on the observation of children's visiting behavior, we find that although in the open space layout, children still tend to experience each exhibit one by one. Therefore, it is not meaningful to use attracting power parameter to measure the characteristics of IDE.

3.2 Observation Procedure

Firstly, the timing and tracking observation is adopted to analyze visitor's behavior, route and total experience time in a specific exhibition hall. All visitors from six years old to eleven years old are eligible to be observed in each exhibition hall. The children are selected by random sampling method, that is, the observer stands at the entrance of the exhibition hall. Once a qualified visitor (6–11 children) is found to enter the exhibition hall, the observer will write down the entrance time on the paper and then follow the visitor through the exhibition. The child was observed through the whole exhibition and the exit time will be recorded, thus the total time spent in the exhibition hall is calculated. According to the results of the tracking observation, the space design of the exhibition hall will be analyzed (Table 1).

Table 1. The average holding time of the 60 IDEs

Code	IDE name	AHT	Code	IDE name	AHT
GM1	3D Hologram	15	LM11	Symphony Conductor	187.7
GM2	Chemical Reaction	31.2	LM12	Micro-view of Amoeba	44.6
GM3	Structure of Fuel Cell	47.4	LM13	The Structure of Ribosome	31.8
GM4	LED Magic Board	74.7	LM14	Speed of Sound	49.4
GM5	Interactive Projection	114	LM15	Sound Test	81.1
GM6	Aramid Game	68.2	LM16	Digital Interactive Harp	52.2
GM7	Blood Type Game	115.7	LM17	Multi-user Touch-screen	61.5
GM8	Simulator: UAV	182	LM18	Find Composite Numbers	53.5
GM9	Bernoulli Ball	65.3	LM19	Understanding Ferrofluid	62.4
GM10	The AR Magic Book	45.7	LM20	Golden Ratio of Body	79.8
GM11	Anthropometric Apparatus	56.3	LM21	Brownian Movement	39.1
GM12	Interactive Windmill	41.6	LM22	Time Travel	71.9
GM13	Digital Interactive Harp	31	LM23	Constellation	42.9
GM14	Dinosaur AR Projection	62.7	LM24	Know the Stone	30.9
GM15	Single Player VideoGame	172.6	LM25	Weights on DifferentPlanets	49.3

(continued)

Table 1. (*continued*)

Code	IDE name	AHT	Code	IDE name	AHT
GM16	Game Character Design	331.2	LM26	Face Recognition	62
GM17	Kinect Video Game	315.9	LM27	Story of Survivors	36.7
GM18	Spray Paint Projection	186.7	LM28	Firefighting Experiment	79.9
GM19	3D Projection	25.2	LM29	Driving Simulator Game	144.5
GM20	Real-time Microscope	44.8	LM30	Fire Extinguishers	42.2
LM1	Textile Factory	84.7	LM31	Dinosaur AR Projection	98.7
LM2	Watt Steam Engine	98.7	LM32	Interactive Projection	97.1
LM3	IndustryChemicalReaction	26.9	LM33	What to do?	31.9
LM4	Machine Tool's Operation	102.3	LM34	Mars Probe	75.7
LM5	Aircraft Assembly	50.9	LM35	Coal Unit	52.5
LM6	Chemical Composition	20.9	LM36	The Digital Water Curtain	152.4
LM7	Humanoid Robot	128.7	LM37	Garbage Sorting Game	100.9
LM8	Climbing Robots	91.9	LM38	Driving Simulator Game	156.1
LM9	Michael Faraday	25.6	LM39	Chinese Characters	65.1
LM10	Sound Travel	41.3	LM40	Ceramic Manufacturing	151.7

After the tracking observation on each exhibition hall, focused observation was carried out to investigate IDE through the following steps. Firstly, the observer stands next to the selected interactive digital exhibit at a specified period (10:00–12:00 a.m.) to observe the passing visitors and the visitors who experience the interactive digital exhibits. The age of the experiencer is judged and if the experiencer is a 6–11-year-old child, their experiential time will be recorded by stopwatch and written on paper with a pen. For the purpose of analysis, only those exhibit interactions in which visitors became engaged were recorded. A visitor was considered to be engaged in an exhibit when he or she spent at least 5 s. And the interaction behavior between visitor and exhibit includes reading labels, watching posters and examining, manipulating and touching the exhibit. (In this study, all the observation processes were completed by the author.)

4 The Data Analysis

4.1 The Classification of IDEs

Many previous studies [4, 24] already have developed the classifications of interactive exhibits. These classification researches on interactive exhibits are helpful to analyze and improve the effectiveness of different kinds of interactions and visitor experience. But the limitation of these studies is that they have not carried out detailed research and classification for interactive digital exhibits. And, since most of the people visiting and experiencing the Science and technology Museum are children and more digital technology applied in interactive exhibits, it is more meaningful to study children's experiences and behaviors on interactive digital exhibits and to know how these interactive digital exhibits affect children's experiences. In this study, the new classifications of IDEs were developed by analyzing the 60 IDEs in the two selected science museums.

1) **Classification by Technology Types**

The classification of IDEs by technology types was created and shown in the Table 3. It consists of three groups: Display (No interactive), Interactive + Display, and Interactive (No display). And technology type, description on technology type and the 60 examples in both GM and LM are sorted.

Table 2. Classification of IDEs by technology types

Pattern	Technology type	Description
Display (No Interactivity)	Simple Display or Projection	Display science principle or information by video or animation only. Visitors can only watch the video or animation and they cannot control the progress
		Explain science principle, information or narrative the background of the story by video, movie or animation big screen projection
	3D Display	A 3D hologram is defined as a 3D projection that exists freely in space and is visible to everyone without the need for 3D glasses. It is used to display a fully three-dimensional image of the holographic subject
Interactive + Display	Touch Pad	With multi touch software, we can create tables that are interactive displays, allowing people to touch and obtain information in a way that perfectly supplements the rest of the exhibit
	VR/AR/MR	VR (Virtual Reality) is an interactive computer-generated experience taking place within a simulated immersive environment. AR (Augmented Reality) a real-world environment is "augmented" by computer-generated perceptual information. Similar to AR, MR (Mixed Reality) integrates virtual elements perfectly into the real world
	ICT-based	Information and Communications Technology (ICT) refer to all the technology used to handle telecommunications, broadcast media, intelligent building management systems, audiovisual processing and transmission systems, and network-based control and monitoring functions
	Motion Sensing	Motion sensing device is a kind of visitor-centered installation which enable visitors use their whole bodies and motion to control digital objects on the projection or digital display
Interactive (No display)	ICT-based	The use of Information and Communications Technology (ICT) on the exhibits enables visitors interactive with the installations and some feedback will be given such as sound or change of mechanical mechanism

Group1: Digital Display (No interaction)
The main purpose of these exhibits in this group is to display science information. According to the type of technology, these exhibits are divided into two categories: Simple display and 3D display. Simple display means that these exhibits use monitor or big screen projection to play animations or videos. 3D display uses 3-D display or projection technology such as 3-D hologram projection. Compared with traditional labels, posters or display boards, digital display has the characteristics of low cost and easy maintenance. More importantly, the study found that children don't look at labels or instructions. Children are more likely to focus their attention on screen and get information in this way. Therefore, the use of digital screen is important to explain science concepts and improve children's understanding of scientific knowledge.

Group2: Interactive + Digital Display
The "Interactive + Digital Display" type of exhibit refers to those supporting interaction between users and digital elements on the screens. The exhibits in this group which use a combination of physical interaction and digital display accounts for the largest proportion exhibits throughout the whole museum. The technology types include: touch pad, AR/VR/MR, and Interactive installations based on ICT.

Group3: Interactive (No digital screen)
A small number of exhibits use this interactive and non-display approach. Because there is no digital display, the exhibits in this group look a bit like pure physical interaction. But in fact, these exhibits use ICT technology to achieve interaction or feedback.

2) **Classification by Exhibition Purposes**

Interactive science and technology centers or science museums have been recognized as potential educational resources. The educative value of different types of exhibits has been researched by a few studies [4, 6, 25, 26]. And visitors can meet their interests and accept science explanations by means of entertainment [22]. Therefore, it can be seen that education and entertainment are both attributes of interactive exhibits.

This study focuses only on digital interactive exhibits, and the classification of IDEs by exhibition purposes was created and shown in the Table 3. The interactive digital exhibits are classified into three types according to the purposes of display: Education, Education + Entertainment, and Entertainment. And the content type, description on content type and the 60 examples in both GM and LM are listed by it.

Educational
And Jan Packer [23] documented that "education" includes: being better informed; being mentally stimulated; discovering new things; expanding one's interests. It can be seen from the educational objectives that the learning in science museum is different from the traditional formal study. Children's learning in science museums mainly through interaction with exhibits. Therefore, those exhibits aimed at education can play an important

Table 3. Classification of IDE by exhibition purposes

Exhibition purposes	Types	Description
Educational	Display Objects or Phenomenon	The main purpose of the exhibit is to enable visitors to know the specific science information or knowledge. The visitors can learn or know the exhibit information by watching videos, display boards, posters or labels
	Explain Science Principle or Phenomenon	The main purpose of the exhibit is to demonstrate the science principles or phenomenon. The visitors can learn science knowledge from the exhibits
Educational + Entertaining	Educational Interaction	Interactive exhibits include physical interactivity, digital interactivity and mixed interactivity. By operation and feedback from the system visitors can have both educational and entertaining experience
	Serious Game	Such exhibits designed mainly for education other than pure entertainment. This kind of exhibit presents the content of scientific knowledge in the form of games
Entertaining	Pure Game	Digital games are highly entertaining, interactive and competitive and the use of games in museum can improve visitors' engagement and experience. Combining scientific knowledge with common sense and digital games to enable visitors to learn in the process of games namely "Learn by play"

role in children's learning experience in science museums. According to the observation of 60 selected interactive digital exhibits, educational interactive digital exhibits are classified into two categories: "Display Objects or Phenomenon "and "Explain Science Principle or Phenomenon".

According to the analysis, we found that education is still the main purpose of exhibition in science museums. And most interactive digital exhibits are mainly aimed at displaying scientific information or explaining scientific principle and phenomena. But unlike traditional formal education, science museum pays more attention to "learning by doing". That is to say, through interactive exhibits, visitors can experience and participate in the process of interaction. Ultimately, the transition from hands-on to minds-on or even hearts-on is achieved.

Entertaining

Not all interactive digital exhibits in science museums are educational or combination of education and entertainment. There is no doubt that games or entertaining digital exhibits will attract more children's attention. Therefore, interactive digital exhibits purely for entertainment purpose will play a supporting role for the science museum. The hidden goal of science museums is to entertain, to attract large numbers of people, to increase visitor numbers at a museum [27]. Considering the motivation of children to visit the Science Museum, the entertainment of interactive exhibits is more attractive for them and it's the main reason for their visit.

Educational + Entertaining

Education is not the sole purpose of interactive digital exhibits. More interactive digital exhibits have both educational value and entertainment attributes. Through play children can develop social and cognitive skills, grow mature emotionally, and gain the self-confidence required to engage in new experiences and environments (Kahn and Susan 2013). By assigning selected interactive digital exhibits to different types in both GM and LM, we can see that up to thirteen interactive digital exhibits are both educational and entertaining in GM. And there are only two exhibits are pure entertainment-oriented games. There are five exhibits, which are educational only. The same situation goes for LM. Of the forty interactive digital exhibits in LM, 24 are both educational and entertaining. And the number of pure game exhibits is 2, the same with in GM. The classification and data tell us that most of the IDEs in the two selected science museums are both educational and entertaining.

The classification of interactive digital exhibits gives us a clear understanding of the composition of IDEs by technology types and exhibition purposes. Through the analysis of the total number and average holding time of each category of interactive digital exhibits, the effects of different IDEs category on children's experience can be found. The total number of IDEs and average time spent in each category are shown on Fig. 1. From the holding time of each category of interactive digital exhibit, we can see that children spend most of their time on game-type (both pure game and serious game) IDEs. It means that game-type IDEs in the two selected science museums are attractive, and they give children enjoyment experiences. The average holding time of Serious Game is almost half that of Pure Game, but it is still longer than the average holding time of other categories. Two technology types of IDE, Motion Sensing and AR/VR, have relatively high holding time values. This shows that children spend relatively more time on interactive digital exhibits of technological novelty.

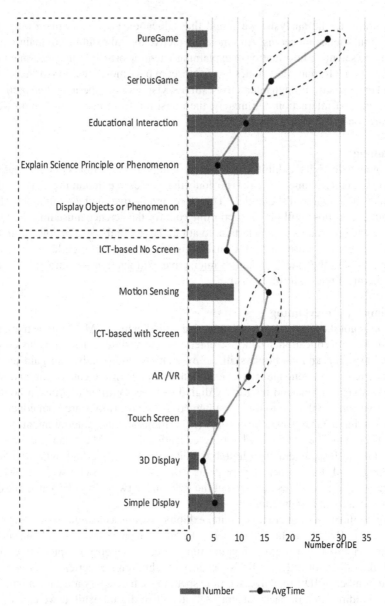

Fig. 1. Total number of IDEs and AHT of each category

4.2 Characteristics of Observed IDEs

Through the observation and study of the 60 interactive digital exhibits in the two science museums, we found some common characteristics of IDEs. These characteristics include a high level of Competition, Narrative, Interactivity, Physical, Visitor Control, Social Interaction, User-centered, Stimulate Senses (see Table 4). And the holding time of each IDE was recorded and the average holding time was calculated. To measure and determine the level of each characteristic of each IDE, the scoring (or grading, weighted scoring) on characteristics of the 60 IDEs will be established. The expert assessment approach was used in this study. In order to avoid subjectivity in the scoring process, detailed scoring criteria are formulated. The scoring criteria based on Likert scale were developed and used to score the characteristics of IDEs.

Table 4. Characteristics of IDE

No.	Dimensions	Description
1	Competition	Competitive elements allow users to compete for high scores
2	Narrative	Narrative with a story and characters
3	Interactivity	The interaction between visitor and installation to make choice by visitors to create respondent content
4	Physical	Physical touch or activity by hands or full body motion over time with the installation
5	Visitor Control	The ability to control the flow of the installation
6	Social Interaction	Communication or exchange information among visitors
7	User-centered	The outcome of the exhibit manipulation involved a representation of or an effect on the user's own information such as body, voice or user-created stuff
8	Stimulate Senses	One or more senses of the visitor are stimulated by elements of exhibit such as visual or sound

4.3 Data Analysis

The analysis of the effect of the eight characteristics on children's experience relies mainly on the relationship between the quantitative measure of characteristics scores and average holding time. The relationships among the dependent variable (Average Holding Time) and the IDE characteristics are determined by correlation analysis. The purpose of correlation analysis is to measure the closeness of the linear relationship between the defined variables. In this study, the Pearson correlation coefficient (Analyzed by IBM SPSS Statistics 24) is used to express the strength of the correlation among the eight characteristics of IDE and children visitors' average holding time (Table 2). The "R" from the SPSS output (Table 5) is the "coefficient of correlation".

Statistical results show that the correlation coefficient of five variables has statistical significance (p-value < 0.05) and other three variables have no statistical significance (p-value > 0.05). It means that there is a significant correlation between children visitors' average holding-time and the six characteristics of IDE. The six characteristics are: Competition, Interactivity, VisitorControl, SocialInteraction, StimulateSenses and User-Centered. From the value of correlation coefficient, we can see that the variable Visitor-Control ($r = 0.517$), has a strong positive linear relationship with average holding-time.

Table 5. Correlation analysis

Variable	R(Correlation coefficient)	p-value
Competition	.439**	0.000
Narrative	−0.251	0.053
Interactivity	.357**	0.005
Physical	0.218	0.095
VisitorControl	.517**	0.000
SocialInteraction	.489**	0.000
StimulateSenses	.387**	0.002
UserCentered	.273*	0.035

Note: **. (2-tailed) Correlation is significant at the 0.01 level.

And other five variables Competition ($r = 0.439$), Interactivity ($r = 0.357$), SocialInteraction ($r = 0.489$), StimulateSenses ($r = 0.387$), and UserCentered ($r = 0.273$) have a moderate positive linear relationship with average holding-time. In other words, the other two characteristics of IDE are independent of or not linear related with children visitors' average holding-time.

In this study, six variables (characteristics of IDE) were found to be linearly correlated with children's average holding time on IDE. However, the correlation analysis does not reveal the extent to which the interaction of all variables working together. Therefore, a multiple linear regression analysis needs to be done in future study to define the pattern between all characteristics of IDE and average holding time.

5   Conclusion

According to the survey of the 60 IDEs in the two science museums, the classifications on IDEs were identified and defined. Based on time-based analysis, the study found that IDEs like video games, which lack educational content, are very attractive to children and take up a lot of time for children's overall visit. In the same time, entertainment IDEs should be more educational, such as Serious Games. Therefore, the Educational IDEs and Entertainment IDEs shouldn't simply put together, but be balanced to provide children an experience in which "Education is entertainment, discovery is exciting, and learning is an adventure". And the new HCI technologies were found can attract and hold children's attention.

Based on the statistical analysis in this study, 6 characteristics have been shown to attract children's attention and improve children's experience and learning. IDEs with technological novelty, with its multi-sensory stimulation, user-centered design, and rich interaction, brings a pleasant even flow experience for children. Therefore, in order to achieve educational purposes, the characteristics of new technologies should be integrated with scientific phenomena and concepts to provide children with interesting, surprising, exploratory and fun experiences, and improving the efficiency of science communication.

References

1. Melton, A.W.: Visitor behavior in museums: some early research in environmental design. Hum. Factors **14**(5), 393–403 (1972)
2. Koran Jr, J.J., Koran, M.L., Longino, S.J.: The relationship of age, sex, attention, and holding power with two types of science exhibits. Curator Mus. J. **29**(3), 227–235 (1986)
3. Leister, W., et al.: Towards assessing visitor engagement in science centers and museums. In: Proceedings of PESARO, pp. 21–27 (2015)
4. Sandifer, C.: Technological novelty and open-endedness: two characteristics of interactive exhibits that contribute to the holding of visitor attention in a science museum. J. Res. Sci Teach. **40**(2), 121–137 (2003)
5. Studart, D.C:. The perceptions and behaviour of children and their families in child-orientated museum exhibitions. Dissertation, University of London (2000)
6. Stocklmayer, S., Gilbert, J.K.: New experiences and old knowledge: towards a model for the personal awareness of science and technology. Int. J. Sci. Educ. **24**(8), 835–858 (2002)
7. Csikszentmihalyi, M., Robinson, R.E.: The Art of Seeing: An interpretation of the Aesthetic Encounter. Getty Publications, Malibu (1990)
8. Falk, J.H., Dierking, L.D.: The Museum Experience. Howells House, Washington, DC (1992)
9. Doering, Z.D.: Strangers, guests, or clients? Visitor experiences in museums. Curator Mus. J. **42**(2), 74–87 (1999)
10. De Rojas, M.D.C., del Carmen Camarero, M.: Experience and satisfaction of visitors to museums and cultural exhibitions. Int. Rev. Public Non Profit Mark. **3**(1), 49 (2006). https://doi.org/10.1007/BF02893284
11. Packer, J., Bond, N.: Museums as restorative environments. Curator J. Mus. **53**(4), 421–436 (2010)
12. Darling-Hammond, L.: Developing professional development schools: early lessons, challenge, and promise. Prof. Dev. Sch. Sch. Developing Prof., 1–27 (1994)
13. Hodgkin, R.A.: Born Curious: New Perspectives in Educational Theory. Wiley, London (1976)
14. Hawkey, R.: Learning with digital technologies in museums, science centres and galleries (2004)
15. Pine, B.J., Glimore, J.H.: Welcome to the experience economy. Harv. Bus. Rev. **76**, 97–105 (1998)
16. Jung, T.H., tom Dieck, M.C.: Augmented reality, virtual reality and 3D printing for the co-creation of value for the visitor experience at cultural heritage places. J. Place Manage. Dev. **10**(2), 140–151 (2017)
17. McCarthy, J., et al.: The experience of enchantment in human–computer interaction. Pers. Ubiquit. Comput. **10**(6), 369–378 (2006). https://doi.org/10.1007/s00779-005-0055-2
18. Gagnebien, A., et al.: Analyse des usages de l'iPad et de la Muséotouch. LabSic, Rapport d'étude pour le musée des Confluences, service développement et stratégie, Nathalie Candito [en ligne] (2011). http://reseau.erasm.org/Evaluation-Ipad-au-museeet
19. Vom Lehn, D., Health, C.: Accounting for new technology in museum exhibitions. Int. J. Arts Manage. **7**(3), 11–21 (2005)
20. Szymanski, M.H., et al.: Sotto voce: facilitating social learning in a historic house. Comput. Support. Coop. Work (CSCW) **17**(1), 5–34 (2008). https://doi.org/10.1007/s10606-007-9067-y

21. Hughes, C.E., et al.: Augmenting museum experiences with mixed reality. In: Proceedings of KSCE 2004, pp. 22—24 (2004)
22. Afonso, A.S., Gilbert, J.K.: Educational value of different types of exhibits in an interactive science and technology center. Sci. Educ. **91**(6), 967–987 (2007)
23. Packer, J.: Learning for fun: the unique contribution of educational leisure experiences. Curator Mus. J. **49**(3), 329–344 (2006)
24. Ghose, S.: From hands-on to mind-on: creativity in science museums. In: Lindqvist, S. (ed.) Museums of Modern Science–Nobel Symposium, pp. 117—127. Science History Publications, Canton (2000)
25. Borun, M., Dritsas, J.: Developing family-friendly exhibits. Curator Mus. J. **40**(3), 178–196 (1997)
26. Boisvert, D.L., Slez, B.J.: The relationship between exhibit characteristics and learning-associated behaviors in a science museum discovery space. Sci. Educ. **79**(5), 503–518 (1995)
27. Russell, I.: Visiting a science center: what's on offer? Phys. Educ. **25**(5), 258 (1990)

Redefining Visual Storytelling for Adaptation of Classic Literature in Immersive Environments: Hölderlin's Echo VR

Hannes Rall[(✉)] [iD]

Nanyang Technological University, Singapore, Singapore
Rall@ntu.edu.sg

Abstract. 2020 celebrates the 250th birthday of the famous German poet Friedrich Hölderlin (1770–1843). The author Hannes Rall co-directs Hölderlin's Echo VR, a serious game for the permanent exhibition in the Hölderlin Tower, in close collaboration with the Hölderlin Museum Tübingen. This paper will unpack the connection between the requirements of adaptation and the design choices that define visual storytelling in immersive space. As such, it aims to create a better understanding of best practice towards methods of adaptation design in VR.

Keywords: Adaptation · Hölderlin · VR

1 Introduction

1.1 Project Background

2020 celebrates the 250th birthday of the famous German poet Friedrich Hölderlin (1770–1843). This legendary and highly romanticized figure spent the latter half of his life isolated in the Hölderlin Tower in Tübingen, which now also houses a museum. Legend has it that this isolation was the immediate result of the failed love affair with married banker's wife Susette Gontard, a.k.a "Diotima", who tragically passed away while the poet was banned from seeing her. It remains highly debated among scholars, if he was truly "mad" during this later period of his life (see McCormick 1973; Dilthey 1993; George 2019). The project *Hölderlin's Echo VR*, supported by the MFG Baden-Württemberg/Digital Content Funding/Prototype Funding, creates an interactive VR experience in an interdisciplinary collaboration between the Centre for Media Competence (ZFM) at the Eberhard Karls University of Tübingen, the Stuttgart Media University (HdM) and Nanyang Technological University Singapore. *Hölderlin's Echo VR* is designed as a serious game: In an artistically-stylized 3D-reconstruction of Hölderlin's historically authentic tower-room, the player can activate and influence "memory rooms", which are designed to provide insight into Hölderlin's literary work and biography through interactive exploration that triggers micro-narratives and gameplay-elements that refer to 5 different time periods in Hölderlin's biography: Childhood, education, study and exploration, forbidden love (Diotima) and later years (spent in the Hölderlin Tower).

© Springer Nature Switzerland AG 2020
M. Rauterberg (Ed.): HCII 2020, LNCS 12215, pp. 229–244, 2020.
https://doi.org/10.1007/978-3-030-50267-6_18

The author has extensively explored the adaptation of classic literature for VR before, in his earlier research project *From Print to Digital: Re-Defining Narrativity for Interactive Digital Media*, funded through a Tier 2 grant by the Ministry of Education (MOE) in Singapore. This project sought to test novel strategies for Shakespeare education by conceiving and testing a wide range of cutting-edge media techniques. It consisted of two major components:

1. An investigation into the relevance of Shakespeare for millennials in Singapore through an animated documentary employing a hybrid between live action and animation: *Shaking a Singapore Spear*.
2. An adaptation of three major Shakespeare plays (*Macbeth*, *The Tempest*; *A Midsummer Night's Dream*) as an abridged narrative hybrid for animated VR: *ShakesVR*. This second animated experiment bears the most resemblance with the approach applied also in *Hölderlin's Echo VR*.

The findings from this previous project have been a major influence for the current adaptation, because they provide experience-based parameters on the creative mechanisms for transforming written source material for immersive visualization.

This meant that there was a solid basis of preliminary research, *Hölderlin's Echo VR* could be built upon Fig. 1 demonstrates some visible parallels between the modes of visual representation that have successfully employed in the framework of *ShakesVR* and therefore could be adopted in similar ways for *Hölderlin's Echo VR*.

Fig. 1. Visual development images for *ShakesVR* (left) and *Hölderlin's Echo VR* (right) demonstrate the high degree of graphic stylization both projects have in common. © Hannes Rall/Nanyang Technological University Singapore.

Most importantly, the idea of artistic interpretation replacing factual replication that has been recognized academically as adequate means of representation.

Fact(s) now can be represented through fiction, as Yip (2016) posits: "In John McGee's Inside—Topologies of Stroke exhibited in the current touring exhibition People Like Us, we are able to walk along cellular paths, like the shrunken submarine crew who venture into the human body in the 1966 sci-fi movie Fantastic Voyage. In McGee's work biology becomes topology; 'we don't necessarily see science, we see landscape', he says, 'we see shape, we see colour, so basically visualising the invisible'."

In the context of adaptation of classic literature this means that a faithful visual replication of period detail in either works or biography of an author can be replaced by a freer approach: The idea that the works of an author or his biography can be adequately represented by poetic visual reinventions that mirror the artistic intent of the written source material.

This paper will unpack the connection between the requirements of adaptation and the design choices that define visual storytelling in immersive space. As such, it aims to create a better understanding of best practice towards methods of adaptation design in VR.

2 Research Aims and Questions

In this paper the author focuses on 3 specific aspects of the practice-based research, which address the role and methods design can provide for adaptation of literature in an educational context and beyond:

- How can fact and fiction be balanced in the context of an animated VR experience that is shown in the context of a museum?
- What is the role and potential of interactive elements to immerse the user in visualized poetry?
- How can the specific properties of animation be employed in particular to express internal states through adequate visualization?

Before addressing the specifics of the research project at hand, a wider investigation into the history and relevance of Hölderlin and the Hölderlin Tower will provide the necessary context.

3 Literary and Historical Context

3.1 Hölderlin's Relevance as a Writer and His Influence on His Contemporaries

As a writer and poet, Hölderlin has been described as a key figure of German romanticism (Warminski 1987, 209). Others debate that: "Johann Christian Friedrich Hölderlin cannot be categorized without doubt as belonging to the epoch of "Classicism", because in his works Hölderlin often spills over into the writing style of the epoch of "Romanticism". However, since his works are partly based on the historical context of Napoleon and that his model was Friedrich Schiller, it can be assumed that he is sometimes a main representative of the "classical" epoch. (Hölderlin 2008, 72) Hölderlin was a contemporary of Schiller and Goethe and in contact with both of them (see Pellegrini 2019, 6). Due to the fact that his poetry is extraordinarily hard to translate into any foreign language, he never reached a similarly high degree of popularity outside of Germany – beyond scholarly circles. The website *Poetry Foundation* does however note that "he significantly influenced modern poetry and philosophy, including the writings of Nietzsche, Rilke, Heidegger, and Celan".

Other scholars emphasize the significant influence Hölderlin had on the development of German philosophy: "Hegel is completely dependent on Hölderlin—on his early efforts to grasp speculatively the course of human life and the unity of its conflicts, on the vividness with which Hölderlin's friends made his insight fully convincing, and also certainly on the integrity with which Hölderlin sought to use that insight to preserve his own inwardly torn life."(Dieter 1997, 139). Olson claims (1992, 39) that, "when Hegel, together with his friends Hölderlin and Schelling, spent quiet hours strolling along the banks of the Neckar receiving the theological education they would eventually challenge and transform through the grand tradition now known as German Idealism."

Of most relevance for the development of the VR experience however was his rather turbulent biography, which itself has served as inspiration for several movies and plays. The crucial turning point in his life proved to be the unhappy love affair with Susette Gontard:

"In order to finance his living, he served as a tutor for the wealthy Gontard family. Here he met his future first love Susette Gontard. After Susette's husband Jakob learned of their relationship, Friedrich Hölderlin fled to Homburg to his old college friend Sinclair out of fear. From there on Hölderlin's life went downhill (…) However, after a few months, Friedrich Hölderlin returned to Württemberg for reasons unknown. It was not until the end of June 1802 that he reached the city of Stuttgart in a completely neglected and confused state, so that he was hardly recognized. As if his situation at the time had not been difficult enough, he was saddened by the news of the death of his only love Susette, who died of rubella in Frankfurt. (…) In 1805 Friedrich Hölderlin was declared insane by the physician and pharmacist Müller: "Hölderlin is broken and his madness has turned into frenzy. In 1806, Hölderlin came to the University Hospital in Tübingen after his friend had asked Hölderlin's mother to take care of him."" (Hölderlin 2008). After being discharged as "terminally ill" from the hospital, the poet then spent the rest of his life in the foster care of the Zimmer-family in the now famous Hölderlin Tower at the banks of the river Neckar in Tübingen.

The Hölderlin Tower: Historical Context

The history of the Hölderlin Tower can be traced back to the 13th century. In 1807 the building was acquired by the master carpenter Ernst Friedrich Zimmer. In the same year Hölderlin was discharged as incurable from the Autenriethsche Klinikum, a local mental hospital. Zimmer agreed to take in Hölderlin, whose *Hyperion* he admired. Hölderlin lived for 36 years in a modestly furnished room on the first floor of the tower. During the time of the tower Hölderlin continued to write - mostly under the pseudonym Scardanelli – and also welcomed visitors, such as the poets and students from the Tübingen monastery Wilhelm Waiblinger and Eduard Mörike. In the year 1874 the master shoemaker Carl Friedrich Eberhardt had the house extended and set up a bathing establishment there. On December 14th of the following year the tower burned down to the ground floor. Soon a new round tower was built on the foundation walls and with a larger adjoining house. In the building plans you can find the name "Hölderlin's Tower" (Fig. 2).

Fig. 2. The floor plan (to the left) and a historical photo of Hölderlin's tower from the late 19th century. © Stadt Tübingen

This historical overview of both, the poet's biography as well as the locale he spent his final days in, has introduced the framework, from which *Hölderlin's Echo VR* emerged. The following sections will now allow a deeper insight into the iterative process that defines pre-production and production. At the stage of writing, pre-production is still ongoing on all gaming levels – but a conceptual artistic framework has already been established.

4   Research Approach

This VR-experience consists of two closely connected main components (Fig. 3):

1. The virtual reconstruction of the tower room:
   Thus, in the physical space of the tower room in Tübingen, the historically authentic version is virtually experienced: This creates an added educational value that can be achieved through traditional exhibition methods alone would be unpresentable.
2. Playful access to Hölderlin's life and work via the 5 windows accessible through the room – Experience the world of Hölderlin through his eyes: The windows become portals in interactive explorable worlds of experience that allow the user to playfully explore Hölderlin's life and work.

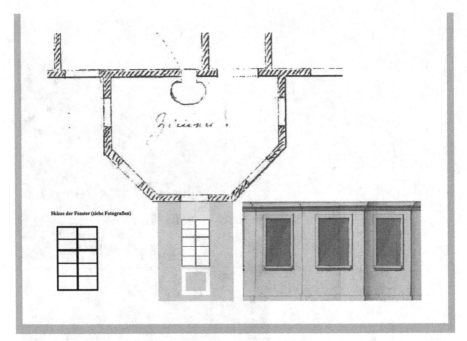

Fig. 3. Visual development for *Hölderlin's Echo VR.* © Hannes Rall/Nanyang Technological University Singapore.

The idea here is to move away from the mere representation of historical data towards an aesthetic reinvention of Hölderlin's written poetry to represent his biography. This transcends common notions of authenticity that are based on photo-realistic-replication. Instead we offer a highly stylized artistic recreation that mirrors the playfulness inherent to the poetry of Hölderlin. All the more so, as his work, particularly in the latter half of his life is nothing but a continuous negotiation between imagination and reality. In that sense, this VR experience aims to be a work of art in and by itself that can stand on its own instead of offering a traditional biography by means of gaming. This makes our project applicable beyond a context in education or museums. A common user might be intrigued by the games concept all by itself without having been immersed into the world of Hölderlin in the context of a museum. Additional potential for distribution opens up, which will allow our experience to be also offered on Internet platforms and in different settings.

While developing our project a possible contradiction appeared to emerge when discussing the project with the representatives of a museum, they appear to be hesitant to accept the idea of a radical artistic reinvention that moves away from factual representation. There is obviously a fear that museum visitors would have difficulties to differentiate between the authentic artifacts presented at the museum itself and the artistic interpretation offered by the VR experience.

Or as Yip (ibid) puts it: "Art galleries, museums and performance spaces are by nature places in which time and space are simulated and suspended, but in these encounters in alternate environments there is a certain amount of system shock. When consciousness becomes materiality, what becomes of the conventions that govern the representation and reception of works of art and the intention of their creators? How are the traditional relationships between audience, artist, artwork and institution reconfigured?"

It took some convincing to establish the idea and to defy the notion of a conflict between stylization and authenticity, when using highly stylized animation for the VR experience. There was an inherent fear that such mediation might result in an inaccurate representation of historical data. But the author has argued before that layers of stylized animation can offer additional depth without endangering the communication of accurate historical data (Weber/Rall 2019).

First of all, any modern spectator has been exposed to the wide variety of digital image manipulation that has become common since the advent of social media and the Internet in general. In other words: the audience would know that if something looks real it doesn't mean it is true all can be seen as an authentic representation of reality.

The point here is that the use of hyperrealism by and in itself will not automatically equal a believable truth as well as a stylized reinvention of biographical data will immediately reveal that it is not even claiming such authenticity. In the context of representing facts versus fiction the stylized approach will honestly declare its artificiality and it is up to the user 2 critically interrogate what is poetic license and what has been based on accurate facts.

If the user is instead immersed in a virtual world that integrates photo-realistic period detail of the time Hölderlin lived in, the danger is much higher that this will be taking for granted as factually accurate information. This applies particularly in the context of a museum. the museum itself suggests a notion of authority on the subject matter. It might seem paradoxical, but to offer an immersive experience that does not claim authenticity through its means of mediation, affords the museum visitor critical autonomy. He or she will first understand that what they see is a literally playful interpretation of a Life and Times of. Due to the strong abstraction, a lot is left to the imagination of the audience and can be filled in with the facts they have learned in the museum exhibition or from other documentation about.

By doing so they will also discover that there are also parts in the experience that have integrated carefully researched measurable data based on historical documentation.

Such is the case with the recreation of Hölderlin's tower room that has been expanded into three dimensions based on the authentic floorplans which are available from the 19th century. This is a good example how the request of the museum experts for historical accuracy can be merged with the idea of creating an artful interpretation of Hölderlin's biography. While the accurate measurements of the room are precisely reflecting that historical data, the rendering of the walls, floor and furniture is carried out in a variety of styles in the experience:

The first version makes an informed guess on how the material might have presented itself in the 19th century based on reference on contemporary window frames, floors and furniture. this was necessary because any contemporary depiction of the interiors of Hölderlin's room was not available. With this being the case, it opened up the possibilities to accentuate the rendering with a bolder graphic style because it would not contradict any accurate information. Yet this version suggests a reliance on fact through its comparatively realistic style (Fig. 4).

Fig. 4. Visual development for *Hölderlin's Echo VR* and a photography of the current windows in the Hölderlin Tower © Hannes Rall/Nanyang Technological University Singapore/Stadt Tübingen.

The second version moves away entirely from any notion of realism other than the underlying measurements as provided by the historical floorplan. The rendering of the walls however, is a pure artistic invention by means of displaying calligraphic excerpts

Fig. 5. Visual development for *Hölderlin's Echo VR*. © Hannes Rall/Nanyang Technological University Singapore.

from Hölderlin's poetry all across (see Fig. 5). This approach literally marries the idea of authentic information with the potential of artistic recreation. A new layer is added that represents the spirit of willful imagination still present in the room today.

This hybrid approach is particularly suitable for the reinvention of the tower room as it provides the gateway for the user into the immersive environment of the game.

4.1   5 Windows to Enter 5 Interactive Animation Worlds: Biographical Stations from Hölderlin's Life

Fig. 6. Visual development for *Hölderlin's Echo VR.* © Hannes Rall/Nanyang Technological University Singapore.

The 5 windows in the room, that represent the different stages of Hölderlin's life, (see Fig. 6) take the user further away from factual replication into fantastic universes that are merely inspired by the historical facts. These segments transparently deny any claim to authenticity, as they reveal their artificiality instantly. Yet they still relate strongly to the work of the poet. This even more so as one might argue that the poets work itself is nothing but a constant negotiation between the requirements of real-life circumstances and notions of pure imagination. As Paul Wells has stated before, animation provides a particularly powerful medium to visualize such imaginary endeavors: Wells (1999, 199) had argued that "animation is after all, a distinctive film-form, which offers to the adaptation process a unique vocabulary of expression unavailable to the live-action film-maker". He further noted that "animation accentuates the intended "feeling" of the text through its very abstractness in the use of colour, form and movement (...) animation simultaneously literalizes and abstracts" (ibid, 208). Ideally, the choice of animation as a medium will not only engage the spectator here, but literally open windows into the soul of the poet (Fig. 7).

The Magical Garden of Childhood. A raven comes to the window knocking vehemently on the glass and thus inviting the user to open up the window. This presents the

Fig. 7. Visual development for *Hölderlin's Echo VR*. © Hannes Rall/Nanyang Technological University Singapore.

first opportunity for interactive intervention and to enter the immersive worlds hidden behind the windows. once the user has opened the window, he will be teleported to the first biographical station in Hölderlin's life: the magical garden of the childhood. It will soon become obvious that the raven was not chosen coincidentally as the guide to invite the user to proceed into his fantastic realm (Fig. 8).

Fig. 8. Visual development for *Hölderlin's Echo VR*. © Hannes Rall/Nanyang Technological University Singapore.

Two years after Hölderlin's birth his father died of a stroke. Two years later, his mother Johanna Christiana Hölderlin married her second husband Johann Christoph Gock, who persuaded his new family to move to his home town of Nürtingen, where he held the office of mayor. As if the past had not already been stressful enough for the family, the stepfather died three years later on March 13th (1779) of a severe pneumonia.

This had a devastating effect on the young Karl Friedrich who was affected by bouts of melancholy. Therefore, this segment of the VR experience seeks to represent the emerging tension between an idyllic paradise, a hidden garden of youth that is already overshadowed by the premonition of impending death. The user will be able to experience this world in a linear path of discovery guided by the recitation of the poem *Als ich ein Knabe war (When I was a boy)*. Colors are changing from light and airy to a stark and monochromatic black and white scheme towards the end of the poem (Fig. 9).

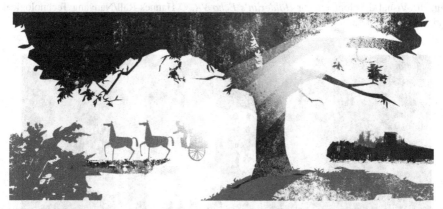

Fig. 9. Visual development for *Hölderlin's Echo VR.* © Hannes Rall/Nanyang Technological University Singapore.

Interactive elements are added along this narrative thread that will allow the user to change the environment upon touching it, which will trigger animated metamorphoses of the surroundings: A sense of magic realism emerges as clouds transform into the face of the beloved stepfather, trees change their shape and lose their colorful leaves to reveal bare branches, mirages appear and disappear.

Ultimately the Raven will return and lend upon the tombstone, which on closer inspection will reveal the name of the stepfather written on it. This element deliberately quotes from the works of Edgar Allan Poe and his famous poem *The Raven* (Poe 1845) where the bird visits the hero as a messenger of death (see Fig. 10). The bold graphic style seeks to avoid any notion of saccharine sweetness often associated with childhood but to provide and imagery that represents this ultimately complicated period in the life of Hölderlin.

Youth and Education. The next segment (accessible through the 2nd window) engages with the education of young Hölderlin (Fig. 11). It shows episodes from his schooling at the monastery of Denkendorf. to differentiate itself from the previous segment the style changes completely: in an approach that pays homage to the animated works of

Fig. 10. Visual development for *Hölderlin's Echo VR*. © Hannes Rall/Nanyang Technological University Singapore.

Denkendorf

Fig. 11. Visual development for *Hölderlin's Echo VR*. © Hannes Rall/Nanyang Technological University Singapore.

Terry Gilliam (Monty Python) contemporary illustrations are brought to life with cut-out-animation. Here a tone of dark humor dominates that is echoed through the awkwardness and stylization of movement.

Romantic Departures. Figure 12 demonstrates the look of the third world that refers to Hölderlin's journeys as a young man. It expresses the romanticism of his poems by introducing the user to a fully immersive world that is resembling the look of contemporary romantic paintings. By clicking on billboards, imaginative animated metamorphoses will take the spectator to different locations in the wildly romantic landscape of the Swabian Alps.

Fig. 12. Visual development for *Hölderlin's Echo VR*. © Hannes Rall/Nanyang Technological University Singapore.

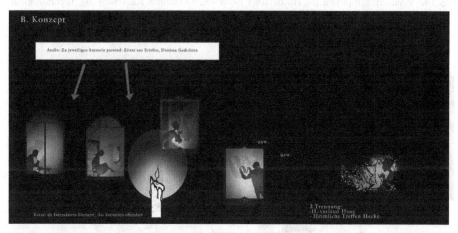

Fig. 13. Visual development for *Hölderlin's Echo VR*. © Hannes Rall/Nanyang Technological University Singapore.

Diotima: A Tragic Love Affair. The 4th window allows the user to witness the tragic love affair between Hölderlin and Susette Gontard through the windows of a stylized house. Here interactivity plays a central role. Only when the user lights the windows with a candle, what is happening inside becomes visible (Figs. 13 and 14). The animations I created in the style that references the work of animation pioneer Lotte Reiniger, who spent her final years in Tübingen.

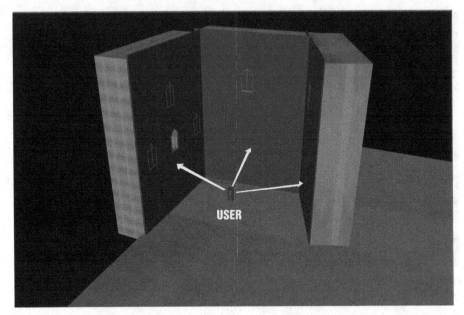

Fig. 14. Visual development for *Hölderlin's Echo VR.* © Hannes Rall/Nanyang Technological **University Singapore.**

Fig. 15. Visual development for *Hölderlin's Echo VR.* © Hannes Rall/Nanyang Technological University Singapore.

Late Life in the Tower. The last immersive world that can be entered in the experience negotiates the final period of Hölderlin's life: After therapy in the clinic had failed,

Friedrich Hölderlin was declared terminally ill and taken in by the Zimmer family. Hölderlin now spent the last 36 years of his life with the family in a tower room (today the Hölderlin Tower) that had been converted for him, until he finally died on 7th June 1843 at the age of 73. During these 36 years he wrote numerous other poems, including a revised edition of his famous novel "Hyperion", written in 1797/1799. In this time period Hölderlin often wrote under the pseudonym Scardanelli, which he adapted as a second personality. The artistic interpretation will mirror this by offering the feature of an ever-changing reflection of him in the Neckar river that runs in front of the tower (see Fig. 15). A fluid instead of a fixed image of identity.

5   Conclusion and Outlook

The preceding sections have demonstrated that animation has specific properties that can answer particularly well to the needs of literature adaptation: Stylization and exaggeration are powerful tools to visualize internal states. What is more, interactivity can further enhance this approach. In *Hölderlin's EchoVR* the user transforms from a passive consumer into an active discoverer of an interactively explorable world of experience, he starts you see the world(s) through Hölderlin's eyes. The literary power of his texts is reflected through interactively triggered animations that poetically resonate with the original texts.

This creates a completely different approach than linear live-action film: The VR-experience opens up numerous possibilities for every user to experience the worlds in and from the room in a completely new and different way. The project attempts an innovative and contemporary form of literary mediation in a time when the reading of complex texts has become a challenge for many people. The author argues that this provides special potential for addressing the generation of digital natives. VR is a state-of-the-art medium that will render the mediation of complex text more accessible.

Therefore, *Hölderlin's Echo VR* has a high potential for use in secondary and tertiary education and museums. It has the capacity to offer a new future for Hölderlin's classical texts. Moreover, the study can demonstrate how the need to create visual equivalents for written narratives can and should strongly inform the design and production process. In doing so, the author hopes that findings can offer meaningful new contributions to scholarship in adaptation, animation, literature and museum studies.

References

Dieter, H.: The Course of Remembrance and Other Essays on Hölderlin, Ed. Eckart Förster, p. 139. Stanford University, Stanford (1997)

Dilthey, W.: Hölderlin and the causes of his madness. Philosophy Today **37**(4), 341–352 (1993)

George, E.E.: Hölderlin's "Ars poetica": A Part-Rigorous Analysis of Information Structure in the Late Hymns, vol. 32. Walter de Gruyter GmbH & Co KG (2019)

Hölderlin, K.H.F.: Johann Christian Friedrich Hölderlin (* 1770–1843). Litoral **245**, 172 (2008)

McCormick, P.: Heidegger on Hölderlin. Philos. Stud. **22**, 7–16 (1973)

Olson, A.: Hegel and the Spirit, p. 39. Cambridge University Press, Cambridge (1992)

Pellegrini, A.: Friedrich Hölderlin: Sein Bild in der Forschung, p. 6. Berlin, Walter de Gruyter GmbH & Co KG (2019)

Poe, E.A.: The Raven. The New York Evening Mirror, New York City (1845)

Poetryfoundation.org (N.d.). Friedrich Hölderlin. https://www.poetryfoundation.org/poets/friedrich-holderlin. Accessed 23 Feb 2020

Warminski, A.: Readings in Interpretation: Hölderlin, Hegel, Heidegger (Theory and History of Literature. 26), p. 209. University of Minnesota Press, Minneapolis (1987)

Weber, W., Rall, H.M.: Comics journalism and animated documentary: understanding the balance between fact and fiction. ImageTexT: Interdiscipl. Comics Stud **11**(1) (2019)

Wells, P.: 'Thou art translated': analyzing animated adaptations. In: Cartmell, D., Whelehan, I. (eds.) Adaptations: From Text to Screen, Screen to Text, pp. 199–213. Routledge, London (1999)

Yip, A.: Virtual reality and the museology of consciousness (2016). https://www.artlink.com.au/articles/4559/virtual-reality-and-the-museology-of-consciousness/. Accessed 23 Feb 2020

Increasing the Museum Visitor's Engagement Through Compelling Storytelling Based on Interactive Explorations

Ana Rodrigues[1](✉), Pedro Campos[1](✉), and Diogo Cabral[2](✉)

[1] ITI/LARSyS, University of Madeira, Funchal, Portugal
`2066213@student.uma.pt, pcampos@uma.pt`
[2] ITI/LARSyS, IST, University of Lisbon, Lisbon, Portugal
`diogo.n.cabral@tecnico.ulisboa.pt`

Abstract. Today, technology offers exciting and news possibilities to bring visitors closer to museums. The museological universe has developed a lot over the last years, presenting today with innovative characteristics thanks to the digital realms, losing the characteristics of traditional and static museums. As a result of this development, the requirements of visitors increased.

In this paper, we introduce a new approach to making the visitor experience more immersive and engaging. We present "StoryWall", a tangible user interface. We created a sensorial experience by presenting the content through touch, vision, and sound. As the main contribution to HCI in museums, we report on the utilization of this interactive installation as a case study.

Preliminary results bring important design implications for this context: how can one develop and implement innovative technology in museums without disturbing the traditional environment and other constraints? We also report on how designers can balance the impact brought by technology in museums and ways to inspire exploratory behaviors as well as promote collaboration among visitors.

Keywords: Interactive museum · Visitor experience · Interactive wall · Tangible user interface · Interaction design

1 Introduction

The use of ambient technologies in different contexts has been vastly increasing over the past years, as these technologies allow for new ways of creating and sharing meaning, as coined by Dourish's seminal work on embodied interaction. New ways of interacting with objects and spaces through interactive systems have been widely used in order to deliver more innovative experiences. In museums, engagement has been recognized as a key driver for improving visitor's satisfaction levels. A new series of technologies are being deployed and evaluated in museums, and interactivity in museums is, therefore, maximizing the physical and real experiencing, offering a more engaged and rich learning experience [1]. Throughout the development of this project, we the use of ambient technologies in different contexts has been vastly increased over the past years, as these

© Springer Nature Switzerland AG 2020
M. Rauterberg (Ed.): HCII 2020, LNCS 12215, pp. 245–254, 2020.
https://doi.org/10.1007/978-3-030-50267-6_19

technologies allow for new ways of creating and sharing meaning, as coined by Dourish's seminal work on embodied interaction. New ways of interacting with objects and spaces through interactive systems have been widely used to deliver more innovative experiences. In museums, engagement has been recognized as a key driver for improving visitor's satisfaction levels. A new series of technologies are being deployed and evaluated in museums, and interactivity in museums is, therefore, maximizing the physical and real experiencing, offering a more engaged and rich learning experience [1]. Throughout the development of this project, we worked closely with the museum manager to identify the main problem points, which are as follows: communication barrier between museum collection and visitor, little information about the sugar manufacturing process and the loss of historical references in the present generation, of the lack of connection (communication) between the museum collection and the visitors that was one of our main motivations. Therefore, our goal was to construct an object (see Fig. 1) that would help minimize the impact of problems encountered through touch, sight, and sound. In this context, we present "Open Sesame", a new tangible user interface that aimed at joining the rich history of Madeira Island (Portugal) in the 15th century, using a "StoryWall". This interactive installation uses BareConductive's Touch Board Starter Kit to implement a wall where visitors interact and actuate digital content. The goal of the approach was to improve learning and promote a more engaging experience to the visitor, bringing a more immersive feel to what would otherwise be a conventional museum featuring artifacts from sugar cane factories of the 15th century. In this article, we start by discussing examples of interactive museums, then describe the whole process of system implementation and prototype construction. Finally, we explain the evaluation to which the project was submitted.

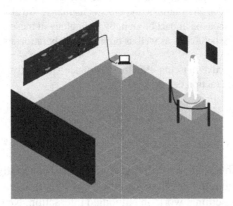

Fig. 1. Vector layout of the interactive installation in the exhibition hall of the museum "A Cidade do Açúcar".

2   Interactivity in Museums

Technology today provides exciting new possibilities for creating more appealing museum experiences, since we can exploit the surprise factor of innovative interaction styles to create an engaging experience that facilitates the learning process [1]. The traditional image of what a computer system is - screen, keyboard and mouse - is changing due to the development of technology incorporated in the real world and this technology allows the user to use their own senses. It is because of these technologies that there are opportunities to create new forms of interaction based on body movement and manipulation of real objects. Museums should seek to bring technology together to capture visitor's attention, evolving interaction design and usability, because incorporating exhibits, objects, interactive installations and people into a network of interconnected systems is a difficult and challenging task [2, 3], given the many factors that make them more attractive and why it is challenging to introduce technology into museums without disturbing the environment.

Interactive installations have grown in the museum world because they have become a support for enhancing the visitor experience and demonstrate their potential to enhance the information contained in exhibitions while educating the visitor.

For example, The Fire and The Mountain [4] is a project in which four digital touchable installations at the Civic Museum of Como (Italy), support tangible interaction and integrate text, video and sound. This project supports what was previously mentioned about interactive installations in museums, as the main objective was to improve the level of learning and understanding about fire culture.

Another example, the PuzzleBeo [5] is an interactive installation implemented at a public maritime museum in Ireland. The installation is comprised of interactive jigsaw, projected motion graphics, sensor technology and multimodal feedback. The focus is on simple interaction through touch, social interaction and learning, because this project presents the story of the sailing and sinking of the RMS Titanic.

Dória et al. [6] developed a project that consists of fifteen sensor-based interactive installations on the endemic forest of Madeira Island, another project in which the focus is on the adopted styles of interaction.

3   Open Sesame

3.1   Design Goals

According to Horn et al. [7], tangible interfaces must be inviting and easy to understand, besides, they must maintain the attention and motivation of the visitors throughout the interaction process. Therefore, we used the five design goals for user interfaces in museological environments to develop our prototype.

Inviting - Interactive installations need to attract the attention of visitors and invite them to interact with them.

Apprehendable - Visitors with no previous experience of interactive facilities should be able to easily learn how to use them.

Engaging - An interactive installation strives to hold the attention of several visitors throughout the exploration process.

Supportive of Group Interaction – Interactive installations should support social learning and group interaction with both active participants and passive observers.

Inexpensive and Reliable - As museums are non-profit institutions and depend on the support of foundations among other supports, the idea is to keep development and maintenance costs low.

We developed the design of the interactive installation based on the design goals and based on the design principles applied in previous works [4].

Emotional Evolvement: Where we make the visitor experience more enjoyable, more engaging, and more meaningful.

Multi-Modality: We support different sensory modalities and involve multi senses: touch, hearing, and sight.

Discovery Learning: We can expose visitors to a variety of content by promoting discovery through direct interaction with the facility.

Social Learning: supporting learning as a social process and fostering mutual collaboration and group discussion.

3.2 Design Rationale

Starting on the theory previously presented, we developed "A Journey in Time". The installation that composes "A Journey in Time" integrates text, icons, videos, and sound. We designed a narrative flow throughout the installation so we developed the timeline (see Fig. 2) so that visitors could understand the whole narrative.

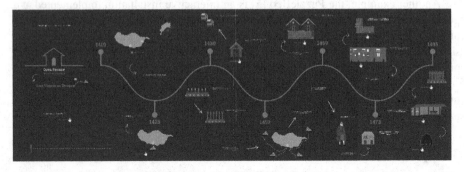

Fig. 2. Interactive installation design

The videos were grouped by themes, a total of eight videos. Three are in 2D and five videos in 3D. The idea was to adopt gestures that people are familiar with in real life so they can watch the videos. Each video is associated with an interactive installation icon, the visitor touches the icon and plays the corresponding video.

The first video demonstrates the discovery of Madeira Island, the second video explains how the settlement was made and the third video how the island developed (see Fig. 3A). These 2D videos have a simple language, based on moving icons.

The 3D videos help minimize the lack of information on sugar manufacturing and 15th century market life. The sugar manufacturing process is grouped into three videos.

The first video explains sugarcane harvesting, the visitor can view a sugarcane field, slaves and animals. The second video and the third video demonstrate and explain how the sugarcane juice was extracted and how the sugar was obtained (see Fig. 3B).

Fig. 3. A) 2D videos frames B) 3D videos frames

The last theme is about the 15th century civil architecture, we built the exterior and interior of a typical century house (see Fig. 4A) and the street environment (see Fig. 4B).

Fig. 4. A) 3D video frames B) 3D video frames

3.3 System Implementation

The prototype was developed using a touch board, conductive ink and crocodile clips that are part of the Bare Conductive Touch Board Starter Kit, a computer, a projector and interactive installation (see Fig. 5). We developed a StoryWall through projection mapping using the touch board. We then use conductive ink to create sensors across the cardboards, painting the conductive ink to the edge of the cardboards and then attaching the crocodile clips to the ink and touch board. When visitors touch the interactive surface, the software triggers digital content, that is, videos, which bring the wall to life, creating a surprising and engaging experience.

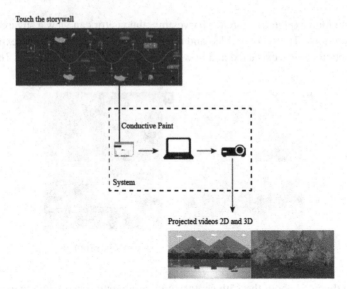

Fig. 5. System architecture

4 Evaluation and Results

4.1 Self – evaluation System

We carry out this assessment because there is a wide range of issues to be assessed in the interactive installation, our goal was to detect usability errors before testing with users (visitors) in order to minimize the impact of errors at the time of testing.

We have submitted our interactive installation for evaluation based on the M-Dimensions framework [8]. This framework was developed by a team of researchers in 2012 to evaluate and compare interactive museum installations. The framework was coined "M-Dimensions" (M stands for Museums) and is composed by ten dimensions (interaction style adequacy, area integration, visibility, feedback, structure, reuse, simplicity, education, entertainment, collaboration), which are evaluated individually by a 5-point Likert scale (1: very weak, 2: weak, 3: reasonable, 4: good and 5: very good score). The goal is to rate each dimension, sum the scores and, finally, divide by the number of dimensions being considered in a specific interactive installation. The result is a final evaluation score between 1 and 5 that is meant to convey the level of the interactivity quality that is present in a given museum interactive installation. For example, if the final result of a specific installation is 1, we can state that the installation is interactively very weak. On the other hand, if the final result of the evaluation is a 4 or a 5, we can assert that the specific installation is good (or very good) in terms of interactivity (Table 1).

As a result, we have to improve the feedback that the system provides to the user and the collaboration between users, it was the parameters that had the lowest scores.

Table 1. M-Dimensions framework applied to the prototype – "A Journey in Time"

Dimensions	Installation	Explanation
Interaction style adequacy	5	A simple and appropriate interaction style (touch) is used, the visitor can control the content viewed
Area integration	5	Prototype was implemented and tested in the museum "The City of Sugar"
Visibility	5	The font style used is readable, all relevant information such as timeline dates are displayed. There is indication on how to enable digital content
Feedback	4,5	The digital displays installation content change but does not indicate when it finishes
Structure	5	The quality of the elements is good, and all follow the chronological order
Reuse	5	Elements follow a pattern and are reused throughout the installation
Simplicity	5	Using the installation is simple, the visitor must follow the dates and the installation indicates where to touch
Learning	5	Appropriate and simple learning content (historical facts) increasing the level of education
Entertainment	5	Digital content is tractive and achieves a greater sense of immersion
Collaboration	4	Only one visitor can use the installation at a time, but we come across multiple visitors

Final Result: 4,85 (Good)

4.2 Collection of Users Tests Data

The museum "A Cidade do Açúcar" authorized the implementation of the prototype and because of this we can perform an *in-situ* evaluation, but due to the limited space, the tests were performed in a support room. The participants were chosen considering the most frequent audience of the museum. A total of 10 participants, 6 females and 4 males, aged 18–32 years (M = 23, SD = 4.4), over 2 days tested our project, underwent observations while interacting with the prototype and then responded to a questionnaire. After the evaluation process, all participants received a flyer with information about the project.

Observations. Observations were performed *in-lock*, we recorded observations through notes and photographic records. During the observations we kept a certain distance so as not to intrude on the interaction between the user and the interactive installation, we started by recording if the interactive installation aroused curiosity, then observing how the user interacts with the installation and how long the interaction lasts.

Questionnaires. The main objective was to gather quantitative data based on visitors' specific opinions by submitting a questionnaire after interacting with the interface. We grouped the questionnaire questions into three groups, according to the themes under analysis: I. Interaction with the installation/II. Presented Content (Videos)/III. Personal Comment.

4.3   Results of Users Tests

The test results with users came only reinforce the results obtained in the self - evaluation performed.

Observations Results. Overall the time of observation was between 7–17 min. Users did not have read order because they did not follow the timeline but read all the information contained in the interface. They watched each video to the end and reread the information and see the icons (see Fig. 6).

Fig. 6. Photographic record of some users testing the prototype

In this evaluation, we detected usability errors, such as the lack of indications along the timeline because for us it makes sense but for the visitor who doesn't know how to make it difficult and the order that the videos follow to be able to tell the story.

Another problem detected was that the distance from the ink to the touch card that is connected to the computer made it a problem because there is a break in communication due to the distance. In this case, some videos didn't work at all. And a system error that we detected, it is necessary to restart the system if the visitor wants to view the videos again.

Questionnaires Results. Questionnaire with a total of 12 questions in which 11 questions are evaluated by a Likert 5-point scale (very poor, poor, fair, good or very good).

First group of questions, participants answered questions about the difficulty they felt interacting with the prototype, whether they found the interaction motivating, whether the prototype is interesting (appealing) and whether it is creative.

In general, the installation is easy to use, appealing and creative.

The second group of questions is about the content presented, the icons and the text of the physical installation and the digital content, the videos in 2D and 3D.

According to the general opinion of the 10 participants, they found the content relevant because the icons and the text had a simple language and the videos were attractive.

In the last group, we asked the participants to describe their personal opinion about the prototype, the opinions of all participants were similar, "creative design", "historical context relevant to the knowledge of island history", "simple and intuitive interface", "interesting idea". Although participants mentioned positive aspects, they also described some fewer positive aspects, "interesting idea, but would like to have tested in the museum environment" and "different ideas, but the icons to touch are confusing".

Initial feedback shows that participants were receptive to the use of innovative technology in the museum.

5 Final Considerations

5.1 Conclusions

In this article, we present Open Sesame, a tangible user interface that is the communication link between the museological estate and the visitors to the museum.

We believe that with the implementation of this prototype we were able to transmit the missing information. It should be noted that this project is still in the development stage because, during the tests carried out, we encounter some errors in the system.

It is a project with innovative technology. The development of 3D elements can become an asset and enrich the project due to the impact it causes because it becomes so real and disseminates information using videos with sound and animation captures the attention of visitors.

5.2 Future Work

For future work, we have to solve the usability and system problems that were detected throughout the observations and In the future we intend to carry out additional assessments to better understand the visitor's learning and engagement process during their visit, to carry out a visit without the tangible user interface and another visit with the tangible user interface. Thus, we will obtain the results that justify the greater use of these technologies in museological environments.

Acknowledgments. This work was partially funded by LARSyS - FCT Plurianual funding 2020–2023.

References

1. Campos, P., Dória, A., Sousa, M.: Interactivity for Museums: Designing and Comparing Sensor-based Installations. Human-Computer Interaction – INTERACT 2009: 12th IFIP TC 13 International Conference, Uppsala, Sweden, 24–28 August 2009, Proceedings, Part I, pp. 612–615 (2009). https://www.researchgate.net/publication/221053740
2. Hakvoort, G.: The immersive museum. In: ITS 2013 Interactive tabletops and surfaces (2013). https://dl.acm.org/citation.cfm?id=2514598
3. Hornecker, E., Stifter, M.: Learning from interactive museum installations about interaction design for public settings. In: Kjeldskov, J., Paay, J. (eds.) Proceedings of the 18th Australia Conference on Computer-Human Interaction, OZCHI 2006, vol. 206. ACM (2006)
4. Rizzo, F., Garzotto, F.: "The Fire and The Mountain": tangible and social interaction in a museum exhibition for children. In: IDC 2007 Proceedings: Tangible Interaction (2007). https://dl.acm.org/citation.cfm?id=1297298
5. Hayes, S., O'Keefee, M., Hogan, T.: Piecing together the past: constructing stories with Jigsaw Puzzles in Museums. In: DIS 2017 Provocations & Works in Progress (2017). https://dl.acm.org/citation.cfm?id=3079123
6. Dória, A., Campos, P. and Fernandes, E.: Designing an interactive forest through sensor-based installations. In: Proceedings of CHI 2008, Florence, Italy (2008)
7. Horn, M.S., Solovey, E.T., Jacob, R.J.K.: Tangible programming and informal science learning: making TUIs work for museums. In: IDS 2008 Papers (2008). https://dl.acm.org/citation.cfm?id=1463756
8. Gonçalves, L., Campos, P., Sousa, M.: M-dimensions: a framework for evaluating and comparing interactive installations in museums. In: Nordi CHI 2012 (2012). https://dl.acm.org/citation.cfm?id=2399027

Semantics-Driven Conversational Interfaces for Museum Chatbots

Dimitris Spiliotopoulos[1](✉) ⓘ, Konstantinos Kotis[2] ⓘ, Costas Vassilakis[1] ⓘ, and Dionisis Margaris[3] ⓘ

[1] University of the Peloponnese, Tripoli, Greece
{dspiliot,costas}@uop.gr
[2] University of the Aegean, Lesvos, Greece
kotis@aegean.gr
[3] University of Athens, Athens, Greece
margaris@di.uoa.gr

Abstract. This work addresses the challenges of creating usable and personalized conversational interfaces for broad, yet applicable, domains that require user engagement and learning, such as museum chatbots. Whether the chatbots are standalone or coupled with virtual agents or real-life robots, the functional requirements for interaction that targets specific learning aspects would be expected to be more or less similar. This work reports on experimental semantics-driven conversational interface design for chatbots in museum settings, targeting visitors to converse about exhibits and learn information about their style, the artists, the era, and other aspects related to them. Depending on the semantics (presentation, learning, exploration), chatbot scenarios were designed and evaluated by participants in a formative evaluation. The evaluation show that user requirement perception manifests in expectations on the semantic level, instead of just the technical level. The results between the scenarios are compared to see how the semantics considered for the design transferred to the implementation and to the user perception.

Keywords: Semantics · Conversational interfaces · Chatbots · Cultural technology

1 Introduction

In the recent years, personal communication via interactive assistants has become mainstream for almost every personal interaction device [1]. Commonly referred to as "chatbots", generic implementations engage natural language communication to interact with the user and allow the user to interact with the system or the device. Chatbots utilize natural language processing, human-computer interaction, dialogue systems, virtual characters and other related technologies [2, 3].

Depending on their use, chatbot design can be classified as task-oriented and non-task-oriented [4]. The former is close-domain, designed for particular tasks and short goal-oriented conversations. The latter is open-domain, generic conversational

© Springer Nature Switzerland AG 2020
M. Rauterberg (Ed.): HCII 2020, LNCS 12215, pp. 255–266, 2020.
https://doi.org/10.1007/978-3-030-50267-6_20

agents that are designed to simulate a conversation and provide personal assistance and communication to users, using broad natural language expressions.

Domain-specific chatbots require very high effectiveness and are evaluated on their ability to perform very well on specific functions, such as learning [5, 6]. Domain-independent chatbots, on the other hand, require broad conversational capacity, using natural language processing and rules or AI for complex interaction [7, 8].

The design of the conversational interface for a chatbot takes into account both the domain (context) and the task (goal). This work aims to investigate how the purpose of the design is perceived between designers and user and how semantics can be used in the formulation of the design.

Based on the above, a relevant research question is how designers and users perceive the design of a relatively complex interaction system. The purpose of the system, as well as the semantics behind its intended use are a key characteristic to user acceptance during first-time introduction and interaction. This work examines the intended design perception between designers and users and reports on the semantics that lead to the design formulation and their impact on the design principles.

The rest of the paper is as follows. Section 2 presents the related work. Section 3 describes the experimental setup and the methodology. Section 4 presents the evaluation results, while Sect. 5 concludes the paper and presents the future work.

2 Related Work

Chatbots are deployed in a multitude of settings and are used for several tasks. For tasks such as e-learning [9], the chatbots may be deployed from a central point and accessed from school, home or on a mobile device. Mobile devices are very suitable platforms since they offer dedicated support for visual, spoken and tactile interaction. Particular chatbot implementations can be designed for primary mobile use, such as the ones for recommendation of tourist sites [10]. Other chatbots may be accessed on specific locations, such as an airport [11]. Turunen et al. (2011) designed chatbots for health and fitness companionship [12].

Ciechanowski et al. (2019) showed that there are differences in human perception of a chatbot depending on the type of chatbot, text-based or avatar [13]. They found that users were more reserved and felt less positively towards the avatar chatbot. Their results show that user emotions change depending on the chatbot type. The type of user and the topic of discussion is also important on the acceptance of the chatbot by the human, as an interaction partner. Studies show that specific user types may prefer to talk to chatbots than to other people for specific topics [14].

Social media settings are different than real life settings. The former can facilitate social interaction with similarly acceptable results as with a real life human for information seeking and learning activities [15]. Regarding the tasks that are the focus of the human-chatbot interaction, specific activities, such as language practice/learning, were found to be more interesting if performed by a human rather than a chatbot instructor [16]. This underlines the limitations of the educational technology – and all the technologies mastered for such tasks - as to the expertise, the abilities and knowledge of the educator. The human educator would clearly possess much higher level of command of language and educational expertise for a better educational experience. Moreover, the language technology required for such tasks is resource heavy, both for natural language analysis [17–19], speech synthesis [20–23] and dialogue [24].

Social norms, such as politeness, are also important factors for the user acceptance of the chatbot [25]. Lee and Choi (2017) measured how a chatbot for movie recommendation established relationships with human users using social communication processes, such as self-disclosure and reciprocity [26].

Cuayahuitl et al. (2019) used deep reinforcement learning using dialogue data to train chatbots [27]. Their human user evaluation showed that the chatbot phrases that were similar to human natural language had high acceptance and triggered engagement. To make chatbot personas more accurate and, therefore, the chatbots more acceptable, data-driven design can be used for creating the chatbot personas as well as the service matching to these personas [28]. Such requirement is important in situations where the chatbot is an all-day companion or partner, such as an emotion-aware wellbeing chatbot [29]. Another recent user experience evaluation study suggests that users expect action cues when interacting with a chatbot [30].

Semantics in general can be utilised to aid the design of the chatbot. Recent works used situational characteristics to tailor the design to specific context [31]. Other works utilised chatbots in settings that traditionally require expert natural language control, such as journalism [32]. In open domain or expert situations, chatbots may succeed in the main tasks they are designed for, but it is a situation where they may also fail to satisfy the natural communication requirements by the users, as in the case of the expert recommender chatbot for Discord failing to provide the conversational behaviour expected by the users [33].

3 Experiment Setup and Methodology

A total of 12 university students (3 female, 9 male), participated voluntarily in the laboratory. The participants were recruited through online-advertisement and the university web forum as well as email invitations. The participants were compensated with Amazon credit vouchers. The participants ranged in age from 19 to 36 with an average age of 26.45 years (SD = 3.48). Regarding computer literacy, they reported a mean experience of 13.32 years (SD = 3.30) and 5.02 h of daily usage (SD = 1.84).

Three chatbot designers were recruited from the human computer interaction lab of the university. They all had degrees in computer science and proven expertise in designing chatbots for postgraduate level computer-human interaction course laboratory exercises. The designers and the users were briefed about the aim and goals of the study and they informed each other on the design idea.

This experiment involved the chatbot designers to design chatbots (all for the same domain of application, a museum) based on the general semantics of purpose. The purpose was chosen between (a) exhibit presentation, (b) exploration and (c) learning. The design itself was a designer choice, each designer selecting a purpose for their design, and using the same chatbot design technology.

The designers provided their vision of the chatbot purpose and the design, which was recorded. Similarly, the users provided their own expectations for chatbot design purpose, for each of the types above. The interpretation of the semantics of the purpose between designers and users was investigated to measure their similarity. The semantics of purpose were also the basis for setting the user expectations and their matching to the design requirements. The summary of the designer and user understanding of the semantics of purpose is provided in Table 1.

Table 1. Designer aims and user expectations.

Purpose	Designer aims	User expectations
Exhibit presentation	Chatbot-directed dialogue	Personalized information
	Allow for level of detail	Show interesting facts
	Suggest more information (same era, same artist, same type of artifact)	Present aspects of the exhibits
Exhibit/museum exploration	Mixed-initiative dialogue	Provide choices for exploration
	Recommend similar exhibits	Show overview of the museum
	Recommend linked objects	Show options
	Plan to present all types of exhibits	Provide a tour
Learning	Chatbot-directed dialogue	Educational content
	Advanced information	Advanced information/questions
	Learning goals and targets	Allow users to ask questions
	Learning outcome metrics	Engaging conversation

The designers had a technical-oriented approach towards the chatbot aims. First of all, they established the type of dialogue the chatbot should have to be able to achieve the core purpose. They opted for chatbot-directed dialogue for exhibit presentation and learning and mixed initiative dialogue for exploration. Regarding the latter, they envisioned that exploration would be open for the user to steer, based on the user input, questions and directions, as well as the chatbot recommendations for similar or semantically linked artifacts. The designers also reported on the core design decisions on how to implement each design. For example, the learning scenario would have to account for advanced information to be provided to the user by the system, especially when there are follow up questions by the users.

The users also discussed and agreed on their main expectations for each purpose. The aforementioned example is also valid for the user perspective, in which case the users expected to pose questions to the system during their interaction for learning about an exhibit. Therefore, they also expected to have advanced information available to them.

The designers, informed about the user requirements, designed the chatbots, that is the chatbot conversational interfaces. For the purpose of this work, they designed short interaction scenarios and not complete designs.

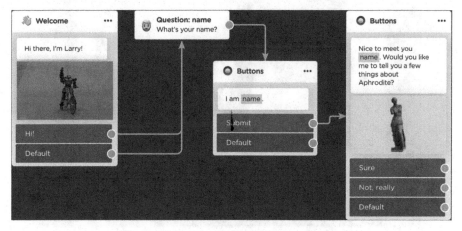

Fig. 1. Chatbot design for exhibit presentation.

Figure 1 depicts a screenshot from the design environment for the exhibit presentation. In this scenario, the user is interested in the Venus de Milo, the statue of Aphrodite of Milos, now on permanent display in the Louvre Museum in Paris. The chatbot makes the introductions and asks the user if they are interested to find out more about Aphrodite.

The designers provided a breakdown of their design principles which were communicated to the participants in a focus group setting. The outcome was recorded for use in the formal evaluation.

4 Evaluation

All 12 participants took part in the evaluation sessions where they immersed in the three semantic-driven chatbot scenarios. The scenarios were presented at random, two for each participant. The participants completed the conversation and provided subjective feedback through online evaluation questionnaires. The aim was to see whether the semantics of purpose, as perceived by the users and the designers, matched their expectations of the chatbot-human interaction. Moreover, the participants were asked to rate the user experience in terms of friendliness and acceptance.

The first point of interest was from the user feedback regarding the type of chatbot. Each participant interacted with two (out of three) scenarios and reported on the perceived purpose of the chatbot. The reason for the user interaction with two rather than all three scenarios was to avoid plain reasoning and deduction of the third scenario.

Figure 2 shows a commonly used, simple and usable way to start a friendly conversation. At this point the actual dialogue is still in the initial stage and the users do not have enough information to differentiate between the possible scenarios.

Fig. 2. One of the simplest and accurate ways to introduce an exhibit, according to the user feedback. Does it provide a hint as to the purpose of the chatbot?

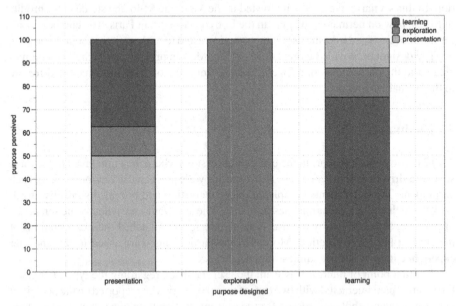

Fig. 3. User-perceived purpose after interaction

Figure 3 shows how the users perceived the purpose of each chatbot scenario. The presentation was perceived accurately by 50% of the participants, while three of them (37.5%) perceived it as learning. The justification given by the users was that the presentation had a lot of information about the exhibits making it quite accurate to their expectations. On the other hand, the learning was perceived accurately by 75% of the participants, while the remaining two reported one of the other purposes each. The justification that was given by the designers was that the learning chatbot interaction failed to trigger the rule-based intelligence many times for the two participants and, therefore, did not provide even the detailed information and show its purpose. The exploration was perceived accurately by all participants. All parties agreed that the expectations were met. The designers were convinced that the choice of mixed initiative dialogue was an apparent reason for the participants to perceive the purpose as it was intended.

The users provided feedback on the friendliness and overall acceptance of the chatbot design. In order to gain insight into the way that semantics of purpose may be relevant to design and acceptability of chatbots, we compared the user feedback after the interaction. The comparison was in terms of user-reported friendliness and overall acceptability evaluation between the designer and the user-perceived purpose distribution. Friendliness was selected since it was one of the main characteristics that help conversational agents achieve their goals as well as a key component to user satisfaction.

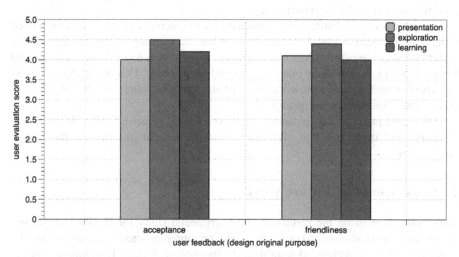

Fig. 4. User feedback aggregated by purpose from the designers

Figure 4 shows the average user evaluation scores (Likert scale 1-5) for each design (as designated by the designers) regarding friendliness and acceptance. The exploration design achieved the highest scores, while the other two were quite close between them.

Figure 5 shows the average user evaluation scores (Likert scale 1-5) for each design (as perceived by the users) regarding friendliness and acceptance. The exploration design achieved the highest scores, although it aggregated the scores of the designer-intended

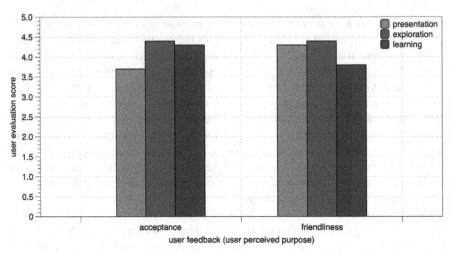

Fig. 5. User feedback aggregated by user perceived purpose

exploration designs (all users agreed with the designers on the exploration purpose assignment) plus two instances (one presentation and one learning) where the users reported them as exploration purposed.

The main perceptual difference between the user-perceived and the designer-intended designs can be seen in Fig. 5 for the presentation and learning user evaluation scores. The distance between the scores is much larger, presentation had lower acceptance and higher friendliness. It was the other way around for learning. This shows that the users perceived friendliness as a presentation attribute, while learning was attributed with a more formal communication quality.

The above indicate that semantics of purpose can be perceived differently between designers and users and that may lead to subtle expectations beyond the formal requirements.

5   Conclusion and Future Work

This work reported on the results of an experimental study for chatbot design perceived purpose. Designers and users shared their requirements and expectations, but the semantics were comprehended from their distinct points of view. The main task of the participants was to report their perceived purpose of the chatbot from their interaction. The reported evaluation showed that for users and designers alike, the formulation of acceptance and design criteria, respectively, is manifested on a semantic level.

The limitations of this work are mainly identified on the low number of participants and the distinct use of design and evaluation for the purpose of the experimental study. Formal evaluation of conversational systems requires rigorous protocols and high number of participants in appropriate experimental settings. The choice of evaluating overall acceptance and friendliness, instead of a meticulous usability evaluation using standard tests, was conscious and deliberate, since the designs were not finalized or field tested, but rather specifically produced for the study.

This work may find use in chatbot design. Specifically, the user perception of purpose and the parameters that may affect that could be useful for the design of socially-adaptive chatbots [34] and works in semantics for communication [35, 36].

Future work includes the use of the proposed methodology with recommender systems [37–39] and especially combination with collaborative filtering techniques [40–44]. Finally we are planning the proposed approach to be incorporated in social and tourist related recommendation applications [45–49].

References

1. Hachman, M.: Battle of the digital assistants: cortana, siri, and Google Now. PCWorld (2014)
2. Marcondes, F.S., Almeida, J.J., Novais, P.: A short survey on chatbot technology: failure in raising the state of the art. Adv. Intell. Syst. Comput. **1003**, 28–36 (2020). https://doi.org/10.1007/978-3-030-23887-2_4
3. Daniel, G., Cabot, J., Deruelle, L., Derras, M.: Xatkit: a multimodal low-code chatbot development framework. IEEE Access. **8**, 15332–15346 (2020). https://doi.org/10.1109/access.2020.2966919
4. Hussain, S., Ameri Sianaki, O., Ababneh, N.: A survey on conversational agents/chatbots classification and design techniques. In: Barolli, L., Takizawa, M., Xhafa, F., Enokido, T. (eds.) WAINA 2019. AISC, vol. 927, pp. 946–956. Springer, Cham (2019). https://doi.org/10.1007/978-3-030-15035-8_93
5. Huang, W., Hew, K.F., Gonda, D.E.: Designing and evaluating three chatbot-enhanced activities for a flipped graduate course. Int. J. Mech. Eng. Robot. Res. **8**, 813–818 (2019). https://doi.org/10.18178/ijmerr.8.5.813-818
6. Liu, Q., Huang, J., Wu, L., Zhu, K., Ba, S.: CBET: design and evaluation of a domain-specific chatbot for mobile learning. Univ. Access Inf. Soc. (2019). https://doi.org/10.1007/s10209-019-00666-x
7. Fogliano, F., Fabbrini, F., Souza, A., Fidélio, G., Machado, J., Sarra, R.: Edgard, the chatbot: questioning ethics in the usage of artificial intelligence through interaction design and electronic literature. In: Duffy, V.G. (ed.) HCII 2019. LNCS, vol. 11582, pp. 325–341. Springer, Cham (2019). https://doi.org/10.1007/978-3-030-22219-2_25
8. Androutsopoulos, I., Spiliotopoulos, D.: Symbolic authoring for multilingual natural language generation. Methods Appl. Artif. Intell. **2308**, 131–142 (2002). https://doi.org/10.1007/3-540-46014-4_13
9. Bahja, M., Hammad, R., Hassouna, M.: Talk2Learn: a framework for chatbot learning. In: Scheffel, M., Broisin, J., Pammer-Schindler, V., Ioannou, A., Schneider, J. (eds.) EC-TEL 2019. LNCS, vol. 11722, pp. 582–586. Springer, Cham (2019). https://doi.org/10.1007/978-3-030-29736-7_44
10. Arteaga, D., Arenas, J., Paz, F., Tupia, M., Bruzza, M.: Design of information system architecture for the recommendation of tourist sites in the city of Manta, Ecuador through a Chatbot. In: Iberian Conference on Information Systems and Technologies (CISTI) 19–22 June 2019 (2019). https://doi.org/10.23919/CISTI.2019.8760669
11. Carisi, M., Albarelli, A., Luccio, F.L.: Design and implementation of an airport chatbot. In: ACM International Conference Proceeding Series, pp. 49–54 (2019). https://doi.org/10.1145/3342428.3342664
12. Turunen, M., et al.: Multimodal and mobile conversational Health and Fitness Companions. Comput. Speech Lang. **25**, 192–209 (2011). https://doi.org/10.1016/j.csl.2010.04.004

13. Ciechanowski, L., Przegalinska, A., Magnuski, M., Gloor, P.: In the shades of the uncanny valley: an experimental study of human–chatbot interaction. Futur. Gener. Comput. Syst. **92**, 539–548 (2019). https://doi.org/10.1016/j.future.2018.01.055
14. Crutzen, R., Peters, G.J.Y., Portugal, S.D., Fisser, E.M., Grolleman, J.J.: An artificially intelligent chat agent that answers adolescents' questions related to sex, drugs, and alcohol: an exploratory study. J. Adolesc. Health **48**, 514–519 (2011). https://doi.org/10.1016/j.jadohealth.2010.09.002
15. Edwards, C., Beattie, A.J., Edwards, A., Spence, P.R.: Differences in perceptions of communication quality between a Twitterbot and human agent for information seeking and learning. Comput. Hum. Behav. **65**, 666–671 (2016). https://doi.org/10.1016/j.chb.2016.07.003
16. Fryer, L.K., Nakao, K., Thompson, A.: Chatbot learning partners: connecting learning experiences, interest and competence. Comput. Hum. Behav. **93**, 279–289 (2019). https://doi.org/10.1016/j.chb.2018.12.023
17. Demidova, E., et al.: Analysing and enriching focused semantic web archives for parliament applications. Futur. Internet **6**, 433–456 (2014). https://doi.org/10.3390/fi6030433
18. Antonakaki, D., Spiliotopoulos, D., Samaras, C.V., Ioannidis, S., Fragopoulou, P.: Investigating the complete corpus of referendum and elections tweets. In: Proceedings of the 2016 IEEE/ACM International Conference on Advances in Social Networks Analysis and Mining, ASONAM 2016, pp. 100–105 (2016). https://doi.org/10.1109/ASONAM.2016.7752220
19. Antonakaki, D., Spiliotopoulos, D., Samaras, C.V., Pratikakis, P., Ioannidis, S., Fragopoulou, P.: Social media analysis during political turbulence. PLoS One **12** (2017). https://doi.org/10.1371/journal.pone.0186836
20. Spiliotopoulos, D., Xydas, G., Kouroupetroglou, G.: Diction based prosody modeling in table-to-speech synthesis. In: Matoušek, V., Mautner, P., Pavelka, T. (eds.) TSD 2005. LNCS (LNAI), vol. 3658, pp. 294–301. Springer, Heidelberg (2005). https://doi.org/10.1007/11551874_38
21. Xydas, G., Spiliotopoulos, D., Kouroupetroglou, G.: Modeling emphatic events from non-speech aware documents in speech based user interfaces. In: Proceedings of Human Computer Interaction, pp. 806–810 (2003)
22. Spiliotopoulos, D., Stavropoulou, P., Kouroupetroglou, G.: Acoustic rendering of data tables using earcons and prosody for document accessibility. In: Stephanidis, C. (ed.) UAHCI 2009. LNCS, vol. 5616, pp. 587–596. Springer, Heidelberg (2009). https://doi.org/10.1007/978-3-642-02713-0_62
23. Spiliotopoulos, D., Xydas, G., Kouroupetroglou, G., Argyropoulos, V., Ikospentaki, K.: Auditory universal accessibility of data tables using naturally derived prosody specification. Univ. Access Inf. Soc. **9** (2010). https://doi.org/10.1007/s10209-009-0165-0
24. Alexandersson, J., et al.: Metalogue: a multiperspective multimodal dialogue system with metacognitive abilities for highly adaptive and flexible dialogue management. In: Proceedings - 2014 International Conference on Intelligent Environments, IE 2014, pp. 365–368 (2014). https://doi.org/10.1109/IE.2014.67
25. Carolus, A., Muench, R., Schmidt, C., Schneider, F.: Impertinent mobiles - effects of politeness and impoliteness in human-smartphone interaction. Comput. Hum. Behav. **93**, 290–300 (2019). https://doi.org/10.1016/j.chb.2018.12.030
26. Lee, S.Y., Choi, J.: Enhancing user experience with conversational agent for movie recommendation: effects of self-disclosure and reciprocity. Int. J. Hum Comput Stud. **103**, 95–105 (2017). https://doi.org/10.1016/j.ijhcs.2017.02.005
27. Cuayáhuitl, H., et al.: Ensemble-based deep reinforcement learning for chatbots. Neurocomputing **366**, 118–130 (2019). https://doi.org/10.1016/j.neucom.2019.08.007
28. Hwang, S., Kim, B., Lee, K.: A data-driven design framework for customer service chatbot. In: Marcus, A., Wang, W. (eds.) HCII 2019. LNCS, vol. 11583, pp. 222–236. Springer, Cham (2019). https://doi.org/10.1007/978-3-030-23570-3_17

29. Ghandeharioun, A., McDuff, D., Czerwinski, M., Rowan, K.: EMMA: an emotion-aware well-being chatbot. In: 2019 8th International Conference on Affective Computing and Intelligent Interaction ACII 2019, pp. 15–21 (2019). https://doi.org/10.1109/ACII.2019.8925455
30. Liu, R., Dong, Z.: A study of user experience in knowledge-based QA chatbot design. In: Karwowski, W., Ahram, T. (eds.) IHSI 2019. AISC, vol. 903, pp. 589–593. Springer, Cham (2019). https://doi.org/10.1007/978-3-030-11051-2_89
31. Chaves, A.P., Doerry, E., Egbert, J., Gerosa, M.: It's how you say it: identifying appropriate register for chatbot language design. In: Proceedings of the 7th International Conference on Human-Agent Interaction HAI 2019, pp. 102–109 (2019). https://doi.org/10.1145/3349537.3351901
32. Veglis, A., Maniou, T.A.: Embedding a chatbot in a news article design and implementation. In: ACM International Conference Proceeding Series (2019). https://doi.org/10.1145/3368640.3368664
33. Cerezo, J., Kubelka, J., Robbes, R., Bergel, A.: Building an expert recommender chatbot. In: Proceedings of the 2019 IEEE/ACM 1st International Workshop on Bots Software Engineering BotSE 2019, pp. 59–63 (2019). https://doi.org/10.1109/BotSE.2019.00022
34. Feine, J., Morana, S., Maedche, A.: Leveraging machine-executable descriptive knowledge in design science research – the case of designing socially-adaptive chatbots. In: Tulu, B., Djamasbi, S., Leroy, G. (eds.) DESRIST 2019. LNCS, vol. 11491, pp. 76–91. Springer, Cham (2019). https://doi.org/10.1007/978-3-030-19504-5_6
35. Pino, A., Kouroupetroglou, G., Kacorri, H., Sarantidou, A., Spiliotopoulos, D.: An open source/freeware assistive technology software inventory. In: Miesenberger, K., Klaus, J., Zagler, W., Karshmer, A. (eds.) ICCHP 2010. LNCS, vol. 6179, pp. 178–185. Springer, Heidelberg (2010). https://doi.org/10.1007/978-3-642-14097-6_29
36. Risse, T., et al.: The ARCOMEM architecture for social- and semantic-driven web archiving. Futur. Internet 6, 688–716 (2014). https://doi.org/10.3390/fi6040688
37. Margaris, D., Vassilakis, C.: Exploiting rating abstention intervals for addressing concept drift in social network recommender systems. Informatics 5, 21 (2018). https://doi.org/10.3390/informatics5020021
38. Aivazoglou, M., et al.: A fine-grained social network recommender system. Soc. Netw. Anal. Min. 10, 8 (2020). https://doi.org/10.1007/s13278-019-0621-7
39. Margaris, D., Vassilakis, C., Spiliotopoulos, D.: Handling uncertainty in social media textual information for improving venue recommendation formulation quality in social networks. Soc. Netw. Anal. Min. 9, 64 (2019). https://doi.org/10.1007/s13278-019-0610-x
40. Margaris, D., Vassilakis, C.: Improving collaborative filtering's rating prediction accuracy by considering users' rating variability. In: Proceedings of the IEEE 16th International Conference on Dependable, Autonomic and Secure Computing, IEEE 16th International Conference on Pervasive Intelligence and Computing, IEEE 4th International Conference on Big Data Intelligence and Computing and IEEE 3rd Cyber Science and Technology Congress, DASC-PICom-DataCom-CyberSciTec 2018 (2018). https://doi.org/10.1109/DASC/PiCom/DataCom/CyberSciTec.2018.00145
41. Margaris, D., Vassilakis, C.: Improving collaborative filtering's rating prediction quality by considering shifts in rating practices. In: Proceedings of the 2017 IEEE 19th Conference on Business Informatics, CBI 2017 (2017). https://doi.org/10.1109/CBI.2017.24
42. Margaris, D., Georgiadis, P., Vassilakis, C.: Adapting WS-BPEL scenario execution using collaborative filtering techniques. In: Proceedings of the International Conference on Research Challenges in Information Science (2013). https://doi.org/10.1109/RCIS.2013.6577691
43. Margaris, D., Vassilakis, C.: Enhancing rating prediction quality through improving the accuracy of detection of shifts in rating practices. In: Hameurlain, A., Wagner, R. (eds.) Transactions on Large-Scale Data- and Knowledge-Centered Systems XXXVII. LNCS, vol. 10940, pp. 151–191. Springer, Heidelberg (2018). https://doi.org/10.1007/978-3-662-57932-9_5

44. Margaris, D., Vassilakis, C.: Improving collaborative filtering's rating prediction quality in dense datasets, by pruning old ratings. In: Proceedings of the IEEE Symposium on Computers and Communications (2017). https://doi.org/10.1109/ISCC.2017.8024683

45. Margaris, D., Vassilakis, C.: Exploiting Internet of Things information to enhance venues' recommendation accuracy. Serv. Oriented Comput. Appl. **11**, 393–409 (2017). https://doi.org/10.1007/s11761-017-0216-y

46. Margaris, D., Vassilakis, C., Georgiadis, P.: Query personalization using social network information and collaborative filtering techniques. Futur. Gener. Comput. Syst. **78**, 440–450 (2018). https://doi.org/10.1016/j.future.2017.03.015

47. Margaris, D., Vassilakis, C., Georgiadis, P.: Knowledge-based leisure time recommendations in social networks. In: Alor-Hernández, G., Valencia-García, R. (eds.) Current Trends on Knowledge-Based Systems. ISRL, vol. 120, pp. 23–48. Springer, Cham (2017). https://doi.org/10.1007/978-3-319-51905-0_2

48. Margaris, D., Spiliotopoulos, D., Vassilakis, C.: Social relations versus near neighbours: reliable recommenders in limited information social network collaborative filtering for online advertising. In: Proceedings of the 2019 IEEE/ACM International Conference on Advances in Social Networks Analysis and Mining (ASONAM 2019), pp. 1160–1167. ACM, Vancouver (2019). https://doi.org/10.1145/3341161.3345620

49. Margaris, D., Vassilakis, C., Georgiadis, P.: Recommendation information diffusion in social networks considering user influence and semantics. Soc. Netw. Anal. Min. **6**, 108 (2016). https://doi.org/10.1007/s13278-016-0416-z

3D Virtual Reconstruction and Sound Simulation of an Ancient Roman Brass Musical Instrument

Zezhou Sun[1], Antonio Rodà[2(✉)], Emily Whiting[1], Emanuela Faresin[3], and Giuseppe Salemi[3]

[1] Computer Science Department, Boston University,
111 Cummington Mall, Boston, MA 02215, USA
{micou,whiting}@bu.edu
[2] Department of Information Engineering, University of Padova,
via Gradenigo 6b, 35131 Padova, Italy
roda@dei.unipd.it
[3] Deparment of Cultural Heritage, University of Padova,
Piazza Capitaniato 7, 35139 Padova, Italy
giuseppe.salemi@unipd.it

Abstract. Digital technologies based on 3D models are always more used to document archaeological remains and obtain hypothetical reconstructions when these remains are more or less heavily damaged. This work addresses the case of remains of ancient musical instruments, and in particular the case study of a brass instrument from the Roman Empire period, found in Voghenza (Italy). The pieces composing the instrument were first digitized by means of a structured light system, then virtually restored and recomposed applying a on-purpose developed algorithm. Finally, some sounds coherent with the geometry of the reconstructed model were simulated using a physically-based synthesis approach.

Keywords: 3D model · Virtual reconstruction · Sound simulation musical cultural heritage

1 Introduction

For millennia, music culture has been handed down orally, since the first detailed written music documents are relatively recent [14]. Therefore, what we know about the music of the past is due to indirect documents, such as literature, music theory treatises, and iconography. In this context, archaeological finds of musical instruments such as ancient flutes or harps coming from ancient Egypt [1,2] or Greek-Roman areas are a very important direct source of information. Unfortunately, these instruments are often seriously damaged and cannot be played anymore. Therefore, observing these artefacts we can have an idea of the global shape and analyse the materials they are built from, but we can not listen to their sound and have experience of the performing practice.

© Springer Nature Switzerland AG 2020
M. Rauterberg (Ed.): HCII 2020, LNCS 12215, pp. 267–280, 2020.
https://doi.org/10.1007/978-3-030-50267-6_21

Traditionally, playable copies of ancient instruments were built by craftsmen. This approach has several limits: a) the manufacturing process is usually slow and expensive; b) often one or few copies only can be built, limiting access to the instrument; c) when the reconstruction is uncertain, due to the poor state of conservation of the artefact, it is difficult to test and evaluate different possibilities.

The digital technologies based on 3D models overcomes these limits. The reconstruction is virtual, therefore many different hypotheses can be tested; FEM techniques [15] and physically informed algorithms allow to simulate the sounds produced by the artefacts, giving also a basis for evaluating the different reconstructions; virtual models can be easily shared, making possible global access to the heritage; finally, additive printing technologies offer the opportunity to have physical copies at relatively low costs. Nevertheless, methods and algorithms to obtain a virtual reconstruction of musical instruments in an automatic or semi-automatic way are still missing; several algorithms were developed in the past years for simulating the sound of known instruments, but these algorithms need to be modified and improved to meet the requirements of these ancient and almost unknown instruments; 3D printing processes need to be tuned to take into account the influence of materials and textures on the sound generation. These issues will be discussed and several solutions will be proposed in reference to the case study of an ancient Roman musical instrument, found in Voghenza, close to Ferrara (Italy) and now hosted in the archaeological section of the Civic Museum of Belriguardo. This instrument is the subject of an ongoing multidisciplinary project, that aims to analyse, reconstruct, and valorise this important musical heritage. A 3D model of the pieces composing the Voghenza instrument were first acquired and then subjected to two kinds of numerical elaboration. The first one aims to repair small holes and deformations, by means of filters and numerical interpolation, and is particularly suited for pieces with less severe damages. The second one aims to estimate the geometric parameters of the trumpet, also in case of very corrupted pieces. In particular, an original algorithm was developed to estimate the central axis of the curved tube of the trumpet and its increasing diameter.

2   3D Model

2.1   Acquisition

The trumpet, made of a metal alloy (probably bronze), is broken into 8 pieces and each piece further suffers from large holes and damages.

The 3d model of each piece was acquired by means of a structured light system that uses light patterns (or codes) and is based on digital cameras and projector. The projector shines a single pattern or a set of patterns onto the surface of an object; the camera then records the patterns on the surface. If the surface of the object under scanning is planar, then the pattern acquired by the camera would be similar to the pattern illuminated by the projector. However, if the object has some variations on the surface, the pattern acquired by the camera would be distorted compared to the projector pattern. Therefore, the 3D shape of the object can be reconstructed by comparing the projected patterns acquired by the camera. The structured light systems have several advantages: they are fast, can be used for large areas, are able to reconstruct the geometry and to acquire texture of the 3D objects, at high resolution with high accuracy. However, they are sensitive to ambient illumination and they are also not suitable for scanning reflective and transparent surfaces [10]. The instrument used for the acquisition is Cronos Dual, a structured light system by Open Technologies, with an accuracy of 10–40 μm; camera resolution: 2 × 1.3 MPixels. The acquisition and post processing software is Optical RevEng 2.4 SR 8 Pro. In order to guarantee the better overlapping, an automatic turntable synchronized with the scanner was used. The rotation angle was set at 20° for each scan and 18 scans for set were made in order to complete the 360° rotation angle (Fig. 1).

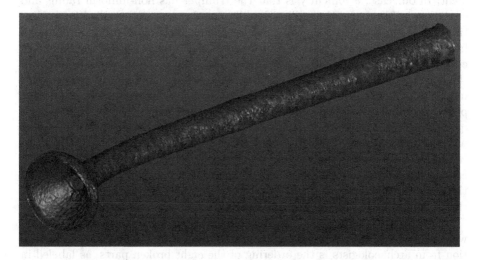

Fig. 1. The data collected by the scanner are X, Y, Z coordinate triplets of each single point acquired, taking a set of partially overlapping range scans. Different colours represent the contribution of each different scan. (Color figure online)

The pipeline of the processing phases is:

- Range map alignment: in order to put all the range maps into a common coordinate system where all the scans lie aligned on their mutual overlapping region. The pairwise ICP alignment algorithm, followed by a global registration, was used. An automatic pre-alignment technique was applied during the acquisition phase to improve this task and to verify, in real time, the acquisition quality.
- Range map merger (or fusion): to build a single, non-redundant triangulated mesh.

- Mesh editing: to improve the quality of the computed mesh. This step requires to order to correct the topological mistakes like cross section triangles or anomalous vertices.
- Mesh decimation: to accurately reduce the huge number of triangles, producing geometrically correct 3D models with different decimation factors (100%, 75%, 50% and 25%).
- Mesh export in STL (Standard Triangulation Language) format used for rapid prototyping in computer aided manufacturing.

2.2   Restoration

The two main tasks for restoration are to fix damaged areas and arrange the parts in the correct position and alignment. In previous work, Avanzini et al. [2] restored Pan flute damaged pipes by using cylinders generated from measurement. In our case, a difficulty is that the trumpet has non-uniform radius and curvature in 3D space. Hole filling for 3D scanning is a well studied field. Centil et al. [5] introduced a method to interpolate an implicit function obtained from a Poisson reconstruction which preserves the input mesh and the boundary curves. Liepa [11] proposed a procedure to interpolate the shape and density of the surrounding mesh to fill gaps. Both approaches achieve good performance in hole filling. But for our instrument model, severely damaged areas should not preserve boundaries. Example-based 3D scan completion [13] provides a high quality method to fill interior and large gap areas with the support of a dataset which contains many complete and similar objects. Dai et al. [8] proposes to complete the shape through a neural network classifier and a U-Net shape 3D-encoder-predictor through a well trained neural network. One challenge to apply these algorithms to our model is that we don't have a large dataset, and further, the arrangement of parts is not considered.

Our restoration approach combines domain knowledge from archaeologists with 3D geometric analysis to find an estimation of its shape. A core assumption from archaeologists is the ordering of the eight broken parts, as labeled in Fig. 2. Observation from archaeologists on less damaged parts also tells us that the trumpet has a curved cylinder-like shape with elliptical cross-section and changing radius. Based on these insights, we developed a computational approach to automatically determine parameters of the elliptical cross-sections, as well as to estimate a central line that will aid in global alignment of the parts. Our pipeline (see Fig. 3) first estimates the central line of each part and performs part alignment. We then filter out less damaged areas and apply ellipse fittings. The final step is to reconstruct the complete instrument from the fitting result.

Estimate Central Line. We propose a computational method to align the individual parts into the global instrument shape. We compute an alignment based on estimating the central line of each individual part, assuming the instrument's central line lies on a plane.

To get the central line for the instrument we used an iterative algorithm. We first place all mesh parts coarsely along the x-axis (see Fig. 4). We then initialize k_i parallel cutting planes $P_j^{(i)}, j \in [1, k_i]$ (normal $(1, 0, 0)$) evenly spaced along the x-axis. Each cross-section is then given by $\psi_{ij} = \left\{ P_j^{(i)} \cap M_i \right\}$, where $M_i, i \in [1, 8]$ is the ith mesh part. Then Update ψ_{ij} by rotating them to XY plane, we simplified a 3D ellipse fitting to a 2D ellipse fitting problem. In 2D an ellipse can be expressed in general conic form

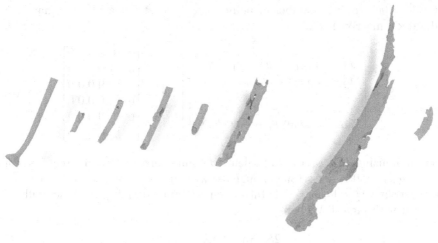

Part 1   Part 2 Part 3   Part 4   Part 5   Part 6   Part 7   Part 8

Fig. 2. Eight parts we get out of 3D scanning. From left to right are our part one to eight.

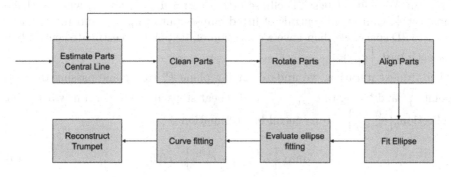

Fig. 3. Our restoration pipeline

Fig. 4. All parts placed in order along x-axis.

$$D(X,a) = X \cdot \mathbf{a} = 0 \tag{1}$$

for $a_1^2 - 4a_0a_2 < 0$. Here, coefficient vector $\mathbf{a} = [a_0, a_1, a_2, a_3, a_4, a_5]^T$, and $X = [x^2, xy, y^2, x, y, 1]$. Then we need to minimize

$$\Gamma(a, \psi_{ij}) = \sum^{p \in \psi_{ij}} [D([p_x^2, p_xp_y, p_y^2, p_x, p_y, 1], \mathbf{a})]^2 \tag{2}$$

Let $n^{(i)} = |\psi_{ij}|$ be the number of points in ψ_{ij}, construct a $n^{(i)} \times 6$ matrix S and a 6×6 matrix A

$$S = \begin{bmatrix} x_1^2 & x_1y_1 & y_1^2 & x_1 & y_1 & 1 \\ x_2^2 & x_2y_2 & y_2^2 & x_2 & y_2 & 1 \\ \vdots & \vdots & \vdots & \vdots & \vdots & \vdots \\ x_{n^{(i)}}^2 & x_{n^{(i)}}y_{n^{(i)}} & y_{n^{(i)}}^2 & x_{n^{(i)}} & y_{n^{(i)}} & 1 \end{bmatrix}, A = \begin{bmatrix} 0 & 0 & 2 & 0 & 0 & 0 \\ 0 & -1 & 0 & 0 & 0 & 0 \\ 2 & 0 & 0 & 0 & 0 & 0 \\ 0 & 0 & 0 & 0 & 0 & 0 \\ 0 & 0 & 0 & 0 & 0 & 0 \\ 0 & 0 & 0 & 0 & 0 & 0 \end{bmatrix} \tag{3}$$

Then minimizing $\Gamma(a, \psi_{ij})$ is equivalent to minimizing $\|Sa\|^2$. The requirement of $a_1^2 - 4a_0a_2 < 0$ is not strong enough, so without loss of generality we can set the constraint $a_1^2 - 4a_0a_2 = -1$. Introducing Lagrange multiplier λ, we will get a best fit with largest λ where:

$$2S^TSa - 2\lambda Aa = 0 \\ \mathbf{a}^TAa = 1 \tag{4}$$

Transformed to $\frac{1}{\lambda}\mathbf{a} = (S^TS)^{-1}Aa$, this can be solved as a standard eigenvalue problem. We will get best 2D ellipse fitting vector $a_{min,ij}$ for ψ_{ij} when we have smallest $\frac{1}{\lambda}$. Collect all centrals of fitted ellipses out of $a_{min,ij}$ and rotate them back to 3D space, we then have a collection of 3D points to estimate central line for each part $\left\{c_j^{(i)}\right\}$.

Then in next iteration, we update cutting plane P_j^i to a plane passing through point $c_j^{(i)}$ and facing to $c_{j+1}^{(i)} - c_j^{(i)}$ and repeat steps above to get a new 3D point collection $\left\{c_{new,j}^{(i)}\right\}$. Stop central line estimation if

$$\max\left\{\|c_{new,j}^{(i)} - c_j^{(i)}\|\right\} \leq 0.5 \tag{5}$$

Otherwise let $c_j^{(i)} \leftarrow c_{new,j}^{(i)}$ and repeat this procedure.

We approximate our central lines for each part as $C_i = \left\{c_{new,j}^{(i)}\right\}$. In our experiment, three iterations is enough to give a reliable central line estimation (Fig. 5).

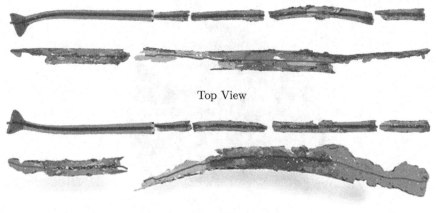

Top View

Front View

Fig. 5. Parts with estimated central lines (red) (Color figure online)

Clean Parts. 3D scanning is intended to scan the exterior surface area for each part. However, for severely damaged parts, the gaps expose interior surfaces during 3D scanning as well (yellow areas in Fig. 6). The difficulty is that the interior surfaces have a slightly smaller radius due to the thickness of the material, which leads to offsets in the ellipse fitting routine. We take an additional step to clean our meshes. For any triangle face f_n in M_i with centroid c_n, we define a condition

$$c_n \cdot \operatorname*{argmin}_{p \in C_i}(c_n - p)^2 > 0 \tag{6}$$

If (6) stands, then face f_n belongs to the interior surface and is neglected. After removal of interior triangles for M_i, we filter out the region with the largest number of connected triangles through a flood-fill algorithm. We update our M_i to these cleaned parts and run the central line estimation to get our new C_i for each part.

Rotate Parts. Our part alignment approach consists of two steps: rotate parts to the same plane and align parts in 2D. In the rotation step, given an estimation of part's central line $C_i = \left\{ c_j^{(i)} = (c_{jx}^{(i)}, c_{jy}^{(i)}, c_{jz}^{(i)}), j \in [1, k_i] \right\}$, we want to find a best fit plane. We define a plane $b_0 x + b_1 y + b_2 z + b_3 = 0$ and denote $Q = (\frac{b_0}{b_2}, \frac{b_1}{b_2}, \frac{b_3}{b_2})^T$, $P_j = (c_{jx}^{(i)}, c_{jy}^{(i)}, 1)$. Then to find best fitting plane we minimize:

$$E(Q) = \sum_{j}^{k_i} (c_{jz}^{(i)} - P_j Q)^2 \tag{7}$$

Fig. 6. Interior surfaces are sometimes included in the 3D scan (yellow) when visible through gaps. This affects our fitting and needs to be removed. (Color figure online)

Let

$$Y = \begin{pmatrix} c_{1z}^{(i)} \\ c_{2z}^{(i)} \\ \vdots \\ c_{k_i z}^{(i)} \end{pmatrix}, X = \begin{pmatrix} c_{1x}^{(i)} & c_{1y}^{(i)} & 1 \\ c_{2x}^{(i)} & c_{2y}^{(i)} & 1 \\ & \vdots & \\ c_{k_i x}^{(i)} & c_{k_i y}^{(i)} & 1 \end{pmatrix} \tag{8}$$

For non-negative and convex function $E(Q)$, its minimum value locate at $\nabla E(Q) = [0,0,0]^T$. Then we get when $Q = (X^T X)^{-1} X^T Y$, we have minimum $E(Q)$. This Q will give us the best fit plane for central point samples.

After getting best fitting plane with normal vectors n_i for $C_i, i \in [1,8]$, we rotate mesh part $j \in [2,8]$ along axis $n_j \times n_1$ about angle $\arccos(n_j \cdot n_1)$ to make all parts lie on the same plane with part one. Then our alignment problem simplified to rotate mesh parts one the same plane.

Align Parts. After placing all parts on the same plane, our next step is to align them in order. We start at estimating each part starting and ending orientation. Orientation at any central line point $c_j^{(i)}$ is $c_{j+1}^{(i)} - c_j^{(i)}$ approximately. Then we apply Kriging algorithm [12], a Gaussian process regression to estimate orientation at starting point $c_1^{(i)}$ and ending point $c_{k_i}^{(i)}$. Denote the orientation at these two points as $o_1^{(i)}, o_{k_i}^{(i)}$. Once we get an estimation of parts orientations, for each M_i we use n_1 as rotation axis and rotate about $\arccos(o_1^{(i)} \cdot o_{k_i}^{(i-1)})$. Then translate it about $-c_1^{(j)} + c_{k_i}^{(j-1)}$ to align parts in order.

We call these new transformed mesh parts as M_i^* and all mesh parts together as M^*.

Fit Ellipse Along Central Line. After alignment of all parts, part i central point sample list will be transformed to C_i^*. Merge all these list in order we will get a new list C^*, which is a collection of points on an estimated central line for the entire instrument. With these points we can define $k*$ planes $\rho = \{P_1^*, P_2^*, ..., P_{k*}^*\}$, which are orthogonal to estimated central line and spaced evenly on it. Their intersections with mesh M^* will give us a collection of points collection: $\{\{P \cap M^*\} | P \in \rho\}$. Now we apply our 3D ellipse fitting algorithm to each points collection $\{P \cap M^*\}$, it will return us an ellipse central point collection $\lambda = \{(c_{xi}^*, c_{yi}^*, c_{zi}^*) | i \in [1, k*], i \in \mathbb{Z}\}$, a collection of semi-major axes $\mu = \{a_i^* | i \in [1, k*], i \in \mathbb{Z}\}$ and a collection of semi-minor axes $\nu = \{b_i^* | i \in [1, k*], i \in \mathbb{Z}\}$.

Evaluate Fitting. Considering that severely damaged areas will bring us biased ellipse fitting, we need to filter out them. An evaluation of fitting quality is required here. For cutting plane P_i^*, we know its intersection with mesh $\{P_i^* \cap M^*\}$ and its fitting ellipse is centered at $(c_{xi}^*, c_{yi}^*, c_{zi}^*)$ with semi-major axis a_i^* and semi-minor axis b_i^*. Let $d(p, (c_{xi}^*, c_{yi}^*, c_{zi}^*), a_i^*, b_i^*)$ be the shortest euclidean distance between point p to this fitting ellipse. We measure fitting quality through

$$Q(P_i^*) = \frac{\sum^{p \in \{P_i^* \cap M^*\}} d(p, (c_{xi}^*, c_{yi}^*, c_{zi}^*), a_i^*, b_i^*)}{|\{P_i^* \cap M^*\}|} \qquad (9)$$

Computing $d(p, (c_{xi}^*, c_{yi}^*, c_{zi}^*), a_i^*, b_i^*)$ in 3D space is costly, but we can simplify it if transformed to 2D. Apply the same transformation which transforms ellipse to XY plane at origin with semi-major axis lay on X axis to both point and ellipse. Point p will be transformed to p^*. Because the symmetry of ellipse, we can transform point p^* to p' which is in the first quadrant by changing all its coordinate sign to positive, then solve for $t \in [-(b_i^*)^2, \infty]$ in

$$\left(\frac{a_i^* p_x'}{t + (a_i^*)^2}\right)^2 + \left(\frac{b_i^* p_y'}{t + (b_i^*)^2}\right)^2 - 1 = 0 \qquad (10)$$

This will give us a point $(\frac{(a_i^*)^2 p_x'}{t + (a_i^*)^2}, \frac{(b_i^*)^2 p_y'}{t + (b_i^*)^2})$ on the ellipse whose distance to p' equals the shortest euclidean distance between $p*$ projection point on XY plane and the ellipse. This quartic equation can get an approximation root using iterative Newton method. To transform back to 3D space, we take p^*'s Z coordinate into consideration and compute Euclidean distance between p^* and closest point on ellipse, this is the shortest distance between p and ellipse in 3D space.

In the last step in this stage, for any plane P_i^*, if $Q(P_i^*) > 2.0$ we will filter out all corresponding ellipse fitting results in λ, μ, ν.

Curve Fitting. For every collection $\beta \in \{\mu, \nu\}$, we construct pairs $(c_{xi}^*, \beta_i), i \in [1, b], i \in \mathbb{Z}$, define a nonlinear model

$$H(x, (t_0, t_1, t_2)) = t_0 + t_1(x) + t_2(x)^2 \qquad (11)$$

and define a function to minimize

$$G((t_0, t_1, t_2)) = \sum_i^{i \in [1,k^*]} [\beta_i - H(c_{xi}^*, (t_0, t_1, t_2))]^2 \tag{12}$$

We need to solve $\operatorname{argmin}_{(t_0, t_1, t_2)} G((t_0, t_1, t_2))$. This is a curve fitting problem, where we apply the Levenberg–Marquardt algorithm.

Once we get a curve fitting minimized $G((t_0, t_1, t_2))$, we will generate a corresponding function $F(t), \mathbb{R} \to \mathbb{R}, t \in [\min(\{c_{xi}^*\}), \max(\{c_{xi}^*\})]$ to represent that fitting. For the central line, we apply the same curve fitting for each coordinate separately and combine the fitting result, giving $F_{central}(t), \mathbb{R} \to \mathbb{R}^3$ in the end. The fitting result for semi-major and semi-minor axes is plotted in Fig. 7.

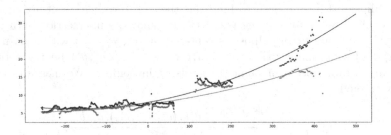

Fig. 7. Semi-major axis and semi-minor axis fitting

Reconstruct Trumpet. After curve fitting, for parts 2 to 7 we acquire an explicit function $F_{central}(t), \mathbb{R} \to \mathbb{R}^3$ which gives us an estimation of their central line. $F_{major}(t), \mathbb{R} \to \mathbb{R}$ and $F_{minor}(t), \mathbb{R} \to \mathbb{R}$ represent an estimation of the semi-major and semi-minor axes of the corresponding fitted ellipse. Then for given $t \in [t_s, t_e]$, the instrument central line length can be computed as

$$L = \int_{t_s}^{t_e} \|F'_{central}(t)\| dt \tag{13}$$

At here we pick the t value where our have $F_{central}(t)_x = C_{x1}^*$ as t_s, and approximate central line length L on model. Then we can solve out our t_e by using Eq. 13.

Let t_i step through $[t_s, t_e]$ with constant interval t_c and $i \in [0, \frac{t_e - t_s}{t_c}]$. For every t_i, we first create ellipse points collection on XY plane.

$$\epsilon_i = \{(F_{major}(t_i) \cos(\theta), F_{minor}(t_i) \sin(\theta), 0) | \theta \in [0, 2\pi)\} \tag{14}$$

Let $D_i = normalize(F_{central}(t_{i+1}) - F_{central}(t_i))$, apply rotation to ϵ_i along axis $[0, 0, 1] \times D_i$ about angle $\arccos([0, 0, 1] \cdot D_i)$ and continue with translation $F_{central}(t)$, we will get ϵ_i^*. Construct triangles between ϵ_i^* and ϵ_{i+1}^* with $i \in [0, \frac{t_e - t_s}{t_c} - 1]$ and turn all triangles to mesh N^*, we will have an estimation of instrument part 2–7 exterior.

Our last step is to turn meshes with only exterior area to watertight meshes. We bring in Autodesk Meshmixer® to do rest job. Thickness of instrument can be measured at severe damaged area where both interior and exterior area are scanned and distance between them will give us an approximate thickness 1.2 mm. As for Part 1, it is preserved pretty well so we can use its 3D scanned mesh exterior as for final mesh generation directly. So we select exterior surface of M_1^* and N_* and applied 'offset' operation about '-1.2 mm' to generate watertight meshes. Generated mesh with aligned raw parts drawn at Fig. 8.

3   Sound Simulation

Having estimated the 3D model of the recomposed instrument, the aim of this section is to describe and simulate the set of tones that a musical instrument with that geometry can produce. The mouthpiece, very similar to that of modern trumpets, trombones and horns, reveals that the Voghenza instrument certainly belongs to the brass family. The modalities of sound generation of these instruments, that is how the acoustic waves are generated and propagate inside the cavity, are widely described in literature (e.g. [9]). From an acoustic point of view, brass instruments are generally divided in three parts: a mouthpiece, a cylindrical section, and a conical section ending with a more or less flared bell. The pitched sound is first generated by the lips that, leaning to the mouthpiece, are vibrated by the air emitted by the musician's respiratory system. The acoustic waves produced by the vibrating lips propagates through the cylindrical part, the length of which can be modified in many brass instruments by means of holes (as in the cornetto), valves (as in the trumpet) or a sliding mechanism (as in the trombone). Finally, the waves reach the ending flared section, where part of the acoustic energy is radiated to the outside the instrument and part is reflected inside the bore.

To what we can observe from the remains, the Voghenza instrument has no holes, valves or sliding parts, therefore the fundamental frequency of the tones that can be produced depend largely by the peaks of the acoustic impedance of the bore. This impedance can be estimated analytically, starting from the well known wave equation and solving it in the case of a wave propagating in a bore with an increasing diameter. The solution lets to the following Eq. [6] that allows the estimation of the frequencies f_n corresponding to a local maximum of the acoustic impedance:

$$f_n = \frac{c}{2(l + X_i)} \left[n - \frac{1 - \nu}{2} \right] \tag{15}$$

where c is the sound speed propagation, l is the length of the cylindrical part, X_i is the length of the flared part, ν is a coefficient related to the shape of the flared part, and n is an integer number. To estimate the ν coefficient, the flared part is usually modeled by a Bessel function ([6,9]). In particular, being x the length of the central axis from the mouthpiece to a specific point of the bore, the radius of the bore is assumed to vary as a function of x according to the following equation:

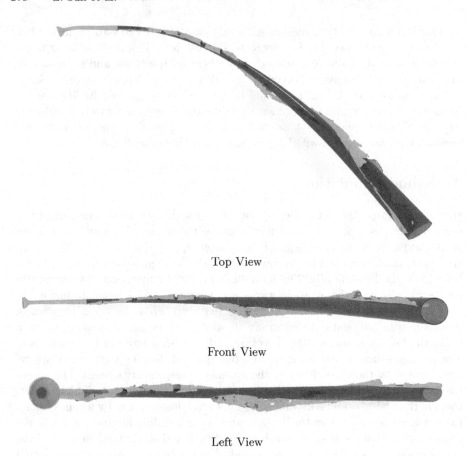

Top View

Front View

Left View

Fig. 8. Aligned trumpet parts from 3D scanning(green) and restored trumpet (blue) (Color figure online)

$$r(x) = \frac{b}{(x_a - x)^\nu} \tag{16}$$

where x_a is the distance between the end of the bore and the asymptote abscissa, b is a scale constant, and ν is a parameter that takes into account how rapidly the radius increases. The three unknown parameters of Eq. 16 were estimated fitting the geometry of the bore, as reconstructed in Sect. 2.2. Fitting the data obtained from the reconstructed model in a least-square sense ($R^2 = 0.91$, $df = 185$), we obtained the following values: $x_a = 1.3$, $b = 1000$, $\nu = 0.71$. Then, the frequencies of the natural resonance of the instrument ware estimated from Eq. 15 (see Table 1). Finally, a sample of these sounds[1] were generated by a physically-informed algorithm based on a waveguide model [7].

---

[1] Examples of the sounds can be listen at http://dei.unipd.it/~roda/brass.

Table 1. Natural resonant frequencies estimated by the geometry of the reconstructed 3D model of the instrument.

n	freq.[Hz]
1	123
2	266
3	409
4	553
5	696
6	839
7	982
8	1126
9	1269
10	1412

4   Conclusions

The 3D model of an ancient brass instrument was reconstructed starting from several partially damaged archaeological remains hosted in the Civic Museum of Belriguardo (Italy). The pieces were first digitized by means of a structured light system, then virtually restored and recomposed applying a on-purpose developed algorithm. Finally, some sounds coherent with the geometry of the reconstructed model were simulated using a physically-based synthesis approach. The results showed in this paper have several limitations that will be faced with further research and experimental work.

In restoration step, we assemble parts together based on estimated central line orientation at part ends and the approximation error of it in severely damaged area cannot neglect. The main reason of it is that least square based ellipse fitting don't perform very well in these areas. We can improve our restoration if change to a better ellipse fitting algorithm. Furthermore, for parts with nearly straight central lines, we neglected their rotation along central lines.

As concern the generated sounds, the Eq. 15 is only an approximated solution of the wave equation in an horn shaped bore and the approximation error increases for lower frequencies. We are going to evaluate this errors comparing the results with the ones obtained two methodologies: a) following a numerical approach based on the Finite Element Method; b) estimating the acoustic impedance of the bore by means of experimental measurements on a printed copy of the reconstructed model. Moreover, the sound simulation neglects at the moment the acoustic coupling with the player's mouth and all the aspects related to music performance, such as vibrato or amplitude envelope [3,4].

References

1. Avanzini, F., et al.: Virtual reconstruction of an ancient greek pan flute. In: Proceedings International Conference Sound and Music Computing (SMC 2016), pp. 41–46 (2016)
2. Avanzini, F., et al.: Archaeology and virtual acoustics. a pan flute from ancient Egypt. In: Proceedings of the 12th International Conference on Sound and Music Computing, pp. 31–36
3. Canazza, S., De Poli, G., Rodà, A.: Caro 2.0: an interactive system for expressive music rendering. Adv. Hum. Comput. Interact. **2015**, 1–13 (2015). https://doi.org/10.1155/2015/850474
4. Carnovalini, F., Roda, A.: A multilayered approach to automatic music generation and expressive performance, pp. 41–48 (2019). https://doi.org/10.1109/MMRP.2019.8665367
5. Centin, M., Pezzotti, N., Signoroni, A.: Poisson-driven seamless completion of triangular meshes. Comput. Aided Geometric Des. **35**, 42–55 (2015)
6. Chaigne, A., Kergomard, J.: Acoustics of Musical Instruments. Springer, New York (2016). https://doi.org/10.1007/978-1-4939-3679-3
7. Cook, P.: Tbone: an interactive waveguide brass instrument synthesis workbench for the NeXT machine. In: Proceedings International Computer Music Conference, pp. 297–299 (1991)
8. Dai, A., Ruizhongtai Qi, C., Nießner, M.: Shape completion using 3D-encoder-predictor CNNS and shape synthesis. In: Proceedings of the IEEE Conference on Computer Vision and Pattern Recognition, pp. 5868–5877 (2017)
9. Fletcher, N.H., Rossing, T.D.: The Physics of Musical Instruments. Springer, New York (2012). https://doi.org/10.1007/978-0-387-21603-4
10. Laga, H., Guo, Y., Tabia, H., Fisher, R.B., Bennamoun, M.: 3D Shape Analysis: Fundamentals, Theory and Applications. Wiley, Hoboken (2018)
11. Liepa, P.: Filling holes in meshes. In: Proceedings of the 2003 Eurographics/ACM SIGGRAPH Symposium on Geometry Processing, pp. 200–205 (2003)
12. Metheron, G.: Theory of regionalized variables and its applications. Cah. Centre Morrphol. Math. **5**, 211 (1971)
13. Pauly, M., Mitra, N.J., Giesen, J., Gross, M.H., Guibas, L.J.: Example-based 3D scan completion. In: Symposium on Geometry Processing, pp. 23–32 (2005)
14. Tomlinson, G.: Musicology, anthropology, history. In: The Cultural Study of Music, pp. 81–94. Routledge (2012)
15. Umetani, N., Panotopoulou, A., Schmidt, R., Whiting, E.: Printone: interactive resonance simulation for free-form print-wind instrument design. ACM Trans. Graph. **35**(6), 1–14 (2016). https://doi.org/10.1145/2980179.2980250. http://dl.acm.org/citation.cfm?doid=2980179.2980250

"Talking" Triples to Museum Chatbots

Savvas Varitimiadis[1], Konstantinos Kotis[1] , Dimitris Spiliotopoulos[2(✉)] ,
Costas Vassilakis[2] , and Dionisis Margaris[3]

[1] Department of Cultural Technology and Communication, i-Lab, University of the Aegean,
Mytilene, Greece
`{svaritimiadis,kotis}@aegean.gr`
[2] Department of Informatics and Telecommunications, University of the Peloponnese,
Tripoli, Greece
`{dspiliot,costas}@uop.gr`
[3] Department of Informatics and Telecommunications, University of Athens, Athens, Greece
`margaris@di.uoa.gr`

Abstract. The paper presents recent work on the design and development of AI
chatbots for museums using Knowledge Graphs (KGs). The utilization of KGs as
a key technology for implementing chatbots raises not only issues related to the
representation and structuring of exhibits' knowledge in suitable formalism and
models, but also issues related to the translation of natural language dialogues to
and from the selected technology for the formal representation and structuring of
information and knowledge. Moreover, such a translation must be as transparent
as possible to visitors, towards a realistic human-like question-answering process.
The paper reviews and evaluates a number of recent approaches for the use of
KGs in developing AI chatbots, as well as key tools that provide solutions for
natural language translation and the querying of Knowledge Bases and Linked
Open Data sources. This evaluation aims to provide answers to issues that are
identified within the proposed MuBot approach for designing and implementing
AI chatbots for museums. The paper also presents Cretan MuBot, the first experimental KG/Ontology-based AI chatbot of the MuBot Platform, which is under
development in the Heracleum Archaeological Museum.

Keywords: Knowledge Graphs · RDF triples · NLP · Chatbots · Museums

1 Introduction

The paper presents recent work on the design and development of AI chatbots for
museums using KGs. A KG mainly describes real world entities and their interrelations, organized in a directed graph [1, 2]. This new interactive technological trend for
museums has been driven by recent observations and studies reporting that museum
visitors are not impressed in the long-run by simple virtual guided tours or tours that
use high-tech technological applications such as Augmented, Virtual and Mixed Realities (AR/VR/MR), but they are interested in gaining knowledge about the exhibits in a
human-like, interactive and conversational manner [3, 4]. Furthermore, in comparison

© Springer Nature Switzerland AG 2020
M. Rauterberg (Ed.): HCII 2020, LNCS 12215, pp. 281–299, 2020.
https://doi.org/10.1007/978-3-030-50267-6_22

with Machine Learning (ML) systems, KGs and their integration to AI chatbots in every domain provides to the AI chatbots better rational dialogues that could eventually lead to more meaningful AI applications. ML focuses on prediction accuracy and scoring learning algorithms. Common sense knowledge or reasoning is out-of-scope of ML systems and for this drawback ML systems are lacking in credibility [5–7]. However, the combination of KGs and ML is an intriguing future research work.

In a museum visiting experience, visitors must be able to chat with 'smart' exhibits, ask questions in natural forms (through text or voice) and receive audible or written answers. The utilization of KGs as a key technology for implementing chatbots in this setting raises not only issues related to the representation and structuring of exhibits' knowledge in suitable formalism and models, but also issues related to the translation of natural language dialogues to and from the selected technology for the formal representation and structuring of information and knowledge [8]. Moreover, such a translation must be as transparent as possible to visitors, towards a realistic human-like question-answering process [4].

For chatbot framework/application to be effective and useful for the museum or any other domain, it must combine recent AI technological advances (Semantic Web, Linked Open Data, Knowledge Graphs, Natural Language Processing/Generation, Machine Learning) with museum needs and purposes. Natural Language Processing (NLP) and Natural Language Generation (NLG) techniques enable computers to segment, assign meaning, and analyze human communication in its natural forms and to give the users the ability to chat with the smart exhibits in a natural way [9, 10].

A museum chatbot must fulfill several specific requirements and characteristics. It must be simple, informative, accurate and precise. It must have strong conversational skills and provide meaningful content. It may be entertaining and should be able to engage the audience in the whole experience/tour duration. It may be positive if there is a capability by the chatbot to provoke users to find and learn more, but at the same time to be sensitive and understanding on human emotions [11–13].

Engineers must be able to configure the chatbot for 'talking' in human-like manner, and at the same time 'taking' in triples i.e., to retrieve and present structured knowledge utilizing Resource Description Framework (RDF) triple stores and the Linked Open Data (LOD) cloud. Furthermore, it must be available anytime, have an attractive interface and to be easy to use/interact with [11–13]. RDF and Web Ontology Language (OWL) are the two basic descriptive Semantic Web technologies that play a crucial role in the formal representation and structuring of data, information and knowledge [14].

The presented work aims to address challenges related to the following questions:

1. How can museum visitors 'talk' to museum exhibits in the most natural way, to learn about them?
2. How can human-exhibit dialogues be used for the user to retrieve the exhibit knowledge about themselves and about other related/connected exhibits, utilizing linked and open datasets?
3. What is the most appropriate technological trend to use for the most efficient conversation between visitors and 'smart' exhibits?

In relation to the above questions, the contribution of this paper is threefold:

1. To introduce the novel concept and interactive technological trend of AI chatbots for museums, as an alternative to the high-tech technological AR/VR/MR applications, towards supporting the learning of knowledge about their exhibits in a human-like, interactive and conversational manner,
2. To review the approaches and necessary tools for KG/Ontology-based AI chatbots and Query/Answering (QA) systems, as an alternative candidate to the ones based on ML techniques (e.g. Dialogflow),
3. To introduce a novel KG-based framework for chatbot-human interaction in a smart museum environment and the MuBot approach to the design, implementation and evaluation of such a framework.

The rest of the paper is structured as follows: Sect. 2 presents the related work concerning the development and use of AI chatbots and QA systems based on KGs and/or ontologies. Also, this section provides a critical description of key tools for NLP/NLG and KGs/Ontologies transformation/translation. Section 3 presents the MuBot approach, the main purpose, the special features, and the architectural design. In Sect. 4, the Cretan MuBot is presented, the first experimental chatbot of the MuBot approach, as an evaluation case study in the Heracleum Archaeological Museum. Section 5 discusses future steps in the development of the MuBot approach and concludes the paper.

2 Related Work

In this section, selected related approaches to AI chatbots/QA systems that are based on KGs and/or ontologies, as well as selected research and commercial tools for NLP/NLG and KGs/Ontologies transformation/translation, are presented. The aim of our work is to evaluate all these approaches and tools for their usability and effectiveness, in the context of the proposed MuBot approach.

2.1 Related Approaches to AI Chatbots/QA Systems Based on KGs and/or Ontologies

KGs are considered as a new AI technological trend that originates to the basic principles of the Semantic Web and the construction of Knowledge Bases (KBs). As KGs are in an evolution process, several definitions can be found [1, 2]. A definition quoted from recent literature is: "A knowledge graph (i) mainly describes real world entities and their interrelations, organized in a directed graph, (ii) defines possible classes and relations of entities in a schema, (iii) allows for potentially interrelating arbitrary entities with each other and (iv) covers various topical domains" [15].

The term KG was re-introduced as such at 2012 by Google, which has developed the famous Google's Knowledge Graph [16]. The most famous open and commercial KGs are Freebase, Wikidata, DBpedia, Yago, Google's Knowledge Graph Yahoo!'s Knowledge Graph, Microsoft's Satori and Facebook's Entities Graph [15]. KGs have many advantages and can be used for a variety of tasks such as relationship prediction systems, search engines and question/answering agents [2]. KGs are flexible, can be easily updated and related to new data in a smart way, contain semantic information, rely on ontologies and may be queried in natural language [2, 16]. KGs may also be used in synergy with other available AI-driven technologies such as NLP, NLG, OWL and RDF datasets [2]. KGs have the ability to respond to NLG questions through database query languages. AI chatbots and QA systems can exploit this new opportunity of KGs and become 'smarter' by gaining unlimited access to stored and structured knowledge [9].

There are many proposed approaches to the recent bibliography that introduce KGs to AI chatbots and QA systems. Hallili [10] has proposed the SynchroBot, a dialog system that a) has connectivity to robust and flexible KBs and KGs for extracting information, and b) could use NLP tools to interpret user's questions and NLG techniques to provide proper answers. This ability differs from other QA systems which are either focusing in providing a logical conversation ability to the users, without caring for the richness of their knowledge source, or, on the other hand, can only provide accurate answers without any conversation skills.

OntBot was an earlier ontology-based chatbot that relied on the approach proposed by Hallili [17]. OntBot used the Protégé platform [18] in order to develop an ontology template which gathers knowledge from e-commerce website APIs. Users can place their questions to a dialog manager that uses NLP such as Facebook Wit.Ai. The dialog manager connects to the ontology template with Python language, searches the KBs and KGs and provides the proper answer to the user with the help of NLG techniques from the dialog manager [19].

Another similar approach was implemented for the healthcare domain and the goal was to produce a framework that can assist patients by providing them an AI chatbot with strong conversational skills and a robust Knowledge Base source [20, 21].

A clear statement of KGs as a part of AI chatbot is provided at the proposed approach of 'GRANK.AI.' KGs platform. GRAKN.AI is described as a KG database that uses machine reasoning to simplify data processing for AI Chatbots and other applications. Question querying is done through Graql, a knowledge-oriented graph query language for retrieving information, and for performing graph analytics and automated reasoning. The proposed approach is using DialogFlow with all its NLP, NLG, ML components, as the dialogue manager component. DialogFlow is connected to GRAKN.AI KGs and searches for the proper answer to the user's question [9]. It is a good example approach for demonstrating the combination of KGs and ML technologies.

Summarizing, the integration of KGs to AI Chatbots and Q/A systems is a task that can boost the AI chatbots effectiveness. More crucial though is the development and evaluation of NLP/NLG components that could become a reliable interpreter of natural language input or output.

2.2 Tools for NLP/NLG and KGs/Ontologies Translation

The tools that are presented and reviewed in this paper are covering key parts of the proposed approach and focus on the following questions:

1. How to recognize the entities and their relationships in a statement?
2. How to translate natural language text to a KG/ontology?

3. How to translate natural language questions to SPARQL queries?
4. How to translate RDF triples (returned from the SPARQL query) to natural language text?

Name Entity Recognition

Word Sense Disambiguation (WSD) and Name Entity Recognition (NER) for the learning of ontologies from text, are difficult tasks to accomplish and automate. Several tools were developed that can recognize the entities and the classes of given user statements in natural language.

The NLP group at Stanford University developed the Stanford Named Entity Recognition (NER), a Java-based tool used for information extraction from users' text. NER tries to find and classify atomic entities in text into predefined categories such as the names of persons, organizations, locations, expressions of times, quantities, monetary values, percentages, etc. [22]. An online demo is published at http://nlp.stanford.edu:8080/ner/. Using the example expression "Snake Goddess figurine was found at Knossos palace in Crete" as input to the tool, entity *"Location"* for the words "Knossos, Crete" and *"Organization"* for the words "Snake Goddess" respectively, were recognized.

A more advanced tool for parsing plain text is Stanford CoreNLP which provides a set of grammatical analysis NLP tools developed by Stanford NLP group, such as the part-of-speech (POS) tagger, the named entity recognizer (NER), the parser, the open information extraction tool (OPENIE) and others [23, 24]. An online demo of the CoreNLP tool is found at http://corenlp.run/. The tool was evaluated with the expression "Snake Goddess figurine was found at Knossos Palace, in Crete" and successfully returned a set of outputs by every integrated subtool i.e., NER tool recognized the entities as described above, while OPENIE analyzed and recognized the relationships between them.

Another tool is Babelfy which implements a graph-based approach to Name Entity Recognition and Linking, and WSD, based on a light identification of the possible meanings presented in graphical semantic interpretations. Babelfy is demonstrated in an online tool at http://babelfy.org/. When the phrase "Snake Goddess figurine was found at Knossos palace in Crete" was used as input, the tool successfully recognized the entities and the concepts, searched for them to LOD cloud sources such as Wikipedia, Babelnet and DBpedia, and fetched the definitions of every entity organized in a graph representation [25].

Natural Language Text to KGs/Ontologies

Protégé is the most popular and widely used free software for easily building and maintaining ontologies for any domain. Users can edit domain ontologies, share their ontology to others, create a knowledge graph representation of them, connect them with external sources, design and implement SPARQL queries, export the developed ontologies in several formats such as RDF/XML, RDF/OWL and others [18]. Protégé is also a Web service for registered users at https://webprotege.stanford.edu [26]. Protégé has been used in our use case scenario to manually create the Cretan MuBot evaluation knowledge base (schema and museum data). The output is available at https://github.com/KotisK/muBotOnto-example. Protégé is providing excellent services in manually building a knowledge base but lacks automation in the creation of ontology schemas from user input statements.

FRED is a tool for automatically producing RDF/OWL ontologies and linked data from natural language sentences. It is implemented in Python and is available as Representational state transfer (REST) service [27] and as a Python library suite. FRED is using a big set of established NLP components to produce RDF/OWL ontologies and knowledge graphs. The provided results are enriched with NER and WSD techniques [28]. FRED tool is available online at http://wit.istc.cnr.it/stlab-tools/fred/demo/ and was used to produce RDF/OWL ontology and a KG for the expression "Snake Goddess figurine was found at Knossos palace in Crete". The example output is included at https://github.com/KotisK/muBotOnto-example. The FRED tool provided an RDF ontology that has some basic similarities with our custom-made Protégé ontology, as entities, classes and properties are similarly recognized to both ontologies. FRED is using RDF triples that are only derived from DBpedia KB, while our Protégé ontology uses custom-made properties and entities. FRED tool is been used in several semantic web applications and will be considered as a component to the proposed MuBot approach.

Natural Language Text to SPARQL Queries
AutoSparql was developed by the Research Group Agile Knowledge Engineering and Semantic Web (AKSW) at University of Leipzig (http://aksw.org/Projects/AutoSPARQL.html). Its main goal is to provide users an easy way to place questions to a knowledge base. Specifically, AutoSparql can convert a natural language question to a SPARQL query, which can then retrieve the answer from a given RDF triple store. The software uses the Query Tree Learner (QTL) algorithm which is described by its creators as a light-weight learning algorithm [29]. The QTL algorithm can use various NLP techniques for creating sophisticated semantic representations of the given questions. In addition, the system and the algorithm can be trained and become smarter in providing the proper SPARQL queries. Furthermore, the user can connect with open RDF resources such as DBpedia and others [29–31]. AutoSparql software is not active now but its code is available at https://github.com/AskNowQA/AutoSPARQL. During evaluation, runtime errors were reported at compile time. Future work includes fixing and testing the tool in order to be used as candidate component of the proposed MuBot approach.

FREyA software is an interactive natural language interface that is used for querying ontologies. FREyA uses syntactic parsing in combination with the ontology-based lookup in order to interpret the question of the user. FREyA is also able to use Linked Open Data such as DBpedia. In addition, the user gets further involved and trains the system as his choices are used in order to improve its performance over time [32, 33]. This strong involvement of the user in the training of the system is consider as a drawback, as the naivety of the user about certain complex issues of data modelling, without any assistance, may not lead to the best results [30]. FREyA is not fully active now but its code is available at https://github.com/danicadamljanovic/freya. The code is outdated (Sesame java framework has evolved to Eclipse RDF4J framework which requires further installation efforts, which are left for future work).

QUEPY is a python framework that can transform natural language questions to SPARQL queries. The transformation from natural language to SPARQL queries is done by using at first a special form of regular expressions and then using a convenient way to express semantic relations. The input question is parsed using a library called

REfO (Regular Expressions for Objects). The rest of the transformation is handled automatically with the use of the Natural Language ToolKit (NLTK), a python platform that is included in the QUEPY framework and other techniques, to finally produce RDF triples and SPARQL queries [34, 35]. The QUEPY demo is not fully developed and supported. The code and the documentation of the tool is found at https://quepy.readth edocs.io/en/latest/. The software needs significant effort in order to be installed and work properly.

In our future work we aim to reuse and proceed to any modifications to the abovementioned tools in order to make them functionable components of our approach.

SPARQL Query and RDF Triples to Natural Language
SPARQL2NL is a tool that was developed by the Agile Knowledge Engineering and Semantic Web (AKSW) research group at University of Leipzig (http://aksw.org/Pro jects/SPARQL2NL.html). The SPARQL2NL tool allows the verbalization of SPARQL queries by converting them into natural language. The tool uses LOD sources such as DBpedia and performs several improvements to the given results of the queries that help users to choose the suitable answer in a natural way, without getting involved with ontologies and SPARQL queries' syntax [29, 36]. The SPARQL2NL project is not active now but its code is available at https://github.com/AKSW/SPARQL2NL. The installation of SPARQL2NL software encountered the same compile errors as the AutoSparql software.

The Spartiqulator system provides a similar functionality as the SPARQL2NL tool. Its main scope is to verbalize SPARQL queries in order to create natural language expressions that are readable and understandable by the common user. The Spartiqulator system refers only to RDFa and RDFS sources and uses several NLG techniques for the verbalization of SPARQL queries to suitable answers for the users [37, 38]. There is an active online demo of the tool at https://aifb-ls3-kos.aifb.kit.edu/projects/spartiqul ator/. The tool has been tested with SPARQL queries from our Cretan MuBot use case scenario. For our example SPARQL query (*Where was Snake Goddess found?*), which can be found at https://github.com/KotisK/muBotOnto-example, Spartiqulator system provided the answer "*Found ats of snake goddess*". The given answer has obvious syntax and grammatical mistakes and also lacks the *location* property which is derived from http://dbpedia.org/ontology/ that is not supported by the Spartiqulator system. The same limitations were also noticed with other example SPARQL queries that have been used for testing the tool.

SPARQLtoUser is a tool that can produce a representation of a provided SPARQL query to the end-users. The tool supports multilingual input and refers to any domain. The tool tries not only to verbalize the query, but also to find a more schematic representation of it. The user can choose the SPARQL query that provides the most accurate answer. SPARQLtoUser code can be found at https://github.com/WDAqua/ SPARQL-toUser [39]. SPARQLtoUser tool is also used as a QA webservice available at http://www.wdaqua.eu/qa. The webservice is accepting input from the users in NLG and is providing them several possible answers along with their SPARQL queries, allowing them to select the most suitable one. It also provides a probability score to each answer, asking users to affirm it or not. The QA webservice refers and gets its answers from Wikidata, DBpedia, DBLP and OpenStreetMap KDs, but cannot understand all user's questions and answer them directly and in a sophisticated way. SPARQLtoUser tool returned *"no answer"* for our example query *"Where was Snake Goddess found at?"*. However, for the term *"Snake Goddess"* the tool returned the correspondent Wikipedia data entry.

Sparklis is a Semantic Web tool that helps users to explore SPARQL endpoints by guiding them in the interactive building of questions and answers, from simple ones to complex ones. There is an online tool at http://www.irisa.fr/LIS/ferre/sparklis/osparklis. html. Users can build a query without having any knowledge of the SPARQL language. Users can see the SPARQL query that has been created and get a proper answer [40, 41]. The tool has been evaluated with the questions from our Cretan MuBot use case. Unfortunately, due to the fact that the tool uses only profound SPARQL endpoints such as DBpedia, it could not provide proper answers. The user is not able to place a free question and must follow a guided structure [42]. The tool works well only if you shape a query such as "Give me an island in Greece?". The tool can retrieve the possible answers by providing all the islands in Greece. But in the case of questions such as "I want to find the most famous island in Greece?" the tool fails.

LD2NL is an open-source holistic NLG framework that facilitates the verbalization of the three key languages of the Semantic Web (RDF, OWL, and SPARQL) into NL. LD2NL framework builds upon the open source code of SPARQL2NL tool, which presented in a previous paragraph [43]. The LD2NL can generate either a single sentence or a summary of a given resource, rule, or query [44]. The LD2NL is an ongoing project that is not fully released as a portable application. Its code could be found at https://git hub.com/dice-group/LD2NL.

We aim to reuse and proceed to any modifications to the abovementioned tools in order to make them functionable components of the proposed MuBot approach.

3   The MuBot Approach

The architecture of the MuBot approach that is proposed in this paper relies on three main components:

- a Knowledge Base component that utilizes Semantic Web technology (RDF, SPARQL query language, OWL ontologies) for knowledge representation, linking, reasoning and querying,
- NLP component for interpreting users input from natural language to RDF/SPARQL,
- NLG component for creating the proper well-defined human-like answers.

The aim of the approach is to develop an AI chatbot able to conduct dialogues/conversations, such as the following:

- **User:** Where was the Snake Goddess figurine found?
- *Chatbot:* The Snake Goddess was found at Knossos Palace.
- **User:** And where is Knossos Palace located?
- *Chatbot:* Knossos Palace is in Crete.

Moreover, an additional objective of the proposed approach is to customize such a conversation in a way that it looks like discussing with the exhibit itself, in case where visitors are found to be nearby (in close range) with it. In this case, the chatbot takes over the role of the exhibit (it becomes the exhibit). For instance, the following dialogue is presented in a museum visitor standing close to the Snake Goddess exhibit, where the chatbot now has taken over the role of the Snake Goddess exhibit:

- **User:** Where were *you* found?
- *Snake Goddess (as chatbot):* I was found at Knossos Palace.
- **User:** And do you know where Knossos Palace is located?
- *Snake Goddess (as chatbot):* I do. Knossos Palace is located in Crete.

Providing a personality trait to an AI chatbot, contributes towards a more engaging experience for the visitors as first person communication is always more effective [45]. In future work authors will evaluate and reuse tools that can provide personality traits to the MuBot approach.

3.1 KG-Based Chatbot-Human Interaction in a Smart Museum Environment

In the following paragraphs, the interaction (questioning/answering) between a chatbot of a smart museum and its visitors that want to interactively learn about its exhibits, is presented.

For demonstration purposes, Fig. 1 depicts the interaction of two visitors (human entities) and the chatbot (software entity) about two exhibits. This choice has been made in order to point out the capacity of the proposed approach to setup the chatbot in a way that can lookup/search for the requested knowledge in a distributed manner, i.e., among the network of interconnected/interrelated exhibits. Such a network is built offline by the curators that are familiar with the 'stories' that each exhibit can tell the visitors. This interconnection/interrelation is formally put in a knowledge index structure that the chatbot has access for lookup/search during the QA processing. So, if a question cannot be answered by the chatbot, due to lack of knowledge that a smart exhibit may have (i.e., its KG is missing the related RDF triples), the chatbot may lookup/search this index for relative knowledge that resides in the KGs of another smart exhibit or in the LOD cloud.

The following entities 'live' in the example smart museum environment:

- Human (H): the visitor in the museum,
- Chatbot (CH): the chatbot software agent,
- Exhibit (Exh): the actual artefact in a museum e.g., a painting, a figurine, etc.,
- Smart Exhibit (SExh): the virtual exhibit in the smart environment of a museum, a virtual entity represented in a conceptual model and encoded in a formal language such as OWL.

In terms of data, information and knowledge, the following are considered to be the required in such a setting: a) Knowledge Graph (KG), b) Natural Language Question (NL-Q), c) Natural Language Answer (NL-A),d) Formal Language Question (FL-Q),

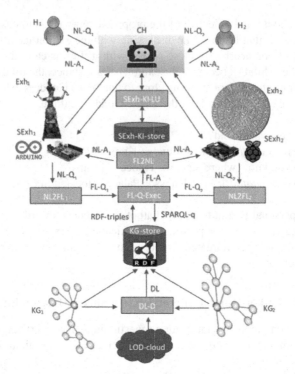

Fig. 1. Visitors interaction with Smart exhibits through the CH application

e) Formal Language Answer (FL-A), f) SPARQL query (SPARQL-q), g) RDF triples (RDF-triples), h) Data Links (DL).

In terms of storage, the setting involves: a) Knowledge Graphs in RDF triples store (KG-store), b) a "Smart Exhibits" Knowledge Index store (SExh-KI-store), and c) the Linked Open Data cloud (LOD-cloud).

Finally, the processing of data, information and knowledge requires the following components: a) Natural to formal language conversion (NL2FL), b) Formal to natural language conversion (FL2NL), c) Smart Exhibits' Knowledge Index Lookup (SExh-KI-LU), d) Formal Language Question Execution (FL-Q-Exec), e) Data Links Discovery (DL-D).

In Fig. 1, an example representation of how two museum visitors interact through the chatbot dialog manager with two "smart" exhibits is depicted. The process is as follows:

1. The visitors, as they use the chatbot application and reach the exhibit of their interest (Exh1, Exh2), interact with the CH by setting a NL-Q.
2. The CH searches at the SExh-KI-store, with the use of SExh-KI-LU, and finds the stored basic information about the exhibits.
3. The CH, with its NL2FL component, translates the NL-Q (1, 2) of the visitors to a formal syntax and sends them to the FL-Q-Exec. The NL2FL component is using NLP techniques as the NER.

4. At the FL-Q-Exec, FL-Q (1,2) are transformed to SPARQL-q which are looked-up to KG-store for retrieving the right answer.
5. KGs, that are designed for the description of the SExhs, are stored at the KG-store (as RDF triples). If an answer could not be found to the exact matched stored SExhs KGs at the KG-store, an additional search could be conducted to other SExh KGs of the museum KG-store or with the use of the DL-D component to connected LOD cloud sources.
6. When the matched RDF triples are retrieved, the FL-Q-Exec sends the FL-A to the FL2NL component.
7. At the FL2NL component, NLG techniques are used for the transformation of the FL-As to NL-As for the SExHs.
8. Finally, the visitors receive the NL-As through the CH app and could proceed to the next NL-Q.

3.2   The MuBot General Architecture

The proposed MuBot approach aims to provide museums the opportunity to create simple, interactive and human-friendly chatbots for their visitors. Visitors will be able to use a chatbot application that will be created through the MuBot platform, to chat with a 'smart' exhibit when they are in front of (or close to) it. They will be able to ask questions through text or voice (in natural language) and receive audible or written answers. The basic components of the proposed general MuBot architecture are presented in Fig. 2 and are described in brief at the following paragraphs.

Dialogue Manager
The dialogue manager is the first component of the proposed architecture and it consists of the front-end graphical user interface that the museum visitors use in order to have a conversation with the chatbot or the exhibits, in contrast to the back-end infrastructure. The dialogue manager could be implemented either as a custom-made solution or reuse a commercial (or free) existing chatbot interface that follows all the UX and UI standards for creating chatbots.

NLP
The NLP component is a crucial part of the architecture as it takes the natural language questions (NL-Qs) and transform them to machine-readable formal questions (FL-Qs). Related work [10, 46] describes three aspects of NLP identification:

- Expected Answer Type (EAT), which in the proposed architecture is handled by the Content Type Recognizer (CTR), represents the answer to the question,
- the property that relates the question with the possible answer, and
- the recognized NE (Named Entity) which in the proposed architecture is handled by the Content Entity Recognizer (CER) and represents the subject of the question made.

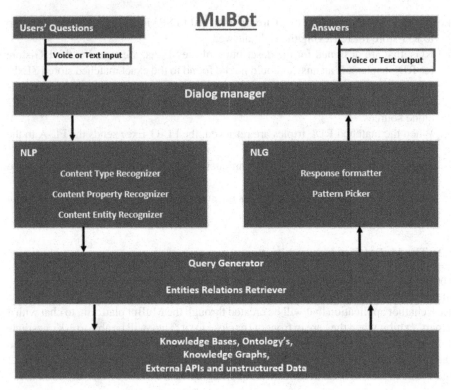

Fig. 2. The MuBot general architecture.

Query Generator and Knowledge Base Retriever
This component transforms the FL-Qs to SPARQL-queries with the FL-Q-Exeq component and searches the KGs Store or the LOD cloud for the proper knowledge. The FL-Q-Exeq receives the provided knowledge in RDF triples and transform it to FL-As.

Knowledge Base (KB)
The KB store is the storage of the KGs. If the search to the KB does not return any results, the DL-D tool will search for possible answers from external Data Links and the LOD cloud. When the knowledge is retrieved, the right answer returns to the FL-Q-Exeq as RDF triples. The connection/linkage of the MuBot architecture with external KGs, such as DBpedia, and the reasoning engine (inferencing mechanism) provides/adds a range of additional (inferred) RDF triples that multiplies the ability of CH in understanding users' questions.

NLG
This component of the proposed architecture uses NLG techniques in order to pick a response pattern that matches with the query-provided triples and proceeds to the final answer formatting by providing user the proper human-like NL-As.

4   Evaluation

The proposed MuBot architecture is under deployment and evaluation with example cases in the Archaeological Museum of Heraklion. Specifically, the Cretan MuBot use case scenario has the visitors chatting with a famous exhibit of the museum, the "Snake Goddess" figurine. For the specific scenario an example ontology was manually engineered and stored to the knowledge base. An example model (in .owl and .ttl serializations) and related queries in SPARQL can be accessed at https://github.com/KotisK/muBotOnto-example. In the following paragraphs, the Cretan MuBot use case scenario and the related queries that have been engineered for this purpose are demonstrated.

4.1   Knowledge Base

The KB uses an example MuBot ontology engineered with the use of the Protégé tool for the specific scenario, with IRI: http://i-lab.aegean.gr/ontologies/mubotOnto/ and prefix "mbo". It uses ontologies that are derived from external sources such as the DBpedia ontology, with IRI: http://dbpedia.org/ontology/ and prefix "dbo" (Fig. 3).

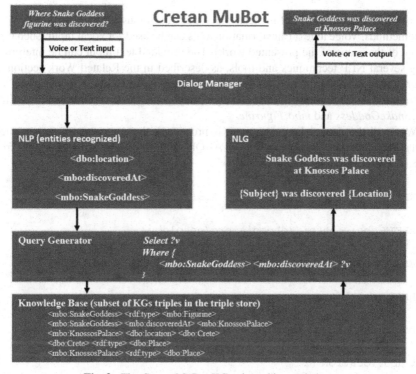

Fig. 3. The Cretan MuBot KG-oriented instantiation.

The MuBot experimental ontological model data is described in the triples form <subject> , <predicate> , <object> . In our example, the statement *"Snake Goddess figurine was discovered at Knossos Palace"* is expressed with the following RDF triples:

a) *<mbo:SnakeGoddess> <rdf:type> <mbo:Figurine>*
b) *<mbo:SnakeGoddess> <mbo:discoveredAt> <mbo:KnossosPalace>*

By extending and enriching the model with external DBpedia semantic data and the MuBot ontology, the following triples can be added:

c) *<mbo:Figurine> <mbo:discoveredAt> <dbo:Place>*
d) *<mbo:KnossosPalace> <dbo:location> <dbo:Crete>*
e) *<dbo:Crete> <rdf:type> <dbo:Place>*
f) *<mbo:KnossosPalace> <rdf:type> <dbo:Place>*

The classes that are produced for the example instantiation are: *mbo:Figurine* and *dbo:Place*, and the properties are: *mbo:discoveredAt, rdf:type,* and *dbo:location.* Furthermore, synonyms could be added to the classes and properties, allowing the system to be able to understand different questions with the same meaning.

4.2 Question Understanding with NLP

The users of the MuBot platform can place their questions through textual or vocal input methods. Voice to text transformation tools can be used for vocal input (such tools are out of the scope of the presented work). The provided text input can be interpreted using several NLP techniques and tools, as described in the Related Work section. In the presented example the question made is *"Where Snake Goddess figurine was discovered?".* The CTR is *mbo:location,* the property is *mbo:discoveredAt* and the CER is *mbo:SnakeGoddess* and *mbo:Figurine.*

When all the natural language input is processed, the component is generating a formal language query (in our case in SPARQL) that produces results (answers) from the KB. The example formal query follows:

```
PREFIX mbo: <http:/i-lab.aegean.gr/ontologies/mubotOnto/>

PREFIX dbo: <http://dbpedia.org/ontology/>

SELECT? v? z

WHERE {

mbo: SnakeGoddess mbo:discoveredAt ?v.

?v dbo:location ?z.
}
```

After query execution and pattern matching, the following triples are matched and returned:

a)   <mbo:SnakeGoddess> <mbo:discoveredAt> <mbo:KnossosPalace>
b)   <mbo:KnossosPalace> <dbo:location> <dbo:Crete>

In a more elaborated example engineered to demonstrate the inferencing/reasoning capabilities of the proposed approach, the following statement is defined (in terms of properties and property hierarchy):

c)   *<mbo:discoveredAt> <rdfs:subPropertyOf> <mbo:foundAt>*

The restriction of *mbo:foundAt* object property has as domain the class *mbo:Figurine*, and as range the class *dbo:Place*. Inferencing will add the following inferred triple in the model:

d)   *<mbo:SnakeGoddess> <mbo:foundAt> <mbo:KnossosPalace>*

This allows for querying the inferred model (tested in Snap SPARQL plugin of Protégé 5.5) with the following queries also:

I. *"Where Snake Goddess figurine was found?"*:

```
PREFIX mbo: <http:/i-lab.aegean.gr/ontologies/mubotOnto/>

PREFIX dbo: <http://dbpedia.org/ontology/>

SELECT ?v ?z

WHERE {

        mbo:SnakeGoddess mbo:foundAt ?v.

        ?v dbo:location ?z.
}
```

The returned data in variables are: ?v = mbo: KnossosPalace, z? = mbo:Crete.

II. *"What was found in Crete?"*:

```
PREFIX mbo: <http:/i-lab.aegean.gr/ontologies/mubotOnto/>

PREFIX dbo: <http://dbpedia.org/ontology/>

SELECT ?s ?v
```

```
WHERE {

        ?s mbo:foundAt ?v.

        ?v dbo:location mbo:Crete.

}
```

The returned data in variables are: ?s = mbo:SnakeGoddess, v? = mbo: Knos-sosPalace, allowing for NLG module (described in next section) to provide answers such as *"Snake Goddess was found in Knossos Palace, in Crete"*.

The example Cretan Mubot model (in .owl and .ttl serializations) and the related queries in SPARQL can be accessed from https://github.com/KotisK/muBotOnto-exa mple.

4.3 NLG Answers

The last step of the process in the MuBot architecture is the creation/formation of the appropriate answer to the given question(s).

In the presented example, the NLG component will be able to generate the following answers:

a) *"Snake Goddess was found at Knossos Palace"*
b) *"Knossos Palace is located in Crete"*

Or better, by synthesizing the two statements above:

c) *"Snake Goddess was found at Knossos Palace, in Crete"* (replacing 'is located in' with, 'in').

The generation processes could be more creative if it can exploit additional semantic properties that, for example, could return multimedia files like a video of the figurine, as a response.

5 Conclusion

The design and development of an AI museum chatbot with the use of KGs is a big challenge as there are several distinct tasks to be considered in order to provide credible answers to questions in a human-like manner. The provided review of key tools and KGs-based AI chatbot approaches aims to provide knowledge related to the proposed architectural components that must be considered for the implementation and deployment of the MuBot approach. AI chatbots must be designed in a way that museum visitors will be facilitated to interact with exhibits the way they could possibly interact with a museum curator or a guide. Moreover, museum chatbots should have strong conversational skills in order to engage users in their cultural experience. This can be achieved by seamlessly accessing and consuming knowledge through KGs stores and the LOD cloud.

The deployment of the Cretan MuBot use case provides the opportunity to evaluate the proposed approach and highlight the steps to future work. Such work is focusing in further evaluating NLP/NLG related modules i.e., evaluation of key tools that transform natural language (visitor questions) to SPARQL queries and the returned triples (knowledge) back to natural language (answers to visitor), in the most effective and human-centered manner. In addition, further work should be conducted in defining the needs and the requirements of museum visitors and museum curators by the proposed AI museum chatbot approach. This might be considered as the most intriguing part of our future work as MuBot approach must not only provide credible answers in a human-like manner but should also develop personality traits and skills that will engage the users and assist them in the understanding of the presented museum/cultural knowledge.

References

1. Yan, J., Wang, C., Cheng, W., Gao, M., Zhou, A.: A retrospective of knowledge graphs. (2018). https://doi.org/10.1007/s11704-016-5228-9
2. Bonatti, P.A., Decker, S., Polleres, A., Presutti, V.: Knowledge graphs: new directions for knowledge representation on the semantic web. Rep. Dagstuhl Semin. **8**, 29–111 (2019). https://doi.org/10.4230/DagRep.8.9.29
3. Roussou, M., Perry, S., Katifori, A., Vassos, S., Tzouganatou, A., McKinney, S.: Transformation through provocation? 1–13 (2019). https://doi.org/10.1145/3290605.3300857
4. Schaffer, S., Gustke, O., Oldemeier, J., Reithinger, N.: Towards chatbots in the museum. In: CEUR Workshop Proceedings, vol. 2176, pp. 1–7 (2018)
5. Tresp, V., Ma, Y., Baier, S.: Machine learning with knowledge graphs. In: Proceedings of the Twelfth International Workshop on Neural-Symbolic Learning Reasoning, vol. 2017, pp. 1–48 (2014)
6. Nickel, M., Murphy, K., Tresp, V., Gabrilovich, E.: A review of relational machine learning for knowledge graphs. Proc. IEEE **104**, 11–33 (2016). https://doi.org/10.1109/JPROC.2015.2483592
7. Pommellet, T., Lécué, F.: Feeding machine learning with knowledge graphs for explainable object detection. In: CEUR Workshop Proceedings, vol. 2456, pp. 277–280 (2019)
8. Androutsopoulos, I., Spiliotopoulos, D., Stamatakis, K., Dimitromanolaki, A., Karkaletsis, V., Spyropoulos, C.D.: Symbolic authoring for multilingual natural language generation. In: Vlahavas, I.P., Spyropoulos, C.D. (eds.) SETN 2002. LNCS (LNAI), vol. 2308, pp. 131–142. Springer, Heidelberg (2002). https://doi.org/10.1007/3-540-46014-4_13
9. Orth, A.: Building chatbots with dialogflow and GRAKN.AI. https://blog.grakn.ai/chatbots-and-grakn-ai-67563c64cfde
10. Hallili, A.: Toward an Ontology-Based Chatbot Endowed with Natural Language Processing and Generation Amine Hallili, vol. 7271 (2014). To cite this version: HAL Id: hal-01089102
11. Akma, N., Hafiz, M., Zainal, A., Fairuz, M., Adnan, Z.: Review of chatbots design techniques. Int. J. Comput. Appl. **181**, 7–10 (2018). https://doi.org/10.5120/ijca2018917606
12. Radziwill, N.M., Benton, M.C.: Evaluating quality of chatbots and intelligent conversational agents (2017)
13. Shawar, B.A., Atwell, E.: ALICE chatbot: trials and outputs. Comput. Sist. **19**, 625–632 (2015). https://doi.org/10.13053/CyS-19-4-2326

14. Cahn, B.J.: Chatbot literature review. Thesis (2017)
15. Paulheim, H.: Knowledge graph refinement: a survey of approaches and evaluation methods. Semant. Web **8**, 489–508 (2017). https://doi.org/10.3233/SW-160218
16. Stichbury, J.: WTF is a Knowledge Graph? (2017)
17. Al-Zubaide, H., Issa, A.A.: OntBot: ontology based ChatBot. In: 2011 4th International Symposium on Innovation in Information and Communication Technology, ISIICT 2011 (2011). https://doi.org/10.1109/ISIICT.2011.6149594
18. Musen, M.A.: The protégé project. AI Matters. **1**, 4–12 (2015). https://doi.org/10.1145/275 7001.2757003
19. Vegesna, A., Jain, P., Porwal, D.: Ontology based chatbot (for E-commerce website). Int. J. Comput. Appl. **179**, 51–55 (2018). https://doi.org/10.5120/ijca2018916215
20. Kamateri, E., Meditskos, G., Symeonidis, S., Vrochidis, S.: Knowledge-based intelligence and strategy learning for personalised virtual assistance in the healthcare domain. In: 13th International Conference on Advanced Semantic Processing (2019)
21. Meditskos, G., et al.: Towards an ontology-driven adaptive dialogue framework. In: MARMI 2016 - Proceedings of the 2016 ACM 1st International Workshop Multimedia Analysis and Retrival for Multimodal Interaction, Co-located with ICMR 2016, pp. 15–20 (2016). https://doi.org/10.1145/2927006.2927009
22. Krishnan, V., Ganapathy, V.: Named entity recognition (2005)
23. Manning, C., Surdeanu, M., Bauer, J., Finkel, J., Bethard, S., McClosky, D.: The stanford CoreNLP natural language processing toolkit, pp. 55–60 (2015). https://doi.org/10.3115/v1/p14-5010
24. Angeli, G., Premkumar, M.J., Manning, C.D.: Leveraging linguistic structure for open domain information extraction. In: ACL-IJCNLP 2015 - 53rd Annual Meeting Association for Computational Linguistic and 7th International Joint Conference on National Language Processing. Proceedings Conference on Asian Federation National Language Processing, vol. 1, pp. 344–354 (2015). https://doi.org/10.3115/v1/p15-1034
25. Moro, A., Raganato, A., Navigli, R., Informatica, D., Elena, V.R.: Entity linking meets word sense disambiguation: a unified approach, vol. 2, pp. 231–244 (2014)
26. Horridge, M., Gonçalves, R.S., Nyulas, C.I., Tudorache, T., Musen, M.A.: WebProtégé: a cloud-based ontology editor. In: Web Conference 2019 - Companion World Wide Web Conference WWW 2019, pp. 686–689 (2019). https://doi.org/10.1145/3308560.3317707
27. Neumann, A., Laranjeiro, N., Bernardino, J.: An analysis of public REST web service APIs. IEEE Trans. Serv. Comput. (2018). https://doi.org/10.1109/TSC.2018.2847344
28. Gangemi, A., Presutti, V., Reforgiato Recupero, D., Nuzzolese, A.G., Draicchio, F., Mongiovì, M.: Semantic web machine reading with FRED. Semant. Web **8**, 873–893 (2017). https://doi.org/10.3233/SW-160240
29. Lehmann, J., Bühmann, L.: AutoSPARQL: let users query your knowledge base. In: Antoniou, G., et al. (eds.) ESWC 2011. LNCS, vol. 6643, pp. 63–79. Springer, Heidelberg (2011). https://doi.org/10.1007/978-3-642-21034-1_5
30. Unger, C., Bühmann, L., Lehmann, J., Ngomo, A.C.N., Gerber, D., Cimiano, P.: Template-based question answering over RDF data. In: WWW'12 - Proceedings of the 21st Annual Conference on World Wide Web, pp. 639–648 (2012). https://doi.org/10.1145/2187836.218 7923
31. Höffner, K., et al.: TBSL question answering system demo. In: Proceedings of the 4th Conference on Knowledge Engineering Semantic Web (2013)
32. Damljanovic, D., Agatonovic, M., Cunningham, H.: Natural language interfaces to ontologies: combining syntactic analysis and ontology-based lookup through the user interaction. In: Aroyo, L., et al. (eds.) ESWC 2010. LNCS, vol. 6088, pp. 106–120. Springer, Heidelberg (2010). https://doi.org/10.1007/978-3-642-13486-9_8

33. Damljanovic, D., Agatonovic, M., Cunningham, H.: FREyA: an interactive way of querying linked data using natural language. In: García-Castro, R., Fensel, D., Antoniou, G. (eds.) ESWC 2011. LNCS, vol. 7117, pp. 125–138. Springer, Heidelberg (2012). https://doi.org/10.1007/978-3-642-25953-1_11
34. Bansal, R., Chawla, S.: An approach for semantic information retrieval from ontology in computer science domain. Int. J. Eng. Adv. Technol. (IJEAT) **4**(2), 2249–8958 (2014)
35. Sæbu, T.S.: OptiqueNLQF: A natural language query formulation system based on semantic technologies (2015)
36. Ngomo, A.C.N., Bühmann, L., Unger, C., Lehmann, J., Gerber, D.: SPARQL2NL - verbalizing SPARQL queries. In: WWW 2013 Companion – Proceedings of the 22nd International Conference on World Wide Web, pp. 329–332 (2013)
37. Ell, B., Vrandečić, D., Simperl, E.: SPARTIQULATION: verbalizing SPARQL queries. In: CEUR Workshop Proceedings, vol. 913, pp. 50–60 (2012)
38. Ell, B., Harth, A., Simperl, E.: SPARQL query verbalization for explaining semantic search engine queries. In: Presutti, V., d'Amato, C., Gandon, F., d'Aquin, M., Staab, S., Tordai, A. (eds.) ESWC 2014. LNCS, vol. 8465, pp. 426–441. Springer, Cham (2014). https://doi.org/10.1007/978-3-319-07443-6_29
39. Diefenbach, D., Dridi, Y., Singh, K., Maret, P.: SPARQLtoUser: did the question answering system understand me? In: CEUR Workshop Proceedings, vol. 1932, pp. 1–8 (2017)
40. Ferré, S.: SPARKLIS: a SPARQL endpoint explorer for expressive question answering. In: CEUR Workshop Proceedings, vol. 1272, pp. 45–48 (2014)
41. De Beaulieu, C.: What' s new in SPARKLIS, pp. 1–4 (2016)
42. Ferré, S.: Sparklis: an expressive query builder for SPARQL endpoints with guidance in natural language. Semant. Web **8**, 405–418 (2017). https://doi.org/10.3233/SW-150208
43. Ngonga Ngomo, A.-C., Bühmann, L., Unger, C., Lehmann, J., Gerber, D.: Sorry, I don't speak SPARQL, pp. 977–988 (2013). https://doi.org/10.1145/2488388.2488473
44. Ngonga Ngomo, A.-C., Moussallem, D., Bühmann, L.: A holistic natural language generation framework for the semantic web, pp. 819–828 (2019). https://doi.org/10.26615/978-954-452-056-4_095
45. Zumstein, D., Hundertmark, S.: Chatbots: an interactive technology for personalized communication and transaction. Int. J. WWW/Internet **15**, 96–109 (2018)
46. Cabrio, E., Cojan, J., Aprosio, A.P., Magnini, B., Lavelli, A., Gandon, F.: QAKiS: An open domain QA system based on relational patterns. In: CEUR Workshop Proceedings (2012)

Acoustic Experiences for Cultural Heritage Sites: A Pilot Experiment on Spontaneous Visitors' Interest

Vincenzo Norman Vitale[1], Marco Olivieri[2], Antonio Origlia[1], Niccolò Pretto[3], Antonio Rodà[3(✉)], and Francesco Cutugno[1]

[1] Department of Electrical Engineering and Information Technology,
Federico II University of Naples, Naples, Italy
{vincenzonorman.vitale,antonio.origlia,cutugno}@unina.it
[2] Department of Electronics, Information and Bioengineering,
Politecnico di Milano, Milan, Italy
marco5.olivieri@mail.polimi.it
[3] Department of Information Engineering, University of Padova, Padova, Italy
{niccolo.pretto,antonio.roda}@dei.unipd.it

Abstract. Providing technologies to support the visiting experience in cultural venues of artistic value is an important issue that needs to be addressed by considering the delicate nature of the places. Architectural heritage and visual arts are two valuable examples: the most sensible choice for augmenting the comprehension and the experience concerning this kind of cultural heritage is through audio cues (e.g., using audio guides). This work describes a pilot experiment to evaluate the impact of soundscapes and environmental acoustics reconstruction in the visitors' experience. We proposed, to the visitors, an audioguide integrated with an optional experience presenting a comparison between a choir recorded in an anechoic chamber and the same choir as it would have sounded in the Church of the San Martino Charterhouse, using a preliminary acoustic survey. Experiments were conducted with real visitors to maximise the ecology of the collected data and results show that people are significantly interested towards the proposed experience, motivating further efforts to improve the quality and depth of the contents provided with this strategy.

Keywords: Cultural heritage experience · Audioguide · Environmental acoustic reconstruction · Impulse response measurement

1 Introduction

In recent years, new technologies offer unprecedented opportunities to promote and improve understanding of cultural heritage by engaging visitors in new personalised experiences. There are several approaches to enhance the visitors' experience (e.g., smartphone applications, interactive multimedia installations [1,2],

M. Rauterberg (Ed.): HCII 2020, LNCS 12215, pp. 300–311, 2020.
https://doi.org/10.1007/978-3-030-50267-6_23

virtual, augmented [29] or mixed realty [22] applications, projections [9]), based on several interaction methods, such as sensor-based, device-based, tangible, collaborative, multimodal, and hybrid interaction methods [4]. From a design point of view, however, the main focus must not be represented by the technology itself, but by the place, the collection or the object that needs to be promoted [23]. In this sense, technological intervention must be designed to be integrated in cultural experience, accompanying it without ever interfering with it. Often the environment where the artefact is exhibited or the site we want to enhance cannot be altered for preservation or respect reasons. In such cases, personal and/or wearable devices (such as smartphones or VR headset) represent a good opportunity for intervention.

Our case study, the church of the San Martino Charterhouse in Naples, has this constraint and, furthermore, it is a visually rich environment that should not be superimposed with other visually impacting contents. It also has an important peculiarity: a sound box under the wooden choir, designed to enhance the singing voices of the monks. This echo chamber is connected to the choir through three grated holes in the floor and its effect cannot be easily perceived during the visit without disturbing the other visitors, as it would require sounds to be played in the environment. Considering these requirements, an augmented audioguide based on smartphone was designed in order to enhance the visit of the Charterhouse. The first prototype of the audioguide includes a partial reconstruction of the acoustic profile of the church. A full reconstruction of the environment response to acoustics is, of course, a complex and delicate task so, a preliminary investigation is presented, in this work, to evaluate the spontaneous interest that would arise in the Charterhouse visitors, towards a sound comparisons experience complementing the standard narrative approach. Tests were conducted in the real environment by proposing the audioguide experience to visitors who spontaneously came to visit the Charterhouse to maximise data ecology and provide a good indicator to establish if the effort of performing a complete acoustic survey of the church environment meets the interest of the people.

After the following section concerning related works, the case study is presented in Sect. 3. Section 4 provides the description of the audioguide, while Sect. 5 describes how the audio scene was created. Then, the test and its results are presented. Lastly, Sect. 7 presents our conclusions.

2   Related Works

The expression *smart tourism* describes the increasing reliance of tourism destinations, tourists and related industries, on emerging Information and Communication Technologies (ICT) [5,14] that allow for massive data collection and value extraction. So, visitors will enjoy a wide range of personalised services, experiences and more, aimed at cultural heritage promotion. Indeed, with the spreading of smartphone and Internet of Things (IoT) devices [6], cultural sites can easily collect information at finer grades, reducing the risk to interfere with visitors. Moreover, cultural sites can leverage this information to offer personalised and context aware experiences. This way is possible to create an integrated and personal "lifelong" visitor model providing a starting point for lifelong experiences personalisation [16]. In this direction several efforts have been made, for user model definition [10] aiming at the integration of pre, during and post visit experiences [11,18]. Anyway to build such models, we need some information about visitors and visits. The collection process must respect visitors privacy, avoiding any interference with visits and related experiences. So these systems have been devised to "accompanies the visitor and augments her overall museum experience" [28], being designed like informative, not obtrusive, frames surrounding the interaction with the exhibit in cultural sites. The audio-guide perfectly reflect the above description, it is one of the most diffused information sources for visitors in cultural heritage sites, accompanying visitors in their experiences without obstructing the visual channel. Anyway, the classic audio-guide concept has been improved in order to enable data collection, at different grades and interaction levels. Some location-aware mobile audio-guides have been deployed in Hecht museum, at University of Haifa [17,19], allowing visitors to receive the right information at the right place. On the other hand, those audio-guide produced information about visitor behaviour inside the museum, allowing curators to evaluate the effectiveness of exhibits, on the basis of indicators like *Attraction Power* and *Holding Power* [19]. A further version of a mobile audio guide has been integrated with an eye-tracker [20], providing the user with the possibility to receive information about an exhibit and/or a specific part of it, relieving him/her with the necessity to request specific information,

Concerning the acoustic experience, the first concept to consider is the *auralisation*, the audio equivalent of 3D visualisation, which enables quantifiable acoustic properties of buildings, sites and landscapes captured via measurements or recreated through computer based modelling, to form the basis of an audio reconstruction and presentation of a space. For acoustic heritage it helps to build a more multi-sensory picture of our past, and the experience of being present within it [21]. These reconstructions create a "acoustical photography", which is preserved for posterity (becoming precious in case of alteration of the original space) [13] and could be used in studio sound processing for musical productions or 3D games. Computer modelling is the only possible solution in case of missing building, as in [26]. The most common method for collecting the acoustic properties of a building is the extraction of room impulse responses (RIRs) from on-site acoustic measurements. Several techniques could be used, however, one of the most robust and used is based on Exponential Sine Sweep [12,15].

3   Case Study

The San Martino Charterhouse is a monumental monastery, built to meet the specific requirements of the carthusian monastic rule, based on the benedictine motto *ora et labora*. Built at the beginning of the XIV century but renovated several times, this impressive and stunning monastic complex hosted the works of generations of craftsmen and artists from all over Europe. After losing its religious function, it has been converted in a museum in 1867 because it could in itself well represent the art, craft and architecture in Naples through the centuries. Since then, it has become a sort of museum of the city of Naples, it started to acquire several collections of very different items (nativity scenes, coaches, pottery, paintings, drawings, coats of arms, etc.), all of them connected in different ways to the history of the city. The Charterhouse, thus, represents a sort of meta-museum, constituted by the Charterhouse itself plus all the collections it hosts. Considering the complexity of this *communication system*, designing well-integrated technologies to enhance the quality of the experience of such a rich place is clearly a challenge.

While the venue itself is large, in this work we concentrated on the church and its immediately connected environment, which represent a sub-visit concentrating on the most artistically rich parts of the Charterhouse. Specifically, the application presents contents about four points of interest (POI):

1 "Parlatorio" (Parlor): a room to receive external visitors.
2 "Sala del Capitolo" (Chapter Hall): the decision room for monastic order representatives.
3 "Coro dei Padri" (Fathers' Choir): choir for the monks.
4 "Sala del Tesoro Nuovo" (New Treasure Hall): the room in which the monastic order kept their belongings (Fig. 2).

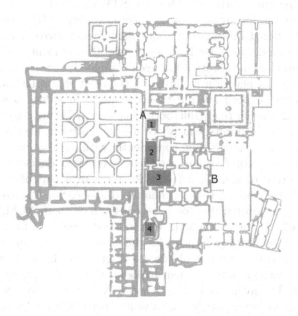

Fig. 1. A map of San Martino Charterhouse in Naples

Fig. 2. A view of the choir

4   Audio Guide

The audioguide *"Caruso"* [8] is an Android smartphone application offering a location aware information layer to cultural sites visitors. It has been proposed for the first time during the Or.C.HE.STRA project [3], as an interactive personal audioguide, for an outdoor augmented reality (AR) experience. In its first version, it offered information about monuments surrounding the visitor, along with 3D soundscapes, for improved cultural enjoyment [7,8]. During the CHROME project, the application has been completely rewritten and extended, in order to provide a platform to integrate the most recent technologies developed for 3D sound experience and to be deployed in indoor scenarios. Using different kinds of sensors (e.g. Bluetooth beacons, RFID tags, etc.) and instrumented/technological exhibits, Caruso locates the visitor inside the cultural site, presenting contents to the visitors, consistently with the context.

The indoor positioning system for Caruso, is based on Bluetooth beacons technology. In order to identify a particular room or a part of it, one or more beacons have been placed in every monitored space. So, Caruso searches for signals issued by monitored Bluetooth beacons and, with an ARMA RSSI filter, it determines whether a visitor is in a monitored area for which contents are available. Caruso automatically provides the visitor with the appropriate audio content as he/she enters the area of interest to let people know they are entering a relevant area without forcing them to look at the smartphone, which is an action we wanted to avoid as a design choice. As done in some previous works [19], for different purposes, every time a visitor reaches/leave an area of interest Caruso updates a report. In our specific case, the report will be updated also on every interaction with multimedia contents, by reporting, for instance, every time an audio content starts or stops.

5   Acoustic Measurements

The architectural complexity of the church of the San Martino Charterhouse and the inaccessibility of the echo chamber impede the creation of a precise physical model of the church. Therefore, the room impulse response (RIR) was preferred for reconstructing the acoustic of the site. This method considers a room as a black box system and assumes it is linear and time invariant (LTI, Fig. 3). By introducing an input signal $x(t)$, we obtain an output $y(t)$, which represents the signal perceived by a listener in the room and this is the sum of the generated noise, $n(t)$, and the deterministic function of the input signal:

$$y(t) = n(t) + F[x(t)] \tag{1}$$

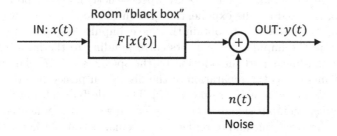

Fig. 3. LTI system

Therefore, it is possible to study the function $F[x(t)]$ as the convolution between the input signal and the impulse response $h(t)$, which is the response of the system after being excited by the Dirac delta:

$$y(t) = n(t) + x(t) \otimes h(t) \tag{2}$$

As said in the related work section there are several ways to measure the acoustic response of a room. Most of them uses speakers to emit a particular input signal $x(t)$ generated by the computer (Fig. 4): this is not an impulse signal because the speakers, having limited power, cannot emit a Dirac delta so as to obtain the impulse response, therefore usually a long signal is reproduced which diffuses energy over time while the microphone records the response of the room, $y(t)$. It is then necessary a further processing step to obtain the impulse response $h(t)$ through an appropriate deconvolution technique.

Nowadays it is possible to have speakers with an almost completely flat frequency spectrum, so you can obtain very precise results. On the other hand, the use of these speakers introduces a non-linear distortion of the signal, so the room is not excited by the input signal $x(t)$ but by a signal already distorted $w(t)$. However, there are some electroacoustic measurement methods, which differ for the input signal $x(t)$ with which the environment is excited that are able to relax this problem.

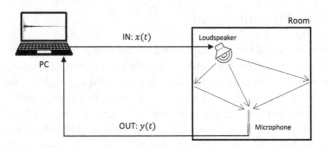

Fig. 4. RIR measurement

Among the various methods of measurements, such as the *MLS* (Maximum-Length-Sequence) or *TDS* (Time Delay Spectrometry), the Exponential Sine Sweep, *ESS*, is based on the exponential growth of the frequency sweep in the input signal $x(t)$ and allows to obtain the linear impulse response of the system separated from the impulse components corresponding to the harmonic distortions of the non-linear part introducing by the speakers [15, 27]. The main purpose of this method is the separation of the distortion peaks, due to non-linear components, from the acoustic response [12]. The underlying idea of this method is to generate as an input signal, $x(t)$, a sine sweep with an exponential variation of the frequency over time and to replace the circular deconvolution with a linear convolution over time. In order to follow this approach, we need to generate an inverse filter $\xi(t)$, that is able to incorporate the input signal $x(t)$ into the delayed function of the Dirac $\delta(t)$ and then perform the convolution between the output signal $y(t)$ with the inverse filter in order to obtain the acoustic response $h(t)$:

$$x(t) \otimes \xi(t) = \delta(t) \tag{3}$$

$$h(t) = y(t) \otimes \xi(t) \tag{4}$$

The following equation describes the input sine sweep signal as an exponential variation from f_1 and f_2 in a total time T:

$$x(t) = \sin \left[\frac{2\pi f_1 T}{\ln \left(\frac{f_2}{f_1} \right)} \left(e^{\frac{t}{T} \ln \left(\frac{f_2}{f_1} \right)} - 1 \right) \right] \tag{5}$$

All the measurements were made using the plug-in suite Aurora[1], that in addition to the generation of the acoustic response, offers the possibility of analysing and manipulating the wave and obtaining summary parameters for each band of octave frequencies. The following list describes the equipment used for the measurements:

– *Behringer ECM8000*: omni-directional microphone with XLR output and ultra-linear frequency response.

---

[1] pcfarina.eng.unipr.it/Aurora_XP (Last accessed: Feb 20th, 2020).

- *Genelec 8030B*: monitor with a fairly flat frequency response between 50 Hz and 25 kHz. Tweeters of 19 mm diameter and woofers of 130 mm diameter.
- *Edirol UA101*: Roland USB sound card with 8 inputs including two XLRs and 8 jack outputs.
- *Samsung Ultrabook*: PC for measurements with Audition 3.0 (the version supported by the Aurora plug-in).
- Stands to support the microphone and the speaker.

Using Aurora, we generated the sine sweep signal with sampling frequency of 48000 Hz and 32 bit resolution, start and end frequency respectively at 22–22000 Hz and duration of 15 s. In this way Aurora can automatically generates the correspond inverse filter, $\xi(t)$, required to obtain the impulse through convolution (4).

The measure was made with the microphone perpendicular to the floor and the tip pointing upwards with a height of approximately 160 cm from the floor in order to simulate the listener point. The height of the speaker with its support has remained fixed at 150 cm, in order to simulate the voice of a singer. The speaker stand was positioned in the choir section that is parallel to the high altar, whereas the microphone was positioned near to the ancient wooden bookrest in the centre of the choir.

The acquired signal was processed to achieve the response of the environment. Through the tools provided by Aurora the impulse responses were obtained by separating the distorted components from the linear impulse useful for the analysis.

6   Field Test

The experiment involved 45 visitors who spontaneously visited the San Martino Charterhouse. The experimenters provided them the audio guide "Caruso" and then they started the visit from one of entry points, *A* or *B*, shown in Fig. 1. The experimenters provided a brief explanation about how to use the application and let the visitors roam freely in the environment, reducing the impact of the experience on natural behaviour. No visitors needed intervention from the experimenters and visited the environment with their own times. The target item, the audio 3D reconstruction, was presented as an optional content integrating the narrative explanation of the sound box, in the "Coro dei Padri". Also, the application let users decide which sounds to listen to, so that indicators of interest towards the full experience could be collected.

In Fig. 5, the visitors distribution per age group is reported, while in Fig. 6 the average visits' length per age group is reported. Collected data show that, in general, the visitors were interested in the contents provided by the audioguide and, specifically, they showed interest in the experience provided by the sound box effect reconstruction: the majority of the visitors, in fact, listened to both the anechoic singing and the simulated version, as shown in Table 1. Furthermore, most of the people (89%) listened to both files for their entire length (15 s). This indicates a high interest, in accessing to the experience, proving its value

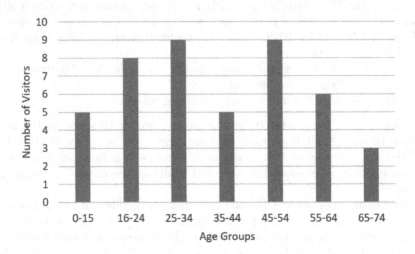

Fig. 5. Number of visitors per age group.

Table 1. Summary of the visitors' behaviour

Did not listen	Listened 1	Listened 2
10	4	31

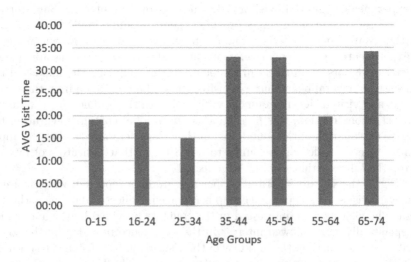

Fig. 6. Average visit time per age group

with respect to the rest of the narrative. This motivates a further effort to improve the experiences through a more precise 3D acoustic reconstruction of the environment, aiming at enriching the narrative in the final audioguide. In general, the application design appears to be functional towards the complexity of the environment and meets the interest of the visitors without presenting contents that superimpose with the rich visual experience provided by the Charterhouse itself.

7   Conclusion

The introduction of cutting-edge technological elements in cultural heritage, brought a great number of opportunities to promote tourism, knowledge and cultural sites too. In this work we show that is possible leverage such technological elements, to promote new experiences, without interfering with channels significant for visual arts, architecture and more. Moreover, we showed that soundscapes and environmental acoustics reconstruction have a great impact on visitors' experience. After this experimental study, many possible evolution can be envisioned. We clearly need to experiment on longer and different soundscapes. Furthermore, with a better indoor positioning system, we will be able to provide users with a better engaging experience, for example by improving the virtual acoustic reconstruction (necessarily based on an extended set of measurements). Finally, the measurement of the room impulse response could be improved using a microphone array [24,25] instead of a single omni-directional microphone. This method allows indeed a time as well as a spatial separation of the elements of the impulse response.

Acknowledgments. This work is partly funded by the Italian PRIN project Cultural Heritage Resources Orienting Multimodal Experience (CHROME) #B52F15000 450001.

References

1. Avanzini, F., et al.: Virtual reconstruction of an ancient Greek pan flute. In: 13th Sound and Music Computing Conference, Proceedings (SMC 2016), pp. 41–46 (2016). https://doi.org/10.5281/zenodo.851179
2. Avanzini, F., et al.: Archaeology and virtual acoustics, a pan flute from ancient Egypt. In: Proceedings of the 12th International Conference on Sound and Music Computing, pp. 31–36 (2015)
3. Barile, F., et al.: ICT solutions for the OR. C. HE. STRA project: from personalized selection to enhanced fruition of cultural heritage data. In: 2014 Tenth International Conference on Signal-Image Technology and Internet-Based Systems (SITIS), pp. 501–507. IEEE (2014)
4. Bekele, M.K., Champion, E.: A comparison of immersive realities and interaction methods: cultural learning in virtual heritage. Front. Robot. AI **6**, 91 (2019). https://doi.org/10.3389/frobt.2019.00091.   https://www.frontiersin.org/article/10.3389/frobt.2019.00091

5. Buhalis, D., Amaranggana, A.: Smart tourism destinations enhancing tourism experience through personalisation of services. In: Tussyadiah, I., Inversini, A. (eds.) Information and Communication Technologies in Tourism 2015, pp. 377–389. Springer, Cham (2015). https://doi.org/10.1007/978-3-319-14343-9_28

6. Chianese, A., Piccialli, F.: Improving user experience of cultural environment through IoT: the *beauty or the truth* case study. In: Damiani, E., Howlett, R.J., Jain, L.C., Gallo, L., De Pietro, G. (eds.) Intelligent Interactive Multimedia Systems and Services. SIST, vol. 40, pp. 11–20. Springer, Cham (2015). https://doi.org/10.1007/978-3-319-19830-9_2

7. D'Auria, D., Di Mauro, D., Calandra, D.M., Cutugno, F.: Caruso: interactive headphones for a dynamic 3D audio application in the cultural heritage context. In: 2014 IEEE 15th International Conference on Information Reuse and Integration (IRI), pp. 525–528. IEEE (2014)

8. D'Auria, D., Di Mauro, D., Calandra, D.M., Cutugno, F.: A 3D audio augmented reality system for a cultural heritage management and fruition. J. Digit. Inf. Manag. **13**(4), 203 (2015)

9. De Feo, E., Russo, A., Venier, E., Breschigliaro, M., Pretto, N.: PAMU: a multimedia park to enhance the renaissance walls of Padua. DISEGNARECON **11**(21), 7 (2018)

10. Dim, E., Kuflik, T., Reinhartz-Berger, I.: When user modeling intersects software engineering: the info-bead user modeling approach. User Model. User-Adapt. Interact. **25**(3), 189–229 (2015)

11. Falk, J.H., Dierking, L.D.: The Museum Experience Revisited. Routledge, Abingdon (2016)

12. Farina, A.: Advancements in impulse response measurements by sine sweeps. In: Audio Engineering Society Convention 122 (May 2007). http://www.aes.org/e-lib/browse.cfm?elib=14106

13. Farina, A., Ayalon, R.: Recording concert hall acoustics for posterity. In: Audio Engineering Society Conference: 24th International Conference: Multichannel Audio, The New Reality (June 2003). http://www.aes.org/e-lib/browse.cfm?elib=12277

14. Gretzel, U., Sigala, M., Xiang, Z., Koo, C.: Smart tourism: foundations and developments. Electron. Mark. **25**(3), 179–188 (2015)

15. Holters, M., Corbach, T., Zölzer, U.: Impulse response measurement techniques and their applicability in the real world. In: Proceedings of the 12th International Conference on Digital Audio Effects (DAFx-09) (2009)

16. Kuflik, T., Kay, J., Kummerfeld, B.: Lifelong personalized museum experiences. In: Proceedings of Workshop on Pervasive User Modeling and Personalization (PUMP 2010), pp. 9–16 (2010)

17. Kuflik, T., et al.: Indoor positioning: challenges and solutions for indoor cultural heritage sites. In: Proceedings of the 16th International Conference on Intelligent User Interfaces, pp. 375–378. ACM (2011)

18. Kuflik, T., Wecker, A.J., Lanir, J., Stock, O.: An integrative framework for extending the boundaries of the museum visit experience: linking the pre, during and post visit phases. Inf. Technol. Tour. **15**(1), 17–47 (2015)

19. Lanir, J., Kuflik, T., Dim, E., Wecker, A.J., Stock, O.: The influence of a location-aware mobile guide on museum visitors' behavior. Interact. Comput. **25**(6), 443–460 (2013)

20. Mokatren, M., Kuflik, T., Shimshoni, I.: Listen to what you look at: combining an audio guide with a mobile eye tracker on the go. In: AI* CH@ AI* IA, pp. 2–9 (2016)

21. Murphy, D., Shelley, S., Foteinou, A., Brereton, J., Daffern, H.: Acoustic heritage and audio creativity: the creative application of sound in the representation, understanding and experience of past environments. Internet Archaeol. **44**, (2017). https://doi.org/10.11141/ia.44.12
22. Plecher, D.A., Wandinger, M., Klinker, G.: Mixed reality for cultural heritage. In: 2019 IEEE Conference on Virtual Reality and 3D User Interfaces (VR), pp. 1618–1622 (March 2019). https://doi.org/10.1109/VR.2019.8797846
23. Pretto, N., Micheloni, E., Gasparotto, S., Fantozzi, C., De Poli, G., Canazza, S.: Technology-enhanced interaction with cultural heritage: an antique pan flute from Egypt. ACM J. Comput. Cult. Herit. (JOCCH) **13**(2) (2020)
24. Salvati, D., Canazza, S., Rodà, A.: A sound localization based interface for real-time control of audio processing, pp. 177–184 (2011)
25. Salvati, D., Rodà, A., Canazza, S., Foresti, G.: A real-time system for multiple acoustic sources localization based on ISP comparison (2010)
26. Segura-Garcia, J., Montagud-Climent, M., Mirasol-Menacho, S., Oleza-Simó, J.: Theatrical virtual acoustic rendering with head movement interaction. Artif. Intell. Eng. Des. Anal. Manuf. **33**(3), 359–368 (2019). https://doi.org/10.1017/S0890060419000192
27. Stan, G.B., Embrechts, J.J., Archambeau, D.: Comparison of different impulse response measurement techniques. J. Audio Eng. Soc. **50**, 249–262 (2002)
28. Stock, O., et al.: Adaptive, intelligent presentation of information for the museum visitor in peach. User Model. User-Adapt. Interact. **17**(3), 257–304 (2007)
29. Tscheu, F., Buhalis, D.: Augmented reality at cultural heritage sites. In: Inversini, A., Schegg, R. (eds.) Information and Communication Technologies in Tourism 2016, pp. 607–619. Springer, Cham (2016). https://doi.org/10.1007/978-3-319-28231-2_44

A Robot in the Library

Evgenios Vlachos$^{(\boxtimes)}$ ⓘ, Anne Faber Hansen ⓘ, and Jakob Povl Holck ⓘ

University Library of Southern Denmark, University of Southern Denmark, Campusvej 55,
5230 Odense, Denmark
evl@bib.sdu.dk

Abstract. If robots are to be beneficial and appealing within an international
library setting, useful to patrons and cooperative with library personnel, then
library culture becomes an important issue. Human-robot interaction designers
need to consider technological factors, the library culture, as well as expectations
from users to develop a solution that could withstand the fall of time and not atone
when enthusiasm is lost. We reviewed the recent literature and performed qualitative analyses of our findings to explore the tasks that are proven to have been
robotized in a library, and to investigate current cultural and technological barriers
that would decrease acceptance rates of robots in a library. Search of Scopus, Web
of Science, IEEEXplore, and LISTA databases was conducted complemented with
Google searches. Articles with scientific content were included if they described
the use of a robot in a library setting, were written in English, and were published
within 2016–2018. We identified 1037 references and after title, abstract and full-
text screening according to the eligibility criteria we included 18 records in our
analysis. We summarize the main roles of library robots as: robots for navigation,
book location and placement; robots as information desks; and robots in education. Barriers towards robotic acceptance was found to be: anxiety and fear among
librarians of being replaced by robots; the lack of resources (time, money, space)
for maintaining a robot and the cost of organizational restructuring; maintaining
the enthusiasm around it over time; and the patrons' need for human contact.

Keywords: Robot · Library · Literature search · Technological benefits ·
Cultural barriers

1 Introduction

In many parts of society, robots have been found to be able to replace physically demanding, dangerous, or repetitive human routines. The development within the field of Artificial Intelligence (AI) seems to hold the potential for more and more complex robotic
task solutions which may not only mimic human, or "natural" movement, but also human
decision making. In the library field, we are not quite there yet.

Some of the larger libraries around the world already have automated storage and
retrieval systems (ASRS). This, for instance, applies to the Joe and Rika Mansueto
Library at the University of Chicago [1] that introduced an ASRS capable of shelving
3.5 million volumes underground by size rather than classification, and the Bodleian

© Springer Nature Switzerland AG 2020
M. Rauterberg (Ed.): HCII 2020, LNCS 12215, pp. 312–322, 2020.
https://doi.org/10.1007/978-3-030-50267-6_24

Libraries' book storage facility at the University of Oxford [2] using an ASRS holding 8 million items. In a world that produces 2.5 quintillion bytes of data every day according to IBM consumer Products[1], vast amounts of information – and consequently huge quantities of printed material – are produced every single day. Automated library systems come in handy as part of manageable logistics solutions at larger libraries, whether the materials to be handled are books, or collections. Naturally, the ASRS facilities are an example of a controlled environment where the library users are completely absent and where only maintenance personnel will come close to the moving parts of the system. Smaller libraries don't have the need for ASRS but could -in theory- have other tasks robotized. Perhaps, a socially assistive robot (SAR) [3–5] designed to move autonomously among humans and capable of socially interacting with them could potentially have the skills to respond to the dynamic environment of a library.

To find out whether a robot could provide valuable assistance at any given library, one would have to initially look at the different routines and tasks at the library in question – and break every library task down into simple movements, or operations that a robot with the current technology would be expected to be able to execute. The handling and circulation of materials is one thing. But there are many other traditional librarian tasks to consider like the acquisition of materials that are to be cataloged, classification of materials, replacement of materials to more modern ones as part of the overall maintenance, and bibliographical support of researchers and students to name a few. Some academic libraries also provide bibliometric analyses at multiple levels and guidance on how to achieve scientific impact, anti-plagiarism support as well as information on research data management.

According to the rankings Frey and Osborne [6] have developed showcasing the job occupations and their probability of computerization, the profession of the librarian has a probability of 65% of being automated. The increasing technicalization of libraries is leading to a wide cultural diversification of patrons, library personnel and services. If a robot is to be usable, useful, and appealing to such a wide range of users, culture becomes an important issue.

The aim of this work is twofold. We explore the recent literature and perform qualitative analyses of our findings *to examine in practice the task areas that are proven to have been robotized in a library setting, and to investigate current cultural and technological barriers that would decrease acceptance rates of robots in the library of the future.* In the following sections we will describe our method and search strategy, present our results and discuss our findings.

2 Method

2.1 Search Strategy

A systematic literature search was performed [7], including the following bibliographical databases in order to maximize inclusion and to represent both robotic and information

---

[1] IBM Consumer Products Industry Blog. https://www.ibm.com/blogs/insights-on-business/consumer-products/2-5-quintillion-bytes-of-data-created-every-day-how-does-cpg-retail-manage-it/, last accessed 2020/01/21.

science literature: Scopus, Web of Science (WoS), IEEE Xplore Digital Library (IEEE) and Library, Information Science & Technology Abstracts (LISTA). The search query was composed of two components: the intervention (robot) and the context (library) taking into consideration of course the defined keywords as described in specific for each of the chosen databases. Free-text terms for the intervention search included: "robot*", "social* robot*", "personalis* robot*", "assistive robot*", and "artificial intelligence", while for the context search terms like "information specialist*", "librar*"and "librarian*" were included. The search was conducted in January 2019.

2.2 Study Selection and Inclusion Criteria

Three reviewers independently screened the articles in a three-step process: first the title, then the abstract, and finally the full-text. An article was considered eligible if it described the use of a robot in a library setting. The studies were grouped together depending on the purpose the robot served in the library, and the grouping was done retrospectively and independently of the original articles. In particular, articles were included if they had scientific content; were published within 2016, 2017 and 2018; and if they were written in English.

3 Results

The initial search resulted in 1037 references: 571 from IEEE, 171 from LISTA, 99 from Scopus, 195 from WoS, and 1 from individual Google searches. After removal of duplicates, articles with no scientific content or irrelevant content, and after screening on title and abstract level 58 publications remained to be assessed for eligibility. A schematic flowchart of included references is shown in Fig. 1. A tricky part in the screening of articles was that many studies were referring to "software libraries", which are collections of data and programming code used to develop programs and applications. Hence, the high number of articles with no content. Articles with no scientific content, essays, debate articles, newspaper articles, or with irrelevant contents were excluded from the final search result, leaving 18 articles for the analysis. Table 1 below outlines the purpose the robot served, the benefits of the library by implementing a robotic solution, and the cultural and technological barriers reported.

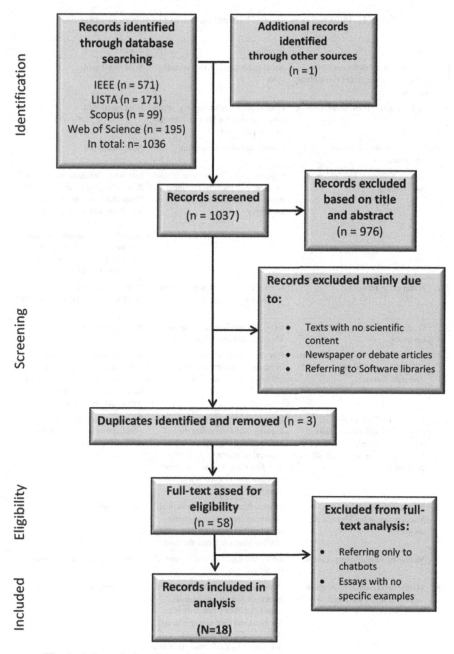

Fig. 1. Schematic flowchart of the review process, search method and results.

Table 1. Purpose, benefits and barriers on the use of robots in libraries.

Ref.	Purpose	Benefits	Barriers
[8]	Pick-and-place intelligent robot using an arm connected to the library database	Avoid tedious and time-consuming tasks	None mentioned
[9]	Self-navigating book finder robot	Finding books autonomously, saving time, and ideal for libraries with not enough personnel	None mentioned
[10]	Library management robotic system – pick-and-place	Lessen curator inconvenience	None mentioned
[11]	Robotic assistance for children in book locating	High efficiency, shorter time of book locating, user friendly, providing interesting navigation experience in the library	Patron's unfamiliarity with robots. Robotic "strong guidance" could "limit children's opportunities of wondering and free browsing". The child users projected their expectations of human librarians onto the robots and expected them to have the same intelligence and professional skills
[12]	Makerspace: robotics	Library events – building, inventing, sharing and learning	Coding and programming vs. building a robot? Funding and staff time?
[13]	Guiding robot, mascot of the university	Interactive guidance at the university library, acceptance of robots	None mentioned
[14]	Intelligent agents to assist librarians and enable users' better access to their information	Free librarian time and enable increased reference support or even off-hours support for users	Understanding what intelligent agents are, and their uses, is important for libraries for keeping up with the ever-changing technology landscape
[15]	To gain insight into the information-seeking behaviors of patrons and to understand their perception of the library via affective computing	Increased patron engagement and learning. Software senses the emotions of a user and provides appropriate response. To combine with for example an android robot acting as a team-mate in a learning situation	Ethical, privacy, and cost effectiveness issues are at the top in a list of concerns
[16]	Autonomous Book Location Management in big libraries. Robot on wheels	Monitor book locations throughout the library, automatically detect book misplacements, and by camera help the loaner to locate the book	None mentioned
[17]	Mobile humanoid library assistant	Interactive guidance and support at the library	How to maintain the enthusiasm?
[18]	Mobile library assistant to search, locate and notify the user to collect the book	With the increasing number of books, magazines and journals, running of library manually is a laborious and time-consuming task. Also, some books might get overlooked by the human eye. Good substitute for the manual work done by the users	None mentioned

(*continued*)

Table 1. (*continued*)

Ref.	Purpose	Benefits	Barriers
[19]	Automatic shelf-scanning and self-navigating book finder robot	Finding miss-shelved and lying-down books, liberating librarians from intensively manual labor	Potential threat to replacing the librarian
[20]	Telepresence robot for remote navigation and meetings	Library tours, and online conversations with encounters, fostering communication within the libraries	Potential threat to the librarians' job situation. People's fear of the robots turning evil. Technophobia, a sense of being monitored, or unfamiliarity with the intended purpose of the robot
[21]	Recognize and manipulate books, localize itself and navigate using RFID tags	Guide library users to a reference suitable source when a librarian is not available	The state of library development in the use of AI in the field of public, technical, and management services
[22]	Enhance library services and help improve students' information literacy skills	Complement librarians' work and alleviate some of the burdens placed on librarians that will allow them to focus on more complex and time-consuming obligations	Should academic law librarians consider using agent systems with the ever-changing legal environment and budgetary constraints that plague many of our libraries?
[23]	Placement of an AI lab in the library	Students majoring in different fields, from philosophy to computer science and biomedical engineering, will visit the lab and use it to brainstorm about important social and ethical issues today and create cutting edge projects	The very disruptive nature of any new technology could be viewed as a threat to many institutions, including the mission of the library
[24]	Introduce young children to programming logic with the help of robots	Libraries hold a unique position in our communities as informal learning platforms, and are perfectly positioned to bring our communities together. Robots are a great visual expression of writing a set of code to perform a task and make for a very interactive coding experience	None mentioned
[25]	Help bring technology fluency by coding with LEGO robotics courses to residents through digital literacy trainings	The TechMobile is a fully-equipped computer lab on wheels, offered as a mobile outreach service of the library to people of all ages and abilities throughout the City of San Francisco for their recreational, educational and lifelong learning needs. Mobile Outreach brings the library to you!	None mentioned

4 Discussion

4.1 Task Areas and Benefits

The articles collected constitute different approaches to – and views on – the use of robots in a library setting and have the potential of revealing world trends in the adaptation of robot technologies in libraries. Reading through our results in Table 1, we could identify three major task areas which will be further discussed in the subsections below:

- robots for navigation, book location and placement [8–11, 16, 19, 21];
- robots serving as an information desk [13, 14, 17, 18, 20]; and
- robots in education [12, 22–25].

Article [15] describes many adoption cases of robots in the libraries and does not fit into these areas, as it examines mainly artificial agents analyzing the information-seeking behavior of patrons for law libraries.

Robots for Navigation, Book Location and Placement

The automation aspect clearly plays an important part: If librarians/library staff can avoid tedious and time-consuming tasks – like detecting book displacements, putting books back on their shelves, finding lying-down books, or helping the loaners to locate their books – then they can spend their time doing more complex assignments [8, 9, 13, 16, 19, 21]. This is recommended for small libraries or libraries short of personnel and especially with a focus on high-volume repeatable assignments [10] while offering an "interesting navigation experience" [11].

Robots Serving as an Information Desk

With the use of robots as information providers, the notion of high efficiency in a busy environment is stressed, complimented with the very modern experience *per se* of having robot technology in the library. The latter is described with buzz phrases like "interactive guidance" [13], or "a robot using intelligent agent-based software" [14]. These phrases imply, generally speaking, that robots are a futuristic experience and – depending on their type and functions of course – that they will engage the patrons in a welcoming, intelligent and creative way, adding value to the library activities as a whole [17]. Robots in this task area could act as telepresence robots for remote navigation and virtual meetings [20], as assistants to search, locate and notify the user to collect a book [18], or even as a university mascot [13].

Robots in Education

Many libraries today host creative, interdisciplinary, informal makerspaces [12], AI and robotic labs [23, 24], or even have computer labs on wheels [25] with the purpose of educating and bringing robotic fluency to the public they serve. There is a plethora of benefits in having an AI or robotic lab in the library [12, 23–25]: it offers students of various levels the opportunity to learn robotics through tutorials and workshops; students majoring in different fields can brainstorm together; librarians can benefit as AI can make library collections FAIR (findable, accessible, interoperable and reusable) in new ways; and introduce young children to programming logic and coding with robotics. Intelligent personalized courses [22] with the assistance of intelligent agents can also help students improve their information literacy skills by making them more active participants in the learning process.

4.2 Cultural and Technological Barriers

By "cultural barriers" we understand ideas, customs and behavior among both library staff and patrons that may complicate, or even prevent the adaptation of a new mindset and, subsequently, a new way of doing things, a culture shift – in this case concerning the integration and use of robots in the library.

Depending on the perspective of library management and on the library resources at hand, one could speculate that tedious and time-consuming tasks would always be best handled by a robot. Nevertheless, we need to be reminded that the authors of the reviewed articles are mainly engineers who have come up with a robot solution to a library problem without necessarily considering the robot's impact on both the library patrons and the library services. Also, one would not expect the engineers to include harsh criticism of their own solution in their own publication – especially not, if the presented robot technology is supposed to be introduced to the market for library supplies and equipment. Therefore, *author bias* affected eight articles [8–10, 13, 16, 18, 24, 25] which had neither barrier nor limitation mentioned. The remaining ten articles from Table 1 indicate several cultural barriers for such an endeavor.

Most likely, some of the library's patrons will be quite *stressed or afraid when interacting with robots.* As reported in [11], robots caused anxiety and fear to children users as children were unsure of how to communicate within this unfamiliar environment. Children at a certain age could expect a robot to act as a human librarian and would possibly be very disappointed by a lesser performance [11, 22]. Also, it could be uncomfortable for patrons as well as library staff to be monitored by a robot [20] that may store personal data concerning human emotions and behavior [15].

Another cultural barrier reported is the library staff's need to *familiarize itself with the robots* in order to gain the best out of them [12] and be able to keep-up with such disruptive technologies [12, 14]. The many choices upon creating a makerspace and having to deal with coding, programming, and even building robots, may end up being a turnoff for library personnel. In many cases, and depending on the robot type and model, gaining the necessary robotics' skills [21] will be time-consuming. *Technophobia* [20] could in this case be seen as an example of a nonreceptive culture among librarians who may, or may not, have been part of the decision-making concerning acquiring a robot. In addition, the robot would demand working hours for its' operation, maintenance and administration that could act as a cultural barrier, if the library staff is unfamiliar with such technology, and economical barrier in case the library struggles with budgetary constraints [22]. Another barrier reported is the *maintenance of patron's enthusiasm* with the same robot after a couple of years [17], meaning that library personnel should come up with new ideas and tasks perfectly executed to maintain interest.

As shown in the articles [11, 15], robots and their corresponding computing technologies may come with severe limitations when compared to the capacity of a librarian. If a robot must work among the library patrons and employees, the robot must be completely safe with no risk of inflicting damage to humans, or to the library interior. *Maintenance and development costs* should be at a minimum and transparent for the library management [15].

Without any doubt, there is another important human factor to consider: In many libraries around the world, you will see shelving and book picking routines as tasks that are providing job opportunities for students and young people, modified duty work or flexible positions for people with disabilities and are engaging senior citizens at libraries in volunteer work. It goes without saying that a robot for shelving and shelf scans [19] would *deprive the opportunity of creating job positions* that are proven to be beneficial to society. As stated in [18], robots will "prove as a very good substitute for the manual work", and such statements is natural to invoke emotions of fear for librarians. *Fear*, of course, can generate resistance [20]. From a union perspective, one should consider whether the introduction of a robot would de facto lead to unemployment for members of the library staff, or disrupt employment contracts, and current work descriptions [20]. The library management should consider whether personnel to be replaced by a robot could easily be transferred to other duties, or retrained – and if not, what would be the consequences. From a psychological perspective, depending on the employee(s) in question, all sorts of negative emotional reactions could occur, possibly inflecting on the work environment in general [20, 23].

Another issue to be of some concern is – in addition to the arguments listed above – that especially students who gain work experience at a university library may, later, choose educational pathways that would eventually lead them back to the library world, even to a position at the very same library. From a recruiting perspective, this is of great importance to both the library management, and to the young employee. If student workers at the library were to be replaced by robots it would destroy the potential of this type of future recruitment. However, we should be reminded that "we do not have libraries just to create jobs for librarians" [26]. Furthermore, people with positive experiences from library work as mentioned above will tend to act as ambassadors for the library in question. At the present stage of robot technology, this is not likely to occur. Robots cannot speak fondly of libraries, unless they are programmed to do so, or are in fact operated by a human (telepresence robotics).

Robots could definitely assist librarians in their tasks, but librarians' tasks could never be automatized to the fullest degree [24, 27]. Librarians, first and foremost, are considered as intermediaries of communities as well as trustworthy, and humane advisers, they have to put up with people who are rude, or angry – even with people who are crying. Lastly, some patrons still prefer the "traditional" face-to-face-talk [20].

5 Conclusion

The adaptation of robot technology in a library may be furthered by inherent library needs, local/national and international trends, patron demands, and staff/management demands. Currently, libraries with positive attitudes to new technologies and even prior experience with robotics seem to be inclined to invest in robots that could: autonomously navigate, locate and place books; serve as information desks; assist in the education of students and the patrons. Obstacles towards a robotic adaptation proved to be stress and fear among the library staff of being gradually replaced by robots, an unsatisfying level of robotic functionality and/or a simple reluctance to implement new and advanced library task solutions that, in turn, would demand retraining the library staff and perhaps even an organizational restructuring. The general lack of resources (staff time, money, space) would of course present an obstacle, as well as the cost of maintaining the patron's enthusiasm with robots in the long term. Finally, the smartness of robots has to be weighed up against the need for human contact – especially, regarding elderly people and young children.

References

1. The Joe and Rika Mansueto Library. https://www.lib.uchicago.edu/mansueto/tech/asrs. Accessed 21 Jan 2020
2. Bodleian's Book Storage Facility, https://www.bodleian.ox.ac.uk/bodley/news/2015/oct-19. Accessed 21 Jan 2020
3. Breazeal, C.: Social interactions in HRI: the robot view. IEEE Trans. Syst. Man Cybernetics **34**(2), 181–186 (2004). IEEE
4. Tan, Z.-H., et al.: iSociobot: a multimodal interactive social robot. Int. J. Soc. Robot. **10**(1), 5–19 (2017). https://doi.org/10.1007/s12369-017-0426-7
5. Vlachos, E., Schärfe, H.: Social robots as persuasive agents. In: Meiselwitz, G. (ed.) SCSM 2014. LNCS, vol. 8531, pp. 277–284. Springer, Cham (2014). https://doi.org/10.1007/978-3-319-07632-4_26
6. Frey, C.B., Osborne, M.A.: The future of employment: how susceptible are jobs to computerisation? Technol. Forecast. Soc. Chang. **114**, 254–280 (2017)
7. Bartels, E.M.: How to perform a systematic search. Best Pract. Res. Clin. Rheumatol. **27**, 295–306 (2013)
8. Pujari, T.S., Deosarkar, S.B.: Design of intelligent and robotic library system. In: 2017 2nd IEEE International Conference on Recent Trends in Electronics, Information & Communication Technology (RTEICT), pp. 1903–1908. IEEE (2017)
9. Rashid, M.R., Uzzaman, N., Hossain, S., Shuvra, N.K.D.: Development of a self-navigating algorithm for library book finder robot. In: 2017 3rd International Conference on Electrical Information and Communication Technology (EICT), pp. 1–6. IEEE (2017)
10. Angal, Y., Gade, A.: Development of library management robotic system. In: 2017 International Conference on Data Management, Analytics and Innovation (ICDMAI), pp. 254–258. IEEE (2017)
11. Lin, W., Yueh, H.P.: Evaluating children's performance and perception of robotic assistance in library book locating. In: 2018 27th IEEE International Symposium on Robot and Human Interactive Communication (RO-MAN), pp. 1185–1189. IEEE (2018)
12. Kroski, E. (ed.): The Makerspace Librarian's Sourcebook. Facet Publishing, London (2017)
13. Tanaka, M., Okada, K., Wada, M.: Guiding robot at entrance hall of university library. In: 2017 IEEE International Conference on Consumer Electronics-Taiwan (ICCE-TW), pp. 269–270. IEEE (2017)
14. Herron, J.: Intelligent agents for the library. J. Electron. Res. Med. Libraries, **14**(3–4), 139–144. Taylor & Francis (2017)
15. Brigham, T.J.: Merging technology and emotions: introduction to affective computing. Med. Ref. Serv. Q. **36**(4), 399–407. Taylor & Francis (2017)
16. Pham, H., Giordano, A., Miller, L., Giannitti, J., Mena, M., DiNardi, A.: A ubiquitous approach for automated library book location management. In: Proceedings of the 2018 International Conference on Computing and Big Data, pp. 78–82. ACM (2018)
17. Stahl, B., Mohnke, J., Seeliger, F.: Roboter ante portas? about the deployment of a humanoid robot into a library. In: Proceedings of the IATUL Conferences, Paper 6 (2018)
18. Animireddy, S.P., Singh, K.P., Natarajan, V.: Robotic library assistant. In: 2018 Second International Conference on Inventive Communication and Computational Technologies (ICICCT), pp. 1443–1447. IEEE (2018)
19. Liu, J., Zhu, F., Wang, Y., Wang, X., Pan, Q., Chen, L.: RF-scanner: shelf scanning with robot-assisted RFID systems. In: IEEE INFOCOM 2017-IEEE Conference on Computer Communications, pp. 1–9. IEEE (2017)
20. Guth, L., Vander Meer, P.F.: Telepresence robotics in an academic library: a study of exposure and adaptation among patrons and employees. Library Hi Tech, **35**(3), 408–420. Emerald (2017)

21. Asemi, A., Asemi, A.: Artificial Intelligence (AI) application in library systems in Iran: a taxonomy study. Library Philosophy and Practice (2018)
22. Talley, N.B.: Imagining the use of intelligent agents and artificial intelligence in academic law libraries. Law Libr. J. **108**, 383–401 (2016)
23. Massis, B.: Artificial intelligence arrives in the library. Inf. Learn. Sci. **119**(7/8), 456–459. Emerald (2018)
24. Prato, S.C.: Beyond the computer age: a best practices intro for implementing library coding programs. Children and Libraries, 15(1), pp. 19–21. Association for Library Service to Children (2017)
25. The TechMobile. https://sfpl.org/index.php?pg=2000795701. Accessed 13 Jan 2020
26. Calvert, P.: Robots, the quiet workers, are you ready to take over? Public Library Quarterly, **36**(2), 167–172. Routledge (2017)
27. Vlachos, E., Faber Hansen, A., Holck, J.P.: The essence of being a librarian in disruptive times. In: IFLA WLIC 2019 - Athens, Greece - Libraries: dialogue for change, Session 113c - IFLA Poster Session (2019)

Preservation of Local Cultures

Preservation and Promotion of Opera Cultural Heritage: The Experience of La Scala Theatre

Federico Avanzini⬡, Adriano Baratè⬡, Goffredo Haus⬡,
Luca A. Ludovico(✉)⬡, and Stavros Ntalampiras⬡

LIM – Laboratorio di Informatica Musicale, Dipartimento di Informatica
"Giovanni Degli Antoni", Università degli Studi di Milano,
Via G. Celoria 18, 20133 Milano, Italy
{federico.avanzini,adriano.barate,goffredo.haus,luca.ludovico,
stavros.ntalampiras}@unimi.it

Abstract. This paper focuses on music and music-related cultural heritage typically preserved by opera houses, starting from the experience achieved during the long-lasting collaboration between La Scala theater and the Laboratory of Music Informatics of the University of Milan. First, we will mention the most significant results achieved by the project in the fields of preservation, information retrieval and dissemination of cultural heritage through computer-based approaches. Moreover, we will discuss the possibilities offered by new technologies applied to the conservative context of an opera house, including: the multi-layer representation of music information to foster the accessibility of musical content also by non-experts; the adoption of 5G networks to deliver spherical videos of live events, thus opening new scenarios for cultural heritage enjoyment and dissemination; deep learning approaches both to improve internal processes (e.g., back-office applications for music information retrieval) and to offer advanced services to users (e.g., highly-customized experiences).

Keywords: Cultural heritage · Digital technologies · Machine learning · Music · Opera · Preservation · Promotion

1 Introduction

The impact of digital technologies on the preservation, restoration, and fruition of tangible and intangible cultural heritage is indisputable [7]. Music cultural heritage has also been part of this digital revolution.

A particular emphasis has been given to the preservation and fruition of audio documents, which poses non-trivial challenges, as these document require several layers of contextual information to be preserved along with the audio signal. Preservation of audio documents can be categorized into *passive* preservation, meant to protect the original documents from external agents without

M. Rauterberg (Ed.): HCII 2020, LNCS 12215, pp. 325–337, 2020.
https://doi.org/10.1007/978-3-030-50267-6_25

alterations, and *active* preservation, which involves the data transfer from the analogue to the digital domain. Despite initial concerns about the use of digital recordings and digital storage media for long-term preservation, the traditional "preserve the original" paradigm has progressively shifted to the "distribution is preservation" idea of digitizing the content and making it available in digital libraries [11].

The categories of passive and active preservation may be extended to the field of physical artifacts, e.g., musical instruments [2]. Here active preservation involves virtual simulations enabling new means of interaction with objects that are otherwise not accessible, with important implications for museum exhibits in particular. Presenting artifacts to the general public is a complex task: interactive museum installations can increase the engagement and participation of visitors [23], and enforce new forms of learning. Ultimately, applying new technologies to interactive museum installations can create stronger consensus and interest for the preservation of cultural heritage [27].

This paper presents the results of a long-standing project [15] on a specific case study, the historical archive of the La Scala theatre of Milan (*Teatro alla Scala di Milano*), one of the best known musical temples of the world. This is a particularly interesting and challenging case, due to the richness and the heterogeneity of the documents and artifacts that are typically found in an opera archive. The results achieved by the project so far provide the basis for reflecting on the added values of digital technologies applied to the preservation and exploitation of opera cultural heritage, and for proposing further developments building on current research advancements.

The rest of the paper is structured as follows: Sect. 2 will describe the background of the project, Sect. 3 will report the main results achieved by the 10-years cooperation between La Scala and the LIM, Sect. 4 will present a number of scenarios where digital technologies can help the preservation and exploitation of opera cultural heritage, Sect. 5 will focus on machine learning as a promising technology to give new value to archive materials, and Sect. 6 will draw conclusions.

2   Background

In its 35 years of activity, the *Laboratorio di Informatica Musicale* (LIM) of the Department of Computer Science, University of Milan has established collaborations with relevant institutions active in the fields of music production, research, and cultural heritage. Examples include, to cite but a few, Bolshoi Theatre (Moscow), Ricordi Historical Archive (Milan), Bach Archiv (Leipzig), and Paul Sacher Stiftung (Basel).

A particularly important partnership was the one with La Scala theatre of Milan. Such a cooperation lasted more than one decade (from 1996 on) and involved different competences and professional skills available in the LIM staff, ranging from researchers dealing with sound and music computing to students enrolled in the course of Music Informatics.

The performing activities of La Scala embrace operas, concerts, recitals, and a number of other cultural events such as presentations and conferences. Along with production, this theater has also the goal of preserving its cultural heritage, distributed across different organizational structures: the Music Archive (hosting both scores and audio recordings), the Photo/Video Archive, the Sketch Archive, the Costume Archive, the Set Design Archive, and the Properties Archive.

When the joint project started, the ICT revolution was in an early phase.[1] As a consequence, most of the information contained in the archives was either on paper or stored in magnetic tapes. In 1997, a pool of international sponsors (Accenture, HP, Oracle, TDK, etc.) funded a project whose ultimate goal was recovering, restoring and preserving the musical heritage of La Scala theater, through a comprehensive digitization campaign and the creation of an on-line database for their retrieval.

In this framework, the cooperation between the LIM and La Scala mainly achieved three results:

1. The preservation and restoration of the historical audio archive, counting about 5000 open-reel magnetic tapes recorded since 1950;
2. The release of advanced computer-based solutions to foster quick and effective access to information. This part of the project included both a comprehensive relational database to federate heterogeneous contents coming from different archives and an experimental platform aimed at providing multimodal access to information (e.g., via queries by humming, symbolic inputs, etc.);
3. The design and implementation of an integrated asset management system, called *LaScalaDAM*, embracing all the archives of the theatre. The idea was to provide full network access via intranet to La Scala authorized staff, and a filtered view (e.g., only selected items, at lower resolution and higher compression, with watermarking, etc.) to the web users of a dedicated portal.

Even if focusing on different aspects – i.e. digitization, information retrieval, and dissemination – all these experiences share a common goal, namely the preservation and promotion of the rich and heterogeneous cultural heritage owned by an opera house or a similar institution. The mentioned activities will be described in detail in Sect. 3.

3   Achieved Results

This section focuses on the state of the art of the collaboration between La Scala and the LIM, reporting the most relevant results achieved in the field of opera-related cultural heritage.

---

[1] If, on the one hand, the CD-DA standard for audio was available since 1980, on the other the birth of the World Wide Web dated back to just 5 years before, and digital cameras were not widely adopted in a professional context.

3.1 Digitizing with the Aim to Preserve

The digitization campaign began in 1996 with a rescuing project addressing the audio archive. This first step involved about 5000 open-reel magnetic tapes containing opera, ballet and symphonic-music recordings from 1950 onward. To this end, the LIM set up a digitization environment in a dedicated space at the Department of Computer Science (see Fig. 1).

In detail, a staff of experts prepared the tapes and – when needed – restored them through thermal pre-treatment (see Fig. 2), acquired audio content through professional devices, converted and transferred them to digital media, and collected and organized the corresponding metadata. Thanks to this joint effort, about 10000 h of music were recovered and preserved. Such recordings include performances by world-renowned singers (e.g., Maria Callas, Giuseppe Di Stefano, Mario Del Monaco, Plàcido Domingo, Mirella Freni, Luciano Pavarotti, Joan Sutherland, Renata Tebaldi, etc.), great conductors (e.g., Claudio Abbado, Daniel Barenboim, Pierre Boulez, Victor De Sabata, Carlo Maria Giulini, Herbert von Karajan, Carlos Kleiber, Riccardo Muti, Arturo Toscanini, etc.), and famous dancers and choreographers (e.g., Roberto Bolle, Alessandra Ferri, Carla Fracci, Rudolf Nureyev, Roland Petit, etc.).

Since 1998, the digitization project was incrementally extended to all theater's archives, namely the costumes and accessories warehouse, the sketches and costume-designs archive, the props warehouse, the photos and posters archive. Currently, the digitized heritage of La Scala embraces about 24000 sketches and costume designs, 45000 costumes, 60000 accessories (including jewels, clothing, footwear, wigs and hats), and 80000 props. Moreover, the theatre's activity is documented in 17000 posters and in more than one million photographs taken from the stage, rehearsals and back-stage.[2] For each category, great artists are involved; to cite but a few: Alberto Burri, Dino Buzzati, Salvatore Fiume, Renato Guttuso, and Mario Sironi as sketch and costume designers; Caramba, Emanuele Luzzati, and Franca Squarciapino as fashion designers; Alessandro and Nicola Benois, Ezio Frigerio, Pier Luigi Pizzi, and Robert Wilson as set designers and directors.

The number of digitized objects, the heterogeneity of the acquired materials, and the stature of the artists involved make the cultural implications of this activity evident. This is even more true since the long-term goal was not only to preserve digital objects and their metadata, but also to organize, analyze and disseminate them, as explained in next sections.

3.2 Analyzing and Structuring

Following the chronological order, in this section we will describe the two main initiatives that characterized the collaboration between La Scala and the LIM concerning the access to digital cultural heritage.

A first step, experimental and highly innovative at that time, was represented by the *Music Archive Information System* (MAIS) initiative [12]. The goal of

---

[2] Source: http://www.teatroallascala.org/en/archive/the-historical-archive.html.

Fig. 1. Devices for open-reel magnetic tapes in the LIM digitization studio: from left to right, Revox A77, Revox B77 MKII and Otari MX-55.

MAIS was to allow content-based queries on available scores and audio materials, so as to support artists in the preparation of a performance already present in the archive. In detail, it was possible to retrieve all the scores and/or audio which contained an exact sequence of notes or a similar one.

From a technical point of view, MAIS was a hardware, software and network environment based on an Oracle 8 object-relational technology. Such a solution was multi-platform, running under Unix, Windows NT and Macintosh operating systems, and distributed, supporting 10 workstations. The environment included also a CD-audio jukebox able to contain up to 224 compact discs and to provide quick access to their content via network (see Fig. 3).

The MAIS overall architecture is shown in Fig. 4. The database was organized around single events (i.e., performances), and stored and linked related metadata, audio materials (CD-DAs and tapes), and music scores. Both traditional and audio-based queries could be used to retrieve information. Designing MAIS posed several challenges, ranging from large storage requirements to the intrinsic complexity of the database, being the scenario characterized by a large amount of music and multimedia unstructured data stored in a variety of formats.

If on one side the MAIS project was an experimental environment addressing the theatre's staff, a later initiative, called *La Scala DAM* (Digital Asset Management), targeted a wider audience. This project, developed in cooperation with the LIM and other technological partners, equipped the theater with an integrated management system to access its huge digital heritage, from the

Fig. 2. The Heraeus UT6200 oven used to thermally pretreat magnetic tapes.

Fig. 3. The CD-R jukebox in use in the MAIS project.

second decade of the 20th Century to present. In 2006, La Scala DAM was connected to the theater's intranet, thus supporting the everyday activities of every sector and constituting an internal authoritative source for the creation, production and documentation of each show. Based on a relational database, whose structure is described elsewhere [14], La Scala DAM supplied integrated views on performances that included metadata, sketches and costume designs, costumes, footwear, jewellery, head-dress, props, fliers and posters, photographs and audio recordings. A key page of the intranet application is shown in Fig. 5, that provided a synoptic view of events with easily accessible links towards all related metadata and materials. A second example is illustrated in Fig. 6: from this view focusing on photographic material, it was possible to jump to detailed photo descriptions, to enlarge images and to follow links towards other sections (e.g., all the materials related to a given opera, all the titles in that season, all the pictures taken in a date or by a photographer, etc.).

3.3   Disseminating

The cooperation between La Scala and the LIM paved also the way toward the public availability and dissemination of preserved cultural heritage. In fact, an evolution of La Scala DAM project mentioned in Sect. 3.2 was the opening of the historical-archive section, called *ArchivioLaScala*, within the institutional web site of the theater.[3] Even if limited and simplified with regard to the huge quantity of information contained in the complete archive, ArchivioLaScala represents the web-accessible page of La Scala DAM. The initiative addresses a worldwide audience of scholars and enthusiasts who now have the opportunity to access a relevant part of the cultural heritage of La Scala.

---

[3] http://www.teatroallascala.org/archivio/.

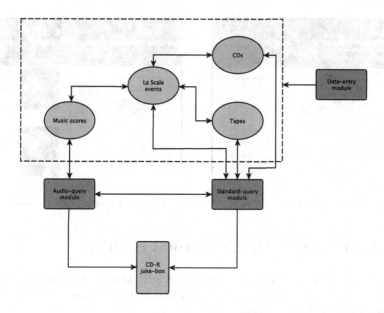

Fig. 4. The MAIS architecture.

This kind of approaches has many practical consequences. The most obvious one is to open cultural heritage archives usually accessible to experts and insiders only. In addition to satisfying the curiosity of regular opera attendees, a long-term goal concerns the involvement of a new audience. At La Scala this aim is pursued by showcasing materials from the past together with teasers about current productions.

Moreover, a suitable combination of digital materials and advanced technologies can be the first step towards information sharing for the constitution of semantic networks capable to offer new services and improved user experience [5]. Such an approach implies the concept of *openness*, in terms of accessibility of knowledge, technology and digital resources. Unfortunately, cultural heritage stakeholders often do not recognize the advantages offered by a shared access to information, rather fearing the infringement of intellectual property and, more in general, the loss of control over their own assets.

Conversely, once the digitization chain is established and tested, benefits may come at a very little cost for the institution. For example, the cooperation between the LIM and Archivio Storico Ricordi, aiming once again at the preservation and promotion of music cultural heritage, has resulted in a number of significant and profitable projects, including the publishing of high-quality reprints of manuscripts and the organization of technology-empowered exhibitions around the world.

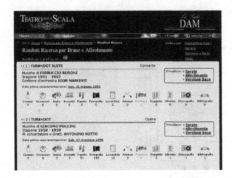

Fig. 5. The synoptic view of events.   **Fig. 6.** A result page for photos.

4   Added Value of Opera Cultural Heritage

From the experience acquired working with La Scala and other musical institutions, it is possible to infer the advantages that an opera house can expect from the adoption of ICT approaches.

First, it is fundamental to preserve the past, also with the aim to provide new value to cultural heritage and exploit archive materials. In this sense, digitization campaigns conducted through professional devices and following international standards are only the first step to take. For example, an underestimated aspect is the need to monitor continuously the conservation status of media: contrary to what common sense suggests, "digital" does not mean "everlasting". As pointed out in [9], preserving digital information is plagued by short media life, obsolete hardware and software, slow read times of old media, and defunct standards.

The availability of cultural heritage in digital format can open previously unexplored commercial opportunities to opera houses, going beyond traditional editorial initiatives and merchandising. For example, new media products can be conceived, containing a number of historical performances of the same opera, all synchronized with different versions of the score. This scenario is made possible by a multi-layer environment (i.e., a format plus an application) for the description of music information, such as the one mentioned in [4].

One further goal of a modern opera house is to enlarge its audience, and, in this perspective, young spectators represent the future. Meeting the expectations of digital natives implies implementing novel ways to let them experience the show and offering advanced services. Moreover, the use of suitable techniques to record live performances and the adoption of new network technologies to broadcast them can extend the potential audience by overcoming the limits of space and time distance. An example is *augmented opera* [5], i.e. the application of augmented reality to opera live experience. An ad-hoc application installed on users' devices could present features such as automatic score and libretto following with multi-language translation, dynamic identification of characters, links to user-tailored content and external services, etc. In this way, the ongoing show is enriched by already-available archive materials (e.g., scores, librettos, on-stage photos from the past, stage maps, etc.) in order to offer a more comprehensive and engaging user experience.

A technology that in the near future will foster the promotion of opera cultural heritage, embracing both new productions and archive materials, is the one of 5G networks. Thanks to the expected characteristics of 5G – namely improved bandwidth, reliability, and density of devices in an area – it will be possible to release innovative services for mobile devices rich in multimedia content, supporting multimodal interaction, and highly customizable depending on users' requirements and special needs. The applications are manifold, ranging from multi-angle and multi-track experience of opera to immersive navigation inside performances [3]. Materials from the past can be integrated with ad-hoc recordings and new digital objects within a unique environment, for both entertainment and educational purposes [3].

It is worth emphasizing that, nowadays, a considerable problem for opera houses is the economic sustainability of their activities. For example, La Scala is still far from the goal of financial self-sufficiency, rather relying on significant public and private funding to achieve a balanced budget. In this sense, both the promotion of the preserved cultural heritage and the release of new services and products based (also) on archive materials can be a low-cost solution to generate income from already available assets.

5   Future Perspectives: Machine Learning for MIR Purposes

In this section, we will focus on the application of machine learning to music information retrieval (MIR) for opera cultural heritage, since it can represent a promising approach both for scientific investigation (e.g., musicological analysis) and for practical aims (e.g., multilayer content navigation and retrieval).

In this context, technologies can be employed to automatically process the above-mentioned data sources in either a mono- or multi-modal way following the line of thought described in [24]. In such a context, the MIR framework can elaborate either on a single data source alone or on multiple ones at the same time and facilitate several applications. With the noticeable exception of the experimentation conducted in the MAIS project, indexing, retrieval and navigation within the La Scala dataset is being carried out in a manual fashion so far without efficient description of music content. Indexing and retrieval services can automatically return information related to queries such as "locate measure x in all the available recordings of a given piece", "retrieve the performances more similar to the one of a given soloist/conductor", "find all a-capella music pieces", etc. Such queries need an internal characterization of music content enabling tagging information related to melody, rhythm, harmony, expression, etc.

During the last decades, MIR has been receiving ever-increasing attention including on-line music services able to reply to such queries via interpretation of musical content. Recognition of musical content, similar to generalized sound recognition, is based on the fact that each music piece has a characteristic way of distributing its energy on its frequency content, which constitutes its so-called signature [21]. MIR technologies offer automatic extraction of information by processing the available audio signals as the main modality as well as complimentary ones such as music scores, video of the performances, etc. Thus, it paved the way for novel applications in the context of an opera house, such as:

- *Music genre classification*—Genre is one of the most widely-used descriptions of music. The literature typically includes genres such as classical, reggae, jazz, rock, etc. [18], but in the case of La Scala archive we can include a more detailed characterization in terms of historical period, style, cultural influences, etc. Such a categorization is subjective up to a certain extent, but in this dataset we looked for overall agreement between experts of this type of music. In general, music signals belonging to the same category share several properties (instrumentation, rhythmic and harmonic structure, etc.) allowing us to assume that each category groups pieces that sound similarly. Features of particular interest here try to capture information associated to instrumentation, rhythm, pitch, harmony, timbre, etc. [26].
- *Music transcription*—This specific application involves mapping the audio signals of the La Scala archive to its complete score [6]. Such algorithms typically estimate the pitch and form the symbols accordingly. However, there are several obstacles here, such as multiple notes emitted by the same instrument or orchestral group, temporal overlapping of several instruments, etc. For example, a reliable algorithm for music transcription could automatically obtain the score of an improvisation (e.g., the extemporaneous *cadenza* by a soloist), the underlying symbolic representation in queries by humming, the audio-driven transcription of non-traditional graphical scores into common western notation.
- *Performer recognition*—It is widely accepted that great soloists and conductors are characterized by their own performance style. Even though there is no formal and explicit definition of what style is, we can trace it back to expression-related parameters like variations in dynamics (loudness) and agogics (tempo), characterization of certain notes/passages, etc. This type of information is not included in the music score, so its investigation is particularly interesting. Despite the subjectivity of the task, there are many researchers who have employed low-level features and machine learning algorithms to identify performers [10].
- *Instrument recognition*—This application encompasses the recognition of both type and number of instruments included in a music piece [13,17]. Such a high-level description comprises a useful information towards improved organization/searching of the La Scala archive, since the ensemble can characterize a piece, genre, historical period, etc. At the same time, such information can boost the signal processing front-end facilitating multi-pitch analysis, source separation, synchronization, and transcription [21].
- *Music emotion recognition*—This application domain is concerned with the prediction of the emotion perceived by the audience of a specific music piece.

Music, as a means of communication, evokes certain emotional responses. Identification of the emotion on the listener's side may be indicative of the respective human reaction. To this end, appropriate signal processing and pattern recognition algorithms can by employed [19].

This is a non-exhaustive list of scenarios, as the richness of the La Scala archives is still under exploration and emerging applications might arise targeting the particular character of such a cultural-defining theater. Interestingly, all the above-mentioned applications as well as emerging ones can be viewed by means of a chronological prism towards a historical analysis of various aspects including how specific performers, performances, compositions, etc. have been evolved with the passage of time.

As a general comment, feature extraction is typically carried out on small parts of audio data (frames) where we assume that the signal holds stationary properties. This assumption is not restrictive as vocal articulators, musical instruments, singers, etc. have an inertia that prohibits instantaneous changes in the frequency content of the sound. As mentioned above, there are several features serving various applications while a rather exhaustive summary is offered in [1]. Interestingly, during the last years, following the boom of Deep Learning, several researchers have tried to address MIR-related problems in an end-to-end fashion, i.e. without any preprocessing/feature extraction step utilizing the audio signal alone with promising results [20]. Such approaches remove the need of designing handcrafted features based on domain knowledge since they elaborate directly on the time and/or frequency domain [25] with the ability to automatically characterize musical content [22].

Finally, deep networks allow generation of musical content as well [8,16], which could be a fruitful direction considering the relevance of La Scala performances.

6   Conclusion

In this paper we have summarized the activities a long-standing project on the historical archive of the La Scala theatre of Milan, emphasizing the most interesting and challenging aspects of this specific case study, and focusing on the main results achieved so far. Based on these, we have proposed a reflection on the implications of this work, in terms of improved access to this heritage, augmented experiences of operas, and novel commercial opportunities. Finally, we have discussed a particularly promising direction of research, which leverages on recent developments in the field of machine learning to support a variety of music information retrieval tasks that can be fruitfully applied to several application scenarios and open up new forms of interaction with opera cultural heritage.

References

1. Alías, F., Socoró, J., Sevillano, X.: A review of physical and perceptual feature extraction techniques for speech, music and environmental sounds. Appl. Sci. 6(5), 143 (2016). https://doi.org/10.3390/app6050143

2. Avanzini, F., et al.: Virtual reconstruction of an ancient Greek pan flute. In: Proceedings of International Conference Sound and Music Computing (SMC 2016), Hamburg, pp. 41–46 (2016)
3. Baratè, A., Haus, G., Ludovico, L.A., Pagani, E., Scarabottolo, N.: 5G technology and its applications to music education. In: Multi Conference on Computer Science and Information Systems, MCCSIS 2019 - Proceedings of the International Conference on e-Learning 2019, pp. 65–72. IADIS Press (2019)
4. Baratè, A., Ludovico, L.A.: IEEE 1599 applications for entertainment and education. In: Baggi, D., Haus, G. (eds.) Music Navigation with Symbols and Layers: Toward Content Browsing with IEEE 1599 XML Encoding, pp. 115–132. Wiley, Hoboken (2013). https://doi.org/10.1002/9781118494455.ch7
5. Baratè, A., Ludovico, L.A.: Local and global semantic networks for the representation of music information. J. e-Learning Knowl. Soc. **12**(4), 109–123 (2016)
6. Benetos, E., Dixon, S., Duan, Z., Ewert, S.: Automatic music transcription: an overview. IEEE Signal Process. Mag. **36**(1), 20–30 (2019). https://doi.org/10.1109/MSP.2018.2869928
7. Cameron, F., Kenderdine, S.: Theorizing Digital Cultural Heritage: A Critical Discourse. MIT Press, Cambridge (2007)
8. Chemla-Romeu-Santos, A., Ntalampiras, S., Esling, P., Haus, G., Assayag, G.: Cross-modal variational inference for bijective signal-symbol translation. In: Proceedings of the 22nd International Conference on Digital Audio Effects, DAFx 2019, Birmingham, UK, pp. 1–8, September 2019
9. Chen, S.S.: The paradox of digital preservation. Computer **34**(3), 24–28 (2001)
10. Chudy, M., Dixon, S.: Towards music performer recognition using timbre. In: Proceedings of the 3rd International Conference of Students of Systematic Musicology, pp. 45–50 (2010)
11. Cohen, E.: Preservation of audio in folk heritage collections in crisis. In: Proceedings of Council on Library and Information Resources, pp. 65–82 (2001)
12. Ferrari, E., Haus, G.: The musical archive information system at Teatro alla Scala. In: Proceedings IEEE International Conference on Multimedia Computing and Systems, vol. 1, pp. 817–821. IEEE (1999)
13. Gururani, S., Sharma, M., Lerch, A.: An attention mechanism for musical instrument recognition. CoRR abs/1907.04294 (2019)
14. Haus, G., Ludovico, L.A.: The digital opera house: an architecture for multimedia databases. J. Cult. Herit. **7**(2), 92–97 (2006). https://doi.org/10.1016/j.culher.2006.02.007
15. Haus, G., Pelegrin Pajuelo, M.L.: Music processing technologies for rescuing music archives at Teatro alla Scala and Bolshoi theatre. J. New Music Res. **30**(4), 381–388 (2001)
16. Kumar, K., et al.: Melgan: generative adversarial networks for conditional waveform synthesis. In: Wallach, H., Larochelle, H., Beygelzimer, A., d'Alché Buc, F., Fox, E., Garnett, R. (eds.) Advances in Neural Information Processing Systems 32, pp. 14881–14892. Curran Associates, Inc. (2019)
17. Nagawade, M.S., Ratnaparkhe, V.R.: Musical instrument identification using MFCC. In: 2017 2nd IEEE International Conference on Recent Trends in Electronics, Information Communication Technology (RTEICT), pp. 2198–2202, May 2017. https://doi.org/10.1109/RTEICT.2017.8256990
18. Ntalampiras, S.: Directed acyclic graphs for content based sound, musical genre, and speech emotion classification. J. New Music Res. **43**(2), 173–182 (2014). https://doi.org/10.1080/09298215.2013.859709

19. Ntalampiras, S.: A transfer learning framework for predicting the emotional content of generalized sound events. J. Acoust. Soc. Am. **141**(3), 1694–1701 (2017). https://doi.org/10.1121/1.4977749

20. Pons, J., Nieto, O., Prockup, M., Schmidt, E.M., Ehmann, A.F., Serra, X.: End-to-end learning for music audio tagging at scale. CoRR abs/1711.02520 (2017)

21. Potamitis, I., Ganchev, T.: Generalized recognition of sound events: approaches and applications. In: Tsihrintzis, G.A., Jain, L.C. (eds.) Multimedia Services in Intelligent Environments. SCI, vol. 120, pp. 41–79. Springer, Heidelberg (2008). https://doi.org/10.1007/978-3-540-78502-6_3

22. Roman, M., Pertusa, A., Calvo-Zaragoza, J.: A holistic approach to polyphonic music transcription with neural networks. In: Proceedings of the 20th International Society for Music Information Retrieval Conference, ISMIR, Delft, The Netherlands, pp. 731–737, November 2019. https://doi.org/10.5281/zenodo.3527914

23. Simon, N.: The Participatory Museum. Museum 2.0 (2010). Creative Commons

24. Simonetta, F., Ntalampiras, S., Avanzini, F.: Multimodal music information processing and retrieval: survey and future challenges. In: 2019 International Workshop on Multilayer Music Representation and Processing (MMRP), pp. 10–18, January 2019. https://doi.org/10.1109/MMRP.2019.00012

25. Simonetta, F., Chacón, C.E.C., Ntalampiras, S., Widmer, G.: A convolutional approach to melody line identification in symbolic scores. In: International Society for Music Information Retrieval Conference, pp.1–8 (2019)

26. Sturm, B.L.: A survey of evaluation in music genre recognition. In: Nürnberger, A., Stober, S., Larsen, B., Detyniecki, M. (eds.) AMR 2012. LNCS, vol. 8382, pp. 29–66. Springer, Cham (2014). https://doi.org/10.1007/978-3-319-12093-5_2

27. Styliani, S., Fotis, L., Kostas, K., Petros, P.: Virtual museums, a survey and some issues for consideration. J. Cult. Herit. **10**(4), 520–528 (2009)

How to Utilize the HuValue Tool for Daily Life Product Design

Shadi Kheirandish[1,2](✉) and Matthias Rauterberg[2]

[1] Department of Industrial Design, Alzahra University, Tehran, Iran
S.Kheirandish@tue.nl
[2] Department of Industrial Design,
Eindhoven University of Technology, Eindhoven, The Netherlands
G.W.M.Rauterberg@tue.nl

Abstract. To support designers considering human value in their design process, the HuValue tool was developed. This tool is instanciated as a tangible, card-based design toolkit including a value wheel, 45 value words, and 207 picture cards, grounded in a comprehensive value framework. Using this toolkit can enable designers to be aware and sensitive to human values and consider various value aspects of their design challenge through different types of values, even if they personally do not value them. To know whether our tool is useful in a design process, we conducted a quasi-experimental study with 64 first year bachelor students in the context of a project based course of an industrial design program. We supported randomly selected students in 12 group projects with four students each, to use our tool during their whole design process (phases: vision, ideation, conceptualization, realization, and validation). Six project groups received the toolkit, an introduction and also guidance during the semester about how to use it in different design phases (Trained Groups). The remaining six of these 12 project groups received the toolkit and an introduction to its usage (Introduction Groups). Additionally, four project groups without any support for human values were used as benchmark (Control Groups). It was up to the students in all 16 groups if at all, and if so when and how to use our tool. We evaluated all the 16 project groups' final designs whether they used the HuValue tool in their design process, if so, how and in which part they used our tool. This setting gave us the opportunity in gaining insights how to propose relevant usage of our tool. The results showed that nine out of the 16 in total (=56%) and eight out of the 12 tool-based (=67%) project groups reported using our tool during their design process for different purposes. Even one of the control groups got - beyond our control - access to our toolkit and used it. The project groups which used the tool applied it in the following phases: vision, ideation, conceptualization and validation, but not realization.

Keywords: Human values · Design tool · Product design · Value-based design · Quasi-experiment

1 Introduction

Products play a mediating role between human beings and the world to anticipate the future, since they co-shape the existence and experience of us and consequently our

© Springer Nature Switzerland AG 2020
M. Rauterberg (Ed.): HCII 2020, LNCS 12215, pp. 338–357, 2020.
https://doi.org/10.1007/978-3-030-50267-6_26

lifestyle [1]. On the other hand, human values guide human actions and behaviours in daily situations and give expression to basic human needs [2]. An extensive literature review showed that despite the significance of human values in everyday life and consequently, in product design, they mostly remain implicit and unarticulated in design projects [3]. Only few design approaches concentrate on human values and aim to address them in their design [4–6]. Nonetheless, there is a very little agreement between them to identify values. In this respect, the lack of an established and accepted fundamental grounding [7] and a comprehensive list of values [8] can be considered as a major unresolved issue. Accordingly, with the intention of supporting designers to embed human values consciously and explicitly in the design process, we developed a comprehensive value framework [9] and provided a tool for overcoming this shortage [10].

To design our HuValue toolkit, we first proposed a comprehensive value framework to raise designers' awareness about human values; and then a card-based design tool, containing a value wheel (Fig. 1), 45 value words and 207 picture cards (Fig. 2). These tangible objects should facilitate using the value framework in a design process. Our value framework was created and developed via research with various theoretical, empirical and design-based approaches to compile, classify and structure the existing value lists, including Rokeach [2], Peterson and Seligman [11], Schwartz [12], and 10 more value lists from the last century [10]. This value framework provides a holistic view of the values of different aspects of human life [13]. In our HuValue toolkit, our value framework is illustrated in a circular form as the value wheel, which is a circle with nine value clusters. Each value cluster is represented by an icon, a label, a mood board, a descriptive sentence, five key values, and some relevant terms. In the wheel, each value cluster can be ranked in their order of importance through a 5-point rating scale: from 'Extremely important' to 'Not important'. Each value is represented by a two-sided card with the value word on the front and its relevant value cluster at the back. All value clusters are developed through an empirical investigation and a cluster analysis [10]. The picture cards (see Fig. 2), as complementary to the value wheel, are examples of representative activities, personas and products/services. Despite the simplicity of their presentation, these cards link the abstract human values to concrete everyday life issues. In fact, the cards are supposed to be applied for expressing human values in practice. The *activity cards* are some examples of concrete valuable behaviours, which can be used to express what does a specific value/group of values mean and how it can appear in real life. The *persona cards* are the examples of iconic people, who can be representative of acting based on a specific value or group of values. The *products/services cards* provide some examples that can be used to express how using a product/service in daily life can straighten or weaken such a value or group of values. The cards are samples of everyday life experiences to clarify how to disclose the underlying values of a daily life situation. Indeed, asking "why is this experience/behaviour important?" is the way to reveal the human value(s) behind daily experiences, and asking "How can this value be actualised?" is the way to express human values within everyday life experiences. Clarifying this relation would be helpful for designers to translate human values into design requirements, which have a guiding role in a design process [14].

Applying our tool during a design process is supposed to be effective for enriching design concepts with human values [15]. Indeed, as evidenced by a quasi-experimental

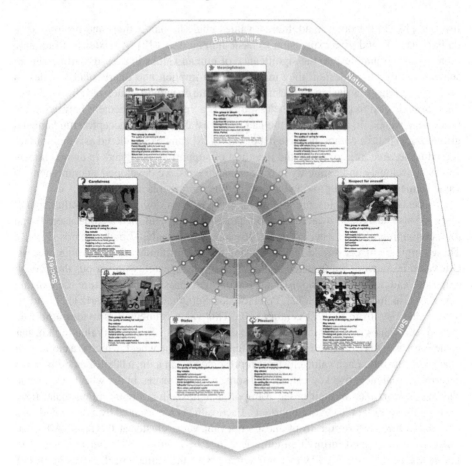

Fig. 1. Value wheel (original size is A2), with nine value clusters and five-point Likert-type scales.

study, we claim that the tool is capable of being used in different design areas. For instance, we proposed using the tool in game design [16], and the current article provides first insights in the way the tool can be used for designing daily life products.

2 Methodology

To study how the HuValue tool can be used in a design project, we conducted a quasi-experiment with design students of a first-year bachelor industrial design program. First, we selected randomly project groups and then we executed a workshop with them to introduce the HuValue toolkit and its potential usage in design. We also supported students to use the toolkit in their design project during the whole semester. In the end, we analysed the project groups' final design whether they used the HuValue tool in their design process, if so, how and in which part they used the tool. The result of the whole experiment is qualitatively and quantitatively analysed, discussed and concluded in another article [15]. The current article intends to study practical ways of using the

Value Words   **Picture Cards**

Fig. 2. Examples of value words and picture cards: (left) two-sided cards (size: 5 × 7 cm) with a value word on the front and its relevant value cluster at the back; (right) three different types of picture cards (size: 7 × 10 cm) including activity, persona, and product/service. The first number on the left side of picture cards means 1 = activity, 2 = persona, and 3 = product/service; the second number represents the position inside each group of activity/persona/product (e.g. for sorting cards).

HuValue tool in design projects. This setting can give us the opportunity of learning from students to propose relevant usages for the tool.

2.1 Participants

The study was designed in the context of the first project of undergraduate design students (called "Project-1-Design"), running in the semester from February until June 2017. To achieve the goal of the study, we selected randomly two project themes, 'Sleep' and 'IoT' (out of 10 themes), with an equal number of project groups to use the tool during their whole design project (2 project themes × 8 project groups × 4 students = 64 first-year design students out of ca. 180 students). The participants were divided randomly into three categories (independent variable, IV):

1. *Trained Groups* (TG): Six project groups received the tool, introduction in the tool's usage during a special workshop, and also more guidance during the semester about how to use it in different design phases (in group meetings).
2. *Introduction Groups* (IG): Six project groups received only the tool and introduction to its usage (in the workshop).
3. *Control Groups* (CG): Four project groups without any support for human values were saved as control groups.

All 180 'Project-1-Design' students were asked to select one out of ten project themes based on their interests. At the end of the semester, every project group delivered a poster and a final report. With a poster presentation they introduce their final design concept; in the final report, they described (a) their design process, (b) their design iterations, (c) their decisions, and (d) relevant arguments to justify their design decisions as occurred during the project.

2.2 Introduction Workshop

We conducted once a specially set-up workshop to introduce our HuValue tool to the selected six TG and six IG project groups. During this workshop, at least three out of four members of each project group were present, and all group members received a complete set of the toolkit. In this workshop, we introduced the HuValue toolkit and its components through a playful group activity. Furthermore, they followed a simple instruction to make their value-board (see Fig. 3 as a fictive example):

1- Rank the groups of values in their order of importance to you.
2- Find important values (between value words) for you.
3- Find important activities (between picture cards) for you.
4- Assign your important activities to groups of values.
5- Assign your values to your important activities.
6- Capture the result in a photo as your value-board.

This procedure can be applied by designers not only to define their personal values but also to discover the common values of the team and also other stakeholders. Via those activities with the toolkit, we guided students to think deeper about values and possible links to their daily life. In addition, they tried to use the tool for defining what is important for them and for understanding what is important for their groupmates. To conclude the activities, by pointing to their values-board as examples, we showed them how this visualisation could help them to reflect on their own value system and highlight their important values, to clarify their vision and goal and also to be sensitive about differences in values with others. Moreover, by mentioning some simple examples, we showed them how they could apply the tool to look at anything from different perspectives and analyse and evaluate them from a value point of view. For instance, in a design project it can be a person as a designer (to define her/his vision) or as a user (to identify her/his needs, wants and ideals), or an existing product or service (to know which value(s) will be supported/conflicted by using the selected product), or a situation and context of use (to clarify the design challenge and to define the design goal), or a design concept or an idea (to evaluate the concept). Finally, we briefly mentioned that the tool could also be used as a source of inspiration for generating ideas and criteria for evaluating them.

2.3 Group Meetings

The six TGs were guided step by step in group meetings to use the tool during their design process. As this study was conducted in the context of a first year bachelor design project in an engineering-focused university, we had to follow the pre-defined structure of the whole course: A design process was considered to have four phases: (1) ideation, (2) conceptualisation, (3) realisation, and (4) evaluation. Additionally, at the start of the semester, students had to formulate their vision and identity, as well as their learning goal in a personal development plan.

The main purpose of our group meetings was to guide and support students to apply the tool in their design process for specifying important human values in their design situation and designing for them. Four group meetings, 30 min per project group, were

Fig. 3. A concrete example of a value-board made by the first author of this paper

arranged over the semester. Since the students were familiar with the tool and possible applications for ideation phase, the first group meeting (Week 4) was allocated for analysing the design situation and context of use from a value point of view, using the Five W's [17]. During this meeting, we explained how they could apply the tool to look at their topic from different perspectives. The second meeting (Week 6) was about defining the design challenge from a value point of view, in which they were encouraged to highlight human values in their design story. The third group meeting (Week 7), which was just before mid-term demonstration day, was appointed for value specification. In that meeting, we asked them to clarify the link between their concept and the intended values from previous meetings. The fourth group meeting (Week 14) was about evaluating concepts from a value point of view.

During the group meetings, we mostly used the HuValue tool to show how the intended goals such as 'analysing design situation and context of use from a value point of view' are practically achievable. For each meeting, we have some relevant examples, which was fixed for all project groups and were not close to any of their project ideas. We used the toolkit to explain these examples, and then asked the students to follow the idea and use it for reflecting on their own projects. We did try to form the questions in their mind, but we did not provide answers for them since they were supposed to find their own ways. In each meeting, depending on the goal of that meeting, we mentioned some possible ways of using the toolkit, for instance, visualizing "what is important in their design" with making a value-mood-board or a value-storyboard. For this, we suggested making new relevant picture cards of activities, products, and personas to their project or simply use the existing cards of the HuValue tool (see more in Table 1). Meanwhile, we used the toolkit components, including value wheel, value words and picture cards, and post-it notes during the meetings to facilitate the discussion.

According to the plan of 'Project-1-Design', after seventeen weeks of ideation, conceptualisation, realisation and validation, students were supposed to present their outcomes to the public and a week after they had to deliver their final reports. In these final reports they described their design process, and how the iterations contributed to their end results. After collecting students' final reports, we read and analysed their reports to find out whether they applied the tool in their project. If this was the case, we tried to find out in which phase and for what purpose the tool was used. Furthermore, we tried to understand how the tool was utilized. For this purpose, we semi-automatically searched the reports of all TG, IG, and CG groups via search option with the keywords of 'human values', 'value tool', 'value workshop', and also with any of our 45 value items.

3   Results

According to our search results in the final reports of participants, nine out of 16 groups mentioned using human values in their design process: six TGs (=100%), two IGs (=33%), and one CG (=25%); six of them reported to use the HuValue tool in their design process (the tool was mentioned in the text and/or shown in photos) and three of them used the HuValue perspective in their design process (the workshop and/or the workshop leader's name, as well as "values", were mentioned in the reports). Seven other groups did not mention human values in their report; five of them used value words unclearly (without identifying those words as values). Two other groups did not mention anything about values at all.

To know how students used human values in their design process, we went to relevant parts in the reports, which mentioned human values, and highlighted their purpose of usage. These usages can be labelled as 'Defining design goal', 'Choosing final idea', 'Searching for what is important for the design and make a list of values', 'Discovering common value(s) of the group', 'Developing the concept to cover the intended values', 'Being inspired by value words or related activities/ products/ personas', 'Presenting intended values in a mood board', and 'Using intended values for user test'. We analysed this information based on the design phases, as such (0) Vision, (1) Ideation, (2) Conceptualization, and (4) Validation. Realisation phase (3) is excluded, since no value use were reported in this phase at all.

3.1   Vision

As a result, 'Defining design goal' was the most popular purpose of using human values during their design process. Seven groups reported defining their design goals based on values:

Table 1. Four group meetings were arranged over the semester to support project groups in TG with step by step training how to apply the tool in different parts of their project.

Description
Meeting 1 **Goal:** Analyse design situation and context of use from value point of view **Context:** Week 4 - Project-1-Design **Content:** They received some general information about analysing the design situation with the Five W's questions and specifically, how each question can be answered from a value point of view. So, we asked them to make some examples of common and relevant activities or behaviours of their target group in the situation as keywords, and also some examples of existing products in that context. (Those examples can be picture cards, or simply, photos or even drawings and texts on post-its.) We used the examples to facilitate the discussion and to review how different values and groups of values play a role in their design situation. **Tool application:** We presented how to use the tool to find relevant values for anything including the keywords and examples.

Meeting 2
Goal: Define the design challenge from a value point of view.
Context: Week 6 - Project-1-Design
Content: They received some general information about how to use the answers of the Five W's questions to tell a story about their design and how to define their design challenge in a brief question. We stressed on "WHY" question. In addition, we asked them to make a list of important values in their design:
- Find important values for:
  the target group (generally)
  the target group (specifically in the context of use)
  the context of use
  the problem/challenge
  the solution(s)
  the design goal
- Find relevant examples for those values.
- Find relations between those values.
Tool application:
We used the tool to find relevant values for their answers to the Five W's questions.
We showed them how to use the tool for interviewing the user.
We used picture cards as examples to show how to find relevant examples of the intended values and how to make this link clear and understandable.

Meeting 3 **Goal:** Value specification **Context:** Week 7 - Project-1-Design **Content:** They received some general advice for presenting their concept and specifically about how and where to show the important values for their design during the mid-term demonstration day. In addition, we checked together what they made based on last discussions and how to improve them. For instance, we suggested making a value-mood-board or a value-story-board for visualizing "what is important in their design". **Tool application:** We used the tool to make some examples of specifying values in their presentation.
Meeting 4 **Goal:** Evaluate the concept from a value point of view **Context:** Week 14- Project-1-Design **Content:** After reviewing relevant values for their design, they received some guidance about how to use the values for evaluating their concept in validation phase and discussed how to specify abstract values and criteria in more clear and understandable statements. **Tool application:** We showed them how to use the tool as a questionnaire to review which human values can be supported by their concept. We mentioned that this could be done by themselves or the user.

"Based on a workshop we had on values, we defined the values of TU/e students. We used our own knowledge to do this. We found that the most important values were

creativity, pleasure, self-discipline, intelligence, success, ambition. Apart from these, TU/e students also value freedom, helpful, self-awareness, environment, security, varied life and independent." (Final report, project group IoT.3, IG)

"From our personal wishes, we focused on what our stakeholders; students in LaPlace find important regarding sociality in the study space. These values, which were checked in evaluation, made us state our final project goal. The important values within our project are personal development and pleasure. We want our users to focus finding seats on their social environment preference and to stimulate playful interaction with the ceiling. Our project goal is to design a study space that communicates with its user to stimulate personal development and pleasure." (Final report, project group IoT.5, TG)

"[...] the concept is in line with important values, the device will be enjoyable to use, improve the working environment of students, be sustainable and be respectful to all users that interact with it." (Final report, project group IoT.4, TG)

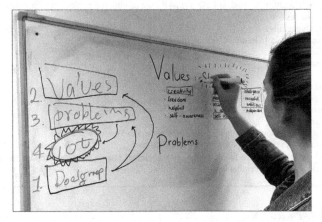

Fig. 4. Defining design goal (Image is adopted from final report, IoT.3, IG)

Regarding this purpose, one project group expressed defining their design goal by focusing on user's needs and wants and linking them to values (see Fig. 4):

"We did not want to focus on making large changes in people's lifestyles, because we think that new designs should not interfere with one's ordinary life too much, and instead improve their lifestyle. Therefore, we focused more on the human values, because those influence the user experience and whether a person would use it. Paying attention to human values would help our product to be more personal and accessible for everybody." (Final report, project group Sleep.5, TG)

Also, three project groups reported that they discovered common values for the team, however, each in their own way, such as by ranking value words individually and then compared (see Fig. 6):

"To get to know each other better and to get a clear image of our joined vision, we used the value cards we got during the human value workshop. We divided the value cards among our team. By ranking these value cards, we could see what value was especially important for whom. We calculated the points each value got from each team member and made a joint value ranking for the whole team. We found out that personal development was a value we had in common, carefulness was a close second. We discovered that our least important value was meaningfulness. The overall score of all 5 first values did not vary a lot. In conclusion, we have a lot of different values in our team. This is something to keep in mind during our design process." (Final report, project group Sleep.1, TG)

Or by making a group Value-board (see Fig. 5):

"With the technique that we learned at the workshop we had from [author], we first started thinking about what our vision was for this project and what our values were. By placing pictures and words on a circle we found that pleasure, respect for others and self-development were important to us and therefore we wanted to include that in our design. [...] When doing the human value test [Fig. 5], we found out that we ourselves find self-development and pleasure very important. In addition, we want to stimulate the students in divergent thinking, this is one of the few external ways to influence creativity of humankind 2. In conclusion, we want to inspire them and stimulate their creativity." (Final report, project group IoT.2, IG)

Or by finding important values and then clustering and ranking them (see Fig. 6):

"To start getting our minds on the same track, we explored values. What do we find important? What do we find interesting? Where do we want to work on? Do we find the same things interesting? Can we convince each other? How can we work together? Then, we clustered all the values that are related to either efficiency, business, user, innovation, design or environment together. For example, "sustainable", "eco-friendly" and "not harmful for the environment" are all in the group "environment". Next step was to rank the group to importance with numbers from 1 to 6. With 6 the least important and 1 the most important. These values will be used for the QOC later on. After doing this, we started brainstorming again. With a better understanding of our common values and goals we could now focus on generating ideas. [...] We agreed to overwork our values in another way. We made a collective of all values, piled them up and drew a round target on the table. Important values get placed in the bull's eye and the importance decreases the further away they are. We realized the importance of this exercise and repeated it when all members of the group were present. It showed the diverse viewpoints of the members and their personal view on where to go with our project. Not that our previous work was less valuable, but it could have been more effective. Of course, new ideas came up during these exercises, which were more of an unstructured collection of thoughts [...] This exercise of ranking values was therefore useful in a way that we now knew what area interested our team the most so we could now focus on that." (Final report, project group IoT.6, TG)

Fig. 5. Discovering common value(s) of the group (Image is adopted from final report, Sleep.1, TG)

Fig. 6. Discovering common value(s) of the group (Image is adopted from final report, IoT.2, IG)

3.2 Ideation

Three project groups reported brainstorming around picture cards and used them as inspiration (see Fig. 7):

> *"We used cards with all kind of different activities as a brainstorming technique. By putting a set of 9 to 12 cards on the table, we had to think about ideas, products*

or target groups that had to do with sleeping and with what you could see on the card. We ended up with 18 ideas for target groups, products and design areas. We invented the idea of brainstorming this way for ourselves. We used the cards we got during the human value workshop from [author]." (Final report, project group Sleep.1, TG)

Fig. 7. Inspiration by value words or related activities/ products/personas (Image is adopted from final report, IoT.2, IG)

One project group of CG, who was supposed to have no access to the tool, received the tool from their friends in TG and used it. Although in an interview they mentioned that they did not have any information about the tool or its function and possible application(s) in design, they used the picture cards as inspiration in the ideation phase:

"We used a couple of different methods for brainstorming: [...] Cards with images [...]. We used this method to look into different users, situations and places. We borrowed these cards from another group at our coach meeting. Each card had a picture printed on it. These pictures could be of anything, they did not have a specific theme. For each card we tried to identify a user-group, for example celebrities, people who suffer depression, taxi drivers and stewardesses. We also tried to identify in what places (for example at work) their sleeping problems might occur and what the problems are. This method helped us a lot with the idea generating, because we had a clearer overview of possible users and problems." (Final report, project group Sleep.2, CG)

Another project group mentioned they started ideation from values:

"[...] we also discussed what self-development meant for us. We wrote this down on a big sheet for everybody personally so we could discuss it afterwards." (Final report, project group IoT.2, TG)

They also used their intended values for choosing final idea:

"[...] At this point, we had to choose our final idea, we did this by making a QOC analysis. We asked the following four questions: Is it educational related? Is it connected to the Internet of Things? Does it fit our values and vision? Is it realizable?" (Final report, project group IoT.2, TG)

"An important iteration that we made was deciding that our final concept was going to be a project board and then going back, realigning our values and refining our final ideas again to come out with the bin. This was a very important step as it outlined our path for the rest of the project and gave us a direction that we were passionate about." (Final report, project group IoT.4, TG)

Some project groups reported assigning values to generated ideas to find more important ideas for them and more relevant ideas to intended values (see Fig. 8).

"This image [Fig. 8] shows a mind map on education. What we considered to be very useful after having made a mind map was to place post-its on the spots we found most important, according to our own values. This way, we could take everyone's values into account and already get rid of some directions within education we all didn't want to focus on." (Final report, project group IoT.5, TG)

Fig. 8. Choosing final idea (Image is adopted from final report, IoT.5, TG)

"As a designer it is important to focus on the human values of your design. There-fore we, at the end of each cycle, reflected on the design specifically focusing on human values. For this part we received help from [author] who was doing her PhD about this subject." (Final report, project group IoT.6, TG)

"Implementing values as a way to brainstorm: After deciding the target group and defining IoT we started an individual brainstorm. In this matrix we used what we learned about values during the workshop of [author] to rate the ideas partly on our visions and values. [...] We started the ideation by each brainstorming to acquire at least 25 ideas per person. We categorized these ideas to see in which areas our interest was. We used these categories to selectively broaden our idea field. Since the use of values worked out very good in the pressure-cooker, we used this again to brainstorm, together with the goals we had set for this project. (Final report, project group IoT.3, IG)

3.3 Conceptualization

Four project groups mentioned searching for what is important for their design and making a list of values (see Fig. 9), for instance:

"[...] we did research about the human values of our target group. [...] An overview of our research is in the picture [Fig. 8]." (Final report, project group Sleep.1, TG)

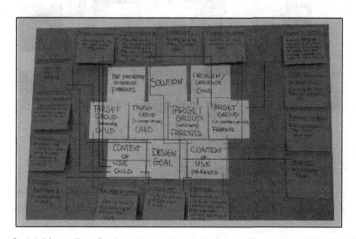

Fig. 9. Making a list of values (Image is adopted from Final report, Sleep.1, TG)

"We found important values for different categories. To start we looked for impor-tant values for the target group. This could be divided into two categories itself: generally and via a questionnaire. Also we thought of important values for the context of use. Furthermore we found values for the problem/challenge and what

values the solution should meet. At last we looked at what would be the most important values our design goal should have. [...] During the conceptualisation of our project, we set up some values for the user of our project. These include, among others, a better health, a better discernment and more self-control. [...]" (Final report, project group Sleep.7, TG)

One of those project groups also made a mood board of relevant activities, products and values (see Fig. 10):

"We also thought about the human values that were important in our concept. We used [author]'s tool to a great extent for this. We came to the conclusion that important human values are: status, self-reflection, inner harmony and meaning-fulness. The first two are negative values that the users have now and the last two are values that are important for our product and a mood board was made to show the human values in the form of pictures and some keywords." (Final report, project group Sleep.5, TG)

Fig. 10. Presenting intended values in a mood board (Image is adopted from Final report, Sleep.5, TG)

Furthermore, three project groups specified that they considered their intended values for developing their concepts (see Fig. 11):

"BinK [our concept] would have the possibility to interact with the users by greeting them and asking them for some help. [...] the product bring a smile to everyone's faces. [...] These aspects cover the values which were decided to be

the most important in the ideation phase. Also the four compartments of BinK instead of the two compartments right now in LaPlace and the fact that BinK eventually will be programmed to be respectful to the users will cover the other values, respectively sustainability and respect." (Final report, project group IoT.4, TG)

Fig. 11. Developing the concept to cover the intended values (Image is adopted from final report, IoT.6, TG)

"By using pictures and cards we found the human values and designs related to our concept 'SEE', and used them to develop the concept." (Final report, project group IoT.6, TG)

"Now that we have our idea, the Fixcloud, it is time to turn this idea into a concept. This means that we have to elaborate the idea by asking questions like 'What is the purpose of our design?' [...] The meetings with [author] helped us answering these questions and made us also look at the human values our design supports. [...] During the meetings with [author] we looked at the human values our design contained. We assigned the values to categories for which certain values are important or applicable. We first looked at the values that are important for our target group. [...] Then we looked what values the context of our design contains (working in the study spaces). [...] At last we looked at the values that are connected with the design goal. [...] The relation between those values is: taking the values respect for others, justice and personal development into account, you create a study environment that is nice to work in. This stimulates the personal development and makes studying in this environment a nice experience which stimulates the value pleasure. This supports our design goal. Ultimately we looked at how these values play role in our design. We want to achieve this by [...]" (Final report, project group IoT.5, TG)

3.4 Validation

One project group used their intended values for evaluation by user testing:

> *"The statements [of the questionnaire] were based on our design goal and human values. Before validating, we made sure we had the right values for our concept. Values that we find important for our users. We would then test if these values are important for them as well, in the first part of the test. We divided all our discussed values into a target group general value-set which centers the values for the entire target group and then we have a value-set for the target group in context of use. This guided the statements for user evaluation 2. This evaluation exists of three parts. In total we tested 11 students. 0% on the sliders means that the user could not identify his or her-self with that statement, and 100% means that it totally suited the user's perception. [...]" (Final report, project group IoT.5, TG)*

All in all, a general look at the results indicates that using human values was with ten groups most reported in conceptualisation (=83%). Both ideation and defining vision with nine groups stand in second place (=75%), and validation with five groups is third (=42%). None of the groups used value words in the realisation phase.

4 Discussion

As our results show, nine out of 16 project groups reported using the tool during their design for different purposes; all six groups of TG, who were present in the workshop and received guidance for using the tool in the group meetings; two introduction groups (IG), who were present in the workshop but not in the latter group meetings; and one group of CG, who was supposed to do not have access to the toolkit. In fact, although they mostly preferred to follow their own personal and creative way, they still used the toolkit for the same purposes as we discussed during the workshop and group meetings. We proposed using the toolkit to generate valuable and creative ideas, and to analyse and valuate anything, such as a person, an object, even an activity or a context, from a value point of view.

We emphasise on - before making any decision - defining design challenge clearly with considering human values. For this, the designer is supposed to start from analysis phase to define vision and design goal and to identify the user and the context of use from a value perspective. Our suggestion for facilitating this is a technique of using our toolkit with the value wheel and the cards, which can be applied for different purposes. For instance, for defining the vision, the designer should consider him/herself in the centre of the value wheel and visualize his/her important values, as mentioned in Sect. 2.2 above. Afterwards, the designer is supposed to consider this visualisation as her/his value-board and conclude it with answering "What is important for me?", "Why I am doing this design?" and "What do I want to achieve?", Furthermore, s/he can link her/his vision to design goal and ask "What is the goal of design?" and "Why a new design is needed?". The designer also can use the same technique for identifying the user. For this, s/he is supposed to moderate a meeting with some people from the target group, ask them to make their own value-boards, and discuss "What is important for them in life?", "What are their needs, wants and dreams?" and "What are their values and anti-values?" In continue, these general questions can be specified about the context of use from the user view and clarify "How do they see the current situation?", "What is right and what is wrong there?", "What is important for them in that context?", and "What is an ideal situation for them?" In this meeting, the value-wheel is supposed to be a ground for discussing and making relevant examples, and the value words and the picture cards could be helpful for this sake. In addition, we suggested that designer could prepare more relevant cards to their topic and put them between the picture cards. To summarise the collected information, we suggest visualising the results in a mood-board or story-board. Also, the designer is asked to make a list of requirements including important human values as guidance for the design phase and as criteria for the evaluation part. By this, we mean to specify important human value not only for the designer but also for the user and the context of use.

We also suggest some creativity techniques with human values to diverge ideas. "Value-based mind mapping", "Random value" and "Value-based participatory" are simple techniques to generate ideas around human values. For instance, in "Value-based mind mapping" shared values can be starting points for ideation: we suggest designer starts with marking relevant values for the project's designer, employer, end user, and other stakeholders in different colours. Then, they were supposed to find shared and different values between those groups. In next step, designer is asked to put their challenge in the middle of the framework and start doing mind-map with human values. For this, they were asked to pick one of the shared values and find an example for that in daily life. S/he is supposed to imagine him/herself as a person who cares a lot about that value, try to link the value to the goal of the project and find a solution. S/he is asked to write or draw their idea on the mind-map as a new branch for that value and try to grow the map like a tree. Designer is supposed to ask him/herself "how to motivate people with this value to use my design?" and/or "How to help people to reach this value as their goal?" In "Random value", the designer is supposed to pick a value word at random, create associations between the random value and her/his design challenge, and use the associations to find new ideas. The idea in "Value-based participatory" is to co-design with two or more persons from the target group and do ideation together around human values. We also suggest that after generating enough ideas, they can cluster them in terms of values. By this, they can focus more on relevant ideas to their vision and design goal, and develop them with combining ideas even from less important groups. For selecting the final idea, we suggest using "Decision matrix", in which the list of requirements including important human values considered as criteria. In this phase, the main application of the tool components is inspiring discussions and idea generations.

For evaluating any object such as a design concept or product, the tool can function the same. For instance, the designer can put the final concept or its picture in the centre of the wheel, ask the user(s) to rate the relevance of value groups to the concept, and then open a discussion to understand "What is the main value of this design from user's view?", "Which value(s) would become stronger with using this concept?" and "Which value(s) would become weaker?". This co-evaluation meeting(s) can help the designer to know whether the design covers the requirements and goals, or not. The same approach can be applied to an existing product in the market to assess and understand the current trends.

Studying the reported usages by students indicated that not only the HuValue tool but also its value point of view can be applied in a design process. This means after knowing the tool and its perspective, designer can apply the view, even without using the toolkit, in different design phases. Widening designers' views in terms of human values and facilitating using this concept in a design process can be helpful for enriching their design concepts with human values. The results of the whole experimental study with design students is published in another article [15]. There we provide empirical evidence that the project groups who were supported with the HuValue toolkit addressed *significantly* stronger human values in their design concepts compared to the control groups.

5   Conclusion

Our HuValue toolkit, consisting of the value wheel and the cards, provides tangible materials to investigate everything from a human value perspective. Due to the flexibility of our components, this function can be fulfilled in many ways and for many purposes. Based on our empirical results, we suggest several possible usages of our tool in a design process as informative examples. These usages are as follows: for defining vision, guiding during ideation, support focus in conceptualisation, and provide criteria in validation. Usage of our tool helps in uncovering the human values of designers behind their needs, goals, motivations and actions in a design process. In this respect, we applied well-known design techniques, and added the important but often neglected *value point of view* to them. In other words, although our comprehensive framework of human values is borrowed from philosophy and social sciences, by revealing the place of our framework in every design discussion, our tool introduces and represents human values as substantiated terms in design, not only as a moral and ethical concern, but also as an essential aspect of design discussions and practice.

Acknowledgement. We are grateful for the PhD scholarship of the Ministry of Science, Research and Technology of Iran, the additional scientific and financial support from the two departments of Industrial Design from Alzahra University (Tehran, Iran) and from Eindhoven University of Technology (Eindhoven, The Netherlands). We are also very grateful for the participation, support and contributions of all students and their project coaches, and in particular the program director Prof S. Wensveen.

References

1. Verbeek, P.P.: What Things Do: Philosophical Reflections on Technology, Agency, and Design. Penn State Press, Pennsylvania (2005)
2. Rokeach, M.: The Nature of Human Values. The Free Press, New York (1973)
3. Steen, M., van de Poel, I.: Making values explicit during the design process. IEEE Technol. Soc. Mag. **31**(4), 63–72 (2012)
4. Friedman, B., Kahn, J.P.H.: Human values, ethics, and design. In: Andrew, S., Jacko, J.A. (eds.) The Human-Computer Interaction Handbook, pp. 1177–1201. CRC Press, Boca Raton (2003)

5. Halloran, J., Hornecker, E., Stringer, M., Harris, E., Fitzpatrick, G.: The value of values: resourcing co-design of ubiquitous computing. CoDesign 5(4), 245–273 (2009)
6. Iversen, O.S., Leong, T.W.: Values-led participatory design: mediating the emergence of values. In: Proceedings of the 7th Nordic Conference on Human-Computer Interaction: Making Sense Through Design, Copenhagen, Denmark (2012)
7. Boztepe, S.: The notion of value and design. In: Proceedings of the Asian Design International Conference, Tsukuba, Japan (2003)
8. Borning, A., Muller, M.: Next steps for value sensitive design. In: Proceedings of the SIGCHI Conference on Human Factors in Computing Systems 2012, Austin, Texas (2012)
9. Kheirandish, S., Funk, M., Wensveen, S., Verkerk, M., Rauterberg, M.: A comprehensive value framework for design. Technology in Society, under review (2020)
10. Kheirandish, S.: HuValue: a tool to enrich design concepts with human values, Eindhoven, The Netherlands: (Doctoral Dissertation), Eindhoven University of Technology (2018)
11. Peterson, C., Seligman, M.E.: Character Strengths and Virtues: A Handbook and Classification, vol. 1. Oxford University Press, Oxford (2004)
12. Schwartz, S.: Universals in the content and structure of values: theoretical advances and empirical tests in 20 countries. Adv. Exp. Soc. Psychol. 25, 1–65 (1992)
13. Verkerk, M.J., Hoogland, J., Van der Stoep, J., de Vries, M.J.: Philosophy of Technology: An Introduction for Technology and Business Students. Routledge, London (2015)
14. Poel, I.: Translating values into design requirements. In: Michelfelder, D.P., McCarthy, N., Goldberg, D.E. (eds.) Philosophy and Engineering: Reflections on Practice, Principles and Process. PET, vol. 15, pp. 253–266. Springer, Dordrecht (2013). https://doi.org/10.1007/978-94-007-7762-0_20
15. Kheirandish, S., Funk, M., Wensveen, S., Verkerk, M., Rauterberg, M.: HuValue: a tool to support design students in considering human values in their design. Int. J. Technol. Des. Educ. (2019)
16. Kheirandish, S., Rauterberg, M.: Human value based game design. In: Proceedings of 2nd National and 1st International Digital Games Research Conference: Trends, Technologies, and Applications (DGRC), Tehran, Iran, pp. 6–16 (2018)
17. Hart, G.: The five W's: an old tool for the new task of audience analysis. Tech. Commun. 43(2), 139–145 (1996)

A Study on Symbolic Aesthetics of China's Splashed Ink Freehand Landscape Painting

Liming Liu[1,2(✉)]

[1] Zhuhai College of Jilin University, Zhuhai, People's Republic of China
23528476@qq.com
[2] Shinawatra University, Bang Toei, Thailand

Abstract. Splash painting and splashing ink landscape painting has been a hot issue in the field of Chinese painting. In the study of the symbolic aesthetics of splashed and splashed ink landscape painting, we find its identity and difference with the symbolic aesthetics of western landscape paintings. In today's fierce collision of Chinese and Western cultures, which penetrate and merge with each other, the study of the aesthetics of splashed ink and landscape symbols will broaden our research horizon of painting innovation, and also help us to return to ourselves and see art and people clearly. And the complexity and richness of the subject's reproduction of the objective scene.

Keywords: Splashed ink landscape painting · Chinese culture · Objective scene reproduction · Aesthetic essence of artistic conception

1 Introduction

Splashing ink is a unique and important method of ink painting in Chinese painting. It is also a concentrated embodiment of the freehand concept and aesthetics of literati painting. Although the use and creation of ink-spattering techniques have become a common phenomenon in the history of paintings in the Ming and Qing dynasties, especially after the middle and late Tang Dynasty, the research and writings on the formation mechanism, occurrence trajectory, aesthetic characteristics, and historical significance of the concept of ink-spattering in early ink paintings are not detailed. Based on this reason, this article starts from the initiation period of Tang Dynasty's ink-spray painting, and also examines the content of literary and poetic works, art forms, regional characteristics, aesthetic psychology, etc. at that time. It mainly focuses on the formation of the history of early ink-spray painting and cultural opportunities. The influence of splashed ink on the creative ideas of freehand of future ink painting.

M. Rauterberg (Ed.): HCII 2020, LNCS 12215, pp. 358–370, 2020.
https://doi.org/10.1007/978-3-030-50267-6_27

Zhang Daqian, Four Screens of Mountains and Waters, 173cm × 356cm, Color on paper, 1955

Although Zhang Yanyuan was prejudiced against ink splashing in the late Tang Dynasty, from the perspective of the entire painting history, the ink splashing method in the Tang Dynasty is not a contingent skill, it is not a grotesque legend, nor is it a flashy limited aesthetic acceptance. It has a continuous evolution process and aesthetic ideal. The early ink-spraying paintings showed the state of artistic exchanges between scholars and doctors, and the process of ink-spraying became the scene of artistic soul communication. For example, in the process of splashing ink by Gu Kuan, Wang Qia, Zhang Zhihe, etc., the actions of the viewer and the singer and dancers were all part of the ink splash creation. Painting became the common aesthetic discovery and creation of the artistic subject and the recipient. Far-reaching influence on spiritual creative ideas,"By leveraging the power of indulgence, splashing with ink, not being stubborn with form, and free from restraint. When painting, there is not a fixed image, but on the basis of wiping and sweeping, with its shape, and then write a relative specific image with pen and ink. Wang Mozhe doesn't know who he is, nor does he know his name. He splashes ink on landscapes, and is often referred to as Wang Mo. He travels between rivers and lakes, often painting landscapes, turquoise stones, and mixed trees. Draw obstacles, drink first. After splashing, use ink splashes. Or laugh or sing, wipe your hands with your feet. Or wave or sweep, or light or thick, according to its shape, as mountains for stones, clouds for water. The hand is free, and if it is natural.

2   Research Model Design

Since modern times, style theory in western painting studies has been introduced into Chinese painting studies, especially since the 1980s. With the introduction of a large number of overseas Chinese studies on Chinese painting studies, style studies have become an important way for Chinese painting studies It has strongly promoted the modern transformation of Chinese painting research. First, "style" as understood by western style theory takes form as its core, and style analysis is mainly form analysis, while the vital characteristics of Chinese painting are obvious and form factors are weak. The formal analysis of Chinese painting is often powerless and difficult to reach the subtleties of Chinese painting. Second, people in the style understood by Western style theory are people in the Western cultural context. They have psychology, personality, class, and power. And so on. Compared with the discouragement, chest order, temperament, and spirituality in Chinese painting aesthetics, the cultural connotation is obviously different.

2.1 Symbol Extraction Principle

The aesthetics of Chinese painting is influenced by the evaluation of human objects, and it tends to regard paintings as organic living organisms like human bodies, with its shape, wind, and character. The stability characteristic of this life form is style. Therefore, the style we understand also has three levels of form, Fengshen, and character. Among them, there is lightness of "shape" and emphasis on "god", and it has the value evaluation of character. The concept of style in Chinese painting aesthetics basically comes from the evaluation of human objects. "Body" is the earliest concept of style. Other important style concepts include lattice, style, style, style, and style. In specific applications, different style concept groups have been derived, and different groups can be combined to generate new style concepts, which is very flexible. complex. This is determined by the dynamic sense of life in Chinese painting style.

2.2 Technique of Writing

Hooking is one of the main techniques of gongbi and freehand drawing. In comparison, more brushwork is used Gongbi hooks are mainly centered and require neatness and rigor, similar to the regular script in calligraphy.

Wipe

Point

Dyeing

- Wipe: The brush stroke is not clear. The wiping is the continuation of the "cun" process, and it is a supplement to 其, the purpose of which is to make the picture effect stronger.
- Point: The expression method of surface modeling, freehand drawing is more commonly used, and there is also a method of boneless staining in gongbi painting. The dots and dyes of gongbi are inseparable, so they are called dot dyes.
- Dyeing: Another way to enhance the effect of the picture. Dyeing in Meticulous painting can be divided into two types: hook dyeing and baking dyeing. The stroke is

formed by strokes. The strokes include three parts: strokes, movements, and receipts. Strokes must be strong.

2.3 Mofa

There are seven main methods of using ink: thick ink method, light ink method, coke ink method, old ink method, broken ink method, ink accumulation method, and ink splash method.

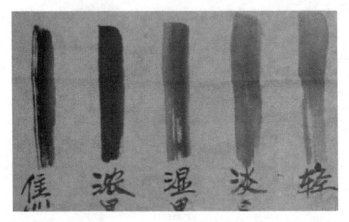

Dense ink method, dipped in thick ink with a pen and sketched quickly. Coke method. The key to the use of burnt ink is that the pen root still needs a certain amount of water. During the squeeze of the brush, the water leaks out of the burnt ink. Ink stain method. Commonly used loose smoke ink, stained ink into the painting. Accumulation of ink. Different layers of ink are used to dye, which is called accumulated ink. Splash ink method. One is that the ink is directly spilled on the paper, and based on the natural bleeding ink, use a pen to add appropriate dots. The other is the ink-spray method. Washing method. After painting with ink, rinse with water at a speed of wet to make the ink ooze naturally. Sumo method. The scum is contained due to the degumming of the ink, and the ink is exposed. Therefore, when using the pen, pay attention to virtual spirits, looseness, and not to drag. Ink breaking method. The direction of using the pen should also pay attention to the change, straight pen penetrating with pen, pen penetrating with pen. Light ink method. There are two kinds of wet and dry.

2.4 Classification of Chinese Painting Symbol Expressions

Mountain painting

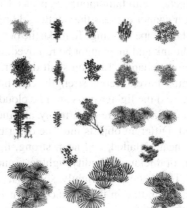

Water painting   **Tree painting**

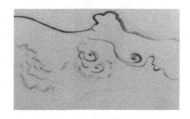

云卷云舒，轻盈曼妙，所以在勾云时注意线条
的流畅和轻盈。

勾云法关键在用笔，线条的运用提中带力，灵动随和，要符合
云的轻柔飘逸的特性。注意留白的疏密。

Cloud   **painting**

2.5 Form and Content Analysis

The characteristics of the composition of Chinese landscape paintings. The composition of landscape paintings, also called chapters or layouts, is called the business position in the six methods of Chinese painting. The painters of all ages have attached great importance to composition. Zhang Yanyuan of the Tang Dynasty said, "As for the business position, painting is always necessary." (Zhang Yanyuan's "Historical Paintings of Different Dynasties" Volume 1) A certain understanding, I realize that composition has a great relationship with a landscape painting: To be able to make full use of the composition method to make the layout of the picture very reasonable, you must first understand the Chinese painters' observation of natural landscapes and the perspective of Chinese painting.

Regarding the main and sub-levels of the composition of Chinese landscape painting, first of all, it is the subject and guest. There is a main part in a painting, or a relatively major part. This refers to the component of the specific scene shape. The main part is not necessarily the important part., Or the location of the vicinity is not restricted, the other small parts are matched with faint mountain peaks. Clear levels make you feel ethereal. Without levels, you cannot express the depth and breadth of natural space. So level is very important in landscape painting. To make the picture layered, the ink and ink can be removed first. If the ink and ink cannot be removed, there will be no emptiness if there is a layer. On the other hand, "Linluan shall deliver, and Qing shall be the law." The tops of each part must have different strengths. The houses in the mountains and forests are slightly lighter, and the lighter parts are like clouds and smoke. Each part is thicker and lighter, and the other parts are in harmony, and the changes of the lighter and richer levels are enriched. Different objects must be described according to the principles of near large, small, near, detailed, and near, strong, light, and light. They must also be matched with pens of thickness, rigidity, lightness, and speed. The same should be used for drawing trees. The distance is slightly, such as a small tree in the vicinity, although it is not large, but a building in the distance, but it is large in the distance. This is to express the scene with the layers of pen and ink of near and far, so that the picture and layers are richer.

The picture structure is the same as writing an article. The paragraph structure and organization arrangement must have a unified concept. The scene in front of me is just a part, and a painting should be a whole, which is concentrated, refined and generalized. It is like arranging arrays, which is to process natural materials in an organized way, and form a complete and unified whole on the screen.

2.6 Middle Hall

The middle hall is also called the vertical axis, vertical frame, and horizontal frame, which is named for hanging in the middle of the hall. Both sides of the middle hall can be paired with couplets. This frame is suitable for panoramic composition.

Through the screen

Long roll

Banner

Folding fan

- Long roll: Long rolls are also called horizontal rolls, with lengths ranging from a few meters, tens of meters, or even hundreds of meters. There is no fixed size for the length of the long roll, which is very flexible. It uses scatter perspective and more global composition.
- Banner: Banners are also called horizontal drapes. It can be long or short, wide or narrow, suitable for various composition forms.
- Folding fan: There are two kinds of composition for folding fan painting: one is to draw the horizon of the picture horizontally regardless of the radian of the upper and

lower sides of the fan; the other is to keep the painted scene parallel to the arcs of the upper and lower sides of the fan, namely Move with fan.

- Group fan: The group fan is mostly circular or oval, and the content drawn is mostly small landscapes. Therefore, the composition advocates simplicity and charm, and rarely takes complicated composition forms.

3   Research Application

3.1   Chinese Landscape Painting

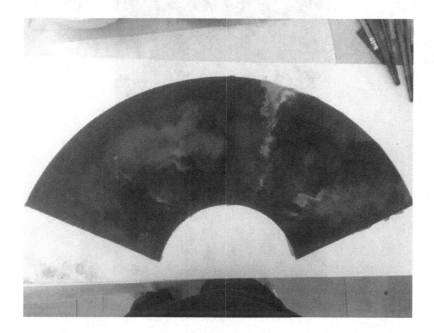

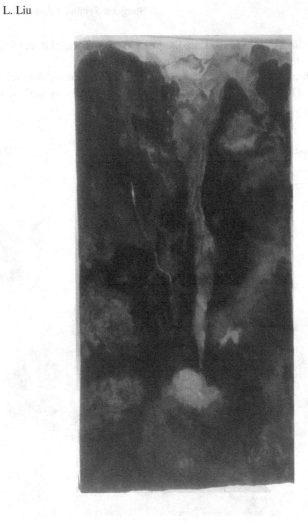

3.2 3D Animation Effect Application

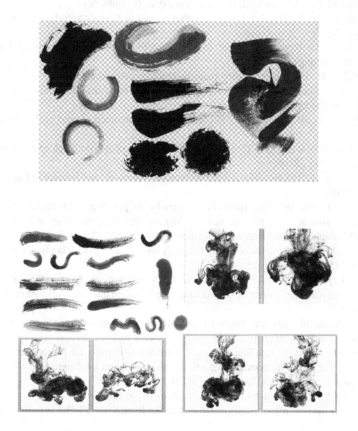

4 Conclusion

Ink splashing surpasses the level of painting skills and becomes a freehand symbol of Chinese art. It has reached the poetic nature of self-existence through the simplest and most direct ink splashing. The process of ink painting means spirituality and unlimited free imagination, becoming China's unique art way of expression. In terms of the creative and spiritual freedom of art, splashing ink is a painting presentation of Chinese cultural tradition and aesthetic ideals, and its freehand expression and aesthetic inspiration are important values to be adhered to in modern and contemporary Chinese painting.

References

1. Guo, D.: On the causes and artistic differences of Zhang Daqian and Liu Haisu's splashing ink and color. J. Nanjing Univ. Arts (Fine Art and Design) (2015)
2. Liao, J., Huang, Z.: The causes and evolution of Zhang Daqian's splashed ink and splashed color art form. Searching (2012)

370   L. Liu

3. Li, K., Wang, X.: The formation of Zhang Daqian's splashed ink and splash of color landscape painting and its artistic value. Beauty and the Times (in Chinese)
4. Shao, X., Rong, B.: The Academic Contribution of Liu Haisu's Splashed Color Landscape Painting (2017)
5. Dong, X., Qi, L.: Beyond the image: interpretation of Hou Beiren's "Abstract Splash Color" landscape paintings (2017)
6. Liu, Z., Liu, H.: Pioneer innovating painting language. Artworks. 2017
7. Zhang, X.: Characteristics of western impressionist painting from Liu Haisu's ink and color splash. J. Heihe Univ. (2016)
8. Cen, X., Ye, R.: Responsibility of cultural person—remembering teacher. J. Literat. History (2016)
9. Li, C.: Exploration of Zhang Daqian's artistic technique of splashing ink and splashing color. Western Leather (2016)
10. Wang, X., Rong, B.: One millenary in one hundred years—a brief account of Liu Haisu's Art Road (2016)
11. Wang, Y.: On song Wenzhi's splash-colored landscape painting. Art Educ (2015)
12. Luo, L.: Traveling to the poor in water, sitting and watching the clouds rise—Liu Zhibai's life and his splashing landscapes. J. Guizhou Univ. (Art Ed.) (2015)
13. Wan, Y.: The artistic features of Zhang Daqian's ink and splash color landscape painting. Big Stage (2015)
14. Liu, D.: Exploring pen and ink language in sketching. Shenyang Normal University (2012)
15. Cao, Y.: A preliminary study of the ink language of ink characters. Hubei Academy of Fine Arts (2019)
16. Sui C.: Pen and ink language features of contemporary post-70 s ink and wash figure paintings. Shandong Normal University (2019)
17. Wei, Y.: The report of "Lou Shan Xiongzi". Guizhou University for Nationalities (2019)
18. Chen, L.: The modeling performance and the use of pen and ink language in the creation of "Shuixieweiyu". Yangzhou University (2018)
19. Rao J.: Ku Ying made a mess. Chinese Academy of Art (2018)
20. Wang, H.: Effects of reform and opening on the "Xu Jiang System". Henan Normal University (2018)
21. Yan, S.: Talking about Zhejiang School Figure Painting—Li Zhenjian's Pen and Ink Language. Hangzhou Normal University (2018)
22. Chen, J.: Traditional Chinese Education and Simple Chemical Engineering. Nanjing Art Institute, Nanjing (2018)
23. A Study of the Brush and Ink Language in the Creation of Freehand Flower and Bird Paintings
24. Li, G.: Painting, Painting and Nature. Fudan University Press (2012)
25. Taixiangzhou: Look Up at the Vertical Image. Zhonghua Book Company (2011)
26. Pan, G.: Pan Tianshou Talks Art Records. Zhejiang People's Fine Arts Publishing House (2011)
27. Chen, Z.: Essentials of Paintings in Stone Pots. People's Fine Arts Publishing House (2010)
28. Yin, X.: Essentials of Ancient Landscape Painting. People's Fine Arts Publishing House (2010)
29. Ren, M.: Dan Qinghuan. Wuhan University Press, Beijing (2009)
30. Wang, S.: Research on Chinese Painting Theory. Guangxi Normal University Press, Guilin (2009)
31. Yu, J.: History of Chinese Painting. Southeast University Press, Nanjing (2009)
32. Zhang, J.: History of Chinese Paintings. Shandong People's Publishing House, Jinan (2008)
33. Li, T.: The Contemporary Significance of Lao Zi's Aesthetic Thoughts. China Social Science Press (2008)

Study on the Development of Ruichang Bamboo Weaving Patterns Based on Computer Graphics and Machine Learning

Miao Liu⬤, Chenyue Wang(✉), and Jiale Zhou

East China University of Science and Technology, Shanghai 200237, China
183787975@qq.com, 691352768@qq.com

Abstract. Ruichang bamboo weaving in Jiangxi Province, known as one of China's significant intangible cultural heritages (ICH), faces multiple problems such as old-fashioned and monotonous patterns due to a lack of inheritors, uncreative design and low efficiency. This study applies machine learning and computer graphics to the generation of new Ruichang bamboo weaving patterns, or more specifically, it generates new patterns by establishing the Generative Adversarial Networks (GAN) algorithm model, inputting reasonable parameters and applying Python and Tensorflow frameworks. This study develops and diversifies bamboo weaving patterns through machine deep learning, providing new approaches and ideas for the ICH protection.

Keywords: Machine learning · Generative Adversarial Networks · Bamboo weaving patterns · Intangible cultural heritage protection

1 Introduction

Ruichang bamboo weaving is among the list of national intangible cultural heritages. As the "hometown of Chinese folk art", Ruichang is located northwest of Jiangxi Province, China and on the south bank of the middle reaches of the Yangtze River. More than 60,000 acres of mangosteen grow here with nearly ten varieties such as moso bamboo, bambusa and fishscale bamboo. Ruichang bamboo weaving craft is so time-honored that bamboo baskets transporting the ore have been completely unearthed from local Shang-Zhou ancient copper smelting site. Now it has formed its own unique style after thousands of years of inheritance and development by countless craftsmen.

The completely handmade Ruichang bamboo weaving is hard to be produced by modern machines due to its complicated process, high weaving standards, difficult weaving skill and great varieties. In Ruichang, bamboo weaving is everywhere and closely related to everyday life. Main products include bed, desk, chair, stool and cabinet. In recent years, more than one hundred kinds of new products have been developed, such as flower basket, bamboo weaving birds and animals (chicken, duck, turtle, etc.), fruit basket, gift box. Exquisite, beautiful and useful, these bamboo weaving products are exceptional crafts.

© Springer Nature Switzerland AG 2020
M. Rauterberg (Ed.): HCII 2020, LNCS 12215, pp. 371–385, 2020.
https://doi.org/10.1007/978-3-030-50267-6_28

The Jiangxi Provincial Government in China issued the Blue Book of Jiangxi Culture - Annual Report on the Development of Jiangxi Intangible Cultural Heritage (2016), pointing out that "there exist urgent outstanding problems in the protection of Jiangxi intangible cultural heritage, such as an extreme lack of professional talent teams and decreased strength of innovation in protection and utilization of intangible cultural heritage." As for Ruichang bamboo weaving, on the one hand, the craft is complicated and hard to grasp, most young people are not willing to learn and inherit, while elder craftsmen are unable to continue working, so with a lack of inheritors and a bleak prospect, it needs urgent protection; on the other hand, the bamboo weaving product patterns are old-fashioned and monotonous, the artificial designs are uncreative and low-efficient.

To solve these problems, this study leverages the advantage of GAN models that they can generate images, and generates the patterns of Ruichang bamboo weaving by computer deep learning after field sampling.

Goodfellow, et al. [1] mentioned the GAN model in 2014. Currently, the GAN has been widely applied in the data generation, image completion, high-resolution image reconstruction of deep learning, transfer learning, reinforcement learning, etc. In addition, it has been used for image generation, image translation, interactive image generation, etc. [2].

GAN learns the generative model of data distribution in an adversarial way (Fig. 1). It provides a brand new technology and method for the computer vision application and generates high-quality samples through unique zero-sum game and adversarial training with stronger feature learning and feature expression than traditional machine learning algorithm. Now it achieves remarkable success in machine vision, especially in sample generation [3]. GAN includes large amounts of apps because it can learn and simulate almost any types of data distribution. In general, it can handle ultra-low-resolution images and generate any types of images, etc.

2 Study Purpose

This study aims to apply computer graphics and machine learning to the generation of new bamboo weaving patterns based on the GAN model, protect the ICH in a digital way, enrich the Ruichang bamboo weaving pattern database through GAN technology, and prevent the loss of ICH due to a lack of inheritors.

3 Study Tools and Theories

3.1 Basic Tools

Python language and Tensorflow framework have been adopted in this experiment.

Python is a computer programming language and an object-oriented dynamically typed language initially designed for the writing of automated scripts (shell). With the updated versions and added functions of language, it has been increasingly applied to the development of independent and large-scale projects.

TensorFlow is a deep learning framework with leading market shares and user amount. It can carry out high-performance distribution numerical computing on the CPU

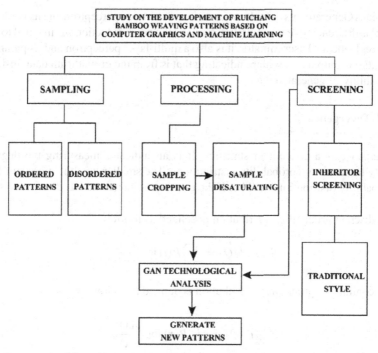

Fig. 1. Framework of the study on the development of Ruichang bamboo weaving patterns based on computer graphics and machine learning

or GPU based on the data flow graphs. The TensorFlow2.0 launched in 2019 simplifies the deep learning API, takes Keras as its advanced deep learning API, better integrates with Python through Eager Execution, and greatly facilitates the machine learning of Python language [4].

With its unique advantages, Python becomes the most popular language in machine learning that can easily yet efficiently accomplish the machine learning tasks by virtue of Scikitlearn, TensorFlow, etc.

3.2 Mathematical Theories of GAN

GAN involves large amounts of mathematical formulas. For the convenience of descriptions, mathematical symbols mentioned below are listed as follows:

data: groundtruth
pdate: groundtruth distribution
z: noise (input data)
p_z: distribution of original noise
p_g: data distribution after generator
G(): Generative mapping function
D():Discriminant mapping function

G means Generator, its default structure is a multi-layer perceptron and its parameters are θ_g. (;) is the generative mapping function and the noise reduction z is mapped to a new data space. D means Discriminator, it is also a multi-layer perceptron and its parameters are θ_d. $(x;\theta_d)$ is output as a scalar, indicating that is from the groundtruth data, instead of the probability of generated data.

3.3 KL Divergence

KL divergence is a concept in statistics. It is an indicator measuring the degree of similarity between two probability distributions. The smaller it is, the more similar the two probability distributions will be. If the two are the same, the KL divergence should be 0.

The discrete probability distribution is defined as follows:

$$D_{KL}(P\|Q) = \sum_i P(i) \log \frac{P(i)}{Q(i)} \tag{1}$$

The continuous probability distribution is defined as follows:

$$D_{KL}(P\|Q) = \int_{-\infty}^{+\infty} P(x) \log \frac{p(x)}{q(x)} dx \tag{2}$$

KL divergence is not commutative, so it cannot be understood as the concept of "distance", it measures not the distance between two distributions in space, more accurately, it measures the information lost of one distribution in comparison with the other. By continuously changing the parameters of estimated distributions, different KL divergence could be achieved. When the KL divergence reaches the minimum value within a certain range of change, corresponding parameter is the desired optimal parameter. This is the optimization procedure of KL divergence. The tasks performed by the neural networks are function approximators to a large degree. So the neural networks can be used to learn many complex functions. The key to the learning process is to set an objective function to measure the learning effect, i.e., train the networks by minimizing the loss of the objective function.

3.4 Maximum Likelihood Estimation

One of the key mathematical theories for the GAN is maximum likelihood estimation, which is a kind of mathematical statistical method that can obtain the parameters of relevant probability density function of a sample set.

If the population X is discrete:

We assume that the distribution law is $\{X = x\} = p(x;\theta)$, is the parameter to be estimated, and $p(x;\theta)$ represents the probability of the occurrence of when the estimated parameter is

$$L(\theta) = L(x_1, x_2, \ldots, x_n) = \prod_{i=1}^{n} p(x_i; \theta) \tag{3}$$

If the population X is continuous:

Assume that the probability density is f (;), is the parameter to be estimated.

$$L(\theta) = L(x_1, x_2, \ldots, x_n) = \prod_{i=1}^{n} f(x_i; \theta) \tag{4}$$

Among them, (θ) is named the sample likelihood function.

When the sample values are: $x_{1,2,\cdots},x$,

If:

$$L(x_1, x_2, \ldots, x_n; \widehat{\theta}) = \max_\theta L(x_1, x_2, \ldots, x_n; \theta) \tag{5}$$

That is, when the parameter $\theta = \widehat{\theta}$, the maximum value can be assigned to the likelihood function, then the θ is the maximum likelihood estimation value of $\widehat{\theta}$.

To apply the maximum likelihood estimation to the GAN, first a probability distribution function $P_{\text{mod el}}(x; \theta)$ for the generative model shall be defined, which means that this distribution function is determined by the parameter θ. In practice, we hope to continuously optimize the parameters so that the probability distribution function of the generative model $P_{\text{mod el}}(x; \theta)$ can be as close to the groundtruth distribution as possible.

The sample values can be obtained by collecting original data. We assume that the data are $\{x^1, x^2, \ldots, X^m\}$. Then we can obtain the probability distribution function $P_{\text{mod el}}(x^{(i)}; \theta)$ of multiple sample values according to the data sample, finally the likelihood function of generative model can be obtained through above-mentioned maximum likelihood estimation:

$$L = \prod_{i=1}^{m} P_{\text{mod el}}(x^{(i)}; \theta) \tag{6}$$

Now the objective is to obtain the maximum likelihood estimate θ^* of the likelihood function through the maximum likelihood estimation.

To simplify the operation, now we calculate the logarithm of all the $P_{\text{mod el}}(x; \theta)$ and transform the multiplication to the sum.

$$\theta^* = \arg\max \prod_{i=1}^{m} P_{\text{mod el}}(x^{(i)}; \theta)$$

$$= \arg\max \log \prod_{i=1}^{m} P_{\text{mod el}}(x^{(i)}; \theta)$$

$$= \arg\max \sum_{i=1}^{m} \log P_{\text{mod el}}(x^{(i)}; \theta) \tag{7}$$

For the above formula, we can approximately transform the sum to the expected value and then obtain the integral expression of the formula:

$$\theta^* = \arg\max E_{x\sim pdata} \log P_{\text{mod el}}(x; \theta)$$

$$= \arg \max_{\theta} \int p_{data}(x) \log p_{\text{mod el}}(x; \theta) dx \qquad (8)$$

By adding a constant term $\int p_{data}(x) \log p_{\text{mod el}}(x; \theta) dx$ unrelated to θ in the above integral formula, following derivations can be further obtained:

$$\theta^* = \arg \max_{\theta} \left(\int p_{data}(x) \log p_{\text{mod el}}(x; \theta) dx - \int p_{data}(x) \log p_{data}(x) dx \right)$$

$$= \arg \max_{\theta} \int p_{data}(x) \log \frac{p_{\text{mod el}}(x; \theta)}{p_{data}(x)} dx \qquad (9)$$

After the above transformation, according to the definition of KL divergence:

$$KL(P\|Q) = \int p(x) \log \frac{p(x)}{q(x)} dx \qquad (10)$$

We can transform the above integration formula into the form of KL divergence:

$$\theta^* = \arg \min_{\theta} KL(p_{data}(x) \| p_{\text{mod el}}(x; \theta)) \qquad (11)$$

$P_{\text{mod el}}(x; \theta)$ can be obtained by the prior probability distribution:

$$P_{\text{mod el}}(x) = \int_z P_{prior}(z) I_{[G(z)=x]} dz \qquad (12)$$

Among them, I represents an indicative function and its expression is:

$$P_{\text{mod el}}(x) = \begin{cases} 0 \; G(z) \neq x \\ 1 \; G(z) = x \end{cases} \qquad (13)$$

3.5 Framework

The study on the development of Ruichang bamboo weaving patterns based on computer graphics and machine learning can be divided into 4 parts: Sampling, sample processing, screening, and application (see Fig. 1).

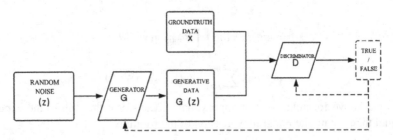

Fig. 2. Basic framework of GAN

4 Basic Components of GAN

GAN is a deep generative model containing two competitive neural network models: Generative model G and discriminant model D. The former aims to learn the distribution of groundtruth samples and generate the generative samples with the similarity close to the groundtruth samples, the latter aims to discriminate whether the domesticated samples come from groundtruth samples or the generative samples. To put it simply, through continuous adversarial training, the model G maximizes the generation of false generative samples, and the model D minimizes the probability of its false discrimination [5] (see Fig. 2).

4.1 Generative Model

In probability theory and mathematical statistics, the generative model is defined as follows: Under the premise of some known hidden parameters, a model of raw data is randomly generated, and the relationship between observations and labeled data sequences can be represented by a joint probability distribution. In machine learning, the generative model can be used to directly model the data, such as sampling the data according to the probability density of a certain variable, or carry out aided modelling with conditional probability. The conditional probability distribution can be derived from Bayes' theorem. The name of generative model is obtained because the model directly represents the generation relationship that a given input X generates an output Y. Common generative models include Naive Bayes, Mixed Gaussian Model, Hidden Markov Model, etc.

Naive Bayes Generative Model: Use the maximum likelihood estimation (using the data distribution in the sample to fit the actual distribution probability of the data) to obtain the prior probability. By learning the prior probability distribution ($Y = c_k$) and conditional probability ($X = x|Y = c_k$),

the corresponding posterior probability is:

$$P(Y = c_k|X = x) = \frac{P(X = x|Y = c_k)P(Y = c_k)}{\sum_K P(x = x|Y = c_k)P(Y = c_k)} \tag{14}$$

Mixed Gaussian Model: The Gaussian model is an extension of the probability density function of single Gaussian model. It uses multiple Gaussian probability density functions (normal distribution curves) to accurately quantify the distribution. It is a statistical model decomposing the variable distribution into multiple Gaussian probability density function (normal distribution curves) distributions.

The discrete probability density of mixed Gaussian model is:

$$P(y|\theta) = \sum_{k=1}^{k} \alpha_k \phi(y|\theta_k) \tag{15}$$

The continuous probability density of mixed Gaussian model is:

$$\phi(y|\theta_k) = \frac{1}{\sqrt{2\pi}\sigma_k} \exp\left(-\frac{(y - \mu_k)^2}{2\sigma_k^2}\right) \tag{16}$$

Hidden Markov Model (HMM) is a statistical model that uses a hidden Markov chain to randomly generate observation sequences. HMM is a probability model of time series. It describes the process of randomly generating unobservable state random sequences from a hidden Markov chain, and then generating an observation from each state to generate an observation random sequence. It contains three elements: the initial state probability vector pie, the state transition probability matrix A, and the observation probability matrix B.

4.2 Discriminant Model

Discriminant model is also called conditional model, or conditional probability model, which estimates conditional probability distributions. For conditional probability ($y|x$), the basic idea is to establish a discriminant function under the condition of limited samples and directly study the prediction model. The task of the discriminant model is to discover the optimal classification surface among different classes, reflecting the differences among heterogeneous data. Common discriminant models include logistic regression, SVM traditional neural network, k-proximity method, decision tree, etc.

4.3 Globally Optimal Solution of GAN ($p_g = p_{data}$)

First, we obtain the optimal discriminator D under the known generator G. For the fixed generator G, the optimal discriminator D is:

$$D_G^*(x) = \frac{p_{data}(x)}{p_{data}(x) + p_g(x)} \tag{17}$$

4.4 Derivative Model of GAN

We summarize the classification of common GAN derived models from the loss function, application and improvement of models, etc. of GAN models, as shown in Table 1.

Here we mainly introduce the DCGAN and WGAN-GP in the study:

Radford, Luke Metz and Soumith Chintalahave attempted to solve the problem of instability of GAN training by using supervised learning based on convolution neural network architecture [9] to extend GAN. Convolution neural networks feature higher performance in deep learning tasks, and combine GAN with convolution neural network architecture. For the construction of GAN, they only used existing supervised learning tools to construct Deep Convolution Generative Adversarial Networks (DCGAN), greatly reducing the duration of network construction and improving the efficiency of model construction and operation. Finally, they discovered an architecture that can stably train various datasets and generate higher-resolution images, which is called DCGAN.

Arjovsky et al. [10] proposed WGAN, which abandoned the JS divergence definition of traditional GAN and used Earth Mover distance (EM distance) to calculate the distance between two distributions. The EM distance is used to monitor the quality of the model, so as to solve the problems of GAN training, such as instability and model collapse. However, this method sometimes could only generate poor samples.

Table 1. Classification of GAN derived models.

Improved GAN based on the loss functions	f-GAN, Least-Square GAN, Loss-sensitive GAN, WGAN,WGAN-GP,WGAN-LP, DRAGAN, BEGAN, Fisher GAN, EBGAN, etc.	
Improved GAN based on the model application	Improved GAN based on the network architecture	CGAN, DCGAN, InfoGAN, StackGAN, ALGAN, ASGAN, etc.
	Improved GAN based on encoder	BEGAN,VAE-GAN, BiGAN, tDCGAN, [6], [7], [8], etc.
	Other improvements of GAN	LAPGAN, MGAN, 3D-GAN, SRGAN, ESRGAN, etc.

In view of the shortcomings of WGAN, Gulrajani et al. [11]. proposed an improved version (WGAN-GP) of WGAN. The improved WGAN-GP solved the problems such as parameter concentration, gradient explosion and gradient disappearance, which arose from the weight clipping of WGAN.

5 Study Materials

5.1 Sampling

Collect existing Ruichang bamboo weaving patterns. From July to August 2019, we went to Ruichang, Jiangxi Province, China (115.65 longitude, 29.68 latitude) to inspect the protection of the ICH of bamboo weaving in Ruichang and collect samples of bamboo weaving patterns. We visited Ruichang Nanyi Bamboo Weaving Factory, local museums, local folk museums etc., and collected 210 samples of bamboo weaving patterns by taking pictures.

5.2 Sample Processing

Crop the sample images of Ruichang bamboo weaving patterns. Firstly, we divided one image into 9 zones, each of which is a 1×1 square with a resolution of 1420×1420. As shown in Fig. 3, a complete pattern image can be divided into 9 sub-images with the same size and different unit patterns. When processing samples, the size and resolution of each sample image must be consistent. There were 300 sample images available after processing. Due to the limited length of article, Fig. 4 only shows sample images numbered 1–60.

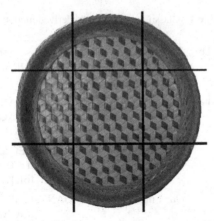

Fig. 3. Bamboo weaving pattern sample zonation

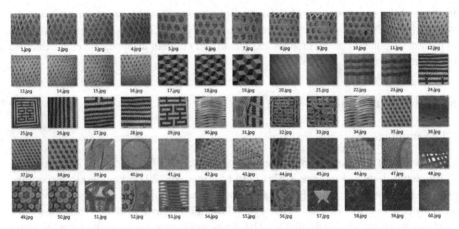

Fig. 4. Sample images numbered 1–60

6 Experiment and Results

6.1 Experimental Environment Configuration

Machine Configuration: During the experiment, the computer was equipped with Windows system. Due to the support of the motherboard, the computer was equipped with two graphics cards. Main graphics card: NVidia GTX1080Ti; the secondary graphics card: NVidia GTX1070; Running memory: 32 GB; CPU: Intel i7-9700 K.

Software and IDE configuration: The programming language was the Python (a mainstream language in recent years). The version number was Python 3.7.3 and the release date is March 25, 2019. The TensorFlow version was TensorFlow 2.0 Alpha and the release date is March 7, 2019. Python's IDE was Pycharm community edition January 1, 2019.

6.2 Training Process

In the file model.py, first define the DCGAN class. The methods include build_model (self), sigmoid_cross_entropy_with_logits (x, y), train (self, config), discriminator (self, image, y = None, reuse = False), generator (self, z, y = None), sampler (self, z, y = None), load (self, checkpoint_dir)

Prepare the dataset:

(1) Create a new folder named data in the root directory of the DCGAN project;

(2) Create another folder named TRAIN_DATA in this folder;

(3) Copy the Ruichang training images to the TRAIN_DATA folder;

Enter the command in the terminal: python main.py –dataset TRAIN_DATA –train for network training.

Among them:

-dataset TRAIN_DATA means using the data in the TRAIN_DATA folder for training;

-train means training DCGAN, the command without this parameter means testing DCGAN.

The following code in the main.py file outputs the images generated by DCGAN:

142 if FLAGS.visualize;

143 OPTION = 1

144 visualizs(sess, dcgan, FLAGS, OPTION, FLAGS.sample_dir)

Note that when defining the DCGAN class, the internal parameters need not be adjusted, and its parameters have been written in the main program main.py.

Results can be generated after training and processing 300 samples obtained through field inspection and sampling.

6.3 Results Generation

After using DCGAN to train the CPU for 500 rounds, the computer generated 113 new Ruichang bamboo weaving pattern images. The resolution of DCGAN output image was 64 × 64. The new representative Ruichang bamboo weaving patterns generated by DCGAN are shown in Figs. 5, 6 and 7.

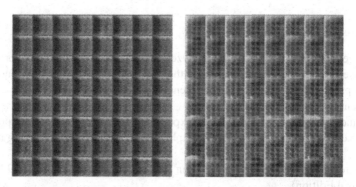

Fig. 5. Brown square patterns generated by DCGAN (Color figure online)

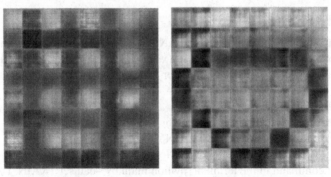

Fig. 6. Linear and heart-shaped patterns generated by DCGAN

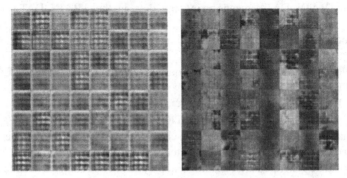

Fig. 7. Yellow square patterns generated by DCGAN (Color figure online)

It can be seen from the new patterns that the colors of new images are richer and more varied than traditional Ruichang bamboo weaving patterns. After zooming in, the texture is still visible. Compared with traditional Ruichang bamboo weaving patterns, newly generated pattern images feature multiple paths while most traditional Ruichang bamboo weaving patterns show only one path, but the image quality of the new patterns is not high enough.

6.4 Improved Experiment

After the generation of DCGAN, we analyzed the generated Ruichang pattern images and discovered that the image quality of the new patterns was not high enough. To solve this problem, the improved experiments adopted WGAN-GP. The experimental environment was configured as follows:

Machine configuration: During the experiment, the computer is equipped with Ubuntu 16.04 system; CPU: i7-8700 k; graphics card: Nidia 2080Ti; running memory: 16G.

Software and IDE configuration: Python IDE is PyCharm February 2019 February (Professional Edition)

Prepare the dataset: Put the training images in/data/pic in the root directory of the file, the specific form is./data/faces/*.jpg

Commands for network training:

CUDA_VISIBLE_DEVICES = 0 python train.py –dataset = pic –epoch = 500 –adversarial_loss_mode = gan –gradient_penalty_mode = 1-gp

Among them, CUDA_VISIBLE_DEVICES = 0: uses GPU for training

Running code of python train.py: train.py

dataset: select the dataset for training

epoch: number of training rounds

adversarial_loss_mode: loss function type for network training

gradient_penalty_mode: gradient penalty method for network training

In train.py, the following codes output the images generated by the network:

```
# sample
if it_g % 64 = 0:
x_fake = sample(z)
x_fake = np.transpose(x_fake.data.cpu().numpy(), (0,2,3,1))
print('shape:',x_fake.shape)
for i in range(0,25):
img = im.immerge(x_fake[4*i:4*(i + 4),:,:,:],n_rows = 4).squeeze()
im.imwite(img,py.join(sample_dir, 'iter-%09d-%03d.jp'%(it_g,i)))
```

6.5 Improved Generation Results

After using WGAN-GP to train the CPU, the computer generated a total of 825 new Ruichang bamboo weaving pattern images. The quality of the bamboo weaving pattern image output by WGAN-GP was higher than that of the images generated by the previous DCGAN. The new images showed richer curves and circular shapes than the pattern images generated by the DCGAN previously. The improved experiment generated new representative patterns of Ruichang bamboo weaving, as shown in Figs. 8, 9 and 10.

Fig. 8. Green arc and yellow circular patterns generated by WGAN-GP (Color figure online)

The improved images of the new patterns of Ruichang bamboo weaving can be applied to the actual pattern weaving and the production of bamboo handicrafts after being screened by bamboo weaving craftsmen.

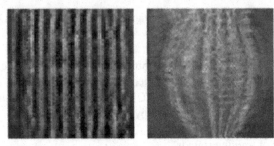

Fig. 9. Black stripes and red spindle-shaped patterns generated by WGAN-GP (Color figure online)

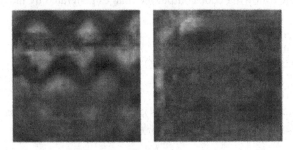

Fig. 10. Zigzag and stripe patterns generated by WGAN-GP

7 Summary

DCGAN is suitable for most image generations and can be trained with only natural images. It can run on the CPU with a low implementation cost. It refines and improves the GAN. The DCGAN generator and discriminator use convolution neural networks; the Jiangxi Ruichang bamboo weaving pattern images generated by DCGAN are diverse, but their image quality is not high enough and the model training is unstable. After improving the experiment and using the WGAN-GP to train the CPU, the image quality is higher than before. The weaving patterns generated by the GAN model also possess the characteristics of high efficiency, high utilization rate, high quality, etc.

This study creatively introduces machine learning and computer graphics into the innovation and inheritance of ICH, enriching the Ruichang bamboo patterns in Jiangxi Province, China. It establishes a GAN algorithm model, inputs reasonable parameters, and uses Python and Tensorflow frameworks to generate new machine patterns.

We adopt computer graphics and machine learning to bring widespread publicity to Jiangxi ICH at home and abroad, and accelerate the application of digital technology in ICH. The new generated patterns can be widely used in industry-academia cooperation, culture, economic industries, etc. to assist the bamboo weaving enterprises in Ruichang, Jiangxi Province to efficiently and rapidly produce more innovative Ruichang bamboo weaving products. The application of new patterns in the cultural and economic industries is as follows: 1. In terms of physical cultural and creative design and virtual weaving experience in local museums, it can bring local culture to the world and attract tourists to yield economic benefits. 2. In terms of design education, new patterns can be used to cultivate the discernment of bamboo weaving inheritors. 3. The expanded new patterns can enrich Ruichang bamboo weaving pattern database and apply computer technology to the protection of ICH.

Meanwhile, it provides new approaches and ideas for the application of GAN technology in the development of traditional crafts and the protection of ICH.

References

1. Goodfellow, I.J., Pouget-Abadie, J., Mirza, M., et al.: Generative adversarial nets. In: 21st International Conference on Neural Information Processing Systems, Malaysia (2014)
2. Ge, S., Fan, B., Zhe, Y.: Review of studies based on generative adversarial networks. Comput. Knowl. Technol. **15**(25), 197–198 (2019)
3. Cao, Y., Jia, L., Chen, Y., Lin, N., Li, X.: Review of generative adversarial networks and computer vision application. J. Graph. Images **23**(10), 1433–1449 (2018)
4. Xu, Y., Su, B.: Features of Python language and its application in machine learning. Computer Products and Distribution **2019**(12), 142 (2019)
5. Wu, S., Li, X.: Review of study progress of generative adversarial networks. Front. Comput. Sci. Technol. **1**(13), 13 (2020)
6. Donahue, J., Krähenbühl, P., Darrell, T.: Adversarial feature learning. In: 5th International Conference on Learning Representations, ICLR, France (2017)
7. Perarnau, G., van de Weijer, J., Raducanu, B., et al, F.: Invertible conditional gans for image editing. CoRR abs, **16**(11), 6–7 (2016)
8. Li, Y., Swersky, K., Zemel, R.S.: Generative moment matching networks. In: 32nd International Conference on Machine Learning, ICML, France (2015)
9. Heidi, L., Tero, K., Antti, M., Jorma, V.: Novel glass welding technique for hermetic encapsulation. In 5th Electronics System-Integration Technology Conference (ESTC), Finland (2014)
10. Arjovsky, M., Chintala, S., Bottou, L.: Wasserstein GAN. CoRR abs, **17**(1), 75–78 (2017)
11. Gulrajani, I., Ahmed, F., Arjovsky, M., et al.: Improved training of Wasserstein GANs. In: 30th Advances in Neural Information Processing Systems 30: Annual Conference on Neural Information Processing Systems, USA (2017)

Prakempa: The Colour Music
of the Balinese Calendar

Vibeke Sørensen[1]([✉]) and J. Stephen Lansing[2,3,4]

[1] School of Art, Design and Media, Nanyang Technological University,
Singapore 637371, Singapore
`vsorensen@ntu.edu.sg`
[2] Santa Fe Institute, Hyde Park Road, Santa Fe, NM, USA
`lansing@santafe.edu`
[3] Complexity Science Hub Vienna, Josefstädter Str. 39, Vienna 1080, Austria
[4] School of Anthropology, University of Arizona, Tucson, AZ, USA

Abstract. We explore the Balinese concept that an underlying structural pattern of interlocking cyclical patterns *(tatotekan)* may be the key not only to music and time, but to the experience and propagation of social harmony. The Balinese permutational uku calendar, the most complex known to anthropology, appears to have had a profound influence on the evolution of Balinese gamelan music, and on key developments in Western musical composition. In 1986 a Balinese ethnomusicologist, Dr. Made Bandem, translated a traditional lontar manuscript called Prakempa from Balinese into Malay. This manuscript explicitly links the five and seven tone scales of the gamelan to colours and the sacred geometry of the microcosm and macrocosm. Working with Dr. Bandem, we use Pure Data software to translate the ten dimensional uku calendar into colour music, generative computer music and animation, and explore the possible musical inspiration for the calendar offsets that shape the social and ritual cycles of life in Bali. How does the progression of dissonance and harmony in Balinese music relate to their understanding of the meaning of time? And how much of this system of thought remains opaque to those whose experience of time is shaped by the one dimensional calendar of the European tradition? We describe experiments in dome immersion at the Future Design Symposium of the Beyond Festival, held at the Experimenta Science Dome in Heilbronn Germany from 25–27 September 2019, and color music on a sand table at the Sharjah Archtecture Triennal 2019 in the United Arab Emirates (9 November 2019–8 February 2020), designed to convey the multi-dimensional harmonies of Balinese aesthetics to Western audiences.

Keywords: Gamelan music · Cyclical time · Immersive media

1 Introduction

The Balinese *uku* calendar is the most mathematically complex of all calenders. It has many functions in Balinese life. But to a musician its most striking feature

© Springer Nature Switzerland AG 2020
M. Rauterberg (Ed.): HCII 2020, LNCS 12215, pp. 386–395, 2020.
https://doi.org/10.1007/978-3-030-50267-6_29

is that it is naturally polyrhythmic, and so might be intrinsically musical. To explore this idea, we created a visual model to understand the logic of the calendar and visualize the rhythms by assigning a colour to each note and a note to each day (Fig. 1). Each day becomes a chord of notes representing what day it is on each of the ten weeks. Then we took the entire 210 day uku calendar and sped it up, so that each day lasts a quarter of a second. The result was delightfully musical. Inspired by the work of Dr. Made Bandem, a renowned Balinese composer and ethnomusicologist, we sought new ways to communicate the deeper harmonies celebrated in Balinese manuscripts about aesthetics, which associate sounds with colors, elements, emotions and the relationship between microcosm and macrocosm. Here we describe the works of art created by Sørensen for exhibition at the Experimenta Science Dome in Heilbronn, Germany; and at the Sharjah Architectural Triennale 2019 as colour music on a sand table. We begin with an introduction to the relationship between time, calendars and gamelan music in Bali.

2 Interlocking Cycles in Balinese Concepts of Time and Music

The *uku* calendar is the principal instrument used by the farmers to manage staggered irrigation flows into their terraced rice fields [2]. This hybrid instrument grafts a permutational calendar of 10 concurrent weeks, which vary in duration from 1 to 10 days, to the ancient luni-solar Icaka calendar. The *uku* calendar is depicted in *tika*, which are wooden or painted grids resembling matrices, that show 210 days arranged in 30 seven-day weeks called *uku*. The traditional duration of the main rice crop is also 210 days. Each week has a name, and most Balinese can easily recall the names of the weeks from memory. But this is only the first and simplest classification of time portrayed on the *tika*. In addition to these 30 seven-day weeks, the tika also keeps track of nine other weeks, each of different lengths. Thus there is a three day week, consisting of the days Pasah,

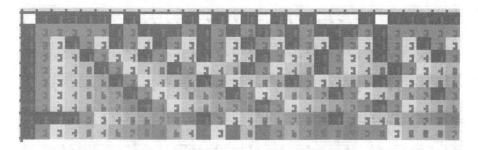

Fig. 1. A section of the days of the (tika) calendar colored as notes on the pentatonic scale. The first day of the first week is at the top left corner. Immediately below it is the second day of the first week. Credit: Guy S. Jacobs

Beteng and Kajeng, which repeat without pause. The three day week is concurrent with the seven day week, so that if today is Sunday on the 7 day week, it will also be one of the days of the 3 day week. Symbolic notations (lines, dots, crosses etc) are used to superimpose the days of the three day week on the grid of 30 seven day weeks displayed on the tika. Eight more weeks are also included in the tika, which range in duration from one to ten days. The 8 day week or

test weeks 1 2 3 4 5 6 7 8 9 10 using6conjunctions fast240 slendro

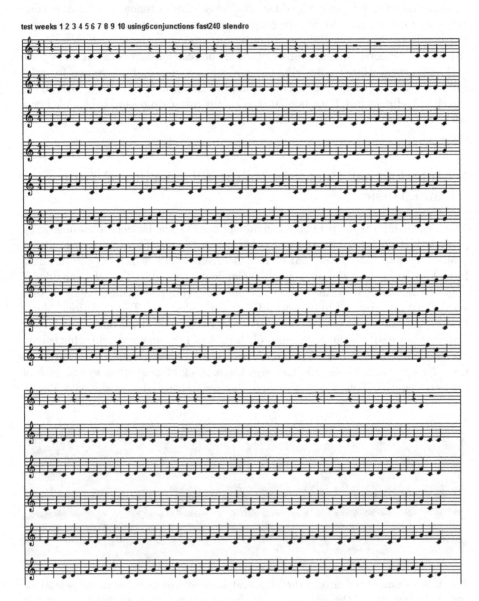

1

Fig. 2. First part of a musical score for the *u*ku calendar, by Guy S. Jacobs

Astawara, for example, consists of eight named days. Each of these days has its own use and meaning. For example, when a child is born, the parents check what day it is on the tika, because the infant's Astawara birthday is a clue to his or her identity in their previous life:

- Day 1 (Sri) -> reincarnation of female ancestress from Mother's side
- Day 2 (Indra) -> reincarnation of male ancestor from Father's side
- Day 3 (Guru) -> reincarnation of brother of male ancestor from Father's side
- Day 4 (Yama) -> reincarnation of male ancestor from Father's side
- Day 5 (Ludra) -> reincarnation of female ancestress from Mother's side
- Day 6 (Brahma) -> reincarnation of male ancestor from Father's side
- Day 7 (Kala) -> reincarnation of someone who died as a child
- Day 8 (Indra) -> reincarnation of sister of female ancestor from Mother's side

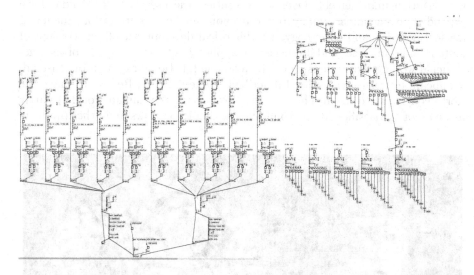

Fig. 3. The PureData visual music program to create and play the music of the uku calendar, by Sorensen.

3   Structure of the (tika) Calendar

Each of the 201 cells in the tika calendar represents a day on each of the ten concurrent weeks. The idea is not unlike "Friday the 13th", a day that is special in the Anglo-American calendar because of the intersection of two cycles, the week and the month. On the tika, there is a one-day week that consists of a single day, (Luang). In principal, every day is (Luang), but there are exceptions where the one day slot is empty. As we will explain below, we suggest that the reason for such exceptions has to do with the harmonies created by the concurrent cycles of days, which resemble the cyclical musical patterns of Balinese gamelan music.

There is also a two day week, consisting of two days, (Menge) and (Pepet), which follow in an endless progression. The first day of the tika calendar is Day One (Menge) of the two day week, Day One (Pasah) of the three day week, and so forth. However, weeks 4 and 10 begin later in their respective cycles. As we will show, when the days of the weeks are played as musical notes, this offset transforms the calendar from a monotonous sequence of notes to one that has a compelling complex structure.

4   The Experience of Cyclical Time

The *uku* calendar enables groups of farmers who share a common water source to organize complex interlocking irrigation schedules, composed of varying combinations of water turns and planting schedules, and is the main instrument for irrigation management. Over the centuries, the uses of this calendar have expanded to encompass many other phenomena besides irrigation, including musical notation and cosmology. The historical development of this concept of nested temporal cycles and its successive application to many aspects of the phenomenal world is not well captured by a simple functional explanation. Instead, it appears to reflect what Hegel described as the desire of Reason to make the world congruent to itself. Thus, as Hegel observed, the human world is partly made up of "objectified ideas" (buildings, technologies, laws and other products

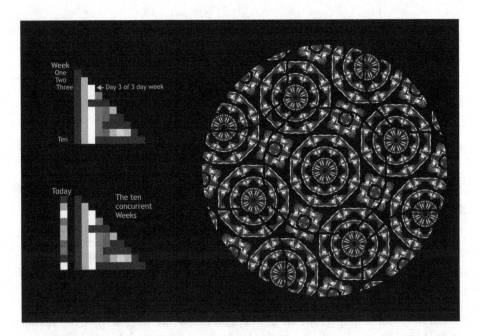

Fig. 4. Frames from the Prakempa Dome Film exhibition at Experimenta in Heilbronn. Left: explaining the logic of the calendar. Right: an image from the colour music.

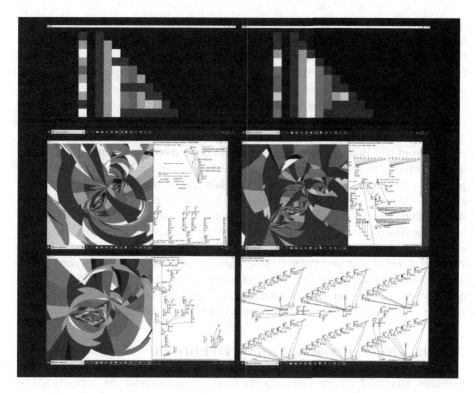

Fig. 5. Photos of the real-time Pure Data version of the Prakempa immersive dome film, produced for the Future Design Symposium of the Beyond Festival 2019.

of mental activity). Progressive history in the Hegelian sense occurs as the mind encounters its own creations. This process gathers historical momentum as the world appears to become more orderly and comprehensible. In Bali, the concept of nested cycles was extended to personal identity through the adoption of teknonyms (in which a person's name changes at each step in the life cycle, as they become parents, grandparents and great-grandparents) and birth order names, which cycle from first to fourth born and then repeat (thus the same birth order name is used for the first and fifth born child in a family). Similarly, Balinese literature is full of references to temporal cycles, and the regularity of cyclical progressions is a major theme in Balinese literature. The consistent application of this abstract notion to so many aspects of the Balinese world contributed to a mental and physical landscape of perceptible coherence, in which (to borrow again from Hegel) the workings of Reason appear to pervade the phenomenal world: "only then did they feel a real interest in the universe, when they recognized their own Reason in the Reason that pervaded it" (Figs. 2 and 3).

The purpose of the *uku* calendar is nominally religious. However, although the religion of Bali is a form of Hinduism, the calendar is more than a way to schedule religious rites. The Balinese, like the ancient Romans, imported an entire pantheon of fully scripted foreign gods, like Zeus, Athena, Dionysius and Hephaestus. But while these deities became the pillars of the state religion of Rome, they were largely absent from the Roman countryside. As in Bali, the Roman gods worshipped in the annual calendar of agrarian rites lacked any personality or mode of existence except for instrumental names, which 'imprisoned them', as Dumezil observes, 'in the minor definition of a function, in an act or a fraction of an act, gods like Sarritor (weeding), Occator (harrowing) and Messor (harvesting)' [5]. Unlike both the Greek and Hindu gods, the imagined capacities of the Balinese agrarian deities do not exceed their named functions, and their mode of worship consists in the performance of calendrical rites, which provide a ritual template for agricultural labour. In the Balinese countryside, the colourful and capricious personalities of the foreign gods of Hinduism are backgrounded in favour of the clockwork regularity of the calendrical rites and irrigation schedules. It is the farmers, rather than the gods, who thus assert control over their managed landscape. This interpretation is consistent with the views of Cicero, who recognized these gods as personified abstractions: 'what shall we say of Ops (fortune)? What of Salus (well-being)? Of Concordia, Libertas, Victoria? As each of these things has a power too great to be controlled without a god, it is the thing itself which has received the title of god' [4].

5   The Dome Presentation at Heilbronn

Sørensen analyzed the musical aspects of the uku calendar by extracting the musical cycles, paying special to the offsets of several weeks, which yielded mathematical structure. Notes from the Balinese pentatonic scale were assigned to the days, with different octaves for different periods of the calendar. Colours were assigned to the notes as prescribed by the Prakempa manuscript, which emphasizes this association of musical notes with the colors of flowers used in offerings. For visualization, a grid-like structure was created with the PureData and GEM software, which uses OpenGL, to create real-time animation precisely synchronized with the underlying mathematics, which linked the audio synthesis and the computer-generated moving colour imagery. When the program runs, the progression of lines of colours and days appear to be visually similar to traditional Balinese ikat weaving, suggesting possibilities for further research on weaving and the calender.

An 8K dome film entitled Prakempa was created and premiered at the Future Design Symposium at the Beyond Festival 2019 in Heilbronn, Germany (Figs. 4 and 5).

6   The Sand Table Exhibition at Sharjah

Following the Heilbronn dome premiere, Søorensen created a Prakempa sand table installation for the inaugural Sharjah Architecture Triennale, in the United Arab Emirates. The theme of the Triennial was the "Rights of Future Generations". The Architecture School of ETH Zurich organized a series of installations "ranging from films, archival documents, music, models and interactive displays that trace the history of Bali's Subak rice farming heritage".[1] These installations were named "Priests and Programmers", after Lansing's 2007 book. [6]

7   Discussion: Immersive Media

The Balinese calendar and ancient Balinese manuscripts such as Prakempa, describe a pervasive order that permeates their world. It took centuries to

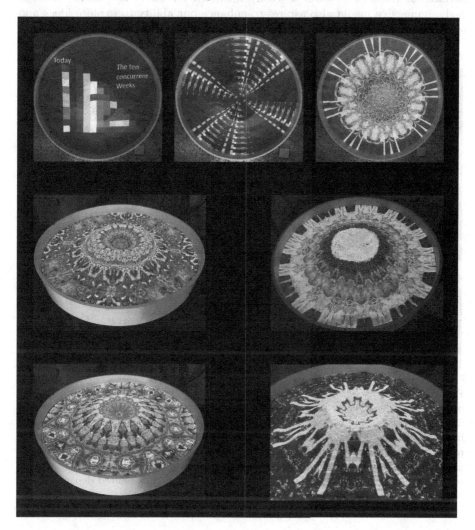

Fig. 6. Frames from the sand table installation of Prakempa at the ETH "Priests and Programmers" exhibition at the inaugural Sharjah Architecture Trienniale, in the United Arab Emirates.

---

[1] Adam Kleinman, "The First Sharjah Architecture Triennial: Can Art Be an Applied Science?". FRIEZE, 26 November 2019.

create, as both the macrocosm of the island and the human microcosm gradually came to embody the interlocking cyclical patterns of time. Balinese children hear gamelan music from infancy and many learn to play in the gamelan orchestra, which normally occupies a place of honor in the great temple of each village.

Much, perhaps most of this is simply invisible to foreign visitors to Bali, despite their attraction to Balinese culture. The Balinese are clearly immersed in their world, but how are foreign visitors to discern what lies beneath the surfaces of Balinese culture, so easily mistaken for mere decoration? Intriguingly, immersive media also aspires to enhance our ability to explore ideas and experiences that connect in unexpected and aesthetic ways (Figs. 6, 7 and 8).

Fig. 7. Baskets of offerings at a village temple. The colors and shapes form cyclical mandalic patterns that correspond to the musical cycles of the gamelan orchestra. Subaks are self-governing assemblies of farmers, which hold regular meetings and assess fines on members who do not abide by their decisions. However, in surveys, farmers report that punitive fines and sanctions are seldom needed. From their perspective, the most important responsibility of the subaks is the performance of calendrical rites in water temples. By encouraging the farmer's awareness of their shared dependence on Nature's bounty, these rites clearly have functional significance.

Fig. 8. A shrine marks the place where irrigation flows for two villages are divided, and coloured offerings are placed for local agrarian deities. In Bali, water is regarded as a public good, the gift of the Goddess of the Lakes. Rice is grown in paddy fields fed by irrigation systems dependent on rainfall. Rainfall varies by season and in combination with groundwater inflow determines river flow. By virtue of their location, upstream farmers can influence how much water reaches their downstream neighbors. Across the island, farmers recognize two management systems. In tulak sumur ("reject the wellspring"), everyone is free to plant whenever they like, which gives upstream farmers an advantage over their downstream neighbors. Alternatively, in kerta masa ("lawful/good timing"), farmers agree to adopt synchronized irrigation schedules.

References

1. Hegel, G.W.F.: Lectures on the Philosophy of World History: Introduction, Reason in History (translated from the German edition of Johannes Hoffmeister from Hegel papers assembled by H. B. Nisbet), p. 440. Cambridge University Press, New York (1975)
2. Lansing, J.S.: Perfect Order: Recognizing Complexity in Bali. Princeton University Press, Princeton (2006)
3. Guermonprez, F.: La religion balinaise dans le miroir de l'hindouisme. Bulletin de l'E'cole francaise d'Extreme- Orient **88**, 271–293 (2001). https://doi.org/10.3406/befeo.2001.3517
4. Cicero, M.T.: De Natura Deorum. 45 B.C.E., 2.61
5. Dumezil, G.: Archaic Roman Religion, pp. 32–33. University of Chicago Press, Chicago (1966)
6. Lansing, J.S.: Priests and Programmers: Technologies of Power in the Engineered Landscape of Bali. Princeton University Press, Princeton (2007)

Virtual Cinematic Heritage for the Lost Singaporean Film *Pontianak* (1957)

Benjamin Seide[✉] and Benjamin Slater[✉]

School of Art, Design and Media, Nanyang Technological University,
Singapore 637458, Singapore
{bseide,baslater}@ntu.edu.sg

Abstract. In 1957, Cathay-Keris Studio in Singapore released "Pontianak", the first of a hugely popular series of horror films featuring the female vampiric ghost based on Malay folk mythology. The visual transformation of the lead actress Maria Mernado into the Pontianak creature amazed the audience in cinemas (Mustafar, 2012) [1]. The *Pontianak* trilogy by Cathay-Keris was ground-breaking for the genre at that time and registered several firsts in Singapore: *Pontianak* was the first Malay film to be dubbed into Mandarin, while *Sumpah Pontianak* is the first local CinemaScope (widescreen) film. The 1957 film is also considered the first depiction of the Pontianak in a film [2]. Despite their relatively wide distribution in 1957 both films are believed to be lost, with no prints or copies surviving (Barnard, 2011) [3]. Film Heritage in the conventional way of 'restoration' being impossible, this project investigates the novel approach of creating a *Virtual* Cinematic Heritage application. In this paper, we outline our current work in progress from historical film research to recreating a scene from the lost film as a Virtual Reality experience.

Keywords: Film Heritage · Virtual Heritage · Pontianak

1 Introduction

Cinematographic works are an essential component of our Cultural Heritage and therefore deserve full protection. Film or Cinematic Heritage aims to preserve tangible cultural property in the form of film copies, photos and manuscripts. In the widest sense, film preservation assures that a movie will continue to exist in as close to its original form as possible. A film for which not one single copy can be preserved is considered lost, much like a historic site, which has been fully destroyed.

Virtual Cultural Heritage explores techniques such as laser scanning, CGI animation, 360° imagery and photogrammetry, aiming to create photorealistic and accurate representations of historic environments (Zara 2004) [4]. The goal of being as realistic as possible has not been fully accomplished, but considering the rate of improvement, virtual environments and augmented vision will eventually become indistinguishable from reality. Inhabiting such photorealistic virtual environments with realistic-appearing actors will enable Virtual Heritage to attract a broader audience beyond researchers, creating accessible reconstructions for museum installations and edutainment. The term

© Springer Nature Switzerland AG 2020
M. Rauterberg (Ed.): HCII 2020, LNCS 12215, pp. 396–414, 2020.
https://doi.org/10.1007/978-3-030-50267-6_30

'walk-in movie' could be used to describe a Virtual Reality environment, in which the viewer can freely explore, with a headset in a room-scale VR setup, while a narrative with actors unfolds around them. In such a scenario, the audience of a Virtual Heritage application could be enabled not only to virtually encounter a historic site but also an important historic event happening at that site.

Considering the fundamental role of visual components in Cultural Heritage, Virtual Reality is particularly suitable (Bocci et al. 2010) [5], and extensive research has been accomplished on the application, but the implication is, that for the benefit of Cultural Heritage, developments in Virtual Reality filmmaking are highly relevant aspects to explore. Bogdanovych et al. (2010) [6] argue that populating a Virtual Heritage site with virtual agents could bring heritage preservation to a new level but found that previous attempts were unsatisfying as they "are not involved into historically authentic interactions" and "that the agents are not behaving in a way that the relevant cultural knowledge is authentically presented to the human observer". The MIRALab mixed-reality project of Magnenat-Thalmann and Papagiannakis experiments with "animated characters acting a storytelling drama on the site of ancient Pompeii" [7] and they conclude that "dramaturgical notions" could help to "develop an exciting edutainment medium" from their Virtual Heritage application. Researchers are aware that the audience's narrative involvement is relevant for a successful Virtual Heritage application.

The research project aims to investigate if approaches used in Virtual Heritage, such as the creation of virtual environments of historic sites, and developments in the field of Virtual Reality filmmaking, such as inhabiting virtual environments with actors and stories, can be utilised to create Virtual Cinematic Heritage for films, which are considered lost and for which Film Heritage, in form of film preservation, is not an option.

As a case study, the research has begun the process of creating a Virtual Cinematic Heritage application for the historic Malayan *Pontianak* films produced in Singapore, originating in 1957 and originally starring Maria Menado as the titular supernatural creature from the oral folklore of Malaya. The first two films in this hugely popular trilogy – *Pontianak* and *Dendam Pontianak*, both produced and released by the Cathay-Keris Studio in 1957, directed by B.N. Rao, and starring Maria Menado, are believed to be "lost films" despite their relatively wide distribution in 1957.

According to Barnard (2011), the first film was so well received that it "even appealed to the Indian and Chinese communities – a first for a Malay film". Released in Malay, then later in a Chinese language version, *Pontianak* was screened in cinemas for over a month, an unusual occurrence for a Malay film at the time. Adrian Yuen Lee (2015) [8] argues, regarding the success of the films, that "the already existing beliefs, mythologies and superstition has allowed Malaysians and Singaporeans to develop a deep sense of 'cultural verisimilitude' that invokes a deep sense of plausibility, motivation, justification and belief due to familiarity with the pontianak in these films".

The choice of the Cathay-Keris *Pontianak* trilogy as a case study for the Virtual Cinematic Heritage application requires the project to conduct research into the films' history and based on those findings - to investigate the recreating of key scenes of the film as a virtual representation. While both investigations are ongoing, the project has created new knowledge by unearthing previously uncollated details of the lost films. In this paper, we share our preliminary findings and outline our process of creating a virtual reality experience for the lost film (Fig 1).

Fig. 1. Pontianak film poster © 1957, Cathay-Keris

2 The Pontianak Film(s)

2.1 Background - Pontianak Folklore

The traditional folk culture of Malayan Archipelago is rich in superstition and belief in mythical beings, which persist in the popular imagination until today. They were first 'recorded' in English by English Anthropologist Walter Skeat at the end of the 19th century in his seminal volume - Malay Magic, first published in 1900.

In this work, Skeat describes a female figure called the Langsuyar or Langsuir, a woman who has died in childbirth who returns from death as an owl-like "flying demon" and a "woman of dazzling beauty" who later transforms in grief into a Pontianak, a "ghostly form" which is still feminine, wearing a robe, brandishing long nails, long dark hair, and a gaping hole in the back of her neck. This creature sucks the blood of children or pregnant women, which is why it has often viewed as analogous to the Western Vampire. Skeat goes on to explain that if captured the Pontianak can be made "tame and indistinguishable from an ordinary woman" (by stuffing the neck-hole with her hair and cutting her nails) (Skeat 1900) [9].

Skeat notes that the word "Pontianak" contains elements of "mati anak", which means "dead child" in Bahasa Melayu, and therefore it follows that "Pon" is likely a corruption of the Malay "Puan" an honorific for Woman/Wife. So Pontianak literally means "Woman of a dead child" (Skeat 1900) [10].

What's important to note here is the Pontianak is a feminine figure whose origins are tragic, and that she is subject to multiple transformations: from corpse to beautiful woman, to flying winged creature, grotesque long-nailed monster, and back again.

Today, the Pontianak is an iconic and instantly recognisable figure in popular culture in Malaysia, Singapore and Indonesia; she has appeared in novels, comics, collections of supernatural tales, video games, and most predominantly in films.

However, we can argue that the official 'birth' of the Pontianak as an icon of Southeast Asian horror occurs only in April 1957, with the premiere of the Singapore-produced, Malay language film *Pontianak* - the subject of our research.

2.2 History of the Film

Background to the Malay Film Industry in Singapore. The Malay-language film industry in Malayan-era Singapore has its origins prior to the Second World War, but came to prominence in the period shortly after 1945 and had a period of great productivity, oft-referred to as a "Golden Age" from 1947 to 1965.

The films they produced were shot largely in studio interiors with additional location shooting rural and urban in Singapore; they stared ethnically Malay talent from Singapore, Malaya and Indonesia; the directors were initially imported from India, and also to a lesser extent, Indonesia and the Philippines. The films initially drew on Malay musical and theatrical traditions, such as bangsawan (a form of Malay folk opera) as well as being heavily influenced by popular Indian cinema of the time.

Pontianak was directed by B.N. Rao, a veteran Indian director who'd been brought to Singapore by the Shaw Brothers to make Malay films in 1953, but left to join Cathay-Keris in 1956.

Pontianak arises out of a creative collaboration between its lead actress - Maria Menado, and its screenwriter, her husband, Abdul Razak. Maria Menado, originally Liesbet Dotulong, was born in Dutch-colonised Indonesia and arrived in Singapore to work as a model in 1950, where she married boxing promoter Razak, before he brought her to the attention of the Malay film studios. According to Maria Menado, she helped her husband write the story for *Pontianak*, based on her own knowledge of the supernatural from rural Indonesia (Zieman 2007) [11].

They created a story set approximately a century earlier in rural Malaya, located in the jungle and in and around a traditional Malay village, which we will refer to by the Malay term "kampong". This environment was deeply rooted in the world of rural Malay folklore that Walter Skeat described, although Razak and Maria Menado fabricated their own origin story for the Pontianak.

There are numerous accounts of the film's phenomenal box office success. Film historian Mustafar A. R. provides an account of its distribution in Singapore, running from late April to mid-May and then revived again in August, screening for 41 days altogether, which was "a major achievement of the time" unrivalled by even the most popular Malay films. (Mustafar 2019) [12].

The first sequel, *Dendam Pontianak* was rushed into production almost immediately. By November 1957, both Cathay-Keris and its rival studio MFM/Shaw were announcing multiple Pontianak films in production.

MFM/Shaw managed to release their first rival Pontianak film, *Anak Pontianak* (with a story also by Abdul Razak), in February 1958, before Cathay-Keris's third Pontianak film, *Sumpah Pontianak*, came out in April 1958. These two titles are the earliest Pontianak films in existence, still available in the archives. However, *Pontianak* and *Dendam Pontianak* (both 1957) are classified as 'lost films'.

The Loss of *Pontianak* and *Dendam Pontianak*, 1957. The question of how a film actually becomes 'lost' is debatable. Edmundsen and Pike offer a succinct definition of this "relative term": *"(It) Usually means one < film > that no longer exists or, at least is not identified among the holdings of a film archive, production company, distributor, or publicly known organisation or collection. In other words, it is not in one of the places where one might normally seek to find it."* (Edmundsen & Pike 1982) [13].

By this standard, the first two *Pontianak* films are lost. There is no definite record of them ever being screened after their theatrical runs in Singapore, Malaya, Borneo, Hong Kong or Indonesia (where it was retitled *Chomel*).

In 1960 Ho Ah Loke and Loke Wan Tho broke up Cathay-Keris, so that Ho could set up a new film studio in Kuala Lumpur. In the official Cathay version of the events (Lim & Yiu 1991) [14], the two men "drew lots" to determine who could keep ownership of which films, and among those that Ho kept, were the first two *Pontianak* films (but not the third).

In 1963 Maria Menado, who had declared her marriage to Abdul Razak void, became the wife of the Sultan of Pahang, a member of the Malay royal family. After this, by her own account, her films were not permitted to be screened, "no cinema or TV station could play them", she said in 2007 (Zieman 2007) [15].

Then, as Lim and Yiu write: "Wherever he (Ho Ah Loke) moved, the films would be brought along and usually packed under a staircase. Then years later… perhaps in a fit of depression, he ordered removers to take the cans of film away in a lorry…. (They) are believed to be at the bottom of a lake somewhere in Malaysia." (Lim & Yiu 1991) [16].

This speculation about Ho's "depression" was supported by a memoir by a former Cathay-Keris employee Hamzah Hussin, published in 1997, where he posits that Ho acted out of "disappointment and defiance" (Uhde 2005) [17]. Barnard goes on to explicitly make the link between the act of disposing of the films in a lake or river with the fact that Maria Menado's royal status made the films commercially unusable (Barnard 2011) [18].

This version of the story has since become the oft-repeated 'legend' of the film's loss, supported by further details supplied by Maria Menado since the 2000s. She told an interviewer in 2005 that after the Sultan's death in 1974 she successfully applied to the Royal Council for permission to have her films screened again and contacted Ho Ah Loke to view the first *Pontianak* film. He told her it had been thrown into a mining pool.

"I didn't ask him which lombong (mining pool) it was because I was already too upset. I was speechless when he told me about it." (Koay 2005) [19].

L. Krishnan has repeatedly debunked the notion that Ho was angry or depressed when he disposed of the films. He states that Ho needed space in his house and removed many of his films (presumably canisters containing negatives as well as distribution prints), of not only the two *Pontianak* films [20].

The story is further complicated by an interview that Maria Menado gave in 2013 on Malay television in Singapore [21], where she states that upon request Ho Ah Loke did supply her with a print of *Pontianak*, for her own personal viewing, but it was dubbed into Mandarin (the film was re-released with Mandarin dialogue in July 1958). This contradicts the earlier, and oft-told, anecdote that Ho told her they were thrown away.

Another complicating element is the assumption that Ho Ah Loke was the sole possessor of prints of his films. Given that multiple prints would have been struck and released in multiple territories (where they would have been stored by the film's local distributors), it is certain that other prints existed elsewhere.

However, in at least three decades of believing the first two *Pontianak* films to be lost, there has been no account of anyone seeing the films since their initial theatrical runs, and not a single trace of a copy or print has ever been unearthed.

2.3 Unearthing the Synopses of the Lost Pontianak Films

For the purposes of our research the primary task was to find out as much as possible about the content of the two lost films, and what follows is a summary of research completed so far, although it is still ongoing.

Available sources included newspaper articles, interviews and books, essays and articles on Malay cinema. Key sources for the 'narrative' of the first *Pontianak* (1957) include:

1. Maria Menado herself, from an interview she gave in 2005 in which she described the film's plot in some detail
2. The website of Malaysian film historian Mustafar A. R. and his recently published book, *50 Years of Film in Malaysia and Singapore*, which includes his personal reminiscences of watching the film
3. A short, but complete synopsis of the film published as part of promotional material for the Mandarin dialogue for the film in 1958
4. A review of the film in English published in The Straits Times, Singapore's main English language broadsheet, at the time of its release in 1957
5. References to prior aspects of the story that are present in the final film of the initial trilogy, *Sumpah Pontianak*, 1958

One discovery we made was that over the years, books and articles that covered the lost *Pontianak* films invariably focussed on the first film, so that there was almost no available information regarding the sequel, *Dendam Pontianak*.

Attempts to contact Maria Menado, and her *Pontianak* co-stars, for new interviews were unsuccessful, but are ongoing. Interviews with other individuals associated with the Malay film industry, contemporaneous to the films, led to very little information on the content of the films, although valuable context was supplied.

An attempt to canvass social media for memories of the first two films, in collaboration with the marketing of a new Pontianak film in Singapore and Malaysia - also called *Dendam Pontianak* (2019) - led to very little information despite a great many enthusiastic responses.

However, through the key sources referred to above, an outline of the first film's narrative presented itself:

- The film begins with a reclusive old man, Wak Dolah, a bomoh (Malay Shaman) picking herbs in the jungle where he discovers an abandoned baby. He brings her to his home (which is either a cave or a hut - depending on the source), where he names her Chomel (translated as 'Cute') and raises her as his own daughter.
- Years pass and Chomel grows up and is revealed to be an "ugly" young woman with a hunch-back, who is mocked and reviled by the villagers she encounters. Wak Dolah teaches her his medicinal skills.
- Eventually, Wak Dolah dies of old age, but before that he makes Chomel promise to burn all his books of magic. She dutifully carries out his wishes, until she notices a book that contains a spell to make its possessor beautiful. Unable to resist she follows the instructions, creates a potion (to be drunk during the full moon) and becomes beautiful. The book states that after her transformation, she must never drink human blood.
- The 'new' unrecognisable Chomel enters the village and meets the son of the Village Chief, Othman, who falls in love with her and soon they are married, and Chomel gives birth to a daughter, Maria.
- One day, while taking a walk outside, Othman is bitten by a poisonous snake. He asks Chomel to suck the poison from his wound. Reluctantly, Chomel obeys and once she's tasted blood continues to drink her husband's blood until he dies. At this point, Chomel transforms again - this time into a deformed, fanged creature in a white robe with long fingernails and hair - the Pontianak!

From this point, the narrative becomes less clear:

- The appearance of the Pontianak strikes fear among the villagers.
- Chomel hides in the jungle beside the village for many years.
- Years pass and Maria grows up to be a young woman. Chomel, in her form as a beautiful woman, brings her fruits.
- She kills some men from the village.
- When she turns 18, Chomel brings Maria to a cemetery with the intention of turning her into a Pontianak too. This plan fails.
- The village bomoh tries to stop or kill the Pontianak, but this fails as well.
- The village Doctor, Tabib Razak, drives a nail into the back of her neck, and she transforms back into "ugly" Chomel.
- She flees into a hut in the village - pursued by the villagers - who set fire to the hut, burning it down and thus destroying Chomel.

Mustafar, on his website (Mustafar 2012) [22], referred to a publication related to the film, published by a company called Harmy, a Malay publisher based in Singapore in the 1950s and '60s that was (among other things) a publisher of film synopses (Nasri 2017) [23].

These synopses were both promotional materials and film merchandise designed to appeal to film fans, by reproducing the stories of films they'd just seen at the cinema (or were about to see), complete with film stills.

Synopses were published in written Malay and Jawi (an Arabic script form of written Malay). Knowing that a Harmy *Pontianak* synopsis existed, we set about searching for it. Public archives, libraries, and rare book dealers in Singapore and Malaysia did not have it, and neither did the British Library. However, we did find a blog belonging to a collector of Malay movie memorabilia that featured six images of what we realised was the Harmy synopsis, in a combination of Malay and Jawi.

Although it's not complete, through translation we have learnt several more details that weren't previously established, including a reference to Gunung Ledang (Mount Sophir) which locates the story between Johor and Malacca, where the herbs grow that "Chomil" (not Chomel in this first synopsis) picks to create the concoction that will make her beautiful. We also learn that Chomel's daughter Maria is the one who discovers the corpse of her father after his blood has been drained by her mother.

We have since acquired two versions of full synopses for *Dendam Pontianak* and now know many details of this previously forgotten, lost and undocumented film, bridging the narrative between *Pontianak* and *Sumpah Pontianak*.

3 The Virtual Cinematic Heritage Application

3.1 Project Outline

Based on the findings described in the previous chapter, we identified several key moments of the first *Pontianak* (1957) film of which the "snake bite scene" is considered the most iconic moment: Mustafar describes its effect on the audience at the time: *"At that moment, the cinema went absolutely silent since they knew what was going to happen next. The change from Maria Menado's beautiful face into that of the scary Pontianak shocked the audience, even causing a slight commotion for a while. When the shock died down, silence came again."* (Mustafar 2019) [24].

Location of the Snake Bite Scene. According to film descriptions, the scene happens in a backyard area (the Malay "tanam" describes a garden or space beside a home) and in earshot of their daughter and the head of the village who come to the scene to find the dead Othman, Chomel's husband. It is likely that the snake bite scene happened in proximity to the jungle that surrounds the kampong.

The process stages of recreating the 'snake bite scene' as a virtual reality experience can be described as follows:

- Script: Writing a detailed film script based on the findings describing the scene
- Visual Concept: References from the films
- Environment: Creating the village and surrounding jungle

- Characters: Creating at least 3 characters; beautiful Chomel, Othman, the Pontianak and the snake.
- Story and Interactivity: Animation layout based on script and design of viewer's logic
- Character Animation and Realism: Capturing actors' performances, research and development of hair and cloth simulations, skin shaders, realistic lighting and recreating the look of the film
- Sound design: Recreating the aural atmosphere of the film
- Evaluation and refinements

In the following, we will describe key considerations and preliminary findings of some of the above processes.

3.2 Script, Story and Interactivity

A detailed film script based on preliminary findings describing the scene in question has been developed. In short, the story goes as follows.

Story. Beautiful Chomel and her husband Othman stroll in conversation from the village into a path leading into the jungle. Othman is suddenly attacked and bitten by a poisonous snake. Othman begs Chomel suck out the poison from his wound. To save her husband Chomel sucks the poison out of Othman's leg, but in doing so tastes his blood, and the one thing cursed Chomel is not allowed to do is drink human blood. Fulfilling the curse means something terrible is going to happen: Chomel kills her husband and transforms into the Pontianak.

Considerations. To realise the snake bite scene as a 'walk-in movie' we must consider several aspects and possible issues:

- The viewer can walk and look around freely and might not be in range or within a viewing angle to see the action.
- With a pre-recorded animation we have limited control over re-positioning our actors into the field of view of the user.
- How can we be sure that certain key moments such as the transformation of Chomel into the Pontianak are not missed by the viewer?

Approach. The viewer can walk and look around freely in the Kampong. Chomel and Othman will appear and leave one of the houses if the viewer has their house in focus for more than 3 s. Chomel and Othman will start their 90 s long walk on a predefined path to the snake bite location. After 16 s a "user tracking logic" will be activated to verify that Chomel is in the user's field of view, or in range. If the viewer is too far away or loses unobstructed line of sight, of either one for more than 5 s, the viewer is teleported to the nearest checkpoint and forced facing Chomel. If the viewer is still far away after 75 s, the line of sight is not considered anymore and the viewer will be forced to a checkpoint to assure he/she won't miss the snake bite scene at second 90 and following that, the transformation of Chomel into the Pontianak.

3.3 Visual Concept

In the film, the actress Maria Menado plays three characters: "Ugly" hunchback Chomel, beautiful Chomel and the scary Pontianak (see Fig. 2). In the snake bite scene beautiful Chomel transforms into the Pontianak after sucking the poison from her husband's leg.

Fig. 2. Maria menado in three roles © 1957, Cathay-Keris

The most accurate visual references are film stills found in the synopsis booklet (Harmy, 1957) [25]. A still shows Chomel and her husband in conversation (see Fig. 3), and assuming that this image shows the couple just moments before the snake bite, we know that the scene happens in daylight in an exterior scene in or around the kampong houses. The book *Cathay 55 Years of Cinema* (Lim & Yiu, 1991) [26] includes a high-resolution film still from *Dendam Pontianak* showing the Pontianak in action, strangling a villager. We have visual references for all three characters involved in the snake bite scene: Beautiful Chomel, her husband Othman (played by M. Amin) and the Pontianak itself (see Fig. 3).

Fig. 3. Film stills from *Pontianak* (1957) and *Dendam Pontianak* (1957) © 1957, Cathay-Keris

Kampong Villages in the Film. None of the available film stills provides a useful visual reference to the kampong environment.

The existing third film, *Sumpah Pontianak* was released in April 1958, just eight months after the second film's release in August 1957 and 12 months after the first film, so we can assume that locations and film sets would have been re-used between all three, and it can be a key reference for our virtual kampong.

In *Sumpah Pontianak*, several scenes play out in studio sets of a kampong (see Fig. 4), these are mainly the longer dialogue scenes. In addition, several scenes are shot in real kampong villages; according to researcher Toh Hun Ping, the main village used was Kampong Siglap at the east coast close to today's junction of Siglap Road and Upper East Coast Road [27]. In *Sumpah Pontianak*, the Satay man, a comedic character played by Wahid Satay (who also features in the first two films), strolls around singing, followed by a group of boys from one village along a pathway to a second village. During the Satay man's stroll, we can see various Kampong houses, and, although the film editing implies continuous action over a total of 9 shots, continuously following the Satay man crossing the screen from right to left, none of the shots appear to be geographically continuous at one location but rather shot at several different locations, eventually ending at a studio set at which a longer dialogue scene begins [28].

Fig. 4. Stills from sumpah pontianak. Left on location, right studio set © 1958, Cathay-Keris

3.4 Environment – The Kampong

Kampong in Virtual Reality. Our virtual kampong consists of around 10 different houses modelled in Autodesk Maya (see Fig. 5). These houses take visual reference from those seen in *Sumpah Pontianak* but are not exact replications. As it would be common for the period, the village houses in *Sumpah Pontianak* have palm leaf roofs. As the film was shot in the 1950s but set in the past, there are some exceptions of buildings without palm leaf roofs hidden in the background or at the edge of the frame. Regarding the building materials of the house walls, the village houses in *Sumpah Pontianak* appear to have either palm leaf, vertical or horizontal wooden planks. All three options are reflected in our 3D models (Fig 6).

Vegetation. Singapore is famous for its rich tropical vegetation with huge trees and high species diversity. According to the National Park Board, Singapore has "over 2000 recorded native plant species" with "two million trees planted on roadsides, in parks

Fig. 5. 3D modelled houses for virtual village © 2020, B. Seide

Fig. 6. Virtual kampong village © 2020, B. Seide

and nature areas" [29]. The kampong sets in *Sumpah Pontianak* feature an equality high species diversity, ranging from angsana, sea apple, palm, banana leaf, malayan banyan trees to ixora shrubs. The vegetation used in and around our virtual village consists of 18 species (see Fig. 7). These assets are dynamic and react to wind.

Fig. 7. Vegetation assets used in and around our virtual village

3.5 The Characters

For the project we created 3D character models of the Pontianak, beautiful Chomel and her husband, Othman. In that process an initial approximation of beautiful Chomel was designed in Reallusion Character Creator which served as a foundation for the sculpting of the Pontianak face in Pixologic zBrush (see Fig. 8) and texturing in Adobe Substance. The model was then tested in Reallusion iClone for consistency of the facial rig before designing the costume in CLO Virtual Fashion Marvelous Designer and evaluating the entire character in Epic Unreal Engine.

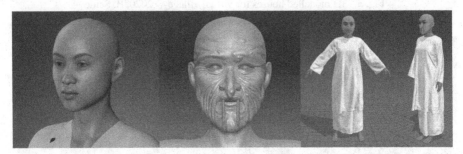

Fig. 8. Modelling stages of pontianak © 2020, B. Seide

3.6 Character Animation and Realism

Many factors contribute to the realism of a Computer-generated (CG) character, and while huge advancements have been made in recent years, creating a photorealistic CG character for a real-time environment is still a hugely challenging task. The most important contributing factors are: The skin and eye textures and shaders, the hair and cloth simulation, the character's level of detail and the character animation in general. In 2018, Epic demonstrated with their Andy Serkis and Siren Digital Human projects, that "crossing the uncanny valley in real time" [30] is possible. For these projects, "Epic Games teamed with 3Lateral, Cubic Motion, Tencent and Vicon to take live-captured digital humans to the next level". These demonstrations were ground-breaking in several regards, not only was the CG character convincingly realistic but in addition this was achieved in a real-time environment.

Based on these demonstrations, the project team decided to utilise facial and body motion capture techniques for all main characters to achieve a high level of realistic motion. Consequently, the motion would be pre-recorded and simply played-back in the virtual reality experience, with very limited possibilities to react to the users action, thus making the experience passive to a certain degree. As the primary aim of the project is to recreate scenes from a film, its structure is linear by design. So, while still posing uncertainties, the aforementioned limitation seemed acceptable.

Body Motion Capture. Our research facilities offer a professional Vicon motion capture system, set-up as a circle of 14 cameras at a height of 2.5 m. This camera-based set-up can produce high quality results, but often introduces errors on ground level when parts of the feet are occluded, a limitation of the one-circle set-up, requiring a time-consuming clean-up post-process of the captured data. At the time of writing, the project team is evaluating a lower-cost system from Rokoko, which in contrast to the camera-based Vicon system, is an inertial sensor-based system. Skogstad and Nymoen analyse both concepts and conclude "If high positional precision is required, OptiTrack (a camera-based system) is preferable over Xsens (a sensor-based system), but [...] Xsens provides less noisy data without occlusion problems" [31]. Our comparison of the two concepts is ongoing but our recordings indicate that for our snake bite scene, the husband falling to the ground after being bitten by the snake poses the biggest challenge for both systems. As our two main characters, Chomel and her husband walk in an area spanning 40 by 25 m, the portable sensor-based system appears more practical for our use case.

Facial Motion Capture. The project team is currently evaluating two systems, Rokoko facial capture and the Reallusion iClone Motion LIVE software. Both are iPhone FaceID-based systems. "The iPhone tracks faces with a depth map and analyses subtle muscle movements transforming the iPhone into a powerful 3D biometric mocap camera" (Reallusion) [32].

Cloth Simulation. Cloth and hair simulation are still huge challenges in real-time environments. Epic's Unreal Engine is improving constantly, and in 2017 implemented NVIDIA's NVCloth physics, a low-level clothing solver in version 4.16. The project evaluated the use of NVCloth and Marvelous Designer to simulate the long robe of the Pontianak character. In our initial tests, Marvelous Designer created fewer artefacts and a more detailed simulation, whereas NVCloth produced some intersection artefacts.

Hair Simulation. The project team tested two different approaches to simulate the long hair of the Pontianak character. Although the Pontianak character would not act with extreme movements in our snake bite scene, a solution for the hair simulation should provide a level of flexibility for a range of movements. After analysing Epic's Paragon game character projects which used NVCloth to simulate hair using low polygon proxy ribbons wrapped to original denser high poly hair, we evaluated to combine this technique into the photorealistic hair of Epic's Digital Human project [33] which uses Mike Seymor as a case study. This approach could work for the Pontianak character, if the long hair would not be moving too much.

With the release of version 4.24 in December 2019, Unreal Engine introduced Niagara's new "Strand-based Hair Rendering and Simulation System". Our initial simulation results of the long hair, generated in XGen and imported as Alembic file, are remarkable regarding the simulation accuracy in comparison to the NVcloth/proxy approach: The Strand-based Hair approach did not show artefacts or geometry intersections (see Fig. 9). Unfortunately, at the point of writing the Strand-based Hair approach is not yet usable for a virtual reality experience as it is not rendered stereoscopically for both eyes.

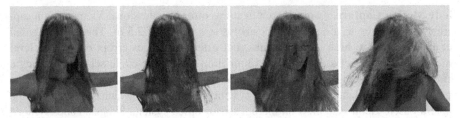

Fig. 9. Strand-based hair rendering and simulation system, © 2020, B. Seide

3.7   Film Look and Result

Film Look. The first colour films in Singapore were shot in 1952 and 1953 by Cathay-Keris Studio. *Pontianak* and its sequels (1957–1958) were shot in black and white. To recreate the cinematic look as close as possible for the virtual reality experience, we've utilised real-time post-processing effects to simulate the quality of the film, such as rendering the experience in black and white, adding film grain and a shallow depth of field. To evaluate the cinematic look of our VR experience, our approach was to first recreate an iconic moment of the existing third film *Sumpah Pontianak* (1958) (see Fig. 10), which is, apart from a few still photographs, the main source of visual references for the films. This approach allowed us to adjust the lighting and depth of field to get convincingly close to the original look of the trilogy (Fig 11).

Preliminary Results. The VR experience is compiled for a SteamVR/HTC Vive Pro setup in which the user can freely walk and teleport to explore the kampong and the path leading away from the village into the jungle; the jungle itself is restricted and can not be entered. In our draft result, the music and sound design, a recreation of the aural atmosphere of the film, has not been added yet. The story logic has been fully implemented and as such, Chomel and Othman leave one of the houses and we are free to follow them to witness the snake bite scene and Chomel's transformation (see Fig. 12).

Fig. 10. *Sumpah Pontianak* (left, © 1958 Cathay-Keris), VR Pontianak (© 2020, B. Seide)

Fig. 11. Stills from VR experience: pontianak in environment © 2020, B. Seide

Fig. 12. Still from VR experience: the snake bite scene © 2020, B. Seide

4 Discussion and Conclusion

This project arises out of a key question - In Film Heritage, how do you bring to life that which is apparently lost? Authentic recreation of a lost film is clearly impossible, even with anecdotal accounts of the film, synopses of the stories and scenes, detailed knowledge of its aesthetics and style, there are still far too many variables in terms of filmic construction that can't be definitively resolved. Instead we have taken a different approach, to create a virtual immersive environment that places the viewer into the narrative world of a lost film, and in one particular key scene.

This approach is a theatrical one, in that we are drawing attention to the difference between the lost object and the new work that we are making that is inspired by the lost original. We are using the latest advancements of narrative in moving image and applying them to a film from 1957, that only exists as memory and documentation.

In shifting the media, we hope to evoke and explore the lost film rather than to attempt to strictly emulate it. We aim to create an experience that activates the imagination and will animate the lost *Pontianak* both for audiences familiar with the Pontianak myth (and the myth of the film), and for those who are completely new to the story.

In preparing the material that can be used for the Virtual Reality Heritage Project, we have gone further than previous researchers in assembling information about the narrative content of the Pontianak films, as well as questioning some of the assumptions about the films that have been repeated in many histories of Malay film-making of that era. There is still much work to be done to learn more about both of the lost films, and we will continue to gather material.

Our visual reconstruction in form of the Virtual Cinematic Heritage application is a unique approach and at the time of writing still a work in progress, and this paper can be considered a preliminary report of our findings. The project aims to recreate a scene of the lost film as a walk-in VR experience in the most realistic way. The technical challenges are plenty and diverse, from creating a realistic environment to the even more demanding aspect of creating realism for three individual characters, including animation and simulation. Although creating near photorealism for such advanced tasks has become de facto possibility and is in reaching distance, it still poses a tremendous challenge for a small research team with limited resources. Our creations of the kampong environment and the three CG characters can be considered as possessing a high level of detail which supports the visual fidelity of the experience but the ultimate goal of reaching near photorealism has not been achieved yet. Even without full photorealism, the ability to freely explore an iconic film scene of a lost film within a historic setting alone is a unique experience, presenting an original approach to Cinematic Heritage.

As of today, there are no other virtual kampong reconstructions in existence. Panorama photos exist, i.e. of Singapore's Kampong Buangkok, but in regard to walk-in/room-scale Virtual Reality, our project presents the first virtual Malay-Singaporean kampong for audience exploration. As the audience's narrative involvement is highly relevant for a successful Virtual Heritage application, the research team aims to further develop the virtual kampong reconstruction into a fully inhabited village with authentically behaving and realistic appearing virtual humans.

Acknowledgements. This research has been made possible through the kind support of an MOE grant in Singapore and ADM, School of Art, Design and Media, NTU Singapore. We also express our gratitude to Toh Hung Ping, the Asian Film Archive, Dr. Rohana Said, Allan Koay, Wong Han Ming and Tay Ying Hui. We would also like to thank Justin Cho, Syaza Arinah Bte Muhammad Sham, Gerald Wee, Amber Chan, Clemens Tan, Jessabel Teng and Zhu Chuan for their contributions, Naga Thummanapalli and Ramalingam Sivakumar for their technical support and Joshua Tan and Sishuo Yang of CraveFX (Singapore) for their kind support.

References

1. Mustafar, A.R., Zaini, Y.: *Pontianak* Film Review (2012). http://filemklasikmalaysia.blo gspot.com/2012/10/pontianak-1957.html. Accessed 14 Dec 2019

2. Wikipedia website. wikipedia.org/wiki/Pontianak_(folklore). Accessed 14 Dec 2019
3. Barnard, T.P.: Films of change in early Singaporean film history. In: Y. Michalik (ed.), Singapore Independent Film. Marburg (Germany): Schüren. Call no.: RSING 791.43095957 SIN; Barnard, pp. 47–48 (2011)
4. Zara, J.: Virtual reality and cultural heritage on the web. In: 7th International Conference on Computer Graphics and Artificial Intelligence, pp. 101–112 (2004)
5. Bocci, F., Bonfigili, M.E., Calori, L., et al.: Virtual reality and cultural heritage: some applications. In: Conference: EVA 2000 Florence, Volume: Electronic Imaging and the Visual Arts: Il Nuovo Rinascimento, Atti della conferenza, Firenze – 27–31 marzo (2000)
6. Bogdanovych, A., Rodriguez-Aguilar, J.A., Simoff, S., Cohen, A.: Authentic interactive reenactment of cultural heritage with 3D virtual worlds and artificial intelligence. Appl. Artif. Intell. **24**(6), 617–647 (2010)
7. Magnenat-Thalmann, N., Papagiannakis, G.: Virtual Worlds and Augmented Reality in Cultural Heritage Applications, p. 2, 9 (2005)
8. Lee, A.Y.B.: The Digital Villain: Mapping Cross-Cultural Fears of the Pontianak in Malaysian, Singaporean And Indonesian Cinemas (2015)
9. Skeat, W.: Malay Magic: An Introduction to the Folklore and Popular Religion of the Malay Peninsula, pp. 325–326. Macmillan and Co., London (1900). Reprint: Barnes and Noble, New York (1966)
10. Skeat, W.: Malay Magic: An Introduction to the Folklore and Popular Religion of the Malay Peninsula, p. 325. Macmillan and Co., London (1900). Reprint: Barnes and Noble, New York (1966)
11. Zieman: A role she will always be remembered for. The Star, Malaysia, 19 August 2007. https://www.thestar.com.my/opinion/letters/2007/08/19/a-role-she-will-always-be-remembered-for. Accessed 18 Feb 2020
12. Mustafar, A.R.: 50 Tahun Filem Malaysia & Singapura (19301980), p. 114. Pekan Ilmu Publications, Malaysia (2019)
13. Edmundsen, R., Pike, A.: Australia's Lost Films: The Loss and Rescue of Australia's Silent Cinema, p. 22. National Library of Australia (NLA), Canberra (1982)
14. Lim, K.T., Yiu, T.C.: Cathay 55 Years of Cinema, p. 126. Landmark Books for Meileen Choo, Singapore (1991)
15. Zieman
16. Lim & Yiu, pp. 126
17. Uhde, J., Uhde, Y.,: The Exotic Pontianaks in Fear Without Frontiers: Horror Cinema Across the Globe. In: Schneider S.J. (ed.) pp. 125. FAB Press, London (2003)
18. Barnard, T.P.: Films of change in early Singaporean film history. In: Michalik, Y., (ed.) Singapore Independent Film. Marburg (2011). Call no.: RSING 791.43095957 SIN; Barnard, p. 48
19. Koay, A.: Famed Foe, The Pontianak. The Star, Malaysia, 5 August 2005. (No longer online)
20. Interview with Ben Slater, 2 December 2019. Unpublished
21. Television Interview with Maria Menado. *Bicara*, 7 February 2013. https://youtu.be/rOdNb9 7bNww. Accessed 18 Feb 2020
22. Mustafar, A.R., & Zaini Yusop
23. Shah, N.: A walk through kampong gelam. Muse SG **10**(1), 34 (2017). No.35, National Heritage Board, Singapore
24. Mustafar, A.R.: 50 Tahun Filem Malaysia & Singapura (19301980), p. 113. Pekan Ilmu Publications, Malaysia (2019)
25. Razak, A.: Pontianak, p. 13, Harmy, Singapore (1957)
26. Lim, K.T., Yiu, T.C.: Cathay 55 Years of Cinema. Landmark Books for Meileen Choo, Singapore (1991)

27. Toh, H. P.: Singapore Film Locations Archive, Sumpah Pontianak. https://sgfilmlocations. com/2014/12/26/sumpah-pontianak-the-curse-of-pontianak-1958/. Accessed 14 Dec 2019

28. Loke, H. A., Rao, B. N., Razak, A.: Sumpah Pontianak (1958). Cathay Organisation, Keris Film Production, Singapore (1958)

29. National Park Board Homepage. https://www.nparks.gov.sg/activities/family-time-with-nat ure/recommended-activities/know-10-trees. Accessed 17 Jan 2020

30. Unreal Engine news blog, April 2018. https://www.unrealengine.com/en-US/events/siren-at-fmx-2018-crossing-the-uncanny-valley-in-real-time. Accessed 17 Jan 2020

31. Skogstad, S., Nymoen, K., Høvin, M.: Comparing inertial and optical MoCap technologies for synthesis control. In: Proceedings of the 8th Sound and Music Computing Conference, SMC (2011)

32. Reallusion Face Mocap. https://mocap.reallusion.com/iclone-motion-live-mocap/iphone-live-face.html. Accessed 17 Jan 2020

33. Epic, Digital Human project, Unreal Engine website. https://docs.unrealengine.com/en-US/ Resources/Showcases/DigitalHumans/index.html. Accessed 17 Jan 2020

Interactive Rakuchu Rakugai-zu (Views in and Around Kyoto)

Naoko Tosa[1], Ryohei Nakatsu[1(✉)], Makoto Nagao[1], Naoko Iwasaki[1], Tsumiki Wada[1], Futoshi Saegusa[2], Tsuyoshi Kishigami[2], Katsunori Ishikawa[2], Masato Takaba[2], and Kohei Nishino[3]

[1] Kyoto University, Kyoto, Japan
{tosa.naoko.5c,ryohei.nakatsu.7r,
iwasaki.naoko.4c}@kyoto-u.ac.jp, maknag@fm2.seikyou.ne.jp,
wada.kit@gmail.com
[2] Toppan Printing Co., Ltd., Tokyo, Japan
{futoshi.saegusa,tsuyoshi.kishigami,katsunori_1.ishikawa,
masato.takaba}@toppan.co.jp
[3] Kyoto Seika University, Kyoto, Japan
nishino@cybermanga.com

Abstract. Rakuchu Rakugai-zu is a screen painting illustrating in and around Kyoto created from the beginning of 16th century until 17th century. As in the Funaki Version of Rakuchu Rakugai-zu everyday lives of over 2,000 people in Kyoto are vividly painted, the painting is a good material to learn their customs in early 17th century in Kyoto. However, it is difficult to understand the details of the painting, if background information is not provided. How to document such information and how to provide people such information would be crucial for the future of museums. To cope with this, we are carrying out a project to develop the interactive Rakuchu Rakugai-zu, Funaki Version. Firstly, we digitize the painting with ultra-high resolution. Secondly, using historical books regarding the customs of that era., we identify clothes and behaviors of each person in the painting and linked them to the person in the painting. Thirdly, we develop the technology to provide such information interactively using text or voice. Fourthly, we develop present Funaki Version including various manga characters so that we can compare old and present customs of people. Integrating these contents and technologies we are now developing the interactive Rakuchu Rakugai-zu, Funaki Version.

Keywords: Rakuchu Rakugai-zu · Funaki Version · Cultural heritage · Interactive museum · Interactive viewing · Online museum

1 Introduction

In order to preserve art works and cultural heritage for everyone to enjoy and for future generations, digitizing and archiving have been often achieved. In particular, with the development of high-definition digital technology, it has become possible to give viewers the feeling as if they are looking at real things [1]. Also, as new devices such as

© Springer Nature Switzerland AG 2020
M. Rauterberg (Ed.): HCII 2020, LNCS 12215, pp. 415–427, 2020.
https://doi.org/10.1007/978-3-030-50267-6_31

high-definition large-screen displays and projectors have emerged, it is now possible to reproduce these contents on a large screen/display. In the past, museums used to make efforts to let people visit with the primary objective of appreciating the real thing, but recently they are actively archiving their own content digitally and open them on the Internet. This would give people the desire to see the real thing, which is expected to increase the number of visitors to museums.

For example, at the National Museum of Japan, high definition digitalization of national treasures and important cultural properties are made public on the Web with the name of eNational Treasures [2]. Since printing companies have advanced high-definition digital technologies, there are many cases where printing companies have partnered with museums to digitize and archive their artworks. For example, Toppan Printing, with the name of Toppan VR, has been showing internal structure of buildings that do not exist anymore or that cannot be opened from the viewpoint of security, work protection, etc. [3]. Also, the Louvre Museum, in partnership with DNP (Dai Nippon Printing), digitizes and archives their artworks and actively open them to public [4].

When people appreciate cultural heritages and artworks, their understanding will be deepened if there is a guide that explains these heritages and artworks. The conventional method for such guidance is to prepare an explanatory document for each artwork. But, as many visitors often stop in front of the explanatory document, often it is difficult to read it. Another method adopted by many museums is that audio explanation of each work is prepared in advance, and the corresponding explanation is provided by voice when a viewer comes in front of the work [1].

However, if a story progression is drawn such as in the case of a painting scroll, or various contents are drawn in a single drawing such as an old city map, the present methods are not efficient enough. Rauchu Rakugai-zu (Views in and around Kyoto) [5] treated in this paper draws various famous spots in Kyoto, that was once the capital of Japan, and it depicts a very large number of people and buildings. As it is impossible to explain each of them in a single explanatory document, it is desirable to provide information regarding to each landmark, individual structure, and also the individual people drawn in the painting. Then viewers can deepen their understanding regarding the customs and so on of the era.

How to document information of a painting with such complex content and how to convey the information to viewers is an important issue. In this paper, we will describe a system that can, by interactively providing explanations about a painting with complex content, let viewers understand it well.

This paper is organized as follows Sect. 2 explains related papers Sect. 3 explains what the Rakuchu Rakugai-zu and its Funaki Version are Sect. 4 describes in detail the interactive Rakuchu Rakugai-zu Funaki Version, that can interactively provide the viewer with its contents, including the concept, the system configuration, and the content of each part consisting the system. Section 5 describes the exhibit of the developed system. Finally, the conclusion is given in Sect. 6.

2 Related Works

There is an opinion that artworks and cultural heritages should withstand appreciation well even without explanation. However, for a deeper understanding, it is better to know culture and art history of each country regarding these works. For example, modern abstract paintings cannot be easily understood without knowing the history of Western art. Therefore, it is more convenient to have explanations and guidance for understanding artworks and cultural heritages. Some of the research to realize the understanding and appreciation of artworks and cultural heritages easier are as follows.

2.1 Virtual Museum

In a virtual museum a 2D or 3D model of a museum is developed and viewers can appreciate artworks by freely moving around in the virtual museum. One good example is the virtual Louvre museum in which the interior of the Louvre museum is prepared as a panoramic image, and a viewer can freely walk around the museum to appreciate each artwork [4]. It is well done as a virtual museum, but has the disadvantage that the descriptions of the exhibits are simple and easy to get bored. A lot of research has been conducted on the design of virtual museums, such as changing the explanation for each individual in order to prevent viewers from getting bored [6, 7].

2.2 Interactive Museum

For virtual museums, even in actual museums, conventionally, explanations have always been fixed, and research has been conducted such as changing explanations in accordance with the knowledge of visitors and selecting exhibits to be explained according to their preferences [8–13]. One direction is to make a smartphone of a viewer as a guide by downloading an application to the smartphone. In these studies, it is important how to know the visitor's preference and degree of knowledge.

In addition, instead of tablets and smartphones, research is being conducted to make robots, especially a humanoid robot, act as a guiding agent. It is considered effective to use a humanoid robot as a guide, since humans are easy to feel familiar with a humanoid robot. However, since it is necessary for such robots to perform human interaction with humans through natural language and gestures, research on such human-robot interactions is actively conducted [14–16].

3   Rakuchu Rakugai-zu and Its Funaki Version

3.1   Rakuchu Rakugai-zu

Kyoto was the capital of Japan during the Heian period (794–1185), and after the transfer of political power from the emperor to the samurai, it continued to be the cultural center as the emperor lived there until the end of the Edo period, and is still the center of Japanese culture. The Rakuchu Rakugai-zu [5] is a painting depicting the scenery and customs of the city (Rakuchu) and the suburbs (Rakugai) of Kyoto, which cultural, historical, and academic values have been highly valued. Two of them have been designated as national treasures and five of them designated as important cultural properties. They were produced from the early 16th century, when groups of warriors from all over Japan fought for supremacy, to the Edo period, when the political control by the Tokugawa

Shogunate was established. Among the existing ones, 30 to 40 works are well preserved. Figure 1 shows an example of Funaki Version, which is preserved as two sets (left wing and right wing) of Byobu (folding screen) [20].

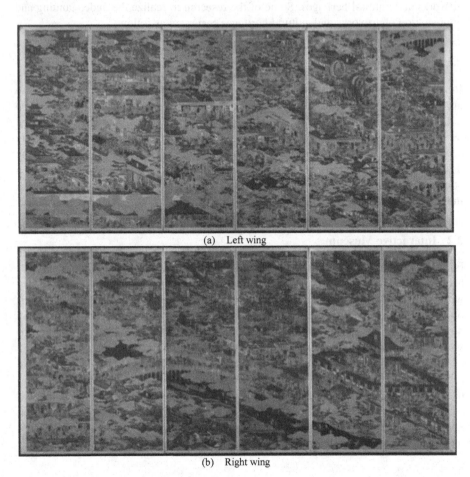

(a)   Left wing

(b)   Right wing

Fig. 1. Rakuchu Rakugai-zu Funaki Version

The era in which the Funaki Version was drawn is a politically unstable one in Japan. However, as mentioned above, Kyoto has been the center of Japanese culture for a long time and people used to enjoy their stable lives. Also, Kyoto have attracted many tourists from all over Japan. Especially, the desire to visit Kyoto was high among people living in rural areas. Therefore, Rakuchu Rakugai-zu made people aware of the center of Japanese culture and also served as a tourist guide.

More than 2,000 people are drawn on Rakuchu Rakugai-zu, and their personality, occupation, clothing, hairstyle, etc. are important research subjects. It is general that the Rakuchu Rakugai-zu is drawn as the two folding screens; east side of Kyoto on the right wing, and west side of Kyoto on the left as a bird's-eye view. In the early

Rakuchu Rakugai-zu the landscape of the Sengoku-jidai (Warring States period) [18] is drawn. In the right half the down town of Kyoto including the Kamo River, the Gion Shrine, and Higashiyama areas are drawn. The left half includes famous places such as the samurai residences, the Funaokayama Hill, the Kitano Tenmangu Shrine, etc. In the Edo era, many Rakuchu Rakugai-zu drew the Kouho-ji Temple, that was famous by its big Buddha stature, on the right wing and the Nijo Castle on the left wing.

3.2 Rakuchu Rakugai-zu Funaki Version

Rakuchu Rakugai-zu Funaki Version (hereafter the Funaki Version) is one of many Rakuchu Rakugai-zu. More than 2,000 of people are drawn in it in extremely detailed and dynamic way, and the daily lives and manners of the people of Kyoto are drawn well.

It is said that the Funaki Version was painted by a painter Iwasa Matabei, and the time of painting is around 1614. It is the time when political power in Japan was being transferred from the Toyotomi administration established by Toyotomi Hideyoshi, who achieved national reunification, to the Tokugawa government established by Tokugawa Ieyasu. As Toyotomi family will be destroyed in the two battles called the "1614 and 1615 Osaka Battles," what is depicted in the Funaki Version is the scenery of Kyoto just before the battle. On the left side of the left wing drawing is Nijo Castle, which shows off the authority of the Tokugawa Shogunate. At the same time, however, as opposed to it, the Hokoji Buddha built by the Toyotomi family boasts the dignity at the right end of the right wing. It shows that the power of the family is still great. Under such historical background, a group of samurai warriors who hurry up and a scene of tension with people fighting with a sword or a spear is also depicted. However, despite of such a political situation, it looks that everyday life of people in Kyoto is normal and usual. And the city is filled with the energy of such people.

Fig. 2. Zoom-up view of the Rakuchu Rakugai-zu Funaki Version

Iwasa Matabei is an excellent painter for drawing people's lively expressions and movements. While viewers watch the drawing from a distant position, it is difficult to notice this, but when they approach the drawing, the lively expressions and actions of people in the drawing become distinctive. By looking at the details of the Funaki Version, viewers would be interested in the lifestyles and customs of the people of Kyoto in the early 17th century. Figure 2 shows several examples of enlarged views of persons drawn in the Funaki Version.

4 Interactive Rakuchu Rakugai-zu

4.1 Concept

In the Funaki Version, the clothes, actions and expressions of over 2,000 people are drawn in detail and they are very intriguing. Viewers would have questions as to what kind of occupation and status they are, what kind of clothes they are wearing, and what they are doing now. By knowing these things, viewers can know the lives of people at that time, and they can know what the daily lives of these people were during the unstable political situation at that time. Furthermore, from the standpoint of studying society and customs at that time, it is required that the system can answer questions such as what kind of occupation people are engaged in and what is the proportion of each occupation.

Since the knowledge that viewers want to know is different from person to person, it is necessary for the system to be able to interactively give such information. Based on this consideration, we are developing an interactive system of the Funaki Version.

After completion, we aim to open the platform on the Internet so that various people can search for information and freely exchange information, and so on.

4.2 Digital Funaki Version

In order to develop an interactive Funaki Version, firstly it is necessary to digitize and archive the original Funaki Version. The original Funaki Version is currently stored at the Tokyo National Museum. Toppan Printing Co., Ltd., to which several of the authors belong, cooperates with the Tokyo National Museum and has developed a system that converts the Funaki Version into high-definition digital data with 2.21 billion pixels. The system has the function of moving the viewpoint to any position by a mouth or a finger, and zooming-in with an arbitrary size. Although the size of each person drawn in the original drawing is at most a few centimeters, when viewers zoom it up about 100 times and watch it on a big screen of several hundred inches, they can watch very detailed view of people in the drawing including their face expressions, closes, action, etc. as shown in Fig. 2.

4.3 Database

The aim of this interactive system is to realize the function to answer viewers' various questions regarding persons and buildings drawn in the Funaki Version. For that purpose, we have designed and developed the architecture of the database as follows.

Database Structure

The painting is divided into sets of appropriate square boxes and systematic 2D address was given to each of the boxes. Also, multiple names were given to each box regarding the place, object, and event such as the Shijo Bridge, the Shijo Street, the Gion Festival, etc. These multiple names are used to link each place/object/event and its position.

Contents of the Database Regarding Place/Object/Event
Regarding each of places and objects such information as shrine/temple/house, vehicle, goods, their meanings, etc. was prepared and given. For event name, such information as content of event, season, etc. was given.

Contents of the Database Regarding Person
For each person, viewers would be interested in such information as the kind of occupation or position of the person, what the person is wearing, and what he/she is doing. For that purpose, we prepared data of the following structure for each person.Tile number, location, gender, occupation, clothing, hat, hairstyle, mustache/beard, belongings, actions, and comments.

Such information was prepared and given to each of more than 2,000 persons drawn in the Funaki Version. Table 1 shows a part of the database regarding person.

How to Get Information
It is a time consuming work to get various information shown in Table 1 for more than 2,000 persons drawn in the Funaki Version. We have asked several Kyoto University researchers and students studying Japanese history to do this. They identified such information based on their expertise and when it is difficult for them to do this, they identified such information by referring to various history books stored in the Kyoto University Library. Also, we have carried out several interviews with persons whose family live long time in Kyoto and know various old stories about Kyoto.

4.4 Dialogue Function

The above database structure makes it possible for the system to do the following dialogue based interaction.

(1) By indicating a person or an object in the painting shown on a tablet PC, viewers can ask what it is, what it is doing, whether there are other similar persons, and so on.

- Pointing of a position: pin pointing and area pointing are possible.
- Information display: If the indicated object has information, an appropriate natural language based answer is composed and is displayed on a pop-up window.
- Search for similar things: If the indicated thing has a description, it can search other ones with the same descriptions and display their images.

(2) If a viewer asks a question by text, the system searches and displays corresponding object with a zoom-in view. (So far, the system accepts only text input, but speech input will become possible soon.)

Table. 1. Example of the database

Tile number	Place	Gender	Occupation	Clothing	Hat	Hairstyle	Mustache/Beard	Belongings	Actions	Comments
U3-1-1	Kiyomizu Temple	Male	Samurai	Men's Kimono	Straw hat	Invisible	Mustache	None	Standing and waching	
U3-1-1	Kivomizu Temple	Male	Monk	Clerical dress	None	Bold	None	None	Sitting and sightseeing	
U3-1-1	Kivomizu Temple	Female	Unknown	Woman's Kimono	None	Binded at the back	None	None	Standing and talking	
U3-1-4	Bion Temple	Male	Samurai	Kimono and hakama	None	Samurai style	Mustache	Sword	Walking	
U3-1-4	Gion Temple	Male	Samurai	Kimono and hakama	Straw hat	Samurai style	None	Sword and fan	Talking while walking	
U3-1-4	GiotiTemple	Female	Unknown	Woman's Kimono	None	Natural style	None	Battle of sake	Sittng and drinking	
U3-1-6	Tokuhara Temple	Female	Shop rtaff	Woman's Kimono	None	Natural style	None	Mortar	Sitting and cooking	
U3-1-6	Tokuhara Temple	Female	Shopaaff	Woman's Kimono	None		None	None	Sitting and watching	
...	...	...	...	...	...	...	...	...	...	

Hakama: Japanese style trouser used by Samurai

- Question on place: Gosho (Imperial house), Gojo Bridge, Shijo Street, etc.
- Question on action: festival, prayer, rice planting, fight, etc.
- Question on types of goods: cattle, bells, swords, etc.
- Combination of these questions: example: "Where is vehicle being drawn at Gion Festival?"

(3) By combining (1) and (2), viewers can continue dialogue with the system.

In order to be able to achieve the above interaction, a dialogue system shown in Fig. 3 was developed.

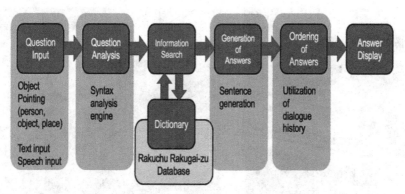

Fig. 3. Block diagram of the dialogue system

4.5 Present Funaki Version

When viewers look at the Funaki Version, they will be interested in the fact that the everyday lives of people are vividly depicted in almost every part of the drawing, and they will also be interested in what these places look now. When we exhibited the system, which will be described in Sect. 5, we received many questions and comments such as "What does this place in the Funaki Version look now?" or "It would be great if I could compare the time of the Funaki Version and present." In order to meet such hopes, we decided to produce a present version of Funaki Version.

Firstly, among various places drawn in the original Funaki Version, we have identified several places where viewers would be particularly interested such as the Shijo Street, the Gosho (emperor house), etc. In addition, we have decided to draw several representative events, which could survive long history and remain until today, such as the Gion Festival, to compare them with those drawn in the Funaki Version. Furthermore, in order to compare the appearance/dress of people of those days depicted in the Funaki Version with those of the present people, we also have decided to draw present people. Because persons in the Funaki Version are drawn in a deformation way regarding to their expressions/actions, which actually attracts our interest, it is better to draw a cartoon based character rather than to draw a present person as a realistic person. Based on this consideration, we have asked students of Manga (comic) Department of Kyoto Seika University to create such characters.

Figure 4 shows characters, vehicles, events of the present version superimposed on the original Funaki Version.

In Fig. 4 (a), to illustrate the difference between the Funaki Version's era and the present, Shinkansen (Japanese bullet train) and the Gojo Street, where many cars come and go, are drawn. Also, in Fig. 4 (b), vehicles used in the Gion Festival, that are moving along the Kawaramachi Street, are drawn.

The followings were recognized through the development of the present Funaki Version.

(a) Shinkansen (bullet train) and Gojo street   (b) Kawaramachi Street and Gion Festival

Fig. 4. Present Funaki Version overlapped on the original version

(1) Modern buildings are too large compared to the houses/buildings at the time of the Funaki Version and therefore, they would not match when superimposed on the original version. Therefore, it is better to limit the drawing of modern buildings only to such characteristic buildings as the Kyoto Tower. Also, it is not relevant to strictly consider the size ratio.

(2) It is better to use modern characters not only simply but also more aggressively when putting them in the original Funaki Version. There are several ways to realize this. For example, it is relevant to draw as if modern characters are participating in events such as Hanami (cherry blossom viewing) and the Gion Festival in the original Funaki Version. Another idea is that a viewer manipulates the modern character by itself in the original Funaki Version and let it speak to persons of the original version. (In other words, modern characters would play the role of "player characters" in a game). Anyway, we plan to decide an appropriate way while exhibiting the system and listening to viewers' comments.

5 Exhibition

The above system is currently under development. But it is important to obtain various opinions from viewers by exhibiting the system even at the development stage, and to feedback the obtained opinions for future system development. As a part of this effort, we exhibited the system at an international conference called the Art Science International Symposium held at Kyoto University in March 2019 [21], and the system was well appreciated by …. Figure 5 shows the scenes of the exhibition.

(a) Exhibition of the original Rakuchu Rakugai-zu.   (b) Exhibition of the developed interactive system.

Fig. 5. Exhibition of the original and interactive Rakuchu Rakugai-zu.

Figure 5(a) shows a scene of exhibiting a full size high-definition copy of the original Rakuchu Rakugai-zu. Many people enjoyed the appreciation of the original version with ultra-high definition. Figure 5(b) is a scene in which the interactive system is displayed. A tablet PC was provided for a viewer, which has the function of allowing the viewer to freely move to an arbitrary place on the map and zoom-in or out. Also, when a specific person in the drawing is tapped, information on the person is displayed in a separate window. Furthermore, by displaying the screen of the tablet PC on a large screen using a projector, how the interaction is going on could be appreciated by other people. We received various opinions from the viewers, and now are analyzing them for the future development.

In addition, since a VR type exhibition would give the immersive impression of actually entering into the world of the Funaki Version, VR exhibition of the interactive Funaki Version would be very effective. We are planning to carry out such VR exhibition as shown in Fig. 6.

Fig. 6. VR exhibition of the interactive Funaki Version.

6 Conclusion

In the 16th and 17th centuries in Japan, various Rakuchu Rakugai-zu (Views in and around Kyoto) were created as drawings depicting the city and the surrounding areas of Kyoto. Among them the Funaki Version is well-known, as it draws more than 2,000 persons, each of whom is drawn vividly. We are developing the interactive Rakuchu Rakugai-zu Funaki Version, with the purpose of providing viewers better understanding of the original Funaki Version by interactively providing information on persons, buildings, famous places, and so on.

In this paper, we first explained what the Rakuchu Rakugai-zu is and described the features of the well-known Rakuchu Rakugai-zu Funaki Version. Then, we described the details of the interactive Funaki Version, focusing its database, dialogue function, and its present version to be overlapped on the original one. We also described our experience of exhibiting the system and how it attracted the interest of many people.

This system is now being improved based on the viewers' comments and opinions obtained at the exhibition. At the stage of completion, we aim it to be open on the Internet and also aim it to become an online intellectual space where many people can gather and exchange opinions.

References

1. Bay, H., Fasel, B., Gool, L.C.: Interactive museum guide. In: Proceedings of UbiComp 2005 (2005)
2. http://www.emuseum.jp/top?d_lang=en
3. http://www.toppan-vr.jp/mt/en/
4. http://www.dnp.co.jp/eng/
5. Christie's: A Magnificent Rakuchu Rakugai Screen New York October 16, 1990, Christie's (1990)

6. Haskins, E.: Between archive and participation: public memory in a digital age. Rhetor. Soc. Q **37**, 401–422 (2007)
7. Sylaiou, S., et al.: Exploring the relationship between presence and enjoyment in a virtual museum. Int. J. Hum Comput Stud. **68**(5), 243–253 (2010)
8. Ciolfi, L, Bannon, L.J.: Designing interactive museum exhibits: enhancing visitor curiosity through augmented artefacts. In: Proceedings of ECCE11 (2001)
9. Hindmarsh, J., Heath, C., Lehn, D.V., Cleverly, J.: Creating assemblies in public environments: social interactive, interactive exhibits and CSCW. Comput. Support. Coop. Work **14**, 1–41 (2005)
10. Caultom, T.: Hands-On Exhibitions: Managing Interactive Museums and Science Centres. Routledge, London (2006)
11. Sandifer, C.: Technological novelty and open-endedness: two characteristics of interactive exhibits that contribute to the holding of visitor attention in a science museum. J. Res. Sci. Teach. **40**(2), 121–137 (2003)
12. Bitgood, S.: Suggested guidelines for designing interactive exhibits. Visitor Behav. **VI**(4), 4–11 (1991)
13. Hornecker, E., Stifter, M.: Learning from interactive museum installations about interaction design for public settings. In: Proceedings of OZCHI200618, pp. 1–8 (2006)
14. Burgard, W., et al.: The interactive museum tour-guide robot. In: Proceedings of AAAI-1998 (1998)
15. Shiomi, M., Kanda,T., Ishiguro, H., Hagita, H.: Interactive humanoid robots for a science museum. In: Proceedings of HRI 2006, pp. 305–312 (2006)
16. Thrun, S., et al.: Probabilistic algorithms and the interactive museum tour-guide robot minerva. Int. J. Robot. Res. **19**(11), 972–999 (2000)
17. Mason, R., Caiger, J.: A History of Japan. Tuttle Publishing, North Clarendon (2004)
18. Sengoku period. https://en.wikipedia.org/wiki/Sengoku_period
19. Chaplin, D.: Sengoku Jidai, Nobunaga, Hideyoshi, and Ieyasu: Three Unifiers of Japan. Createspace Independent Publishing Platform, Scotts Valley (2018)
20. https://en.wikipedia.org/wiki/Byōbu
21. http://art.gsais.kyoto-u.ac.jp/index-en.html

Research on the Regenerated Design of Blue Calico Based on Computer Image Processing

Yuanyuan Wang and Rongrong Fu[✉]

East China University of Science and Technology, Shanghai, China
ecust_wyy@163.com, muxin789@126.com

Abstract. As a traditional handicraft printing and dyeing product of the Han nationality, blue calico has been included in the first batch of national intangible cultural heritage list. Blue printed pattern is famous for its blue and white color characteristics. However, due to monotonous and old pattern design, lack of innovation and other factors, blue calico cannot adapt to the contemporary aesthetic habits, resulting in difficulties in inheritance and regeneration. In order to solve this problem, this paper aims at redesigning and activating the blue calico by combining the traditional pattern with the modern graphic design pattern through machine learning and computer image processing technology. With Inception Score and user satisfaction survey as the evaluation metrics, feasibility of computer image processing technology for the reconstruction of intangible cultural heritage image generation is verified. Finally, design value of generated patterns is proved, and a research model of the relationship between computer image processing technology and intangible cultural heritage design is established.

Keywords: Computer image processing · Computer vision · Intangible cultural heritage regeneration · Blue calico

1 Introduction

Due to the simple and unsophisticated blue and white color combination, colorful patterns, abundant connotative themes and ingenious craftsmanship, blue calico has been included in the first batch of national intangible cultural heritage list. Its unique art form, folk aesthetic concept of advocating auspiciousness and completeness, as well as the decorative implication full of good luck, provide ideas and inspiration for artistic creators [1]. However, with the development of the times, its strong rural and folksy flavor do not accord with the tone of modern life, and the use has become single with certain limitations. Many blue calico products gradually withdrew from public view. Therefore, it is necessary not only to appreciate the craft and aesthetic characteristics of blue calico, but also to think about improvement and innovation of the monotonous and old traditional pattern elements. According to the needs of the times, new expression methods and artistic ideas are explored. Characteristics of modern graphic design patterns can be integrated. Modern forms of expression are mainly point, line and surface, repetition, emission, gradient, space of contradiction, contrast, texture, as well as the combination

© Springer Nature Switzerland AG 2020
M. Rauterberg (Ed.): HCII 2020, LNCS 12215, pp. 428–438, 2020.
https://doi.org/10.1007/978-3-030-50267-6_32

of virtual and real. Therefore, there are broader and more diverse themes and contents of blue calico pattern [2].

At present, computer image processing technology has been widely applied in the field of intangible cultural heritage. The construction of digital protection platforms, such as intangible cultural heritage database, image restoration, image classification and image simulation research have made tremendous contributions to inheritance and protection of intangible cultural heritage. However, in order to comply with the development trend of the times, intangible cultural heritage should not only play a role of inheritance and protection, but also put forward innovations to adapt to the aesthetic needs of modern people. Nevertheless, there are few relevant studies on the redesign of intangible cultural heritage images and the creation of new vitality by using computer image technology. On this basis, this paper improves the Deep Convolutional Generative Adversarial Network in aspects of sample construction and loss function, and verifies the feasibility of computer image processing technology in the generation and redesign of intangible cultural heritage image. In addition, this paper explores whether the generated pattern has design value and whether a new relationship between computer image processing technology and intangible cultural heritage design can be established.

2 Related Work

In terms of combination of computer image processing technology and blue calico, literature includes the study from Jia X. et al. [3], which identifies different patterns from images by the method of deep learning, and uses the improved and optimized structure and parameters of VGGnet-16 convolutional neural network. Moreover, a classification model of blue calico patterns based on Convolutional Neural Network is established to realize a proper classification of patterns and lay a foundation for the inheritance and innovation of digital blue calico. Chen S. et al. [4] use specific elements of Julia set graphics and Photoshop software to carry out a secondary design of patterns, and reconstruct patterns of blue calico. Julia set graphics can not only create new patterns combining traditional and modern design, but also greatly improve the diversity, fashion and technology of traditional pattern design.

In addition, research on computer image processing includes image classification, image generation, image captioning and other emerging technologies. Among them, as a new type of computer image processing technology, GAN [5] has been widely applied in the field of image generation, which can accurately generate face and other target objects [6], generate high-resolution images from low-resolution images [7], and generate images from simple text descriptions [8], etc. The Deep Convolutional Generative Adversarial Network (DCGAN) is a new type of GAN improved by Redford et al. [9] in 2015, which takes advantage of the convolutional network's better ability to extract image features. Furthermore, emerging image translation technologies such as pixel2pixel [10] and CycleGAN [11] can realize the conversion of image style. However, the premise is that the images before and after need to be isomorphic, such as zebra and horse, male face and female face, etc., which is not applicable for graphic design scenes full of transformation. To sum up, although computer image processing technology has become a new trend, it still has not fully played its unique advantages in the recreation design of intangible cultural heritage blue calico.

Therefore, this paper proposes to improve the deep convolutional generative adversarial network in terms of sample construction and loss function. The convolutional network can better capture the contour details of blue calico pattern and modern graphic art pattern, and generate redesigns, thus realizing the modernization extension and innovation of traditional blue calico patterns. The research work mainly includes network construction, sample collection, sample data pre-processing, training evaluation, generating results preliminary screening, user satisfaction survey, and building a model of the relationship between computer image processing technology and intangible cultural heritage design.

3 Methods

3.1 Neural Network Design

Generative Adversarial Network [5] consists of two networks, generator (G) and discriminator (D). Generator generates images from random noise while discriminator judges whether input image is real data or generated data. In the training process, task of generator is to generate pictures as real as possible so as to confuse discriminator. Task of discriminator is to distinguish the pictures generated by generating network G from real pictures as accurate as possible. These two networks constitute a dynamic game until Nash equilibrium is achieved [5]. Figure 1 shows how GAN works.

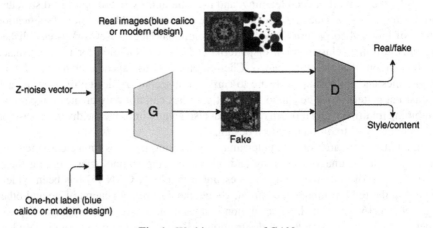

Fig. 1. Working process of GAN

In this paper, DCGAN, an improved version of GAN is adopted. We used a full connection layer to reshape 100-d random noise to a 16384-d vector, then the vector is reshaped to a 4*4*1024 tensor. Transposed convolution is used to reshape tensor to 8*8*512, 16*16*256, 32*32*128 and finally 64*64*3. Generator's network structure is shown in Fig. 2.

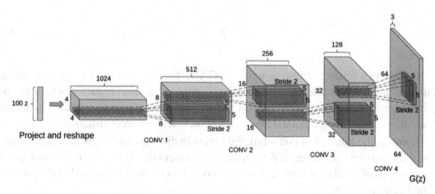

Fig. 2. Network structure of generator G in DCGAN

3.2 Loss Function

DCGAN has the same loss function as Gan, Eq. (1) shows GAN's loss function is made up of loss from generator and loss from discriminator.

$$\min_G \max_D V(D, G) = E_{x \sim p_{data}(x)}[\log D(x)]$$

$$+ E_{z \sim p_z(z)}[\log(1 - D(G(z)))] \tag{1}$$

Discriminator D tries to maximize the probability of correctly classifying real image and generated image. Optimization of discriminator is achieved through maximizing V(D,G). V(D,G) is the object function for discriminator. The first term represents the mathematical expectation that a sample from real images is classified as a real sample by the discriminator. For samples in real data, probability should be as close to 1 as possible, thus we want maximize this term. The second term represents expectation of the negative logarithm of the prediction probability for the generated image. When this term goes bigger and close to 0, discriminator has better judgement.

Optimization for generator is done through minimizing the maximum of V(D,G). Generator minimizes the maximum value of discriminator's objective function, which represents JS divergence between real data distribution and generated data distribution. JS divergence can measure similarity between two distributions, and the closer two distributions are, the smaller the JS divergence is. Therefore, objective for generator's optimization is to make the distribution of generated data as close as possible to that of real data.

In this paper, for the regenerated scenario, loss function is upgraded by referring to the idea of calculating loss function for style and content in style transfer. Upgraded loss function is as Eq. (2) [12].

$$\min_G \max_D V(D, G) = E_{x \sim p_{data}(x)}[\log D(x)]$$

$$+ E_{z \sim p_z(z)}[\log(1 - D(G(z)))]$$

$$+ \alpha \sum_j^L y \ell_{style}^{\phi, j}(\hat{l}_j, l_j)$$

$$+ \beta \sum_{j}^{L} (1 - y) \ell_{feat}^{\phi,j}(\hat{l}_j, l_j) \tag{2}$$

The first two terms are loss function in GAN. The last two term is the loss added relative to label. When discriminator is being optimized, if label equals 1, which means input image is blue calico, style reconstruction loss plays a role and if label equals 0, which means input image is modern design image, feature reconstruction loss plays a role. L means the number of convolutional layers in discriminator. $\hat{l}_j$ is the output value of the j-th convolutional layer. α, β are hyper-parameters that keep loss at the same order of magnitude and balance content loss and style loss. Content loss and style loss are defined detailed below.

Content Loss

$$\ell_{feat}^{\phi,j}(\hat{y}, y) = \frac{1}{C_j H_j W_j} ||\phi_j(\hat{y}) - \phi(y)||_2^2 \tag{3}$$

$\phi_j(\hat{y})$ represents output after the j-th convolutional layers. Equation (3) means pixel-level mean squared error of convolutional output between a generated image and a real image.

Style Loss

$$\ell_{style}^{\phi,j}(\hat{y}, y) = ||G_j^{\phi}(\hat{y}) - G_j^{\phi}(y)||_F^2 \tag{4}$$

Style loss is obtained by taking the Frobenius norm after taking the difference through Gram matrix. G represents Gram matrix and F represents Frobenius norm. Gram matrix describes features of a image, defined as Eq. (5)

$$G_j^{\phi}(x)_{c,c'} = \frac{1}{C_j H_j W_j} \sum_{h=1}^{H_j} \sum_{w=1}^{W_j} \phi_j(x)_{h,w,c} \phi_j(x)_{h,w,c'} \tag{5}$$

$\phi_j(x)$ represents output after the j-th convolutional layers and h and w and c represent height, width and channels. Style loss function focuses more on structure of the whole image and describes image style through correlation of features. Although style loss and content loss are added to loss, the network update method does not change accordingly. Parameters in network is updated by back propagation. Discriminator update is based on its loss function and so is generator.

4   Experiments

4.1   Original Data

First, sample images are collected and processed. There are many kinds of point and line in blue calico, such as big mixing point, small mixing point, pepper point, meson point, plum point and horizontal point, etc. Also shapes of line include round, fan, triangle, rectangle and irregular shape. Samples are selected to cover each pattern, in order to make original data as complete as possible to represent the various patterns of blue calico. Therefore, selected samples of blue calico should be clear and representative of its various patterns. On the other hand, modern design patterns are mostly composed of changes in point, line and surface, and also involve effects such as emission gradient. In modern design pattern selection, considering that complex contours may cause difficulty in training neural networks, simple contours are used as much as possible.

Finally, 200 samples were collected through fieldwork and Internet search, including 100 blue calico patterns and 100 modern graphic design patterns that meet requirements above. Sample illustrations of blue calico and modern graphic design are shown in Table 1 (partial display):

Table 1. Blue calico and modern design legends

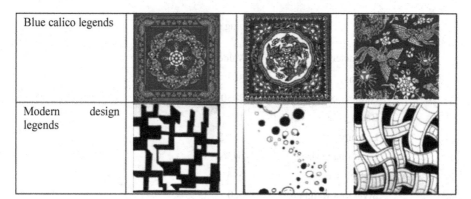

4.2 Data Pre-processing and Data Augmentation

Data pre-processing is vital in computer image processing. Proper pre-processing can make network training easier and generated images more reasonable. Since there is no ready-made data set, number of samples is limited by manual collection and selection. Data augmentation contributes a lot to convergence of deep learning and can yield more data from a limited number of samples. The following pre-processing and data augmentation methods are adopted in this paper:

- Uniform resize: all data is clipped to a uniform size (64*64).
- Filter: some blue prints have stains, median filtering processing is done to remove unclear dots.
- Random cropping: randomly cut 20*20 pieces and enlarge to the uniform size.
- Random occlusion: blue calico images mostly have repetitive textures. Random occlusion can enhance the robustness of the network.
- Contrast adjustment: texture information is unrelated to color changes, so changing contrast can enlarge training data set without hurting convergence of the network.

- Brightness adjustment: texture information is unrelated to color changes, so similar images sharing different rightness can all be training samples.

After nested combination of the above data augmentation methods, size of the original dataset was expanded from 200 to 2030. 98% of the blue calico patterns and all the modern design patterns were randomly selected and shuffled as the neural network training set, and the rest 2% of the blue print related patterns were used as the evaluation set.

4.3 Training Details

GPU is NVIDIA GeForce MX150, python environment is python 3.6. TensorFlow version is 1.14.0. Table 2 shows detailed training parameters.

Table 2. Training parameters

Parameter	Value
Epochs	30
Number of training images	2030
Batch_size	1
Learning rate	2e−5
Input image size	64*64*3
Kernel size	5*5
Style loss weight α	5e0
Content loss weight β	5e2
Initialization	N (0,0.2) random initialization

Algorithm flow includes: random noise is transmitted to the generator, and the generator network converts the noise into G(z) through multiple deconvolutional layers; Discriminator D combines generator's output, input real image and label to calculate content loss, style loss, generation loss and discrimination loss; Using Adam optimizer [13], the network parameters are updated by back-propagation algorithm. Multiple epochs are trained until the network converges.

Corresponding solutions are adopted to solve problems in experiments, such as unclear generated pictures and bad generating performance. Here are some examples:

- Generated pictures by DCGAN are not clear enough. This is a common problem in the training GAN, because the network cannot fully fit the picture details, resulting that output patterns are not clear and include much noise interference. In the follow-up evaluation of user satisfaction, clarity also has an impact on user perception. Therefore, quadric spline interpolation and Kalman filtering are used to eliminate noise in generated images and smooth image features.

- The loss of the discriminator quickly drops to a value very close to 0, and the loss of the generator changes very little. This is caused by the discriminator beating the generator too fast. Change parameter update frequency to: discriminator: generator = 1:2 to overcome this trouble.

After the training is completed, the neural network has the ability to generate creative patterns. Eventually 100 blue calico patterns are generated, and Fig. 3 are legends for generated patterns. (Partial displayed.)

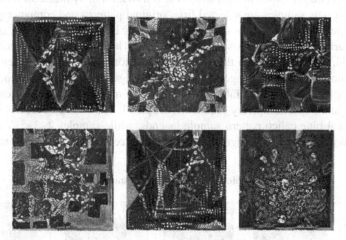

Fig. 3. Legends of generated patterns

4.4 Generated Samples Evaluation

In accordance with the principles of graphic design, 92 valid samples are finally selected after eliminating those that violate visual principles or are ambiguous. The effectiveness of the valid samples is verified from two perspectives, computer rational scoring and user satisfaction survey. One is measurement on diversity of network's generated images by Inception Score, and the other is user satisfaction survey. The higher the Inception Score is, the more diverse the images are. In this case, valid samples of the blue calico and images of original traditional blue calico are inputs to the Inception net to calculate the Inception Score and obtain Table 3.

Table 3. Inception Score

Real images	Generated images
3.64 ± 0.71	4.22 ± 0.67

From the average value, generated blue calico samples have higher Inception Score, indicating that the diversity of generated pattern is stronger than that of the original patterns. Through combination of modern design and traditional blue calico design, neural networks can have more diverse artistic expressions.

4.5 User Satisfaction Survey

In order to verify feasibility and effectiveness of the research on regeneration design of blue calico based on computer image processing technology, a user satisfaction survey on the final generated patterns is evaluated from the creativity dimension through user interview method. The specific operation is as follows. First, by means of random sampling, 5 interview samples are selected from original patterns and computer-generated patterns respectively. Second, the author visits Nantong Blue Calico Museum, and invites 5 staff to participate in the user satisfaction survey. They are all aged between 25 and 50 years old, and familiar with the development history and pattern characteristics of the blue calico. Third, the average scores of the 5 judges in each category under the 10 pattern samples are shown in Table 4 (on a scale from 1 to 5, with 1 indicating very dissatisfied and 5 indicating very satisfied). Samples 1, 4, 6, 9 and 10 are selected from the traditional blue calico pattern sample legends, while samples 2, 3, 5, 7 and 8 are selected from the computer image processing generated pattern sample legends.

Table 4. User satisfaction survey

Evaluation Metric\Image			
	sample 1	sample 2	sample 3	sample 4
creativity	1.6	4	3.8	1.8
Evaluation Metric\Image			
	sample 5	sample 6	sample 7	sample 8
creativity	2.4	2.2	3.4	4
Evaluation Metric\Image			
	sample 9	sample 10		
creativity	2.4	2.2		

According to the interview results, in terms of creativity, satisfaction of the computer-generated pattern samples is mostly higher than that of the traditional patterns. Computer-generated patterns break the single symmetrical layout of the traditional blue calico, which are more personalized and imaginative. During the user interview, some experts point out that the sample 3 looks like gorgeous star trails, sample 5 looks like scattered ginkgo leaves, and sample 8 looks like fantasy feathers, giving users infinite imagination. Based on the survey, it is well qualitatively and quantitively verified that generated patterns that integrates pattern characteristics of traditional blue calico and modern design has certain creative value and a sense of rhythm. Regenerated design is in line with the aesthetic taste of modern people. However, this paper still has limitations. Compared with the traditional blue calico pattern, the computer-generated pattern is not clear enough, which needs to be further studied.

Therefore, the creative characteristics of the blue calico pattern generated by computer image processing technology can be well applied to the design field, such as redesign of home textiles, redesign of blue calico, redesign of packaging and redesign of cultural creative products, etc. Generally, a typical blue calico designer designs a new pattern of blue calico in a few hours or even days, while the computer generates a new pattern in only 16 s. The application of computer image processing and regeneration technology can not only improve the work efficiency of designers, but also provide designers with a certain source of inspiration. On the basis of the computer-generated patterns, designer can further optimize. Finally, computer image processing technology can assist designers to do the design, achieving the effect of integration of science and art.

5 Conclusion

Through a fusion of rationality of computer image processing technology and sensibility of user satisfaction survey, new creative patterns combining traditional sense and modern sense are created, which effectively updates the blue calico pattern library. A new model of constructing computer image processing technology to assist designers to redesign is proposed. Next, designers apply regenerated blue calico patterns to related cultural and creative products, which can enhance user purchase interest. Then this will inject new vitality into the economy of Nantong, and provide new development ideas for the regeneration and creation of other intangible cultural heritages.

References

1. Xiaojing, T.: Analysis on the aesthetic characteristics and innovative application of traditional blue calico patterns. In: Art and Design Theory, pp. 130–132 (2016)
2. Jianan, C., Hanyi, W.: Study on the pattern of nantong blue calico. In: Western Leather, pp. 18–22 (2019)
3. Xiaojun, J., Hongtao, D., Zihao. L., Lihua, Y.: Classification of blue calico patterns based on VGGNet convolutional neural network. In: Optoelectronics Laser, pp. 867–875 (2019)
4. Shan, C., Wenjin, H.: Design method of blue calico patterns based on julia set graphics. In: Textile Review, pp. 88–90 (2018)
5. Goodfellow, I.J., et al.: Generative adversarial networks. arXiv preprint arXiv:1406.2661 (2014)

6. Karras, T., Laine, S., Aila, T.: A style-based generator architecture for generative adversarial networks. In: Proceedings of the IEEE Conference on Computer Vision and Pattern Recognition, pp. 4401–4419 (2019)

7. Ledig, C., et al.: Photo-realistic single image super-resolution using a generative adversarial network. In: Proceedings of the IEEE Conference on Computer Vision and Pattern Recognition, pp. 4681–4690 (2017)

8. Zhang, H., et al.: StackGAN: text to photo-realistic image synthesis with stacked generative adversarial networks. In: Proceedings of the IEEE International Conference on Computer Vision, pp. 5907–5915. 2017)

9. Radford, A., Metz, L., Chintala, S.: Unsupervised representation learning with deep convolutional generative adversarial networks. arXiv preprint arXiv:1511.06434 (2015)

10. Isola, P., Zhu, J.Y., Zhou, T., Efros, A.A.: Image-to-image translation with conditional adversarial networks. In: Proceedings of the IEEE Conference on Computer Vision and Pattern Recognition, pp. 1125–1134 (2017)

11. Zhu, J.Y., Park, T., Isola, P., Efros, A.: Unpaired image-to-image translation using cycle-consistent adversarial networks. In: Proceedings of the IEEE International Conference on Computer Vision, pp. 2223–2232 (2017)

12. Gatys, L.A., Ecker, A.S., Bethge, M.: A neural algorithm of artistic style. arXiv preprint arXiv:1508.06576 (2015)

13. Kingma, D.P., Ba, J.: Adam: a method for stochastic optimization arXiv preprint arXiv:1412.6890 (2014)

WeChat Redesign for Foreigners Living in China from Culturally Adaptive Design Perspective

Qinyan Zhang[✉]

Aalto University, 00076 Espoo, Finland
qinyan.zhang@aalto.fi

Abstract. As an approach of human-centered design, the culturally adaptive design is flexible to integrate cultural specific attributes into design thinking. This study chooses WeChat to exemplify how to resign from a culturally adaptive view. WeChat has become a universal social media tool in the Chinese market, with 960 million users. However, the lack of culture adaption in interaction interfaces results in some usability problems for foreigners. To be globally accepted, the design should adapt to different users' cultural preferences. In this paper, we conducted a systematic research focusing on incorporating cultural factors, and Human-Computer Interaction factors into mobile interface design. It consists of five main steps include data collection, problem definition, ideation, prototype implementation, and evaluation. The statistical evaluation metrics of evaluation illustrates that interfaces that accommodate culture can significantly increase the user experience. The design process also provides deep insights into how WeChat can improve its interaction ways, which will enhance foreigners' satisfaction and their future usage intentions.

Keywords: Culturally adaptive interfaces · WeChat redesign · Cultural usability

1 Introduction

Large companies like Google, Microsoft, and IBM have spent an increasing amount of money on adapting their software applications to users from different countries [12], which contributes to improving customer loyalty in global market places. Reinecke and Bernstein [11] have previously proposed an approach called 'cultural adaptivity' to bridge this dichotomy between the need for internet products that cater to individual culture.

WeChat, similar to the Facebook app, released in 2011 by Tencent, Inc., has become the most frequently used application in China, with 900 million daily active users. Besides some usual functions such as instant messaging, video calls, posting moments, and mobile payment, the powerful app offers many services for daily life. The following are some representative examples: users can hail an Uber car or order delivery food by WeChat; citizens can pay the telephone, electricity, and water fees by the app; customers can book any tickets including train, flight and movie tickets with the help of it; even

© Springer Nature Switzerland AG 2020
M. Rauterberg (Ed.): HCII 2020, LNCS 12215, pp. 439–449, 2020.
https://doi.org/10.1007/978-3-030-50267-6_33

they can purchase stocks and insurances from WeChat [3]. Therefore, it is inevitable for people living in China to rely on WeChat for social communication and life services.

Nowadays, WeChat has a strong influence and has landed in many countries and regions. The survey in [14] indicated that foreign WeChat users are distributed in all age groups but relatively concentrated in 20–29 years old (44.0%) and 30–39 years old (25.5%). About 60.0% of foreign WeChat users have stayed in China for more than one year. The overwhelming majority of exotic users have a higher educational level; 84.2% of the respondents have undergraduates degree or higher education level. Non-Chinese WeChat users living in China send 60% more text messages than typical users. They send 45% more stickers or emoji. The research also indicates that foreigners send ten red pockets a month, and 64.4% of expats use WeChat Pay.

WeChat aims to expand the overseas market and attract more expats, but it is unwise to design one universal app interface for local and exotic audiences. The target user of our study is international students living in China. At the ideation and prototype stage, we consider the influence of aesthetic and internal emotions differences between East and West on interface design and then use statistical methods of measuring experience to compare different ideas. In the final evaluation, with ten users of distinct cultural backgrounds, the majority of subjects preferred their culturally adaptive interaction ways compared to the current version.

2   Literature Review

As we know, besides the language-translation function, WeChat has not applied cultural adaptive factors into the app design. With developments in globalization and world cultural communication, cross-cultural adaptation has become one of the concerns of researchers in different fields. The anthropologist Hofstede [7] conducted comprehensive research about classification with five cultural dimensions: Power Distance (PDI), Individualism (IDV), Masculinity (MAS), Uncertainty Avoidance (UAI), and Long Term Orientation (LTO). Heimgärtner [8] demonstrated cultural models to serve as a basis for the identification of cultural distance between countries, shown in Table 1.

Table 1. Cultural dimensions between countries [7].

Factor	Western	China
Power distance	Low	High
Individualism	High	Low
Uncertainty avoidance	Medium	Low
Long-term orientation	Low	High
Context	Low	High
Time perception	Mono	Poly

Zurich researchers [11] have developed a "culturally adaptive" system using an approach to cultural adaptivity, acquiring the influences mentioned above storing in a personal user model instance, and mapping onto user interface adaptations. Also, Australia researchers connected essential HCI elements such as information speed and Information density with cultural dimensions [8], illustrated in Table 2. The references of cultural adaption dimensions provided the empirical baseline to support the new cross-cultural redesign guidelines.

Table 2. The connections HCI factors and cultural distance dimensions [8].

HCI factors	PDI (L)	IDV (L)	UAI (L)	LTO (L)	CTX (L)
Information speed	Low	High		Low	Low
Information density				Low	Low
Information frequency	Low	High	High	Low	Low
Information sequentiality	Low	High		Low	Low
Interaction frequency	Low	High	Low	Low	High
Interaction speed	Low	High		Low	Low

3 Methods

In this study, we propose a culture adaption design framework for foreigners living in China. Five main steps are included, which are separately addressed as follows. This study adopts triangulation methods for data gathering.

3.1 Data Collection

The step aims to gather data and explore the WeChat usage scenario in order to find cross-cultural usability problems.

Firstly, ten foreign participates (half male and half female) are respectively invited to fill in a questionnaire about their demographic information. Subsequently, each respondent is interviewed approximately 15 min and answers the following opening questions: the frequency and aim of using WeChat; the most commonly used functions of WeChat; the shortcomings of WeChat.

Secondly, based on interviews, we explore that the WeChat use scenarios mainly focus on the following three aspects, contacting people, using the mobile payment to buy things, and sharing personal life. After analyzing survey results, the usability problems of foreign users are summarized below in Table 3.

3.2 Problem Definition

As clearly stated by the level connection of HCI and cultural factors, we map the cultural factors of the western and China to HCI factors. From Table 1 and Table 2, we conclude

Table 3. Summary of experience problems for international users.

Number	Summary
1	WeChat should be a service tool for life, not a social media tool (notifications interrupt them)
2	Cross-cultural users can't understand how to trigger a function quickly (deep hierarchy of mobile payment)
3	WeChat own a great deal of unnecessary functions for foreigners
4	Too many operations (sharing pictures from Moments, paying by WeChat pay)
5	The function button is not obvious and does not conform to the mental model of western friends (like group creation, and payment)
6	The icon does not consider the usual western semantics (like '+' in main page)

that information density, interaction speed, and interaction frequency are low in some western countries. However, China, in contrast, has been shown efficiently filter such dense information. Therefore, high complexity is often comprehended as information overload by Westerners [9]. After initially sorting out, we plan to redesign interfaces closely related to Problems 2, 4, and 6, which helps foreigners utilize functions of WeChat smoothly. Then, according to the previous survey, we take a functional icon '+' of the home interface as a redesign example. '+' is a collection of the most routine functions, as shown in Fig. 1, which does not conform to the cognitive model of expats.

Fig. 1. Home page of WeChat. It shows the function of '+'. Users can create a new group with others, add new friends by QR code, scan code for entering anything and pay.

3.3 Ideation Process

In the phase of ideation, the reason for cultural preferences is analyzed from culture adaptive theories and aesthetic perspective.

Fig. 2. Two final alternatives after sorting from five solutions. One is arranged directly and another adopts an icon stack arrangement.

Due to the cultural dimensions like higher PDI, lower IDV, although eastern users cannot understand the meaning of a design at first, they rarely tend to refuse it and will accept it.

From an aesthetic perspective, the Chinese emphasize abstract aesthetic feeling rather than the description of the actual shape of things [11]. In contrast, Western pursue the accurate meaning and linguistic world. Most importantly, the western interface layout has more horizontal information. Traditional culture influences the form of the interface layout. For example, the ancient Chinese used to go from top to bottom, While Greek-speaking sloping field called "boustrophedon" from the horizontal view [5].

Supported by Nielsen's ten usability heuristics [10], designers must make objects and options visible. The aim of the redesign is to make icon design consistent with the standard semantics of foreign users and also select one usual function to optimize like the payment process. The research in [15] demonstrated that user evaluations are better if users can compare several alternatives. Under the guidance of this analysis and principles, we design five solutions and invite eight participants to vote for the favorite one. Figure 2 shows that the two most popular sketches that we choose.

Table 4. Advantages and shortcomings of prototypes.

No.	Advantages	Disadvantages	Improvement
Alternative 1	Succinctly describes function	Unintentional triggering, distracts attention	Redesign how icons are presented
Alternative 2	Space-saving icons, low learning cost, and intriguing interaction	Smaller touch targets, weak contrast in icon and background	Sufficient contrast for buttons that convey information

At the evaluation of the ideation phase, participants are required to score from 1–10 for the two design alternatives, and we use a statistical method named paired sample t-test to compare means and know whether there is a difference between the two prototypes. As with the independent sample's output, the p-value is 0.004411518, indicating that there is a significant difference between the two designs since this number is smaller than 0.05. Combining the analysis of Table 4 and metrics data, we select the No. 2 design as a prototype implementation.

3.4 Prototype

Comparing icon design of the most popular Chinese apps with that of Instagram, Stem, and Facebook, we find that the semantics of '+' function means creating a new activity rather than function storage.

The prototype follows metaphor and affordance principles proposed respectively by Jakob Nielsen [10] and Naoto Fukazawa [6]. For example, one of the screens (shown in Fig. 3) applies principles mentioned above to prototype implementation. This user interface matches the virtual system and the real world, which gives users instantaneous knowledge about how to interact with it. The stacked icons (used in the current version) creates affordances that provide users with stronger cues and hints for how to interact with the object.

Fig. 3. The comparison between two versions.

3.5 Evaluation

This evaluation mainly employs observation and quantitative methods to obtain the user's feedback on each step of operation [1].

WeChat payment is selected as one of the tasks and set up a simple usage scenario for users: when buying a large coke in the KFC, you pay it by the WeChat payment code as Fig. 4 shows.

We choose combined metrics to exemplify how to conduct user tests, through which the whole test procedure can be explained. Independent completion rate, the number of operation paths, and user satisfaction and are utilized to evaluate the availability, accessibility, and applicability of the improved version. An independent completion rate can measure the difficulty of tasks by completing a task in a limited time. The number of operation paths means how many clicks or slides users have to trigger the function. User satisfaction could partly reflect the user experience with the help of a 5-point SUS system scale.

Starting point   Ending point

Fig. 4. We set up a simple usage scenario for users: when buying a large coke in the KFC, you pay it by the WeChat payment code.

4 Results

The outcomes from Table 5 indicate that a culturally adaptive version greatly improves usability performance over the current version. The rate of independent completion goes up to 100%, and the number of path operand immensely declines.

Table 5. The comparison of usability performance between two versions.

Version	Completion rate	Path operand	Overall satisfaction	Aesthetics satisfaction	Perception satisfaction
Universal	60%	6.5	2.6	3.5	3.2
Adaptive	100%	3.0	3.6	3.4	4.0

It can be seen from the table below that the culturally adaptive statistical data of aesthetics satisfaction is not significantly different from the universal system (Table 6).

In order to find out the reason for statistically insignificant difference in aesthetics satisfaction, we conduct hierarchical task analysis, a way in which researchers collect usability problems for a range of practical applications including interface design and evaluation. Coupled with the observation for users' operations and interviews in experiments, the whole process of paying by QR code is reorganized and divided into four steps

Table 6. P-value of paired two sample t-test: for universal and adaptive version.

Measures	Universal version	Adaptive version	P-value
Overall satisfaction	–	+	0.0018810
Aesthetics satisfaction	=	=	0.7221858
Perception satisfaction	–	+	0.0000610

from opening WeChat to tapping the payment button, leading to a map of hierarchical task analysis, as shown in Fig. 5.

This subsequent analysis details users operating process and interactive patterns. After listing every step problem, we find that the most confusing part for participants is about stack icons and they are not able to perceive the stacked form as the semantics of unfolding with limited time. To address the triggering problems for payment, we change the color of different icons when overlapping and unfolding.

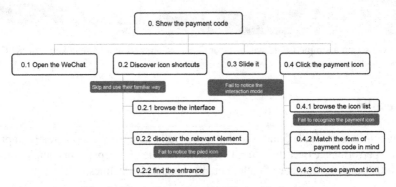

Fig. 5. The problems listed of hierarchical tasks.

Fig. 6. The problems listed of hierarchical tasks.

Figure 6 shows the improvements made in adjusting the size of icons appropriately to increase the range of touch and the optimized function structure. In the new adaptive version, the foreigner users can easily understand the operational metaphor of the stacked icon at the right corner since the icon redesign eliminates unnecessary confusion on the main page. Foreign users trigger the commonly used functions more efficiently by simpler information architecture and fewer information density.

5 Discussion

This discussion section comprises two parts. Firstly, we revisit the levels of cultural attributes in western countries and China and review the correlations between culturally dimensional levels and HCI factors. Secondly, we compare the usability test results and analysis to cited theories about the connections of cultural elements and HCI factors.

5.1 Applications of Previous Theories

The research integrates the cultural attributes in different countries and the correlations of those and prominent design metrics, which contributes to understanding possible usage difficulties and confusion. The model explains the contribution towards HCI and the cultural influences. Based on the research [8], the interaction frequency (the number of interactions per time unit) shows a negative correlation with individualism and uncertainty avoidance and a positive correlation with power distance and long-term orientation. To contrast with Asian, western users represent high individualism and uncertain avoidance, but lower power distance and long-term orientation. Therefore, we can deduce that the level of interaction frequency is relatively low. Low interaction frequency constitutes layout, visual display, navigation and hierarchy related principles. To summarize, it can be seen that these levels of culturally different dimensions and characteristics [7] in different countries, can perfectly match the corresponding cultural level in theory [8] so that the corresponding level of HCI factors can be further deduced. These HCI indicators, to a greater extent, are broken down into key design elements. Similarly, due to the corresponding relationship between two complicated models, we can draw an inference about other HCI factors in the usage of the western scenario. For example, when compared with the standardized universal WeChat interaction, the culturally adaptive version of WeChat provides a time saving alternative to reach the commonly used functions. Thus, the improved version reduces the number of interactions and optimizes the way how buttons are presented in order to give additional support in a structured way and rebuild an easier hierarchical structure resulting in a lower cognitive load.

5.2 Validation of Previous Theories

The prior works and theories provide a shortcut for researchers and designers to find cultural usability problems quickly and make redesign assumptions easily. Conversely, subjective feedback and quantitative data from user tests confirm the validity and reliability of prior theoretical models. According to usability performance in Table 5, the improved version shows fewer operations and better overall satisfaction performance.

Also, participants reflected that the understandable analogy and additional details eliminate confusion. The hierarchical task map indicates that exotic users are still not accustomed to a new interactive mode and need to rely on more explicit information. we can verify relations and connections between culture, HCI factors, and design elements.

6 Conclusion

In an overall comparison of the two versions, our result demonstrates that culturally adaptive user interfaces can reflect different preferences owing to cultural background. Also, it proves that cultural adaptation of user interfaces makes a huge difference in enhancing the efficiency and acceptance in a diverse traditional context. This research selects the interactive design of the functional icon as an example, and the next phase will be to redesign the information structure and interactive flow, which can adapt to foreigners' preferences.

References

1. Albert, W., Tullis, T.: Measuring the user Experience: Collecting, Analyzing, and Presenting usability Metrics, 2nd edn. Morgan Kaufmann, San Mateo (2013)
2. Alexander, R., Murray, D., Thompson, N.: Cross-cultural web design guidelines. In: The 14th Web for All Conference on the Future of Accessible Work Proceedings, p. 10. ACM (2017)
3. Introduction for WeChat. http://www.baike.baidu.com/subview/5117297/15145056.html. Accessed 27 Oct 2019
4. Cyr, D., Trevor-Smith, H.: Localization of web design: an empirical comparison of German, Japanese, and United States web site characteristics. J. Am. Soc. Inf. Sci. Technol. 55(13), 1199–1208 (2004)
5. Chai, J.X., Fan, K.K.: Analyzing the differences of design between Chinese and Western social media. In: 2016 International Conference on Advanced Materials for Science and Engineering (ICAMSE), pp. 136–138. IEEE (2017)
6. Ding, F., Wei, W.: Naoto Fukasawa and his without thought design theory. J. Hunan Univ. Technol. (Soc. Sci. Ed.) 16(2), 138–141 (2011)
7. Hofstede, G., Hofstede, G.J., Minkov, M.: Cultures and Organizations: Software of the Mind, vol. 2. Mcgraw-Hill, New York (2005)
8. Heimgärtner, R.: Reflections on a model of culturally influenced human–computer interaction to cover cultural contexts in HCI design. Int. J Hum. Comput. Interact. 29(4), 205–219 (2013)
9. Marcus, A., Baumgartner, V.-J.: A practical set of culture dimensions for global user-interface development. In: Masoodian, M., Jones, S., Rogers, B. (eds.) APCHI 2004. LNCS, vol. 3101, pp. 252–261. Springer, Heidelberg (2004). https://doi.org/10.1007/978-3-540-27795-8_26
10. Nielsen, J.: Ten usability heuristics (2005)
11. Reinecke, K., Bernstein, A.: Improving performance, perceived usability, and aesthetics with culturally adaptive user interfaces. ACM Trans. Comput. Hum. Interact. 18(2), 1–29 (2011)
12. Reinecke, K., Bernstein, A.: Culturally adaptive software: moving beyond internationalization. In: Aykin, N. (ed.) UI-HCII 2007. LNCS, vol. 4560, pp. 201–210. Springer, Heidelberg (2007). https://doi.org/10.1007/978-3-540-73289-1_25
13. Reinecke, K.: Culturally adaptive user interfaces. Dissertation, University of Zurich (2010)
14. A report about what are most active WeChatters Out-WeChatting. https://www.thebeijin ger.com/blog-/2017/05/18/for-eigners-are-out-wechatting-chinas-most-active-wechatters. Accessed 27 Oct 2019

15. Tohidi, M., Buxton, W., Baecker, R., Sellen, A.: Getting the right design and the design right. In: Proceedings of the SIGCHI Conference on Human Factors in Computing Systems, pp. 1243–1252. ACM (2006)
16. Zhu, X.Y., Chhachhar, A.R.: Descriptive analysis regarding use of WeChat among university students in China. Asian Soc. Sci. **12**(2), 151 (2016)

A Methodological Reflection: Deconstructing Cultural Elements for Enhancing Cross-Cultural Appreciation of Chinese Intangible Cultural Heritage

Shichao Zhao[✉]

Bournemouth University, Bournemouth BH12 5BB, UK
szhao@bournemouth.ac.uk

Abstract. This paper presents a practical method of deconstructing cultural elements based on the Human Computer Interaction (HCI) perspective to enhance cross-cultural appreciation of Chinese Intangible Cultural Heritage (ICH). The author pioneered this approach during conducting two case studies as a means to enhance appreciation and engagement with Chinese ICH, such as the extraction of elements from traditional Chinese painting and puppetry with potential to support cross-cultural appreciation, as well as the establishment of an elements archive. Through integrating a series of HCI research methods, this approach provides a specific foundational framework that assists non-Chinese people to better understand the cultural significance of Chinese ICH.

Keywords: Digital cultural heritage · Research through design (RtD) · Design ethnography · Experience-centred design (ECD) · Co-design

1 Introduction

In recent years, the exhibition of intangible cultural heritage (ICH) has attracted increased attention from pertinent organisations [1]; at the same time, however, globalisation and modernisation threaten the safeguarding and development of various aspects of ICH, such as cultural customs, practises, artistic expression, and knowledge. There are plenty of Chinese ICH areas, such as traditional handicraft skills, folk acrobatics, minority music and dance, and sacrificial activities, which are becoming endangered. The Chinese government and academics have stepped up efforts to safeguard ICH [2], but despite these attempts, many cultural practices are in danger of being lost or forgotten. On the other hand, in an increasingly internationalised world, exposure to 'international' art forms is becoming common, and there is broad interest in maintaining such creative practices, which might otherwise die out. Compared to the practice of Chinese ICH, the aesthetic appreciation is a more appropriate approach to engage audiences with Chinese ICH in their initial experience and potentially attract their interests to Chinese ICH itself [3, 4].

However, for foreign audiences, cultural differences bring about specific challenges for the appreciation of Chinese ICH. Therefore, this paper reviews some methodological

© Springer Nature Switzerland AG 2020
M. Rauterberg (Ed.): HCII 2020, LNCS 12215, pp. 450–459, 2020.
https://doi.org/10.1007/978-3-030-50267-6_34

considerations from two designed interactive applications (one application explored Chinese painting, the other Chinese puppetry) that supported cross-cultural audiences' appreciation of Intangible Cultural Heritage (ICH). Throughout two case studies, the author adopted a practical method of deconstructing cultural elements based on the Human Computer Interaction (HCI) perspective to enhance cross-cultural appreciation of Chinese ICH. This approach integrates aesthetics, anthropology, psychology, and other related areas.

In the first case study, the author conducted a cultural appreciation undertaken by qualitative and quantitative fieldwork to classify colours and subjects and expanded the content of each category to explore the available transferable design components for the design study. Then the author designed a mobile application incorporating the elements archive with multi-touch engagement to support cross-cultural appreciation of traditional Chinese painting. Based on the user experience study, which was inspired by experience-centred design (ECD) [5], the author relied on contrastive workshops and in-depth interviews of focus groups to consider the design suggestions and comments from the evaluation. The findings illustrated that the elements archive combines with multi-touch gestural engagement to effectively help application users analyse the meaning of colours and themes in order to express their understanding of Chinese painting. As well as this, they actively explored relevant knowledge through discussions with other users or searched for information online, including the artists' background story, related Chinese history, and material on Chinese religions.

In the second case study, the author adopted an approach that utilises design ethnography [6, 7] and co-design [8, 9] to conduct fieldwork with Chinese puppetry professionals, learners, and amateurs. The author gained insight into the barriers between puppetry performance and cross-cultural audiences; different languages or dialects were identified as the main obstacles to understanding [10–13]. Then, the author designed and developed an interactive system called the Digital Gesture Library, which uses a three-perspective archive of puppetry gestures and a tangible interface to support cross-cultural audiences. Through this interactive system, the author employed a mixture of questionnaires, focus groups, and workshops to promote reflection on certain aspects of audience members' experiences.

These two studies posit a series of fundamental design strategies addressing revealed hindrances to the cross-cultural appreciation of Chinese painting and puppetry. First, integrating the colours and themes of Chinese painting as design elements could help non-Chinese viewers develop a more reasonable knowledge of them and ability to appreciate them. Moreover, colours – being a component of a non-Chinese viewer's appreciation approach – would not conflict with their inability to comprehend the genres [3, 14]. Second, for the appreciation of puppetry, digital design may be used as a tool to integrate gestural resources that support audiences in forming a more systematic understanding of puppetry. Furthermore, showing audiences different gestures or movements from various visual dimensions could help viewers from distinct cultural backgrounds accurately interpret puppets' gestures.

2 Methodology Review

2.1 Research Methods in Heritage Studies

In this section the author discusses the methods that have been traditionally used in heritage studies. Since the 1980s, heritage studies have become a well-defined, independent research area [15]. Text analysis and archival research are frequently used techniques to grasp the essence of past occurrences and to trace the changing meanings of heritage [16]. In particular, they are used to analyse relevant historical records and archives to aid the introduction of traditional Chinese painting and puppetry and foster cultural and aesthetic appreciation of these art forms among cross-cultural interviewees; in this research, these methods were also used in the fieldwork, to analyse the data from the interviews with professionals and stakeholders.

The research focus of ICH has transferred from specific cultural products to excavating the wealth of knowledge and skills held by artists and local communities [17]. Some scholars have adopted investigative techniques from other realms, such as sociology, psychology, art and anthropology, to support their research on ICH. Ethnography is a primary social–anthropological approach that is frequently employed in combination with in-depth interviews, workshops, or other techniques to examine the significance of traditional ICH [18]. Some scholars believe that ethnography is the study of heritage [19]. For this research, the purpose of ethnography is to grasp the artists' point of view and vision of their world [20], as well as to help the author understand the bigger picture of traditional ICH. Specifically, the author used ethnography in the fieldwork to gain familiarity with the performance of traditional Chinese puppetry, as well as to become involved with the puppetry lectures and the performing experiences outside China of professionals and stakeholders.

2.2 Research Method in Case Studies

This section provides a detailed description of the methodologies adopted in the two case studies, which includes research through design (RtD) to form the theoretical basis; aesthetic experience approaches and design ethnography for use in the fieldwork; as well as experience-centred design (ECD) for design and evaluation studies and co-design for exploring the future design studies.

Research Through Design (RtD). Research about design by engaging in that very activity has become widely recognised and utilised in the field of HCI and interaction design. Frayling [21] provided an interpretation in 'Research through Art and Design': 'research where the end product is an artefact – where the thinking is, so to speak, embodied in the artefact, where the goal is not primarily communicable knowledge in the sense of verbal communication, but in the sense of visual or iconic or imagistic communication'. In short, the process of making artefacts or designing systems should all be regarded as various outcomes of design research. From the perspective of HCI, Zimmerman [22] and Gaver [23] identified their works as 'research through design' (RtD). Zimmerman, Stolterman, and Forlizzi [24] defined RtD as 'a research approach that employs methods and processes from design practice [sic] as a legitimate method of inquiry'.

This research utilises this approach to conduct a series of practise-led case studies in order to comprehend how cross-cultural viewers/audiences engage with ICH. As an overarching technique, RtD pursues several ends within this research. Fundamentally, RtD offers a mode of generative inquiry: to conduct heuristic work; to review existing research with a critical eye; and to seek the possibilities and design insights of the cross-cultural appreciation of Chinese ICH. Furthermore, RtD provides an efficient theoretical foundation and framework for linking various research methods in a coherent manner in order to contribute to research questions.

Approaches for Aesthetic Experience. The research adopts a series of methods as a theoretical foundation to understand the viewers' aesthetic appreciation and experience of traditional Chinese painting, as well as to reflect the content of the workshop and questionnaire. Based on the interviews with museum professionals and other relevant stakeholders on their thoughts about aesthetic occurrences, Csikszentmihalyi developed the theory of optimal experience, also known as 'flow' experience, which integrates knowledge, memory, emotion, sensation, and perception [25]. Csikszentmihalyi developed questionnaires based on his four dimensions of the aesthetic experience through open-ended discussion with professionals and stakeholders. He also emphasised that subjective interpretation is key in understanding the aesthetic experience, explaining that art museum visitors (for example) have more expectations in terms of opportunities to embed their personal thoughts or emotions into the artwork, however, such expectations also entail that visitors themselves need to have a greater understanding of cultural and historical context, which should be presented to them. Lankford [26] commented that flow experience stresses holistic engagement and thus is more suitable for a global cultural experience. In the study on cultural appreciation, the author adopted Beardsley's five criteria [27] and flow experience [28] as theoretical references to design the workshop and questionnaire.

Design Ethnography. Unlike traditional ethnography, design ethnography integrates design and ethnography to form a specific method that transfers users' perceptions into design insights. As Genzuk [29] explains, 'the key aspect of adopting ethnographic practice in design is to ultimately understand more of the user's perception of the object, environment, system, or service the user is engaged with'. The timescale of design ethnography is normally limited to only a few days (or an even shorter period of time). Traditional ethnographers more intend to engage with societies and become a part of them; meanwhile, design ethnographers are more focused on observing and interviewing people from outside. Design ethnography does not require researchers to collect and build an enormous dataset, but only to create a 'just enough' analysis to test risky assumptions [19].

Blomberg [30] suggests that actively participating in fieldwork will help designers formulate an explicit goal for the design process that will make users' behaviour and experiences more relevant to the design itself. Blomberg also states that designers should bring their knowledge of design strategies and methods to collaboration within fieldwork: 'User partnership in developing and evaluating the technology in relation to current and imagined work activities should be aided by designer participation'. In addition, the understanding and findings of design ethnography can potentially be reflected in design artefacts even if they cannot be embodied in written statements.

In the second study (Puppetry), the author employs design ethnography to collects data from traditional puppetry professionals and stakeholders to explore the design concepts and insights that may support cross-cultural appreciation of the art form. The author also adopted this method for collecting the puppetry gestures that supported the non-Chinese audience's cross-cultural appreciation of the art forms. Furthermore, this research uses design ethnography to carry out in-depth observations and understand the user experience of digital applications in the design study and the user study.

Experience-Centred Design (ECD). The author adopted ECD, developed by Wright and McCarthy [5], to conduct the design study for two case studies. This method helped obtain deep and targeted understanding of the audiences'/viewers' user experience from the angle of ICH. The design process, which is supported by interactive technology, is used as a tool to comprehend how these viewers engage with traditional Chinese heritage—the main principle for this research. This entails the need for a technique to aid in capturing and analysing audiences'/viewers' experience and putting the findings into practise.

Wright and McCarthy believe that understanding users' experiences requires not only designers' observations but also their involvement, values, and sensibilities. Kearney [31] argues that 'when the events of our lives, our experiences, are transformed into story … we become agents of our history'. Wright and McCarthy [5] explain several other frequently used methods that are employed in ECD. For instance, cultural probes are a strategy for experimental design to explore people's lives, cultural environments, and technology [32]. The experience prototype helps designers understand, explore, and communicate with the product, space, or system of the prototype [33]. It can also engage users and designers to experience the application directly, which potentially avoids forming the indirect user experience (e.g. hearing about or seeing somebody else's experience of it). Fictional inquiry uses shared narratives to create fictional settings, artefacts, and circumstances [34], as do drama and role-play [35] and technology biographies [36].

In the two case studies, storytelling and cultural probes are adopted to help cross-cultural viewers/audiences integrate experience from their personal lives, cultural context, aesthetic habitus and feelings to describe the challenges of appreciating traditional Chinese heritage, in preference to just developing abstract descriptions to summarise their experience. This gave the author a needed opportunity to delve into cross-cultural appreciation and determine the reasons for the challenges. Furthermore, drawing on ethnographic tools (such as participant observation, interviews, and video-recording), the experience prototype and fictional inquiry are both used to engage traditional heritage stakeholders in the design phase and elicit their perspectives for the evaluation of the interactive applications.

Co-design. Co-design has been employed in various realms of human–computer interaction, in digital heritage studies, co-design is often applied by designers to enhance museum visiting experiences based on reflections emerging from participatory development of interaction concepts and prototypes with cultural heritage professionals [8]. Co-design also carries a wide range of resources around shared cultural, historical, and thematic interests to contribute ideas and offer creative input [9]. In general, co-design is used to form and assess prototypes, systems, and services; it may involve the opinions of users, designers and stakeholders, applying them to improve the accessibility and usability of digital applications. The key point of co-design is to focus on identifying common values and gather feedback (rather than pursue agendas and solutions) [37].

In the case study of traditional Chinese puppetry, the author's responsibility as designer was to participate in, organise, and facilitate a series of co-design activities with professional puppeteers and puppetry stakeholders. The co-design activities are interspersed into the puppetry fieldwork. As a participant and organiser, the author engaged and conducted a series of co-design activities with Chinese and European puppetry professionals and researchers in the UK and China. The author used this interspersed approach as the author believed that the special features of Chinese puppetry performance could help the author easily to follow the perspectives of the professionals and probe the subtle design details of their communication and interactions during the co-design activities.

3 Reflection

First, the author analysed traditional literature and traditional cultural materials such as performance repertoire to become familiar with certain forms of ICH. During this step, the author employed text analysis and archival research as the two main strategies to grasp the historical origin, background knowledge, subject classification, and other information related to aesthetics literature on traditional Chinese painting and puppetry. Second, the author conducted a series of investigation-based activities with potential cross-cultural audiences and amateurs to explore how they appreciate Chinese painting and puppetry, as well as the barriers they face. The author intended to extract the cultural elements from the first step and gather elements that would be easier for cross-cultural audiences to understand. Third, the author carried out a series of fieldwork activities with ICH stakeholders and professionals. Fieldwork is commonly used to research a specific event or population in anthropology, psychology, and HCI. During this step, the author utilised fieldwork to achieve three main goals:

(1) Classify the components of Chinese painting and puppetry based on suggestions from stakeholders and professionals in order to explore representative elements;
(2) Reflect upon the findings from the investigation-based activities (which were conducted with potential cross-cultural audiences and amateurs) to the stakeholders and professionals. Then integrate and summarise the constructive design strategies derived from the stakeholders and professionals' suggestions;
(3) Discuss and select elements that could deepen cross-cultural audiences' understanding of aesthetic meaning.

Through these three steps, the author deconstructed Chinese painting and puppetry based on the criterion of cross-cultural appreciation, and applied the results to the elements archive in order to integrate into its interactive techniques using digital devices. These three steps also provide a template that can be adapted to other kinds of ICH. Although this approach refers to other research methods, such as participation design and co-design in HCI, the deconstruction of cultural elements offers not only a design strategy but one that incorporates multidisciplinary research techniques to deconstruct ICH. This method is centred on exploring the theoretical foundations of a design strategy; in other words, it requires the designer and researcher to take on an additional role as aesthetic researchers throughout the entire design project. The figure shows each step of the method of deconstructing cultural elements (see Fig. 1).

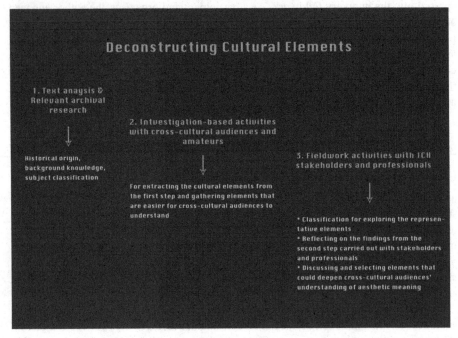

Fig. 1. Steps of the method for deconstructing cultural elements.

Furthermore, the author's role transformations as a researcher are tremendously critical in the process of elemental deconstruction. Based on the theoretical framework of RtD, the author conducted at least four role transformations and role advancements within this research: 1. layman; 2. cross-cultural viewers/audiences and amateurs; 3. reflective thinker and coordinator; and 4. designer. Each role change provided a variety of research aims and achievement of specific research targets. For most of the researchers in digital cultural heritage, it is productive to be a layman-researcher of ICH to spend more time immersed in external literature, and as a beginner, to get familiar to a specific area of ICH. In these case studies research, the author adopted analysing the traditional literature with plenty ethnography experience of ICH, in order to support the author to finish the role of 'layman of ICH'. While implementing the investigation with cross-cultural viewers/audiences and amateurs, the author's role as a researcher grew from 'layman' to 'potential cross-cultural viewer of traditional Chinese painting and audience of traditional Chinese puppetry'. This role transformation potentially engages the author so that the author may experiences how to appreciate ICH from the perspective of cross-cultural viewers/audiences and amateurs. It is worth mentioning that this role also helped the author (as a Chinese person) to abandon the conventional understanding of traditional Chinese cultures. More importantly, this role also helps the author to perceiving the barriers in their appreciation, as well as their habitual appreciation methods.

The next role transformation is from 'cross-cultural viewers/audiences and amateurs' to 'reflective thinker and coordinator'. This role also offered a directive strategy for conducting the fieldwork with professionals and stakeholders of Chinese ICH. By directly collaborating with professionals and stakeholders, the author might obtain a more professional and accurate element deconstruction, as well as avoid the oversimplified ICH to a certain extent. However, as a reflective thinker and coordinator, it is extremely significant to reflect the barriers of cross-cultural appreciation with professionals and stakeholders and engage in a discussion with them. More specifically, as the 'reflective thinker and coordinator', the author also has the opportunity to be more practically involved with the barriers of cross-cultural appreciation as an aspect to be considered in the deconstructing of cultural elements. As a representative of a cross-cultural viewer/audience, the author could now understand the deconstruction of elements, and could therefore communicate with professionals and stakeholders to adjust the acceptability of cultural elements.

The last role transformation is the author as a 'designer' to explore the potential design strategies and techniques based on the frameworks of element deconstruction. In this role, the author as the designer of this research would still be affected by subjective and individual understandings of traditional Chinese painting and puppetry, however, the previous roles with a series of relevant activities, fundamentally offered the author opportunities to explore how to design the interactive technology to support the appreciation of ICH from a cross-cultural perspective, which also avoids the esoteric or oversimplification of cultural elements.

4 Conclusion

The safeguarding of ICH requires sustained efforts. As such, this entire research not only focuses on the evaluation and iterative design of interactive applications. Supported by the theoretical framework of RtD, this research is also dedicated to constantly enhancing the cross-cultural appreciation of ICH with the support of interactive technology. This research does not intend to directly design interactive technology to safeguard ICH. Compared to the protection of tangible cultural heritage (TCH), promotion, enhancement and transmission are more significant for safeguarding ICH and for understanding how to appreciate it. Deconstructing cultural elements based on the HCI perspective provides potential sustainability for safeguarding ICH, as well as avoiding the threat that interactive technology might simplify the original forms of ICH. Although the author adopted a low-cost design strategy instead of creating complex interactive technology, users' appreciation of the application was still enhanced effectively. This research does not stop here. For example, based on deconstructing cultural elements, the author may wish to draw from sustainable research to inform the curatorial practises of other ICH, or to foster RtD-based discussions on concerns surrounding cross-cultural appreciation.

References

1. William, S.L.: Closing pandora's box: human rights conundrums in cultural heritage protection. In: Silverman, H., Ruggles, F. (eds.) Cultural Heritage and Human Rights, pp. 33–52. Springer, New York (2007). https://doi.org/10.1007/978-0-387-71313-7_2
2. Zhicong, L., Michelle, A., Mingming, F., Daniel, W.: "I feel it is my responsibility to stream": streaming and engaging with intangible cultural heritage through livestreaming. In: Proceedings of the SIGCHI Conference on Human Factors in Computing Systems, pp. 1–14. ACM: Association for Computing Machinery, Glasgow Scotland (2019)
3. Zhao, S.C., Kirk, D., Bowen, S., Wright, P.: Enhancing the appreciation of traditional chinese painting using interactive technology. Multimodal Technol. Interact. 2(2), 1–16 (2018)
4. Zhao, S.C., Kirk, D., Bowen, S., Chatting, D., Wright, P.: Supporting the cross-cultural appreciation traditional chinese puppetry through a digital gesture library. Comput. Cult. Herit. (JOCCH) 12(4), 1–28 (2019)
5. McCarthy, J., Wright, P.: Experience-Centred Design: Designers, Users, and Communities in Dialogue, 1st edn. Morgan & Claypool Press, Williston (2010)
6. Raijmakers, B., Gaver, W.W., Bishay, J.: Design documentaries: inspiring design research through documentary film. In: Proceedings of the 6th Conference on Designing Interactive Systems, pp. 229–238. ACM: Association for Computing Machinery, University Park (2006)
7. Dijk, G.V.: Design Ethnography: Taking Inspiration from Everyday Life, 1st edn. BIS Publishers, Amsterdam (2011)
8. Ciolfi, L., et al.: Articulating co-design in museums: reflections on two participatory processes. In: Proceedings of the 19th ACM Conference on Computer-Supported Cooperative Work & Social Computing, pp. 13–25. ACM: Association for Computing Machinery, San Francisco (2016)
9. Popple, S., Mutibwa, D.H.: Tools you can trust? Co-design in community heritage work. In: Borowiecki, K.J., Forbes, N., Fresa, A. (eds.) Cultural Heritage in a Changing World, pp. 197–214. Springer, Cham (2016). https://doi.org/10.1007/978-3-319-29544-2_12
10. Xu, Z.M., Xin, X.F.: The Phylogeny of Chinese Puppet Show, 1st edn. Literature of Shandong Press, Shandong (2007)
11. Zhao, S.C., Kirk, D.: Using interactive digital media to support transcultural understanding of intangible Chinese cultural heritage. In: Proceedings of CHI 2016 Conference Workshop—Involving the CROWD in Future MUSEUM Experience Design, pp. 1–3. ACM: Association for Computing Machinery, San Jose (2016)
12. Zhao, S.C., Kirk, D., Bowen, S., Wright, P.: Cross-cultural understanding of Chinese traditional puppetry: integrating digital technology to enhance audience engagement. Int. J. Intang. Herit. 14(1), 140–156 (2019)
13. Zhao, S.C.: Exploring how interactive technology enhances gesture-based expression and engagement: a design study. Multimodal Technol. Interact. 3(1), 1–13 (2019b)
14. Zhao, S.C.: An analysis of interactive technology's effect on the appreciation of traditional Chinese painting: a review of case studies. Int. J. New Media, Technol. Arts 14(3), 1–12 (2019a)
15. Sørensen, M.L.S., Carman, J.: Heritage Studies: Methods and Approaches, 1st edn. Routledge, Abingdon (2009)
16. Soderland, H.A.: The history of heritage: a method in analysing legislative historiography. In: Sørensen, M.L.S., Carman, J. (eds.) Heritage Studies: Methods and Approaches, pp. 55–84. Routledge, Abingdon (2009)
17. Giglitto, D.: Using wikis for intangible cultural heritage in Scotland: suitability and empowerment. Ph.D. Thesis, University of Aberdeen, UK (2017)

18. Palmer, C.: Reflections on the practice of ethnography within heritage tourism. In: Sørensen, M.L.S., Carman, J. (eds.) Heritage Studies: Methods and Approaches, pp. 123–139. Routledge, Abingdon (2009)
19. Travis, D., Hodgson, P.: Think Like a UX Researcher, 1st edn. Routledge, Abingdon (2019)
20. Malinowski, B.: Argonauts of the Western Pacific: An Account of Native Enterprise and Adventure in the Archipelagos of Melanesian New Guinea. Taylor & Francis e-Library, London (2005). [1922]
21. Frayling, C.: Research in Art and Design-Royal College of Art Research Papers 1, 1st edn. Christopher Frayling and Royal College of Art, London (1993)
22. Zimmerman, J., Forlizzi, J., Evenson, S.: Research through design as a method for interaction design research in HCI. In: Proceedings of the SIGCHI Conference on Human Factors in Computing Systems, pp. 493–502. ACM: Association for Computing Machinery, San Jose (2007)
23. Gaver, W.: 2012. What should we expect from research through design. In: Proceedings of the SIGCHI Conference on Human Factors in Computing Systems, pp. 937–946. ACM: Association for Computing Machinery, Austin (2012)
24. Zimmerman, J., Stolterman, E., Jodi, F.: An analysis and critique of research through design: towards a formalization of a research approach. In: Proceedings of the 8th Conference on Designing Interactive Systems, pp. 310–319. ACM: Association for Computing Machinery, Aarhus (2010)
25. Csikszentmihalyi, M.: Flow: The Psychology of Optimal Experience, 1st edn. Harper Perennial Modern Classics, New York (1990)
26. Lankford, E.L.: Experience in constructivist museums. J. Aesthet. Educ. 36(2), 140–153 (2002)
27. Beardsley, M.C.: The aesthetic point of view. In: Beardsley, M.C., Wreen, M.J. (eds.) The Aesthetic Point of View: Selected Essays, pp. 15–34. Cornell University Press, New York (1982)
28. Csikszentmihalyi, M., Robinson, R.E.: The Art of Seeing: An Interpretation of the Aesthetic Encounter, 1st edn. Getty Publications, Los Angeles (1990)
29. Genzuk, M.: A Synthesis of Ethnographic Research, 1st edn. University of Southern California, Los Angeles (2003)
30. Blomberg, J., Giacomi, J., Mosher, A., Pat, S.W.: Ethnographic field methods and their relation to design. In: Schuler, D., Namioka, A. (eds.) Participatory Design: Principles and Practices, pp. 123–155. CRC Press, Boca Raton (1993)
31. Kearney, R.: On Stories (Thinking in Action), 1st edn. Routledge, London (2002)
32. Gaver, W., Dunne, A., Pacenti, E.: Cultural probes. Interactions 6(1), 21–29 (1999)
33. Buchenau, M., Suri, JF.: Experience prototyping. In: Proceedings of the 6th Conference on Designing Interactive Systems: Processes, Practices, Methods, and Techniques, pp. 424–433. ACM: Association for Computing Machinery, New York (2000)
34. Dindler, C., Iversen, O.S.: Fictional inquiry: design collaboration in a shared narrative space. J. Co-Des. 3(4), 213–234 (2007)
35. Newell, A., Carmichael, A., Morgan, M., Dickinson, A.: The use of theatre in requirements gathering and usability studies. Interact. Comput. 18(5), 996–1011 (2006)
36. Blythe, M., Monk, A., Park, J.: Technology biographies: field study techniques for home use product development. In: Proceedings of Extended Abstracts on Human Factors in Computing Systems, Minneapolis, pp. 658–659. ACM: Association for Computing Machinery, Minnesota (2002)
37. Ferretti, V., Gandino, E.: Co-designing the solution space for rural regeneration in a new world heritage site: a choice experiments approach. Eur. J. Oper. Res. 268(3), 1077–1091 (2018)

Author Index

Printed in the United States
By Bookmasters